FRONTIERS
OF
CREATIVITY
RESEARCH

Beyond The Basics

Edited By
Scott G. Isaksen

bearly limited

Copyrights & Permissions

Grateful acknowledgment is made to the publishers, authors, and other copyright holders named below for their permission to reprint the following material.

About The Editor

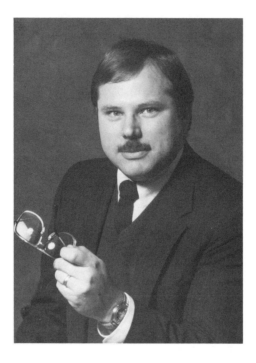

Scott G. Isaksen, Ed.D. currently directs the Center for Studies in Creativity at the State University College at Buffalo. In addition to this role, he serves as a faculty member, advises graduate students, and conducts research in the areas of creativity and innovation.

Dr. Isaksen holds adjunct appointments at the Center for Creative Leadership (Greensboro, North Carolina) and the Department of Learning and Instruction at the State University of New York at Buffalo. He consults regularly with educational, governmental, industrial, and business organizations throughout the world.

In addition to numerous articles, Dr. Isaksen's publications include *Creative Problem Solving: The Basic Course, The Handbook of Creative Learning,* and *Frontiers of Creativity Research: Beyond the Basics.*

Dedication

This book is dedicated to all those who have been and will be involved in creativity research. All royalties derived from the sale of this book will be utilized to promote creativity research at the Center for Studies in Creativity at the State University College at Buffalo.

Acknowledgments

In order for a book of this size and scope to be completed, the work, cooperation and support of many individuals was necessary. The contributors invested much time and energy to write their selections. They were patient and supportive during the seemingly endless editorial process. Early editorial assistance was provided by Susan Tannehill. A great deal of patience was shown by Sharon McGrath who did much of the typing of the manuscripts and correspondence. The bulk of the editorial assistance was provided by Michael Zich, whose untiring and dedicated efforts made this book a reality. Assistance was provided by Carol Keck and Karen Hardie from the Center for Creative Leadership's Library in tracing down some illusive references. My colleagues (Don, Roger, Ed, Pat, Gerard, Mary and Andy) and students were indispensible resources in providing encouragement and patience during the preparation of this book. The indexing challenge was accomplished by Jon Michael Fox. Ultimately, although many have provided help, I must accept responsibility for the errors.

Important support and guidance from Buffalo State's Vice President for Academic Affairs, Dr. Richard A. Wiesen, and the Associate Vice President for Academic Affairs, Dr. Gerald Accurso, rekindled the motivation so necessary in accomplishing such a challenging task. My career-long mentor, Dr. Ruth B. Noller, provided the initial spark of interest in reading the creativity literature during my very first creativity course in 1970. Her guidance, listening and caring has been felt during the editing and writing associated with this book. Contact and encouragement from Dr. Guilford, Dr. Torrance, Dr. MacKinnon and Dr. Stein has been invaluable. William Lambert, Tom Carter, Stan Gryskiewicz, and Anne Faber have provided much assistance in helping me to understand the importance of the applications for creativity research. Finally, the writer's family, Marves, Kristin and Erik, tolerated the temporary loss of attention from their husband and father, but they will never lose his love and appreciation.

Table of Contents

Preface

About seventeen years ago, I took my first course on creativity. I had received an invitation to be involved in an experimental program designed to teach creative problem solving to undergraduate students at Buffalo State College. This program had a profound influence on my life and is one of the main reasons I continue to be involved in searching for better approaches, applications and implications of the concept of creativity.

When I began reading about creativity it became clear to me that there were no universal definitions or approaches. On the one hand this provided many challenges and some confusion; on the other hand, it provided a sense of excitement and reinforced the idea that creativity was a developing line of inquiry.

Over the past seventeen years, I have been very fortunate to meet many others who have an interest in understanding creativity. This book has been assembled by those who have already engaged in examining creativity for the benefit of those who may discover the concept in the future. In a sense, the book provides an opportunity to take stock through examining the past and current findings and questions in order to better understand and shape the future work in this field.

Some individuals and groups have discovered the concept of creativity and have assumed that they are the first to stumble into the area. Frequently, they end up not too far from where their predecessors were. This book has been written to provide a historical viewpoint as well as a glimpse into the future because the need and usefulness in understanding creativity is great; but the resources and energy currently available are few. We cannot afford to waste these valuable but limited resources solely on unnecessary rediscovery.

It is my hope that this book may promote better coordination, communication and cooperation to better understand creativity and more effectively use the resources to be focused on the concept. We need to be more creative about the way in which creativity research is conducted. Although some remarkable progress has been made over the past thirty-seven years, there are many important questions needing multivariate, complex, and longitudinal research approaches.

Through my work as a classroom teacher, administrator, college professor, creativity researcher, consultant and trainer to businesses and organizations; I have become increasingly concerned with bridging the existing gap between theory and practice. Some wish to focus only upon theory or research; others only look for application and what they can do or use within the short term to increase effectiveness or profitability. My work in a variety of contexts has shown that these apparently conflicting orientations can be mutually supportive and beneficial. This book reflects that belief, so there will be information derived from traditional academic or theoretical perspectives as well as from those concerned with educational, organizational and industrial applications. In fact, I hope this combined perspective will enhance the likelihood of those in business and education working together with creativity researchers. Those using psychological research approaches and behavioral science need to work with trainers, teachers, managers, and others concerned with finding new and better approaches to identifying and developing creativity.

Finally, the reason for the emphasis on "frontiers" is that I do not believe we have managed to answer all the questions or even identify all the productive avenues for exploring creativity and innovation. This book has been designed to get to a "higher level of ground" from which the explorer can identify existing settlements and the wild territories. It is my hope that we will be able to expand and improve the existing settlements and routes, as well as explore the vast territories remaining to be examined by cutting some new routes. This may take some improved methods of "transportation," better "maps," and a great deal of courage, but I am confident that the significance of the benefits to be derived will mobilize the necessary commitment and resources.

Scott G. Isaksen
Buffalo, New York

Foreword

David Campbell
Smith Richardson Senior Fellow
Center for Creative Leadership
Greensboro, North Carolina

There are many reasons for staying far, far away from the study of creativity, or from the applications of its principles in problem solving. The creative process is usually murky, often messy, occasionally, at the extreme, dangerous or disastrous. People while creating are often prickly and self-centered, hard to live with, hard to manage, hard to love. There are no formula guidelines showing you how to put X units of creativity in to get Y units of progress out.

More distressingly, creativity, by its very nature, guarantees change, and most of us most of the time want stability, predictability, and continuity. For example, we want the people around us to dress as we expect them to, and the more responsibility they have for our affairs, the less creativity we want to see in their attire. We want our doctors and dentists in white coats, our lawyers and pension fund managers in corporate dress, and our airline pilots in conservative uniforms. Oh, we believe in freedom of expression, all right, but we do not want to see any wild T-shirts or cutoffs in the cockpit, operating room, or executive suite. We want our experts to know their place, and to demonstrate their sense of responsibility.

Furthermore, we want the inanimate objects in our lives to be equally orderly and responsible. We do not want any surprising innovations from our telephones, automobiles, lawn mowers, or food processors. We want them to do exactly what we expect them to do, with no fanciful flights of imagination. One cringes at the prospect of living in a house with, say, a creative water heater.

Why, then, in the face of these problems, do we find this continual obsession with creativity, its definition and its well-springs, demonstrated by the twenty authors of the following chapters, the hundreds of other writers and researchers whom they cite, the thousands of organizational managers who want to manage innovative work places, the tens of thousands of teachers who want to stimulate students to deal with life both effectively and creatively, and the millions of parents who want to see their children using their imaginations to cope successfully with the challenges of development.

With hopeless over-simplicity, I suggest there are two main reasons for our durable fascination with creativity, the first being pragmatic, the second philosophic.

The pragmatic reason is starkly simple; it is survival. All individuals, all groups, all organizations, all societies, and all environments are at all times in a state of change. Change requires adaptation, and adaptation often requires creativity, or at least a willingness to depart from "the way we have always done it." People or groups who live stodgy lives will inevitably be confronted with challenges that their talents and experience will not be sufficient to meet. In the 70th Anniversary issue of *Forbes* magazine (July, 1987), the editors list the 100 largest corporations in America 70 years ago and their eventual disposition. Today, only 17 of them survive unchanged; the rest have gone bankrupt, merged, or disappeared in some other manner. A similar pace of change has undoubtedly occurred in most other social or organizational categories.

Consequently, those individuals or organizations who do not wish to be at the mercy of the disintegrating forces of change had best study the insights in this book for protection. This is a marvelous collection of both classic and modern writings on creativity, and, in one book, covers a broad scope. It is not written as a survival manual, in the sense that I have just suggested, so readers will have to dig for their own lessons, but the organization imposed by the editor, Scott Isaksen, makes the task easier, especially when aided by his excellent opening chapter which provides an historical context for each of the sections.

The second reason for our fascination with creativity is both more personal and more abstract; it is a blend of various motivations such as curiosity, inspiration, admiration, and stimulation from the work of others, and the quest for personal achievement, visibility, and self-actualization through our own efforts. Some writers have used the umbrella concept, "intrinsic motivation," and argue that it is central to all creative work. "We do what we want to do — we strive to be what we can be — we create what we are driven to create." Goethe, the poet, said it in a more mystical fashion, "I did not make my songs, my songs made me."

Both of these themes — society's need to create for changing conditions, and the individual's need to create for personal satisfaction — run continually through the historical and contemporary writing presented in each section. The breath of coverage and the historical framework in this milestone book on creativity will amply reward those willing to spend time studying it, and then pondering the implications of where we have been in the past, where we are now, and where we are going in the areas of personal and organizational creative problem solving.

David Campbell
Colorado Springs, CO

Introduction: An Orientation to the Frontiers of Creativity Research

Scott G. Isaksen
Center for Studies in Creativity
State University College at Buffalo

What created our current interest in creativity? Why do people actually research such a broad topic? If we were to compare other, more established, disciplines like mathematics or philosophy, the scientific investigation of creativity would be a relatively recent and scanty development.

This is a book on creativity. Specifically, this book reviews the progress that has been made by the individuals and groups who have inquired into this complex and important area. This book is, by no means, the first attempt to review creativity research (Arieti, 1976; Bloomberg, 1973; Guilford, 1977; MacKinnon, 1978; Parnes & Harding, 1962; Rothenberg & Hausman, 1976; Stein, 1974; Taylor & Getzels, 1975; and Torrance, 1979 and 1986). What makes this volume different from the previous reviews are the following major purposes:

1. To provide a current, comprehensive review of the major research findings and trends through the 1980's;
2. To examine some new and emerging lines of inquiry for the creativity researcher and a sampling of the type of research within these newer approaches; and
3. To provide a needed resource for those interested in creativity research by identifying trends, issues, questions, and challenges for the future of this emerging line of inquiry based upon more established lines of research.

The purpose of this introduction is to provide: a rationale for the importance of studying creativity; a historical review of the early developments of this relatively new area of inquiry; some information on the definitional issues and the facets of the area of study; and the current scope of inquiry. In addition, this introduction will place the other selections of the book within the larger context of the creativity literature. A more complete listing of the selections and their contributors will be found in "The Selections and their Contributors" on pages 26 to 31.

Why Study Creativity?

Before going into the historical development of creativity research, it may be useful to reflect on some assumptions individuals would have to make in order to pursue the study of such a complex, abstract, or "fuzzy," concept. If one were viewing the area of creativity research from the relatively well-defined territory of an established discipline, one may question why anyone would venture into such a tenuous endeavor. There appears to be a widespread and natural resistance to studying a concept like creativity. Some of this type of resistance can actually stimulate areas of productive inquiry. At times, however, this resistance can also stifle new or emerging areas of work. Much of this resistance is caused by what I would call the mythology associated with creativity. As in human history, people often resort to myths to explain that which defies the use of traditional tools or methods of explanation. Let's examine some of the assumptions necessary to deal with a few of these myths about creativity.

Some would assert that creativity is a *mysterious* phenomenon, one which defies systematic analysis. Afterall, these individuals may point out, "I have yet to see an acceptable, widely-utilized definition of this concept, how can you study something which is not clearly defined?" This very lack of definitional consensus embraces another, closely related, area of resistance to studying creativity. This line of thinking suggests that creativity is a *mystical* concept which is elusive, challenging, explicit or scientific study. Both of these assertions about the qualities of creativity are based upon a rather rigid view of what a field must look like in order for valid scientific inquiry to take place. The conflicting assumption a creativity researcher must make is that creativity is an important human phenomenon which is multi-faceted (complex; but not impossible to study), and universal (it exists within art and science as well as business and education). This assumption creates conflicts with unitary views of the scientific method. Kaplan (1964) supported the value of non-traditional lines of inquiry and the struggles these emerging areas promote. He indicated:

> For the most part, these struggles may come to nothing; but the few which do succeed contribute markedly to the expansion of the frontiers of science. It is less important to draw a fine line between what is "scientific" and what is not than to cherish every opportunity for scientific growth. There is no need for behavioral science to tighten its immigration laws against subversive aliens. Scientific institutions are not so easily overthrown (p. 28).

The historian Toynbee (1964) pointed out the importance of this type of inquiry by stating that "To give a fair chance to potential creativity is a matter of life and death for any society (p. 4)."

Another major source of resistance to studying creativity is the belief that creativity is a *magical* phenomenon. This line of thinking holds that only a few precious (or infamous) individuals have *real* creativity. These gifted geniuses have been given a special gift or have been given a Muse. Rather than attempt to find out the nature of this gift or how to nurture this gift in others, it is more productive to simply appreciate the manifestations of genius. Perhaps our emphasis on studying persons who exhibit high levels of creativity (such as Einstein, Michelangelo and Copernicus) feeds the myth of magic by placing these individuals on a pedestal which separates them from the bulk of humankind. If we better understood how or why these individuals made their contributions, they may be knocked off their pedestals and the awe surrounding them would disappear. This could be similar to losing the appreciation or impact of a magic trick once the trick is exposed or explained. This line of resistance would promote simply allowing and enjoying the amazement, rather than conducting inquiry into the source of the wonder or surprise. In addition, those who believe that creativity is magical may promote the notion that it involves trickery or sleight of hand, not substance. The creativity researcher must again hold a conflicting assumption. Rather than being a magical phenomenon, one which occurs only by divine intervention or can only be appreciated; creativity needs to be seen as a natural human characteristic that is not ruined, lessened or destroyed by inquiry. Support for this assumption comes from a variety of sources, but Arieti (1976) provided a succinct summary:

> Whether it is considered from the viewpoint of its effects on society, or as one of the expressions of the human spirit, creativity stands out as an activity to be studied, cherished, cultivated (p. ix).

A third area of opposition to studying creativity comes from the belief that to be creative, you must be *mad,* weird, neurotic or at least unusual. Creativity is equated with pure novelty, which, by definition, must be outside the realm of what is acceptable, traditional, or standard. As a result, that which is creative threatens and disrupts established systems. The overemphasis on novelty promotes the view that creativity must involve madness. Creative behavior is seen as totally undisciplined and spontaneous. Although this view of creativity seems to be popular at times, the creativity researcher often assumes that creativity is a natural human phenomenon, one which everyone possesses and may choose to manifest in varying levels or degrees as well as in differing styles. If creativity is not seen this way, then the focus of creativity research would be limited to only the pathological applications of personality. Although there is no single mold into which all who are creative will fit, MacKinnon (1978) indicated:

> The full and complete picturing of the creative person will require many images. But if, despite this caution, one still insists on asking what most generally characterizes the creative individual as he has revealed himself in the Berkeley studies, it is his high level of effective intelligence, his openness to experience, his freedom from crippling restraints and impoverishing inhibitions, his esthetic sensitivity, his cognitive flexibility, his independence in thought and action, his unquestioning commitment to creative endeavor, and his unceasing striving for solutions to the ever more difficult problems that he constantly sets for himself (p. 186).

The issue of the relationship between creativity and mental health still remains somewhat open, but there is no clear evidence to suggest that to be creative, a person must also be neurotic or psychologically disturbed.

There are good reasons for the pervasiveness of these mythologies. The field of creativity research is plagued by an overabundance of conflicting definitions and words used synonymously that have very different meanings. This condition promotes the view that creativity is mysterious or mystical. Much research and public attention on our geniuses and the very highest level creative persons have fostered the myth of magic. The use of the word "creative" to describe such things as divorce, financing which is illegal or unethical, or any form of behavior which we might find repulsive, feeds the myth of madness. Despite the wide diffusion of these beliefs, the creativity researcher has made some different basic assumptions in an effort to understand this complex and important concept.

The following collection of beliefs forms the basic rationale for pursuing research into creativity. These beliefs account for the growth of interest and acceptance of this line of inquiry.

Creativity is Important.

There are many challenges within many facets of society in which an immediate or single correct response cannot be found. These real-life situations call for a more creative type of thinking. As Rogers (1959) indicated:

> Unless man can make new and original adaptations to his environment as rapidly as his science can change the environment, our culture will perish. Not only individual maladjustment and group tensions but international annihilation will be the price we pay for a lack of creativity (p. 70).

In addition, there is widespread belief that innovations (the practical results of creativity) are needed in all areas of human endeavor. As Rothenberg and Hausman (1976) asserted:

> The investigation of creativity is at the forefront of contemporary national inquiry because it potentially sheds light on crucial areas in the specific fields of behavioral science and philosophy and, more deeply, because it concerns an issue related to man's survival: his understanding and improvement of himself and the world at a time when conventional means of understanding and betterment seem outmoded and ineffective (p. 5).

The Nature of Knowledge.

The increasing accumulation of factual information makes the comprehensive awareness of what is known more difficult, if not totally impossible. Developing awareness of creativity, helps to examine the imaginative and productive applications of knowledge. The focus is more upon the dynamic process of knowing and less on the static recall and memorization of data. In this way, creativity builds on knowledge because all creativity occurs in some context. For example, it would be very unlikely that a chemist would be called a creative chemist without some basic (or perhaps thorough) understanding of the field of chemistry. Basic knowledge may be a necessary condition for creativity, but not a sufficient condition. The creativity researcher may view the imaginative and meaningful application of knowledge as more important in explaining creativity. Rogers (1959) provides a succinct rationale for creativity research in relation to the nature of knowledge.

> In a time when knowledge, constructive and destructive, is advancing by the most incredible leaps and bounds into a fantastic atomic age, genuinely creative adaptation seems to represent the only possibility that man can keep abreast of the kaleidoscopic change in his world . . . . Consequently, it would seem to me that investigations of the process of creativity, the conditions under which this process occurs, and the ways in which it may be facilitated, are the utmost of importance (p. 70).

The Need for Transferable Skills.

From all sectors of our society, there are calls for students, teachers, employees, managers, citizens, and leaders who know how to think critically and creatively. Since it is impossible to accurately predict what knowledge or information will be needed in the long-range future, it is important to focus on the development of skills which help individuals become more adaptable to new and changing circumstances. The ability and facility of using knowledge are more generalizable and more widely applicable than memorization of data. Skills and abilities are more permanent and related to the process of solving problems. Focusing on the development of creative problem-solving skills can have short and long-term impact on dealing more effectively with challenges and opportunities. Further support for this focus is provided by those concerned with what the future will demand from our educational system. For example, Combs (1981) indicated:

> An educational system unable to predict the knowledge or behaviors demanded by the future will have to concentrate instead on producing persons able to solve problems that cannot presently be foreseen. Tomorrow's citizens must be effective problem-solvers, persons able to make good choices, to create solutions on the spot. That is precisely what intelligence is all about (p. 369).

Creativity is a Natural Human Phenomenon.

To enable the study of creativity to progress beyond those extreme examples of genius and eminence, the creativity researchers must assume that creativity is a widely-held characteristic upon which individuals may differ. Some may possess very high levels of potential or accomplishment; others may show lower levels of possibility or attainment. In addition, people may differ in the way they choose to demonstrate or manifest their level of creativity. As Hilgard (1964) indicated:

> The capacity to create useful or beautiful products and to find ways of resolving perplexity is not limited to the highly gifted person, but is the birthright of every person of average talent (p. 162).

Creativity as Mental Health.

This notion of the naturalness of this human characteristic provides support for another aspect of studying creativity. That is, creativity is related to the natural development of human potential. Releasing creativity is healthy. Maslow (1959) described this aspect of creativity being related to health when he stated:

> *Self-actualizing creativeness is hard to define because sometimes it seems to be synonymous with health itself. And since self-actualization of health must ultimately be defined as the coming to pass of the fullest humanness, or as the "Being" of the person, it is as if self-actualizing creativity were almost synonymous with or a sine qua non aspect of . . . essential humanness* (p. 94).

Literature and Research on Creativity Exists.

One final rationale exists which supports the further study of the concept of creativity. There is a large and increasing body of literature related to the concept of creativity. In addition, " . . . useful research has been and can be done on many different aspects of creativity . . . it can no longer be said that fruitful research cannot be done . . . . Instead, there are now many leads to pursue at this relatively early period of serious scientific research . . . (Taylor & Barron, 1963, p. xix)." More currently, Treffinger (1986b) has asserted that:

> *Through more than thirty years of research and development, creativity has continued to be a topic of considerable interest and concern to educators as well as to social and behavioral scientists* (p. 19).

Despite the many areas of resistance, creativity remains an important area within which to conduct research. In order to adequately examine the current status of the field of creativity research the next section will provide a historical overview.

Historical Background

Some Early Developments.

Some could argue that the study of creativity began with the dawn of human civilization. However, most people who have reviewed the status of deliberate and explicit research on the concept of creativity frequently highlight the year 1950 as a significant starting point. It was during this year that J. P. Guilford gave his presidential address to the American Psychological Association (APA). Guilford (1950) pointed out the neglect of the study of creativity and backed up his claim by indicating that only 186 out of 121,000 titles listed in *Psychological Abstracts* (that's only two-tenths of one percent) had anything to do with creativity. He encouraged his colleagues to inquire into this complex area of human behavior. Guilford's complete address is reprinted in the first selection of this book, along with his twenty-five year summary of progress and a vista for future creativity research.

Although there were some attempts to study creativity before 1950 (Galton, 1911; James, 1890; Patrick, 1937; Ribot, 1900; Rossman, 1931; Spearman, 1931; Wallas, 1926; and others), the bulk of creativity research has been conducted during the thirty-some years since 1950. There are many reasons for this relatively infrequent examination of creativity until mid-twentieth century. Since the major discipline within the behavioral sciences that was likely to have been engaged in this work was psychology, it will be helpful to understand some of the rationale for the scant treatment of creativity as a research area prior to 1950.

MacKinnon (1975) explained that during the late 1800's, psychology was focusing on simpler aspects of human behavior in order to establish itself as an empirical and experimental science. He described the emphasis that followed to be that of behaviorism which placed the nature of man and his personality outside the scientific domain of psychology. He states " . . . a psychology that paid little or no attention to persons and to which the concept of a personality was largely foreign could hardly tackle the concept of creativity (p. 60)." Following the behavioral school, the Freudian emphasis on psychoanalysis promoted a psychopathological focus which did manage to bring the person into the field of psychology. However, psychoanalysis followed the medical model of curing the sick, rather than optimizing the healthy.

By the late 1930's there were a number of changes within the field of psychology which broadened the field to potentially include the study of creativity (Kendler, 1981, and Sanford, 1963, provide a more thorough treatment). There was a development of a third type of psychology; where the "normal" and more favorable manifestations of personality were introduced into academic psychology (Allport, 1937; Murray, 1938). In addition, Gestalt psychologists were demonstrating that some complex processes of thought and behavior could be examined in the psychological laboratory. Finally, the area of personality and intelligence assessment was beginning to become popular.

The Search for Effective Intelligence.

Since it was the area of the assessment of human abilities which was central to the historical development of the study of creativity, it is important to examine the early attempts to investigate human intelligence. Although the early measures of intelligence were developed as a result of interest in those on the lower end of that scale, a great deal of interest has been focused on those with the highest degree of intelligence. Willerman (1979) has indicated that:

> *Perhaps there are no more fascinating subjects in the study of human individual differences than those who represent the highest extremes on measures of achievement. Their extraordinary accomplishments earn for them a place in the pages of history, to be admired and revered. For want of a better term, we shall call such individuals geniuses* (p. 321).

One of the earliest contexts within which we can see the search for creativity is in the area of examining exceptional talent or genius. Sir Francis Galton's (1869) study of the inheritability of high intelligence was one of the earliest examples of this type of inquiry. Later, Terman (1925) began his classic studies of intellectual superiority by identifying and studying California school children with Stanford Binet IQ scores of 135 or more. This group has been followed longitudinally in an effort to comprehensively characterize their social and academic attainments throughout their lives. Catherine Cox (1926) estimated the IQ's of great geniuses to determine if creative people are more intelligent than others. Regarding Cox's findings, Hayes (1978) indicated that "despite the faults of these IQ estimates, their very high average suggests strongly that the eminent are superior in intelligence to the general public (p. 220)."

Other researchers have continued this line of inquiry (Albert, 1983; Goertzel, Goertzel & Goertzel, 1978; and Terman, 1954). Simonton (1984, 1986) has studied the same populations of earlier investigators and had written an extensive review of the historiometric findings. Selection Two by Dr. Simonton provides an example of a current approach to the study of genius and eminence.

Related to the study of genius was the study of great individuals and the method of thought which led to innovative breakthroughs (Gruber, 1981; Kuhn, 1970; Wallas, 1926; and Wertheimer, 1945).

Since no purely historical study of genius can actually measure natural mental abilities, many studies have focused on measuring the significant contributions of those who have been assigned the label of "genius." How the researchers defined and measured this term has varied widely, causing some confusion among those using the same word. An examination of intellectual and creative achievers has been provided by Bullough, Bullough and Mauro (1981) along with some suggestions regarding alternative research approaches.

The search for genius was very often accomplished through the use of IQ measurements. Although the early work in this area treated intelligence as a monolithic characteristic, the work of Gardner (1983), Guilford (1967a) and Sternberg (1985) has done much to broaden our conception of effective human intelligence. There has been sufficient analysis and critique of traditional psychometric approaches to intelligence (Gould, 1981; Meichenbaum, 1980; Raaheim, 1984; Treffinger & Renzulli, 1986; and Wallach, 1985) to promote this more comprehensive view of giftedness and intelligence.

In describing the early psychometric interests in creativity, Guilford (1967b) pointed out that psychologists concerned with how persons differ on various characteristics could not avoid the problem of creativity. Among the characteristics upon which people differ are those that prepare some individuals for higher levels of performance with regard to invention and innovation. Guilford explained the historical reason for separating creativity from the mainstream of intelligence testing:

> The first successful tests of intelligence, from Binet to Terman and others, were aimed at prediction of academic achievement at the elementary level, where almost no attention was given to self-initiated ideas when it came time to evaluate achievement. The selection of abilities to be measured in the first Stanford revision of the Binet scale omitted those especially relevant to the assessment of creative potential, due to an incidental result in a faulty experiment . . . . Thus, over the years, tests of creative qualities have been almost nonexistent in intelligence scales (p. 4).

Although some creativity researchers asserted that creativity was ruled out of the domain of intelligence, a major amount of inquiry has been focused on the relationship between creativity and intelligence. Investigators like MacKinnon (1961), Getzels and Jackson (1962), Wallach and Kogan (1965), and Wallach and Wing (1969) studied the relationship between these two concepts and their measures. It appears that there is a basis for differentiating creativity from intelligence, but the exact relationship appears to be very complex. Selection Three in this volume, written by Dr. Getzels, provides an examination of this area of study and how the idea of "problem finding" has emerged as a more current focus of inquiry. Selection Four by Dr. Treffinger provides a general overview of how creativity has been assessed and some future directions necessary for improved creativity assessment.

Centers of Research.

There were undoubtedly other factors which could help account for the growth of the field of creativity research. For example, much of the research on creativity during the past thirty years has been produced through the efforts of various centers. These centers were frequently well-funded and were able to sustain some very important lines of research.

One of the earliest centers was at the University of Southern California where Guilford conducted the Aptitudes Research Project during the late 1940's (Guilford, 1967a). This project was initially funded by the Office of Naval Research to study the aptitudes of high-level personnel. Guilford (a student of Thurstone) rejected the prevailing doctrine of intelligence being a single monolithic characteristic. Perhaps the best known outcome of Guilford's work is the development of the Structure of the Intellect Model (SOI) which theoretically identifies a wide variety of intellectual attributes (Guilford, 1977).

The Institute of Personality Assessment and Research (IPAR) was another major early center for creativity research. This center was established on the Berkeley campus of the University of California in 1949, with the primary purpose of investigating the characteristics of persons who are highly effective in their personal lives and professional careers. IPAR was made possible by a grant from the Rockefeller Foundation. The stimulus for the development of this center was the assessment program of the Office of Strategic Services. IPAR was responsible for a large amount of research into the creative personality and continues to promote this area of research. Selection Five by Dr. MacKinnon provides an overview of some of the critical issues remaining for future creativity research.

Another of Thurstone's students was responsible for another center for inquiry into creativity. Taylor began a series of international creativity research conferences at the University of Utah in 1955. These Utah Conferences were sponsored by the National Science Foundation and the focus was upon the identification of creative scientific talent. The results of these conferences are reported in Taylor (1964b); Taylor & Barron (1963) and Taylor & Ellison (1975). Selection Six by Dr. Taylor provides an overview of some of the implications of the work done at the University of Utah.

One of the earliest writers to popularize what was known about creativity was Alex Osborn. In 1948, he wrote *Your creative power;* in 1952, he wrote *Wake up your mind;* and in 1953, he wrote *Applied imagination.* In 1955, the first annual Creative Problem Solving Institute was held at the University of Buffalo and co-sponsored by Osborn's Creative Education Foundation. The University had begun offering courses as early as 1949. After some early course development, Parnes moved the program to the State University College at Buffalo and began, with his colleague Ruth Noller, the Creative Studies Project (Parnes & Noller, 1972). This project, along with the work of the faculty, ied to the development of the Center for Studies in Creativity at the State University College at Buffalo. This center continues to offer a prototype undergraduate program as well as a graduate program leading to a Master of Science degree. Selection Seven by Dr. Parnes provides an extensive review of the Creative Studies Project.

Another major force in the field of creativity research has been E. Paul Torrance. His first work was done at the Minnesota Studies of Creative Behavior (1958-1966); and then at the Georgia Studies of Creative Behavior (now called the Torrance Center for Creative Studies). The primary focus of this center has been the development of the Torrance Tests of Creative Thinking (TTCT) and working on the development of creative potential. Torrance's centers have been responsible for advancing the educational implications of creativity research (Isaksen, In press; Torrance, 1979). Selection Eight by Dr. Torrance provides a reprint of an earlier study by Torrance to answer the question: Can we teach creativity? In addition, this selection provides an overview of some recent developments and research findings since this earlier study was completed.

A few more recent centers have been developed. The Center for Creative Leadership in Greensboro, North Carolina, contains a Creativity Development Division which was first headed by Irving Taylor and is currently directed by Stanley Gryskiewicz. There are other centers outside the United States within which creativity research is being undertaken. Some of these include: The Manchester Business School in England (Rickards, 1985); the Norwegian Management Institute (NILA) in Oslo, Norway (Grøholt, 1985); The University of Bergen (Kaufmann, 1980); The Swedish Council for Management and Work Life Issues (Ekvall, 1983); Project Industrial Innovation in the Netherlands (Buijs, 1984); and the Battelle Institute in Frankfurt, Germany (Alter, Geschka, Schaude & Schlicksupp, 1973).

In sum, there have been a variety of centers for the development of creativity research projects. The development of these centers can be traced to the early explicit creativity research which emerged during the second half of the twentieth century. These centers are spread across the United States and have emerged on an international basis.

Definition: The Many Facets of Creativity

Before providing an overview of the current findings and levels of interest in creativity research, some attention will be focused on the definitional issues surrounding creativity.

A Multi-Faceted Phenomenon.

It is probably most productive to view creativity as a multi-faceted phenomenon rather than as a single unitary construct capable of precise definition. Guilford's address provided an impetus to many to undertake creativity research. The address also provided renewed encouragement to those who were already involved in such research. As the creativity literature began to expand so did the number of definitions used for the concept. Only nine years following Guilford's address Taylor (1959) found in excess of one hundred definitions of creativity in the literature. These definitions are varied and some could be considered conflicting. Welsch (1980) reviewed twenty-two definitions of creativity to find elements of agreement and disagreement. She was searching for a definition that would be applicable to a variety of creative activities and stated:

> The definitions of creativity are numerous, with variations not only in concept, but in the meaning of subconcepts and of terminology referring to similar ideas. There appears to be, however, a significant level of agreement of key attributes among those persons most closely associated with work in this field. Significantly for this study, the greater disagreements occur in relation to aspects that are less relevant to educational purposes. On the basis of the survey of the literature, the following definition is proposed: Creativity is the process of generating unique products by transformation of existing products. These products, tangible and intangible, must be unique only to the creator, and must meet the criteria of purpose and value established by the creator (p. 97).

Of course, not everyone associated with creativity research would agree with this definition.

One of the major reasons for the complexity of the field of creativity research is the diversity of theoretical perspectives upon which the research is based (Treffinger, Isaksen & Firestien, 1983). Many of these theoretical approaches are intertwined which adds to the semantic confusion. For example, the concepts of problem solving and creative learning are frequently linked together. Guilford (1977) defined problem solving as facing a situation with which you are not fully prepared to deal. Problem solving occurs when there is a need to go beyond the information given, thus there is a need for new intellectual activity. Guilford (1977) reported that:

> ... problem solving and creative thinking are closely related. The very definitions of those two activities show logical connections. Creative thinking produces novel outcomes, and problem solving involves producing a new response to a new situation, which is a novel outcome (p. 161).

This definition is also very closely related to a framework for describing the process of creative learning put forth by Torrance and Myers (1970). They described the creative learning process as:

> ... becoming sensitive to or aware of problems, deficiencies, gaps in knowledge, missing elements, disharmonies, and so on; bringing together available information; defining the difficulty or identifying the missing element; searching for solutions, making hypotheses, and modifying and retesting them; perfecting them; and finally communicating the results (p. 22).

The fact that there is no widely-held and uniformly applied definition of creativity has added fuel to the argument that creativity is a difficult field to study.

About ten years after Guilford's address, Rhodes (1961) responded to the criticism leveled at those attempting to study creativity due to the loose and varied meanings assigned to the word "creativity." Rhodes set out to find a single definition of the word by collecting in excess of fifty-six different definitions. Despite the profusion of those definitions, he reported:

> ... as I inspected my collection I observed that the definitions are not mutually exclusive. They overlap and intertwine. When analyzed, as through a prism, the content of the definitions form four strands. Each strand has unique identity academically, but only in unity do the four strands operate functionally (p. 307).

The four strands Rhodes discussed included information about the: *person* (personality, intellect, traits, attitudes, values and behavior); *process* (stages of thinking people go through when overcoming an obstacle or achieving a goal); *product* (characteristics of artifacts or outcomes of new thoughts, inventions, designs, or systems); and *press* (the relationship between people and the environment, the situation and how it affects creativity). Each of these four strands operates as identifiers of some key components of the larger, more complex, concept of creativity.

This classification scheme has been used quite extensively in the creativity literature and helps to provide some frame of reference in studying creativity (Hallman, 1981; MacKinnon, 1978; and Welsh, 1973). This general approach to the definition of creativity appears to be more fruitful than attempting to specify a single definition which would be appropriate for all contexts. Keeping the definition rather general does feed the notion that creativity is a complex concept. Selection Nine provides a reprint of the Rhodes article so that you can start with an understanding of these four basic strands of creativity.

Although creativity research may not always be conclusive, there does appear to be sufficient evidence to warrant the consideration of its various implications. The study of creativity, rather than being an exact science, appears to be more like a diamond. It is certainly worthwhile, and you can see the entire jewel, or you can focus on one of its many facets. When your attention is directed at only one of the facets, care must be taken to avoid the tendency to forget that you are only looking at one part and not the whole. Real value, operationally, occurs when all the facets are taken into consideration. Even then, there remain many critical issues to be investigated to shed further light on the conceptions of creativity and their many implications. Investigation and analysis of creativity is facilitated when consideration is given to each of its facets. The following subsections will focus on the four facets of creativity identified by Rhodes.

The Creative Personality.

The questions within the area of the creative personality include the identification of traits or characteristics to differentiate creative persons from their less creative peers. The major response to this type of question has been research through biographical descriptive and empirical methodologies utilizing readily identified "creators" and attempting to distill their attributes. The end products of these investigations are lists and tests of characteristics and traits that have something to do with being creative (Torrance, 1974; Williams, 1980). These lists do not provide a comprehensive picture of the creative personality. As MacKinnon (1978) has emphasized, " . . . there are many paths along which persons travel toward the full development and expression of their creative potential, and there is no single mold into which all who are creative will fit. The full and complete picturing of the creative person will require many images (p. 186)."

Many psychological theorists have provided a diversity of characteristics of the creative person (Fromm, 1959; Maslow, 1959; and Rogers, 1959). Torrance (1979) introduced a multi-faceted model for thinking about the search for creative behavior. This model " . . . takes into consideration, in addition to creative abilities, creative skills and creative motivations . . . high level(s) of creative achievement can be expected consistently only from those who have creative motivations (commitment) and the skills necessary to accompany the creative abilities (p. 12)." Other multi-faceted models for dealing with the creative personality have been put forth by Amabile (1983), Gowan (1972), and Renzulli (1978).

Within the scope of research into the creative personality, the questions concerning why people choose to create are central. Amabile (1983) also refers to a three-faceted model for examining creativity. Hers includes domain-relevant skills, creativity-relevant skills and task motivation. She focuses her attention on the former and promotes the hypothesis that intrinsic motivation is important for creativity. Selection Ten by Dr. Amabile provides a more thorough treatment of this area of research.

An emerging line of research becoming increasingly connected to the study of the creative person is the area of study of the human brain. Immunology, microbiology, and many of the neurosciences are attempting to better understand the linkages between mind and body (Dixon, 1986; Frank, 1984). Of the many lines of inquiry emerging from these interests, one is examining the effects of brain growth on cognitive development (Grennon, 1984; and Toepfer, 1982). Selection Eleven by Dr. Toepfer provides an overview of some of this research and discusses implications for creativity.

Another aspect to the study of the creative person relates to knowing more about the personal orientation toward problem solving and creative thinking. Isaksen and Treffinger (1985) suggest that it is helpful for individuals to have information regarding their learning and thinking style when learning how to use creative problem solving. Some of the current research within this area focuses on studying different styles of creativity and how these styles may effect different elements of creativity (Kirton, 1976; and Myers and Myers, 1980). Certain personality characteristics will influence preferences regarding what type of information people pay attention to, how they collect and analyze that data, and how they choose to use the information. Most previous literature on the creative personality focused upon the difference in level of tendency or achievement. It is the area of style of creativity which provides an entirely new lens to utilize regarding the study of the creative person. The new focus is upon how people differ in their approach to using their creativity; not upon their level of qualitative factors. Selection Twelve provides an overview to this emerging line of style of creativity through the work of Kirton (1976).

The Creative Process.

One of the earliest descriptions of the creative process was provided by Wallas (1926). He described four stages for this process including: preparation, incubation, illumination and verification. Research regarding the creative process has relied upon retrospective reports, observation of performance on a time-limited creative task, factor analysis of the components of creative thinking, experimental manipulation and study of variables presumably relevant to creative thinking and simulation of "creative" processes on computers.

Some of the questions relating to the creative process include: What are the stages of the creative thinking process? Are the processes identical for problem solving and for creative thinking? What are the best ways to teach the creative process? How can the creative process be encouraged? Is the creative process similar in different contexts?

The previously mentioned description of creative learning (Torrance & Myers, 1970) is sometimes equated with what is meant by the creative process. In both, there is a description of various stages of thinking and problem solving when an individual is confronted with a challenge or opportunity. These stages provide the basis for the creative problem solving (CPS) process. Current thinking about the CPS process describes the process as having two mutually-important types of thinking. Osborn (1953) originally referred to these as imaginative and evaluative. Current language for these types of thinking is creative and critical, respectively. Creative thinking involves making and communicating meaningful new connections to: think of many possibilities; think and experience in various ways and use different points of view; think of new and unusual possibilities; and guide in generating and selecting alternatives (Isaksen & Treffinger, 1985). Critical thinking involves analyzing and developing possibilities to: compare and contrast many ideas; improve and refine promising alternatives; screen, select, and support ideas; make effective decisions and judgments; and provide a sound foundation for effective action (Treffinger, 1984). These two types of thinking are seen as mutually important components of effective problem solving. Although much of the historical emphasis within programs which teach CPS has been on the development of divergent thinking, there is an increasing emphasis on providing a balanced approach including the development of both divergent and convergent thinking skills. This more balanced approach is consistent with recent research in the problem solving and intelligence fields (Hellesnes, Raaheim & Bengtsson, 1982).

Much of the emphasis regarding the creative process involves the teaching or training of explicit methods and techniques in order to help solve problems and think more effectively. A major question underlying this emphasis is whether or not these strategies and skills will be of assistance across disciplinary boundaries. In short, are there generic problem solving skills that cut across fields?

A review of research with this exact question was supported by the Program Planning Research Council of the Educational Testing Service (Baird, 1983). Despite the difficulties inherent in the problem-solving literature (research based on highly artificial problems, a wide variety of tasks and studies, and others), several lines of inquiry appeared fruitful:

> First, there is some evidence that various heuristics are used by effective problem solvers in many areas of activity when confronted by new types of problems and that these heuristics can be identified. Second, there are converging lines of evidence that a major role is or can be played by a managerial function that selects strategies and plans attacks on problems. Finally, the study of how problem solvers within specific fields learn to solve the field-specific problems they face suggests several generic skills that cut across fields (p. 19).

These findings are qualified by pointing out that the actual field or context within which the problem solving occurs provides the requisite knowledge as well as the procedures and outlets necessary to implement the generic skills. More detailed reviews of this line of research are provided by Chipman, Segal and Glaser (1985), Dansereau (1985) and Derry and Murphy (1986).

Findings regarding the generality of thinking skills relates to the current writing on metacognition (Costa, 1984 and Nickerson, Perkins & Smith, 1985). The abilities associated with the managerial function are remarkably similar to those of metacognition. Both seem related to an individual's ability to make his or her thought process more explicit and deliberate.

The connections which exist between the creative process and teaching for thinking are well-documented in a vast collection of literature (Treffinger, Isaksen & Firestien, 1982, p. 18). There are many historical antecendents for this type of teaching. One of the earliest spokespersons of the importance of the deliberate development of thinking was Dewey (1933). He charged teachers with the responsibility to know the process of reflective thought and facilitate its development, indirectly, in students by providing appropriate conditions to stimulate and guide thinking. This approach was described in even more detail by Hullfish and Smith (1961). They reported:

> Where there is no problem, where no snarl appears in the normal flow of experience, there is no occasion to engage in thought . . . it is important that teachers understand the intimate relationship between problem solving and thought (p. 212).

Dewey's work continues to be a focal point for those concerned with the development of thinking skills (Baron, 1981).

Many methods and techniques have been presented in the literature (Feldhusen & Treffinger, 1985; Isaksen & Treffinger, 1985; Parnes, Noller & Biondi, 1977; and VanGundy, 1981). These techniques have been developed through some association with aspects of the stages of the creative process. Extensive reviews of the research surrounding these techniques and procedures are available in the literature (Stein, 1974 & 1975).

Within the strand of the creative process, and the development of creative problem solving techniques, there are at least two lines of inquiry which appear to be taking on importance.

The first of these is the effort to become more informed regarding the appropriate application of various techniques. This means finding out what techniques work best under what types of circumstances and for whom. Some work is already being done to test the effectiveness of specific techniques under various conditions (Ekvall & Parnes, 1984; and Necka, 1984). An example of this line of inquiry is provided in Selection Thirteen by Dr. Gryskiewicz. This selection focuses on gaining more information on the qualitative outcomes of various idea-generating techniques.

Another emerging line of inquiry within the broad area of the creative process is the concept of mental imagery and its place in creative problem solving. There is a growing amount of information regarding the concept of imagery (Fleming & Hutton, 1983; Kaufmann, 1980; Khatena, 1984; and Sheikh, 1983) and visualization (Samuels & Samuels, 1975). Although much of the early emphasis within creative problem solving was the development of cognitive, rational and semantic aspects of creativity, there is an increasing awareness that the creative process cannot be limited to just those elements. Selection Fourteen by Dr. Khatena provides an overview of some of the research done in this area and outlines a few areas of importance for future inquiry into imagery.

The Creative Product.

The centrality and importance of studying the creative product has been pointed out by MacKinnon (1978). He stated:

> *In a very real sense . . . the study of creative products is the basis upon which all research on creativity rests and, until this foundation is more solidly built than it is at present, all creativity research will leave something to be desired* (p. 187).

Although many researchers acknowledge the importance of this line of investigation, there appears to be a paucity of empirical investigation on the topic of creative products. One of the possible explanations for the lack of research in this area is the opinion that the problem is too easy. In other words, the identification of creative products is "obvious." Everyone knows a creative product when they see one. MacKinnon (1975) pointed out that this view might account for the scarcity of scientific investigation of creative products:

> *In short, it would appear that the explicit determination of the qualities which identify creative products has been largely neglected just because we implicitly know—or feel we know—a creative product when we see it* (p. 69).

There are some who have conducted investigations of creative products (Amabile, 1982; Besemer & Treffinger, 1981; Pearlman, 1983; Taylor & Sandler, 1972; and Ward & Cox, 1974). Much of this work has dealt with creative products in specific contexts. Very little has been done beyond individual disciplines and contexts to gain a more general picture of the characteristics of creative products. Selection Fifteen by Besemer & O'Quin reviews the extension of some earlier research (Besemer & Treffinger, 1981) and the development of a measuring tool for identifying creative products. Further research on this newly-developed instrument is reported in Besemer & O'Quin (1986). Although much emphasis has been placed on the need for a creative product to be novel; it is interesting to note that the current trend is to include aspects of relevance and appropriateness to the description of the creative product. As Briskman (1980) pointed out:

> *. . . the novelty of a product is clearly only a necessary condition of its creativity, not a sufficient condition: for the madman who, in Russell's apt phrase, believes himself to be a poached egg may very well be uttering a novel thought, but few of us, I imagine, would want to say that he was producing a creative one* (p. 95).

A related, and more thoroughly-researched area of study dealing with creative products involves the diffusion of innovations. There appears to be a general increase of interest in how new ideas or products are communicated or accepted by others. An increased interest in the process of innovation has also increased concern for studying communication to promote acceptance of new ideas. This area of study is called the diffusion of innovations.

When the book *Diffusion of Innovations* was first published in 1962, there were 405 publications about this topic available in the literature (Rogers, 1983). By the end of 1983, there were more than 3,000 publications about diffusion, many of which were scientific investigations of the diffusion process. Rogers (1983) described diffusion as an information exchange occurring as a convergence process involving interpersonal networks. He asserted that the diffusion of innovations is a social process for communicating information about new ideas. The study of this process has examined specific attributes of innovations (such as relative advantage, compatibility, complexity, trialability, and observability) and how they influence acceptance (Rogers, 1983).

These attributes of innovations may account for many of the reasons for their acceptance, but there are other variables which must also have an effect on the diffusion of new ideas and inventions. Other variables would include: the number of people involved in making a decision; the type of communication used; the environment or culture; and who is supporting or selling the new idea or product. Selection Sixteen by Dr. VanGundy reviews the literature on organizational innovation and identifies some areas upon which to focus future research efforts.

The increasing importance of this emphasis on the development of new products has spawned a new journal to publish literature relating to product innovation management. In short, this journal draws articles from a variety of disciplines and functions as a forum for the exchange of ideas for this area of management. As the editors indicated:

> . . . *management is critically questioning strategies, organizational structures, basic objectives, and present operating systems in a search for increased success in new products management in the global environment* (Crawford & Hustad, 1986, p. 2)

The Creative Press.

The term press refers to the relationships between individuals and their environments. This facet of creativity includes the study of social climates conducive or inhibitive to the manifestation of creativity, differences in perception and sensory inputs from varying environments, and the various reactions to certain types of situations. The questions guiding study within this area include understanding the environmental conditions that have an effect on creative behavior, how these conditions effect creativity and how they can be used to facilitate creativity. The research approaches have included case study, interview and survey techniques with small groups and organizations.

Torrance (1962) synthesized the findings of various investigators and listed the following as necessary conditions for the healthy functioning of the preconscious mental processes which produce creativity:

1. *The absence of serious threat to the self, the willingness to risk;*
2. *Self awareness . . . in touch with one's own feelings;*
3. *Self-differentiation . . . sees self as being different from others;*
4. *Both openness to the ideas of others and confidence in one's perceptions of reality or ideas; and*
5. *Mutuality in interpersonal relations . . . balance between excessive quest for social relations and pathological reflection of them* (p. 143).

Investigation into creative environments has included attention to the educational and organizational areas. There has been much recent attention to the climate conducive to creativity and innovation from the business and industrial community (Abetti, 1986; Amabile, 1983; Amabile & Sensabaugh, 1985; Ekvall, 1983; and Steffire, 1985). The emphasis of this research has been to identify those factors, in certain organizations, that account for creative behavior. The findings from business and education are somewhat similar in that the climates in both types of organizations appear to be supportive of the intrinsic motivation hypothesis put forth by Amabile (1983; see also Selection Ten).

The popular literature contains many lists of suggestions for creating an environment conducive to creativity (Amabile, 1984; Isaksen, 1984; and VanGundy, 1984). VanGundy (1984) identified three categories of factors that determine a group's creative climate. They are: the external environment, the internal climate of the individuals within the group, and the quality of the interpersonal relationships among group members. He acknowledged that there would be considerable overlap among these categories and that each category would include suggestions that deal with both task and people-oriented issues.

A common thread running through all these suggestions is the encouragement of group involvement and increasing the level of ownership over activity and decisions. Although there are plenty of times a leader would not care to use group resources when making a decision, the climate literature suggests the decision to use or not to use a group should be based on more than personal preference. Situational variables such as: the needed quality of decision; the amount of information available; the needed level of commitment to the decision; the amount of conflict in existence; and many other factors could have an impact on deciding when and where to use group resources. When examining the many suggestions to establish a creative climate it is important to keep the concept of balance in mind. Taking as many factors into consideration when using those suggestions will help to moderate the many variables effecting their appropriate application.

A related factor to consider when attempting to provide a creative climate is the type of leadership role required for the situation at hand. There are different kinds of leadership appropriate for different kinds of situations (Fiedler, Chemers & Mahar, 1976; and Hersey & Blanchard, 1982). In considering the kind of environment within which creativity flourishes, it becomes apparent that a different type of leadership role is necessary. Some use the term "facilitator" to describe this leadership style (Isaksen, 1983b & 1986; Parnes, 1985; and Wittmer & Myrick, 1974). Others use the term "mentor" (Frey & Noller, 1986; Noller & Frey, 1983; and Torrance, 1984b).

Another common theme within the climate literature is that the kind of environment which is supportive of creativity and innovation will allow individuals to be aware of their own blocks to creative thinking. The focus is on providing a climate where these can be minimized. Some of these blocks can be personal (such as the inability to take risks), problem solving (such as working only within a fixed "set"), or situational (like a great deal of emphasis on negative criticism). Taking time within a group or organization to develop an orientation to these inhibitors may provide reinforcement of the groundrules for the creative environment and may reduce the likelihood of the manifestation of blocks.

Creativity's Current Scope of Interest

One of the factors contributing to the complexity of the study of creativity is the interdisciplinary nature of the concept. No single discipline can legitimately claim to have exclusive rights to the study of creativity. Creativity research is found in the arts (Barron, 1972; Barron & Welsh, 1952; Getzels & Czikszentmihalyi, 1976; and Patrick, 1935 & 1937), as well as in the sciences (Aris, Davis & Stuewer, 1983; Mansfield & Busse, 1981; Roe, 1951 & 1953; Taylor, Smith & Ghiselin, 1963). In addition, within the disciplines there are many possible contexts within which to study creativity (Isaksen, Stein, Hills, & Gryskiewicz, 1984). Selection Seventeen by Dr. Hausman provides an overview of philosophical inquiry into creativity.

Creativity has been studied in managerial, business and industrial areas (Basadur, 1981; Basadur & Thompson, 1986; Ekvall & Parnes, 1984; and Johansson, 1975), in disciplines such as engineering (Arnold, 1959; and Rubinstein, 1975), mathematics (Helson & Crutchfield, 1970; Schoenfeld, 1982; and Schoenfeld & Herrmann, 1982), philosophy (Hausman, 1984; Lamb, 1981; and Lipman, Sharp & Oscanyan, 1980), physics (Larkin, 1980), and English (Elbow, 1983; Langer, 1982; and Olson, 1984); and in teacher preservice and inservice educational programs (Brookes, 1984; Gibney & Meiring, 1983; Krulik & Rudnick, 1982; and Martin, 1984) as well as in the general counseling process (Heppner, 1978).

On the basis of these lines of research, there is increasing evidence that specific and deliberate actions can be taken to impact creativity. Torrance (1981) made the following assertion:

> A few years ago, it was commonly thought that creativity, scientific discovery, the production of new ideas, inventions, and the like had to be left to chance. Indeed many people still think so. With today's accumulated knowledge, however, I do not see how any reasonable, well-informed person can still hold this view. The amazing record of inventions, scientific discoveries, and other creative achievements amassed through deliberate methods of creative problem solving should convince even the most stubborn skeptic. (p. 99).

Educational Interest.

The educational interest in creativity stems from a vast collection of literature (Gowan, Demos & Torrance, 1967; Gowan, Khatena & Torrance, 1981; Isaksen, in press; Isaksen, 1983a; Torrance, 1975 & 1986; and Stein, 1986). Guilford (1980) provided support for the importance of the educational context for creativity research:

> Of all the environmental influences on development of creativity, education has received special interest. It is the business of education more than any other institution to determine to what extent creativeness and creative production can be improved and how this shall be done. It is apparently no longer doubted that there can be improvement in creative thinking and problem solving. There is increasing realization of education's responsibility in this direction (p. viii).

One of the reasons for the increasing interest in creativity within education is that there is mounting evidence that creativity can be assessed systematically and scientifically (Amabile, 1983; Biondi & Parnes, 1976; Khatena, 1982; and Torrance, 1974). In addition, a related finding is that creativity can be enhanced through deliberate instructional procedures (Goor & Rapaport, 1977; Heppner, Neal & Larson, 1984; Mansfield, Busse and Krepelka, 1978; Parnes & Noller, 1972; Reese, Parnes, Treffinger and Kalsounis, 1976; Rose & Lin, 1984; and Torrance, 1972 & 1986).

Two selections in this volume provide much more in-depth information about the status of research on the deliberate development of creativity and on an example of a two-year study of the development of creative problem-solving skills (see Torrance's Selection Eight and Parnes' Selection Seven).

In general, there appears to be a growing recognition that the traditional educational system needs to be more responsive to individual creativity and to move beyond the focus on recall and memorization. Indeed, if what Goodlad (1983) reported is true, then not much has changed in American education since the early 1900's despite the increased research on creativity in education. Goodlad reported that schools appear to be spending most time, energy and resources to provide for lower level thinking and recall through lecture and recitation methodology. This phenomenon has been well documented by those in the fields of mathematics (Carpenter, Lindquist, Mathews & Silver, 1983; and NCTM, 1980), reading and literature (Berkenkotter, 1980; Glatthorn, 1982; and NAEP, 1981) and in teacher questioning practices (Dillon, 1984; and Gall, 1984).

Those who resist the current trend toward reaching out to the higher mental processes point out their concern in terms of what might be lost if precious time is taken away from teaching for thinking. It appears that, as long as the new focus is on creative learning, the loss is non-existent. Gains can be found in reading and mathematics (Brandt, 1982), SAT scores (Worsham & Austin, 1983) and in overall school achievement (Johnson, Maruyama, Johnson, Nelson & Skon, 1983). These recent findings are consistent with earlier research findings reported from the Eight-Year study (Aiken, 1942).

Educational interest in creativity can be traced to some well-established historical antecedents (Kilpatrick, 1918; and Rugg & Shufmaker, 1928). As Judd (1936) indicated:

> Memorization of facts frequently fails to result in the development of higher mental processes. If the higher mental processes of application and inference are really to be cultivated, learning conditions appropriate for their cultivation are necessary (p. 17).

Recent inquiry into how to plan to provide these appropriate learning conditions seems to indicate that the planning for the development of creative learning needs to be deliberate and explicit (Isaksen, 1983a, 1984; Isaksen & Parnes, 1985; and Whitman, 1983). It would appear that if we really want to bring a more creative trend to education it will be necessary to plan deliberately for the attainment of that goal.

Another major aspect of the educational interest in creativity is the focus on giftedness and talent development. There is a growing literature on the characteristics of giftedness in children (Gowan, Khatena & Torrance, 1979; Horowitz & Obrien, 1985; Stein, 1986; and Tannenbaum, 1983). This literature provides support for special efforts within the educational setting to provide for the needs of these learners (Renzulli, 1986). There is also some current concern with coordinating the special activities for the special learners with the total school program (Treffinger, 1986a). In all these areas, the implications of creativity research are central.

Organizational Interest.

There is an increasing interest in the literature of management, business and industry on innovation and dealing with changes in organizational structure to make them more supportive of innovation and creative thinking (Bennis, Benne, Chin & Corey, 1976; Lundstedt & Colglazier, 1982; Rothberg, 1981; and Vedin, 1980). Smeekes (1986) reported that in a 1985 survey of almost one thousand senior executives from the US, Europe and Japan, 90% indicated a growing need for innovation in their companies and 75% felt that special skills and knowledge are required to effectively manage the innovation process. For example, Drucker (1985) asserted that it was time to develop the principles, practice and discipline of innovation in much the same way management became a "science" thirty years ago. Regarding the practice of innovation by organizations, he stated:

> Innovation is the specific tool of entrepreneurs, the means by which they exploit change as an opportunity for a different business or a different service. It is capable of being presented as a discipline, capable of being learned, capable of being practiced. Entrepreneurs need to search purposefully for the sources of innovation, the changes and their symptoms that indicate opportunities for successful innovation. And they need to know and to apply the principles of successful innovation (p. 19).

Lawrence and Dyer (1983) reviewed the need to renew American industry by organizing for both efficiency and innovation. They indicated that:

> Although organizations can get by for a time being only efficient or only innovative, over the long term there must be a simultaneous achievement of both efficiency and innovation (p. 267).

It has been easier for organizations to organize themselves for efficiency rather than for innovation. There appears to be a natural bias to want to increase the ability to control and manage existing lines of work rather than to create new and changing approaches to work. Peters and Austin described the "messiness" of innovation in their book *A Passion for Excellence* (1985):

> The course of innovation . . . is highly uncertain. Moreover, it is always messy, unpredictable, and very much affected by the determined ("irrational"?) champions, and that is the important point. It's important, because we must learn to design organizations . . . that take into account, explicitly, the irreducible sloppiness of the process and take advantage of it, rather than systems and organizations that attempt to fight it (p. 155).

One of the major areas of concern within organizations is how to structure themselves for innovation. In addition, they are increasingly concerned with providing training to managers to promote their abilities to deal with their own creativity and the creativity of their employees. Selection Eighteen by Dr. Basadur provides a current overview to the status of research in this area and points out a few areas for increased future attention.

In a recent in-house publication (Frey, 1986) a major industrial manufacturing company reported the results of a study done by its corporate training and development department. In response to what employees thought was lacking in current training, they indicated:

> Training in innovation and creativity were consistently requested by all division and all personnel levels . . . people here are hungry to learn how to think more creatively (p. 4).

International Interest.

It appears that creativity research is growing in a variety of ways in the educational contexts, as well as within organizational contexts. There is also strong international interest in creativity research. About thirty years after his presidential address, Guilford (1980) wrote the foreword to a book devoted to the international perspectives on creativity research. He stated:

> This volume provided substantial evidence that there is indeed a creativity movement and that it now has nearly world-wide proportions. This is a hopeful situation, for a world population of creative problem solvers should be more productive and happy as well as more self-confident and more tolerant and, therefore, more peaceful (p. v).

The international interest in creativity can be reflected in the emergence of many centers to study innovation and assist organizations in applying the results of this research (Smeekes, 1986). In addition, there is increasing literature providing information on research trends from various countries (Onda, 1986). Torrance (1984a) also found evidence of a growing international concern for applying creativity research to educational contexts. He compiled a bibliography with the assistance of over twenty different countries and found:

> . . . that almost every country in the world is concerned about stimulating and developing the creativity of its gifted and talented children, and that each country has something important and unique to offer the rest of the world (p. 19).

Conclusion

Creativity research has managed to become increasingly available and relevant to many different people and contexts. Although there is a bulk of research available, there are still many more questions and challenges than answers and completed lines of inquiry. Selection

Nineteen by Dr. Stein provides a discussion of issues and suggestions for those who may contemplate studying this important concept.

It appears that enough scientific inquiry has occurred to enable the rejection of the myths of mystery, magic and madness discussed earlier in this introduction. The creativity literature has demonstrated a change from nearly restrictive use of the term "creative" to describe the work of the "Creator," to an extremely wide application of that term for all sorts of human activity. The abundant creativity and innovation literature offers a robust assortment of challenging questions and areas for inquiry. In reviewing the literature contained in this volume, one general observation is that once definitional concerns have been identified and focused, significant progress has been made in better understanding the nature of the creative act or outcome, personality, setting and process. In addition, it appears quite plausible that creativity, as a dynamic concept, can be impacted and nurtured by various means.

Looking ahead, creativity research can be viewed as an emerging frontier of interdisciplinary inquiry. What seems to be necessary is less "reinventing" of the established lines of inquiry, and a more coordinated, collaborative and complex effort. The future of creativity research may rely greatly on our ability to bring elegant simplicity to the scientific approaches to examining creativity, recognizing that we may never reduce creativity to a totally predictable or controllable concept.

References

Abetti, P. A. (1986). Fostering a climate for creativity and innovation in business-oriented R&D organizations: An historical project. *Creativity & Innovation Network, 12,* 4-16.

Aiken, W. M. (1942). *The story of the eight year study.* New York: Harper & Brothers.

Albert, R. S. (Ed.) (1983). *Genius and eminence: The social psychology of creativity and exceptional achievement.* New York: Pergamon Press.

Allport, G. W. (1937). *Personality: A psychological interpretation.* New York: Holt.

Alter, V., Geschka, H., Schaude, G. R., & Schlicksupp, H. (1973). *Methoden und organization der ideefinding.* Frankfurt, Germany: Battelle Institute.

Amabile, T. M. (1982). Social psychology of creativity: A consensual assessment technique. *Journal of Personality and Social Psychology, 43,* 997-1013.

Amabile, T. M. (1983). *The social psychology of creativity.* New York: Springer-Verlag.

Amabile, T. M. (1984). Social environments that kill creativity. In S. S. Gryskiewicz, J. T. Shields, & S. J. Sensabaugh (Eds.), *Blueprint for innovation* (pp. 1-18). Greensboro, NC: Center for Creative Leadership.

Amabile, T. M. & Sensabaugh, S. J. (1985). Some factors affecting organizational creativity: A brief report. A paper presented as a part of the Creativity Innovation & Entrepreneurship Symposium at The George Washington University, Washington D.C.

Arieti, S. (1976). *Creativity: The magic synthesis.* New York: Basic Books, Inc.

Aris, R., Davis, H. T. & Stuewer, R. H. (1983). *Springs of scientific creativity: Essays on founders of modern science.* MN: University of Minnesota Press.

Arnold, J. E. (1959). Creativity in engineering. In Smith, P. (Ed.), *Creativity: An examination of the creative process* (pp. 33-46). New York: Hastings House.

Baird, L. L. (1983). *Research report: Review of problem solving skills.* Princeton, NJ: Educational Testing Service.

Baron, J. (1981). Reflective thinking as a goal of education. *Intelligence, 5,* 291-309.

Barron, F. (1972). *Artists in the making.* New York: Seminar Press.

Barron, F. & Welsh, G. S. (1952). Artistic perception as a possible factor in personality style: Its measurement by a figure preference test. *Journal of Psychology, 33,* 199-203.

Basadur, M. S. (1981). Research in creative problem solving training in business and industry. *Creativity Week IV Proceedings.* Greensboro, NC: Center for Creative Leadership, 40-59.

Basadur, M. S. & Thompson, R. (1986). Usefulness of the ideation principle of extended effort in real world professional and managerial creative problem solving. *Journal of Creative Behavior, 20,* 23-34.

Bennis, W. G., Benne, K. D., Chin, R. & Corey, K. E. (1976). *The planning of change.* NY: Holt, Rinehart & Winston.

Berkenkotter, C. (1980). Writing and problem solving. In T. Fulwiler & A. Young (Eds.), *Language connections: Writing and reading across the curriculum* (pp. 33-44). Urbana, IL: National Council of Teachers of English.

Besemer, S. P. & O'Quin, K. (1986). Analyzing creative products: Refinement and test of a judging instrument. *Journal of Creative Behavior, 20,* 115-126.

Besemer, S. P. & Treffinger, D. J. (1981). Analysis of creative products: Review and synthesis. *Journal of Creative Behavior, 15,* 158-178.

Biondi, A. M. & Parnes, S. J. (1976). *Assessing creative growth.* Buffalo, NY: Creative Education Foundation.

Bloomberg, M. (Ed.). (1973). *Creativity: Theory and research.* New Haven, CT: College and University Press.

Brandt, A. (1982, September). Teaching kids to think. *Ladies Home Journal,* pp. 104-106.

Briskman, L. (1980). Creative product and creative process in science and art. *Inquiry, 23,* 83-106.

Brooks, M. (1984). A constructivist approach to staff development. *Educational Leadership, 42,* 23-28.

Buijs, J. (1984). *Innovatie en interventie.* Uitgeverij, Norway: Kluwer.

Bullough, V., Bullough, B. & Mauro, M. (1981). History and creativity: Research problems and some possible solutions. *Journal of Creative Behavior, 15,* 102-116.

Carpenter, T. P., Lindquist, M. M., Mathews, W. & Silver, E. (1983, December). Results of the third NAEP mathematics assessment: Secondary school. *Mathematics Teacher,* 652-659.

Chipman, S. F., Segal, J. W. & Glaser, R. (Eds.). (1985). *Thinking and learning skills: Research and open questions* (Volume 2). Hillsdale, NJ: Lawrence Erlbaum Associates.

Combs, A. W. (1981). What the future demands of education. *Phi Delta Kappan, 62,* 369-372.

Costa, A. L. (1984). Mediating the metacognitive. *Educational Leadership, 42,* 57-62.

Cox, C. M. (1926). *Genetic studies of genius.* Stanford: Stanford University Press.

Crawford, C. M. & Hustad, T. P. (1986). From the editors. *The Journal of Product Innovation Management, 3,* 2-4.

Dansereau, D. F. (1985). Learning strategy research. In J. W. Segal, S. F. Chipman & R. Glaser (Eds.), *Thinking and learning skills: Relating instruction to research* (Vol. 1, pp. 209-239). Hillsdale, NJ: Lawrence Erlbaum Associates.

Dellas, M. & Gaier, E. L. (1970). Identification of creativity: The individual. *Psychological Bulletin, 73,* 55-73.

Derry, S. J. & Murphy, D. A. (1986). Designing systems that train learning ability: From theory to practice. *Review of Educational Research, 56,* 1-39.

Dewey, J. (1933). *How we think: A restatement of the relation of reflective thinking to the educative process.* Lexington, MA: Heath & Co.

Dillon, J. T. (1984). Research on questioning and discussion. *Educational Leadership, 42,* 50-56.

Dixon, B. (1986, April). Dangerous thoughts: How we think and feel can make us sick. *Science,* pp. 63-66.

Drucker, P. E. (1985). *Innovation and entrepreneurship: Practice and principles.* New York: Harper & Row.

Ekvall, G. (1983). *Climate, structure and innovativeness of organizations: A theoretical framework and an experiment.* The Swedish Council for Management and Work Life Issues. Stockholm, Sweden: FA Radet.

Ekvall, G. & Parnes, S. J. (1984). *Creative problem solving methods in product development: A second experiment.* The Swedish Council for Management and Work Life Issues. Stockholm, Sweden: FA Radet.

Elbow, P. (1983). Teaching thinking by teaching writing. *Change, 15,* 37-40.

Feldhusen, J. F. & Treffinger, D. J. (1985). *Creative thinking and problem solving in gifted education - Third edition.* Dubuque, IA: Kendall/Hunt.

Fleming, M. L. & Hutton, D. W. (Eds.). (1983). *Mental imagery and learning.* Englewood Cliffs, NJ: Educational Technology Publications.

Fiedler, F. E., Chemers, M. M. & Mahar, L. (1976). *Improving leadership effectiveness: The leader match concept.* New York: John Wiley & Sons.

Frank, M. (Ed.). (1984). *A child's brain: The impact of advanced research on cognitive and social behaviors.* New York: The Haworth Press.

Frey, B. R. & Noller, R. B. (1986). Mentoring: A promise for the future. *Journal of Creative Behavior, 20,* 49-51.

Frey, P. (1986, May, 3-5). Opening the door to creativity. *Moonbeams.*

Fromm, E. (1959). The creative attitude. In: H. H. Anderson (Ed.), *Creativity and its cultivation* (pp. 44-54). New York: Harper & Brothers.

Gall, M. (1984). Synthesis of research on teacher's questioning. *Educational Leadership, 42,* 40-47.

Galton, F. (1869). *Hereditary genius.* London: Macmillan.

Galton, F. (1911). *Inquiries into human faculty and its development.* New York: Dutton.

Gardner, H. (1983). *Frames of mind: The theory of multiple intelligences.* New York: Basic Books, 1983.

Getzels, J. W. & Csikszentmihalyi, M. (1976). *The creative vision: A longitudinal study of problem finding in art.* New York: Wiley.

Getzels, J. W. & Jackson, P. W. (1962). *Creativity and intelligence: Explorations with gifted students.* New York: Wiley.

Gibney, T. C. & Meiring, S. P. (1983, March). Problem solving: A success story. *School Science and Mathematics, 83 (3),* 194-203.

Glatthorn, A. A. (1982). *A guide for developing an English curriculum for the eighties.* Urbana, IL: National Council of Teachers of English.

Goertzel, M. G., Goertzel, V. & Goertzel, T. G. (1978). *300 eminent personalities.* San Francisco, CA: Jossey-Bass.

Goodlad, J. I. (1983). A study of schooling: Some findings and hypotheses. *Phi Delta Kappan, 64,* 465-470.

Goor, A. & Rapaport, T. (1977). Enhancing creativity in an informal educational framework. *Journal of Educational Psychology, 69,* 636-643.

Gould, S. J. (1981). *The mismeasure of man.* New York: W. W. Norton.

Gowan, J. C. (1972). *Development of the creative individual.* San Diego, CA: Robert R. Knapp.

Gowan, J. C., Demos, G. D. & Torrance, E. P. (1967). *Creativity: Its educational implications.* New York: Wiley.

Gowan, J. C., Khatena, J. & Torrance, E. P. (Eds.). (1979). *Educating the ablest: A book of readings on the education of gifted children.* New York: Peacock Publishers, Inc.

Gowan, J. C., Khatena, J. & Torrance, E. P. (1981). *Creativity: Its educational implications.* Dubuque, IA: Kendall/Hunt.

Grennon, J. (1984). Making sense of student thinking. *Educational Leadership, 43,* 11-16.

Grøholt, P. (1985). *Bevisst Ledelse.* Oslo, Norway: Bedriftsøkonomens Foriag.

Gruber, H. E. (1981). *Darwin on man: A psychological study of scientific creativity.* Chicago: The University of Chicago Press.

Gryskiewicz, S. S. (1980). Targeted innovation: A situational approach. *Creativity Week Proceedings* (pp. 1-27). Greensboro, NC: Center for Creative Leadership.

Guilford, J. P. (1950). Creativity. *American Psychologist, 5,* 444-454.

Guilford, J. P. (1967a). *The nature of human intelligence.* New York: McGraw-Hill.

Guilford, J. P. (1967b). Creativity: Yesterday, today and tomorrow. *Journal of Creative Behavior, 1,* 3-14.

Guilford, J. P. (1977). *Way beyond the IQ.* Buffalo, NY: Bearly Limited.

Guilford, J. P. (1980). Foreword. In M. K. Raina (Ed.), *Creativity research: International perspective* (pp. v - viii). New Delhi, India: National Council of Educational Research and Training.

Hadamard, J. (1954). *The psychology of invention in the mathematical field.* New York: Dover.

Hallman, R. J. (1981). The necessary and sufficient conditions of creativity. In J. C. Gowan, J. Khatena, & E. P. Torrance (Eds.), *Creativity: Its educational implications* (pp. 19-30). Dubuque, IA: Kendall/Hunt.

Hausman, C. S. (1984). *A discourse on novelty and creation.* Albany, NY: State University of New York Press.

Hayes, J. R. (1978). *Cognitive psychology: Thinking and creating.* Homewood, IL: The Dorsey Press.

Hellesnes, T., Raaheim, K. & Bengtsson, G. (1982). Attempts to predict intelligent behavior: The relative importance of divergent and convergent production. *Scandinavian Journal of Psychology, 23,* 263-266.

Helson, R. & Crutchfield, R. S. (1970). Creative types in mathematics. *Journal of Personality, 38,* 177-197.

Heppner, P. P. (1978). A review of the problem solving literature and its relationship to the counseling process. *Journal of Counseling Psychology, 25,* 366-375.

Heppner, P. P., Neal, G. W. & Larson, L. M. (1984, May). Problem solving training as prevention with college students. *The Personnel and Guidance Journal,* 514-519.

Hersey, P. & Blanchard, K. (1982). *Management of organizational behavior: Utilizing human resources.* Englewood Cliffs, NJ: Prentice-Hall.

Hilgard, E. R. (1964). Creativity and problem solving. In H. H. Anderson (Ed.), *Creativity and its cultivation* (pp. 162-180). New York: Harper & Brothers.

Horowitz, F. D. & O'Brien, M. (Eds.). (1985). *The gifted and talented: Developmental perspectives.* Washington, DC: American Psychological Association.

Hullfish, H. G. & Smith, P. G. (1961). *Reflective thinking: The method of education.* New York: Dodd & Mead.

Isaksen, S. G. (1983a). A curriculum planning schema for the facilitation of creative thinking and problem solving skills. Unpublished doctoral dissertation. State University of New York at Buffalo.

Isaksen, S. G. (1983b). Toward a model for the facilitation of creative problem solving. *Journal of Creative Behavior, 17,* 18-31.

Isaksen, S. G. (1984). Implications of creativity for the middle school education. *Transescence: The Journal on Emerging Adolescent Education, 12,* 13-27.

Isaksen, S. G. (1986). Facilitating small group creativity. In S. S. Gryskiewicz & R. M. Burnside (Eds.), *Blueprint for innovation: Creativity Week VIII proceedings* (pp. 71-84). Greensboro, NC: Center for Creative Leadership.

Isaksen, S. G. (In press). Educational implications of creativity research: An updated rationale for creative learning. In G. Kaufmann & K. Grønhaug (Eds.), *Innovation: A cross-disciplinary perspective.* Oslo, Norway: Norwegian University Press.

Isaksen, S. G. & Parnes, S. J. (1985). Curriculum planning for creative thinking and problem solving. *Journal of Creative Behavior, 19,* 1-29.

Isaksen, S. G., Stein, M. I., Hills, D. A. & Gryskiewicz, S. S. (1984). A proposed model for the formulation of creativity research. *Journal of Creative Behavior, 18,* 67-75.

Isaksen, S. G. & Treffinger, D. J. (1985). *Creative problem solving: The basic course.* Buffalo, NY: Bearly Limited.

James, W. (1890). *The principles of psychology - Volume I.* New York: Henry Holt and Co.

Johansson, B. (1975). Creativity and creative problem-solving courses in United States industry. Special project funded by the Center for Creative Leadership, Greensboro, NC.

Johnson, D. W., Maruyama, G., Johnson, R., Nelson, D. & Skon, L. (1981). The effects of cooperative, competitive, and individualistic goal structures on achievement: A meta-analysis. *Psychological Bulletin, 89,* 47-62.

Judd, C. H. (1936). *Education as cultivation of the higher mental processes.* New York: MacMillan.

Kaplan, A. (1964). *The conduct of inquiry: Methodology for behavioral science.* San Francisco, CA: Chandler Publishing Co.

Kaufmann, G. (1980). *Imagery language and cognition.* Bergen, Norway: Universitetsforlaget.

Kendler, H. H. (1981). *Psychology: A science in conflict.* New York: Oxford University Press.

Khatena, J. (1982). Myth: Creativity is too difficult to measure. *Gifted Child Quarterly, 26,* 21-23.

Khatena, J. (1984). *Imagery & creative imagination.* Buffalo, NY: Bearly Limited.

Kilpatrick, W. H. (1918). *The project method: The use of the purposeful act in the educative process:* New York: Teacher's College Bulletin.

Kirton, M. J. (1976). Adaptors and innovators: A description and measure. *Journal of Applied Psychology, 61,* 622-629.

Kneller, G. F. (1965). *The art and science of creativity.* New York: Holt, Rinehart and Winston, Inc.

Krulik, S. & Rudnick, J. A. (1982, February). Teaching problem solving to preservice teachers. *Arithmetic Teacher,* 42-45.

Kuhn, T. S. (1970). *The structure of scientific revolutions.* Chicago: The University of Chicago Press.

Lamb, M. L. (Ed.). (1981). *Creativity and method: Essays in honor of Bernard Lonergan.* Milwaukee, WI: Marquette University Press.

Langer, J. A. (1982). Reading, thinking, writing and teaching. *Language Arts, 59,* 336-341.

Larkin, J. H. (1980). Teaching problem solving in physics: The psychological laboratory and the practical classroom. In D. I. Tuma & F. Reif (Eds.), *Problem solving and education: Issues in teaching and research* (pp. 111-126). Hillsdale, NJ: Lawrence Erlbaum Associates.

Lawrence, P. R. & Dyer, D. (1983). *Renewing American industry: Organizing for efficiency and innovation.* New York: The Free Press.

Lipman, M., Sharp, A. M. & Oscanyan, F. S. (1980). *Philosophy in the classroom.* Philadelphia, PA: Temple University Press.

Lundstedt, S. B. & Colglazier, E. W. (1982). *Managing innovation.* New York: Pergamon Press.

MacKinnon, D. W. (1961). The personality correlates of creativity: A study of American architects. In G. S. Nelson (Ed.), *Proceedings of the XIV International Congress of Applied Psychology* (pp. 11-39). Copenhagen: Munksgaard.

MacKinnon, D. W. (1975). IPAR's contribution to the conceptualization and study of creativity. In I. A. Taylor & J. W. Getzels (Eds.), *Perspectives in creativity* (pp. 60-89). Chicago: Aldine.

MacKinnon, D. W. (1978). *In search of human effectiveness: Identifying and developing creativity.* Buffalo, NY: Bearly Limited.

Mansfield, R. S. & Busse, T. V. (1981). *The psychology of creativity and discovery: Scientists and their work.* Chicago: Nelson-Hall.

Mansfield, R. S., Busse, T. V. & Krepelka, E. J. (1978). The effectiveness of creativity training. *Review of Educational Research, 48,* 517-536.

Martin, D. S. (1984). Infusing cognitive strategies into teacher preparation programs. *Educational Leadership, 42,* 68-72.

Maslow, A. (1959). Creativity in self-actualizing people. In H. H. Anderson (Ed.), *Creativity and its cultivation* (pp. 83-95). New York: Harper & Brothers.

Meichenbaum, D. (1980). A cognitive-behavioral perspective on intelligence. *Intelligence, 4,* 271-283.

Miles, M. B. (1964). *Innovation in education.* New York: Teachers College Columbia University.

Murray, H. A. et al. (1938). *Explorations in personality.* New York: Oxford University Press.

Myers, I. B. & Myers, P. B. (1980). *Gifts differing.* Palo Alto, CA: Consulting Psychologists Press.

National Assessment of Educational Progress. (1981). *Reading, thinking and writing.* Denver, CO: NAEP.

National Council of Teachers of Mathematics. (1980). *An agenda for action: Recommendations for school mathematics of the 1980's.* Reston, VA: The Council.

Necka, E. (1984). The effectiveness of synectics and brainstorming as conditioned by socio-emotional climate and type of problem. *Polish Psychological Bulletin, 19,* 41-50.

Nickerson, R. S., Perkins, D. N. & Smith, E. E. (1985). *The teaching of thinking.* Hillsdale, NJ: Lawrence Erlbaum Associates.

Noller, R. B. & Frey, B. R. (1983). *Mentoring: An annotated bibliography.* Buffalo, NY: Bearly Limited.

Olson, C. B. (1984). Fostering critical thinking skills through writing. *Educational Leadership, 42,* 28-39.

Osborn, A. F. (1953). *Applied imagination.* New York: Scribners.

Onda, A. (1986). Trends in creativity research in Japan: History and present status. *Journal of Creative Behavior, 20,* 134-140.

Parnes, S. J. (1985). *A facilitating style of leadership.* Buffalo, NY: Bearly Limited.

Parnes, S. J. & Harding, H. (1962). *A sourcebook for creative thinking.* New York: Scribners.

Parnes, S. J. & Noller, R. B. (1972). Applied creativity: The creative studies project - Part II: Results of the two-year program. *Journal of Creative Behavior, 6,* 164-186.

Parnes, S. J., Noller, R. B. & Biondi, A. M. (1977). *Guide to creative action.* New York: Scribners.

Patrick, C. (1935). Creative thought in poets. *Archives of Psychology, 26,* 1-74.

Patrick, C. (1937). Creative thought in artists. *Journal of Psychology, 4,* 35-73.

Pearlman, C. (1983). Teachers as an informational resource in identifying and rating student creativity. *Education, 103,* 215-222.

Perkins, D. N. (1981). *The mind's best work.* Cambridge, MA: Harvard University Press.

Peters, T. & Austin, N. (1985). *A passion for excellence: The leadership difference.* New York: Random House.

Raaheim, K. (1984). *Why intelligence is not enough.* Bergen, Norway: Sigma Forlag.

Raina, M. K. (1980). *Creativity research: International perspective.* New Delhi, India: National Council of Educational Research and Training.

Reese, H. W., Parnes, S. J., Treffinger, D. J. & Kaltsounis, G. (1976). Effects of a creative studies program on structure-of-intellect factors. *Journal of Educational Psychology, 68,* 401-410.

Renzulli, J. (1978). What makes giftedness. *Phi Delta Kappan, 60,* 180-251.

Renzulli, J. (Ed.). (1986). *Systems and models for developing programs for the gifted and talented.* Mansfield Center, CT: Creative Learning Press.

Rhodes, M. (1961). An analysis of creativity. *Phi Delta Kappan, 42,* 305-310.

Ribot, T. (1900). The nature of creative imagination. *International Quarterly, 1,* 648-675, and *2,* 1-25.

Rickards, T. (1985). *Stimulating innovation: A systems approach.* London, Frances Pinter.

Roe, A. (1951). A psychological study of eminent physical scientists. *Genetic Psychology Monograph, 43,* 121-239.

Roe, A. (1953). A psychological study of eminent psychologists and anthropologists and a comparison with biological and physical scientists. *Psychological Monographs, 67,* 1-55.

Rogers, C. (1959). Toward a theory of creativity. In H. H. Anderson (Ed.), *Creativity and its cultivation* (pp. 69-82). New York: Harper & Brothers.

Rogers, E. M. (1983). *Diffusion of innovations (3rd Ed.).* New York: The Free Press.

Rose, L. H. & Lin, H. T. (1984). A meta-analysis of long-term creativity training programs. *Journal of Creative Behavior, 18,* 11-22.

Rossman, J. (1931). *The psychology of the inventor: A study of the patentee.* Washington, DC: The Inventors Publishing Co.

Rothberg, R. R. (Ed.). (1981). *Corporate strategy and product innovation.* New York: The Free Press.

Rothenberg, A. & Hausman, C. R. (1976). *The creativity question.* Durham, NC: Duke University Press.

Rubinstein, M. F. (1975). *Patterns of problem solving.* Englewood Cliffs, NJ: Prentice-Hall.

Rugg, H. & Shumaker, A. (1928). *The child-centered school.* New York: World Book.

Samuels, M. & Samuels, N. (1975). *Seeing with the mind's eye: The history, techniques and uses of visualization.* New York: Random House.

Sanford, N. (1963). Personality: Its place in psychology. In S. Koch (Ed.), *Psychology: A study of science - Volume 5: The process areas, the person, and some applied fields: Their place in psychology and in science* (pp. 488-592). New York: McGraw-Hill.

Schoenfeld, A. H. (1982). Measures of problem solving performance and of problem solving instruction. *Journal for Research in Mathematics Education, 13,* 31-49.

Schoenfeld, A. H. & Herrmann, D. J. (1982). Problem perception and knowledge structure in expert and novice mathematical problem solvers. *Journal of Experimental Psychology: Learning, Memory and Cognition, 8,* 484-494.

Sheikh, A. A. (Ed.). (1983). *Imagery: Current theory, research, and application.* New York: Wiley & Sons.

Simonton, D. K. (1984). *Genius, creativity and leadership: Historiometric inquiries.* Cambridge, MA: Harvard University Press.

Simonton, D. K. (1986). Biographical typicality, eminence and achievement styles. *Journal of Creative Behavior, 20,* 14-22.

Smeekes, H. (1986). The innovation program. *Issues & Observations, 6,* 9-10.

Smith, P. (Ed.). (1959). *Creativity: An examination of the creative process.* New York: Hastings House.

Spearman, C. E. (1931). *The creative mind.* New York: Appleton-Century.

Steffire, V. (1985). Organizational obstacles to innovation: A formulation of the problem. *Journal of Product Innovation Management, 2,* 3-11.

Stein, M. I. (1974). *Stimulating creativity: Individual procedures - Volume I.* New York: Academic Press.

Stein, M. I. (1975). *Stimulating creativity: Group procedures - Volume II.* New York: Academic Press.

Stein, M. I. (1986). *Gifted, talented and creative young people: A guide to theory, teaching and research.* New York: Garland.

Sternberg, R. J. (1985). Instrumental and componential approaches to the nature and training of intelligence. In S. F. Chipman, J. W. Segal & R. Glaser (Eds.), *Thinking and learning skills: Volume 2 - Research and open questions* (pp. 215-243). Hillsdale, NJ: Lawrence Erlbaum Associates.

Tannenbaum, A. J. (1983). *Gifted children: Psychological and educational perspectives.* New York: Macmillan.

Taylor, C. W. (Ed.). (1964a). *Creativity: Progress and potential.* New York: McGraw-Hill.

Taylor, C. W. (Ed.) (1964b). *Widening horizons in creativity.* New York: Wiley.

Taylor, C. W. & Barron, F. (Eds.). (1963). *Scientific creativity: Its recognition and development.* New York: Wiley & Sons.

Taylor, C. W. & Ellison, R. L. (1975). Moving toward working models in creativity: Utah creativity experiences and insights. In I. A. Taylor & J. W. Getzels (Eds.), *Perspectives in creativity* (pp. 191-223). Chicago, IL: Aldine Publishing Co.

Taylor, C. W., Smith, W. R. & Ghiselin, B. (1963). The creative and other contributions of one sample of research scientists. In C. W. Taylor & F. Barron (Eds.), *Scientific creativity: Its recognition and development* (pp. 53-76). New York: Wiley.

Taylor, I. A. (1959). The nature of the creative process. In P. Smith (Ed.), *Creativity: An examination of the creative process* (pp. 51-82). New York: Hastings House.

Taylor, I. A. & Getzels, J. W. (Eds.). (1975). *Perspectives in creativity.* Chicago, IL: Aldine.

Taylor, I. A. & Sandler, B. J. (1972). Use of a creative product inventory for evaluating products of chemists. *Proceedings of the 80th Annual Convention of the American Psychological Association, 7,* 311-312.

Terman, L. M. (1925). *Genetic studies of genius: Mental and physical traits of a thousand gifted children.* Palo Alto, CA: Stanford University Press.

Terman, L. M. (1954). The discovery and encouragement of exceptional talent. *American Psychologist, 9,* 221-230.

Toepfer, C. F. (1982). Curriculum design and neuropsychological development. *Journal of Research and Development in Education, 15,* 1-11.

Torrance, E. P. (1962). *Guiding creative talent.* Englewood Cliffs, NJ: Prentice-Hall.

Torrance, E. P. (1972). Can we teach children to think creatively? *Journal of Creative Behavior, 6,* 114-143.

Torrance, E. P. (1974). *Torrance tests of creative thinking: Norms and technical manual.* Lexington, MA: Personnel Press/Ginn-Xerox.

Torrance, E. P. (1975). Creativity research in education: Still alive. In I. A. Taylor & J. W. Getzels (Eds.), *Perspectives in creativity* (pp. 278-296). Chicago, IL: Aldine Publishers.

Torrance, E. P. (1979). *Search for satori and creativity.* Buffalo, NY: Bearly Limited.

Torrance, E. P. (1980). Georgia studies of creative behavior: A brief summary of activities and results. In M. K. Raina (Ed.), *Creativity research: International perspective* (pp. 253-271). New Delhi, India: National Council of Research and Training.

Torrance, E. P. (1981). Creative teaching makes a difference. In J. C. Gowan, J. Khatena, & E. P. Torrance (Eds.), *Creativity: Its educational implications* (pp. 99-108). Dubuque, IA: Kendall/Hunt.

Torrance, E. P. (1984a). International contributions to the study of creativity. In A. B. Crabbe, et al. (Eds.), *New directions in creativity research* (pp. 19-24). Ventura, CA: Ventura County Superintendent of Schools Office.

Torrance, E. P. (1984b). *Mentor relationships: How they aid creative achievement, endure, change, and die.* Buffalo, NY: Bearly Limited.

Torrance, E. P. (1986). Teaching creative and gifted learners. In M. C. Wittrock (Ed.), *Handbook of research on teaching* (Third ed.) (pp. 630-647). New York: MacMillan.

Torrance, E. P. & Myers, R. E. (1970). *Creative learning and teaching.* New York: Dodd-Mead.

Toynbee, A. (1964). Is America neglecting her creative minority? In C. W. Taylor (Ed.), *Widening horizons in creativity* (pp. 3-9). New York: Wiley.

Treffinger, D. J. (1980). *Encouraging creative learning for the gifted and talented.* Ventura, CA: Ventura County Schools/LTI.

Treffinger, D. J. (1984). Critical and creative thinking. Mutually important components of effective problem solving. Unpublished paper prepared as a part of a series of papers on Gifted Education for the Language and Learning Improvement Branch of the Division on Instruction of the Maryland State Department of Education.

Treffinger, D. J. (1986a). *Blending gifted education with the total school program - Second edition.* East Aurora, NY: D.O.K. Publishers.

Treffinger, D. J. (1986b). Research on creativity. *Gifted Child Quarterly, 30,* 15-19.

Treffinger, D. J., Isaksen, S. G. & Firestien, R. L. (1982). *The handbook of creative learning.* Honeoye, NY: Center for Creative Learning.

Treffinger, D. J., Isaksen, S. G. & Firestien, R. L. (1983). Theoretical perspectives of creative learning and its facilitation: An overview. *Journal of Creative Behavior, 17,* 9-17.

Treffinger, D. J. & Renzulli, J. S. (1986). Giftedness as potential for creative productivity: Transcending IQ scores. *Roeper Review, 8,* 150-154.

VanGundy, A. B. (1981). *Techniques of structured problem solving.* New York: Van Nostrand Reinhold Co.

VanGundy, A. B. (1984). *Managing group creativity: A modular approach to problem solving.* New York: American Management Association.

Vedin, B. (1980). *Current innovation: Policy, management and research options.* Stockholm, Sweden: Almqvist & Wiksell International.

Wallach, M. A. (1985). Creativity testing and giftedness. In F. D. Horowitz & M. O'Brien (Eds.), *The gifted and talented: Developmental perspectives* (pp. 99-123). Washington, DC: American Psychological Association.

Wallach, M. A. & Kogan, N. (1965). *Modes of thinking in young children: A study of the creativity-intelligence distinction.* New York: Holt, Rinehart & Winston, Inc.

Wallach, M. A. & Wing, C. W. (1969). *The talented student: A validation of the creativity-intelligence distinction.* New York: Holt, Rinehart & Winston, Inc.

Wallas, G. (1926). *The art of thought.* New York: Franklin Watts.

Ward, W. C. & Cox, P. W. (1974). A field study of nonverbal creativity. *Journal of Personality, 42,* 202-219.

Welsch, P. K. (1980). The nurturance of creative behavior in educational environments: A comprehensive curriculum approach. Unpublished doctoral dissertation, University of Michigan.

Welsh, G. S. (1973). Perspectives in the study of creativity. *Journal of Creative Behavior, 7,* 231-246.

Wertheimer, M. (1945). *Productive thinking.* New York: Harper & Brothers.

Whitman, N. (1983, February, 9-13). Teaching problem solving and creativity in college courses. *AAHE Bulletin: Research Currents.*

Willerman, J. R. (1979). *The psychology of individual and group differences.* San Francisco, CA: W. H. Freeman & Co.

Williams, F. E. (1980). *Creativity assessment packet.* Buffalo, NY: DOK Publishers.

Wittmer, J. & Myrick, R. D. (1974). *Facilitative teaching: Theory and practice.* Pacific Palisades, CA: Goodyear Publishing.

Worsham, A. W. & Austin, G. R. (1983). Effects of teaching thinking skills on SAT scores. *Educational Leadership,* November, 50-57.

The Selections and their Contributors

The selections within this volume have been chosen based on their matching the broad purposes of the book. Each contributor has recognized expertise within a specific area of inquiry and the ability to recognize future issues, questions and needed research along the emerging boundaries of creativity research. Each selection's content is briefly introduced along with a short description of the contributor. The word "selection" is being used instead of chapter because some selections may contain numerous chapters or articles. Each selection provides an overview and summarizes the historical developments along a particular line of inquiry. Each selection also includes some current updating and writing to identify issues and challenges for future research within that particular area of interest.

Introduction. **"An Orientation to the Frontiers of Creativity Research."** The introduction of this book serves to locate the nineteen selections within the broad field of creativity research. A rationale for studying creativity is provided with historical and definitional background information to assist the reader in choosing appropriate selections for study.

Dr. Isaksen is the editor of this volume and currently serves as the Director for the Center for Studies in Creativity at the State University College at Buffalo. He was an experimental subject in the Creative Studies Project conducted during 1970-1972, earned one of the first Master of Science degrees in Creative Studies offered by the Center, and now serves as a graduate faculty member and administrator for the Center.

Selection one. **"Creativity Research: Past, Present and Future."** This selection contains three separate writings by Dr. J. P. Guilford. The first is a reprint of the text of the seminal 1950 presidential speech to the American Psychological Association. This work is frequently identified as the "cornerstone" for those interested in creativity research. The second part of the selection is a reprint of an examination of twenty-five years of work done since the 1950 address. The final part is a newly-written reflective view on the current state of affairs with an emphasis on new views and needs for the field.

Dr. Guilford is a pioneer in the field of creativity research. He is a Professor Emeritus from the Department of Psychology at the University of Southern California-Los Angeles and past president of the American Psychological Association. He is the author of many articles and books including: *Psychometric methods* (McGraw-Hill, 1936), *Fundamental statistics in psychology and education* (McGraw-Hill, 1956), *The nature of human intelligence* (McGraw-Hill, 1967), *Intelligence, creativity and their educational implications* (Knapp, 1968), and *Way beyond the IQ* (Bearly Limited, 1977). Dr. Guilford serves as a member of the Board of Trustees of the Creative Education Foundation.

Selection two. **"Genius: The Lessons of Historiometry."** This selection was originally prepared and presented at the Frontiers in Creativity Research Symposium cosponsored by the Center for Studies in Creativity and the Creative Education Foundation. Dr. Dean K. Simonton made the presentation during the Thirtieth Annual Creative Problem Solving Institute (1984) at the State University College at Buffalo. The selection presents information to better understand the foundations of genius.

Dr. Simonton has had access to the Cox data and has pursued the historiometric research approach. He is a professor in the Department of Psychology at the University of California, Davis. He has written extensively in the area of genius and is also known for his work on the American Presidents. One of his recent publications is the book entitled *Genius, creativity and leadership* (Harvard University Press, 1984).

Selection three. **"Creativity, Intelligence, and Problem Finding: Retrospect and Prospect."** This newly-written selection is a synthesis of more than twenty-five years of research and inquiry into the nature of creativity. Although originally noted for his work on studying the creativity-intelligence distinction, Dr. Getzels is currently concerned with the concept of problem finding. This selection traces these developments and identifies several general domains for further research.

Dr. Jacob W. Getzels is the R. Wendell Harrison Distinguished Service Professor at the University of Chicago's Department of Education. He has been a pioneer in the field of creativity research by providing insight into the relationship between creativity and intelligence and pointing to important developing lines of inquiry. His work has been widely published and cited. Along with Csikszentmihalyi, he has written *The creative vision: A longitudinal study of problem finding in art* (Wiley, 1976) and *Creativity and problem finding in art* (Praeger, in press).

Selection four. **"Research on Creativity Assessment."** This selection provides a review of creativity assessment research including: the purposes of creativity assessment; issues of theory and definition, validity, reliability and usability; and areas of needed and continuing research.

Dr. Treffinger is the Director of the Center for Creative Learning at Honeoye, New York and is also a Professor of Creative Studies at the Center for Studies in Creativity at the State University College at Buffalo. He has had wide-ranging experience within the field of educational psychology including holding the chair of the Educational Psychology Department at Purdue University. Dr. Treffinger has published hundreds of articles and books relating to creativity, problem solving and giftedness. He's a Fellow of the American Psychological Association and has been active in the AERA.

Selection five. **"Some Critical Issues for Future Research in Creativity."** This selection is reprinted from Dr. MacKinnon's book *In search of human effectiveness: Identifying and developing creativity* (Bearly Limited, 1978). The original intent of the chapter was to highlight some of the key areas within which future creativity research should focus. Although the listing he provides is not comprehensive, Dr. MacKinnon does outline a rather large agenda for areas needing attention for the creativity researcher.

Dr. Donald W. MacKinnon was the founding director of the Institute for Personality Assessment and Research at the University of California-Berkeley. He had contributed to the creativity research literature since its very beginnings and had been identified as a "Senior Statesman" within the field of creativity research.

Selection six. **"A High-Tech High-Touch Concept of Creativity—with its Complexity made Simple for Wide Adoptability."** This selection provides a newly-written perspective on the nine University of Utah sponsored research conferences on creativity. The historical research supporting multiple talents and some methods and procedures for teaching for multiple talents are shared.

Dr. Calvin W. Taylor is a professor of Psychology at the University of Utah. He has hosted the important Utah Creativity Conferences and had edited a series of the proceedings and reports from these conferences. He is continuing his work on the development of multiple talents and is active in many organizations related to this purpose.

Selection seven. **"The Creative Studies Project."** This selection is newly written for this publication. Dr. Parnes provides a comprehensive synthesis of earlier publications of research surrounding the efforts made by the Creative Education Foundation and the Center for Studies in Creativity at the State University College at Buffalo to provide a program to impact creativity. The two-year program he and his colleagues developed and tested is examined for its ability to make a significant difference in students' lives.

Dr. Parnes is the Chairman of the Board of the Creative Education Foundation and was the founding director of the Center for Studies in Creativity at the State University College at Buffalo. He was the first recipient of the Alex F. Osborn Visiting Professorship in Creative Studies and continues to serve as a Professor Emeritus of Creative Studies. He has written extensively in the field of creativity and is currently working on a variety of international research projects.

Selection eight. **"Teaching for Creativity."** This selection is made up of two parts. The first part is a reprint of an earlier publication in *The Journal of Creative Behavior* entitled "Can we teach for Creativity?" Part two is entitled "Recent trends in teaching children and adults to think creatively" and has been written expressly for this volume. Part two re-answers the question of the teachability of creativity in light of fourteen years of research undertaken since the publication of the first article in 1972. Part two provides extensive support for the earlier findings reported by Dr. Torrance.

Dr. E. Paul Torrance began his extensive creativity research first as the Director of the Bureau of Educational Research at the University of Minnesota and later as the University of Georgia's Alumni Foundation Distinguished Professor in the Department of Educational Psychology. He is the author of the *Torrance tests of creative thinking,* and more than 1000 other publications. Dr. Torrance serves on the Board of Trustees of the Creative Education Foundation.

Selection nine. **"An Analysis of Creativity."** This selection is reprinted from the *Phi Delta Kappan* as it was originally published in 1961. The selection provides information on the four classic categories of the creativity literature. These include the creative: personality, process, press and product. This selection provides the reader a glimpse of the first period of explicit analysis on the area of creativity research and, thus, acts as a reference point for those interested in the "basics" of creativity research.

Dr. Rhodes was an Assistant Professor of Education at the University of Arizona when he wrote the selection. His Ph.D. dissertation was on "The dynamics of creativity."

Selection ten. **"The Motivation to be Creative."** This selection was originally presented at the Frontiers in Creativity Research Symposium conducted during 1984. It provides a restatement of the intrinsic motivation hypothesis as well as some examples of the empirical investigation surrounding this approach. This line of research is based on a comprehensive theory of creativity placing motivation as an important and perhaps "deciding" factor in predicting creativity.

Dr. Amabile is an Associate Professor of Psychology at Brandeis University and a Research Associate at the Center for Creative Leadership in Greensboro, North Carolina. Her work on the influence of social environments on creativity has been widely published. This research has led to the development of a theoretical approach to creativity and to methods for stimulating innovation in business, government and education. Her book on *The social psychology of creativity* (Springer-Verlag, 1983) provides additional information regarding the research approach described in this selection. Dr. Amabile serves on the International Advisory Board of the Center for Studies in Creativity.

Selection eleven. **"Some Needed Research on the Cognitive Limits of Creativity."** This selection provides information regarding contemporary issues from both psychology and neurology and their possible relationships to the concept of creativity. Specific information is identified regarding brain growth periodization and readiness issues for creative thinking. Key questions for further inquiry are shared throughout the selection.

Dr. Conrad F. Toepfer is an Associate Professor of Learning and Instruction at the State University of New York at Buffalo. He has been involved in brain growth periodization research along with Dr. Epstein of Brandeis University and has been especially active in the area of Middle Grades education. Dr. Toepfer is the editor of *Transescence: The Journal on Emerging Adolescent Education* and serves on the International Advisory Board of the Center for Studies in Creativity.

Selection twelve. **"Adaptors and Innovators: Cognitive Style and Personality."** This selection provides information on a relatively new theory which separates the traditional emphasis on level or quality of creativity and identifies a second dimension of style or type of creativity. This work has helped to clarify the literature and the measure of this dimension holds much promise for future creativity research which may focus the application of existing techniques for certain personality types. This approach to examining the creative personality may be able to assist researchers in answering the criterion questions of creativity as well as recognizing the natural bias to consider only one style in searching for the highly creative individual or h/her products.

Michael Kirton is currently the Director of the Occupational Research Center at the Hatfield Polytechnic in Hertfordshire, England. His early work involved studying management initiatives and was conducted while serving in a variety of research positions in the United Kingdom. He serves on the International Advisory Board of the Center for Studies in Creativity. His instrument (KAI) is currently being widely applied and tested.

Selection thirteen. **"Predictable Creativity."** This selection provides a review of an earlier research study in which cognitive style was combined with divergent thinking techniques in order to provide information on what type of outcome to expect from which techniques. The research was conducted at the University of London by Dr. Stanley Gryskiewicz and currently serves as a model for management training at the Center for Creative Leadership.

Dr. Gryskiewicz is the Director of the Creativity Development Division of the Center for Creative Leadership in Greensboro, North Carolina. He has worked at the Center since 1970 and has conducted applied research into how creativity fits into organizations. He has published his work and it has received considerable attention. Dr. Gryskiewicz serves on the International Advisory Board of the Center for Studies in Creativity.

Selection fourteen. **"Research Potential of Imagery and Creative Imagination."** This selection is focused on providing information on the broad area of creative imagination and imagery. Some information regarding how this area has been researched and measured is shared along with some methodologies for stimulating imagery.

Dr. Joe Khatena is the Chairman of the Department of Educational Psychology at Mississippi State University. His work on imagery is well published. The selection is based on his publication of *Imagery & creative imagination* (Bearly Limited, 1984).

Selection fifteen. **"Creative Product Analysis: Testing a Model by Developing a Judging Instrument."** This selection reports the development and testing surrounding an instrument designed to examine the "creativeness" of certain products. The selection provides information on the model and the instrument as well as a few of the early statistical analyses.

This selection has been written by Susan Besemer, currently the Director of Library Services at the State University College at Fredonia and a graduate of the Creative Studies Master's Program, and Dr. Karen O'Quin, an Assistant Professor of Psychology, at the State University College at Buffalo.

Selection sixteen. **"Organizational Creativity and Innovation."** This selection provides an extensive overview of the research surrounding organizational applications of creativity and innovation. The literature is synthesized and many key factors to consider are pointed out in this newly-written selection. Dr. VanGundy also provides a listing of needed research in this important area.

Dr. VanGundy is the Chairperson and Professor of the Human Relations Department of the University of Oklahoma. He has studied and written extensively within the field of creative problem solving and leadership. A few of his recent books include: *Techniques of structured problem solving* (Van Nostrand Reinhold, 1981); *Training your creative mind* (Prentice-Hall, 1982); and *Managing group creativity: A modular approach to problem solving* (AMACOM, 1984). Dr. VanGundy serves on the International Advisory Board of the Center for Studies in Creativity.

Selection seventeen. **"Philosophical Perspectives on the Study of Creativity."** This selection focuses upon how the discipline of philosophy has researched creativity. Rather than providing a comprehensive review of philosophical discourse on creativity, this selection is provided as an example of the type of inquiry the field of philosophy provides surrounding the subject of creativity.

Dr. Carl Hausman is a Professor of Philosophy at the University of Pennsylvania. He has written some major publications within the creativity research field including *The creativity question* (Duke University Press, 1976; along with Albert Rothenberg) and *A discourse on novelty* (SUNY Press, 1984).

Selection eighteen. **"Needed Research in Creativity for Business and Industrial Applications."** This selection was written for this publication and includes information regarding Dr. Basadur's personal perspectives and research into the effectiveness of training in business and industry.

In this selection Dr. Basadur provides the specifications for his training programs and how he developed and carried out the research to test the effectiveness of the programs. Aside from summarizing the research in this area, he also provides some suggestions for future research in this area.

Dr. Basadur is currently an Assistant Professor of Organizational Behavior within the Faculty of Business at McMaster University. He has authored a variety of articles and technical reports in the area of training in creative problem solving for business and industry. He serves on the faculty of the Annual Creative Problem Solving Institute and on the International Advisory Board of the Center for Studies in Creativity.

Selection nineteen. **"Creativity Research at the Crossroads: A 1985 Perspective."** This selection has been newly written to provide a commentary on the thirty-five year span of developments within the field of creativity research. Dr. Stein summarizes the major areas of development and points out some important suggestions for those who may consider researching creativity.

Dr. Morris I. Stein is eminently qualified to provide this critical commentary due to his active production and involvement in creativity research since its beginnings. Some of Dr. Stein's early work was done at the University of Chicago's Center for the Study of Creativity and Mental Health. He has written a number of important syntheses of findings for the field including the two-volume *Stimulating creativity* (Academic Press, 1974, 1975), and the recent *Gifted, talented and creative young people: A guide to theory, teaching and research* (Garland Publishing, 1986). He has also conducted extensive research and has published his work in many journals and reports. Dr. Stein is currently a Professor of Psychology at New York University.

1

Creativity Research:
Past, Present and Future

J. P. Guilford
University of Southern California

PART ONE: The 1950 Presidential Address to the American Psychological Association*

I discuss the subject of creativity with considerable hesitation, for it represents an area in which psychologists generally, whether they be angels or not, have feared to tread. It has been one of my long-standing ambitions, however, to undertake an investigation of creativity. Circumstances have just recently made possible the realization of that ambition. But the work has been started only within the past year. Consequently, if you are expecting answers based upon new empirical research you will be disappointed. What I can do at this time is to describe the plans for that research and to report the results of considerable thinking, including the hypotheses at which my students and I have arrived after a survey of the field and its problems. The research design, although not essentially new, should be of some interest. I will also point out some implications of the problems of creativity in vocational and educational practices.

Some Definitions and Questions

In its narrow sense, creativity refers to the abilities that are most characteristic of creative people. Creative abilities determine whether the individual has the power to exhibit creative behavior to a noteworthy degree. Whether or not the individual who has the requisite abilities will actually produce results of a creative nature will depend upon his motivational and temperamental traits. To the psychologist, the problem is as broad as the qualities that contribute significantly to creative productivity. In other words, the psychologist's problem is that of creative personality.

In defining personality, as well as other concepts preparatory to an investigation, definitions of an operational type are much to be preferred. I have often defined an individual's personality as his unique pattern of traits. A trait is any relatively enduring way in which persons differ from one another. The psychologist is particularly interested in those traits that are manifested in performance; in other words, in behavior traits. Behavior traits come under the broad categories of apptitudes, interests, attitudes, and temperamental qualities. By aptitude we ordinarily mean a person's readiness to learn to do certain types of things. There is no necessary implication in this statement as to the source of the degree of readiness. It could be brought about through hereditary determination or through environmental determination; usually, if not always, by an interaction of the two. By interest we usually mean the person's inclination or urge to engage in some type of activity. By attitude we mean his tendency to favor or not to favor (as shown objectively by approach-withdrawal behavior) some type of

* This material first appeared in the *American Psychologist, 5,* 444-454.

object or situation. Temperamental qualities describe a person's general emotional disposition: for example, his optimism, his moodiness, his self-confidence, or his nervousness.

Creative personality is then a matter of those patterns of traits that are characteristic of creative persons. A creative pattern is manifest in creative behavior, which includes such activities as inventing, designing, contriving, composing, and planning. People who exhibit these types of behavior to a marked degree are recognized as being creative.

There are certain aspects of creative genius that have aroused questions in the minds of those who have reflected much about the matter. Why is creative productivity a relatively infrequent phenomenon? Of all the people who have lived in historical times, it has been estimated that only about two in a million have become really distinguished (Gidding, 1907). Why do so many geniuses spring from parents who are themselves very far from distinguished? Why is there so little apparent correlation between education and creative productiveness? Why do we not produce a larger number of creative geniuses than we do, under supposedly enlightened, modern educational practices? These are serious questions for thought and investigation. The more immediate and more explorable problem is a double one: (1) How can we discover creative promise in our children and our youth? and (2) How can we promote the development of creative personalities?

Neglect of the Study of Creativity

The neglect of this subject by psychologists is appalling. The evidences of neglect are so obvious that I need not give proof. But the extent of the neglect I had not realized until recently. To obtain a more tangible idea of the situation, I examined the index of the *Psychological Abstracts* for each year since its origin. Of approximately 121,000 titles listed in the past 23 years, only 186 were indexed as definitely bearing on the subject of creativity. The topics under which such references are listed include creativity, imagination, originality, thinking, and tests in these areas. In other words, less than two-tenths of one percent of the books and articles indexed in the *Abstracts* for approximately the past quarter century bear directly on this subject. Few of these advance our understanding or control of creative activity very much. Of the large number of textbooks on general psychology, only two have devoted separate chapters to the subject during the same period.

Hutchinson (1931), reviewing the publications on the process of creative thinking to the year 1931, concluded that the subject had hardly been touched by anyone. Markey (1935), reviewing the subject of imagination four years later, reported very little more in the way of a fundamental contribution to the subject.

Some of you will undoubtedly feel that the subject of creative genius has not been as badly neglected as I have indicated, because of the common belief that genius is largely a matter of intelligence and the IQ. Certainly, that subject has not been neglected. But, for reasons which will be developed later, I believe that creativity and creative productivity extend well beyond the domain of intelligence.

Another important reason for the neglect, of course, is the difficulty of the problems themselves. A practical criterion of creativity is difficult to establish because creative acts of an unquestioned order of excellence are extremely rare. In this respect, the situation is much like that of a criterion for accident proneness which calls for the actual occurrence of accidents. The accidental nature of many discoveries and inventions is well recognized. This is partly due to the inequality of stimulus or opportunity, which is largely a function of the environment rather than of individuals. But if environmental occasions were equal, there would still be great differences in creative productivity among individuals.

There are, however, greater possibilities of observing individual differences in creative performance if we revise our standards, accepting examples of lower degrees of distinction. Such instances are more numerous. But even if we can detect and accept as creative certain acts of lower degrees of excellence, there are other difficulties. Creative people differ considerably in performance from time to time. Some writers on the subject even speak of rhythms of creativity. This means that any criterion, and probably any tests of creativity as well, would show considerable error variance due to function fluctuation. Reliabilities of tests of creative abilities and of creative criteria will probably be generally low. There are ways of meeting such difficulties, however. We should not permit them to force us to keep foot outside the domain.

Another reason for the oversight of problems of creativity is a methodological one. Tests designed to measure intelligence have fallen into certain stereotyped patterns, under the demands for objectivity and for scoring convenience. I do not now see how *some* of the creative abilities, at least, can be measured by means of anything but completion tests of some kind. To provide the creator with the finished product, as in a multiple-choice item, may prevent him from showing precisely what we want him to show: his own creation. I am not opposed to the use of the multiple-choice or other objectively scorable types of test items in their proper places. What I am saying is that the quest for easily objectifiable testing and scoring has directed us away from the attempt to measure some of the most precious qualities of individuals and hence to ignore those qualities.

Still another reason for the neglect of the problems of creativity is to be found in certain emphases we have given to the investigations of learning. For one thing, much learning research has been done with lower animals in which signs of creativity are almost nonexistent. For another thing, learning theory has been generally formulated to cover those phenomena that are easiest to order in logical schema. Learning theorists have had considerable difficulty with the behavior known as insight, to which creative behavior shows much apparent relationship (Wertheimer, 1945). It is proper to say that a creative act is an instance of learning, for it represents a change in behavior that is due to stimulation and/or response. A comprehensive learning theory must take into account both insight and creative activity.

The Social Importance of Creativity

There is general recognition, on the part of those outside the academic fold, at least, of the importance of the quest for knowledge about creative disposition. I can cite recent evidences of the general interest in the discovery and development of creative talent. Large industries that employ many research scientists and engineers have held serious meetings and have had symposia written about the subject (Kettering, 1944). There is much questioning into the reasons why graduates from the same institutions of higher learning, with high scholastic records and with strong recommendations, differ so widely in output of new ideas. The enormous economic value of new ideas is generally recognized. One scientist or engineer discovers a new principle or develops a new process that revolutionizes an industry, while dozens of others merely do a passable job on the routine tasks assigned to them.

Various branches of the government, as you all know, are now among the largest employers of scientific and technical personnel. These employers, also, are asking how to recognize the individuals who have inventive potentialities. The most common complaint I have heard concerning our college graduates in these positions is that while they can do assigned tasks with a show of mastery of the techniques they have learned, they are much too helpless when called upon to solve a problem where new paths are demanded.

Both industry and governmental agencies are also looking for leaders. Men of good judgment, planning ability, and inspiring vision are in great demand. How can leaders with imagination and vision be discovered? Can such qualities be developed? If those qualities can be promoted by educational procedures, what are those procedures?

We hear much these days about the remarkable new thinking machines. We are told that these machines can be made to take over much of men's thinking and that the routine thinking of many industries will eventually be done without the employment of human brains.

We are told that this will entail an industrial revolution that will pale into insignificance the first industrial revolution. The first one made man's muscles relatively useless; the second one is expected to make man's brain also relatively useless. There are several implications in these possibilities that bear upon the importance of creative thinking. In the first place, it would be necessary to develop an economic order in which sufficient employment and wage earning would still be available. This would require creative thinking of an unusual order and speed. In the second place, eventually about the only economic value of brains left would be in the creative thinking of which they are capable. Presumably, there would still be need for human brains to operate the machines and to invent better ones.

Some General Theories of the Nature of Creativity

It is probably only a layman's idea that the creative person is peculiarly gifted with a certain quality that ordinary people do not have. This conception can be dismissed by psychologists, very likely by common consent. The general psychological conviction seems to be that all individuals possess to some degree all abilities, except for the occurrence of pathologies. Creative acts can therefore be expected, no matter how feeble or how infrequent, of almost all individuals. The important consideration here is the concept of continuity. Whatever the nature of creative talent may be, those persons who are recognized as creative merely have more of what all of us have. It is this principle of continuity that makes possible the investigation of creativity in people who are not necessarily distinguished.

The conception that creativity is bound up with intelligence has many followers among psychologists. Creative acts are expected from those of high IQ and not expected from those of low IQ. The term "genius," which was developed to describe people who distinguish themselves because of creative productivity, has been adopted to describe the child with exceptionally high IQ. Many regard this as unfortunate, but the custom seems to have prevailed.

There is much evidence of substantial positive correlations between IQ as measured by an intelligence test and certain creative talents, but the extent of the correlations is unknown. The work of Terman and his associates is the best source of evidence of these correlations; and yet, this evidence is not decisive. Although it was found that distinguished men of history generally had high estimated IQs, it is not certain that indicators in the form of creative behavior have not entered into those estimations (Cox, 1926). It would be much more crucial to know what the same individuals would have done on intelligence tests when they were children. Terman's study of the thousand children of exceptionally high IQs who have now reached maturity does not throw much light on this theory. Among the group there is plenty of indication of superior educational attainment and of superior vocational and social adjustment. On the other hand, there seems to be as yet little promise of a Darwin, an Edison, or a Eugene O'Neill, although the members of the group have reached the age level that has come to be recognized as the "most creative years." The writers of that study recognize this fact and account for it on the basis of the extreme rarity of individuals of the calibre of those whom I have mentioned (Terman & Oden, 1947). It is hoped that further follow-up studies will give due attention to criteria of a more specifically creative character.

When we look into the nature of intelligence tests, we encounter many doubts concerning their coverage of creative abilities. It should be remembered that from the time of Binet to the present, the chief practical criterion used in the validation of tests of intellect has been achievement in school. For children, this has meant largely achievement in reading and arithmetic. This fact has generally determined the nature of our intelligence tests. Operationally, then, intelligence has been the ability (or complex of abilities) to master reading and arithmetic and similar subjects. These subjects are not conspicuously demanding of creative talent.

Examination of the content of intelligence tests reveals very little that is of an obviously creative nature. Binet did include a few items of this character in his scale because he regarded creative imagination as one of the important higher mental functions that should be included. Revisions of the Binet scale have retained such items, but they represent only a small minority. Group tests of intelligence have generally omitted such items entirely.

The third general theory about creativity is, in fact, a theory of the entire personality, *including* intelligence. I have defined personality as a unique pattern of traits, and traits as a matter of individual differences. There are thousands of observable traits. The scientific urge for rational order and for economy in the description of persons directs us to look for a small number of descriptive categories. In describing mental abilities, this economy drive has been grossly overdone when we limit ourselves to the single concept of intelligence. Furthermore, the term "intelligence" has by no means achieved logical or operational invariance and so does not satisfy the demand for rational order.

We do not need the thousands of descriptive terms because they are much interrelated, both positively and negatively. By intercorrelation procedures it is possible to determine the threads of consistency that run throughout the categories describing abilities, interests, and temperament variables. I am, of course, referring to the factorial conception of personality. From this point of view, personality is conceived geometrically as a hypersphere of n dimensions, each dimension being a dependable, convenient reference variable or concept. If the idea of applying this type of description to a living, breathing individual is distasteful, remember that this geometric picture is merely a conceptual model designed to encompass the multitude of observable facts, and to do it in a rational, communicable, and economical manner.

With this frame of reference, many of the findings and issues become clarified. The reason that different intelligence tests do not intercorrelate perfectly, even when errors of measurement have been taken into account, is that each test emphasizes a different pattern of primary abilities. If the correlations between intelligence-test scores and many types of creative performance are only moderate or low, and I predict that such correlations will be found, it is because the primary abilities represented in those tests are not all important for creative behavior. It is also because some of the primary abilities important for creative behavior are not represented in the test at all. It is probably safe to say that the typical intelligence test measures to a significant degree not more than a half dozen of the intellectual factors (Jones, 1949). There are surely more intellectual factors than that. Some of the abilities contributing to creative success are probably non-intellectual; for example, some of them are perceptual. Probably, some of the factors most crucial to creative performance have not yet been discovered in any type of test. In other words, we must look well beyond the boundaries of the IQ if we are to fathom the domain of creativity.

Development of Creativity

Before referring to the experimental design and to more specific hypotheses concerning the nature of creativity, I will venture one or two opinions on the general problem of the development of creativity. For I believe that much can be done to encourage its development. This development might be in the nature of actual strengthening of the functions involved or it might mean the better utilization of what resources the individual possesses, or both. In any case, a knowledge of the functions is important.

We frequently hear the charge that under present-day mass-education methods, the development of creative personality is seriously discouraged. The child is under pressure to conform for the sake of economy and for the sake of satisfying prescribed standards. We are told by the philosophers who have given thought to the problem that the unfolding of a creative personality is a highly individual matter which stresses uniqueness and shuns conformity. Actually, the unfolding of the individual along the lines of his own inclinations is generally frowned upon. We are told, also, that the emphasis upon the memorizing of facts sets the wrong kind of goal for the student. How serious these charges are no one actually knows.

We have very little experimental evidence that is decisive one way or the other and such evidence is hard to obtain.

Charles Kettering (1944) one time commented upon a survey in which it was found that a person with engineering or scientific training had only half the probability of making an invention compared with others. His comment was that an inventor should be defined as "a fellow who doesn't take his education too seriously." If the results of that survey represent the actual situation, either creative individuals do not seek higher education in engineering and science, or that kind of education has negative transfer effects with respect to inventiveness.

Many of us teachers assert that it is our main objective to teach students how to think, and this means also to think constructively. Certainly, if we succeeded in this objective, there should be much evidence of creativeness in the end product. I am convinced that we do teach some students to think, but I sometimes marvel that we do as well as we do. In the first place, we have only vague ideas as to the nature of thinking. We have little actual knowledge of what specific steps should be taken in order to teach students to think. Our methods are shotgun methods, just as our intelligence tests have been shotgun tests. It is time that we discarded shotguns in favor of rifles.

We all know teachers who pride themselves on teaching students to think and yet who give examinations that are almost entirely a matter of knowledge of facts. Please do not misunderstand me. I have a strong appreciation of knowledge of facts. No creative person can get along without previous experiences or facts; he never creates in a vacuum or with a vacuum. There is a definite place for the learning of facts in our educational system. But let us keep our educational objectives straight. Let us recognize where facts are important and where they are not. Let us remember, too, that the kinds of examinations we give really set the objectives for the students, no matter what objectives we may have stated.

The confusion of objectives is illustrated by the following incident. The story was told by a former dean of a leading Midwestern University. An old, experienced teacher and scholar said that he tried to encourage originality in his students. In a graduate course, he told the class that the term paper would be graded in terms of the amount of originality shown. One school teacher in the class was especially concerned about getting a high mark in the course. She took verbatim notes, continuously and assiduously, of what the learned professor said in class. Her term paper, the story goes, was essentially a stringing together of her transcribed lecture notes, in which the professor's pet ideas were given prominent place. It is reported that the professor read the term papers himself. When the school teacher's paper was returned, the professor's mark was an A, with the added comment, "This is one of the most original papers I have ever read."

Before we make substantial improvement in teaching students to think, in my opinion we will have to make some changes in our conceptions of the process of learning. The ancient faculty psychology taught that mental faculties grow strong by virtue of the exercise of those faculties. We all know from the many experiments on practice in memorizing that exercises in memorizing are not necessarily followed by improvement of memory in general. We all know that exercises in perceptual discriminations of certain kinds are not followed by improvement of perceptual discriminations in general (Thorndike & Woodworth, 1901). Thorndike and others concluded that the study of courses in high-school curricula did not necessarily result in a general improvement in intellect, but that the increases in test scores could be attributed to learning of a more specific nature (Broyler et al., 1927; Thorndike, 1924). Following this series of experiments the conclusion has often been that learning consists of the development of specific habits and that only very similar skills will be affected favorably by the learning process.

In view of the newer findings concerning primary abilities, the problems of formal discipline take on new meaning, and many of the experiments on the transfer of training will have to be reexamined and perhaps repeated with revised conditions. The experiments just cited do justify the rejection of the concepts of a general memory power, a general perceptual-discrimination power, and perhaps, also, rejection of the concept of a single power called intellect. These findings are in harmony with factorial theory. But the other alternative to the idea of formal discipline is not necessarily a theory of specific learning from specific practice.

There is certainly enough evidence of transfer effects. Experiments should be aimed to determine whether the instances of positive, zero, and negative transfer effects conform in a meaningful way to the outlines of the primary abilities. The work of Thorndike and others that I have just cited does, in fact, actually throw some light on this question. Although this aspect of their findings is usually not mentioned, they reported that high school students' experiences in numerical, verbal, and spatial types of courses—arithmetic and bookkeeping, Latin and French, and manual training—were associated with relatively greater gains in numerical, verbal, and spatial types of tests, respectively.

A general theory to be seriously tested is that some primary abilities can be improved with practice of various kinds and that positive transfer effects will be evident in tasks depending upon those abilities. At the present time some experiments of this type are going on in the Chicago schools under the direction of Thelma Gwinn Thurstone (1948). In one sense, these investigations have returned to the idea of formal discipline. The new aspect of the disciplinary approach is that the presumed functions that are being "exercised" have been indicated by empirical research.

Factorial Research Design

The general outline of the design for a factor-analysis investigation is familiar to many of you. It has been described before but needs to be emphasized again (Thurstone, 1948). The complete design involves a number of steps, not all of which are essential but all of which are highly desirable if the investigator is to make the most efficient use of his time and to achieve results of maximum value. The major steps will be mentioned first, then more details concerning some of them.

One first chooses the domain of his investigation. It may be the domain of memory abilities, visual-perceptual abilities, reasoning abilities, or the domain of introversion-extraversion.

One next sets up hypotheses as to the factors he expects to find in that domain. His preparatory task of hypothesis formation goes further. It includes the framing of several alternative hypotheses as to the more precise nature of each factor. This is necessary as the basis for transforming each factor hypothesis into the operational terms of test ideas. He then constructs tests which he thinks will measure individual differences in the kind of ability, or other quality, he thinks the factor to be. He will want to include in the test battery some reference tests that measure already known factors. One reason for this is that the new tests will almost inevitably also measure to some extent factors that have previously been established, such as verbal comprehension, number facility, and visualization. If such variance is probably going to appear in more than one new test in the battery, it is best to have that variance clearly brought out and readily identifiable. Another reason is that it is possible, after all, that one or more of the hypothesized factors will turn out to be identifiable with one or more of the known factors. The possibility of this identification must be provided for by having the suspected, known factors represented in the battery.

The test battery is administered to a sample of adequate size from a population of appropriate qualifications. Certain kinds of populations are better for bringing out variances in some common factors and other kinds are more suitable for other purposes. There should be relative homogeneity in certain features that might be correlated with the factors, such as sex, age, education, and other conditions. Some thought should be given to whether tests should be speed tests or power tests or something between the two. Some consideration should also be given to the most appropriate type of score for each test.

Factors are extracted and their reference axes are rotated into positions that are compelling because of the nature of the configuration of test vectors in the hyperspace. The psychological nature of each factor is surmised by virtue of the kinds of tests that have substantial variance attributable to that factor in contrast to tests which lack that variance.

In many respects, the complete factor-analysis design has properties parallel to those of a good experiment. In both, we begin with hypotheses. In both, some conditions are held constant while others are varied. In both, the measured outcomes point toward or away from the hypotheses. One important difference is the possibility of a statistical test of significance of the measured result for the experiment but not for the factor analysis. Confidence in the latter case depends upon the compellingness of the factor structure and the repeated verification of a result.

As an illustration of this analogy to an experiment, I will cite the factorial study of the well-known figure-analogies test. In the Army Air Forces research results, the figure-analogies test exhibited variances in three factors denoted as reasoning I, II, and III (Guilford, 1947). They were thus designated because they were peculiar to a number of reasoning tests, but their more precise natures were obscure. Examination of what one does in solving a figure-analogies item suggests several possible psychological functions or activities. First, one has to grasp correctly the relation between figure one and figure two. This suggests an ability to see a relationship between two objects. Second, one must observe the properties of the third figure. Then, one has to see what kind of a fourth figure it takes to satisfy the same relationship between figure three and figure four. Having decided upon the kind of figure needed, one has to find it among four or five that are supplied in the multiple-choice item. This is a kind of classifying act. There is still another possibility. The mislead responses may be so reasonable that considerable discrimination may be needed to select the best figure for the purpose. Considering the figure-analogies item from a more holistic point of view, there may be a primary ability involved in seeing that there is an identity of two relationships when the elements related are different. Or, there may be a general reasoning-by-analogy ability. Transposability of relations may be a key function here. Thus, we have several hypotheses as to the functions involved. There could be others. For every one of them we also have the further question as to whether the ability implied is restricted to the visual perception of figures or whether it is more general, extending to word meanings, numbers, and sounds. And if it is general, what are its limits?

To seek answers by factorial methods, one would construct special tests, each limited, if possible to one kind of act implied by each hypothesis. One would also vary the kind of material in each type of test to explore the scope of generality. The answers to the hypotheses (for each hypothesis is in reality a question) would be to find that the loading for each factor would rise with some of the variations and fall with others as compared to its loading in the traditional figure-analogies test. We would hope to find the changes in factor loadings so marked that we would not feel seriously the lack of t tests or F tests.

The question of the sources of factor hypotheses calls for some comment. In a domain in which there have already been factorial studies, the previous results are always suggestive. This makes it appear that the factorist merely moves from hypotheses to hypotheses. This is quite true. It is a fundamental truth of all scientists, no matter what their methods. Some hypotheses are merely better supported and more generally accepted than others at the time. There is enough uncertainty left in many a hypothesis to invite further investigation. That is what makes science interesting. That is what I think Kettering meant when he stated that the inventor is one who does not take his education (or knowledge) too seriously.

In a personality domain in which there has been little previous illumination of the underlying variables, other sources of hypotheses must be sought. The critical-incident technique of Flanagan (1949) would be one useful exploratory approach. Incidentally, one might say that this method has been used informally in connection with creative people from the "Eureka" episode of Archimedes down to modern times. The literature includes many descriptions of creative events. It would be more correct to refer to these historical reports as anecdotes, however, rather than critical incidents, since they suffer from most of the weaknesses of anecdotes. Where modern writers have attempted to interpret them psychologically, the interpretations have been quite superficial. They abound with vague concepts such as "genius," "intuition," "imagination," "reflection," and "inspiration," none of which leads univocally to test ideas. In the writings of those who have attempted to give a generalized picture of creative behavior, there is considerable agreement that the complete creative act involves four important steps.

According to this picture, the creator begins with a period of preparation, devoted to an inspection of his problem and a collection of information or material. There follows a period of incubation during which there seems to be little progress in the direction of fulfillment. But, we are told, there *is* activity, only it is mostly unconscious. There eventually comes the big moment of inspiration, with a final, or semi-final, solution, often accompanied by strong emotion. There usually follows a period of evaluation or verification, in which the creator tests the solution or examines the product for its fitness or value. Little or much "touching up" may be done to the product.

Such an analysis is very superficial from the psychological point of view. It is more dramatic than it is suggestive of testable hypotheses. It tells us almost nothing about the mental operations that actually occur. The concepts do not lead directly to test ideas. In attempting to distinguish between persons with different degrees of creative talent, shall we say, for example, that some individuals are better incubators than others? And how would one go about testing for incubating ability? The belief that the process of incubation is carried on in a region of the mind called the unconscious is of no help. It merely chases the problem out of sight and thereby the chaser feels excused from the necessity of continuing the chase further.

It is not incubation itself that we find of great interest. It is the nature of the processes that occur during the latent period of incubation, as well as before it and after it. It is individual differences in the efficiency of those processes that will be found important for identifying the potentially creative. The nature of those processes or functions will have to be inferred from performances of the individuals who have been presented with problems, even though the creator is largely unaware of them.

Specific Hypotheses Concerning Creative Abilities

The hypotheses that follow concerning the nature of creative thinking have been derived with certain types of creative people in mind: the scientist and the technologist, including the inventor. The consensus of the philosophers seems to have been that creativity is the same wherever you find it. To this idea I do not subscribe. Within the factorial frame of reference there is much room for different types of creative abilities. What it takes to make the inventor, the writer, the artist, and the composer creative may have some factors in common, but there is much room for variation of pattern of abilities. Some of the hypotheses mentioned here may apply also to areas of creative endeavor other than science, technology, and invention, but others may not. Included in the list of primary abilities that may contribute to creative efforts of these special groups are the reasoning factors, but I shall restrict mention here to other possible thinking factors that are more obviously creative in character.

First, there are probably individual differences in a variable that may be called *sensitivity to problems.* How this variation among individuals may come about will not concern us at this time. Whether it is best regarded as an ability or as a temperament trait will not concern us, either. The fact remains that in a certain situation one person will see that several problems exist while another will be oblivious to them.

Two scientists look over a research report. There are generally acceptable conclusions, but there is one minor discrepancy in the results. One scientist attributes the discrepancy to "experimental error." The other feels uneasy about the discrepancy; it piques his curiosity; it challenges him for an explanation. His further thinking about the matter develops into a new research project from which highly important findings result. Such an incident was reported by Flanagan (1949); it could be found duplicated many times.

There are questions as to the generality of such a variable. Is the supposed sensitivity restricted to a certain kind of situation or a certain kind of problem? Is it a perceptual quality as well as a thought quality? Could it be a general impressionability to the environment? Is it our old friend "curiosity" under a new name? Is it an ability to ask questions? Is it a general inhibition against closure? There may be other hypotheses just as pertinent. Each one suggests possible tests of individual differences.

Examples of possible tests follow. One might present the examinee with a short paragraph of expository material and instruct him to ask as many questions as he can that are suggested by the statements, with relatively liberal time allowed. A large part of the scientist's success depends upon his ability to ask questions, and, of course, to ask the right questions. In another test, one might name common household appliances, such as a toaster, or articles of clothing, such as trousers, and ask the examinee to list things that he thinks are wrong or could be improved. As a perceptual test, one might present pictures of objects or forms that are conventional and regular except for minor irregularities. Can the examinee detect the unusual features or will he overlook them? A third possibility is in the form of what we have called a "frustration test," merely because it is somewhat frustrating to many who have tried it. Contrary to the usual test practice, no task instruction is given: only items, and the very general instruction "do something with each item; whatever you think should be done." Each item is of a different type. One or two examinees have refused to do anything with the test.

There is very likely a *fluency* factor, or there are a number of fluency factors, in creative talent. Not that all creators must work under pressure of time and must produce rapidly or not at all. It is rather that the person who is capable of producing a large number of ideas per unit of time, other things being equal, has a greater chance of having significant ideas. There have been previous results yielding several verbal-fluency factors but I have insufficient time to acknowledge those studies properly here. It is probable that there are a number of fluency factors, nonverbal as well as verbal, yet undiscovered. There is a general problem to be investigated, apart from creativity, whether many of the primary thinking abilities have both a power and a speed aspect somewhat independent of each other. Some work of Davidson and Carroll (1945) suggests this in a result with regard to one of the reasoning factors.

One kind of fluency test would consist of asking the examinee to name as many objects as he can in a given time, the objects having some specified property; for example, things round, things red, or things to eat. In another test, the ideas might be more complex, as in naming a list of appropriate titles for a picture or for a short story. Still more demanding and also more restricting would be the task of naming exceptions to a given statement. Fluency of inferences may be tested by providing a hypothetical statement to which the examinee is to state as many consequences or implications as he can in a limited itme. The statement might be: A new invention makes it unnecessary for people to eat; what will the consequences be? This type of test has been previously proposed by several investigators.

The creative person has *novel* ideas. The degree of novelty of which the person is capable, or which he habitually exhibits, is pertinent to our study. This can be tested in terms of the frequency of uncommon, yet acceptable, responses to items. The tendency to give remote verbal associations in a word-association test; to give remote similarities in a similies test; and to give connotative synonyms for words, are examples of indications of novelty of ideas in the category of verbal tests.

The individual's *flexibility* of mind, the ease with which he changes set, can possibly be indicated in several ways by means of tests. Although there have been disappointments in the attempt to establish a common factor of this type (Guilford, 1947), the concept of flexibility and of its probable opposite, rigidity, will not be downed. In conjunction with some of the fluency tests, there may be opportunities to obtain some indications concerning flexibility. Does the examinee tend to stay in a rut or does he branch out readily into new channels of thought? Tests whose items cannot be correctly answered by adhering to old methods but require new approaches, in opposition to old habits of thinking, would be pertinent here. Certain types of puzzles fit this requirement fairly well, for example, a problem in which the examinee cannot succeed without folding the paper on which he writes, and the idea of doing so must come from him.

Much creative thinking requires the organizing of ideas into larger, more inclusive patterns. For this reason, we have hypothesized a *synthesizing ability.* As a counterpart to this, one might well expect an *analyzing ability.* Symbolic structures must often be broken down before new ones can be built. It is desirable to explore many kinds of both synthesizing and analyzing activities, in both perceptual and conceptual problems, in order to determine the existence of such factors and their numbers and whether they cut across both perceptual and conceptual areas.

From Gestalt psychology comes the idea that there may be a factor involving *reorganization* or *redefinition* of organized wholes (Wertheimer, 1945). Many inventions have been in the nature of a transformation of an existing object into one of different design, function, or use. It may be that this activity involves a combination of flexibility, analysis and synthesis, and that no additional hypothesis of redefinition is really needed, but the possibility must be investigated.

There is a possibility of a dimension of ability that has to do with the degree of *complexity* or of intricacy of conceptual structure of which the individual is capable. How many interrelated ideas can the person manipulate at the same time? The scientist must often keep in mind several variables, conditions, or relationships as he thinks out a problem. Some individuals become confused readily; they can keep only one or two items of structure delineated and properly related. Others have a higher resistance to confusion—a greater span of this type. Such an ability might be identifiable with the hypothesized synthesizing factor, but the study should make possible a separation of the two if the distinction is real.

Creative work that is to be realistic or accepted must be done under some degree of evaluative restraint. Too much restraint, of course, is fatal to the birth of new ideas. The selection of surviving ideas, however, requires some *evaluation.* In this direction there must be a factor or two. The evaluations are conceivably of different kinds, consequently the kinds of possible tests are numerous. In a paragrpah of exposition, we may ask the examinee to say whether every underlined statement is best classified as a fact, a definition, or a hypothesis. He will, to be sure, need some preliminary instruction in these distinctions. In another test, we can present him with a stated problem, then ask him which of several items are relevant to its solution and which ones are not. In still another test, we can give a problem and several alternative solutions, all correct. The examinee is to rank the solutions in the order of degree of excellence or fitness.

The hypotheses mentioned, as was stated earlier, refer more specifically to a limited domain of creative thinking more characteristic of the scientist and technologist. Even so, this entails a factorial study of substantial proportions. Similar studies will need to be made in the domains of planning abilities, in order to anticipate abilities more characteristic of the economic, the political, and the military leader. Still other restricted domains will need to be investigated to take care of the writer, the graphic artist, and the musical composer.

The question will inevitably arise, "How do you know your tests are valid?" There are two answers to this question. The first is that the factorial study of the tests is in itself one kind of validation. It will determine which tests measure each factor and to what extent. That is a matter of internal validity or factorial validity. It answers the question, "What does the test measure?" The second answer will be in terms of which factors are related to the creative productivity of people in everyday life. That calls for the correlation of factor measures with practical criteria. I feel very strongly that only after we have determined the promising factors and how to measure them are we justified in taking up the time of creative people with tests. If a certain factor we discover turns out not to be related to creative production, we have made a bad guess, but we will have discovered a new factor that may have some other practical validity. If a certain factor is not related to the criteria of creative productivity, the tests which measure it uniquely will also prove to be invalid for predicting these criteria. It is better to fail in the validation of a single factor measure than to fail in the validation of a half-dozen tests. If we make a study of the practical validity of every creative test we can think of before it is analyzed, we are bound to exert considerable wasted effort of our own and of our examinees. This statement, incidentally, applies to the validation study of any test.

Creative productivity in everyday life is undoubtedly dependent upon primary traits other than abilities. Motivational factors (interests and attitudes) as well as temperament factors must be significant contributors. Hypotheses concerning these factors in connection with creative people might be fruitful starting points for factorial investigations. The design of the research would be much the same as that described for creative abilities.

Summary and Conclusions

By way of summary, it can be said that pschologists have seriously neglected the study of the creative aspects of personality. On the other hand, the social importance of the subject is very great. Many believe that creative talent is to be accounted for in terms of high intelligence or IQ. This conception is not only inadequate but has been largely responsible for the lack of progress in the understanding of creative people.

The factorial conception of personality leads to a new way of thinking about creativity and creative productivity. According to this point of view, creativity represents patterns of primary abilities, patterns which can vary with different spheres of creative activity. Each primary ability is a variable along which individuals differ in a continuous manner. Consequently, the nature of these abilities can be studied in people who are not necessarily distinguished for creative reasons. Productivity depends upon other primary traits, including interests, attitudes, and temperamental variables.

It is proposed that a fruitful exploratory approach to the domain of creativity is through a complete application of factor analysis, which would begin with carefully constructed hypotheses concerning the primary abilities and their properties. It is suggested that certain kinds of factors will be found, including sensitivity to problems, ideational fluency, flexibility of set, ideational novelty, synthesizing ability, analyzing ability, reorganizing or redefining ability, span of ideational structure, and evaluating ability. Each one of these hypotheses may be found to refer to more than one factor. Some hypothesized abilities may prove to be identical with others or accounted for in terms of others. At any rate, these hypotheses lead to the construction of tests of quite novel types, which is a promising condition for the discovery of new factors. The relation of such factors to practical criteria of creative performance will need to be established. It is likely that the tests have been aimed in the right direction.

Once the factors have been established as describing the domain of creativity, we have a basis for the means of selecting the individuals with creative potentialities. We also should know enough about the properties of the primary abilities to do something in the way of education to improve them and to increase their utilization. These ends certainly justify our best efforts.

References

Broyler, C. R., Thorndike, E. L., & Woodyard, E. (1927). A second study of mental discipline in high schools. *Journal of Educational Psychology, 18,* 377-404.

Cox, C. M. (1926). *Genetic studies of genius,* Vol. II. Stanford, CA: Stanford University Press.

Davidson, W. M. & Carroll, J. B. (1945). Speed and level components in time-limit scores. *Educational and Psychological Measurements, 5,* 411-435.

Flanagan, J. C., et al. (1949). *Critical requirements for research personnel.* Pittsburgh: American Institute for Research.

Giddings, F. H. (1907). *Elements of sociology.* New York: Macmillan Co.

Guilford, J. P. (Ed.). (1947). *Printed classification tests,* Army Air Forces Aviation Psychology Research Program, Report No. 5. Washington, D.C.: Government Printing Office.

Hutchinson, E. D. (1931). Materials for the study of creative thinking. *Psychological Bulletin, 28,* 392-410.

Jones, L. V. (1949). A factor analysis of the Stanford-Binet at four age levels. *Psychometrika, 14,* 299-331.

Kettering, C. F. (1944). How can we develop inventors? In a symposium on *Creative engineering.* New York: American Society of Mechanical Engineers.

Markey, F. V. (1935). Imagination. *Psychological Bulletin, 32,* 212-236.

Terman, L. M. & Oden, M. H. (1947). *The gifted child grows up.* Stanford, CA: Stanford University Press.

Thorndike, E. L. (1924). Mental discipline in high school studies. *Journal of Educational Psychology, 15,* 1-22, 83-98.

Thorndike, E. L. & Woodworth, R. S. (1901). The influence of improvement in one mental function upon the efficiency of other functions. *Psychological Review, 8,* 247-261, 384-395, 553-564.

Thurstone, L. L. (1948). Implications of factor analysis. *American Psychologist, 3,* 402-408.

Wertheimer, M. (1945). *Productive thinking.* New York: Harper & Bros.

PART TWO: A Review of a Quarter Century of Progress (1975)*

Introduction

My impression is that on this unique occasion we are expected to survey, each from his own point of view, man's progress in explorations of creativity during the past quarter century, to offer some evaluations, and to make some extrapolations into the future. Having done this sort of thing three times in recent years (Guilford, 1965, 1967b, 1970), I shall find it a bit difficult to avoid redundancy.

Areas of Development

Taking a broad view of the domain with which we are concerned, I see three areas in which developments can be considered. Probably the most vigorously investigated have been problems of creative disposition, to determine the characteristics of those who exhibit to greater degrees different forms of creative production. It is generally agreed that productions are creative if they have qualities of novelty about them—novelty within the history of the individual's behavior, and probably also within the social context. So long as we maintain the role of

* J. P. Guilford, "Creativity Research: A Quarter Century of Progress" from Irving A. Taylor and J. W. Getzels, editors, Perspectives In Creativity, New York: Aldine Publishing Company. Copyright © 1975 by Aldine Publishing Company. Reprinted by permission.

scientist, we are not concerned with whether or not the products are socially valuable. The technologist is likely to add that specification.

Creative dispositions have been studied from different directions. The aspect with which I have been most concerned is that of intellectual abilities or functions. This does not mean that I have not recognized the importance of other qualities, in the form of motivational and temperamental traits.

The picture of creativity-related intellectual abilities has pointed directly to another important area, that of creative-thinking processes. As so often happens, technology outruns scientific foundations. As long as forty years ago, special strategies for generating novel ideas had been developed and were being taught. Methods that have been more fruitful have survived, and can now be accounted for in terms of basic psychological principles. What we know now could serve as a basis for other strategies and tactics that could be taught.

The broadest, and most heterogeneous, area to be considered is concerned with determiners of creative disposition and creative production. The role of heredity was first considered almost a hundred years ago by Galton, in his studies of genius. There has been very little attention to this problem in recent times, using experimental approaches. On the other hand, there has been much attention to environmental or biographical factors. The relation of creative disposition to IQ, or academic aptitude, has been extensively investigated. Some efforts have been made to remove some of the pressures for conformity in education and to encourage the employment of general and special educational procedures aimed at development of creative skills.

Consequences of Developments

Besides considering progress in these various areas, it is important for us at this time to see the needs for further investigations, and to decide in which directions the more promising and significant progress lies. It is important, also, to note whether what we already know about creativity is being exploited as it should be toward the development of a more creative society.

Intellectual Basis for Creative Production

The human mental abilities that contribute to potential for creative production, and the mental functions that go with them, I consider to be an important part of human intelligence, when that construct is conceived as broadly as it should be. Since much of what follows depends upon features of my structure-of-intellect (SOI) model, for the uninitiated reader, especially, some explanation of that model is in order.

One of the earliest conceptions of intelligence among the Romans equated it to information. To this day, that connection persists in some governmental affairs. In my conception, the connection is also a good one for psychology, except that intelligence is not the information itself but rather a collection of abilities or functions for processing information. Abilities differ with respect to kinds of information, and to kinds of operations we perform with information. I define information as that which we discriminate. Information comes in chunks or items, and every item is different in some way from all other items. No discrimination, no information.

Items of information differ in two ways: substantive differences, or *content,* and regarding form, or *product.* All items of information are constructed by our brains, and the constructs are products. The content categories are like codes or languages. The individual products are like words within those languages.

Kinds of Content. To be more specific, four major kinds of content are recognized. One of them is *figural,* which is generated rather immediately from input from the sense organs as what we call perception. The most important kinds in this category are visual-figural and auditory-figural. It takes different abilities to process these two kinds of information.

Perceptions lead to thoughts, and we have another kind of information called *semantic* in the SOI model. It should be said, however, that thoughts in the form of images would be figural, for they more or less duplicate perceptions. This leaves "imageless thoughts" for the semantic category. But there is still a multitude of items of semantic information.

A third kind of content is called *symbolic.* It is composed of signs or labels that commonly stand for items of other kinds of information. Letters, words, and numbers are the most familiar examples. Symbolic information is the language of the mathematician, but, of course, it is shared by anyone who speaks or reads. It is the important medium of communication.

The fourth kind of content is given the label *behavioral,* because it is concerned with mental events. We can be aware to some extent of what the other fellow is feeling or thinking, or what he intends to do, by means of cues that we obtain from his behavior. Some writers call this mode of communication "body language." Abilities for dealing with this kind of information determine how well we understand other people and how well we can deal with them. The limited "intelligence" represented by an IQ has no provision for this kind of ability. Abilities concerned with behavioral information may be said to compose a "social intelligence."

Products of Information. Within each of the content areas of information we find the same six kinds of products or brain-produced constructs. The basic kind of construct is a *unit.* A unit, like a thing, can stand by itself. It can be analyzed into other units, however, as when the parts of a tree—trunk, branches, twigs, leaves—are constructed as separate units.

Units can be grouped because they are similar, and we have *classes* (or class ideas), another kind of product. Units can be connected in other ways, giving still other kinds of products. One broad kind of connection is seen when one unit suggests another, as when lightning suggests thunder. This somewhat casual, but logical, kind of connection is called an *implication.* It has commonly been known as an "association," but the term "implication" better suggests its logical nature. Other instances of implications are describable as expectations or as predictions, which takes the concept beyond the idea of association.

A more definitive connection between two units is a *relation,* as when we know that "wet" is the opposite of "dry," and "cornea" is a part of the "eye." When more than two things are connected, we have a *system,* such as an organized sentence, a paragraph, a story, or a scientific theory. Any temporal or spatial sequence or arrangement is a system. One of the most interesting products is a *transformation,* which is any kind of change in an item of information, including redefinitions and substitutions. We shall see that transformations have special significance for creativity.

Intellectual Operations. There are five known basic operations that we perform with information. One operation is just knowing it, which means structuring it, and which I have called *cognition.* Technically, we may say that it is a matter of coding, within any one of the content areas and in the form of one of the kinds of products.

Information that we obtain can be put into storage, in an operation that can naturally be called *memory.* That is as far as the SOI meaning of "memory" goes. Getting information out of storage involves two kinds of operation—*divergent production* and *convergent production.* These operations mean the retrieval of stored information for use when it is thought to be needed. The difference between the two is that divergent production is a broad search, usually in an open problem, in which there are a number of possible answers. I also sometimes say that it is the generation of logical alternatives. Fluency of thinking is the name of the game. Convergent production, on the other hand, is a focused search, for, from the nature of the given information or problem, one particular answer is required. I sometimes say that it is the generation of logical imperatives. Actually, the difference between the two productive operations is a relative one, depending upon the degree of restraint or limitation upon the desired answer. One may also indulge in a guessing approach to a convergent problem, which means divergent production on the way to convergent production.

In such a case, especially, there must be decisions as to which answers are best, if not *the* best. This brings in the fifth kind of operation of *evaluation,* or judging the suitability of information. There is a comparing of the known or produced information in the light of certain logical criteria, such as identity, similarity, and consistency. Information that we have cognized or produced is constantly under evaluative checking for satisfaction of requirements.

The Structure-of-Intellect Model. From what I have just been saying about kinds of information and of operation, it might be concluded that there should be broad intellectual abilities, each in line with one of the categories. There is some indication that this is true. But research has indicated much more clearly that each ability or function is concerned with only one kind of content, one kind of product, and one kind of operation. Each little cube or cell in *Figure One* represents such a combination. Thus, we can say that there is a certain ability for cognition of semantic units, which is a fancy name for knowing word meanings, an ability measured by a good vocabulary test. Incidentally, this ability dominates common verbal IQ tests. Another ability would be memory for semantic transformation. An example of this activity would be your putting into memory storage a pun you have just heard so that you could tell the joke later. A pun is a good example of a semantic transformation. Still another ability would be convergent production of a symbolic implication, as in answering questions like 7 x (4 + 2) = ?, where the answer, 42, is implied by the given information.

Figure One.

The SOI Model.

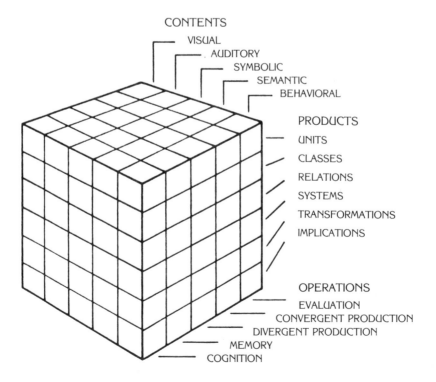

CONTENTS
- VISUAL
- AUDITORY
- SYMBOLIC
- SEMANTIC
- BEHAVIORAL

PRODUCTS
- UNITS
- CLASSES
- RELATIONS
- SYSTEMS
- TRANSFORMATIONS
- IMPLICATIONS

OPERATIONS
- EVALUATION
- CONVERGENT PRODUCTION
- DIVERGENT PRODUCTION
- MEMORY
- COGNITION

Relevance of the SOI Model for Creative Potential

All the intellectual abilities contributing to creative potential should be found represented somewhere in the SOI model. Let us consider the three facets or dimensions of the model in turn.

Informational Content and Creativeness. Consideration of the common fields of creative performance will show that they correspond to these categories of content. Creators specializing in visual-figural information include producers of visual art in any form, architects, engineers, and inventors. Creators in auditory-figural information are composers, arrangers, and stylistic performers of music. In the symbolic category we list mathematicians and cryptographers. The semantic list is a bit longer: writers, speakers, teachers, scientists, and planners. Creative performers specializing in behavioral information are salesmen, politicians, teachers, parents, policemen, lawyers, judges, and probation officers, not that all in these groups are necessarily creative.

If a person shines creatively in two or more fields of everyday activity, it may be that those fields all emphasize the same kind of content, or the person is high in abilities in more than one content area. Being high in more than one content category would be desirable especially in science or drama. But the informational-content categories do seem to present some limitations upon the extensiveness of a person's creativeness.

SOI Operations and Creativeness. Of the five kinds of operations, it is apparently generally recognized that divergent production (DP) has the most to do with creative behavior. In order to give more realism to this operation, let us take a few examples, selected from typical tests in the DP category. All examples are from the semantic-content area. The information processed may be in any kind of product.

In a common task for DP of semantic units, we give a problem like the following: Name all the things you can think of that are white and edible. The search is to be made within a class with the two given specifications. It may elicit responses such as: sugar, salt, snow, bread, flour, foam, and milk.

In a task requiring the production of alternative class ideas, we may present a list of perhaps ten familiar words that can be classified in several different ways by regrouping, with at least three words to a class. Some individuals may produce only one set of classes while others produce several.

For a task of producing alternative relations, we may ask in what different ways a father and daughter are related. For example, they are parent and child, of opposite sex, one is older, stronger, and wiser than the other, and so on.

Tasks given as tests for production of systems often require the composition of sentences. We may ask the person to write as many sentences as he can in each of which three different words are all used, for example, desert, food, and army. He has to interrelate the three concepts in various ways.

A common task for producing alternative transformations asks the examinee to suggest clever titles for a given short story, as if he were writing newspaper headlines. To be clever, a title almost has to involve a transformation, such as by allusion to something well known or by a pun.

A test for producing alternative implications presents a pictorial symbol, such as a bell, and asks for all the possible occupations or kinds of jobs that this symbol might suggest for a person who wears it on his clothing. It should be added that all DP tests are standardized by applying a working-time limit to each problem or set of problems.

As stated earlier, divergent production is the generating of logical alternatives to fit a cognized situation. When I say "logical," in this connection, I mean two things. On the one hand, the information produced is in the form of products, all six kinds of which I regard as logical constructs, basic to a "psycho-logic." This conception of products is clearest in the cases of the products of classes, relations, and implications, but it can be defended in the cases of units, systems, and transformations (Guilford, 1974). All the SOI products are forms of mental constructs or informational structures that have logical properties.

The other meaning of "logical" here is expressed by using the definitive synonym "relevant." Relevance means that there is some reasonable kind of connection between the stimulus information, or input, and the produced information, or output. In this connection, I must comment on the proposition that is sometimes expressed, to the effect that the creative person is "open to the irrational in himself." If this means being "illogical," I do not accept the proposition, for I believe that all intellectual performance is "logical" in the broad sense I have mentioned and is therefore "rational." When someone says that certain information-processing behavior is "irrational," he is displaying failure to see connections that are relevant to the person in question.

What I think the proposition under question really means is that the more creative person is ready to make and to accept more remotely connected output as being relevant. It is also said of the more creative person that he is more ready to take risks; he is not afraid of being wrong; he is willing to try out "long shots."

There is considerable evidence of various kinds to support the alleged relevance of divergent production for successful creative thinking. I have assembled much of that evidence elsewhere (Guilford, 1967a). Evidence has continued to accumulate. Furthermore, differential effects are being demonstrated, showing that different DP abilities or functions are relevant, depending upon the kind of informational content and informational product featured in the immediate task. In the SOI model there are twenty-four places for DP abilities, all of which have been demonstrated by factor analysis at least once. This statement applies when only the six *visual*-figural abilities are taken into account. Theoretically there should also be six *auditory*-figural DP abilities. These auditory-DP abilities represent an unexplored area.[1]

When we view the creative performance in the larger context of problem solving, we find that all the other SOI operations play their roles. Cognition is involved in seeing that a problem exists and is structuring the problem so that it is understood. The known structure of the problem serves as a search model, with which one explores his memory file (or pile), and possibly also his immediate environment, to find what is needed for a solution or to produce a solution from the information he retrieves.

Searching the memory store has already been identified in the form of divergent and convergent production. These operations play key roles, for without them there is no solution. The operation of evaluation plays a number of roles throughout problem-solving episodes. There are evaluative checks on conceptions of the problem as well as on solutions that are produced. And throughout the whole process there is at least short-term memory, a recording of informational events that have transpired, so that we need not repeat our errors and we can remember our more promising attempts.

Contributions of Transformations. Perhaps fully as important for creativeness as the divergent-production functions is another segment of the SOI model that contains the transformation abilities. Although the horizontal transformation layer of the model intersects with the divergent-production column, most of the transformation abilities involve other kinds of operations—cognition, memory, convergent production, and evaluation. In our processes of problem solving, we can see, or cognize, that transformations occur, as in visualizing changes in perceived figures or in revising meanings connected with words. We can remember these changes and later retrieve them, as in divergent and convergent production. And we can reach decisions regarding the adequacy or suitability of the change, in the operation of evaluation.

The chief role of transformations in our creative thinking is that they provide needed flexibility. How often do we persist in trying to solve the wrong problem? There is no headway until our conception of the problem is revised. How often do we persist in trying to use an old solution because it worked before but will not work under even slightly altered conditions? Sometimes a very simple transformation is the key to an important invention, as when the eye of the needle was moved from the blunt end where it had always been to the sharp end where it is needed in the sewing machine.

Other Traits Relevant for Creativeness

What is true of the multivariate nature of intellectual talents is probably also true of nonintellectual qualities. No one person possesses all the favorable qualities. His stronger motivational traits direct his interests and determine to some extent his sources of satisfaction. His temperamental characteristics may help to determine his strategies, and, in general, the way in which his talents are employed. The joint effects of intellectual and nonintellectual qualities may well be observable in what have been called "cognitive styles" or "cognitive attitudes."

Unfortunately, there is no well-recognized taxonomy of either motivational or temperamental traits, as there is in the intellectual domain. The best we can do is to note the more characteristic qualities that seem to be related to creative production. The relevant traits have been observed either from the study of socially recognized creative producers or of those who score high in divergent-production tests. The sources of such information are scattered. In the quick review that follows, the traits are differentiated as motivational and temperamental. The former include needs, interests, and attitudes; and the latter, some qualities describing the manner or style of behavior.

Motivational Qualities. Creative people are reported to be generally highly motivated, and to show a high energy level, with effective work habits. The behavioral signs are often described by saying "dedicated to his work" or "persistent in intellectual tasks." But such qualities are likely to be true of all succcessful people, especially creative or not. In both cases, these qualities are likely to mean that the person has found work that he likes and that gives him satisfaction. As symptoms of creative disposition, therefore, these qualities are ambiguous. Their absence would be more decisive than their presence.

The more creative person is said to have a high level of curiosity. I interpret this quality as a need to know, a desire to learn or to accumulate information. The person with curiosity seeks to have a well-stocked memory store, which he needs in productive thinking. It is no wonder that distinguished creative people often point out the need for a large stock of information.

Along with the need to know, there is likely to be also an interest in reflective thinking, from which satisfaction is derived. Probably most satisfying are the achievements in productive thinking, divergent and convergent. In some of my own research, incidentally, we found that there is a real difference in degree of interest in these two kinds of thinking, and there is a small negative correlation between the two interests.

There are some other qualities that also have intellectual implications, especially where transformations are concerned. The more creative adolescents are said to be less tied to reality, which suggests more readiness to let transformations occur, or even to seek them (Getzels and Jackson, 1962). There is said to be an unusual appreciation of humor and facility for producing humor. I suggest that this probably refers to the variety of humor that depends upon transformations. We have some evidence that associated with at least one DP ability is the need for adventure. This need may also account for the tendency toward risk-taking. A need for variety can also be tied to the high curiosity level. Often reported is a higher level of tolerance for ambiguity. Sometimes there is said to be a preference for disorder, in visual forms, at least. Both these qualities suggest that ambiguous or disordered situations present welcome challenges to the confident, creative thinker. There is also probably a desire to resolve the ambiguity and to organize the disordered information. In both cases, systems of some degree of complexity are to be produced. Much creative production is involved with the organization of new systems.

Other qualities may be summed up in the word "individuality." The creative person is a self-starting creature, with a strong need for autonomy and self-direction. The adolescent shows interests in unconventional careers. There is need for recognition from others for personal accomplishments, yet the standards of evaluation are likely to be the creator's own; he is said to possess independent judgment. In this same area we may cite the commonly low level of sociability and the high level of self-sufficiency. Unlike his peers, he is unwilling to accept things as they are; he seeks improvements. He commonly says or thinks, "There must be a better way." His showing of self-confidence reflects a high evaluation of himself. This quality may go so far as to include self-assertiveness, if not aggressiveness, but this is by no means universal. Rejecting some conventional standards, the creative boy may show some feminine interests, and the creative girl may show some masculine interests. The creative man shows some aesthetic interests, which, of course, are not commonly regarded as being masculine.

From scattered sources (e.g., Kallick, 1962) we gain impressions that those with higher creative potential differ in various other ways from those with lower potential. Individuals with high potential indulge in reading as a favorite pastime. They are more likely to report that they are frequently surprised or puzzled. They think that children should be taught to be different; those with low potential think that children should be taught to conform. The highs think that daydreaming can be fun; the lows think it can be useful. The highs know that they are bright and think that they can control their own destinies; they feel destined for great things.

One description sometimes applied to the creative person is that he is exceptionally "aware of his own impulses." I do not know what this means. It has little communication value except for the initiated.

Temperamental Qualities

Some temperamental qualities of creative persons were touched upon in the discussion of interests, above; for example, the higher levels of self-sufficiency and self-confidence. One quality that could be added here is introversion, what I have called "thinking introversion," which is probably included within the concept of pleasure in thinking also mentioned above. Creative people are sometimes said to be impulsive, and this may be limited to the sphere of thinking activities. It could be an aspect of risk-taking, which was associated above with the trait of need for adventure.

More broadly speaking, the creative person is said to be neither neurotic nor psychotic. The old saying that linked genius with madness is apparently not true. A neurotic condition tends to retard or inhibit thinking. A psychotic condition, although freeing the person to some extent from reality, also yields socially irrelevant responses.

Creative-Thinking Processes

The processes of creative thinking were touched upon in the discussion of divergent-production and transformation abilities, particularly, in connection with the intellectual aspects of creative disposition. Although the abilities or functions in those categories appear to be at the heart of operations of creative thinking, many other functions make their contributions, and they can also be described in terms of concepts of the SOI model.

A larger view of the subject gives us a comprehensive picture of problem solving. There is something creative about all genuine problem solving. Although it is easiest to see problem-solving events in the work of the scientist and technologist, they also abound in everyday personal affairs, and we can say that the artist, of whatever kind, also solves problems. In his case, the problems are concerned with self-expression and communication.

For a general picture of problem-solving events, I have presented an operational model, in which all the SOI operations play roles, and any kind of informational content and product may be involved (Guilford, 1966, 1967a). Cognition operates in seeing that a problem exists and in analyzing and structuring the problem, setting up what Dunker called a "search model." Earlier I used the term "search" in defining productive thinking, either divergent or convergent. Both are concerned with searching the memory store for needed information. Along the way, information is evaluated, bringing in another kind of SOI operation—evaluation. Evaluated (and accepted or rejected) are conceptions of the problem as well as the information retrieved from storage, and any transformations or new construction made of it. The SOI operation of memory, which is concerned only with the putting of information into storage and must therefore be distinguished from the memory store, comes into play in keeping a running account of steps in the problem-solving event. Without this record, we should be helpless.

It is sometimes said that the creative person is "in close touch with his unconscious." This is another of those cryptic, ambiguous statements that mean many things to different people. Attributing certain behavioral processes to an "unconscious" has no explanatory value whatsoever, and is like sweeping things under the rug. At its worst, an animistic conception is introduced. If the expression has any meaning at all, I think it should mean facility in retrieving information from memory storage, which implies divergent- and convergent-production operations. Let us fully admit that a considerable part of thinking activity is unconscious, in the sense that the thinker cannot observe all the steps. It is often said that he "sees the tip of the iceberg." To say that something is unconscious does not relieve us of the responsibility of finding out what the processes are. This we must infer from what we *can* observe, mostly as outsiders. The discovery of the SOI functions has enabled us to make a good beginning in this enterprise.

Determiners of Creative Disposition

Heredity

In considering the question of how creative people "got that way," for other aspects of personality, we look to possible hereditary and environmental sources. Although Galton found that genius tended to "run in families," in his study the hereditary and environmental sources were confounded, and no uncontested conclusions could be drawn. Most studies of hereditary contributions to intellectual abilities have been done with IQ tests. In terms of SOI categories, IQ tests have been much restricted to the operation of cognition, to semantic content, and to the products of units and systems. Because a strong hereditary effect upon IQ is often reported, to the extent that creative performance depends upon IQ, it is accordingly dependent upon heredity. Studies of direct effects of heredity upon divergent-production abilities have been very rare, as yet. Barron's study, the only one I know of, utilizes twins and seems to show some direct relationship, but it is apparently much weaker than that for IQ (Barron, 1970), and it may vary from one DP ability to another.

We have the common observation that creative persons come from homes of higher socioeconomic levels, which could mean that either the heredity behind the homemakers or the nurture that the home provides is the determiner, or both. The other unknown is whether the effect is directly exerted on DP abilities or indirectly through consequences on IQ.

Biographical Circumstances

Biographical features that are associated with socially recognized genius have been studied by Goertzel and Goertzel (1962). Among the parents of geniuses they found a higher incidence of respect for learning and an encouragement of investigation and independent thinking in their children. Again, some of this may have contributed indirectly through effects on abilities represented in the IQ. The parents had strong opinions, which might suggest rigidity, but, on the other hand, they supported minority causes. Fathers, often reported to be unrealistic, were inclined to be dreamers and were often either failures economically or had widely fluctuating fortunes. Some mothers were ambitious and domineering, and others were described as "smothering mothers," who showered their sons with love and affection. The child's home was often a troubled one, with conflicts between parents. There were quite a number of children with physical handicaps, thus providing support for Adlerians. There were an unusual number of deaths in the family, with accompanying traumas. In spite of the parents' respect for learning, the children frequently disliked school, and tutoring at home was common.

It seems to me that the general picture is one of families in which the children encountered unusual numbers of problems to be solved. In their efforts to solve the problems, the children had unusual exercises in creative thinking. They thus developed problem-solving skills. There were conditions that otherwise encouraged individualism, and motivation to make better lives for themselves.

Things Still To Be Done

From this sketchy review of what we know about creativity, what is implied about future needs? In our present-day, enormously complicated human milieu, problems of all kinds arise on every hand. Failure to solve some of them, or postponement of attempts to solve them, may even spell disaster. Are we and our leaders equipped to undertake solutions? What does it take to make better problem solvers?

As a people who have been "going West" for nearly 400 years, Americans have had unusual numbers of problems to solve, and they have generally risen to the occasion. America is recognized historically as a leader in mechanical inventions, and the founding fathers of the United States were also innovative in bringing into the world new forms of government. But the innovations needed to make our social, economic, and legal systems serve us better have been slower to come than those providing for a superb gadgetry. One reason is that while our patent system has richly rewarded the inventor, there has been no comparable system of rewards for innovative social ideas. As Torrance has often said, to get creative behavior, we must reward it. Can we institute any better assurances of rewards for new and workable social ideas that is comparable to that provided by our patent system?

Implications from Knowledge of Creative Dispositions

Knowledge of the characteristics of the more creative person can start us on several roads. If we are concerned with identifying children and youths who have unusual promise, we can assess those qualities that appear to be contributory to future success. Because of the multivariate nature of creative dispositions, we should be able, furthermore, to forecast in which areas the person's talents and inclinations are greatest. We would describe him by means of an individual profile with respect to relevant abilities and other traits. We could probably see in which directions his development could be the most rapid, and also detect some characteristics that, if not given special educational attention, would become unnecessary handicaps.

Assessment of Creative Potential. We are already prepared to do a great deal in the assessment of creative-thinking potential. As elsewhere, I argue strongly against a policy of giving an individual a single value to indicate his level of creative talent, as I have argued against the use of a single score to indicate level of intelligence. In either case, such information is ambiguous. Furthermore, by this approach, much potentially useful information is lost.

Now there will be those who are disappointed in the amount of prediction of a creative-production criterion that can be obtained from a test of any one ability, and they will continue to look for "the philosopher's stone," a single test that will predict at a substantial or high level. They will be doomed to disappointment. The prediction of creative performance of any kind is a multivariate affair, requiring the properly weighted combination of a number of predictors. Jones (1960), Elliott (1964), and others have demonstrated that weighted combinations of only a few DP tests can predict performance criteria as well as academic aptitude tests predict achievement (grade-point averages) of college students.

As in most areas of trait measurement, we lack all the knowledge and the instruments that we need. In the intellectual domain, all of the divergent-production abilities in the SOI model have been demonstrated by factor analysis, with tests available for many of them. Most of the transformation abilities have also been demonstrated, with tests available for some. There are also tests for abilities in other SOI categories, abilities that are contributory to learning and to problem solving.

Having rejected the use of an over-all creativity score, I now retreat a little in saying that there may be some meaningful composite scores, short of an all-inclusive one. Although my associates and I in research have always rotated axes in factor analysis orthogonally, we did not necessarily believe that all the SOI abilities are mutually independent. We didn't have faith in any of the methods of oblique rotation, which are in common use to find correlations between first-order factors. There may well be higher-order divergent-production factors and abilities. If so, my guess is that the second-order factors would be along the lines of the content categories; that is, a visual-figural-divergent-production factor, a semantic-divergent-production ability, and so on. A third-order factor in common to all the DP abilities might also be a fair hypothesis. Indications for higher-order factors along the lines of the product categories are not so clear.

Theoretically, I should say that the higher-order DP factors would depend upon how much the tested population had generalized its DP abilities. G. W. Ferguson (1956) was probably right when he suggested that aptitude factors arise by generalizations of specific practiced skills. The skill in performing any task may be thought to have at least two components. One is a specific affair, unique to the particular task, and there are one or more others of a more general nature, shared with other tasks that are similar to it psychologically.

Limited experimental research has tended to show that drills in certain selected tasks are followed by gains in performance in other tasks that feature the same common-factor ability, but not in tasks for other factors. Generalization in intellectual ability seems limited within operation, content, and product boundaries. One way in which broader generalizations might be effected would be to make the learner aware of the parallels across SOI boundaries, so that he applies what he learns in a task that is salient for one SOI ability to tasks involving parallel abilities. Perhaps some of these parallels are sensed by individuals, without their being taught, and such transfers occur automatically, thus producing high-order factors.

Assessment of Other Qualities. It is commonly recognized that, in general, assessment of traits of motivation and temperament is in a less satisfactory state than assessment of intellectual traits. Although there have been factorial definitions of many variables of needs, interests, and attitudes, and also in the domain of temperament (Guilford, 1959), and some definitive instruments of measurement are available, there has been limited information regarding predictive validity against creative-production criteria. Obtained validity indices have generally shown low relationships with criteria of performance for single trait scores. Again, multiple predictions are needed. Much tedious validation effort will be needed in order to determine which traits and their tests are relevant.

Promoting Creative Development

Knowledge of the traits that enter into creative disposition should help not only to identify and locate potential creative talent but also to give us clues to promote development in creative directions. This is more true of abilities than of other traits, for, as pointed out earlier, the abilities directly suggest certain creative processes. It is not so clear how we should go about improving traits of motivation and temperament, and whether, if we succeeded, gains in creative performance would automatically follow.

Special Training in Creative Thinking. It has been repeatedly demonstrated that exercises designed to increase success in creative thinking have the effect of raising status in the relevant SOI abilities. Torrance's (1972) recent review of studies of effectiveness of various methods of training for creative thinking gives the palm to Alex Osborn's procedures, as described in his book *Applied Imagination* (Osborn, 1963). These procedures have a solid foundation of theory in the creative aspects of the SOI model. This is another instance of technology outrunning basic knowledge, in this case, owing to the rare insights of Alex Osborn.

Results of training experiments also support the multivariate view of creative potential. For any given type of training, certain SOI abilities show improvements while others do not. In a grand educational experiment at the college level, Parnes and Noller (1972) have found that abilities, some outside the divergent-production and transformation categories as well as some within those categories, are affected, much as one should expect, knowing the kinds of exercises given the students.

From this it should follow that in the educational setting, one should give due regard to the SOI abilities probably involved in the behavior skills to be achieved, and he should select his pre- and post-test instruments accordingly, if there is to be evaluation of the generalized effects of the training. There is evidence (Forehand and Libby, 1962) that perhaps even more important than drill in thinking exercises is the step of imparting knowledge of the nature of creative thinking. Information concerning the SOI model and the problem-solving model that is based upon it (Guilford, 1967a) should be useful in this situation.

Considering the special creative-thinking courses known to me, I should say that they fall short of offering a full curriculum. Use of the two models just mentioned would help to evaluate courses as to comprehensiveness. When the goal is aimed at better problem solving, the range of SOI abilities involved is much greater. It is quite natural that the courses should stress semantic content, for that is the kind of information in most common use in our verbal civilization. But I suspect that there is an unexpressed expectation that training in this area will transfer automatically to other areas of information. From what we know about transfer effects, that training would do little for the visual artist or the creative musician, for the mathematician or the politician, unless the analogies are pointed out, and some exercise is given in transfer.

Of all the content categories, that of behavioral information is probably most neglected in exercises in creative thinking, yet in that area are some of the most significant everyday problems. They are encountered not only by politicians, whom I have mentioned, but also by all those who need to influence or control people—parents, teachers, policemen, attorneys, judges, probation officers, social workers—the list is a long one. If these are the kinds of people we are to make more creative thinkers, we should do better by giving attention to solving behavioral problems.

It is not clear, but I am sure that not all the SOI informational products are given due attention. Brainstorming sessions may emphasize units of information unduly. Solutions to problems in daily life may call for new relations or implications, as when a scientist is attempting to decide what the connection is between two things or two variables, or when generating alternative hypotheses to account for some phenomenon. A detective also needs the generation of such products. The need to produce systems is obvious in much creative work, systems such as melodies, story plots, or scientific theories. The unique importance of transformations was emphasized earlier.

In the larger context of problem solving, we need to consider functions outside the category of divergent production. Some attention is given to evaluation, in some instances, but probably not enough. Some attention is given to seeing problems, but the nature of that step is not often realized. Analytical studies have led to the conclusion that seeing that a problem exists is a matter of cognition of implications. We size up an object or a situation and we are aware of a shortcoming of some kind. I once addressed an organization of engineers, who wanted to know how they could more readily translate discoveries in basic science into useful inventions. I pointed out that they must improve their skills in seeing implications. They could start with the nature of the scientific finding and its properties and ask themselves, how, by virtue of these attributes, it leads to new uses. Or they could start with a collection of human needs, needs that could possibly be collected in public polling; they should define those needs in terms of specific requirements, which might lead to things that fit those specifications.

Remembering that productive thinking depends very heavily upon stored information, in a course on problem solving we might give some attention to memory training. This should emphasize how information is put into storage, for how it is stored will make a difference in how efficient the retrieval can be. Things can be retrieved more readily if they are properly organized and labeled, for we get at them by using appropriate cues. The activity is analogous to looking for a book in a library. Organization of the memory store depends upon how items of information are put into storage, and this means the manner in which the information is learned. In order to tag information in a useful way, full advantage must be taken of the logical constructs of classes, relations, implications, and systems–the SOI products. But to be left with flexibility, information needs to be in cross classifications, hierarchies, and other alternative systems. The simple moral for education is that attention should go well beyond the teaching of isolated units.

Creative Education in General. The special approaches to development of creative thinking have never been known to achieve miracles. But, if by any approach we could lift the population's problem-solving skills by a small amount on the average, the summative effect would be incalculable. The special methods of training have been usually applied outside the academic setting. To have any widespread effect on the population, they would need to be utilized within the academic world. But in that connection, the somewhat specialized procedures should be expanded, as suggested earlier. Educational practices should be revamped from the bottom to the top, giving attention to creative problem-solving skills. For this purpose, many suggestions can be made. Many of these ideas have already been recommended and have been put into effect in places, but this reorganization should become more nearly universal.

Some general principles are agreed upon. The student's role must be a more active one. He should be given not only opportunity to pursue learning as a goal, but also personal responsibility for learning. The teacher's role should be to stimulate and to guide, providing a favorable climate and the necessary tools. As much as possible, the student should discover what he learns; he should not just wait for the teacher to tell him the information. Education must be more individualized, each child progressing at his own rate, his goal being to make progress, and when he puts forth the effort, progress should be forthcoming. He should have immediate and adequate feedback information, as the basis for reinforcement that rests on intrinsic, rather than extrinsic, motivation.

In the past, the goal of education has been too much directed toward the stockpiling of information. A well-stocked memory store is, of course, a necessary asset in creative problem solving. But information is by no means sufficient. Viewed in one way, stockpiling of information contributes to exercise of the SOI operations of cognition and memory. This emphasis neglects the productive-thinking and evaluative functions that are so important for creativity. Skills must be developed for *using* information as well as for *storing* it. Instruction should be problem-centered. The student should encounter many problems; problems that are difficult enough to be challenging to him, but not so difficult as to discourage effort. Creative behavior should be rewarded. Intrinsic rewards are best. Skills in evaluation should not be overlooked, but personal criticism should be kept at a minimum. If special weaknesses appear, special exercises should be prescribed. Students should be taught to be flexible in their thinking. In a fast-moving, fast-changing world, the individual must be ready to alter information and habits. Requirements of new problems render both information and skills rapidly out of date.

The setting and the climate for creativity in schools must be favorable. The school administration must be for it, the teachers must be for it, and parents must at least acquiesce. The school housing should be adapted to creative learning. The curriculum should be designed to offer different kinds of problems. The teacher's lesson plans should be adapted to this kind of learning—programming teaching operations with enough flexibility to take advantage of student-initiated trends.

While I am on the subject of education, I cannot refrain from adding some unique suggestions. Using the structure-of-intellect model as the frame of reference, I recommend that every student be given the chance to show what he can do with respect to all the intellectual functions. Each child is thus likely to find areas in which he can do relatively well, and in which learning can be more rapid and more rewarding. He is thus also likely to find areas of stronger interests. Assessments of the status of the student in various SOI abilities would also be informing for teachers and counselors.

I also frequently recommend that as early as the child is ready for it, he be given information regarding the nature of his own intellectual resources. As suggested earlier, this step should be an important basis for effecting transfers of learning, and the broadening of skills. Incidentally, I have been told by a teacher who has tried it, that his group of Negro children in grades four to six could be given some degree of understanding of the SOI model and could apply it effectively in their own learning. As related by Robert Rose, of the San Bernardino, California Schools, after such treatment, the children showed very unusual gains in achievement tests and in IQ.

Needed Basic Research

We know something about what the creative problem solver does in the act of thinking, but we need to know more. We know that a key activity in productive thinking, divergent or convergent, is retrieval of information from memory storage, but we do not know as much as we should about the process of retrieval itself, and the conditions that are favorable or unfavorable. Psychologists have lavishly investigated learning, including the putting of information into storage, while neglecting the process of recall. And when recall has been investigated, it has usually been what I call "reproductive" recall rather than "transfer" recall, which is so likely to be needed in productive thinking (Guilford, 1967a). In transfer recall, an item of information is retrieved in connection with some new cue, not the one in connection with which it was learned.

We need to know more about transformations which have been almost entirely neglected except incidentally by Gestalt psychologists. Why are some people more ready than others to revise their conceptions? The answer is not to be found in a general personality trait of flexibility versus rigidity. Our research has found that even within the realm of thinking, there is more than one trait of this nature. Even each of the 20 transformation abilities in the SOI model has its measure of independence. We may ask some general questions, however. Are there principles to be found to account for particular kinds of changes in information? Can transformations take place in information while it is in storage, or only when it is retrieved? Progress in making fruitful investigations, as usual, depends upon our ability to ask significant questions about the phenomenon.

The last question asked regarding transformations leads to the more general question about the role of *incubation* in problem solving. I doubt that any recognized creative person would deny the fact that incubation occurs and is frequently helpful. This phenomenon, of course, is an observed progress during times when one is not actively pursuing solutions. In experimental studies of the matter over long periods of time, it would be difficult to exert the controls one should desire. A study of short-term incubation (over a period of minutes) has been done (Fulgosi and Guilford, 1968), using a divergent-production task (Consequences). Positive effects upon performance in the task were found to increase during the first 20 minutes. In a second study, it was found that the effects decreased during the next 40 minutes. The possibility of experimental investigation of incubation has thus been demonstrated.

The Use of Biographical Information

One use that has been made of biographical features found to be associated with creative performance in later life is found in Calvin W. Taylor's (IBRIC, 1968) Alpha Biographical Inventory. This purely empirical method has value in identifying youth and adults who have higher probabilities of exhibiting creative behavior. It is useful in selection of personnel in industrial settings and in spotting students with talents that are overlooked by ordinary academic-aptitude tests. It is a "shotgun" approach, lacking basic psychological theory, however, and hence would not be very useful in research where well-defined variables are needed.

Can use be made of any particular biographical features, such as those mentioned by Goertzel and Goertzel (1962)? I doubt that anyone would be heartless enough to recommend the institution of precarious and troubled homes in order to make a child more creative. Nor would one recommend the infliction of a physical handicap. We could tell a mother, perhaps, to be either dominating or loving. But if my interpretation of the effects of the troubled homes is correct, all we would need to do is to see to it that the child has numerous problems to solve. The problems should be paced at a level appropriate for the child at his level of development—problems neither too easy nor too difficult. This would take considerable attention and ingenuity on the part of the parents, who should not only contrive natural problems but also arrange for appropriate rewards for successful solutions. In more general terms, we need to train parents how to be teachers and how to take advantage of situations for teaching as events arise. The right kind of teaching parents could be the most important key to the development of a creative, problem-solving society. A problem-solving society should also be high in status with respect to mental health.

Expectations from Drugs. Probably because of its alleged "mind-stretching" effects and its production of bizarre hallucinations, LSD has received the most attention as a possible augmentor of creative thinking, with lasting as well as temporary consequences. A well-controlled experiment designed to test lasting effects (at least to six months) was conducted by the McGlothlins and Cohen (1967). A large number of different kinds of tests of creative-thinking abilities, of attitudes, and of behavior of different kinds were used in this connection. There was no significant gain in any creative-thinking test, either short-term or long-term in duration. There was a significant increase in self-observed aesthetic interests, and more incidence of attention to art and music, but no improvement in productive performances in those areas. Perhaps the aesthetic interest came from the startling sensory effects of the drug.

Effects of Psychotherapy. There may have been some experimental studies of effects of psychotherapy upon creative production, but I do not happen to be acquainted with any of them. As in studies of other effects of therapy, it may be very difficult to demonstrate positive results experimentally. It is known that individuals who score high on divergent-production tests are inclined to have slightly lower scores on neurotic tendency or emotional immaturity, consistent with the common observation that neurotics are less creative.

Probably the most that can be expected is that therapy would remove some of the blocks that may exist in the way of creative production. An anecdotal bit of evidence comes from E. G. Boring, one of our distinguished psychologists, who underwent psychoanalysis with the hope of performing more creatively as a scientist. From his own evaluation, the results were very disappointing (Boring, 1940). In such an instance, one may conclude either that there were no blocking impediments, or that therapy did not succeed in removing them.

Summary

A survey of psychological research on creativity, with new theory and new methods, during the past quarter century shows substantial progress in several areas—dispositions of the more creative individuals and some of the apparent determiners, the basic nature of creative thinking, and procedures for improving creative performances. The multivariate nature of the contributing qualities of creative persons has been well established, and it involves both intellectual and nonintellectual traits.

Episodes of creative problem solving involve a great many different intellectual functions that are represented in the structure-of-intellect model. Thus, creative abilities are a part of intelligence, not something apart from it. Most critically involved, particularly at the stage of generating ideas, are the divergent-production abilities or functions and those involving transformations of information. The former provide an abundance of alternative ideas; the latter a flexibility in the structuring of information so that alterations and adaptations can occur.

Various procedures for improvement of potential for creative thinking have been tried experimentally. The most successful methods can lay claim to theoretical bases in structure-of-intellect concepts. Teaching individuals the nature of those concepts has also been found to be effective. There is insufficient scientific evidence as yet to lead us to expect much in the way of creative benefits from psychotherapy or the use of drugs.

Further research is needed on basic problems, especially on the process of retrieval of information (recall) from memory storage, which is at the heart of creative thinking. More should be learned regarding the phenomena of transformations, their nature, and their determiners. Experimental investigation of the phenomenon of incubation has been barely started.

Footnote

1. For a condensed history of the research on discoveries of divergent-production abilities, and other abilities, see Guilford and Hoepfner (1971).

References

Barron, F. (1970). Heritability of factors in creative thinking and esthetic judgment. *Acta Geneticae Medicae et Gemellogie, 19,* 204-208.

Boring, E. G. (1940). Was this analysis a success? *Journal of Abnormal and Social Psychology, 35,* 4-10.

Elliott, J. M. (1964). Measuring creative abilities in public relations and in advertising work. In C. W. Taylor (Ed.), *Widening horizons in creativity* (pp. 396-400). New York: Wiley.

Ferguson, G. W. (1956). On transfer and the abilities of man. *Canadian Journal of Psychology, 10*, 121-131.

Forehand, G. A. and Libby, W. L., Jr. (1962). *Effects of educational programs and perceived organizational climate upon changes in innovative administrative behavior.* Chicago: University of Chicago Center for Progress in Government Administration.

Fulgosi, A. and Guilford, J. P. (1968). Short-term incubation in divergent production. *American Journal of Psychology, 81*, 241-246.

Getzels, J. W. and Jackson, P. W. (1962). *Creativity and intelligence.* New York: Wiley.

Goertzel, V. H. and Goertzel, M. C. (1962). *Cradles of eminence.* Boston: Little Brown.

Guilford, J. P. (1950). Creativity. *American Psychologist, 5*, 444-454.

Guilford, J. P. (1959). *Personality.* New York: McGraw-Hill.

Guilford, J. P. (1965). Implications of research on creativity. In C. Banks & P. L. Broadhurst (Eds.), *Studies in psychology presented to Cyril Burt.* London: University of London Press.

Guilford, J. P. (1966). Intelligence: 1965 model. *American Psychologist, 21*, 20-26.

Guilford, J. P. (1967a). *The nature of human intelligence.* New York: McGraw-Hill.

Guilford, J. P. (1967b). Creativity, yesterday, today, and tomorrow. *Journal of Creative Behavior, 1*, 3-14.

Guilford, J. P. (1970). Creativity: Retrospect and prospect. *Journal of Creative Behavior, 4*, 149-165.

Guilford, J. P. (1974). Psychology with act, content, and form. *Journal of General Psychology.*

Guilford, J. P. and Hoepfner, R. (1971). *The analysis of intelligence.* New York: McGraw-Hill.

IBRIC (1968). *The alpha biographical inventory.* Greensboro, NC: Prediction Press.

Jones, C. A. (1960). Some relationships between creative writing and creative drawing of sixth grade children. Doctoral dissertation, Pennsylvania State University.

Kallick, M. (1962). A construct validation of a creativity questionnaire and certain theoretical considerations. Master's thesis, University of Akron.

McGlothlin, W., Cohen, S., and McGlothlin, M. S. (1967). Long lasting effects of LSD on normals. *Archives of General Psychiatry, 17*, 521-532.

Osborn, A. F. (1963). *Applied Imagination* (3rd ed.). New York: Scribner's.

Parnes, S. J. and Noller, R. B. (1972). Applied creativity: The creative studies project: Part II. *Journal of Creative Behavior, 6*, 164-186.

Torrance, E. P. (1972). Can we teach children to think creatively? *Journal of Creative Behavior, 6*, 114-143.

PART THREE: A Vista of Future Research on Creativity

After a review of past research on creativity, what can be said regarding the future of that kind of activity? From the standpoint of one who has been active along these lines, some projections can be made. The following discussion will not attempt to list all particular problems needing attention, but to mention some general shortcomings, with some suggestions on research procedures and on areas of research.

Some Needs in Research

Perhaps the greatest need in investigations involving aptitude for creative performance is to remember that creativity is not just one comprehensible variable. This is the same kind of error that was made regarding "intelligence," of which creative aptitude is a part. Apparently, many of those who do research on creativity still think that if we have found a word for something we are dealing with one unanalyzable thing.

Many of my readers know that my helpers and I have analyzed intelligence, including its creative components, into a very large number of different abilities or functions, and that creative aptitudes occupy two categories of my structure-of-intellect (SOI) model, as shown on Page 48 (Guilford, 1977, 1986). One is the operation category of *divergent production*—abilities concerned with a broad search of the memory store for alternative items of information to fulfill a need and the other is the product category of transformation of items of information—a recognition or a production of a *change* in an item of information. It is noteworthy that Alex F. Osborn recognized these two categories and emphasized them in connection with his brainstorming sessions before they were discovered by factor analysis (Osborn, 1963).

Creative aptitude is indeed a multivariate affair, and in terms of the two categories that I mentioned it includes 30 divergent-production abilities or functions and 25 transformation variables. The former provide for fertility of thinking, offering quantities of ideas, and the latter contribute flexibility or quality of ideas. The five abilities where the two categories intersect in the SOI model have a double reason for claim to membership among creative talents. And when we broaden the picture to include problem solving, many more SOI abilities come into the picture; those involved in seeing that a problem exists, in seeing the nature of the problem, evaluating the steps taken, and in remembering those steps.

As I have pointed out (Guilford, 1982), a serious sin of cognitive psychology has been the ambiguity of so many of its terms, such as "reasoning," and even "verbal." The basic factors of the SOI model provide concepts that are free from ambiguity, each being defined in terms of three specifications, each of which is operationally defined. Thus, experimental results based upon measures of any one SOI function are uniquely labeled. The extent to which conclusions may be generalized will depend upon the SOI categories that two variables have in common: an operation, a content, a product or two such features in common.

This kind of situation suggests that some pairs of SOI variables have some degree of correlation between them, and my recent investigations have borne this out (Guilford, 1981). Experience has shown, however, that such correlations are very small. For example, I found that the estimated correlations among measures of 23 divergent-production abilities ranged below .50. Variables having a correlation of .50 can be represented by vectors that are 60 degrees apart. Smaller correlations indicate larger angles of separation and even less support for generalizing from one variable to another. Thus, generalizing conclusions from one SOI variable to others should be made with appropriate restraint.

I can cite two important pieces of research on creativity that demonstrate the value of working in terms of SOI variables. One was the study by Jones (1960), who found that tests of divergent production with visual content were strongly predictive of success of children in making novel drawings, while semantic tests in the same category predicted success in producing novel stories. The other is the large study using a large number of various tests in predicting success from taking a four-semester sequence of courses on Creative Problem Solving at the State University College at Buffalo (Parnes & Noller, 1972). The results were very much in line with what one would expect from the nature of the course. For example, semantic divergent-production tests tended to be predictive where visual tests of the same sort were not valid. A test for memory ability was not valid.

Basic Research Needed on the SOI Model

Basic research for demonstrating the existence of many SOI abilities is by no means complete. As matters now stand, of the 150 abilities or functions projected by the model, only about two-thirds have been demonstrated (Guilford, 1977). Most in need of attention are the auditory abilities, including the ones most relevant for creative production. The latter should be most important for the musical composer, the arranger, and the performing artists, as well as those concerned with effects in speech—orators and actors.

I have often suggested that the SOI model might be extended, with a slab for kinesthetic abilities, parallel with the visual and auditory ones, although the relevance for such abilities for creativity is not so clear. But there is a glimmer of evidence that there are relevant psychomotor abilities. Two such abilities were found incidentally in our analysis of divergent-production abilities in the behavioral-content area (Hendricks, Guilford, and Hoepfner, 1968). We included a few tests that, instead of calling for the usual written responses, asked the examinees to respond to described emotional situations by producing expressions that were recorded. There were some tests for facial expressions and others for vocal expressions. Each set of expressions determined a new factor, both distinguished from all the factors that called for written responses.

Quite a number of factors had previously been found from tests calling for voluntary movements of different kinds (Guilford, 1958). In one respect, these, too, depended upon the part of the body concerned, suggesting a motor-content category. Finding psychomotor factorial abilities is not surprising, since voluntary movements are organized by our brains, as they organize items of information. The relevance of such abilities for creativity can be seen for acting, choreography, and athletics.

Use of the SOI Variables in Research

An important implication of the SOI model in experimental research is that great care should be taken in the nature of the tasks assigned to subjects who are being employed, in order to control conditions, as we painfully learned in constructing new tests for hypothesized factors. The SOI model pointed clearly at expected abilities in a factor analysis. A well-planned analysis could tell us whether controls were successful. Sample test items for the different abilities may be found in *The Analysis of Intelligence* (Guilford & Hoepfner, 1971). Information is also given as to their factor affiliations; the ability that the test most strongly represents, and how strongly. The tests could serve as models for tasks to be used in research.

Other Areas of Research

In addition to the abilities that prepare a person for creative performance there is an area of traits known as "cognitive styles" to be considered. In intellectual functioning there are a number of traits concerned with which of the many talents the person will favor or apply. My survey of the reports of research on this subject showed that there seem to be two kinds of such variables (Guilford, 1980). They, too, have been determined by factor analysis, when tests are scored in terms of *manners* in which examinees work on them rather than how well they perform, as a rule.

I concluded that those variables lie along the categories of the SOI model, as if the brain has some awareness of the SOI categories. One type of style seems more compulsive than the other. I have referred to them as "intellectual executive functions." A good example, which must be quite relevant for creativity, is Witkin's "field independence versus field dependence" (Witkin, et al, 1962). He first discovered this trait in tasks requiring a person to locate the correct vertical position, either of a line or of his own body, under illusory conditions. He has to change his perception of the vertical position. The same trait has been found to play a role in hidden-figures tests. The examinee has to change the use of certain lines as parts of the larger, inclusive, figure to make them into lines of the smaller figure. This *change* feature gave me the cue to suggest that the trait is a general urge to utilize transformations, hence to apply SOI transformation abilities. The generality of the trait has been shown by evidence for its effects in other kinds of activities. Its relevance for creativity has been mentioned.

The other kind of cognitive styles seems less compulsive. Such styles can be regarded as preferences for, or interests in, different kinds of intellectual activity. These traits also lie along the lines of the SOI categories. There are preferences for applying different kinds of informational content–visual, semantic, or behavioral, for example. These interests have effects in the direction of art, writing, or management.

There seem to be interests along the lines of different kinds of SOI products–classes, relations, or systems, for example. And as to kinds of operations, we found an interest in divergent thinking and an interest in convergent thinking. Interestingly, we found a correlation of -.30 between scores for these two traits. There is a noteworthy interest in evaluation in the hypercritical person. This trait can have a depressing effect on divergent production, as Osborn pointed out in connection with his brainstorming sessions. But it can be of value to the creator who decides which of his ideas are best.

It is quite reasonable that the intellectual interests should lie along the lines of the SOI categories, for a person likes to do what he can do well. He therefore gets more practice in the same functions, improving them, in circular fashion. One implication might be that to increase an individual's ability, encourage him to get more practice in it. I would also recommend that the person be informed as to the nature of his abilities and their role in problem solving as soon as he is ready to comprehend such information.

Development of Creative Dispositions

The mention of development leads to some other directions of thinking. There have been numerous studies of the effects of different kinds of efforts to increase skills in creative thinking, as it should be. But sometimes the objective in development is broadened to include skills in problem solving. This involves much more than the unique creative-thinking skills. All problem solving does include creative elements, for the problem solver must arrive at a solution that is novel to him or her and must therefore be creative. But many more SOI functions are involved, depending upon the nature of the problem and the thinking habits of the individual.

The solver must be aware that a problem exists, and we have shown that the main SOI activity involved is cognition of implications, the kind of content depending on the situation. The solver is aware that objects or conditions are not as they should be; something new is needed. Thus, items of information are suggested by things as they are; in other words, implications. Tasks involving cognition of implications should be applied as training exercises.

Next, the problem solver must see the *nature* of the problem. The SOI operation is again cognition, the SOI content depending upon the situation. Having grasped the nature of the problem, the solver thinks of possible solutions, involving divergent production, or possibly convergent production if the problem is conceived in mathematical terms, for example. Along the way, from the beginning the solver guides his own activity by evaluating results at the various stages. If the solution takes much time he does well to keep in memory storage the steps he has taken, so as to avoid making the same mistakes more than once. If the evaluations show that something is seriously wrong he may take a new start at some point along the way.

The moral of all this is that quite a number of SOI functions need to be exercised in order to gain in skills in problem solving. There are so many skills needed that one answer could be to apply what the Japanese call "intelligence education." For more than 20 years their Learned Society of Intelligence Education has taken the SOI model as a map of intellectual functioning. They have constructed and used exercises and tests for almost all the SOI abilities and have applied them in many of their schools (Chiba, 1985). Their report is that the average child gains 20 points per year in his or her IQ, based on their own SOI tests. Similar exercises and tests have been developed in the USA by the SOI Institute of El Segundo, California. Here they are used more to diagnose learning difficulties of children and prescribing remedies.

In the development of problem-solving abilities, presumably abilities involving semantic content would be most usefully developed, followed by those with visual content. There is a general reason for developing the visual-thinking abilities because of greater efficiency. As an old Chinese saying goes, a picture can be as good as a thousand words.

References

Chiba, A. (1985). *The development of intelligence education.* Tokyo: International Society for Intelligence Education.

Guilford, J. P. (1958). A system of psychomotor abilities. *American Journal of Psychology, 71,* 164-174.

Guilford, J. P. (1977). *Way beyond the IQ: Guide to improving intelligence and creativity.* Buffalo, NY: Creative Education Foundation.

Guilford, J. P. (1980). Cognitive styles: What are they? *Educational and Psychological Measurement, 40,* 715-735.

Guilford, J. P. (1981). Higher-order structure-of-intellect abilities. *Multivariate Behavioral Research, 16,* 411-435.

Guilford, J. P. (1982). Cognitive psychology's ambiguities: Some suggested remedies. *Psychological Review, 89,* 48-59.

Guilford, J. P. (1986). *Creative talents: Their nature, use, and development.* Buffalo, NY: Bearly Limited.

Guilford, J. P., Hendricks, M., & Hoepfner, R. (1968). Solving social problems creatively. *Journal of Creative Behavior, 2,* 155-164.

Guilford, J. P., & Hoepfner, R. (1971). *The analysis of intelligence.* New York: McGraw-Hill.

Hendricks, M., Guilford, J. P., & Hoepfner, R. (1968). Measuring creative social intelligence. *Reports from the Psychological Laboratory, University of Southern California,* No. 42.

Jones, C. A. (1960). *Some relationships between creative writing and creative drawing of sixth-grade children.* Unpublished doctoral dissertation, Pennsylvania State University.

Osborn, A. (1963). *Applied imagination* (3rd ed.). New York: Scribner's.

Parnes, S. J., & Noller, R. B. (1972). Applied creativity: The creative studies, Part I. *Journal of Creative Behavior, 6,* 11-22.

Parnes, S. J., & Noller, R. B. (1972). Applied creativity: The creative studies, Part II. *Journal of Creative Behavior, 6,* 164-186.

Witkin, H. A., Dyk, R. B., Faterson, H. F., Goodenough, D. R., & Karp, S. A. (1962). *Psychological Differentiation.* New York: Wiley.

2

Genius: The Lessons of Historiometry

Dean K. Simonton
University of California at Davis

If we are to judge from the research literature on the subject, creativity and leadership appear to be two very different topics. Creativity appears to attract the attention of personality and educational psychologists, whereas leadership seems to fascinate social and organizational psychologists. This separation is unfortunate, I believe, for in many respects these two phenomena can be subsumed under a single generic definition. Social psychologists are fond of defining a leader as that group member who exerts more influence over group performance and decision-making than other group members. By this definition creators are leaders, too, of a certain kind. A creative scientific researcher, for example, is one whose publications command respect in the scientific community, a respect that is displayed in the citations that the researcher receives in the professional literature. Those scientists who are less creative are not so acknowledged as leaders within their disciplines. The definitional similarity between creativity and leadership becomes particularly pronounced when we turn our attention to those creators and leaders who have in some sense "made history." Clearly if someone is of sufficient importance to be found in encyclopedias, biographical dictionaries, and histories, that person can be said to have stood well above his or her contemporaries in influence, the specific nature of the achievement making little difference. Indeed, if the achievement is big enough, we often label the person a "genius"—as a kind of generic designation for any truly outstanding manifestation of creativity or leadership.

To comprehend the foundations of genius, however, requires a different methodological approach than is the norm. To objectively study historical figures, to scientifically test hypotheses about the "laws of genius," demands that we resort to historiometric techniques. These involve the quantification and mathematical analysis of pertinent historical and biographical data. In my recent book *Genius, Creativity, and Leadership* (Simonton, 1984c) I review the major "lessons of historiometry," but here I can offer an abstract of some of the more provocative findings, including results too recent to have been incorporated in the book. I will specifically discuss birth order, role-models, formal education, intelligence, productivity, age, and zeitgeist.

Birth Order

Francis Galton (1874) pointed out long ago that the first-born child is over-represented among those who attain distinction in scientific endeavors. A number of explanations have been offered for this finding. One possibility is that the first born is the favored child into whose development and education the parents channel most of their resources. Another explanation is provided by Zajonc's (1976) confluence model of intellectual development: The first-born child is exposed to an environment at a higher level of maturity than the later-born children who are over-exposed to literally infantile minds. However, both of these interpretations must face the ugly fact that the last-born child also enjoys a high probability of success, though still not as great as the first born (Ellis, 1904). This finding may suggest that some kind of favoritism is operating in the form of a serial-position effect, the first born being the most spoiled for being first, the last born spoiled the next most for being the last of a series. We must not conclude that the middle children are invariably left out in the cold, nonetheless. The Goertzels' study of over three hundred eminent 20th century personalities found that the politicians in their sample were quite prone to be middle children (Goertzel, Goertzel, & Goertzel, 1978). This result suggests that birth order may be crucial to the development of certain requisite social skills. The middle child, always caught between older and younger siblings, has plenty of opportunity for learning how to negotiate, compromise, and reconcile differences. An only child has no chance at all to nourish these abilities, at least not in the home.

Actually, the connection between birth order and success as a political leader may be a bit more complicated. Stewart (1977) has put forward a theory that the optimal birth order for a potential leader may depend on the political circumstances, or zeitgeist, in which he comes to power (his focus is on males). On the one hand, leadership styles are said to correspond to four unique sibling configurations—the only, first-born, middle, and last-born child. Each configuration gives the child a special set of experiences during early development, experiences that help shape personality. On the other hand, four varieties of crises determine which leadership style is appropriate, namely, the (a) breakdown of social institutions, (b) imperialistic expansion and confrontation, (c) retrenchment and realignment of domestic and foreign commitments and (d) rebellion and revolt. According to Stewart, the first of these crises is the proper province of only children, the second of the first born, and the third of the middle child, and the fourth of the last born. To make the case for his theory, Stewart studied the birth order and political zeitgeist for American presidents and British prime ministers, and obtained statistical endorsement. Curiously, the two leading candidates for the presidency in any given election year display a distinct tendency to be of the same ordinal position in their respective families. Moreover, other researchers have found results consistent with the theory. Revolutionaries, for example, are more likely to be later-born children (Walberg, Rasher, & Parkerson, 1980). Even the Goertzels' conclusion that the politicians in their sample were predominantly middle children bolsters Stewart's theory. Most of the politicians in the Goertzels' study attained their power positions in the post-World War II period, when domestic and foreign commitments were being remade and consolidated—putting a premium on negotiation skills. The days of the first born war leaders were over.

The main point is that birth order may exert an influence on the aspects of personality development which are responsible for achievement, whether as a leader or as a creator. It is of interest to speculate on how creators might fit into Stewart's interactionist theory. Are the revolutionaries in a creative endeavor more inclined to be later-born children? Are those creators who fight their way to dominating positions of prestige and influence more prone to be first borns? And are middle children more disposed to become the administrators in research institutions?

Role Models

An important influence on development has repeatedly been shown to be role models. The development of creative potential, in particular, is dependent on the availability of creative individuals who can serve as models for emulation. For example, one investigation scrutinized the historical distribution of over five thousand Western creators from Ancient Greece to the twentieth century; each creator was assigned to a 20-year period called a "generation" (Simonton, 1975). A time-series analysis indicated that the number of creators in one generation is a positive function of the number of creators in the previous *two* generations—namely the parental and grandparental generations. The impact of role-model availability puts constraints on the ups and downs in historical creativity, for a dearth of potential models implies an impoverished setting for creative development. As a consequence, creative geniuses tend to fall into clusters, or "configurations" (Kroeber, 1944), or "Golden Ages" spaced by "Dark Ages." Creativity does not emerge *de novo*. This intergenerational dependence has been shown to hold for leaders as well. In an inquiry into 342 hereditary monarchs of Europe, the eminence attained by a king was found to be a positive function of the fame attained by the king's father and grandfather (Simonton, 1983b). This study also found that for this modeling process to be effective, the models must be of the same sex. Queens gain nothing from their fathers and grandfathers for example.

Despite the clear significance of role models, there is a darker side, for the presence of a model in the psychological environment can be a mixed blessing. On the one hand, models can stimulate creativity by provoking admiration and emulation. As an illustration, one investigation of 677 classical composers found that the number of models available in childhood was significantly related to the emergence of musical precociousness (Simonton, 1977b). On the other hand, a developing creator may never rise above the temptation of mere imitation and thus become entrapped by models who must be surpassed. The classical composers study accordingly revealed that the presence of models can also serve to stifle the creative productivity of adulthood creators. In a similar way, an examination of 2,012 philosophers in the Western philosophical tradition indicated that even though the number of thinkers in one generation is a positive function of the number of predecessors in the previous generation, truly great intellects seem to require a comparative paucity of role-models for optimal creative development (Simonton, 1976c). If a developing mind has too many opportunities to become a disciple of some master or school, the free quest for alternative viewpoints may be undermined.

A recent study of 772 famous Western artists demonstrates this trade-off between emulation and imitation (Simonton, 1984a). Looking at the differential eminence of painters and sculptors from the Renaissance to the present day, the question was how the artist's eminence is dependent on a matrix of interpersonal relationships that the artist establishes with other artists. One type of relationship that is quite important concerns paragons and their admirers. Is the creative development of an artist facilitated if he or she employs a large number of predecessors as standards of excellence? Moreover, does it make a difference how far removed these paragons are in time? Certainly an artist can benefit from scrutinizing the "grand masters." It turns out that there exists an optimal generational (or age) gap between paragon and admirer for the maximum advantage of accrue from emulation. Furthermore, the optimum itself varies according to the number of paragons the artist admires. Thus, if an artist admires as many as 10 predecessors, they should precede him or her by an average of 136 years for the optimal result. For five paragons the best age gap expands to 162 years, for four 178 years, for three 210 years, and for two 305 years. (Figure One shows the typical case for artists who have three paragons.) Finally, if the artist admires but one paragon, there is no optimum age gap at all, but rather the more historically remote the paragon the better. Obviously, if an artist has a great many paragons the danger of imitating any one is comparatively small, and so they can be more proximate without any detrimental effect. Yet when only a single person is the object of admiration, the sole way that remains for reducing blind imitation is to separate the paragon and the admirer by a wide historical hiatus. The larger the age gap the greater the dissimilarity in styles, aims, and techniques, historical differences that themselves serve to temper any proclivity towards slavish imitation. With more paragons this protection is unnecessary.

To sum up, while it is true that role models contribute to the development of genius, the contribution can be negative rather than positive if the individual never breaks out of the initial pattern of imitation. Truly creative individuals, during the course of their careers, manage

Figure One.

The equation for predicting artistic eminence (A) as a function of the number of paragons (C) and the mean artist paragon age gap (G). The curve is for the typical case of C = 3 (from Simonton 1984a).

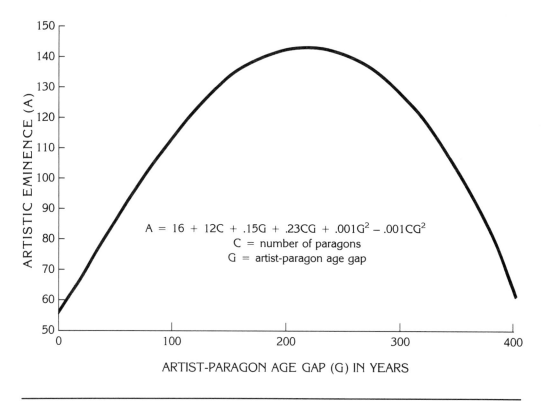

$$A = 16 + 12C + .15G + .23CG + .001G^2 - .001CG^2$$

C = number of paragons

G = artist-paragon age gap

ARTIST-PARAGON AGE GAP (G) IN YEARS

somehow to pass from the apprenticeship of imitation to full-fledged self-actualization (Simonton, 1980d).

Formal Education

The formal training we receive in our schools, colleges, and universities is equally equivocal in effect. On the positive side, we can definitely argue that success in life requires a great many special skills that can only be acquired with an enforced discipline which our educational systems conveniently provide. These skills range from reading to running a linear accelerator. On the negative side, there also can be little reason to doubt that formal education can inculcate a certain conformity of thought, even rigidity, that may hamper innovation. Therefore, it is conceivable that the relation between formal education and achievement follows a curvilinear, inverted-U function. Two studies show this may indeed be the case (Simonton, 1983a).

In the first investigation I re-examined the 301 geniuses collected by Catherine Cox (1926) in her famous study of the association between achievement and intelligence (Simonton, 1976a). This sample included both creators and leaders. They all were scored on achieved eminence using Cattell's (1903) rankings. In addition, a coding scheme was devised for scaling the level of formal education they attained. Then a test was run for curvilinear relationships using a multiple regression analysis. The result appears in Figure Two. For the leaders the relationship was strictly linear, not curvilinear, but *negative.* That is, the most acclaimed (or cursed) leaders were those who had the least formal training. In the case of creators, however,

Figure Two.

The relation between eminence and formal education for the 301 geniuses in the Cox sample (from Simonton, 1983a).

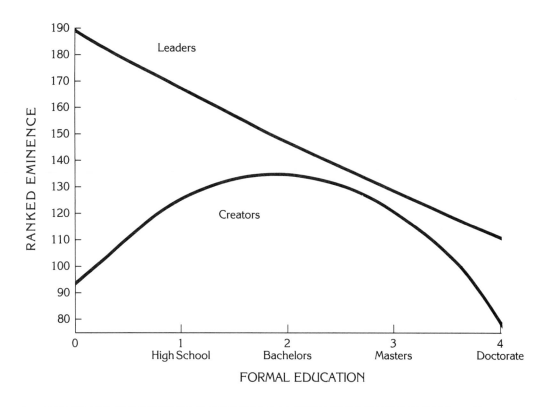

the expected relationship appeared—an inverted-J curve in fact. Recipients of doctoral degrees were at a distinct disadvantage even in comparison to those with no college, and a peak occurred in the level of education that maximally contributed to attainment. That optimum point occurred somewhere between the junior and senior years of college. Up to around the third year, increasing formal education increases the chances of success, but thereafter additional education was negatively associated with achievement.

This finding is interesting, but it should not be accepted without first obtaining corroborating evidence. Such support came from a second study, and from a very unlikely quarter—an inquiry into American presidents (Simonton, 1981b). Maranell (1970) had 571 American historians rate 33 presidents (Washington through Lyndon Johnson, deleting W. Harrison and Garfield) on several dimensions, two of which are pertinent here, namely, flexibility versus inflexibility and idealism versus pragmatism. It turns out that these two dimensions are related: Idealistic presidents tend to be inflexible, pragmatic ones flexible. Accordingly, a single dimension was created which I styled "dogmatism" (i.e., idealistic inflexibility). Now there is much research that suggests that creativity and dogmatism are negatively related (Simonton, 1983a). If so, it follows that the impact of formal education on dogmatism should be the reverse of that on creativity. In other words, the graph for the 33 presidents should be a reflection of that for the Cox creators. That is exactly what is found, as can be seen in Figure Three. The most dogmatic presidents are those with higher degrees, such as Dr. Wilson, the next most dogmatic those with very little formal education, such as the totally unschooled Andrew

Figure Three.

The relation between dogmatism and formal education for 33 American presidents (from Simonton, 1983a).

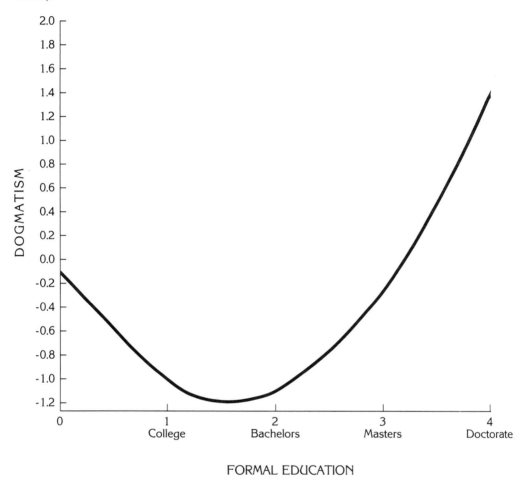

FORMAL EDUCATION

Johnson. The least dogmatic, that is, the most pragmatic and flexible, were those who left college somewhere between their junior and senior years—precisely as was found before. Thus, as unlikely as it seems, the data for the 33 presidents fits almost perfectly that for the creators in the Cox sample. The only assumption we have to make is that creativity and dogmatism are inversely related.

Now I realize that there could be a number of complaints about the above two studies. For one thing, the average birth year for the Cox sample is 1705, that for the 33 presidents 1820, and hence the results may not apply to 20th-century personalities. Moreover, it can be argued that even though the curvilinear relationships hold for some creative activities, other disciplines may require more formal training for maximal chances of success. For example, even if a doctoral degree in the fine arts is detrimental, the sciences require greater technical competence and hence a doctoral degree may be desirable. To handle these two objections I conducted a third study, this time using the 314 eminent 20th Century personalities collected by the Goertzels (Simonton, 1984c, chap. 4). Since their birth years are as recent as 1948 (with an average of 1902), we are dealing with more contemporary subjects. Furthermore, I separated those who attained distinction in the sciences from those who made their names in the arts and humanities. Besides these two domains of creativity, I examined the leaders. Both leaders and creators were then scaled for achieved eminence and formal educational level. In the instance of the leaders a marked contrast was observed with what was found for the leaders in the Cox sample: The function was described by a curvilinear curve with a peak at some modest amount of graduate education. Perhaps the greater complexity of modern political systems requires greater educational attainments, and the peak seems to coincide with the level of training reached by lawyer-politicians in most democratic societies. A similar function was found for scientists, only the peak is shifted a bit later, at some graduate education just shy of a PhD. This result endorses my conjecture that more technical disciplines require more formal training. Finally, the curve for the creators in the arts and humanities exhibits an inverted-U form, too, but in this case the peak falls somewhere between the junior and senior years of college—precisely as learned in the previous two investigations. Hence, I have succeeded in replicating the curvilinear function in a sample of more contemporary subjects, many of whom are still living and active.

To be sure, we do not know why the curvilinear relationship holds. One interpretation would be that excessive formal education actively inhibits creative development by stamping in a conformist perspective. An alternative is to say simply that beyond a certain point formal education becomes merely irrelevant to further creative development and so the more self-directed creators tend to drop out after the irrelevancy becomes apparent. But whatever the explanation, it is fair to say that a maximal amount of formal education is not always the optimal amount.

Intelligence

Intelligence has an immediate association with genius, for genius is often conceived as intelligence manifested to an extreme degree. Nevertheless, the connection between intelligence and the two principal applications of genius, creativity and leadership, is more in doubt, at least insofar as empirical research is concerned. In the case of creativity, for example, it seems that once a person achieves an IQ of around 120, further increments in intelligence represent no corresponding gain in creativity, and in the instance of leadership, the correlation between IQ and leadership is normally only around .25 or so, a modest figure even if a positive one (Simonton, 1985a). Still, it may be argued that most of these investigations concentrated on rather everyday subject pools with very few genius-level creators and leaders. What happens if we examine more exclusive subjects—true historical geniuses?

The classic investigation in this domain was executed by Catherine Cox back in 1926. She carefully collected data on the early childhoods of 301 geniuses, including such leaders as Napoleon and such creators as Beethoven. This data was utilized to calculate an estimated intelligence quotient, based on the definition of IQ as being proportional to the ratio of mental to chronological age. The result was IQ scores like the following: Napoleon 155, Washington 140, Garabaldi 140, Luther 170, Beethoven 165, Michelangelo 180, Voltaire 190, and Kant 175. Cox then addressed the question of whether these IQ estimates correlate in a positive direction with the achieved eminence of the 301 subjects. Though she found such a correlation, and her result has been more recently replicated (Walberg, Rasher, & Parkerson, 1980), a more detailed statistical analysis has revealed that the correlation is too small to satisfy standard levels of significance (Simonton, 1976a). This is not to say that this batch of creators and leaders is not a smart bunch, for the mean IQ is around 164. The problem is clearly that the group represents an elite so selective that the variance in either IQ or eminence is severely truncated, thereby attenuating the correlation. If we could manage to insert less bright and more obscure historical personages into the sample, the opportunity for an enlarged and respectable correlation emerging would be all the greater.

One study in fact accomplished this seemingly impossible addition by switching the study to 342 hereditary monarchs (Simonton, 1983b). The advantage of studying hereditary monarchs is that an individual may succeed to the highest office of a land on no greater right than that of primogeniture, and without any notability to boot. Additionally, the right of inheritance makes it possible for even an incompetent ruler to stay on the throne. Consequently, the variance is much larger. Of course, now the criterion variable is leadership rather than creativity, yet the results can still be instructive: Assessed leadership is indeed correlated with assessed intellectual power. Moreover, the intellectual ability is partly inherited by the principles of genetics, a result that would please Francis Galton, the author of *Hereditary Genius* (1869). If there were some way of expanding the variation in creativity as we can do for leadership using hereditary monarchs, we would no doubt obtain a comparable outcome.

The range in intelligence and criterion variables is not the only consideration however. Another issue has to do with the possibility that the functional relationship between intelligence and creativity or leadership might be curvilinear rather than linear. I have developed a conceptual model of intelligence and personal influence in problem-solving groups that allows us to anticipate a nonlinear connection (Simonton, 1985a). The model is too complex to discuss here, so the barest outline may suffice. It starts with the straightforward postulate that intellectual ability is normally distributed around a mean of 100 and a standard deviation of 16. Two factors then translate this distribution into probabilities of exerting influence. On the one hand, influence is more likely to belong to those members of a group who are intellectually superior, for these brightest will be more effective in problem-solving ability and more articulate in coordinating group activities. On the other hand, an excessively intelligent group member may also be less comprehensible to fellow members, and this intelligibility factor can work to place an upper limit on the amount of intelligence that will prove optimal. These two factors obviously operate in a give-and-take relation, and under certain conditions we obtain the curvilinear function shown in Figure Four. Here the optimal IQ gap between leader and follower is 1.2 standard deviations, or an IQ of 119, for a group consisting of members with a mean IQ of 100. If the average IQ of the group is larger than 100, then the leader will most likely have a higher IQ still (1.2 standard deviations higher in fact). Nonetheless, this case is interesting in that the IQ 119 figure is similar to what is said to mark the point beyond which further increases in IQ have no necessary impact on creativity. If we see Figure Four as applying to small creative problem-solving groups, the model helps us understand why.

Productivity

Thomas Edison took out almost 1300 patents over his career, still more than any other inventor. No wonder, then, that he said that genius was ninety-nine percent perspiration! And Edison's case can be considered fairly typical. Earlier we defined a leader as one who exerts more influence than average, and noted that creators are leaders who exert their influence in the form of notable contributions. A number of researchers have shown, in fact, that a small percentage of workers in any given field of creative activity account for a disproportionate amount of contributions to their discipline (Dennis, 1955; Price, 1963). The top ten percent most productive creators are responsible for about half of all contributions, whereas the 50 percent least productive contributors produce only about 15 percent of the contributions. The most productive contributor is at least a hundred times more productive than the least productive members, and the modal number of contributions is one. This means that the distribution of contributions is highly skewed. The plurality of creative individuals produce only one contribution each, a smaller proportion only two each, and so on, until a mere handful make as many as a 100 contributions or more.

According to Lotka's law, in fact, the number of creators who produce n contributions (e.g., patents, publications, etc.) is inversely proportional to n^2, a function that yields a fast

Figure Four.

The optimum discrepancy between leader IQ and the mean IQ of group for the case of a group of average IQ (= 100) (from Simonton, 1985a).

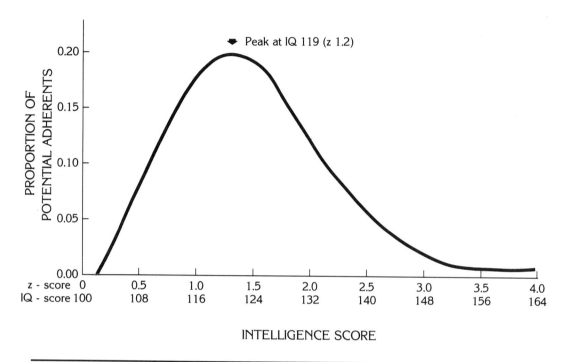

drop-off and a long tail (Lotka, 1926). This formal expression is similar to Pareto's law of income distribution in which income is inversely proportional to $n^{1.5}$ (Price, 1963). Productive output, like income, tends to be unequally distributed, a small, even elite group accounting for a lion's share of the "wealth." Price's law expresses the same idea as Lotka's law in a slightly different but perhaps more instructive way: Half of all contributions to a particular endeavor is produced by the square root of the total number of creators working in that field (Price, 1963). For example, if 100 scientists make up a certain enterprise, ten will be responsible for half of all papers, whereas if 10,000 work in a popular area, 100 will account for half of the publications. Price's law implies that as a creative discipline grows, the proportion of contributors who are responsible for half of all output shrinks. If 100 are in the area, ten percent account for half, but if 10,000, only one percent do. Thus as a field expands it becomes ever more elitist.

We have been speaking of total, lifetime productivity. There are three components to this final score: The creator can begin to produce at an early age, to produce at an exceptionally high annual rate, and to produce until quite late in life. Although there is no mathematical or logical reason for these three components to be associated–indeed, many people subscribe to the folklore belief that those who are prodigiously productive at a precocious age will be subject to early burnout–the three components are in fact positively related to one another (Dennis, 1954a, 1954b; Simonton, 1977b). Those creative individuals who begin their careers earlier tend to end them later, and to maintain high productivity rates throughout their careers (at one period during Edison's long career he was averaging a patent every five days). I have proposed a mathematical theory, too elaborate to discuss here, that predicts that these three components must all correlate due to their common dependence on a variable called "creative potential" (Simonton, 1984b). Another explanation of their interrelationship stems from the doctrine of cumulative advantage (Merton, 1968). Those who publish first will receive rewards first, and those rewards will reinforce further output at higher rates and for a longer duration. In a sense, creative individuals are like rats in a Skinner box receiving food pellets for bar pressing: The first to catch on to the trick and press the lever will get a head start in the rat race for ever more rewards.

Total lifetime output, however generated, is not synonymous with influence, naturally. There are "mass producers" who are prolific but trivial, and "perfectionists" who put out a handful of quality contributions. Even so, empirical research has shown that, these exceptions be what they may, quality tends to be the consequence of quantity (Simonton, 1981a). In fact, a constant-probability-of-success model seems to be operating so that the proportion of hits over misses tends to be relatively even across contributors. Those who produce more masterworks also produce more rubbish. Thus, the best approach is to massively generate ideas in the hope that some pan out. This, of course, is the notion underlying "brainstorming" and similar techniques. This approach also has a theoretical justification in Campbell's (1960) random-variation and selective-retention model of creativity that develops an analogy with the operation of natural selection in the biological world.

The above remarks are based on studies of creators, not leaders. Nonetheless, I think the same principles may apply to leaders, especially to creative leaders. A truly great leader is one who begins generating ideas at an early age, keeps on producing ideas at a prolific rate, and continues the process for many years, never seeming to run out of steam. Even if some ideas prove to be off the mark, the constant-probability-of-success model may assure that enough hits will come to make the effort profitable. The doctrine of cumulative advantage may also prove germane. In the realm of leadership, as in creativity, the rich may indeed get richer, the poor poorer. Initial success breeds further success, and advantage accumulates to those who started off on the right foot. In military leadership, for example, there is an almost perfect correlation between the number of battles fought and the number won (Simonton, 1980a). Finally, it may be that Lotka's and Price's laws may be descriptive of the achievement of leaders too. A small elite may be responsible for a disproportionate number of innovative ideas, whether they be in government or in the private sector.

Age

A creator's lifetime productive output, needless to say, is not distributed evenly throughout a career—nor is achievement generally. Harvey C. Lehman has systematically documented the agewise distribution in his book *Age and Achievement* (1953). In broad terms, creative output in most fields tends to rise fairly rapidly to a peak in the late 30s or early 40s, and thereafter decline somewhat gradually. Recent investigations have established Lehman's chief results (Simonton, 1977a, 1983a). To be sure, the precise nature of the age function is a bit more complicated. In some fields, such as mathematics and poetry, the ascent to an early peak is quite sudden, as is the plunge afterwards. In other disciplines, such as scholarship, the peak occurs much later in life and the decline is virtually nonexistent. For the most part, the 40th year appears to be the highwater mark of creative achievement.

Interestingly, a similar peak may hold for some types of leadership. A study of military success on the battle field found that those generals who were closest to age 45 were more likely to exhibit superior military competence and experience (Simonton, 1980a). Another inquiry into absolute monarchs discovered a peak age for political success around age 42 (Simonton, 1984d). Here, too, the exact placement of the peak depends on the endeavor: Revolutionaries tend to be young, heads of state in established political systems old; founders of religions are usually young, those leaders top in the hierarchy of established faiths old. And in the case of American presidents, the best age for getting elected seems to be in the late 50's (Lehman, 1953). Nonetheless, the early 40s still appears to be a good point estimate, especially in those areas that require creative (rather than traditional) leadership. This may even be true in the economic sphere: 40 years is the approximate peak age of wage attainment for example (Stolzenberg, 1975).

The question that now comes to mind is why achievement tends to be a curvilinear function of age. Though it is impossible to offer a complete answer here, I should briefly describe two theories. The oldest, by Beard (1874), proposes that creativity is a function of two factors, enthusiasm and experience. Enthusiasm without experience produces original work only, whereas experience without enthusiasm produces routine work only. Because enthusiasm rises quickly up to the early thirties and then just as quickly declines, while experience grows continuously, the optimum age emerges in the late 30s where the conjunction is maximal. One nice asset of this theory is that it helps explain why creativity may peak at different ages for various disciplines. Poetry, mathematics, religious innovation, and political revolution all likely require more enthusiasm, but scholarship, religious administration, and political consolidation all demand more experience.

The main drawback of Beard's model may be that it does not make precise predictions. The second theory, recently proposed by myself and mentioned briefly earlier (Simonton, 1984b), is actually a mathematical model which predicts the productivity rate for each year of a creator's career. A typical curve predicted by the model appears in Figure Five. In simple terms, this model assumes that each individual begins with an initial supply of creative potential which then is transformed into actual contributions through a series of cognitive operations. This model explains different peak ages according to the different information processing needs of a given discipline, and, as noted before, accounts for certain features of individual variation in productivity. One intriguing implication of the model is its prediction that creativity never really has to end, even when the creator is quite old. As the model has it, most creators die without fully actualizing their creative potential.

Figure Five.

Predicted curve for creative productivity as a function of career age according to a two-step cognitive model of the creative process (from Simonton, 1984b).

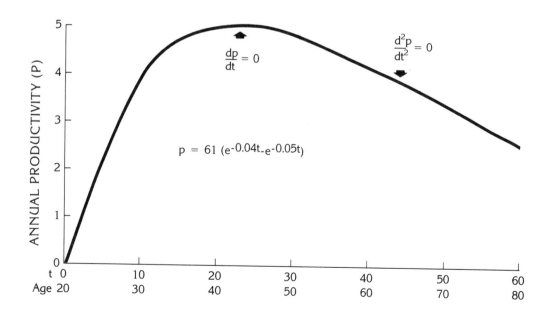

This last point brings us to one final precaution about interpreting the age curves found for achievement. It would be erroneous to discount the contributions of persons simply because they appear to be "over the hill" with respect to the peak age. Previously we spoke of the constant-probability-of-success model that asserts that quality is a repercussion of quantity. This model has been shown to hold across the life span too (Simonton, 1977a, 1985b). That is, the proportion of successful contributions to total output remains constant with age. Hence, even if elderly persons are less prolific than those in their "prime," the probability that any given product will have an impact is not a function of age. The efforts of mature contributors must therefore be taken with equal seriousness to those of their junior colleagues.

Zeitgeist

Up to this point my emphasis has been on the psychological variables behind creativity and leadership. Yet I received my degree in "social psychology," and so it should come as no surprise that I have devoted a considerable part of my own research to discovering how the sociocultural milieu affects the appearance of creativity and leadership. For example, several inquiries have been published into the adverse effect that warfare has on scientific innovation (Simonton, 1976b, 1980b). I have also shown how political violence affects, and is a partial consequence of, the prevailing ideological stance of a generation (Simonton, 1976d). But perhaps the most characteristic studies are those that determine the relative importance of zeitgeist, genius, and chance in creativity and leadership. By "zeitgeist" I mean those social and cultural context (or situational) factors beyond the control of any single individual, while genius is taken to signify an exceptional set of personal qualities. Chance is sort of what is left over—the residual complex of myriad inconsistent effects that defy classification. Political and military leaders have been scrutinized along with musical, philosophical, and scientific creators to weigh the comparative impact of these three factors (e.g., Simonton, 1976c, 1979, 1980a, 1980d, 1984e). The empirical highlights may be given as follows.

Political leadership

A number of investigations have been conducted into the determinants of success in positions of high political leadership. Two specific inquiries deserve attention here. The first has to do with presidential leadership, the second with monarchal eminence. In the first case, a study was done to find out what factors would allow us to predict a president's success in the White House (Simonton, 1981b). Some of the discovered factors were clearly individual in nature. As mentioned earlier in this article, presidential dogmatism was affected by the amount of formal education a president had received. Situational factors have an even larger part to play, however. Presidents who served as wartime commander-in-chief, for example, are automatically rated as "greater" than those who served in peacetime—and the more war years the higher the corresponding greatness rating. Also, some of these situational factors have a potent chance element to them. Most notably, those presidents who succeeded to the presidency via the vice-presidency upon the death (or resignation) of their predecessors tend to perform less well in the White House. Such "accidental presidents" are more prone to see their Cabinet and Supreme Court nominees rejected by the Senate and to see their vetoes overturned by Congress. This disability, moreover, cannot be ascribed to inferior political experience on the part of accidental presidents. No individual differences were found between presidents and their vice-presidents on the most likely background variables (Simonton, 1985c).

The inquiry into the causes of monarchal eminence found further support for the notion that distinction is a product of individual and situational characteristics, with a whimsical influx of probabilistic influences besides (Simonton, 1984e). Certain personality characteristics were again discovered to affect various aspects of a king's or queen's performance on the throne. The monarch's fame was a positive function of assessed intelligence, for example, and such distinction was also a curvilinear U-curve function of assessed morality. Fame via virtue and infamy via vice are the two main routes to leader eminence. Situational factors figure prominently too—in fact, even more so. The single most crucial determinant of monarchal eminence is the number of significant historical events that occurred during the ruler's reign, and the number one determinant of this historical richness is reign span—the main determinant of which is life span. Since historical activity, reign span, and life span were all affected by such situational factors as dynastic rank and whether or not the ruler was a regent, the context in which a leader governs seems critical. This situational input is moderated only slightly by personal characteristics: Intelligence affects both life span and reign span, leadership affects reign span, and morality affects the amount of historical activity. Even more significant is the potential role of chance in the ultimate judgments of posterity. Neither life span nor reign span are subject to complete personal or even institutional control. For instance, less than one quarter of a leader's reign span is due to how long he or she lives, and the vicissitudes of assassination plots and battle deaths implant a capricious element to be sure. A summary of the analysis can be seen in Figure Six.

All in all, the data for monarchs agree with those of presidents: Political leadership is a complex mixture of personal and situational attributes, with a liberal sprinkling of chance events.

Figure Six.

A causal model of monarchal eminence for 342 European kings, queens, and regents. Percentage of variance explained is shown for each determinant along with the nature of the functional relationship (from Simonton, 1984c).

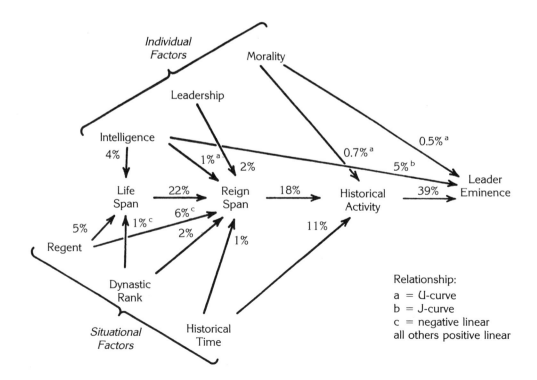

Military genius

In the case of military leadership, both individual and situational factors again prove to be germane to the prediction of tactical victory (Simonton, 1980a). The general who takes the initiative by attacking first has the best odds of success (and younger generals are more prone to be aggressive in this respect than are older generals). On the other hand, the side tends to be more successful that fights under a divided command where two or more generals are equal partners in tactical planning and execution—a situation most likely to arise in allied armies. This fact falls into line with the research on problem solving. For simple problems, individuals working alone do as well as individuals working in groups, but for complex problems individuals do better if they can pool their abilities in a group. The decision-making processes required on the battlefield are complicated if nothing else, and hence it is to be expected that collaborating generals do better than those working alone. In any event, several individual and situational factors emerged as good predictors; though the individual predictors were the best predictors of tactical victory, situational predictors were best predictors of a battle casualty advantage (army size being the most important). In either case, the predictive accuracy was not perfect. The victor, for instance, could only be predicted 71 percent of the time, leaving some room (so far) for chance to operate.

Musical esthetics

The place of chance in the production of notable musical compositions has been intimated earlier when we mentioned the constant-probability-of-success model. Quality has been shown to be a probabilistic consequence of quantity both across composers (Simonton, 1977b) and within composers' careers (Simonton, 1977a). That is, the more productive composers exhibit greater odds of success, and those periods of a composer's life in which he or she produces the most total output are also those periods in which the most masterworks are generated. The individual personality plays a role as well. Certainly individual differences in productivity are a sign of genius. But individual biography affects esthetic success, too, and often in very subtle, personal ways. For instance, the amount of biographical stress a composer must endure—including events like the death of a loved one, the birth of child, a change in residence or place of employ—affects the structure of the melodies composed over the same time interval (Simonton, 1980c). Specifically, the melodies become more original, with more unusual notes (e.g., chromaticism) and more uncommon intervals between notes (e.g., sevenths rather than thirds). This alteration in melodic originality contributes directly to the ultimate esthetic success of a piece (Simonton, 1980d). If we gauge how frequently a work is likely to be performed and recorded, and we look how this "thematic fame" index varies as a function of melodic originality, we obtain the curve represented in Figure Seven. We can see that the most successful compositions are those that feature a moderate amount of melodic originality—just enough to stimulate and even excite. Compositions below this optimum are too boring in their trite predictability, whereas those beyond this optimum are excessively anxiety-producing for most listeners. Interestingly, if the choice is just between boredom and anxiety, the commonplace wins out. Thus the atonal and serial music is fated to be less popular than even the most obvious themes constructed of scale passages.

Since the analysis just discussed was based on 15,618 themes created by classical composers from the Renaissance to the mid-twentieth century, it is possible to run a trend analysis on the melodic originality scores for each theme. The result is shown in Figure Eight. Overall, melodic originality has been increasing, but not at a smooth, monotonic rate. On the contrary, a cyclical pattern is superimposed over the upward trend with two peaks in the early Baroque and the early twentieth century, and low points in the Renaissance and Classical periods. This curve can be taken as the melodic zeitgeist, that is, as the expected or normative melodic structure for each time period. We can then measure a different kind of melodic

Figure Seven.

The relation between thematic fame (or popularity) and repertoire melodic originality for 15,618 themes by 477 classical composers (from Simonton, 1984c).

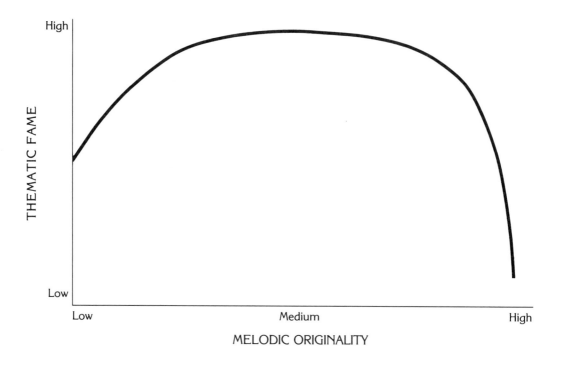

originality based on whether a given theme can be considered typical of other themes composed at the same time. This new measure is called zeitgeist melodic originality (as distinguished from the repertoire melodic originality predicated on the entire classical repertoire). There are two provocative points to be made about this derived indicator. In the first place, it too is connected to the esthetic success of a composition, though in a manner exactly opposite to what holds for repertoire melodic originality. The most successful pieces are those whose melodic structure departs from the prevailing spirit of the times. Furthermore, those that depart in the direction of augmented originality are more successful than those that dissent by being less original than the norm for the age. Hence, value is placed on nonconformity, but the premium is more on being in advance of the age rather than lagging in the rear.

The second finding is closely related: There is an intriguing relationship between the composer's age and melodic originality. In the case of repertoire melodic originality the composer becomes ever more original as his or her career progresses, yet a peak is attained at around the 56th year, after which melodic originality declines. For zeitgeist melodic originality the composer also becomes more and more original with maturity, but no turnaround point is reached. The relationship is simply linear, the older the composer is the more original are the compositions with respect to the musical zeitgeist. Therefore, though the composer appears to begin his or her career immersed in the zeitgeist, the end of the career sees an appreciable increase in nonconformity. In a sense we can say that a composer's career roots itself in the zeitgeist and, through continual self-actualization, ascends into the uninhibited demonstration of unique genius.

Figure Eight.

Result of a trend analysis of how melodic originality varies as a function of composition date, based on 15,618 themes (from Simonton, 1980d).

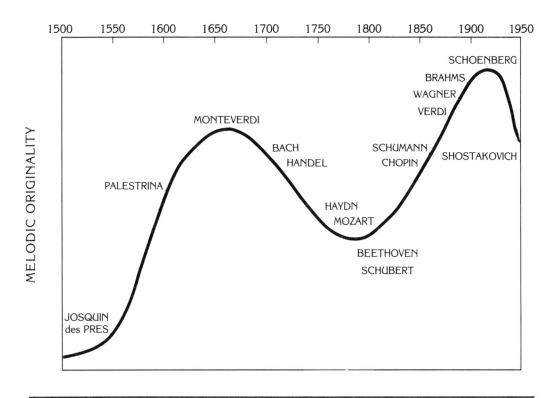

Philosophical eminence

The impact of philosophers on first blush seems quite directly dependent on the milieu in which the thinkers live. It has often been said, for example, that Voltaire's fame as a thinker resulted from his ability to articulate the spirit of his times; he was the voice of his age. A study I conducted on 2,012 philosophers in the Western tradition evaluated this and other related generalizations (Simonton, 1976c). It is true that the distinction of thinkers depends on the political context in which they were born (e.g., political anarchy is detrimental to creative development) and on the number of role-models available to them as they developed. However, there is even more reason to believe that the true philosophical genius is a great dissenter, a rebel against the predominant opinions of the day. First of all, the most highly rated thinkers are less representative of their times than are their more obscure colleagues. On the average, it is the lesser thinker who chooses to conform to the normative views of an era, whereas the greater thinker seems to launch a protest. Curiously, this independence of thought on the part of philosophical geniuses adopts a peculiar form: The master thinker has a closer intellectual affinity with the ideas that preoccupied the previous generation of thinkers. It is as if the most impressive minds are engaged in consolidating, even synthesizing the notions that were being tossed around and argued when they were youths; they are in a sense old-fashioned, behind the times, yet they, in the process, bring the past into an intellectual culmination. Aristotle did this for Greek philosophy, al-Ghazali for the Muslim faith, Chu Hsi for the Confucian tradition, and Thomas Aquinas for the Christian religion. Further, the systems devised by the first-order genius have three additional characteristics that betray a unique personality: The systems cover a much broader range of philosophical issues than average, advocate minority opinions in the context of the entire philosophical tradition, and combine the ideas they present in remarkably unusual ways. All told, the conceptions of the most renowned thinkers tend to be independent, integrative, comprehensive, extremist, and original. Such are the indicators of philosophical genius.

This investigation did not directly assess the participation of chance, but some inadvertent findings have some bearing on this question. For one thing, the equation used to predict philosophical eminence, though it contained a baker's dozen variables, accounted for only 22 percent of the variation in fame. How much of the 78 percent left over variation is due to chance, of course, we cannot say, but there is plenty of room for random influences. Even more suggestive is the effect of modernity. The closer a thinker's ideas are to the favored conceptions of the twentieth century, the greater the assessed eminence. This relationship clearly represents an epochcentric bias, and a transient one at that. When a new set of ideas becomes vogue, the ratings of the past philosophers have to undergo a little reshuffling. Thus a philosopher's standing with posterity is always partially the product of a particular posterity's preferred positions.

Scientific multiples

In scientific creativity, the participation of all three factors is quite evident in the phenomenon of independent discovery and invention—what Merton (1961) calls "multiples." Classic cases include the independent invention of calculus by Newton and Leibniz and the independent formulation of the principle of natural selection by Darwin and Wallace. Proponents of a zeitgeist position have often argued that instances of multiples—and hundreds of cases exist—prove that scientific progress is essentially inevitable, and genius per se is more or less irrelevant to that progress (Ogburn & Thomas, 1922). On first glance this argument certainly looks watertight. Nevertheless, when cases of multiples are subjected to detailed mathematical analysis, a different picture emerges (Simonton, 1978, 1979). In the first place, genius does play a role. For example, the more highly productive scientists also tend to be the ones who participate in multiples. Even more critically, chance seems to play the biggest part in the appearance of multiples. The overwhelming majority of multiples are doublets involving just two independent discoverers, the next most frequent is the triplet, then the quadruplet, and so on. The more scientists involved in a multiple, the more rare the event. This distribution is very peculiar, and, in fact, it can be shown to hold for extremely rare events (viz. it is a Poisson distribution with a small mean). As a consequence, singletons, or discoveries made only once, are more commonplace than doublets and, even more significantly, nulltons, or discoveries never made at all because luck ran out on them, are very common as well. Hence, scientific progress is far from inevitable. Figure Nine shows the typical distribution for this chance model and compares this distribution from what would be expected from pure genius and zeitgeist positions. Although the zeitgeist exerts some influence on the operation of genius (mostly in the rank-ordering of events), chance seems to govern more than anything else what actually ends up in the annals of scientific discoveries and inventions.

The principle conclusion to be drawn from these studies is that creativity and leadership do not function totally at the individual level. Rather, if the situational context moderates the manifestation of even high-level geniuses, can we expect that our own enterprises on a more mundane plane are any less subject to the milieu? And if the history-making leaders and creators are subject at least in part to the whims of luck, certainly we all must take that factor into account. Yet, as we saw in the section on productivity, we can also take advantage of chance for our own purposes: Chance can be an instrument as well as a determinant.

Figure Nine.

The expected distribution of multiple grades for zeitgeist, genius, and chance models. The actual distribution is virtually identical to that shown for the chance model (from Simonton, 1979).

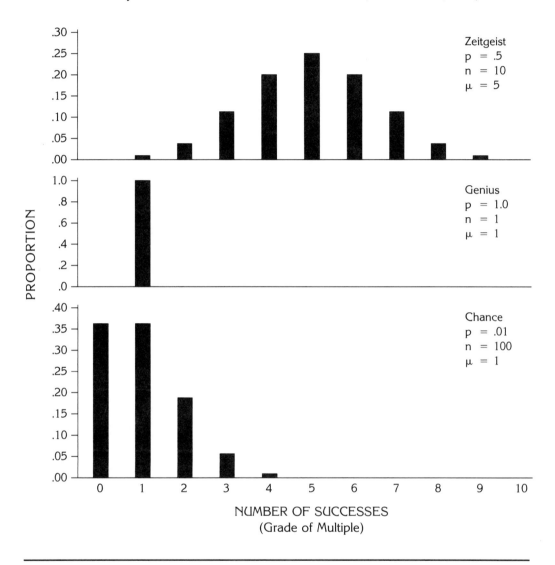

Conclusion

One objection that might be raised against the above review is that much of it is based on historiometric studies of distinguished creators and leaders. How do we know that these results apply to those of us who venture far humbler designs? I maintain that it is merely a matter of degree, not of kind, between geniuses who make history and those of us who leave an innovative mark in some far more subtle fashion. One foundation for this belief is that whenever direct comparison is feasible, the empirical findings for contemporary populations are quite similar to those for historical populations (Simonton, 1984c). The relations between age and achievement, between productivity and influence, between formal education and creativity, and between esthetic originality and appreciation are just a few of many examples. Nonetheless, future research must establish more linkages between genius and less illustrious forms of personal influence. Therein lies one of the frontiers of creativity research in my view. To offer an illustration of what this research might entail, allow me to conclude this chapter with a summary of an investigation as yet unpublished.

The Goertzels, among other concerns of their 1978 study, wondered whether people who achieve in various endeavors can be distinguished regarding certain biographical data. Do leaders stem from backgrounds distinct from those of creators? Are creative scientists biographically distinguishable from creative artists? For the most part, the characteristic biographies do vary from field to field in a systematic way. At the same time, there exist conspicuous individual differences in these matters. Not all artists are the same, for example, for some possess biographies more akin to scientists or even politicians than to their colleagues in the arts. In more general terms, some creators and leaders feature biographies that are typical of achievers in their respective domains, whereas others are atypical or biographically marginal. The question which fascinated me was whether the ultimate eminence that a person attained in a certain endeavor was helped or hurt by being biographically marginal to that endeavor. On the one hand, it could be that the most famous achievers are precisely those who best typify the biographical attributes of most members of their discipline. This would be the case if each field required a unique combination of life experiences for full success so that the closer a person comes to that ideal background the better his or her chances. If so, then the most noteworthy achievers should be just those we should most compare ourselves should we have aspirations whatsoever in a given area, no matter how modest. The less eminent will be less adequate exemplars of the requisite biography. On the other hand, perhaps the reverse is true: The least eminent may be the most biographically typical whereas the most eminent may be the most biographically marginal. This is the expected situation if to accomplish something distinctive one must bring something uncommon into the domain. To be like everybody else may be of no advantage, but to have an offbeat biography may be a distinct asset. What this alternative tells us is that we should *not* look to the great geniuses of the past for any guidance in our own more mundane pursuits, for the most illustrious are the most peculiar. To be sure, a third possibility exists, namely that biographical marginality is simply unrelated to distinction in any endeavor. Perhaps certain biographical experiences provide prerequisites for entering a field, but once in, other factors take over in the determination of eminence, factors that are more general in effect. For instance, each field can require its own characteristic vita, yet differential success in each field may result from individual contrasts in intelligence, persistence of effort, and other generic traits.

Of the three alternatives just presented, by far the most damaging from our current perspective is the middle one. If the most eminent are the most biographically marginal with respect to lesser members of their field, then their utility as models may be seriously vitiated. The lesser figures, even if near nonentities, who are more biographically typical would provide us with superior guides to achievement. In contrast, if the most renown achievers are the most typical, then there is nothing wrong in reading a chapter like the present one for useful clues. Better yet, perhaps, would be a zero correlation, for that would tell us that the most famous have the same biographical characteristics as the least famous. Therefore, we may emulate the great without even aiming for the same heights.

Given the relevance of this question, I was quite pleased when the Goertzels were so kind as to send me their data for 314 personalities. These persons were already classified into 20 different categories of achievement, including realms of both creativity (e.g., fiction authors, nonfiction authors, artists, philosophers, scientists, etc.) and leadership (e.g., politicians, military figures, revolutionaries, reformers, etc.). The Goertzels also quantified over 50 biographical attributes, the same attributes so extensively covered in their book. It was then an easy matter to employ discriminant analysis to pick out which biographical facts go with which endeavors. To give some idea of the contrasts: Nonfiction authors are more likely to come from urban centers, military figures from rural regions; women are more prone to become nonfiction authors and performers, men to become politicians and athletes; scientists, philosophers, and reformers tended to come from happy home environments, whereas authors grew up in less auspicious family circumstances; scientists were more fortunate in having supportive fathers; psychiatrists, in contrast, having endured paternal rejection; some fields evidently require considerable formal education, such as science, others much less so, such as being a mystic or psychic, a labor leader or a business person; and so forth. All told, 17 discriminators were isolated. Using these discriminators one can calculate a "biographical typicalness" score for each of the 314. This score was defined in terms of the probability of a person entering a field that he or she in fact entered given the person's biographical attributes and comparing them with what is the typical biographical profile for the field in question. By comparison, a biographically marginal individual is one whose background would not lead us to predict entrance into the discipline actually chosen. As an example, Rachel Carson, the author of *Silent Spring*, had a biography more typical of poets and, to a lesser degree, reformers, and accordingly was biographically marginal as a scientist, her chosen profession.

The last task was to measure the differential eminence of the 314 personalities. Here I employed the same procedures that worked so well in the studies reviewed earlier in this chapter. A half dozen sources were used to operationalize eminence indicators, and a factor analysis demonstrated that these indicators all tapped a single dimension. A composite eminence measure could thus be pieced together that boasts an internal consistency reliability (coefficient alpha) of .76, a respectable figure. This coefficient proves that the eminence measure has differentiating power even for this elite group of modern personages. Yet it must be said that the Goertzels' 314, though all famous to some degree, differ immensely in comparative eminence. Some, such as Louis Leakey, T. S. Elliot, Jackson Pollock, and Indira Gandhi, are virtually household words, whereas others, such as Rosalind Franklin, Andrei Codrescu, Raphael Soyer, and Estes Kefauver, are much more obscure. In any event, the relationship between this eminence measure and biographical typicalness was assessed using a multiple regression analysis (with numerous control variables). Though the coefficient was not statistically significant, it did lean in the positive, not the negative, direction. Hence, there is absolutely no reason to think that the most eminent creators and leaders are biographically marginal and, if anything, they have a slight propensity for being more typical than their less renowned colleagues. So there is some added justification for believing that studies such as reported in my book may indeed have relevance for all of us with aspirations. The famous are not oddballs or freaks, but people whose biographical characteristics are like others in the same endeavor.

Though I hope that future inquiries will pursue this point further, in a certain sense such a demonstration is impertinent. It is my conviction that historiometric findings possess value even if they cannot be directly applied to more everyday matters. Such factors as birth order, role models, formal education, intelligence, productivity, age, and zeitgeist may or may not be germane to more mundane forms of achievement, yet they certainly are valuable for understanding the biographical foundations of genius. And given that geniuses, whether as leaders or as creators, have shaped our past, currently impact on our present, and will continue to form the future, these individuals are worthy of being comprehended for their own sake, merely because they are there. We do not have to be able to model ourselves after geniuses for geniuses to mold our lives. They do that already, now.

References

Beard, G. M. (1874). *Legal responsibility in old age.* NY: Russell.

Campbell, D. T. (1960). Blind variation and selective retention in creative thought as in other knowledge processes. *Psychological Review, 67,* 380-400.

Cattell, J. McK. (1903). A statistical study of eminent men. *Popular Science Monthly, 62,* 359-377.

Cox, C. (1926). *The early mental traits of three hundred geniuses.* Stanford, CA: Stanford University Press.

Dennis, W. (1954a). Bibliographies of eminent scientists. *Scientific Monthly, 79,* 180-183.

Dennis, W. (1954b). Predicting scientific productivity in later decades from records of earlier decades. *Journal of Gerontology, 9,* 465-467.

Dennis, W. (1955). Variations in productivity among creative workers. *Scientific Monthly, 80,* 277-278.

Ellis, H. (1904). *A study of British genius.* London: Hurst & Blackett.

Galton, F. (1869). *Hereditary Genius.* London: Macmillan.

Galton, F. (1874). *English men of science.* London: Macmillan.

Goertzel, M. G., Goertzel, V., & Goertzel, T. G. (1978). *Three hundred eminent personalities.* San Francisco: Jossey-Bass.

Kroeber, A. H. (1944). *Configurations of culture growth.* Berkeley, CA: University of California Press.

Lehman, H. C. (1953). *Age and achievement.* Princeton, N.J.: Princeton University Press.

Lotka, A. J. (1926). The frequency distribution of scientific productivity. *Journal of the Washington Academy of Sciences, 16,* 317-323.

Maranell, G. M. (1970). The evaluation of presidents: An extension of the Schlesinger polls. *Journal of American History, 57,* 104-113.

Merton, R. K. (1961). Singleton and multiple in scientific discovery: A chapter in the sociology of science. *Proceedings of the American Philosophical Society, 105,* 470-486.

Merton, R. K. (1968). The Matthew effect in science. *Science, 159,* 56-63.

Ogburn, W. K. & Thomas, D. (1922). Are inventions inevitable? *Political Science Quarterly, 37,* 83-93.

Price, D. (1963). *Little science, big science.* New York: Columbia University Press.

Simonton, D. K. (1975). Sociocultural context of individual creativity: A transhistorical time-series analysis. *Journal of Personality and Social Psychology, 32,* 1119-1133.

Simonton, D. K. (1976a). Biographical determinants of achieved eminence: A multivariate approach to the Cox data. *Journal of Personality and Social Psychology, 33,* 218-226.

Simonton, D. K. (1976b). Interdisciplinary and military determinants of scientific productivity: A cross-lagged correlation analysis. *Journal of Vocational Behavior, 9,* 53-62.

Simonton, D. K. (1976c). Philosophical eminence, beliefs, and zeitgeist: An individual-generational analysis. *Journal of Personality and Social Psychology, 34,* 630-640.

Simonton, D. K. (1976d). The Sociopolitical context of philosophical beliefs: A transhistorical causal analysis. *Social Forces, 54,* 513-523.

Simonton, D. K. (1977a). Creative productivity, age, and stress: A biographical time-series analysis of 10 classical composers. *Journal of Personality and Social Psychology, 35,* 791-804.

Simonton, D. K. (1977b). Eminence, creativity, and geographic marginality: A recursive structural equation model. *Journal of Personality and Social Psychology, 35,* 805-816.

Simonton, D. K. (1978). Independent discovery in science and technology: A closer look at the Poisson distribution. *Social Studies of Science, 8,* 521-532.

Simonton, D. K. (1979). Multiple discovery and invention: Zeitgeist, genius, or chance? *Journal of Personality and Social Psychology, 37,* 1603-1616.

Simonton, D. K. (1980a). Land battles, generals, and armies: Individual and situational determinants of victory and casualties. *Journal of Personality and Social Psychology, 38,* 110-119.

Simonton, D. K. (1980b). Techno-scientific activity and war: A yearly time-series analysis, 1500-1903 A.D. *Scientometrics, 2,* 251-255.

Simonton, D. K. (1980c). Thematic fame and melodic originality: A multivariate computer-content analysis. *Journal of Personality, 48,* 206-219.

Simonton, D. K. (1980d). Thematic fame, melodic originality, and musical zeitgeist: A biographical and transhistorical content analysis. *Journal of Personality and Social Psychology, 39,* 972-983.

Simonton, D. K. (1981a). The library laboratory: Archival data in personality and social psychology. In L. Wheeler (Ed.), *Review of Personality and Social Psychology* (Vol. 2). Beverly Hills, CA: Sage Publications.

Simonton, D. K. (1981b). Presidential greatness and performance: Can we predict leadership in the White House? *Journal of Personality, 49,* 306-323.

Simonton, D. K. (1983a). Formal education, eminence, and dogmatism: The curvilinear relationship. *Journal of Creative Behavior, 17,* 149-162.

Simonton, D. K. (1983b). Intergenerational transfer of individual differences in hereditary monarchs: Genes, role-modeling, cohort, or sociocultural effects? *Journal of Personality and Social Psychology, 44,* 354-364.

Simonton, D. K. (1984a). Artistic creativity and interpersonal relationships across and within generations. *Journal of Personality and Social Psychology, 46,* 1273-1286.

Simonton, D. K. (1984b). Creative productivity and age: A mathematical model based on a two-step cognitive process. *Developmental Review, 4,* 77-111.

Simonton, D. K. (1984c). *Genius, creativity and leadership.* Cambridge, MA: Harvard University Press.

Simonton, D. K. (1984d). Leader age and national condition: A longitudinal analysis of 25 European monarchs. *Social Behavior and Personality, 12,* 111-114.

Simonton, D. K. (1984e). Leaders as eponyms: Individual and situational determinants of monarchal eminence. *Journal of Personality, 52,* 1-21.

Simonton, D. K. (1985a). Intelligence and personal influence in groups: Four nonlinear models. *Psychological Review, 92,* 567-582.

Simonton, D. K. (1985b). Quality, quantity, and age: The careers of 10 distinguished psychologists. *International Journal of Aging and Human Development, 21,* 241-254.

Simonton, D. K. (1985c). The vice-presidential succession effect: Individual or situational determinants. *Political Behavior, 7,* 79-99.

Stewart, L. H. (1977). Birth order and political leadership. In M. G. Hermann (Ed.), *The psychological examination of political leaders.* New York: Free Press.

Stolzenberg, R. M. (1975). Occupations, labor markets, and the process of wage attainment. *American Sociological Review, 40,* 645-665.

Walberg, H. J., Rasher, S. P., & Parkerson, J. (1980). Childhood and eminence. *Journal of Creative Behavior, 13,* 225-231.

Zajonc, R. B. (1976). Family configuration and intelligence. *Science, 192,* 227-235.

3

Creativity, Intelligence, and Problem Finding: Retrospect and Prospect

J. W. Getzels
The University of Chicago

The editor has asked me to report on my work in creativity during the past quarter century or more, and to speculate regarding possible work along the same lines in the future. I divide my comments into four parts. I begin with a brief historical note on the status of work in the field at the time I undertook the studies in creativity and intelligence. I then summarize the studies and remark on their unexpected impact to this day. I proceed by describing the shift from the work on creativity and intelligence, conceived primarily as studies in problem solving, to the investigation of *problem finding,* which emerged as a crucial—I was almost tempted to say *the* crucial—but hitherto unexplored feature of creative thought. I end with some suggestions for possible lines of work in the future. Since much of the chapter is a retrospection, I must add a cautionary note. Although with the vantage of hindsight I may put the work together in perhaps not quite the same way as originally, most of what I shall be dealing with, as I warned the editor, is already in print in one place or another.[1]

A Historical Note by Way of Background

The systematic investigation of creativity may be divided historically into three overlapping periods, each period marked by a dominant, albeit not exclusive, focus, namely, genius, giftedness, and originality. Systematic work on the problem was initiated in 1869 with the publication of Galton's *Hereditary Genius: An Inquiry Into Its Laws and Consequences.* During the intervening more than hundred years, the inquiry shifted from the study of genius defined, as Galton had, by recognized achievement to the study of giftedness defined, as Terman (1925) had, by performance on an intelligence test, and from the study of giftedness to the study of originality or more broadly creativity proper defined by a wide range of criteria including recognized achievement and a variety of mental tests.

Although it was possible for Galton to identify genius by the single criterion of recognized achievement and for Terman to identify giftedness by the single criterion of an intelligence test score, it has not been possible to maintain such a dominant single conception of creativity over the past quarter century. The most widely applied conceptions are of three kinds, depending on the relative emphasis given to the product, the process, or the personal experience (Getzels & Madaus, 1969). Whatever the specific emphasis, they have in common the notion of novelty or originality. Some conceptions are formulated in terms of a *manifest product,* which is novel and useful. MacKinnon (1962), for example, suggests that the criterion is a statistically infrequent response or idea that is adaptive and sustained to fruition. Other conceptions are formulated in terms of an *underlying process,* which is unorthodox and fertile. Ghiselin (1952) speaks of creativity as a process of change and development in the psychic life of an individual leading to invention. Still other conceptions are formulated in terms of a *subjective experience,* which is inspired and immanent. Maslow (1963) for one, insists on the importance of the flash of insight—the transcendent sensation itself—without reference to whether it will ever result in anything tangible. Creativity resides not in the "inspired product" but in the "inspired moment."

I myself have attempted to deal with creativity along somewhat different lines, giving primacy to the quality of the *problem* rather than the product or solution (Getzels, 1964). The significant element in creative thinking, as Albert Einstein (1938), Michael Polanyi (1958), and Max Wertheimer (1945) among others have pointed out, is the formulation of the creative problem. For it is the creative question to which the creative solution is the response—an issue and line of work to which I shall return in due course.

The investigation of genius persisted into the first part of the twentieth century; it is reflected in the nearly hundred studies on the subject in the six years following the republication of *Hereditary Genius* in 1914. With the increasing popularity of the intelligence metric and the appearance of Terman's studies of highly intelligent children in the 1920's, the research focus turned from genius to giftedness, although it will be recalled the title given the early studies of giftedness was still *Genetic Studies of Genius* (Terman, 1925). By World War II, genius ceased to be a major focus of inquiry and was replaced by a vast amount of work on children with high IQ's, who were referred to as "gifted." Although the essential portrait of such children had been drawn by 1925-1930 and was not changed substantially thereafter (Miles, 1954), a multitude of investigations continued to rediscover what had already been known for a generation.

In the 1950's the research emphasis shifted once more, from giftedness as measured by IQ to creativity. The shift was dramatic. Only six percent of the references in the authoritative Gowan bibliography on giftedness for the years 1950-1960 dealt with creativity (Gowan, 1961); in the next bibliography for the years 1960-1964, an astonishing fifty percent of the references were listed under creativity (Gowan, 1965).

The dramatic shift was prepared for by a number of circumstances. On the one hand, the mental measurement people were addressing familiar issues with the familiar intelligence tests, and reporting only already familiar observations. On the other hand, the emerging clinical studies of creative artists and scientists in which the intelligence test played little or no part whatsoever were addressing new issues with new methods, and providing new and provocative observations (Roe, 1946, 1953). At the same time, the post-war scientific discoveries were affecting every aspect of life in spectacular ways. They were not only altering the traditional notions of food, fuel, weaponry, and the like; more importantly, they were altering the traditional notions of human potential itself. In the future, power may depend more on the creative use of mind than on the brute control of matter. The term creative ceased to be the province only of artists, poets, scientists, and other such illusive folk who had never had to meet a payroll; it entered the language of the hard-boiled businessman as well. The Chicago telephone directory for 1950 listed 11 business establishments with the name "Creative." By 1966, the number had multiplied to 45, and by 1972, to 80. In 1957, when the Soviet Union surprised the world with Sputnik, creativity became something to be conjured with also in Washington.

No less important, although more subtle, was the impact of the change that the psychological conception of the human being was undergoing. The simple behavioristic notions of the person founded in the equilibrium model of self-maintenance and the drive-reduction theory of action were being supplanted by more complex psychodynamic and cognitive models. In a sense, the ideas of Watson and Thorndike were being replaced or at least modified by the ideas of Freud and Piaget. The human being as a reflexive organism mindlessly reacting to the environment through the operation of stimulus-response mechanisms was giving way to a reflective organism acting upon the environment with purpose and thought. The unidimensional IQ metric no longer loomed as the sovereign criterion of intellect, and it became possible for other ideas of mental functioning, notably for creativity, to emerge out of the shadow of the IQ (Getzels & Csikszentmihalyi, 1975).

Two obstacles to the systematic study of creativity remained, however. One was the lack of a clear conceptual distinction between creativity and intelligence as defined by IQ, and the other was the lack of an instrumental approach comparable to the IQ metric specific to creativity.

Certain historic events, though unrecognized at the time, produce paradigmatic changes that become turning points in a field of study. Guilford's presidential address entitled "Creativity" to the American Psychological Association in 1950 was such an event. Not only was it a statement *ex cathedra* but at one stroke it pointed the way to removing both the conceptual and instrumental obstacles. The concept of divergent thinking provided a dialectical foil to the reigning notion of intelligence and the divergent thinking tests that he and his followers developed provided a foil to the formerly sovereign IQ metric. Guilford bluntly told the American Psychological Association:

> *Examination of the content of intelligence tests reveals very little that is of obvious creative nature . . .*
>
> *Many believe that creative talent is to be accounted for in terms of high intelligence or IQ. This conception is not only inadequate but has been largely responsible for the lack of progress in the understanding of creative people . . .*
>
> *If the correlations between intelligence test scores and many types of creative performance are only moderate or low, and I predict that such correlations will be found, it is because the primary abilities represented in the tests are not all important for creative behavior. It is also because some of the primary abilities important for creative behavior are not represented in the test at all . . . In other words, we must look well beyond the boundaries of the IQ if we are to fathom the domain of creativity* (Guilford, 1950, p. 447).

Guilford's address reformulating the problems of creativity and offering new methods for its study sparked an explosion of work. Issues that had long lain dormant—issues of definition and criteria, theory and procedure—were opened to exploration. Fewer than 200 psychological studies of creativity had appeared altogether in the 25 years preceding the address; within a decade, almost as many were appearing in a single year (Getzels & Dillon, 1973; Parnes & Brunelle, 1967).

Creativity and Intelligence: Studies with Adolescents

It was in this heady climate of conceptual, psychological, and instrumental change that at about mid-century Philip Jackson and I undertook a series of studies to explore the relations among divergent thinking, intelligence, and creative performance in a cohort of highly intelligent students in grades six to twelve at the Laboratory Schools of The University of Chicago (Getzels & Jackson, 1962).

Our interest focused on two experimentally composed groups. One group of 17 boys and 11 girls included students who compared with the same-age peers were in the top 20 percent in IQ but below the top 20 percent in a summative score of five divergent thinking measures. Their mean IQ was 150, with a range from 139 to 179. The other group of 15 boys and 11 girls included students in the top 20 percent in the divergent thinking measures but below the top 20 percent in IQ. Their mean IQ was 127, with a range from 108 to 138. Two things which are often overlooked in reports of the study must be kept in mind. One, there was no overlap in IQ or divergent thinking between the two groups; every student in the Higher IQ/Lower Divergent Thinking group was higher in IQ and lower in divergent thinking than every student in the Higher Divergent/Lower IQ group. Two, the groups were not intended to be low or high either in IQ or divergent thinking in *absolute* terms—neither group was of course low by general population norms; they were high or low *relative* to each other.

The findings for the entire cohort from which the two experimental groups were drawn showed that the measures of divergent thinking and intelligence were positively but not highly related. The range of correlations for the 292 boys was from .131 to .378 with a mean of .261; for the 241 girls the range was from .115 to .393 with a mean of .265. Manifestly, the cohort was not a "normal" one. But Torrance soon replicated the results with eight different samples, comprising a selective school similar to the one in our study, four elementary schools, including a parochial and a rural school, a public high school, and two samples of graduate students (Torrance, 1960).

Findings with respect to the two experimental groups were also novel and unexpected. I recount here only the observations in response to the questions we raised regarding their behavior in school: What was their scholastic achievement? How did their teachers view them?

The measure of scholastic achievement was based on standardized verbal and mathematic achievement test scores available in the records office of the school. For verbal achievement, we computed the average score for all the test data relevant to the English curriculum at each grade level. At the sixth grade level, for example, the average score was based on four grade-related tests: Cooperative English Test C1; Iowa Language Skills, Advanced Form M; Iowa Work Study Skills, Advanced Form C; Stanford Spelling Test, Form F. Mathematics achievement was similarly based on the test data relevant to the mathematics curriculum at each grade level. All scores were transformed to standard scores, and a mean achievement score was obtained for each student. The means of the two experimental groups were compared to the mean of the cohort, excluding the scores of the experimental groups.

The results were quite straightforward. The mean IQ of the 449 students in the cohort was 132 and the achievement score 49.91; the mean IQ of the Higher IQ/Lower Divergent Thinking group was 150 and the achievement score 55.00; the mean IQ of the Higher Divergent Thinking/Lower IQ group was 127 and the achievement score 56.27. That is, despite the 23 point difference in IQ, the achievement scores of *both* experimental groups exceeded the cohort mean at the .001 level of significance (Getzels & Jackson, 1962).

In sum, the first two findings for our subjects were: (1) a positive but not high relationship between intelligence as represented by the IQ metric and creativity as represented by the divergent thinking metrics, and (2) perhaps more importantly and surely more unexpectedly, despite a 23-point difference in IQ, the equal superiority of the high IQ and the high creative thinking groups in scholastic accomplishment as measured by standardized achievement tests.

In view of these observations, we turned to the question, are the two equally-achieving groups perceived equally by their teachers? To answer this question, we asked the teachers to rate all the students in the school on the degree to which they enjoyed having them in class (Getzels & Jackson, 1962). The criterion on which the teachers were to do the ratings read in part as follows:

> This is a student whom the teacher especially enjoys having in class . . . He [she] may or may not be the one who gets along best in the classroom situation, he may or may not be the brightest child in the class, and he may or may not be the one who gets the best grades. But he is liked by you and is the sort of person about whom you are likely to say: 'Of all the children in my class, this is the one I most enjoy'.

When the responses were tallied, the high IQ group stood out as being more desirable than the average student, the high divergent thinking group did not; even though the scholastic performance was the same, the high IQ students were preferred over the average students by their teachers, the high divergent thinking students were not.

In presenting the foregoing three sets of findings with respect to creativity, we were careful to point out the particular intent of the studies–this, for example, is from the book *Creativity and Intelligence:*

> *Let us be clear. We are not saying there is no relationship between IQ and creative thinking. Obviously the feeble-minded by IQ standards are not going to be creative. But at the high average level and above, the two are sufficiently independent to warrant differentiation* (Getzels & Jackson, 1962, p. 26).

Or more generally this:

> *The crucial question in studying the two groups of adolescents is not which is better, or which is more desirable, or which is of greater potential worth to society. Talent in all its forms is admirable and worthy of encouragement. There is no intent here to derogate the IQ metric as such, for it remains one of the best predictors of academic achievement we have. It "selects in," as it is supposed to do, many students who are likely to achieve better than the average. But at the same time—and this is the immediate point—it tends to "select out" some students who are also likely to achieve better than the average. These latter students are in many cases the kind represented by our High Creativity Group. The question for us is not the relative worth of different types of cognitive functioning nor the relative effectiveness of different types of instruments to assess cognitive ability. The crucial issue is how to increase our understanding of all forms of cognition and human excellence, and of the forces that help to produce them* (Getzels & Jackson, 1962, p. 22).

Despite statements of this kind, publication of the findings aroused a storm of protest from among the IQ proponents, who interpreted the study as an attack on the IQ metric rather than as an exploration of types of cognitive giftedness. They said the results went against the grain of all that was known about intellect, had been obtained as a "fluke" with a non-representative sample, and the study would never be replicated in other schools. Fortunately—indeed, at the time it was more appropriate to say mercifully—in short order, E. Paul Torrance published "Educational Achievement of the Highly Intelligent and the Highly Creative: Eight Partial Replications of the Getzels-Jackson Study" (Torrance 1960). He had *not only* replicated the generally low correlations between the creativity and IQ measures to which we have already referred. Using the same method we had used in selecting the High IQ and High Creative students, he also compared the scholastic achievement of the two groups in his eight samples. Despite the sizable differences in IQ, the two groups were equally superior to the population from which they were drawn in six of the eight schools; only in the parochial school and the rural school were there contraindications. In addition, as part of the series of studies, Torrance replicated also our observations regarding the desirability of high IQ and high creative students, and reported: "Two of the most consistent findings are for the high IQ pupils to be better known by their teachers and to be considered more desirable as pupils than the highly creative subjects" (Torrance, 1959, p. 66).

What is remarkable in retrospect is not the findings about the relation between intelligence as measured by IQ tests and creativity as measured by divergent thinking tests, which I believe are now generally accepted with only few modifications. Rather, what is remarkable is that because of the focus on the findings with regard to the IQ, the aspect of the study that seemed to us truly innovative and crucial, namely, the aspect dealing with the *creative performance* of the two groups, attracted so much less notice at the time.

The subjects in both groups completed two tasks of a creative nature. One task was verbal: the pupils, gathered in an auditorium, were required to write brief stories to each of six Thematic Apperception Test (T.A.T.) type pictures shown on a screen, taking about four minutes for each story. The other task was non-verbal: the pupils were required to make a drawing appropriate to the title "Playing Tag in the School Yard," taking as much time as they wished. Writing a story and conceiving a picture obviously entail creative processes and seemed to us to have special merits for observing possible distinctive characteristics of the two groups.

The performance of the groups was startlingly different. The stories of the high divergent students were richer than the stories of the high IQ students in each of these analytic categories: stimulus-free themes, unexpected endings, humor, incongruities, and playfulness. For example, 75% of the former group as against 39% of the latter produced stories marked by stimulus-free themes; 92% of the former group as against 61% of the latter produced stories with unexpected endings; 75% of the former group as against 25% of the latter produced humorous stories, and so on. But the quantitative differences in analytic categories do not alone do justice to the distinctive quality of the stories as wholes, which can only be conveyed by comparing one or two sets of the stories themselves.

Here, for example, to the picture-stimulus perceived most often as a man seated in an airplane are two stories, one by a Higher IQ/Lower Divergent Thinking student and the other by a Higher Divergent Thinking/Lower IQ student (Getzels & Jackson 1962, pp. 39-42). The former writes:

> *Mr. Smith is on his way home from a successful business trip. He is very happy and he is thinking about his wonderful family and how glad he will be to see them again. He can picture it, about an hour from now, his plane landing at the airport and Mrs. Smith and their three children all there welcoming him home again.*

The latter writes:

> *This man is flying back from Reno where he has just won a divorce from his wife. He couldn't stand to live with her anymore, he told the judge, because she wore so much cold cream on her face at night that her head would skid across the pillow and hit him in the head. He is now contemplating a new skid-proof face cream.*

Or here is another set of responses to a stimulus-picture perceived most often as a man working late (or early) in an office.

A high IQ student writes:

> *There's ambitious Bob down at the office at 6:30 in the morning. Every morning it's the same. He's trying to show his boss how energetic he is. Now, thinks Bob, maybe the boss will give me a raise for all my extra work. The trouble is that Bob has been doing this for the last three years, and the boss still hasn't given him a raise. He'll come in at 9:00, not even noticing that Bob had been there so long, and poor Bob won't get his raise.*

A high divergent thinking student writes:

> *This man has just broken into this office of a new cereal company. He is a private eye employed by a competitive firm to find out the formula that makes the cereal bend, sag, and sway. After a thorough search of the office he comes upon what he thinks is the current formula. It turns out that it is the wrong formula and the competitor's factory blows up. Poetic justice!*

The high divergent group typically tended to free themselves from the stimulus, using it largely as a point of departure for self-expression; the high IQ group tended to stick close to the stimulus, using it as an anchor for description. For the high IQ students, if the picture-stimulus was of a man in an airplane, the story was likely to be about travel; if the picture-stimulus was of a man in an office, the story was about work. For the high divergent thinking students, the picture may be of a man in an airplane, but the story they want to tell is of a divorce; the picture may be of an office, but the story they want to tell is of a private eye in a cereal factory. The high IQ student employs predetermined categories, the high divergent thinking student employs emergent categories. Cereal not only snaps, crackles, and pops, it can also bend, sag, and sway; face cream does not only skid, it can also be skid-proof.

The same effects were found in the drawings (Getzels & Jackson, 1962, pp. 44-48). Even a cursory look through the products of the two groups showed unmistakable and compelling differences. When the drawings were analyzed into stimulus-free vs. stimulus-bound categories, 14% of the drawings by the high IQ group but 50% of those by the high divergent thinking group were classified as stimulus-free, or again when the drawings were analyzed into humor-present vs. humor-absent categories, 54% of the drawings by the high divergent thinking group as against 18% of those by high IQ group were in the humor-present category.

But here too, as in the case of the stories, the quantitative categorical analyses do not do full justice to the qualitative differences. For example, one drawing by a high divergent student portrayed a prison yard (metaphor for "school yard?") with guards apparently chasing ("playing tag with?") the prisoners. Another drawing by a divergent thinking student portrayed a group of fantastic fish (a "school" of fish?) or space objects following each other. A third drawing, a quite elaborate one, seemed to represent a play on the word tag—ghosts are tagging the school building with labels ("tags") like "Down with the Faculty," "I hate children," and so on. One of the sheets on which the drawings were supposed to be made came back without any drawing—it was as white as when it had been distributed—but pencilled in lightly following the printed caption "Playing Tag in the School Yard" were the words "in a blizzard." It was by one of the high divergent thinking students. Few of the products by the higher IQ/lower divergent thinking students had the same emergent non-literal quality. Instead, they stayed close to the task they were given in the directions, or perhaps better to the part of the directions which said "draw a picture appropriate to the title 'Playing Tag in the School Yard'," and neglected the part which said "You may draw any picture you like—whatever you may imagine for this theme." Their drawings were recognizably portrayals of children running after each other in a school yard.

A final remark regarding the impact of the series of studies. I have already commented on the initial condemnatory reaction to the work. Yet it is surprising how many of the original results still stand with only minor modifications, so that even the most widely-questioned of the first results—the creativity–intelligence relationship—was confirmed or at least not significantly disconfirmed, and the work grew to have an important influence, especially in the field of giftedness. Indeed, a recent review of the literature on giftedness states:

> Guilford's model brought attention to multiple aptitudes including divergent production or "creativity," as it is sometimes called. His ideas about creativity and its measurement were later adapted by Getzels and Jackson in their comparison of "high creative-low IQ" and "high IQ-low creative" students at the University of Chicago High School. This study had a stunning influence on educational researchers because it announced a breakthrough in the use of so-called "creativity" measure to identify a talent resource that would be overlooked by tests of general intelligence (Tannenbaum, 1979, pp. 8-9).

Another recent review provided by Gallagher (1979) similarly states:

> A broadened concept of giftedness, designed to include more than those characteristics measured by intelligence tests was given additional impetus by the extraordinarily influential study by Getzels and Jackson, who attempted to differentiate between gifted and creative children, and by a decade of work by Torrance focusing on the distinctive characteristics of creative children. Once the magic aura of the intelligence quotient was broken, it became possible to think of other dimensions that should be included in a general definition of giftedness. In addition, the increasing emphasis on the culturally different gifted children spurred the search for other valuable talents beyond the purely academic (pp. 29-30).

Creativity and Problem Finding: Studies with Artists

The study of creativity and intelligence left a number of nagging unresolved issues. One issue was that if we wanted to investigate creativity, why choose children, why not adults? A second and related issue was, why not study talented adults who were engaged in or at least aspired to be engaged in creative work, say, scientists, poets, mathematicians, artists, and the like? A third issue was that we had not really been studying the *process* of creativity at all, only its *correlates*; we had left the question of the creative process itself untouched. Granted, we had observed significant relations between the divergent thinking tests and the creative products, but what do these observations say about how the creative product was attained? Finally, and most importantly, we had explained the differences in the stories and drawings of the two groups in terms of Guilford's distinction between convergent and divergent thinking. He had written regarding the two types of tests:

> In tests of convergent thinking there is almost always only one conclusion or answer that is regarded as unique, and thinking is to be channeled or controlled in the direction of that answer . . . . In divergent thinking, on the other hand, there is much searching about or going off in various directions . . . . Divergent thinking . . . [is] characterized . . . as being less goalbound. There is freedom to go off in different directions . . . Rejecting the old solution and striking out in some new direction is necessary, and the resourceful organism will most probably succeed (Guilford, 1957, pp. 6, 9).

But this formulation did not deal with a crucial aspect of the findings that still needed explanation. True, the divergent thinking students were "rejecting old solutions and striking out in new directions." Yet, after rejecting the old solutions, what is the process through which one strikes out toward *new* solutions? A solution is a response to a problem; an old solution is presumably a response to an old problem. To what is a new solution a response? Is it possible that the high divergent thinking students who were rejecting the old solutions were rejecting also the old problems and discovering *new* problems which triggered the new solutions?

Although the battery of tests used in the study included a "make-up problem" measure, these questions did not emerge immediately after completing the work itself. In 1962, I was asked to do a chapter on "Creative Thinking, Problem Solving, and Instruction" for the 63rd Yearbook of the National Society for the Study of Education entitled *Theories of Learning and Instruction* (Getzels, 1964). After reading the literature on types of "educational objectives," I found myself composing a section entitled "On the Nature of Problems in Learning: Types of Cognitive Problems." I suggested that the prevailing taxonomies of objectives dealt only with *presented* problems and failed to recognize or consider a significant group of problems which may be called *discovered* or created problems. That is, at one extreme there are the *presented problem situations* where the problem has a known formulation, a routine method of solution, and a recognized solution; here a person need only follow established steps ("standard operating procedures") to meet the requirements of the situation. At the other extreme, there are *discovered problem situations* and *created problem situations* where the problem does not as yet have a known formulation, a routine method of solution, and a recognized solution; here the person must identify the problem itself and in fact may devise the problem as the artist does a still-life problem, and there are no established steps to meet the requirements of the situation.

Within these extremes it is possible to differentiate systematically among a number of problem situations varying in what is known and unknown, and the corresponding mental processes from rote memory to creative imagination that are primarily engaged in each situation. For present purposes, it will suffice to distinguish three classes of problem situations:

presented problem situations, discovered problem situations, and created problem situations (Getzels, 1982).

In a presented problem situation, the problem exists, and it is propounded to the problem solver. A teacher teaches that the area of a rectangle is side *a* multiplied by side *b*, and the pupil is given the problem: What is the area of a rectangle whose sides are 3 and 4? Here the problem is presented, and in the particular instance, it has a known formulation, a known method of solution, and a solution known to others if not yet to the problem solver.

Consider now the discovered problem situation. Here the problem also exists, but it is discovered by oneself rather than propounded by another, and it may or may not have a known formulation, known method of solution, or known solution. Roentgen sees a fogged photographic plate as others had before him, but while the others saw it only as a nuisance, he asks: "Why is the plate fogged?"—a self-initiated problem that led to the discovery of the X-ray and a revolution in atomic science. This is clearly different from the presented problem situation.

Consider finally the created problem situation. Here, the problem does not exist until someone invents or creates it. Maier (e.g. 1930) invents a series of problems to test problem-solving abilities. The scientist conceives of the problem of investigating the nature of space and time. The artist creates a still-life problem where no such problem existed before. It makes no sense to think of these situations as anomalies or obstacles that one meets through accident, misfortune, or ignorance. Quite the contrary. These are situations that one strives to bring into being; a well-formulated problem is the result of knowledge, a stimulus to more knowledge, and, most important, it is knowledge itself (Henle, 1971). In Polanyi's words:

> To see a problem is a definite addition to knowledge, as much as it is to see a tree, or to see a mathematical proof—or a joke . . . . To recognize a problem which can be solved and is worth solving is in fact a discovery in its own right (1958, p. 120).

The portion of human activity that is held in highest esteem—pure science, fine art, technological invention, systematic philosophy—is devoted as much to discovering, creating, and formulating problems as it is to solving them. In the words of Einstein and Infeld (1938):

> The formulation of a problem is often more essential than its solution, which may be merely a matter of mathematical or experimental skill. To raise new questions, new possibilities, to regard old questions from a new angle, requires creative imagination and marks real advance in science (p. 92).

This is true not only in science but in all activities calling for thought. Max Wertheimer (1945) generalized Einstein's point as follows:

> The function of thinking is not just solving an actual problem but discovering, envisaging, going into deeper questions. Often in great discoveries the most important thing is that a certain question is found. Envisaging, putting the productive question is often a more important, often a greater achievement than the solution of a set question (p. 123).

Need questions be found? Is not the world already teeming with problems and dilemmas at home and in business, in economics and education in art and in science, and in fact wherever we look, including into ourselves? The world is, of course, teeming with predicaments and dilemmas. But the predicaments and dilemmas do not present themselves automatically as problems capable of resolution or even sensible contemplation. They must be specified and formulated in fruitful and often radical ways if they are to be moved toward productive termination.

Henry Moore (1952) describes the process of problem finding in art in these words:

I sometimes begin drawing with no preconceived problem to solve, with only a desire to use pencil on paper and only make lines, tones, and styles with no conscious aim. But as my mind takes in what is so produced, a point arrives where some idea becomes conscious and crystallizes, and then control and ordering begin to take place (p. 77).

What Moore is describing is the finding and formulating of a problem. Prior to its emergence there is no structure and no task; there is nothing to solve. After the problem is posed, the skill of the artist or of the scientist takes over; control and ordering begin. The crucial step is how the formless situation where there is no problem (or there is only an indeterminate dilemma where the problem is moot) is transformed into a situation where a problem—in this case, an artistic problem—emerges for solution. The quality of the question that is asked is the forerunner of the quality of the solution that will be attained. Transforming the dilemma into a fruitful problem—putting the right question—may be no less a creative achievement than attaining the effective solution once the productive problem is posed.

Despite the manifest role of problems in initiating thought and the function that new problems have in guiding thought toward new solutions, very little is known about how problems are found and formulated. The assumption seems to have been that only answers and solutions count and that only their attainment requires thought and deserves attention. Although there are numerous theoretical statements, psychometric instruments, empirical studies, and training programs in problem solving or what might be called the problem of the solution, there is hardly any work of a similar nature on problem posing or what might be called the *problem of the problem.*

Over a period of some years, a number of my colleagues and students and I have been attempting to investigate the nature of problems and the process of finding and formulating them. We began with problem posing in art along lines raised by Moore's account, and we proceeded to more ordinary problems, including problems in cognition, interpersonal relations, and lately, even administration.

The first study with Mihaly Csikszentmihalyi, and the only one that will be dealt with here, was part of a longitudinal investigation of creative thinking with students from the School of the Art Institute of Chicago, one of the most selective and prestigious American art schools, numbering among its graduates such renowned artists as Georgia O'Keefe and Grant Wood, to mention only two. The detailed description of the subjects, procedures and results for the first two phases of the study are provided in Getzels and Csikszentmihalyi (1976). We began in the usual psychological mode by administering a variety of biographical, perceptual, cognitive, and personality instruments, comparing the responses of the art students with the norms as given by other students, and correlating the observations with grade point averages in studio courses, teacher ratings in originality, and other criteria of creative performance.

We found numerous significant differences in personality between the art students and other students. To mention the observations only with the *Cattel Sixteen Personality Factors Questionnaire,* the male art students differed significantly from the norms on 11 and the female art students on 10 of the 16 factors. On six of the factors both the males and females differed significantly from the norms in the same direction; both groups scored higher in social aloofness, introspection, unconventionality, imaginativeness, experimentalism, and self-sufficiency. We also found significant correlations between certain value constellations of the art students and their creative performance. As an instance, the correlation between low economic values on the *Allport-Vernon-Lindzey Study of Values* and the grade-point average in studio courses was .47.

We were exhilarated by the results as psychologists often are by appropriate significant differences between their subjects and the norms, and even more, by significant correlations between the characteristics of their subjects and measures of performance. But when the first exhilaration was over and we stepped back to survey the results, we were chagrined to discover that despite the significant correlations, we had not come much closer to understanding or even describing the process of creative production. We knew something more about the correlates of creative performance than we did when we started, but we knew nothing much more about our own problem, the processes underlying creative performance. To be sure, there was a .47 correlation between values and creative achievement. But what did that say about the way the creative achievement was attained?

We had fallen into the common research trap. Instead of observing how a creative solution or imaginative work is achieved starting with its inception as a dilemma or problem and concluding with its outcome as a product, which was what we were after, we had followed the familiar expedient in psychological inquiry of correlating a readily obtainable independent variable (in this case, a personal characteristic) with an already available dependent variable (in this case, a grade point average). If we were to explore creative thinking in art, which was our intent, it remained necessary to observe how the creative product—a drawing or painting, say—was achieved from the beginning to the conclusion, and how the quality of the process was related to the quality of the product.

To get at the process of creative thinking and not merely catalogue its biographical or psychometric correlates, we turned to observing how the creative product, the drawing or painting itself, was achieved from its inception to its conclusion. Our observations and conversations with the art students as they worked at their easels were at once fascinating and bewildering. Some worked rapidly, some hesitantly; some flecked bits of color on the canvas, some smeared heavy paint with a trowel. One artist said he painted because it was the only thing he could do, another because he wanted to create a new image of man. Yet despite the manifest differences in the character of what was produced, nothing we saw or heard was related to the creative quality of the products.

But we also observed this—and ultimately it proved crucial. When advertising or industrial artists came to their studios in the morning, someone had given them a problem to work on, sometimes a problem as specific as producing an illustration for a corn flakes box. When fine artists came to their studios, they were faced with only a blank canvas; they had to find or create the problem that they were to work on themselves. In effect, advertising or industrial artists work in the context of presented problems, while fine artists work in the context of discovered or created problems. As Einstein had forewarned in science and Moore in art, problem finding was an integral phase of the creative process. In order to understand the process, we had to study not only how an already identified problem is worked on toward a product or solution, as preceding studies and we ourselves had been doing. We had to study how the problem that was to be worked on is itself, to use Wertheimer's term, "found" (1945, p. 123).

Methods for studying problem solving are readily available. To observe how a person goes about solving a problem, we may administer one of the numerous instruments devised for this purpose—say, the Kohs Blocks, the Vygotsky, the Piaget conservation tasks, or for that matter the Binet or Wechsler Intelligence Tests—and draw inferences regarding the problem-solving process from what the person does and says. But suppose we want to observe how a person finds a problem—how one discovers, invents, poses, or formulates a problem. We were dismayed that despite our diligent search we were unable to locate any existing methods or in fact any prior studies of the subject. We ourselves had to devise a way to observe problem finding just as ways had been devised to observe problem solving.

This is what we did. We furnished a studio at the art school with two tables, a drawing board, paper, and a variety of dry media. On one table we placed twenty-seven objects used at the school to construct still-life problems. We then asked thirty-one fine art students, one at a time, to use one or more of the objects on the first table to create a still-life problem on the second table and produce any drawing they wished of the still-life problem they had created.

We observed what they did in creating the still-life problem before they began the actual drawing and were able to differentiate how they went about formulating their problem on a number of dimensions. One dimension was the number of objects handled, which ranged from two to nineteen. The presumption was that in order to find or create an original problem rather than reproduce an already known or "canned" design, one had to be open to a greater number of possibilities. A second dimension was the extent of exploration of each object. The presumption was that in order to discover a more original problem, one not only had to be open to a greater breadth of objects but to explore the objects in greater depth. Another dimension was the uniqueness of the objects that were selected. An artist can of course create an original work with the most hackneyed of objects, but the presumption was that, other things equal, the more uncommon the objects, the more unique the problem was likely to be.

The supposition was that behavior like handling, exploring, and choosing objects in this problem-finding situation reflected underlying mental processes just as the behavior on the Kohs Blocks, Vygotsky, Wechsler, or Binet is similarly taken to reflect underlying processes in a problem-solving situation. If this supposition, or the assumption about the role of problem finding in creative thought, is unwarranted, the experimental results will "wash out"; there will be no relation between the quality of the problem finding and the quality of the ensuing product.

The procedure for examining the relation between the quality of the problem finding and the quality of the creative product, the completed drawing, was quite simple. We ranked the artists on the quality of their problem finding on the basis of the breadth, depth, and uniqueness of their exploration before they began to draw. Needed next was a measure for judging the quality of the drawings. No contemporary criterion for assessing a work of art is foolproof; only time is the ultimate judge, and even its verdict may vary from generation to generation. Accordingly, we applied the procedure that galleries and museums use under the circumstances—recourse to an expert jury.

We displayed the drawings as in an art exhibit, and asked five artist-critics to rank the drawings on three criteria: graphic skill or craftsmanship, originality, and overall aesthetic value. When the rankings in problem finding before the drawings were begun were correlated with the composite rankings by the artist-critics of the completed drawings, the following results were obtained: for craftsmanship, the relation was positive but not significant; for originality and overall aesthetic value, the relationship was positive and significant. Indeed, for originality the correlation was a robust .54 (sig. at .005 level).

We were of course gratified by the results. But we were also skeptical. Were the effects only a function of the particular experimental situation we had set up? We waited for a half-dozen years after the students had graduated from art school, which was about seven years after the problem finding observations were made, and related the problem finding rankings to the relative success of the former students as professional fine artists. The relation was attenuated but still positive and significant, actually .30 (sig. at .05 level).

Ability in problem finding, even when observed seven years before, did seem to have an impact on creative achievement. More recently in the current phase of the longitudinal study, we correlated the rankings in problem finding now twenty years old with the present status of the former students as professional fine artists, now at mid-life (Csikszentmihalyi & Getzels, in press). The correlation was still a positive and significant .35 (sig. at .05 level). The size of the relation may not be anything one would want to engrave in marble, yet that there should be a consistent relation at all between a measure of problem finding and diverse measures of creative achievement over a period of twenty years is surely noteworthy and calls for continuing work.

Conclusion and a Glance Towards the Future

The study I have reported here and similar studies in areas other than fine art were illuminating beyond our expectations. But at least four caveats that I may have glossed over must be mentioned. First, problem finding and problem solving are not as discontinuous as the necessarily schematic account may have implied. They meld into one another, and the problem may be altered in the very process of its solution. Second, to emphasize the importance of finding and formulating problems is not to diminish the importance of the skills needed for solving problems or the importance of the solution. Third, in observing how a problem is found, it was assumed, as it had been in observing how a problem is solved, that the covert thought processes and the overt behavioral processes reflect one another to some degree; there is of course no intent to imply that pushing many objects about makes one creative. Fourth, it must not be forgotten that the observations depended on experiments, interviews, and judgments of such delicate issues as the originality of drawings and the professional success of fine artists, observations with unavoidable limitations.

Nonetheless, despite these caveats and the necessarily tentative nature of the methods and results of first efforts, a number of things may be said with some assurance. The discovery and formulation of problems can be studied empirically just as problem solving has been. There are individual differences in the discovery and formulation of problems just as there are in the attainment of solutions to problems that have already been formulated. There is a positive relation between the quality of a problem that is found and formulated and the quality of the solution that is attained. And most important, the finding and formulating of problems is a proper subject for investigation not only as an addendum to problem solving, which is typically what has been done when done at all, but as a focus of interest in its own right.

This is surely not the place to design in detail specific further studies. Nor am I capable of doing so for others. Besides, as our studies have suggested, the creative work in this area as elsewhere will be done by individuals who formulate their own research problems, that is, to use our terminology, who work on discovered or created problems rather than presented problems. I can, however, venture to sketch several general domains for further inquiry that would attract me.

The first domain that occurs to me is a study of the sources of problems in science. There are surely many accounts by scientists (or about scientists) regarding how they started with an ambiguous phenomenon or dilemma and the hard work was in formulating the problem for solution. Darwin is reported to have said, "Looking back, I think it was more difficult to see what the problems were than to solve them . . . " (Immegart & Boyd, 1979, p. 2). How then did he come to "see" what the problems were that he ultimately came to solve?

A second domain, also in science, is the formulating of multiple and sometimes contradictory problems in an attempt to resolve the same dilemma, each problem leading to a different or even opposite solution. The issue of course is why did one scientist come to formulate one problem and the other a different problem in response to the identical phenomenon. Here is an actual instance in medical science reported not too long ago:

> Somehow in leukemia the body becomes infected by cells that refuse to age and die naturally the way normal healthy cells do. These harmful cells thus remain trapped in a perpetual state of youth. Current treatment tries to kill these hostile cells by poisoning them. Unfortunately, the drugs are so toxic, they usually also kill the perfectly healthy cells, often causing death by the potent side effects. So Professor Sachs posed a new question. Would it be possible to find a drug that would make the leukemic cells mature and simply die? Professor Sachs' fresh approach was soon to pay dividends in opening a wide range of previously unforeseen possibilities (Griver, 1978, p. 7).

Another domain is an investigation for which a colleague and I have already done some pilot work with encouraging results: How does an executive transform administrative dilemmas into manageable problems? Our subjects were superintendents of schools, but the same principle holds for other executives as well. Asked to describe a difficult decision he had to make, one superintendent gave this account. A school in his district had become overcrowded, and the larger building to replace it would not be completed for two years. In the meantime, seventeen mobile classrooms filled the playground and the parking lot, but they were insufficient for the expected influx of children in the fall. The dilemma was obvious—overcrowding. Discussions among the principals, superintendent, and president of the board of education centered on two problems: Whether to get more mobile classrooms and where to put them, or whether to move the excess children to other less crowded schools and how to transport them there. Typically, the same dilemma had been transformed into different problems. And typically too, the decision was left up to the superintendent with the admonition that the decision should depend on which problem lent itself to easier solution.

As the superintendent tells it, in due course it occurred to him that the problem was really not whether to get more mobile classrooms and where to put them, or whether to get rid of the excess children and how to transport them. The problem was how to get more space. Once this problem was formulated, the solution proved not at all difficult. It was possible to build a temporary classroom structure that could later be converted to commercial use, and this was what was done. In fact, the structure was later sold at a modest profit.

One could go on with numerous other illustrations of bibliographic and empirical studies revolving around the notion of problem finding. But what seems most critical to me is that the idea of problem finding itself remains in need of theoretical clarification. It is this conceptual domain that would attract me.

There are many theories of problem solving: logical-philosophical theories like Dewey's, learning theories of various kinds like those of the Associationists and the Gestaltists, developmental theories like Piaget's and Vygotsky's, information processing theories like Newell and Simon's, and so on. All these deal with the thought processes underlying how a question is answered, a problem solved. None deals with the processes underlying how a question is asked, a problem posed. This despite the fact that, as both scientists and artists testify, the latter aspect of thinking may be the greater achievement in creative work. I suppose if put to it and I had to specify only the one domain for further inquiry that would attract me most, it would be just this: the theoretical clarification of the processes underlying the finding and formulating of problems.

Footnotes

1. Portions of this chapter are drawn from previously published work including: Getzels, J. W. (1964, 1975, 1982), Getzels, J. W. & Csikszentmihalyi, M. (1975, 1976), Getzels, J. W. & Dillon, J. T. (1973), Getzels, J. W. & Jackson, P. W. (1962).

References

Csikszentmihalyi, M. & Getzels, J. W. (in press). Creativity and problem finding in art. In F. H. Farley & R. W. Neperud (Eds.), *The foundations of aesthetics, art and art education.* New York: Praeger.

Einstein, A. & Infeld, L. (1938). *The evolution of physics.* New York: Simon and Schuster.

Gallagher, J. J. (1979). Issues in education for the gifted. In A. H. Passow (Ed.), *The gifted and the talented: Their education and development* (pp. 28-44). Chicago: The National Society for the Study of Education.

Galton, F. (1869). *Hereditary genius: An inquiry into its laws and consequences.* London: Macmillan.

Getzels, J. W. (1964). Creative thinking, problem solving and instruction. In E. R. Hilgard (Ed.), *Theories of learning and instruction* (pp. 240-267). Chicago: University of Chicago Press.

Getzels, J. W. (1975). Problem finding and the inventiveness of solutions. *Journal of Creative Behavior, 9,* 12-18.

Getzels, J. W. (1982). The problem of the problem. In R. Hogarth (Ed.), *New directions for methodology of social and behavioral science: Question framing and response consistency* (pp. 37-49). San Francisco: Jossey-Bass.

Getzels, J. W. & Csikszentmihalyi, M. (1975). From problem solving to problem finding. In I. A. Taylor & J. W. Getzels (Eds.), *Perspectives in creativity* (pp. 90-116). Chicago: Aldine.

Getzels, J. W. & Csikszentmihalyi, M. (1976). *The creative vision: A longitudinal study of problem finding in art.* New York: Wiley.

Getzels, J. W. & Dillon, J. T. (1973). Giftedness and the education of the gifted. In R. M. W. Travers (Ed.), *Second handbook of research on teaching* (pp. 689-731). Chicago: Rand McNally.

Getzels, J. W. & Jackson, P. W. (1962). *Creativity and intelligence: Explorations with gifted students.* New York: Wiley.

Getzels, J. W. & Madaus, G. F. (1969). Creativity. In R. L. Ebel (Ed.), *Encyclopedia of educational research* (pp. 267-275). New York: Macmillan.

Ghiselin, B. (Ed.). (1952). *The creative process.* New York: New American Library.

Gowan, J. C. (1961). *An annotated bibliography on the academically talented.* Washington, DC: National Education Association.

Gowan, J. C. (1965). *Annotated bibliography on creativity and giftedness.* Northridge, CA: San Fernando Valley State College Foundation.

Griver, S. (1979, July 27). Coming close to curing leukemia. *Israel Digest, 22* (No. 14), 7.

Guilford, J. P. (1950). Creativity. *American Psychologist, 5,* 444-454.

Guilford, J. P. (1957). A revised structure of intellect. *Reports of the psychological laboratory, No. 19.* Los Angeles, CA: University of Southern California.

Henle, M. (1971). The snail beneath the shell. *Abraxas, 1,* 119-133.

Immegart, G. L. & Boyd, W. L. (1979). *Problem finding in educational administration.* Lexington, MA: D. C. Heath.

MacKinnon, D. W. (1962). The nature and nurture of creative talent. *American Psychologist, 17,* 484-495.

Maier, N. R. F. (1930). Reasoning in humans: I. On direction. *Journal of Comparative Psychology, 10,* 115-143.

Maslow, A. H. (1963). The creative attitude. *Structuralist, 3,* 4-10.

Miles, C. C. (1954). Gifted children. In L. Carmichael (Ed.), *Manual of child psychology* (pp. 984-1063). Revised Edition. New York: Wiley.

Moore, H. (1952). Notes on sculpture. In B. Ghiselin (Ed.), *The creative process (pp. 73-78).* New York: Mentor Books.

Parnes, S. J. & Brunelle, E. A. (1967). The literature of creativity (Part I). *Journal of Creative Behavior, 1,* 52-109.

Polanyi, M. (1958). *Personal knowledge.* Chicago: University of Chicago Press.

Roe, A. (1946). The personality of artists. *Educational and Psychological Measurement, 6,* 401-408.

Roe, A. (1953). A psychological study of eminent psychologists and anthropologists, and a comparison with biological and physical scientists. *Psychological Monographs, 67,* 1-55.

Tannenbaum, A. J. (1979). Pre-Sputnik to Post-Watergate concern about the gifted. In A. H. Passow (Ed.), *The gifted and the talented: Their education and development* (pp. 5-27). Chicago: The National Society for the Study of Education.

Terman, L. M. (1925). *Genetic studies of genius, Vol. 1. Mental and physical traits of a thousand gifted children.* Stanford, CA: Stanford University Press.

Torrance, E. P. (1959). Explorations in creative thinking in the early school years: A progress report. In C. W. Taylor (Ed.), *The Third (1959) University of Utah Research Conference on the Identification of Creative Scientific Talent.* University of Utah: University of Utah Press.

Torrance, E. P. (1960, September). Educational achievement of the highly intelligent and the highly creative: Eight partial replications of the Getzels-Jackson study. *Research Memorandum BER-60-18,* Bureau of Education Research, University of Minnesota.

Wertheimer, M. (1945). *Productive thinking.* New York: Harper and Row.

4

Research on Creativity Assessment

Donald J. Treffinger
Center for Creative Learning and
State University College at Buffalo

The purposes of this chapter are to review several concerns and recommendations about creativity assessment, to analyze recent progress in creativity assessment research and practice, and to propose some promising directions and persistent difficulties in research on the assessment of creativity.

Although the substantial awakening of interest in creativity research during the last three decades has had many positive consequences, giving rise to the opportunity for a book on "frontiers" in the field, many fundamental problems are still largely unresolved. One such problem, which may be basic to many of the others, is that of identification or assessment of creative talent. Without progress in this area, it will be impossible to provide clear, consistent, and useful answers to many other questions about the nature and nurture of creativity.

Some of the questions for which creativity assessment is essential to researchers include: What is creativity? How does it develop in the individual? From what personal and social sources does it arise? How do individuals or groups vary with respect to degrees or styles of creativity? With what other cognitive and personality variables is creativity importantly related? Through what deliberate training or instructional procedures can creative behavior be nurtured or enhanced? Our ability to find answers to these questions, and many other similar important basic and applied problems, depends greatly upon our solutions for the problem of assessing creativity.

Despite its importance and fundamental status in creativity research, measurement and assessment issues have continued to be particularly vexing challenges. Several reviews of creativity identification and assessment instruments and research have been published during the last two decades (e.g., Crockenberg, 1972; Dellas & Gaier, 1970; Hocevar, 1979a; Khatena, 1973; Torrance, 1976; Treffinger, 1980; Treffinger & Poggio, 1972; Treffinger, Renzulli, & Feldhusen, 1971; Tryk, 1968) and the topic has continued to garner substantial interest among researchers, particularly in education and psychology.

Purposes of Creativity Assessment

A major concern in creativity assessment research has been lack of clarity regarding the purposes or goals for creativity assessment. Why should anyone be concerned with creativity assessment? Creativity testing has never seemed to "catch on" as widely as IQ testing in American educational or organizational practice. The beneficial consequence of this has been that creativity assessment may have been spared some of the misuses and abuses that have often characterized intelligence testing (e.g., Gould, 1981). Less fortunately, however, creativity assessment has continued to be shrouded by confusion, mystery, or even controversy. Intuitively, it is a reasonable notion that people who think creatively might be expected also to display the characteristics commonly or empirically associated with the creative personality, and in turn to *do* things that would ordinarily be regarded as "creative." Thus, one might argue that identifying creativity should be so easy, and the indicators so obvious, that the problem would scarcely warrant three decades or more of theory, research, and development.

Our goal, however, is much more complex than recognizing and appreciating the most obvious instances of creativity. As Gowan (1977) put it:

> Heretofore we have harvested creativity wild. We have used as creative only those persons who stubbornly remained so despite all efforts of the family, religion, education, and politics to grind it out of them . . . As a result of these misguided efforts, our society produces only a small percentage of its potential of creative individuals (the ones with the most uncooperative dispositions). If we learn to domesticate creativity—that is, to enhance rather than deny it in our culture—we can increase the number of creative persons in our midst by about fourfold. (p. 89)

The purposes of creativity assessment should extend well beyond the effort to label or isolate highly creative people from their less creative peers, as has also been argued by Crockenberg (1972, pp. 42-43), Khatena (1977), Rimm (1984), Torrance (1976, 1979a), and Treffinger (1980). Unfortunately, as we consider more complex purposes, it becomes apparent that recognizing creativity is not at all as easy as it might initially seem. In addition, in creativity research, as in most every scientific endeavor, "truth" is usually considerably more complex than "common sense," and much more difficult to document and verify objectively.

Some of the purposes (other than selection of highly creative individuals) for which creativity assessment is important include:

1. Helping to recognize and affirm the strengths and talents of individuals, and making it possible for them to do so as well (Rimm, 1984).

2. Expanding and enhancing our understanding of the nature of human ability and giftedness, considering creativity as a component of assessment that transcends the restricted view of "intellect" as traditional IQ measures (e.g., Gardner, 1983; Guilford, 1977; Renzulli, 1978; Torrance, 1979b). By recognizing that achievement (in any area) is influenced by important factors other than the traditional IQ and achievement measures, we may be better able to explain complex phenomena such as "overachievement."

3. Providing "baseline" data for assessing individuals or groups to guide teachers or trainers in planning and carrying out appropriate instruction. By including creativity data in a profile of a learner's characteristics, we obtain unique and valuable information that will help us to do a better job of defining instructional activities that will be challenging and appropriate (Khatena, 1977; Treffinger, 1980).

4. Obtaining data, such as pre- or post-test data, for group comparisons for research, program evaluation, or assessment of change or growth as a function of instruction or experimental conditions.

5. Helping instructors, counselors, or individuals on their own to discover unrecognized and untapped resources and talents, and providing a language for communicating with others about those aptitudes (Reisman & Torrance, 1980; Torrance, 1979a; Willings, 1980).

6. Advancing research progress in understanding the nature, development, and nurture of creative behavior.

7. Helping to remove the concept of creativity from the realm of mystery and superstition.

Issues of Theory and Definition

Despite our important purposes for creativity assessment, there have been many reasons for its persistence as a formidable problem for researchers. Not the least of these reasons has been our inability to formulate a single, general or unifying theory of creativity, from which a definition could be derived as a foundation for a comprehensive approach to assessment. We suffer, not so much from a shortage of theories and definitions, as from an overabundance (Dacey & Madaus, 1969; Treffinger, Renzulli, & Feldhusen, 1971). Perhaps this diversity is merely indicative of the recency of interest in creativity as a research problem. Or perhaps, as Dacey and Madaus (1969, p. 58) argued, the complexity of creativity itself "mitigates against a universally acceptable definition."

Treffinger, Renzulli, and Feldhusen (1971) contended that in the absence of the unifying and directing effects of a single, generally-accepted theory and definitions, measurement problems are predictable:

> Given the existing array of ideas about creativity . . . it is not in the least surprising that there exists a number of tests, all purporting to be measures of "creativity," but differing in a number of ways. Each instrument mirrors the particular set of beliefs and preconceptions of its developer concerning the nature of creativity. Sadly, the theoretical rationale for such tests is often not sufficient to allow systematic tests of differential predictions (p. 196).

Many researchers have cautioned us of the need to consider creativity as a complex, multi-faceted concept. Guilford (1976) expressed this concern succinctly: "Both intelligence and creative aptitude, which is an important part of intelligence, are multivariate. In either case we must avoid believing that one word means just one thing (p. 169)." Torrance (1979b) has emphasized the need to consider abilities, skills, and motivation in defining creativity, and Amabile (1983) similarly proposed a multidimensional definition, including domain-relevant skills, creativity-relevant skills, and intrinsic motivation. Renzulli (1978), defining giftedness as the potential for creative, productive behavior, also included three similar constructs in his definition (ability, creativity [skills], and task commitment).

With the possible exception of those specifically trained as experimental researchers, most individuals do not consider *operational definitions* when asked to define a complex construct such as intelligence or creativity. A pedagogical example may be useful; we often ask workshop or seminar participants to approach this topic by asking them how they would help an "alien visitor" to understand a new concept, such as "prune." Their responses involve many different approaches to definition: description, stipulation, attribute listing, structural or functional analysis, comparison, example, experience, inclusion and exclusion, or even metaphor, but almost *never* operational (e.g., standards or measurable criteria for being a prune, such as number of wrinkles, moisture, acidity, color, etc.).

Similarly, when we turn our attention to creativity, many different meanings emerge, but they vary widely in their potential for operationalization. Creativity in general (which we're fond of calling, "Big C" Creativity) has many vastly different meanings and implications, reflected in a diversity of philosophical conceptions and values regarding creative talent. Rhodes (1961) emphasized, for example, that views of creativity could be described as emphasizing person, process, product, or (environmental) press. More informally, we have often used the analogy of water in a lake fed by many tributaries to convey the idea of "Big C" Creativity. In the middle of the lake (Creativity), a cup of water might be drawn and described as "lake water." The degree to which it was comprised of specific components from one tributary or another might be nearly impossible to determine in a practical and efficient way. As samples are drawn in or near specific tributaries, however, certain variables might be more readily separated and analyzed (e.g., presence of certain nutrients or silt, etc.). There may be general interest in considering "lake water" (or Big C Creativity), at a broad and philosophical level. But for experimentation and progress at a more exact and empirical level, the researcher is probably operating in or near one of the tributaries (and probably working from a vessel more like a raft or canoe than a yacht!). The challenge, of course, is to be able to learn enough about each of the tributaries to be able to extrapolate intelligently and formulate reasonable hypotheses about the lake water. More formally, Treffinger and Poggio (1972) emphasized this concern in calling for systematic efforts to integrate theories and research on the nature of criteria and for more adequate conceptual and operational definitions.

Progress has been made in these areas, although there is yet no single, widely-accepted or unifying theory. A significant step was made by Gowan (1972) who offered a review of major approaches to creativity organized into five broad categories (which he labelled: cognitive, rational, and semantic; personality and environmental; mental health; Freudian and neo-Freudian; and, psychedelic). Gowan's categories have been used and extended by other reviewers (e.g., Treffinger, Isaksen & Firestien, 1982, 1983) in efforts to bring greater organization and structure to our efforts at understanding the complex nature of creativity. Roweton (1972) and I. A. Taylor (1976) also provided concise overviews and categorizations of major theoretical approaches to creativity. Progress has also been made in the area of identifying and classifying objectives for creativity. Davis and O'Sullivan (1980) proposed a taxonomy of creative objectives, involving four levels: awareness, understanding, techniques, and actualization. Treffinger and Huber (1975) and Isaksen and Treffinger (1985) also proposed specific objectives for each stage of the Creative Problem Solving model.

Despite these efforts at synthesis, a variety of widely divergent creativity assessment instruments has continued to appear in the literature. Surveys of instruments have been reported by Kaltsounis (1971; 48 instruments), Davis (1971; 23 instruments); Kaltsounis (1972; 38 instruments); and Kaltsounis and Honeywell (1980; 77 instruments).

For some researchers creativity continues to be most productively defined and assessed as a cognitive, rational phenomenon. Isaksen and Treffinger (1985), for example, defined creativity as:

Making and communicating meaningful new connections—
– to help us think of many possibilities;
– to help us think and experience in varied ways and using different points of view;
– to help us think of new and unusual possibilities;
– to guide us in generating and selecting alternatives.

In this definition, Treffinger and Isaksen tried to capture enough of the essential aspects of "Big C" Creativity to insure that the definition is logically, intuitively, or experientially reasonable. At the same time, from the perspective of a cognitive, rational orientation, they sought a definition that would have potential for specific operational use. They believe the definition has productive implications for planning training or instruction, for identifying individual characteristics, and for evaluating outcomes appropriately.

Even within the cognitive, rational orientation, however, there is still great diversity in definitions, and hence in operational procedures. Torrance (1974) defined creative talent in relation to abilities, skills, and motivational factors, and emphasized assessment of fluency, flexibility, originality, and elaboration with verbal and figural stimuli. In their "streamlined" scoring procedures (Torrance, 1979b; Torrance & Ball, 1984), additional criteria were introduced, however (including abstract titles, emotional awareness, combining and synthesizing, resisting premature closure, unusual visual perspectives, extending or breaking boundaries, and using humor). Torrance & Hall (1980) considered a variety of expanding dimensions (or "further reaches") of creativity, including empathy and "superawareness" of the needs of another, charisma, sense of future, and others. Guilford (1982) proposed, however, that before turning to "non-scientific" approaches, it would be more promising to examine carefully our known established methods and to explain and assess some of these new constructs. Guilford (1967, 1977, 1983, 1984) has also stressed the need to examine creativity as a factorially-complex structure, emphasizing the need to examine many intellectual facets of creativity, such as the expanded and higher order dimensions of the Structure of Intellect Model. Mednick (1962), still within a cognitive, rational orientation, analyzed creativity from a very different perspective, emphasizing the role of remote associations in creative thinking.

The diversity of definitions and instruments derived from the many "tributaries" feeding Creativity is compounded even more, of course, when orientations other than the cognitive, rational view are considered (e.g., Gowan 1972; Treffinger, Isaksen, & Firestien, 1982, 1983).

An alternative approach to creativity assessment, for example, might emphasize the personality characteristics associated with creativity. Much progress has been made in this area in recent years, in assessment with children (Rimm, 1976), as well as with adolescents and adults (Davis & Rimm, 1977, 1980, 1982; Dellas & Gaier, 1970; Khatena and Torrance, 1976; Rekdal, 1977; Rimm & Davis, 1976, 1980b). Davis (1975) proposed that biographical and personality inventories hold considerable promise for creativity assessment at many age levels. Davis and Rimm (1982) argued:

> The use of personality and biographical information to identify creative talent is not a new idea, but it is one which we feel is under-used. Many studies over the years have shown that creative persons . . . show many common personality and biographical traits . . . To be creatively productive, it is quite possible that a person must possess traits of independence, self-confidence, risk-taking, high energy, attraction to new ideas, curiosity, and visually artistic interests, attraction to complexity, and a better than average sense of humor. It is also not surprising that individuals who have a biographical history of creative activities and hobbies may be expected to be creative in the future as well (p. 56).

Although Williams (1979) described a model for integrating some of the cognitive and affective dimensions of creativity, many studies have reported little success in correlating measures of "creativity" variables drawn from different dimensions (e.g., Gakhar, 1980; Baker, 1978a; Murphy, Dauw, Horton & Fredian, 1976). Guilford (1971) warned of several threats to the validation of any creativity instrument, including the use of inappropriate criteria, poor selection of instruments, or low reliabilities among measures. Researchers must exercise great caution in framing their definition of creativity and selecting instruments that will be appropriate in view of the definition. If one's definition emphasizes the personality characteristics associated with creativity, for example, it is appropriate to look toward instruments that assess those characteristics rather than to instruments based on a definition which emphasizes cognitive skills.

The progress that has been made in recent years has principally enabled us to be more systematic in understanding, describing, and categorizing our theories and definitions, rather than achieving any unification around a single theory or definition. This progress has helped us to address more specifically the implications and concerns of theory and definition for creativity assessment. If we have not solved the problem yet, at least we are better informed about its nature and scope and better prepared to analyze our measurement decisions and their consequences. In view of the diversity of theories and definitions still confronting the researcher, it is scarcely surprising that there are many options and few universals in the area of creativity assessment.

Validity, Reliability, and Usability Concerns

Research on creativity assessment, as with any other human characteristic, begins with some fundamental measurement concerns: developing instruments which are clearly related to the constructs they purport to measure, and which are accurate and useful. These are concerns for the *validity, reliability,* and *usability* of the instruments. We will review these concerns, with particular attention to progress that has been made since Treffinger and Poggio's (1972) survey of needed research in these areas.

Validity

The question of validity—whether or not a measure "really" taps creativity—is one of the foremost concerns for the creativity assessment researcher. No procedure, regardless of its stability, consistency, economy, or ease of use has merit unless there is some unequivocal evidence to support its validity. Psychologists usually consider three major dimensions: content, criterion-related, and construct validity.

Content Validity

In order to demonstrate content validity, it is necessary to present evidence that an instrument provides a representative sample of the domain of concern. Thus, in measuring "creativity," we are presented immediately with a major problem: what *is* the universe from which this sampling should be done?" Torrance (1974) contended:

> Since a person can behave creatively in an almost infinite number of ways, in the opinion of the author, it would be ridiculous even to try to develop a comprehensive battery of tests of creative thinking that would sample any kind of universe of creative thinking abilities. The author does not believe that anyone can now specify the number and range of test tasks necessary to give a complete or even an adequate assessment of a person's potentialities for creative behavior (p.21).

As we have already seen, it is certainly appropriate to view creativity as a complex, multidimensional construct, rather than as a unitary psychological variable; indeed, the term "creativity" itself may be misleading, in that it may suggest that there is only a single universe which must be sampled, rather than several (Treffinger, 1980, 1984; Wallach, 1968, 1971; Wallach & Kogan, 1965). Guilford (1971, 1976, 1984) has warned that creativity should not be associated only with divergent thinking, but that several other Structure of Intellect dimensions are certainly involved, and that divergent production itself is a category which contains as many as 30 different dimensions.

Treffinger and Poggio (1972) called for research on content validity that would involve the development of criteria for new measures of criteria, and for the development of new procedures for implementing those criteria. Considerable progress has been made in many relevant areas, so that our "view" of the many and varied content universes of creativity has been considerably enhanced or expanded. (The progress in this area, however, underscores the importance of caution in generalizing about the "creativity" of particular individuals or groups using data from only one or a very limited set of indicators.) Some notable areas of progress include Besemer's work on creative products (addressed elsewhere in this volume; see also Besemer & Treffinger, 1981); Kirton's research on adaptors and innovators (also addressed in this volume); assessment of creativity characteristics and personality dimensions (e.g., Davis & Rimm, 1980; Khatena & Torrance, 1976; Rimm, 1976; Rimm & Davis, 1980b); development of measures of creative imagery (Khatena, 1984; Khatena & Torrance, 1981; Torrance, Khatena, & Cunnington, 1973); efforts to classify problem solving tasks and develop new criteria for evaluating creative problem solving outcomes (e.g., Speedie, Treffinger & Houtz, 1976; Parnes & Treffinger, 1973); development of new criteria and procedures for scoring tests (Torrance, 1979b; Torrance & Ball, 1984); and, development of new criteria and instruments for assessing creativity in young children (Moran, Milgram, Sawyers & Fu, 1983a, 1983b; Torrance, 1981c).

Criterion-related Validity

The major challenge in establishing criterion-related validity (either *concurrent* or *predictive*) is in the selection of criteria. Against what external indicators of creative behavior can a test be validated? Are there valid general criteria for creativity across age levels, unique criteria for various age groups, or only long-term social acceptance of creativity that requires years or decades to establish and observe? The search for acceptable criteria is not a new problem; indeed, we seem yet to be struggling with many of the same concerns first confronted in the early Utah conferences on creativity (see, for example, Brogden & Sprecher, 1964). In addition, the complexity and diversity of creative behavior discussed in the previous section also make it more difficult to establish criterion-related validity. Consider the case of long-term predictive validity, which has been the most persistent concern of many reviewers and critics. As an example, choose any instrument or test battery that might be administered to school-aged students. As those students progress through life, what factors beyond their creativity ability as measured in childhood would reasonably be expected to have significant impact on their creative development and accomplishments? Will their school experiences ignore, strengthen, or inhibit their potential? In what areas will their interests develop? What cultural and educational opportunities will be made available to them? And, as Torrance (1984) has shown to be of considerable importance, will their creative potential be encouraged and nurtured through mentorship experiences? It is indeed ambitious to expect that early test scores should in themselves account for significant variation in adult creative achievement. In addition, we must keep in mind the explicit cautions of the test developers (e.g., Torrance, 1974; Guilford, 1971) that their instruments do not attempt to assess every possible dimension of creativity and that any selection of tests will necessarily represent only a limited segment of the many universes of creative behavior. Perhaps, then, the critics of creativity tests have established an expectation which is unrealistic and inappropriate. We would do better to recognize the more limited purposes that can be served by the instruments and to adopt more realistic expectations with respect to long-term prediction of creative accomplishments (Treffinger, 1984).

Treffinger and Poggio (1972) called for research on three major aspects of criterion-related validity: defining and using appropriate external criteria, especially for predictive validity; multidimensional and longitudinal studies; and consideration of developmental and cross-cultural perspectives. There is evidence of progress in each of these areas. Predictive validity studies have shown significant correlations between creativity measures and later creative accomplishments over periods ranging from seven to 22 years (Howieson, 1981; Torrance, 1969, 1972, 1974, 1980, 1981a, 1981b; Zegas, 1976). A variety of cross-cultural studies has been conducted in several different countries. Aviram and Milgram (1977) studied creativity and several other variables among children educated in the Soviet Union, the United States, and Israel. Ball and Torrance (1978) studied figural creativity among subjects from nine countries (Japan, China, India, France, Norway, West Germany, the U.S., Canada, and the Virgin Islands). Howieseon (1981) used Torrance tests and Wallach-Kogan's indices of creative accomplishments with Australian students. Milgram and Milgram (1976b, 1978) have investigated intelligence, self-concept and creativity in gifted Israeli children. Minhas (1981) used a variety of creativity and projective personality measures to study factors in creativity, intelligence, and personality among university students in India. Rimm and Davis (1980a) reported international studies over a five year period in which validation evidence for their instruments was obtained from studies in Australia, France, and Israel in addition to the United States. Torrance, Gowan, Wu, and Aliotti (1970) compared the creative functioning of monolingual and bilingual children in Singapore. Willings (1980) reported research and extensive case studies of creativity among adults in England. This sample of cross-cultural studies supports the conclusion that research interest on creativity and its assessment has grown internationally, not merely as a phenomenon unique to American education and psychology.

Construct Validity

The validity of a psychological construct is not established by the results of any single study. Rather, supportive evidence accumulates in small increments as a result of many specific experiments and studies, and the construct is modified and refined as required by the emerging pattern of studies and the evidence they provide. Each research result adds "another piece to the puzzle" which confronts the investigator. The validity of the instrument is "constructed" as a complex framework in which many sources of evidence are woven together into a consistent pattern. Construct validity refers, therefore, to the *total pattern* of research evidence that supports an instrument. It is a very complex challenge. The researcher must be able to clarify the theoretical foundation for the instrument, to describe as completely as possible hypotheses which might be derived from the theory, and to show how those hypotheses differ from those which might be developed from other theories. Construct validity involves the extent to which experimental evidence supports those hypotheses.

Unfortunately, such theoretical analyses are often lacking in investigations of creativity. Given the complex, multidimensional nature of creativity, Treffinger and Poggio (1972) called for research using appropriate multivariate procedures, experimental and quasi-experimental studies with adequate controls, replication studies, long-term studies of creative behavior, and more extensive efforts at theoretical synthesis and analysis to guide the planning and interpretation of such studies. Despite this call, many studies of creativity have continued to be "one shot" projects, lacking in theoretical orientation or sound hypotheses. There are many reports in the literature which are still simple correlations of the investigator's favorite creativity measure with his or her favorite other cognitive or personality instrument, and many simplistic correlations of creativity and intelligence test scores. Such studies add little of consequence to our progress in understanding the phenomenon of creativity.

Fortunately, however, there have been some indications of progress in construct validation. One good example is the work of Khatena (1984), which represents a long-term and systematic program of research on creative imagination and imagery, including many carefully-designed and incremental experiments to provide a framework of evidence supporting the instrument's validity. The research program of Rimm and Davis (summarized well in Rimm, 1984) provides another example of systematic accumulation of research evidence for test validity over a period of more than eight years.

The instruments developed by Torrance, Guilford, Mednick, and Wallach and Kogan have continued to be focal points of many investigations. Even though some studies may represent only a single piece of evidence in themselves, when considered as a group they provide a more extensive contribution to construct validation. With respect to the *Torrance Tests of Creative Thinking* (TTCT; Torrance, 1974), some recent contributions include Baker's (1978a) clarification of the separation between *TTCT* scores and those derived from projective personality measures, and her (1978b) studies of teachers' ratings of creativity among elementary school students in which it was shown that teachers tend to overestimate the creativity of students scoring lowest on the test and underestimate the creativity of those students scoring highest. Belcher and Rubovits (1977) gathered data from ten different instruments, and demonstrated the problems of associating "creativity" with only a single test or factor. Representative studies examining relationships between *TTCT* scores and other measures of creativity-related characteristics include Bolen and Torrance (1978), Davis and Belcher (1971), Glover and Sautter (1977), Halpin, Halpin, and Torrance (1974), Kaltsounis and Higdon (1977), Martin, Blair, and Herrmann (1981), Murphy, Dauw, Horton, and Fredian (1976), Reisman and Torrance (1980), Thies and Friedrich (1977), and Torrance and Horng (1980).

Recent studies involving new and extended correlational and factor analyses of Guilford measures include Guilford's (1983) report on transformation abilities in relation to creativity, his (1984) examination of the varieties of divergent production, Guilford and Christensen's (1973) study of the "one-way relationship" between creativity and IQ, and Richards' (1976) comparison of selected measures with Intelligence and with Wallach-Kogan creativity measures. The Wallach and Kogan measures have also been used in an extensive program of creativity by Milgram and her associates (e.g., Milgram & Arad, 1981; Milgram & Milgram, 1976a, 1976b, 1978; Milgram, Milgram, Rosenbloom, & Rabkin, 1978; Milgram & Rabkin,

1980) and in studies of creativity assessment with young children by Moran and his associates (e.g., Moran, Milgram, Sawyers & Fu, 1983a, 1983b.) McKinney and Forman (1977) also reported support for the validity of the Wallach and Kogan tests through factor analysis of creativity, intelligence, and achievement data.

Additional evidence for construct validation of specific instruments has involved studying the classroom behavior differences among students who scored high or low on the *TTCT* (Bosse, 1979), differences among students in a teen drama program when compared by *TTCT* scores (Clements, Dwinell, Torrance & Kidd, 1982), relationships between creative personality measures and projective test data (Phillips & Torrance, 1977), investigation of group size influences on divergent thinking (Renzulli, Owen & Callahan, 1974), and relation-ships between divergent thinking and Piagetian formal operational thinking in adolescents (Ross, 1976).

Although there are still many isolated, fragmented studies, then, there have also been some promising signs of progress in validating several specific creativity assessment proce-dures.

Reliability

The issue of reliability generally involves three areas of concern: *stability,* or reliability over time (e.g., through "test-retest" reliability); *equivalence* or *comparability,* or the reliability of various forms of an instrument; and *internal consistency,* or the reliability of the various items or components of a test within themselves (Joint Committee, 1974).

There are some very obvious concerns, of course, about the degree to which any creativity instrument will demonstrate a high degree of reliability in the usual psychometric sense. The variability of creativity within the population is extremely great, and many anecdotal reports and case histories of creative people and their work also suggest substantial variations within an individual across brief time periods. Creativity assessment may also be particularly suscep-tible to "intrusive" effects on measurement, such as motivational influences or factors involving the situation, setting, or context for assessment. Alternate forms are difficult to create and document, since there is no single, clearly-defined universe from which items are sampled. Internal consistency is a logical and plausible concern in objective tests (such as true-false or multiple-choice), but is very difficult to consider in relation to open-ended creativity meas-ures. In addition, the important role of the person's interest and experience may play a greater role in creativity test tasks than in objective measures in content areas, so it may not be wise to assume that the person's performance *should* be comparable in all test items or sections. Treffinger and Poggio (1972) called for research that would explore these concerns empirically, but there has been very little discernible progress in this area. Writing six years later, for example, Petrosko (1978) concluded:

> The results showed that a larger proportion of instruments had high correlations
> in test-retest and alternate forms reliability than internal consistency reliability. This
> is the opposite of what usually occurs . . . A possible cause for this unusual finding
> might lie in the almost inevitable heterogeneity of test items in this area of measure-
> ment. Creativity tests often emphasize fluency of production and divergent thinking
> skills . . . With standardized achievement tests . . . there is more orientation toward
> convergent thinking. Achieving homogeneity and internal consistency is probably
> easier with such measures because of their subject matter content and item format
> (p. 117).

The research needs in relation to reliability identified by Treffinger and Poggio (1972) are largely still opportunities. These included: investigation of new methods of determining test accuracy or reliability and specifying "error" components; determining systematic external influences on reliability estimates that may be unique to creativity assessment; critical assessment of the scope and breadth of test batteries in relation to comparability.

Usability

Treffinger and Poggio (1972) identified four areas in which research was needed regarding concerns about the usefulness and practical applications of creativity testing resources. These included studies of the effects of variations in test administration settings and conditions, test scoring procedures, scorer validity and reliability, and norms and interpretation guidelines. There are still many questions, challenges, and unresolved issues, especially in relation to norms and interpretation guidelines. The areas of test administration and test scoring have received considerable attention.

Test Administration

There have been several studies of the overall climate or setting in which tests should be administered. Hattie (1977) provided an extensive review and evaluation of this area. In general, it has been shown that scores on creativity tests will vary as a function of differences in test administration procedures. But it is not clear which testing approach, if any, yields the most accurate or valid results. Variations in test conditions have proven to be difficult to describe and compare, and, although *differences* in scores can be observed, it is not clear how it can be determined which scores are most accurate for an individual. Belcher (1975) reported a curvilinear relationship between stress and test scores, rather than a simple linear relationship. Hattie (1980) reported evidence supporting the administration of creativity tests under relatively standard "testlike" conditions. Treffinger, Torrance and Ball (1980) provided guidelines for training test administrators, to attempt to assure comparable testing conditions in various data collection efforts. Modeling effects on creativity test scores, both beneficial and detrimental, have been reported by Halpin, Halpin, Miller and Landreneau (1979), Mueller (1978), and Trentham (1979). Positive effects of motivation and warm-up exercises on test performance have been reported by Carroll (1980) and Halpin and Halpin (1973). Creativity test scores have also been shown to be influenced by response set (Speller & Schumacher, 1975), group and individual administration (Milgram & Milgram, 1976a), nonverbal administration procedures (McCormack, 1975), and variations in subtest time limits (Torrance & Ball, 1978). Given the variety of test administration factors that surround creativity testing, and in view of this area's continuing resistance to synthesis, it is at least very clear that it should be incumbent upon all test users to report very carefully and thoroughly their testing context and procedures. Those who seek to use creativity assessment instruments in practical situations must also recognize that caution must be taken in interpreting and using test scores in decision-making.

Test Scoring

There has been considerable research since 1972 on test scoring, and particularly on the issue of the relationship between fluency and originality. The confounding effect of fluency on originality has been investigated by Hocevar (1979b, 1979c, 1979d), Hocevar and Michael (1979), and Dixon (1979), although no clearly superior alternative scoring procedure has been demonstrated. Milgram, Milgram, Rosenbloom, and Rabkin (1978) judged quality or cleverness of unusual responses and reported that both popular responses and unusual responses of low rated quality were associated with the production of unusual, high quality, original responses. These findings may not be generalizable to real life problem solving, however, because the researchers recognized the need to distinguish between "lenient" and "stringent" solution standards. In most creativity assessment tasks, virtually all responses are regarded as possible solutions to test problems. In real life problem solving, however, there are more clearly defined and stringent standards for solutions (Milgram and Arad, 1981, p. 568). This study, taking issue with Hocevar's (1979d) argument that originality differences are wholly accounted for by total number of responses, demonstrated that the fluency-originality relationship is more complex, "since the variance explained by unusual low-quality responding far exceeds that explained by popular responding (p. 570)." Total number of responses on a task with a lenient solution standard was significantly correlated with the unusual high-quality score on a stringent solution standard task; however, the total number of responses on a stringent solution standard task was superior as an indicator of unusual, high-quality stringent-standard problem solving. The authors argued that stringent standard tasks are clearly preferable: "Since the quality of real-world creative behaviors is judged by stringent rather than lenient standards, they are probably better predicted by stringent, rather than lenient solution-standard measures (p. 571)." This concern may also reflect the position that effective problem solving demands the ability to employ both critical and creative thinking skills harmoniously (Isaksen & Treffinger, 1985).

Another aspect of research progress on test scoring has been the development of new criteria and simplified or "streamlined" scoring procedures by Torrance and his associates (Ball & Torrance, 1980; Torrance & Ball, 1984). Unfortunately, however, this work presently encompasses only the Figural forms of the Torrance Tests; equivalent work in the Verbal areas would be equally important and valuable.

New Frontiers in Creativity Assessment Research

Although many of the concerns expressed by Treffinger and Poggio (1972) still exist, significant progress has been made in several areas. Treffinger (1980) identified 13 recommendations for creativity assessment practice, based on present knowledge; these were:

1. Clarify goals and objectives for creative learning.
2. Select and evaluate instruments carefully.
3. Avoid using "home-made" instruments.
4. Be alert for many sources of data.
5. Sample student work early and often.
6. Assess complex aspects of creativity.
7. Gather a portfolio of students' creative efforts.
8. Use group tests carefully.
9. Develop a written plan for creativity assessment.
10. Build a data base.
11. Combine clinical and statistical analyses.
12. Don't settle for decisions you can't defend.
13. Retain flexibility about decisions (pp. 28-32).

Treffinger (1980) also identified nine areas of continuing concern and needed research. Many of these continue to be challenges for us, although there are also several "new frontiers" to investigate in the area of creativity assessment. The major areas of opportunity and concern, in the present writer's judgment, are:

1. There is a need for *synthesis* with respect to many practical and technical issues, such as test administration and test scoring.

2. There should be much more interest and attention to studies of creative development across the lifespan; the creativity field has yet to meet its Piaget.

3. Basic research on the biochemistry and neurology of cognitive functions such as creativity should be encouraged, although it is doubtful that progress will be derived from such simplistic and unsatisfactory ("trendy") formulations such as "right and left brain" (see Levy, 1985 and McKean, 1985).

4. Extensive research is necessary to expand norms for creativity assessment instruments, to investigate criterion-referenced measures more thoroughly, and to stimulate new thinking about test use and interpretation.

5. Research could be very beneficial in the area of developing more effective resources, procedures, and guidelines for individual assessment.

6. Although research on creative products has been an area of progress, much more needs to be accomplished to demonstrate the validity and reliability of instruments for evaluating products based on creativity criteria.

7. Research on the use of creativity assessment data for instructional planning or prescription represents a promising area. It has been a concern for several years (e.g., Crockenberg, 1972, called for more emphasis on developing creativity than selecting creative students), but our ability to link assessment data with instructional plans is still limited.

8. We will benefit from continuing research on the distinction between contrived, puzzle-type tasks and real problem solving indicators, or the differentiation of quality and lenient/stringent solution standards in the assessment of fluency and originality.

9. Research must continue to explore the nature of creativity as a complex, multidimensional task. For example, a critical catalogue of creativity instruments would benefit both researchers and practitioners. Studies employing multivariate methods with a variety of creativity instruments (beyond simple correlations of each test with the others), would offer insight into the similarities and differences among creativity test variables across several age levels. It would also be useful to guide us in analysis and synthesis of various theoretical models, definitions, and in instrument selection.

10. Progress in other areas of research, such as learning styles and psychological type, offers promising new opportunities for us to clarify many important aspects of our understanding of creativity, its role in learning and performance, and effective methods of nurture or facilitation.

11. There is a need for long term, multivariate studies in which we explore more systematically the mutually supportive contributions of critical and creative thinking variables to effective problem solving.

In many ways, the field of creativity assessment is demanding and difficult. The creative process is subtle, not readily available to us for immediate observation and inspection. Many years are required to witness the fruition of training efforts or predictive studies, and there are numerous perils along the way. The outcomes themselves may be evidenced in an incredibly diverse array of human activities and products. Nonetheless, the same factors that make our progress difficult are the sources of excitement and wonder; creativity assessment provides a powerful and tantalizing elixir to stimulate the researcher's curiosity.

References

Amabile, T. M. (1983). *The social psychology of creativity.* New York: Springer-Verlag.

Aviram, A. & Milgram, R. M. (1977). Dogmatism, locus of control and creativity in children educated in the Soviet Union, the United States and Israel. *Psychological Reports, 40,* 27-34.

Baker, M. (1978a). The Torrance tests of creative thinking and the Rorschach inkblot test: Relationships between two measures of creativity. *Perceptual and Motor Skills, 46,* 539-547.

Baker, M. (1978b). Teacher creativity and its relation to recognition of student creativity. *Creative Child and Adult Quarterly, 3,* 106-117.

Ball, O. E. & Torrance, E. P. (1978). Culture and tendencies to draw objects in internal visual perspectives. *Perceptual and Motor Skills, 47,* 1071-1075.

Ball, O. E. & Torrance, E. P. (1980). Effectiveness of new materials developed for training the streamlined scoring of the TTCT, Figural A & B forms. *Journal of Creative Behavior, 14,* 199-203.

Belcher, T. L. (1975). Effect of different test situations on creativity scores. *Psychological Reports, 36,* 511-514.

Belcher, T. L. & Rubovits, J. J. (1977). The measurement of creativity: Interrelationships among 10 different creativity tests. *Journal of Creative Behavior, 11,* 209, 220.

Besemer, S. P. & Treffinger, D. J. (1981). Analysis of creative products: Review and synthesis. *Journal of Creative Behavior, 15,* 158-178.

Bolen, L. M. & Torrance, E. P. (1978). The influence on creative thinking of locus of control, cooperation, and sex. *Journal of Clinical Psychology, 34,* 903-907.

Bosse, M. A. (1979). Do creative children behave differently? *Journal of Creative Behavior, 13,* 119-126.

Brogden, H. E. & Sprecher, T. B. (1964). Criteria for creativity. In C. W. Taylor (Ed.), *Creativity: Progress and potential (pp. 155-176).* New York: McGraw-Hill.

Carroll, J. (1980). The effect of warm-up exercises on creativity scores. *Journal of Creative Behavior, 14,* 214, 222.

Clements, R. D., Dwinell, P. L., Torrance, E. P. & Kidd, J. T. (1982). Evaluation of some of the effects of a teen drama program on creativity. *Journal of Creative Behavior, 16,* 272-276.

Crockenberg, S. B. (1972). Creativity tests: Boon or boondoggle. *Review of Educational Research, 42,* 27-46.

Dacey, J. S. & Madaus, G. F. (1969). Creativity: Definitions, explanations, and facilitation. *Irish Journal of Education, 3,* 55-69.

Davis, G. A. (1971). Instruments useful in studying creative behavior and creative talent: Part II. Non-commercially available instruments. *Journal of Creative Behavior, 5,* 162-165.

Davis, G. A. (1975). In frumious pursuit of the creative person. *Journal of Creative Behavior, 9,* 75-87.

Davis, G. A. & Belcher, T. (1971). How shall creativity be measured? Torrance Tests, RAT, Alpha Biographical, and IQ. *Journal of Creative Behavior, 5,* 153-161.

Davis, G. A. & O'Sullivan, M. I. (1980). Taxonomy of creative objectives: The model AUTA. *Journal of Creative Behavior, 14,* 149-160.

Davis, G. A. & Rimm, S. (1977). Characteristics of creatively gifted children. *Gifted Child Quarterly, 22,* 546-551.

Davis, G. A. & Rimm, S. (1980). *GIFFI II: Group inventory for finding interests.* Watertown, WI: Educational Assessment Service.

Davis, G. A. & Rimm, S. (1982). Group Inventory for Finding Interests (GIFFI) I and II: Instruments for identifying creative potential in the junior and senior high school. *Journal of Creative Behavior, 16,* 50-57.

Dellas, M. & Gaier, E. (1970). Identification of creativity: The individual. *Psychological Bulletin, 73,* 55-73.

Dixon, J. (1979). Quality versus quantity: The need to control for the fluency factor in originality scores from the Torrance Tests. *Journal for the Education of the Gifted, 2,* 70-79.

Gakhar, S. & Joshi, J. N. (1980). Creativity within the framework of personological context. *Psychological Studies, 25,* 48-57.

Gardner, H. (1983). *Frames of mind.* New York: Basic Books.

Glover, J. & Sautter, F. (1977). Relation of four components of creativity to risk-taking preferences. *Psychological Reports 41,* 227-230.

Gould, S. J. (1981). *The mismeasure of man.* New York: W. W. Norton.

Gowan, J. C. (1972). *Development of the creative individual* (pp. 5-23). San Diego, CA: R. R. Knapp.

Gowan, J. C. (1977). Some new thoughts on the development of creativity. *Journal of Creative Behavior, 11,* 77-90.

Guilford, J. P. (1971). Some misconceptions regarding measurement of creative talents. *Journal of Creative Behavior, 5,* 77-87.

Guilford, J. P. (1976). Aptitude for creative thinking: One or many? *Journal of Creative Behavior, 10,* 165-169.

Guilford, J. P. (1977). *Way beyond the IQ.* Buffalo, NY: Creative Education Foundation.

Guilford, J. P. (1982). Is some creative thinking irrational? *Journal of Creative Behavior, 16,* 151-154.

Guilford, J. P. (1983). Transformation abilities or functions. *Journal of Creative Behavior, 17,* 75-83.

Guilford, J. P. (1984). Varieties of divergent production. *Journal of Creative Behavior, 18,* 1-10.

Guilford, J. P. & Christensen, P. R. (1973). The one-way relationship between creative potential and IQ. *Journal of Creative Behavior, 7,* 247-252.

Halpin, G. & Halpin, G. (1973). The effect of motivation on creative thinking abilities. *Journal of Creative Behavior, 7,* 51-53.

Halpin, G., Halpin, G., Miller, E. & Landreneau, E. (1979). Observer characteristics related to the imitation of a creative model. *Journal of Psychology, 102,* 133-142.

Halpin, G., Halpin, G. & Torrance, E. P. (1974). Relationships between creative thinking abilities and a measure of the creative personality. *Educational and Psychological Measurement, 34,* 75-82.

Hattie, J. (1977). Conditions for administering creativity tests. *Psychological Bulletin, 84,* 1249-1260.

Hattie, J. (1980). Should creativity tests be administered under test-like conditions? An empirical study of three alternatives. *Journal of Educational Psychology, 72,* 87-98.

Hocevar, D. (1979a, April 12-14). *Measurement of creativity: review and critique.* Review presented at the 1979 Rocky Mountain Psychological Association, Denver. [*RIE:* ED 175916, TM009-556].

Hocevar, D. (1979b). A comparison of statistical infrequency and subjective judgment as criteria in the measurement of originality. *Journal of Personality Assessment, 43,* 297-299.

Hocevar, D. (1979c). The undimensional nature of creative thinking in fifth grade children. *Child Study Journal, 9,* 273-278.

Hocevar, D. (1979d). Ideational fluency as a confounding factor in the measurement of originality. *Journal of Educational Psychology, 71,* 191-196.

Hocevar, D. & Michael, W. B. (1979). The effects of scoring formulas on the discriminant validity of tests of divergent thinking. *Educational and Psychological Measurement, 39,* 917-921.

Howieson, N. (1981). A longitudinal study of creativity: 1965-1975. *Journal of Creative Behavior, 15,* 117-134.

Isaksen, S. & Treffinger, D. (1985). *Creative problem solving: The basic course.* Buffalo, NY: Bearly Limited.

Joint Committee of the American Psychological Association, the American Educational Research Association, and the National Council on Measurement in Education. (1974). *Standards for educational and psychological tests.* Washington, DC: American Psychological Association.

Kaltsounis, B. (1971). Instruments useful in studying creative behavior and creative talent. Part I: Commercially available instruments. *Journal of Creative Behavior, 5,* 117-126.

Kaltsounis, B. (1972). Instruments useful in studying creative behavior and creative talent. Part III: Non-commercially available instruments. *Journal of Creative Behavior, 6,* 268-274.

Katsounis, B. & Higdon, G. (1977). School conformity and its relationship to creativity. *Psychological Reports, 40,* 715-718.

Kaltsounis, B. & Honeywell, L. (1980). Instruments useful in studying creative behavior and creative talent. Part IV: Non-commercially available instruments. *Journal of Creative Behavior, 14,* 56-67.

Khatena, J. (1973, November). *Measurement and identification of the creative potential.* Paper presented at the Southeast Region, National Association of School Psychologists.

Khatena, J. (1977). Facilitating the creative functions of the gifted. *Gifted Child Quarterly, 21,* 218-227.

Khatena, J. (1984). *Imagery and creative imagination.* Buffalo, NY: Bearly Limited.

Khatena, J. & Torrance, E. P. (1976). *Manual for the Khatena-Torrance creative perception inventory.* Chicago, IL: Stoelting.

Khatena, J. & Torrance, E. P. (1981). *Thinking creatively with sounds and words: Norms and technical manual* (Research Edition). Bensenville, IL: Scholastic Testing Service.

Levy, J. (1985, May). Right brain, left brain: Fact and fiction. *Psychology Today, 19,* Number 5, pp. 38-44.

Martin, J. D., Blair, G. E. & Herrmann, W. J. (1981). Correlations between scores on TTCT and Ingenuity subtest of the Flanagan Aptitude Classification Tests. *Psychological Reports, 48,* 195-198.

McCormack, A. J. (1975). Nonverbal administration protocols for figural tasks of the Torrance tests of creative thinking. *Journal of Creative Behavior, 9,* 88-96.

McKean, K. (1985, April). Of two minds: Selling the right brain. *Discover,* pp. 30-41.

McKinney, J. D. & Forman, S. G. (1977). Factor structure of the Wallach-Kogan tests of creativity and measures of intelligence and achievement. *Psychology in the Schools, 14,* 41-44.

Mednick, S. A. (1962). The associative basis of the creative process. *Psychological Review, 69,* 220-232.

Milgram, R. M. & Arad, R. (1981). Ideational fluency as a predictor of original problem solving. *Journal of Educational Psychology, 73,* 568-572.

Milgram, R. M. & Milgram, N. A. (1976a). Group versus individual administration in the measurement of creative thinking in gifted and non-gifted children. *Child Development, 47,* 563-565.

Milgram, R. M. & Milgram, N. A. (1976b). Self-concept as a function of intelligence and creativity in gifted Israeli children. *Psychology in the Schools, 13,* 91-96.

Milgram, R. M. & Milgram, N. A. (1978). *Studies in giftedness and creativity.* Tel Aviv, Israel: Tel Aviv University. Final report.

Milgram, R. M., Milgram, N. A., Rosebloom, G. & Rabkin, L. (1978). Quantity and quality of creative thinking in children and adolescents. *Child Development, 49,* 385-388.

Milgram, R. M. & Rabkin, L. (1980). A developmental test of Mednick's associative hierarchies of original thinking. *Developmental Psychology, 16,* 157-158.

Minhas, L. S. (1981). A factor analytic study of psychometric and projective indices of creativity and those of intelligence and personality. *Personality Study and Group Behavior, 1,* 29-38.

Moran, J. D. III, Milgram, R. M., Sawyers, J. K. & Fu, V. R. (1983a). Original thinking in preschool children. *Child Development, 54,* 921-926.

Moran, J. D. III, Milgram, R. M., Sawyers, J. K. & Fu, V. R. (1983b). Stimulus specificity in the measurement of original thinking in preschool children. *Journal of Psychology, 114,* 99-105.

Mueller, L. K. (1978). Beneficial and detrimental modeling effects on creative response production. *Journal of Psychology, 98,* 253-260.

Murphy, J. P., Dauw, D. C., Horton, R. E. & Fredian, A. J. (1976). Self-actualization and creativity. *Journal of Creative Behavior, 10,* 39-44.

Parnes, S. J. & Treffinger, D. J. (1973). *Development of new criteria for the evaluation of creative studies programs.* Buffalo, NY: State University College. Final report of USOE Region II, Grant No. OEG-2-2-2B019.

Petrosko, J. M. (1978). Measuring creativity in elementary school: The state of the art. *Journal of Creative Behavior, 12,* 109-119.

Phillips, V. K. & Torrance, E. P. (1977). Originality on the Rorschach inkblot test and the creative personality. *Journal of Creative Behavior, 11,* 146.

Reisman, F. K. & Torrance, E. P. (1980). Alternative procedures for assessing intellectual strengths of young children. *Psychological Reports, 46,* 227-230.

Rekdal, C. K. (1977). In search of the wild duck. *Gifted Child Quarterly, 21,* 501-516.

Renzulli, J. S. (1978). What makes giftedness? Reexamining a definition. *Phi Delta Kappan, 60,* 180-184.

Renzulli, J. S., Owen, S. V. & Callahan, C. M. (1974). Fluency, flexibility, and originality as a function of group size. *Journal of Creative Behavior, 8,* 107-113.

Rhodes, M. (1961). An analysis of creativity. *Phi Delta Kappan, 42,* 305-310.

Richards, R. L. (1976). A comparison of selected Guilford and Wallach and Kogan creative thinking tests in conjunction with measures of intelligence. *Journal of Creative Behavior, 10,* 151-164.

Rimm, S. (1976). *GIFT: Group inventory for finding creative talent.* Watertown, WI: Educational Assessment Service.

Rimm, S. (1984). The characteristics approach: Identification and beyond. *Gifted Child Quarterly, 28,* 181-187.

Rimm, S. & Culbertson, F. (1980). Validation of GIFT, an instrument for the identification of creativity. *Journal of Creative Behavior, 14,* 272.

Rimm, S. & Davis, G. (1976). GIFT: An instrument for the identification of creativity. *Journal of Creative Behavior, 10,* 178-182.

Rimm, S. & Davis, G. (1980a). Five years of international research with GIFT: An instrument for the identification of creativity. *Journal of Creative Behavior, 14,* 35-46.

Rimm, S. & Davis, G. (1980b). *GIFFI I: Group inventory for finding interests.* Watertown, WI: Educational Assessment Service.

Rimm, S., Davis, G., & Bien, Y. (1982). Identifying creativity: A characteristics approach. *Gifted Child Quarterly, 26,* 165-171.

Ross, R. J. (1976). The development of formal thinking and creativity in adolescence. *Adolescence, 11,* 609-617.

Roweton, W. E. (1972). *Creativity: A review of theory and research.* Buffalo, NY: Creative Education Foundation, Occasional Paper #7.

Speedie, S. M., Treffinger, D. J. & Houtz, J. C. (1976). Classification and evaluation of problem-solving tasks. *Contemporary Educational Psychology, 1,* 52-75.

Speller, K. G. & Schumacher, G. M. (1975). Age and set in creativity test performance. *Psychological Reports, 36,* 447-450.

Taylor, I. A. (1976). Psychological sources of creativity. *Journal of Creative Behavior, 10,* 193-202, 218.

Thies, C. D. & Friedrich, D. D. (1977). Creativity: Ideational fluency and originality at the verbal and nonverbal production and recognition levels. *Creative Child and Adult Quarterly, 2,* 213-226.

Torrance, E. P. (1969). Prediction of adult creative achievement among high school students. *Gifted Child Quarterly, 13,* 223-229.

Torrance, E. P. (1972). Predictive validity of the TTCT. *Journal of Creative Behavior, 6,* 236-252.

Torrance, E. P. (1974). *Torrance tests of creative thinking: Norms and technical manual.* Bensenville, IL: Scholastic Testing Service.

Torrance, E. P. (1976). Creativity testing in education. *Creative Child and Adult Quarterly, 1,* 136-148.

Torrance, E. P. (1979a). Unique needs of the creative child and adult. In A. H. Passow (Ed.), *The gifted and talented: Their education and development* (pp. 352-371). Chicago: National Society for the Study of Education (78th Yearbook, Part I).

Torrance, E. P. (1979b). *The search for satori and creativity.* Buffalo, NY: Creative Education Foundation.

Torrance, E. P. (1980). Growing up creatively gifted: A 22 year longitudinal study. *Creative Child and Adult Quarterly, 5,* 148-158.

Torrance, E. P. (1981a). Empirical validation of criterion-referenced indicators of creative ability through a longitudinal study. *Creative Child and Adult Quarterly, 6,* 136-140.

Torrance, E. P. (1981b). Predicting the creativity of elementary school children (1958-1980) and the teachers who "made a difference." *Gifted Child Quarterly, 25,* 55-62.

Torrance, E. P. (1981c). *Thinking creatively in action and movement: Administration, scoring, and norms manual.* Bensenville, IL: Scholastic Testing Service.

Torrance, E. P. (1984). *Mentor relationships.* Buffalo, NY: Bearly Ltd.

Torrance, E. P. & Ball, O. E. (1978). Effects of increasing the time limits of the just suppose test. *Journal of Creative Behavior, 12,* 281.

Torrance, E. P. & Ball, O. E. (1984). *Torrance tests of creative thinking: Streamlined (revised) scoring manual, figural A & B.* Bensenville, IL: Scholastic Testing Service.

Torrance, E. P., Gowan, J. C., Wu, J. & Aliotti, N. C. (1970). Creative functioning of monolingual and bilingual children in Singapore. *Journal of Educational Psychology, 61,* 72-75.

Torrance, E. P. & Hall, L. K. (1980). Assessing the further reaches of creative potential. *Journal of Creative Behavior, 14,* 1-9.

Torrance, E. P., & Horng, R. (1980). Creativity and style of learning and thinking characteristics of adaptors and innovators. *Creative Child and Adult Quarterly, 5,* 80-85.

Torrance, E. P., Khatena, J. & Cunnington, B. (1973). *Thinking creatively with sounds and words.* Bensenville, IL: Scholastic Testing Service.

Treffinger, D. J. (1980). The progress and peril of identifying creative talent among gifted and talented students. *Journal of Creative Behavior, 14,* 20-34.

Treffinger, D. J. (1984). *Review of the Torrance tests of creative thinking.* Accession number AN-09032049, Buros Institute Database (Search Label MMYD). Latham, NY: Bibliographic Retrieval Services, Inc. (BRS).

Treffinger, D. J. & Huber, J. R. (1975). Designing instruction in creative problem solving. *Journal of Creative Behavior, 9,* 260-266.

Treffinger, D. J. & Poggio, J. P. (1972). Needed research on the measurement of creativity. *Journal of Creative Behavior, 6,* 253-267.

Treffinger, D. J., Isaksen, S. G. & Firestien, R. L. (Eds.). (1982). *Handbook of creative learning: Volume I.* Honeoye, NY: Center for Creative Learning.

Treffinger, D. J., Isaksen, S. G. & Firestien, R. L. (1983). Theoretical perspectives on creative learning and its facilitation: an overview. *Journal of Creative Behavior, 17,* 9-17.

Treffinger, D. J., Renzulli, J. S. & Feldhusen, J. F. (1971). Problems in the assessment of creative thinking. *Journal of Creative Behavior, 5,* 104-112.

Treffinger, D. J., Torrance, E. P. & Ball, O. E. (1980). Guidelines for training creativity test administrators and scorers. *Journal of Creative Behavior, 14,* 47-55.

Trentham, L. L. (1979). Anxiety and instruction effects on sixth-grade students in a testing situation. *Psychology in the Schools, 16,* 439-443.

Tryk, H. E. (1968). Assessment in the study of creativity. In P. McReynolds (Ed.), *Advances in psychological assessment, Volume I* (pp. 34-54). Palo Alto, CA: Science and Behavior Books.

Wallach, M. A. (1968). Review of the Torrance tests of creative thinking. *American Educational Research Journal, 5,* 272-281.

Wallach, M. A. (1971). *The intelligence/creativity distinction.* Morristown, NJ: General Learning Press.

Wallach, M. & Kogan, N. (1965). *Modes of thinking in young children.* New York: Holt, Rinehart & Winston.

Williams, F. E. (1979). Assessing creativity across the Williams "cube" model. *Gifted Child Quarterly, 23,* 748-756.

Willings, D. (1980). *The creatively gifted.* Cambridge, England: Woodhead-Faulkner.

Zegas, J. (1976). A validation study of tests from the divergent production plane of the Guilford Structure-of-Intellect Model. *Journal of Creative Behavior, 10,* 170-177, 178.

Reference Note

The author expresses his appreciation to Ms. Penny Balance for her assistance in reviewing and searching literature incorporated into this chapter.

5

Some Critical Issues
for Future Research in Creativity*

Donald W. MacKinnon
University of California at Berkeley

As we have seen, empirical research has shed some light on each of the major facets of creativity–the creative product, the creative process, the creative person, and the creative situation. But its illuminations have been spotty and far from complete. There remain critical issues concerning each of these several aspects of creativity which can only be resolved through the findings of future research.

The Creative Product

I would argue that the starting point, indeed the bedrock of all studies of creativity, is an analysis of creative products, a determination of what it is that makes them different from more mundane products. This is the problem of the criterion, and only after we have come to some agreement about the criterion, which I shall argue is the creative product, are we in a position to study the other facets of creativity: the creative process, the creative person, and the creative situation. Each of these must be defined with reference to the creative product:

- The creative process or processes are those that result in creative products.
- A creative person is one who brings into existence creative products.
- The creative situation is that complex of circumstances which permits, and fosters, and makes possible creative productions.

In a very real sense, then, the study of creative products is the basis upon which all research on creativity rests and, until this foundation is more solidly built than it is at present, all creativity research will leave something to be desired (MacKinnon, 1975).

To speak of the creative product as though there were only one kind of product is a gross over-simplification. Creative products range from such concrete and tangible objects as a piece of sculpture or a physical invention to such intangibles as leadership or educational and business climates which permit those in them to express to the full their creative potential. Some have even spoken of the person as a product; for example, the individual who makes his own being and life a work of art. It seems likely that agreement among the experts concerning the creativeness of a product will be greater for those products that are public and relatively permanent.

Considerations such as these led us in the Institute of Personality, Assessment and Research (IPAR) study to draw our subjects from fields of creative endeavor in which the worker creates a public and relatively enduring product. The fields included writing, architecture, mathematics, and physical science and engineering research in industry.

The decision to choose as our criterion objects public and relatively enduring products had been, in part, influenced by our disappointing assessment study of Air Force officers (MacKinnon et al., 1958). Using many of the same tests and procedures which proved so

*Reproduced by permission of The Creative Education Foundation, Inc.

effective in predicting the creativity of architects, mathematicians, and others, we had had little success earlier in predicting the leadership of Air Force officers. In retrospect, it is clear that in the study of Air Force officers it was not the predictors that were at fault but rather the several criterion-measures of leadership.

A critical issue for future research in creativity is to find ways and means of studying creativity that eventuates not in objective, palpable, enduring objects but in subjective, intangible, and sometimes fleeting interpersonal relations, educational, social, business, and political climates which permit and encourage those in them to develop and to express to the full their creative potentials. In such a context the problem of studying the creative person is to identify and come to understand those who exert creative leadership. The study of interpersonal and social creativity is a far more difficult and demanding task than the study of personal creativity which so far has been the main focus of our researches. It is, of course, well to start with the investigation of the simpler problem before undertaking the more complex ones, but the time to begin is now.

What does it mean to speak of a leader, a business manager, a teacher, a governor, a general, a college president who is creative? The creativeness of such persons centers more in the realm of interpersonal and social relations than in the realm of ideas and theoretical problems while obviously not ignoring the latter.

At IPAR we have focused on the creativity of persons too much like ourselves, people whose creative products are somewhat like our own. If one thinks of these in terms of the values described by Spranger (1928), all of the creative groups we have studied have had as their highest values the theoretical and aesthetic—and these are the highest values of academicians too. In order to round out our picture of creativity and of creative persons, we need to study fields of endeavor where the highest values of the practitioners are economic, social, political, or religious, or some combination of these. Or, in fields of economic, social, political, and religious endeavor, will it turn out that the most creative workers also will have as their highest values, the theoretical and aesthetic?

What I am suggesting is that in our studies of creativity we, at least at IPAR, have been rather ethnocentric or at least inclined to draw our subjects from our own subculture. There have been some exceptions, of course; for example, the study of Irish business managers conducted in collaboration with the Irish Management Institute in 1965 (Barron & Egan, 1968). This study provided us an opportunity to assess a most fascinating group of men in Dublin. But the criterion was far from adequate, and I am afraid less light than we would have wished was shed on the creativity of Irish managers to say nothing of managers in general.

The Creative Process

A major problem confronting anyone who undertakes the study of the creative process is that, although the creative act may be of brief duration, it more often is a protracted affair. The moment of insight and inspiration may be sudden and brief, but it comes usually only after prolonged searching. To observe the whole span of creative thought and action would require considerable periods of time; and for such a study, subjects would have to be available, not just for brief periods of observation and assessment, but for months and possibly years of observation and study.

In the absence of such ideal conditions for the study of creativity, investigators have tended to employ other approaches to the study of the creative process: retrospective reports, observation of performance on a time-limited creative task (e.g., writing a poem), factor analysis of the components of creative thinking, experimental manipulation and study of variables presumably relevant to creative thinking, and simulation of creative processes on the high-speed electronic computer.

Another approach worth exploring could be the study of highly creative persons who would be willing to introspect upon their on-going creative processes and allow clinically trained personologists to discover aspects of the creative process upon which they might be themselves unable to report. Combined with this might be a study of the free associations of the creative persons to the significant and germinal ideas in the chain of their creative thinking. The relation of dream content over time to the vicissitudes of the creative process could also be studied.

Still another technique which might be used with highly creative subjects who would be willing to cooperate, would be the induction of hypnosis in order to obtain a hypnotic trance reports on those phases of the creative process which normally go on outside of awareness.

A variation on this technique would be to hypnotize a group of subjects, implanting in each (through hypnotic suggestion) the same emotional complex; for example, a feeling of guilt because of an illegal or immoral act which they are told they have committed. Amnesia for the complex is suggested, but the subject is told that he will dream about the incident the following night. Since the content of the repressed complex is known to the experimenter, he is able to see the relation between this content and the form in which it is expressed in the subjects dreams. Thus he has a powerful technique for studying the varied expressions of a repressed complex, among them the symbolic transformations of elements of the repressed unconscious into that type of active fantasy which we recognize as creative process. Such a study has already been made (MacKinnon, 1971).

Concerning the so-called incubation period of the creative process, little is definitely known. Several hypotheses have been advanced concerning the role and function of the incubation period in arriving at a creative solution. One interprets the time away from the problem as permitting the operation of certain "unconscious processes" in finding a solution—a sort of unconscious cerebration. Another interpretation conceives of the passage of time away from direct and conscious attention to the problem as permitting the "unfreezing" of a fixated and inappropriate way of seeing the problem or its elements. A third interpretation suggests that the period of incubation permits the "retrieval" of information from memory storage, while a fourth theory conceives of the incubation period as permitting the "transformation" of material that is learned or perceived in conventional ways into novel patterns. It is time that experiments be undertaken to determine the relative weight of these and still other alternative interpretations of the incubation period.

The role of accident in the creative and innovative process has been rightly emphasized in the anecdotal literature. There can be little doubt that the "chance" occurrence of an event at the appropriate time during the creative process may be signally important in providing the cue or the material necessary for the creative act. There has been some research in this area but a great deal more needs to be done—and done systematically. The need is for studies to be made of (1) the conditions under which such accidents are more likely and less likely to occur, and (2) the conditions under which such accidents, if they do occur, are more likely to result in the desired creative effect.

A related phenomenon is the use of incidental cues in creative problem solving. First of all, under what conditions are such cues likely to be used? This is a motivational and perceptual problem. And secondly, are there individual and sex differences in the use of incidental cues (Mendelsohn & Griswold, 1964, 1966, 1967; Mendelsohn & Lindholm, 1972)?

Another intriguing problem, as yet little studied, is the relative length of the several phases of the creative process, especially the phase of preparation, including the incubation period, and the phase of execution of the creative product. In some well-known instances of highly creative performance, both the period of preparation for the execution of the creative product and the period of execution itself have both been of extremely short duration—one thinks of Mozart and Schubert. In other cases, the period of preparation, including incubation, has been very long while the period of execution has been short, e.g., Darwin's development of the theory of evolution and Einstein's theory of relativity. In still other notable instances, the periods of preparation including incubation and of execution have both been long, for example, the 20 years it took Brahms to write his First Symphony (Storr, 1972). These observed differences raise the interesting question as to whether the differences are due to the field of creativity, the subject matter of the creative endeavor or to differences in traits of personality and mind, or still other differences. In any case, there are fascinating problems here awaiting future research.

Ernst Kris' (1952) description of the creative person is well-known. He is one who is adept at what Kris called "regression in the service of the ego" or, in other words, movement from *secondary process* (rational, ordered, reality-oriented, purposeful) thinking, to *primary process* (free associative, disordered, reverie-like) thinking. Primary process, according to this view, increases the probability of novel ideas which are subsequently elaborated at secondary process levels.

Rapaport (1957) equated the continuum of states of consciousness from alert, objective thought through fantasy and reverie to dreaming with the secondary process-primary process continuum. Lindsley (1960) has drawn a parallel between differences in level of arousal (as assessed by EEG wave frequency) and the waking-dreaming continuum of states of consciousness. Rapaport's and Lindsley's parallels taken together have suggested to several researchers (Blum, 1961; Dawes, 1966; and Martindale, 1972) that movement from secondary process to primary process thought would be accompanied by decreases in level of arousal.

Martindale, for example, hypothesized that creative individuals would exhibit comparatively low levels of physiological arousal and sought to test the hypothesis by measuring the frequency of alpha rhythm in persons of more and less creativity. The hypothesis was not confirmed, possibly because of the inadequacy of his criterion of creativeness, which was a Composite Creativity Score consisting of the sum of subject's scores on the Remote Associates Test (RAT) and the Unusual Uses Test. Since there is some question as to whether RAT does indeed measure creativity, his criterion measure is, to say the least, questionable.

More basically one can question the hypothesis that creative persons would show a low level of physiological arousal. A more likely hypothesis would be that creative persons possess an above average ability for, or tendency toward, shifting among various levels of arousal. But everyone shifts from higher to lower levels of arousal as they move from alert states of awareness to states of reverie and sleep. Perhaps what characterizes creative persons is not just a tendency to shift among various levels of arousal but a tendency for the timing of the shifts to be different—for example, the states of low arousal may be longer lasting, or the frequency of shifts may be different. Or it may be that creative persons are more interested in and pay more attention to their experiences in lower states of physiological arousal: their hypnagogic visions while falling asleep, their daydreams as well as their night dreams, and their hypnopompic visions when wakening from sleep, reverie, etc.

What I would like to suggest is that this is an area of intriguing research as yet insufficiently pursued, although Martindale (1975) has continued to explore the psychophysiology of creativity. What needs to be done is to obtain the cooperation of truly creative persons—not students whose level of creativity is judged by test performance rather than by outstanding creative achievement—and monitor their levels of physiological arousal over long periods of time and in demonstrated relation to fallow periods and to periods of creative productivity.

For investigation of the relation between the more conscious ego functions and the more primitive layers of the personality, there are two further techniques at hand, beyond those that I have already mentioned. One involves the administration of a mind-altering drug, and the other a marked reduction of the stimulation of the exteroceptors. Both of these techniques have been employed in the study of perceptual and cognitive process, but not intensively enough with specific reference to the creative process. Both procedures have been shown to induce marked changes in consciousness and behavior, and both the degree and quality of change vary greatly from person to person. The relation of these changes to other aspects of personality and especially to creative productivity has not been adequately studied, and cannot be until those who are subjected to such treatment are first thoroughly assessed. The two procedures which I have mentioned offer possibilities for the investigation of the consequences of bombarding the ego with primitive impulse and imagery. It should be noted, however, that such research is not without its hazards and requires, obviously, the closest medical as well as psychological monitoring of the subjects.

There is still much more to learn about the creative process. Most investigators have tended to believe that the creative process is very much the same in all persons, and, to a degree, this is most probably so. However, the question still has to be asked: May there not be different kinds of creative process? To what extent are the creative processes of mathematicians, musicians, painters, entrepreneurs, and business managers, for example, alike and in what respects different? Even within the single field of mathematics, Helson and Crutchfield (1970a, 1970b) have shown that different mathematicians describe their thought processes quite differently, and sex differences have also been revealed (Helson, 1967, 1968). Mathematicians show a significant association between creativity and "sex appropriateness" of creative style. Creative male mathematicians tend to describe their approach to research as purposive, assertive, analytic, etc., revealing the traits of what Erich Neumann (1954) has called *patriarchal* consciousness. Creative women mathematicians, on the other hand, tend to describe their approach to research problems in terms of emotional brooding until an organic growth is realized, reception of ideas from the unconscious, etc., reflecting what Neumann has called *matriarchal* consciousness. Less creative men and women mathematicians each tended, less sharply, in the opposite direction. There is much more to learn about differences in creative style—and much more also, to learn about the differences in content in the creative process.

For example, are there different kinds of imagery, of metaphor, and of analogy used in different fields of creative endeavor? Is the use of geometric symbols more appropriate to the solution of certain problems than the employment of algebraic symbols? Or is the preference for one rather than the other determined by personal and temperamental factors? One thinks of Kurt Lewin's (1936) use of topology in his development of topological psychology, and of Harry Helson's (1964) use of quite different mathematical concepts in his development of adaptation-level theory. As psychologists, both were creatively seeking general laws of human behavior.

I would next like to raise the question as to whether creativity is always a matter of problem solving. I have often argued that it is, pointing out that the creative process starts only when one sees or senses a problem. The beginning of creativeness requires that one becomes aware of something that is wrong, or lacking or incomplete, or mysterious. One of the salient traits of a truly creative person is that he sees a problem where others do not, and this, I have thought, is why a creative person is often so unpopular. He insists on pointing out problems where others wish to deny their existence. A constantly questioning attitude is not an easy one to live with, yet in its absence many problems will not be sensed and consequently creative solutions to them will not be achieved.

But am I correct in so thinking, or is my doing so merely another instance or illustration of my own subculture boundness? Academicians are always raising questions. Their researches start with questions, for implicitly hypotheses are questions which the researcher seeks to answer either affirmatively or negatively. And the subjects whose creativity we have sought to study at IPAR, with the exception of creative writers, were all persons whose creative behavior started clearly with a question which they sought to answer, a problem which they sought to solve.

But is it accurate to say that the creative process in the painter, the sculptor, the musical composer, the poet, the artist in general starts with the conception and formulation of a problem? In the past I have written that "artistic creation no less than scientific creation involves the solving of a problem, e.g., in painting to find a more appropriate expression of one's own experience, in dancing to convey more adequately a particular mood or theme, etc." More recently, Getzels and Csikszentmihalyi (1975) have sought to study the problem-finding activities of painters. Today I'm not so sure. If it is a problem that the artist senses, it typically is not one that is or can be stated verbally.

The artist has a need to express himself, to resolve some tension or imbalance, to do something with the materials of his art. However, does he have a problem to solve, and if he does in what sense is it a problem? This is yet another critical issue in future investigations of creativity.

In what respect is the creativity of a sick and tortured person the same as the creativity of a psychologically sound or of a calm and placid individual, and in what ways different? Maslow is only one of many who have tried to research this problem, but there is much more work that needs to be done in this area.

Many of the questions that can be raised about differences within the creative process become in a larger context questions about variations in style of creative work, different types of consciousness, indeed different types of creative persons, since cognitive processes are not purely cognitive in character but are vitally embedded in the total complex of personality.

The Creative Person

As far as the creative person is concerned, we have discovered traits which differentiate creative persons from their less creative colleagues in a number of fields and professions. But these, for the most part, are group findings which shed little light on the pronounced individuality of creative persons. We at IPAR have been impressed by the generality of our research findings. The design of our study was one that would permit us to say something about what characterizes the creative worker generally, regardless of his special field of endeavor and type of creativity, as well as to delineate the characteristics of the creative worker and his mode of work in each of the areas studied. The difficulty, as I've already pointed out, is that the fields of creative endeavor which we chose to study were too close to one another, too similar in their demands, and too much like our own field of endeavor. We did find differences, as others have between scientists and between different kinds of scientists and those whose creativity is expressed in the realm of art. But there is probably much more in the way of differences between creative practitioners in the varied fields of human endeavor than we have so far been able to even hint at.

We need to go even further in our search for differences among creative persons, focusing our attention upon individuals who are outstandingly creative and upon various types of creative persons, since clearly there is no single mold into which all who are creative will fit. Research on the individuality and typology of creative persons has not been entirely neglected, but it remains largely a task for the future.

We need to know more about the motivation of creativity. "What drives an artist or scientist to engage in his creative activity is a question of great interest, but one which has been somewhat neglected in academic studies of creativity" (Storr, 1972, p. xi)—although not entirely so. In general, academic psychologists have tended to stress and to study the intellective and cognitive skills and abilities as determinants of creativity (e.g., Guilford, 1977), while the psycho-analysis and derivative dynamic psychologists have been more concerned with the dynamics of creation (e.g., Storr, 1972).

The motivational theories of creativity are many and varied. According to some, creativity serves as a defense, just as a neurotic symptom is seen as serving as a defense against primitive impulses or pathological states of conflict whether paranoid-schizoid or depressive. Others see creativity as reflecting a compulsive need to order and control, while others view it as providing expression for the wish-fulfilling fantasies of the dissatisfied. Another view is that man engages in creative activity in an attempt to avoid or overcome feelings of alienation. Some theorists point to such extrinsic factors as fame and wealth as the driving forces behind creative striving. Others are more impressed by such intrinsic motives as enjoyment and pleasure in the exercising of one's skills, or competence motivation. Here the emphasis is upon self-rewarding activities, activities for activities' sake. Need for novelty and need for play have also been proposed as motives leading to creative behavior.

Analytic writers who have studied the motivations of artists and the forces driving their artistic achievements have tended to forget Freud's dictum that all behavior is over-determined and in each case have tended to find and to stress a single motive.

While there are exceptions, the more general rule has been for each investigator demonstrating the role of some motivational factor, earlier neglected, to so stress the motive he has discovered as to seem to deny, at least to overlook, the possible significance and role of other motivational factors and their interaction with the motive upon which he is now focusing.

What is needed, I believe, is a tolerance of multiplicity. Creative behavior is no different from any other form of behavior in being almost certainly the expression of not only one, but many motives. We need not choose among the different motivational theories of creative behavior. We can find confirming cases for each of them. Our need is to seek for still other and as yet unnoticed motivational factors leading to creative striving, and demonstrate, not how each of them is a factor in any given bit of creative behavior for a given person, but how they act in concert in the creative striving of persons.

A similar point can be made in respect to the many approaches to the study of creativity. In his book of readings entitled *Creativity: Theory and Research,* Bloomberg (1973) has grouped the reproduced papers under seven approaches: the psychoanalytic approach, the humanistic approach, the environmental approach, the associative approach, the factorial approach, the cognitive-developmental approach, and the holistic approach. All of these approaches should be pursued, along with still others. The time may come when we will have a single, integrated approach to the conceptualization and study of creativity, but that day, I believe, is far off.

If, as Freud believed, sublimation is the defense against primitive impulses that leads to artistic achievement, it is not clear why he believed that psychoanalysis should heighten an artist's capacity for artistic achievement.

As Storr (1972) has pointed out,

> *Since one of the objects of psychoanalysis is to help people rid themselves of their infantile sexuality, and attain satisfaction by the integration of these remnants of childhood under the supremacy of the genital drive, it is hard to see why the artistic impulse, in successfully analyzed artists, should escape analytic dissolution. Fenichel, for example, is explicit in stating that sublimations are at least partially abolished as a result of psychoanalytic treatment (p.6).*

This contradiction in Freudian theory has long intrigued me. I have fantasied a test of the theory that would not be difficult to execute. All one would have to do would be to gather the names of recognized artists and then determine which of them had ever been analyzed and, if so, precisely when. Some indication of the success or effectiveness of the analysis as judged both by analyst and artist and possibly others would have to be obtained. Further, a sample of artists who had felt the need for analysis but had not carried through for one reason or another would also have to be drawn.

The artists in question would have to be ones who had been productive over a considerable period of time, both before and after their actual or contemplated analysis. The task would then be to get "experts" ignorant of whether the artists had ever been analyzed or considered analysis, and have them rate or evaluate the artistic merit and level of creativeness of the artists' output over time. Mean ratings of the works completed before the analysis could be compared with those done after the analysis, due attention being given, of course, to the judged effectiveness of the analytic therapy.

In recent years there has been an increasing attack upon trait theories of personality for their failure to provide an adequate basis for the prediction of behavior. Those who hold this view, assert that behavior is much more a function of the situations in which individuals find themselves than it is of the presumed enduring traits of personality and character of the individual. The trait theory and the situational theory in their extreme forms are both inadequate in my judgment. Our task, if we are to predict behavior, is to specify both traits and situations; but more important still is the task of studying the interaction between the two classes of variables. This has certainly not been done sufficiently in the study of creativity. A task for the future is to study intensively under experimentally controlled conditions the role of interpersonal and social relations in facilitating and inhibiting creativity and an assessment center offers an ideal setting for such investigations. Subjects who have been thoroughly studied by a multiplicity of assessment techniques can be assigned to groups of known composition, with subsequent observation of the effects of variation in persons, in interpersonal relationships, and in group structures upon the creativity both of individuals in the groups and of groups qua groups in solving problems either undertaken by them or assigned to them.

Such experimental studies of the creative process would have their value and their place, but as previously noted the creative process often requires days, weeks, months, or even years for the full running of its course. What is needed is an opportunity to study creative persons over considerable periods of time in order that fluctuations in creativity can be related to changing life-conditions. Such data would not be obtained entirely or even mainly through the medium of interviews but through observation of the subjects in the natural milieu of their daily lives, with special reference to the conditions under which they work. In such investigations the investigators would be ever-present observers. This brings us to the creative situation.

The Creative Situation

In considering the creative situation, the problem is to discover those characteristics of the life circumstance and the social, cultural, and work milieu which facilitate or inhibit the appearance of creative thought and action.

What kinds of home and educational environments tend to nurture and develop the creative potential of youngsters? If we look only at the generality, ignoring for the moment wide diversity and individual exceptions, we may note that the biographies of our creative subjects reveal several recurrent themes: an early development of interest in and sensitive awareness of their inner experience, and of their ideational, imaginal, and symbolic processes, such introversion of interest often stemming from an unhappiness or loneliness in childhood due to sickness, a lack of siblings or companions, a natural shyness, etc.; the possession of special skills and abilities which the child enjoyed exercising and the expression of which was encouraged and rewarded by one parent or the other or some other adult; aesthetic and intellectual interests of one or both parents similar to those of the child; an unusual freedom for the child in making his own decisions and exploring his universe whether granted by the parents or asserted by the child, in other words, an early and unusual amount of independence both in thought and action; a lack of intense closeness between parent and child so that neither overdependence was fostered nor a feeling of rejection experienced, in short, a kind of parent-child relationship that had a liberating effect on the child; a lack of anxious concern on the part of the parents; the presence of effective adults of both sexes, not necessarily the father or the mother, with whom identification could be made and who offered effective models for the development of positive ego-ideals; frequent moving during the early years, often from abroad to this country, providing both personal and cultural enrichment for the child; and freedom from pressure to establish prematurely one's professional identity.

Beyond the generality of our findings, what needs to be differentiated are the many paths along which persons travel toward the full development and expression of their creative potential. What is needed is a delineation of the many types of life histories that lead to creative productivity.

An example of what I have in mind is such a biographical typology as is to be found in Helson's (1973) study of male writers of fantasies for children. Having described three types of literary genre in these fantasies—the heroic, the tender, and the comic—she was able to relate these patterns of fantasy to types of childhood pathologies found in the writer's life histories. The *heroic* pattern of fantasy appears to have originated in compensation for father-deprivation; the *comic* pattern, on the other hand, appears to reflect early conflict between admiration for the father and reluctance to take his role.

But the clearest model of the kind of analysis I have in mind is to be found in Jack Block's (1971) *Lives Through Time.* Using data from the longitudinal studies of the Institute of Human Development at Berkeley, Block identified types of personality, not at a given point in time but at several points in the life history—childhood, adolescence, adulthood—in other words, types of personality through time. Similar studies need to be conducted with other samples to discover types of personality through time that end up being creative.

This brings us to still another question: What is the nature of the wider social and political climate that is most supportive of and conducive to creative expression? I believe that most of us, on the basis of some experimental work, e.g., Lewin's and Lippitt's (1938) studies of authoritarian, laissez-faire, and democratic group atmospheres as well as our own political sentiments, are inclined to think that creative potential is most apt to come to expression in a democratic rather than an authoritarian state. That may well be so, but before we decide that the matter is all that simple we should recall that German scientists were able to create rocket bombs under Hitler, and that Russian scientists beat American scientists in putting the first satellite into orbit. There is still need for plenty of research before we will haver an adequate or very complete understanding of the role of educational, social, and political factors in facilitating or inhibiting creative potential.

If the fullest possible answer to this question is to be found, the study of creativity will have to become cross-cultural. The main focus of creativity studies has been the United States; increasingly creativity is being researched in Europe, with perhaps the greatest amount of attention being given to such studies in countries behind the Iron Curtain: Czechoslovakia, Poland, Romania, and the USSR. All of these countries, despite other differences, have this in common: they are developed, achieving societies.

But what about creativity in the more primitive and undeveloped countries? Would the definition of creativity generally accepted by European and American psychologists be valid for these other societies and cultures? No one has addressed this question with more insightful understanding than Renaldo Maduro (1976) in his pioneering study of artistic creativity in a Brahmin community of painters called Nathdwara, a sacred pilgrim center in Rajasthan, western India. In this work, Maduro discusses the western psychoanalytic theories of art and creativity in relation to six Hindu folk theories, and in an empirical study of the Hindu Brahmin painters, Maduro successfully applied a research design modeled on my (1962) study of American architects. But this is only the beginning of much work still to be done in studying creativity in more primitive and less developed communities around the world.

Some years ago Jack Conrad, Professor of Anthropology at Southwestern University in Memphis came to IPAR to learn as much about creativity as he could. His purpose in so doing was to prepare himself to study creativity as it expressed itself in African tribes. Part of his research was to identify four different cultures, two of which he would feel justified in labeling creative while the other two would be representative of relatively uncreative cultures. After a year of study of the cross-cultural files at Yale, he picked his four tribes for study, but unfortunately his projected research has not as yet been funded. Such a study, if properly executed, would require, I would think, considerable rethinking of just what creativity is and how it manifests itself in different cultures.

What I am suggesting is that the definition and testing of creativity may be as much based on the same kind of culture-bound presuppositions and biases as are the definition and testing of intelligence. If this is a valid point of view, then research in creativity, although rather intensively pursued during the last quarter century, is in for some rather considerable extension.

References

Barron, F. & Egan, D. (1968). Leaders and innovators in Irish management. *Journal of Management Studies, 5,* 41-60.

Block, J. (1971). *Lives through time.* Berkely, CA: Bancroft Books.

Bloomberg, M. (Ed.). (1973). *Creativity: Theory and research.* New Haven, CT: College and University Press.

Blum, G. S. (1961). *A model of the mind.* New York: Wiley.

Dawes, C. J. (1966). Experiments on selected aspects of "primary process" thinking. Unpublished doctoral dissertation, University of Michigan.

Getzels, J. W. & Csikszentmihalyi, M. (1975). From problem solving to problem finding. In I. A. Taylor & J. W. Getzels (Eds.), *Perspectives in creativity* (pp. 90-116). Chicago: Aldine.

Guilford, J. P. (1977). *Way beyond the I.Q.* Buffalo, NY: Creative Education Foundation; and Great Neck, NY: Creative Synergetic Associates.

Helson, H. (1964). *Adaptation-level theory: An experimental and systematic approach to behavior.* New York: Harper & Row.

Helson, R. (1967). Sex differences in creative style. *Journal of Personality, 35,* 214-233.

Helson, R. (1968). Generality of sex differences in creative style. *Journal of Personality, 36,* 33-48.

Helson, R. (1973). The heroic, the comic, and the tender; patterns of literary fantasy and their authors. *Journal of Personality, 41,* 163-184.

Helson, R. & Crutchfield, R. S. (1970a). Creative types in mathematics. *Journal of Personality, 38,* 177-197.

Helson, R. & Crutchfield, R. S. (1970b). The creative researcher and the average Ph.D. *Journal of Consulting and Clinical Psychology, 34,* 250-257.

Kris, E. (1952). *Psychoanalytic explorations in art.* New York: International Universities Press.

Lewin, K. (1936). *Principles of topological psychology.* New York: McGraw-Hill.

Lewin, K. & Lippitt, R. (1938). An experimental approach to the study of autocracy and democracy: A preliminary note. *Sociometry, 1,* 292-300.

Lindsley, D. B. (1960). Attention, consciousness, sleep and wakefulness. In J. Field (Ed.), *Handbook of physiology, section 1: Neurophysiology.* Vol. III. Washington, DC: American Physiological Society.

MacKinnon, D. W. (1962). The personality correlates of creativity: A study of American architects. In G. S. Neilsen (Ed), *Proceedings of the XIV International Congress of Applied Psychology, Copenhagen, 1961.* Vol. 2 (pp. 11-39). Copenhagen, Munksgaard.

MacKinnon, D. W. (1971). Creativity and transliminal experience. *Journal of Creative Behavior, 5,* 227-241.

MacKinnon, D. W. (1975). IPAR's contribution to the conceptualization and study of creativity. In I. A. Taylor & J. W. Getzels (Eds.), *Perspectives in creativity* (pp. 60-89). Chicago: Aldine.

MacKinnon, D. W., Crutchfield, R. S., Barron, F., Block, J., Gough, H. G. & Harris, R. E. (1958, April). An assessment study of Air Force officers, part I: Design of the study and description of the variables. *Technical Report* WADC-TR-58-91 (1), ASTIA Document No. AD 151-040. Lackland Air Force Base, TX: Personnel Laboratory, Wright Air Development Center.

Maduro, R. J. (1976). Artistic creativity in a Brahimin painter community. *Research Monographs, 14,* 222. Berkely, CA: Center for South and Southeast Asia Studies, University of California.

Martindale, C. (1972). Femininity, alienation, and arousal in creative personality. *Psychology, 9*(4), 3-15.

Martindale, C. (1975). What makes creative people different? *Psychology Today, 9,* 44-50.

Mendelsohn, G. A. & Griswold, B. B. (1964). Differential use of incidental stimuli in problem solving as a function of creativity. *Journal of Abnormal and Social Psychology, 68,* 431-436.

Mendelsohn, G. A. & Griswold, B. B. (1966). Assessed creative potential, vocabulary level, and sex as predictors of use of incidental cues in verbal problem solving. *Journal of Personality and Social Psychology, 4,* 423-431.

Mendelsohn, G. A. & Griswold, B. B. (1967). Anxiety and repression as predictors of the use of incidental cues in problem solving. *Journal of Abnormal and Social Psychology, 6,* 353-359.

Mendelsohn, G. A. & Lindholm, E. P. (1972). Individual differences and the role of attention in the use of cues in verbal problem solving. *Journal of Personality, 40,* 226-241.

Neumann, E. (1954, spring). On the moon and matriarchal consciousness. *Analytical Psychology Club of New York.*

Rapaport, D. (1957). Cognitive structures. In J. S. Brunner et al. (Eds.), *Contemporary approaches to cognition.* Cambridge, MA: Harvard University Press.

Spranger, E. (1928). *Types of men.* P. J. W. Pigors (Trans.). Halle (Saale), Germany: Max Newmeyer.

Storr, A. (1972). *The dynamics of creation.* New York: Atheneum.

6

A High-Tech High-Touch Concept of Creativity—with its Complexity Made Simple for Wide Adoptability

Calvin W. Taylor
University of Utah

The human brain in both its structure and functioning is the most complex "instrument" in the world—especially considering its small size inside the skull. From within this compact complexity, tremendous flexibility and variability of receptivity, thought, and action potentially can and does occur. The greater the number of powers of the brain and other creative attributes that are functioning efficiently together, the higher will be the level of a person's total creative processes. To me, such collective brain powers and other personal powers, acting together, form the most high-tech field that investigators can study. Some scholars of the complex psychological functioning of the brain have questioned whether the human mind will ever be able to comprehend fully the remarkable complexity of the brain.

Practically all of our research studies have been multi-variable and high-tech in nature. They tend to be possibly as complex and technical as any reported in the University of Utah-sponsored series of nine creativity research conferences (which Abe Maslow called the blue ribbon series in creativity). In this chapter, Utah creativity studies plus some challenging and unique features of other past and recent studies will be discussed.

Some critics describe certain creativity research findings as being "heresy." They apparently believe that well-established organizations and widespread practices are almost always the right and the only way that things should be. Occasionally some studies not directly related to creativity will also be mentioned to show that some evidence from these other fields is also felt to be heretical by certain people.

Our policy is to design for the people who will be the *users* of the new measuring and/or training materials. During the process of designing-for-the users, the complexity of the underlying basic research and development can be simplified to produce the materials and approaches needed for implementation. Thus, after obtaining results and insights from complex research studies, we ultimately attempt to simplify in order to obtain widespread applicability and implementation.

Creative Talents of the Mind: Some Historical Research

J. P. Guilford has said that "Creativity is a many splendored thing." This statement describes the complexity involved in our research efforts and findings. Preceding Guilford's work was the work of Thurstone on both factor analysis methodology and its application in analysis of group intelligence test scores. The complexity in our approaches came quite naturally from L. L. Thurstone's work at the University of Chicago. Thurstone, his wife and his students also extended the work beyond the intelligence (IQ) realm into other much more important thinking, producing and creating powers (factors, talents) of the mind.

Thurstone's *The Vectors of Mind* (1935) with the alternate title of "Multiple Factor Analysis for the Isolation of Primary Mental Abilities" is a highly mathematical treatment which opened the way for current computerized procedures to accomplish multiple factor analysis studies.

Further development of this methodology was published over a decade later in his book *Multiple-Factor Analysis: A Development and Expansion of The Vectors of Mind* (Thurstone, 1947). This complex approach (now extremely feasible in our computer age) is well designed to analyze and discover the multiple separate dimensions (variables, factors, abilities, vectors, or talents) of the mind.

He first utilized his own methodology to analyze the group type of intelligence (IQ) tests into seven factors (talents) of the mind which he and Dr. Thelma Gwinn Thurstone, published as "Seven Primary Mental Abilities." Along with his graduate students, he produced further studies on reasoning, perception, scientific, mechanical, and verbal abilities (talents) to yield well over 20 talents—more than twice as many different talent dimensions than there were within the IQ group tests.

Thurstone wrote a general article in the *American Psychologist* about all of these studies and the types of factors of the mind (the different processes of the brain) discovered in his University of Chicago studies. An unnamed donor had given $100 to be awarded to the best *American Psychologist* article of the year and Thurstone's article won that award.

Thurstone was always interested in creativity. Just before his death, he completed a factor analysis project of creativity for A. C. Spark Plug which unfortunately was never widely published (See also his article on "Creative Talent" in L. L. Thurstone (Ed.), *Applications of Psychology*. New York: Harper & Row, 1962). A speech which Thurstone gave in 1953 at an advisory committee meeting of my scientific personnel and fellowship project at the National Academy of Sciences was published later in the fifth of our series of creativity research conferences book, *Widening Horizons in Creativity* (Thurstone, 1964). Its title was "Criteria of Scientific Success and the Selection of Scientific Talent."

Much of this previous research used separate answer sheets and tests. My dissertation was the first in Thurstone's lab which fully moved beyond the use of separate answer sheets. It was focused upon verbal fluency factors and found two new high-level talents described as ideational fluency and expressional fluency (also named verbal versatility).

Many other researchers soon joined in those factor analysis studies. Later, for example, two Educational Testing Service (ETS) research conferences on factor analysis were organized and held in 1951 and 1958 by John French in Princeton, New Jersey, to determine the number of dimensions (factors) of the mind which had been well-established in three or more factorial studies. The number of intellectual factors at the end of the second conference which had been identified and verified had been around 45 in number (not counting physical factors and personality factors). My assigned area of responsibility was communications and creativity.

Further work by Guilford and others has increased this number to at least 100 different high-level intellectual talents (Guilford, 1977). For example, in our continuing studies of communication and creative talents, we found over 40 dimensions by emphasizing writing and talking talents (more than reading and listening), but not including any non-verbal talents in communicating or creating.

These 40 communication talents were definitely important for effective functioning of human beings in the world of work and in lifelong communicative and creative activities (Taylor, 1973; Taylor et al., 1967). Less than a third of these talents however, were ever focused upon and developed in the curriculum areas of English, speech, language arts, and communication courses.

No systematic effort has been made to integrate these talents into Guilford's Structure of Intellect, but, some of them are beyond the 100 plus factors filled into Guilford's model to date.

At our fifth (1962) research conference, Guilford (1964) had filled a bare majority of 61 intellectual factors (specific talents) into the 120 cells. An appendix to his chapter in that report contained verbal titles, three-letter codes plus descriptions and example tests for each of these 61 intellectual factors. The three-letter coding for each cell had been initiated earlier in 1959. A total of 98 cells were filled in before 1977 when Guilford's book *Way Beyond the IQ* was published.

A description of Guilford's work in producing the 120 cell, three dimensional Structure of Intellect (SOI) model by 1959 has been added as a technical appendix to this chapter. An analysis of how he dealt with the simplicity and complexity issues in that mammoth effort is also included in the appendix to this present chapter.

In the course of time, Guilford lost a major source of his funding as he continued to expand the number of factors in his Structure of Intellect. The unexpected and unreasonable explanation given was that each new factor study was just more of the same. The people who made funding decisions presumably did not fully realize that additional new "Elements of the Mind" were being discovered in each new factorial analysis. Guilford's model could be described as being a "Periodic Table of the Mind" with each new factor being analogous to a new element discovered in the Periodic Table of the Elements in physics and chemistry. When found in the physical sciences, a new element has often been given the name of either the finder or the institution where the element was discovered in order to honor its discoverer.

In education, there is a tendency for people to accept simplification of presentations and to resist moving toward greater complexity and potential complications therein. In fact grossly oversimplified explanations may be retained way beyond the time that such oversimplifications have clearly been found to be unjustified and obsolete. In educational and professional areas this has happened especially *in the case of the group-tested intelligence tests* yielding a single, *badly overtitled Intelligence (IQ) test score.* The early studies by the Thurstones and others indicated that such group-tested IQ scores cover only seven or so factor dimensions of the total intellect (total brainpower). Yet the total intellect was estimated in 1959 to be 120 dimensions or "factors of the mind"—without yet considering other sensory content input channels and potential isotopic-like amplification of the 120 factorially separate dimensions functioning in the total mindpower or total brainpower (see Guilford, *Way Beyond the IQ,* 1977). By adding other sensory channels for Content inputs, one realizes that the estimate of the total brainpower could now be even *Way Beyond the IQ.*

Guilford's funding remained largely constant for a considerable period. However, one year, unfortunately, that source permanently folded up its support to his research program. The remaining 22 unfilled cells in his SOI Model are largely in the Behavioral Slab and would thereby underlie a great deal of the vital realms called "Human Relations," "People Reading," and "Non-Verbal Communication." All these areas are certainly worthy of considerable investigation by using factor analysis and other promising approaches. We have discussed this need with Dr. Guilford several times and do hope ways and means will be found soon to complete this 22 cell portion of his unfinished work.

Several Types of Excellence, Particularly in Adulthood

Recently, I have stated that there are *several types of excellence,* especially in adult work. For example, in adult careers and accomplishments, there is a great difference between (1) *Traditional Excellence,* and (2) *Creative Excellence.* The first type maintains a high level of performance and accomplishment by strictly following the patterns of the past. The second type creates new patterns, and produces new performances and accomplishments in the future. That is, in a more excellent future.

Other kinds of excellence are (3) *Research Excellence* in producing new knowledge and new techniques which are improvements over the past, and (4) *Professional Excellence,* displayed in one's career, entirely beyond the formal education required to enter into the profession. Both research excellence and professional excellence are also different from (5) *Academic Excellence* which largely involves reproducing and re-performing (i.e., learning) knowledge and techniques already in existence. Consequently, in studies of ours and others, school grades and aptitude tests used in academic selection programs have been found to be poor predictors of who will excel as researchers. A first such study done in the 1940's and reported much later found essentially a zero (.06) correlation between gradepoint averages and overall research performances in an important government lab (Taylor, 1958, pp. 4-7. Taylor et al., 1963).

The fact is that high grade getters are not the only ones who succeed as scientists. This point is illustrated by a personal communication from a scientist. A university was visited by a large oil company recruiter who asked the scientist, "Have you any more of those fouled-up science students you sent us last year? The last lot of them was pretty good."

Furthermore, in most fields of science, the majority who have completed research doctorates never manage or manage never to do any research again. This suggests that current official selection testing and academic training do not prepare and program persons to become researchers working at the frontiers and continuing out into the unknown.

The academic world and the professional world are also essentially different. Our studies show zero (.00) correlations between grades in medical school with physician performances in practice. The same is true for pre-med grades and even for Medical College Admission Test (MCAT) scores (Price et al. 1964, Price et al., 1971, Nelson et al., 1976). Johns Hopkins Medical School recently announced that they are discontinuing using the MCAT and are advising others to do likewise.

The academic world could be much more in tune and synchronized with all kinds of excellence brought out in the adult and lifetime world of reality. These include the research world, the professional world, the business and industry world, and the world involving other people who are creating new realms and futures around the globe.

PACE can be used as an acronym slogan to describe our desire that the academic world be more in touch with professional excellence. We recommend both of its potential meanings: (1) Programs to Activate Creativity in Everyone and (2) Professional And Creative Excellence.

On the Complexity of Utah's Criterion, Predictor, and Climate Studies

Examples of Creative Studies:
Predictability of Creative and Other Criteria

In our outcome-based criterion studies of contributions of Air Force scientists reported in *Scientific Creativity* (Taylor et al., 1963), we obtained 48 criterion measures. We factor analyzed these criterion scores into 14 criterion factors. Next we administered 14 tests over a two year period to most of our sample of scientists, then correlated these test scores with the criterion factors. The battery of test scores included 42 scores on grade-point average, 12 scores on minimum satisfactory level of aspirations, 10 scores from Cattell's Motivational Analysis Test, 26 scores from Saunders' Personality Research Inventory, 2 scores from our first attempt to develop a Creative Process Check List, and 16 scores from seven aptitude tests.

Three of the initial criteria ("peer rankings on productivity," "supervisory ratings of creativity," and "supervisory ratings of drive-resourcefulness") were retained with the 14 factored criteria to make a total of 17 criteria used in the validation study. Frankly, these three initial criteria were retained mainly to communicate some findings to any readers who were hesitant about accepting findings based upon the factor results.

Next we determined the *predictability of each of these criteria*. The list of the 17 criteria, arranged in order according to the percentage of the 130 psychological scores that were valid for each criterion, is as follows:

Likableness as a Research Team Member (44%)	Scientific and professional society membership (43%)

Current organizational status (38%)	Supervisory rating of creativity (29%)
Judged work output (35%)	Originality of written work (20%)
Supervisory ratings of overall performance (35%)	Visibility (20%)
Peer rankings on productivity (35%)	Recognition for organizational contributions (17%)
Productivity in written work (32%)	Recent Publications (14%)
	Contract monitoring load (11%)
Creativity rating by laboratory chiefs (29%)	Status-seeking, "organizational-man" tendencies (08%)
Supervisory Rating of Creativity (29%)	Quality (without originality) of research reports (02%)

We also completed two major studies of measured physician performance. In the first project, we obtained 77 measures of physician performance plus pre-medical grade point averages and grade point averages for both the first two and the last two years of medical school. The correlations almost universally found between measures in the academic world and measures in the professional physician world were zero (.00) (Price et al., 1971). In our second even larger measurement project, we used five different sources to obtain more than 400 criterion item measurements of physician performances. We again found great complexity of criterion measures which again were unpredictable both by GPA's and by MCAT scores (Taylor et al., 1974) (Lau et al., 1976).

Validation of Different Types of Predictor Tests

The nine main types of predictor measures used in study of Air Force scientists described in the previous section and the number of scores of each type of test are listed in Table One. This table shows the percentage of scores valid for each type of test against the four most creative criteria and against all 17 criteria. One will quickly notice that the biographical scores were more frequently valid than any other type (Henry, 1966), especially against the creative criteria, and that the self ratings ranked second in validity. A predictor score was considered valid each time it correlated .19 or greater (above the .05 level of significance) with a criterion.

A few additional comments are warranted. The overall undergraduate gradepoint average was valid for only four of the 17 criteria and barely valid for three of these four, including one creative criterion. Stated conversely, the grade point average was unrelated to 13 of 17 criteria. In addition, aptitude, personality, and motivational test scores, where significant, were barely significant 7 or 8% of the time against the cut-off of .05 level of significance. Yet professional schools use these school grades and all other types of scores as their main, most heavily weighted selectors.[1]

We therefore wrote a section years ago stating "The Inadequacy of Undergraduate Grades as Substitute Criteria for On-the-job Research Performance" (Taylor et al., 1963, pp. 72-75). It would be even easier to write a section on the inadequacy of undergraduate grades as predictors of Research Performances (Research Excellence) or Professional Performance (Professional Excellence) or Career Excellence, etc. See also the article "Good Scholars Not Always Best," in *Business Week,* February 24, 1962 (pp. 77-78), for three studies where undergraduate grade point averages were unrelated to research performance in scientific

Table One.

Percentage of scores valid for each type of test against creative criteria and against all criteria.

Number of Scores per Type of Test	Type of Test	4 Most Creative Criteria	All 17 Criteria
30	Biographical Inventory (empirically keyed)	63%	47%
12	Biographical Inventory (a priori keyed)	46	34
17	Self Ratings	26	33
1	Grade-point average	25	22
12	Minimum satisfactory level	25	22
10	Cattell's Motivational Analysis Test	7	8
26	Saunders' Personality Research Inventory	7	8
2	Creative Process Check List (a priori)	0	6
16	Intellectual aptitude tests	0	4

work. Similar results are cited in an article titled "NASA Tries New Recruiting Tests," in *Missiles and Rockets,* May 7, 1962 (p. 17).

As a result of the above findings, we have focused on complex biographical inventories as our best predictive devices. Thorough detailed construction and development of a long series of dynamic Biographical Inventories has been the heart of our prediction research together with implementing most of these inventories in organizations with one or more national locations (See Alpha Biographical Inventory Manual, IBRIC, 1968 and Form U Manual, IBRIC, 1978, and Taylor & Ellison, 1967 and 1983).

Over several years, we have completed numerous studies on a variety of predictor tests validated against different criterion measures. While so doing, we have found clues and insights that would increase creativity in individuals and/or groups. Form U Biographical Inventory is now the best prospect available for a world-wide search for talents. It has validity, is administratively and economically feasible as well as showing unbiased cross culture features. So far it has also worked after translation into different languages.

Combining 52 Predictor Scores to Correlate with Scientists' Performances

One chapter in *Widening Horizons in Creativity* produced in teamwork with Brewster Ghiselin, reported a first attempt to construct, score, and validate a Creative Process Check List. Another chapter was on our Air Force Study predicting creative criterion performances from a multiple-test battery of scores, as described above. The results from the study in terms of variance overlap between the battery scores and six criteria are presented in Table Two below in a meaningful new form never displayed before.

From those data, we wanted to know how high the multiple correlations would be when we used a large number of test scores, all of which correlated low but significantly with each

Table Two.

Percentage of creative criteria variance accounted for by each predictor (Beta X r Products) and by all predictors ($100R^2$).

		CRITERIA					
Predictor Scores		Originality of Written Work	Creativity Rating by Laboratory Monitor	Supervisor's Overall Evaluation	Creativity Rating by Supervisor	Productivity of Written Work	Judged Work Output
No.	Name	4	7	8	17	1	6
1	Drive		4	11	3	5	
2	Math ability					-3	-3
3	esourcefulness			3			6
4	Cognition	11	3	4	5		6
5	Integrity				5		
6	Desire for principles		5	3			6
7	Desire for discovery					8	
8	Informative ability						-5
9	Flexibility						4
10	Independence						12
11	Discrimination of value	3		8	3	4	6
12	Intuition			-7	-5		
13	Creation	4					
14	Compulsiveness						
15	Talkativeness						
16	Self-sufficiency						
17	Gregariousness						
18	Aggressiveness			4	7		
19	Belief in rights of individuals						
20	Social consciousness		4				5
21	Status aspiration						
22	Masculine vigor						
23	Progressive vs. conservative	5					
24	Total no. of ideas retained						
25	Per cent correct of marked						
26	Reading skills		4				
27	Writing skills						
28	Quantity of work output					6	
29	Being well liked		7	10		4	
30	Being well known			3			
31	Quantity of reports	5			-3	4	
32	Theoretical contributions				7	6	-3
33	Level of original work						4
34	Total acceptable modifications						
35	Assertion		5				9
36	Self-sentiment						
37	Career					3	
38	Super-ego						
39	States of feeling						
40	Grade-point average		4				
41	Professional self-confidence	3				9	5
42	Emotional restraint		5				5
43	Low sociability			11	12		
44	High self-sufficiency		4		6		
45	Inner directedness			5		7	
46	Dedication to work		-3			5	-3
47	Liking to think		7			10	
48	Intellectual thoroughness					-4	-3
49	Social desirability			3			3
50	Self-reported academic level			6	7		4
51	Modal response	3		4	4	5	
52	Super. vs. scientists rating of job - scatter and shape	11					5
Total per cent of criterion variance overlapped $100R^2$ =		50.0	46.8	70.7	71.0	65.0	65.4 *
Multiple correlation coefficient R =		.707	.684	.841	.843	.812	.809 *

*The last two rows (i.e., $100R^2$ and R) show the values obtained when the Beta X r products are carried to several digits in the computer computations and used for all 52 predictor scores, instead of rounded off to whole numbers, as in the above table. All entries in the table between -3 and +3 have been deleted.

of six criteria in question. Five of these criteria were obtained as criterion factors through factor analysis. These criteria were: Originality of Written Work, Creativity Rating by Laboratory Monitor, Supervisor's Overall Evaluation, Productivity of Written Work, Judged Work Output, and Creativity Rating by Supervisor. The last one was the initial ratings, not a factor-analysis obtained criterion. From our experiences with scoring item alternatives on our complex biographical inventories, we found that many items, collectively, would build up sizeable validity results for the total inventory. This occurs even on cross validation studies, even though all the items have low correlations. Collectively, however, the total inventory has repeatedly shown high cross validation results.

We therefore wondered whether a long set of test scores would yield the same type of results as a long set of biographical items. We found, as seen at the bottom of the Table, that the battery of 52 test scores produced initial multiple correlations of .71, .68, .84, .84, .81, and .81 successively against the six criteria in the sequence arranged in the table. By squaring these multiple R's, 50% or more of the criterion variance was accounted for in all but one of the six cases. Between two-thirds and seven/tenths of the criterion variance was accounted for (overlapped) in four of the six criteria.

This accumulation of high overlap of these criteria occurred even though any single one of the 52 separate tests rarely accounted for more than 10% of the criterion variance. In fact, only eight of the 312 (52 x 6 columns) validities accounted for between 10-12% of the criterion variance in the entire table. (The technique we used to obtain this percent of variance of any particular criterion was by multiplying the beta weight and the validity coefficient for each test score and then summing these products across the scores.) In other words, a large total accumulation occurred from small contributions obtained from a large number of different test scores.

These are the same type of initial validities we have obtained from biographical items and then have found that the big collection of biographical items in the whole inventory, pooled together, produced cross validity results of from .40 to the .60's range. As with a collection of items in biographical inventories, a battery of test scores yields analogous results on the initial validation and we believe it would hold up at a somewhat lower, but certainly noteworthy level of cross validities.

In both cases, we believe that it takes a lot of little oars pulling together collectively in the same broad, but general direction to yield consistently good validity results in cross validation studies. We also believe that no one should lean too heavily on any single oar or any small number of oars, because each one has only a small pull forward in the general direction intended.

The format used in this table provides a "simplified structure" of the results of an earlier investigation of characteristics of scientists functioning in their performances and accomplishments in a large basic science center in our federal government.

Organizational Climates for Creativity

The seventh (1966) creativity research conference was on the topic of Climate for Creativity (Taylor, 1972a). One main point is that climates against creativity are more frequently found than climates for creativity.

My report included four stages or types of leadership in the aging cycles of organizations. At their birth, organizations tend to be started by (1) *Innovators* who make their contributions and tend to be replaced by (2) *Developers*. These leaders expand and develop the organization and deliver it into the hands of (3) *Consolidators* who produce "bigger and better rule books." That is, they rule by rules that control and tend to curtail the range and depth of creativity. At that stage, if a creative idea occurs at the bottom of the organization, what chance does it have to rise and be accepted all the way up to the top of the organization? What chance does an organization have under *Consolidator Leadership* of reversing itself by moving back to the *Developer* or even *Innovator* stage? Instead, the Consolidators tend to prepare the organization well and deliver it into the hands of (4) *Undertakers.* Then the aging has run the full cycle and the organization is dead—unless someone within or from outside becomes another Innovative person by *undertaking a new venture,* a brand new organization to fill the void that the dead one left in the market place (Taylor, 1972b).

From pilot studies, we sensed that the environment—the "atmosphere or climate"—could have positive or negative influences upon the creativeness of people in their work. Perhaps climate measures may have a stronger influence than expected, which would provide major new contributions in predicting how creative people will be. We found our first major opportunity to test these notions in a West Coast Navy laboratory. We were able to construct a lengthy Climate Questionnaire (Inventory), administer it to all the laboratory's scientists, and validate its separate scores against each of the 25 criterion measures.

We used alternative item analysis to determine the validity of each alternative in the Climate Questionnaire. In that way we learned how to score every item alternative against each separate criterion of creative and other accomplishments of each scientist. Then we developed a different scoring key to obtain a best total predictor score for each of the 25 criterion targets. A total of 22 of these 25 climate scores, individualized for each criterion, produced cross validities ranging from the .30's into the .70's. In fact, half of these 25 cross validities were .60 or above with 2 in the .70's. These were extremely promising results—remarkably high validities. This is especially true considering that it was our first time of using this approach to measure the influence of climate conditions on creative and other performances and accomplishments (Ellison et al., 1968) (McDonald et al., 1970).

We have therefore demonstrated that organizational climate scores can provide a strong supplement (not a duplicate) to other typically valid predictor scores. Our further evidence is that such climate scores can be combined with valid biographical inventory scores to account for an increasing amount of on-the-job criterion performances and accomplishments. We believe that this is true not only for scientific research centers, but probably for all other fields of work.

Most of this detailed technical development of biographical, climate, and criterion measurement instruments occurred at the Institute for Behavioral Research In Creativity (IBRIC) founded two decades ago in 1965.

Besides sustaining research work on Biographical Inventories, IBRIC next moved into Management Audit Surveys (or Management Assistance Surveys) (MAS) studies. In the process of producing the MAS measuring instrument, a well-designed factor analysis study was conducted. The resulting rotated factor matrix showed a remarkably clean "simple structure" in the form of an almost perfect step ladder design across the first 15 factors (plus 3 or 4 other more complex factors). This showed both the 15 (or more) dimensional complexity and the underlying separateness and simplicity of the factor structure and the measuring instrument.

From the beginning of the MAS studies, appropriately simplified computer printout scores were provided to different levels of management. Recently, these printouts have changed to more effective graphics rather than numerical printouts to show more clearly any weak areas and the degree of weakness for every supervisor at each level.

After several years of successful MAS studies in research centers and in other business, industry, and government organizations, IBRIC has learned from their experiences of feeding back the survey results that further stage-setting steps are necessary to ensure serious attempts by the organization to improve their management practices. This has led them to describe their approach as a training needs program and to title it more broadly as a total "Management Self-Improvement System." They have also been providing training to management personnel at each level with the training needs being individualized for each manager to be in his greatest area of weakness where improvements are most needed.

Thus, IBRIC's approach is another example of high-tech research and development followed by designing for users. The materials and procedures and instructions and training are produced in a simplified, effective form to ensure as sound implementation as possible. The same emphasis of designing for users has also occurred in IBRIC's biographical inventory studies. Simple Percentile Rank scores have been produced for each student or worker in school and other organizations.

In IBRIC's strong desire to have improvements occur in organizations and management practices, they have taken numerous further frontiering steps. They now ask top management to contract for change by assigning key personnel to put forth the necessary efforts and steps to bring about the changes. Management must also contract that official work time and it will be made available for these key personnel to do this task.

In other words, the call is made for a management action plan, with key personnel freed as needed. The plan moves into action with overseeing and backing by top management. Under such an agreement, a troubleshooting process of change will have a much higher probability of occurring.

These change agents are called *facilitators* who need to be trained and then need to learn to work with management personnel at various levels on how to improve the management practices, especially in areas of weakness. They work with supervisors (1) to help them understand the feedback results measured by the survey, (2) to assist supervisors in using the project manuals on how to improve weaknesses, and (3) to encourage sustained efforts so that full follow-up action is taken.

Another step IBRIC is taking is to have each person who works directly under a supervisor get together as a team with the supervisor and the facilitator. Troubleshooting as a team, they then work through the problems that have been uncovered. They think through and produce many possible ways to try to solve the troubles by using problem solving, even creative problem solving methods to succeed in making the improvements. In these ways, IBRIC is more fully living up to its name of being an Institute for Behavioral Research in Creativity. The final point is that much, if not most of the work accomplished by IBRIC might never yet have been done if IBRIC had not existed.

While studying scientists and the total climate for their best work, one example that intrigued me was the case of a chemist at a large chemical organization. During a period of lengthy reflection, he reached a conclusion about when he had done his best work and had been the best chemist for that organization. It was not when he was in the laboratory, nor when reading in the library, nor when working at his desk. But it was when he rotated his chair away from his desk, put his feet up on the window sill, and was looking out of the window. I suspect a high percentage of supervisors, when seeing a person seated in that position, would interpret that he was definitely not working for the organization or earning his pay during that period. Yet such an interpretation by a supervisor would be 180 degrees different from the way the chemist himself described it.

Challenges from Combining Instructional Media and Creativity

The sixth (1964) creativity research conference was on the unique combination of Instructional Media and Creativity (Taylor & Williams, 1966). An unusual feature of this conference was that both creativity and instructional media can apply "across the board" to all disciplines and areas of human activity. Both topics are therefore almost unlimited in their potential areas of impact, but previously there had never been any serious attempt to put them together. Yet these two topics in combination provide an abundance of rich material for almost endless discussions. The conference proceedings are therefore full of ideas hardly ever worked on before and possibly still full of other ideas with untapped potentials.

Certain unorthodox ways of transmitting information which provoke thinking in readers' minds have occasionally been used in this creativity conference series. For example, at the previous fifth research conference spontaneous discussion was sparked on "Process Vs. Product in Creativity" from a comment by Barron (Taylor, 1964). At the fifth conference only in this spontaneous chapter, each researcher was identified by being named in print as he entered into the discussion. Nearly 100 different comments were produced by the 18 different participants who entered into the discussion one or more times. At one extreme, five persons entered into the discussion only one or two times. At the other extreme, three persons responded more than nine times. For one person, the frequency of responding was 16 times, 12 for another, and 11 for the third person. All but four of the 18 discussants averaged four or less printed lines to make their comments. Across the nearly 100 comments by all participants, the length of all but six comments was less than 10 printed lines. The lengths of these six comments were 17, 17, 13, 11, and 10 lines long.

To produce these creativity research conference volumes, we did not ask each chapter author to produce a paper in advance, nor did we ask them to submit a paper from their notes after the conference. Instead, we went the many extra miles of effort by tape recording them and then transcribing completely their remarks.

In some volumes we also transcribed questions and discussions that occurred. We coded the transcriptions with S representing the speaker and C representing others who commented or raised questions. For occasional chapters, such as the one in the fifth conference described above and in my first chapter in *Instructional Media and Creativity,* we identified accurately the speaker by name and the name of each and every commentor and questioner. This required still greater effort to identify each discussant in the transcript. Readers were able to identify in the printed volume all persons by name as they entered into the discussion. In this way, the readers became better acquainted with each of the participants. The readers of the chapter labeled by S and C acted as if they were participating by making their own comments to themselves as they read the discussions.

In the same spirit of making the volume more interesting and accurate for the readers by identifying those entering into the chapter, we have created another precedent in print which we wish would become universally adopted. For example, whenever we write of the Structure Of Intellect (SOI), we deliberately capitalize and underline (or boldface) each of the key acronym letters, and then add the acronym immediately afterwards in parentheses. This style (1) alerts the readers that we are switching from the fully spelled out name and title to an acronymn which we will start to use later as a code for the full name, and (2) this shows clearly and meaningfully the derivation of the acronym and enables the reader to flip the pages back, if needed, in order to locate, identify, and memorize the full name from which the acronym was derived. This is analogous to the style in mathematics of giving the definition of symbols before using the abbreviated symbol(s) thereafter.

My main experience with this conference and its combined topics will be pointed out by discussing the first three chapters of the book. Sid Parnes helped to set the stage with Thomas Clemens to get creativity researchers and educational media experts together. Shortly before, I had attended an Association for Supervision and Curriculum Development (ASCD) project meeting in St. Louis on a theory of instructional materials (directed by Chandois Reid and supported by the U.S. Office of Education). I was invited in order to be "A watchdog for creativity." In effect, I took a series of "marginal" notes, sparked in me while listening, which proved to be analogous to notes one has jotted in the margins of a book as they popped into one's mind while reading. Afterwards, I expanded each note into a full paragraph so that I had a lengthy paper of new ideas that had come out while listening and thinking throughout the seminar. Such a paper of ideas, especially on these combined topics, might not have emerged if a seminar watchdog-for-creativity had not been present.

In both running a conference and making a presentation, I soon learned to deliver my presentation early in order to be relieved of that burden for the balance of the conference. Consequently, at this sixth conference, mine was the first presentation with an intention of covering my full paper on this topic (Taylor, 1966). However, the session quickly turned out to be a "Discussion of Participants." This session brought about such fruitful discussion that the names of those making comments together with their remarks are included in this chapter as they emerged. Our hunch is that the chapter is more provocative for readers when all the discussion is carefully edited and retained, with each person identified by name in print as s/he entered the discussion. This way of starting the meetings was vital in stirring full discussion among practically all participants, thereby setting the stage for lively meetings thereafter, a more creative conference–indeed, an experience in creativity for participants and later readers alike.

It turned out that I had finished only one-third of my paper when time was up for my speech. Every so often, during my presentation, I was able to break into the discussion tactfully, and add another idea-paragraph from my paper which then sparked the participants to "take the ball away from me" and have another flow of exchanges. During my one hour presentation, I spoke just less than 30% of the time and the other researchers entered in individually and often, so that their total comments and questions occupied over 70% of the time. Three of the dozen other discussants collectively occupied more time than I did as the main presenter by their entering in frequently and/or at length several times. One of them was Carl Rogers, who arrived a little late, but increased the stimulation in the discussion by the depth of his comments. As a consequence of these discussions, the remaining two-thirds of my prepared paper was never presented to the participants, but was published in full as the second (#2) chapter in the published volume.

Guilford (1966) was the next speaker at the conference. He presented his full paper with almost no interruption. Guilford's formal presentation occupied two-thirds of his total period. During the discussions at the end, the other discussants occupied 62% of the remaining time while he occupied 38% of the remaining time by entering in 54 times, averaging three printed lines/time to answer questions and make his own comments. All but four of these answers and/or comments took six lines or less in the text. Whenever he was asked a question, his usual performance was to give a straightforward, thorough-coverage, convergent answer, rarely with much qualification or expansion–a short answer as concise and accurate as possible. As it turned out, he stirred up many questions and much discussion. This suggests that the first presentation of this conference, which was full of exchanges among participants, had set the stage for lively and lengthy discussions to occur in the second presentation by Guilford and throughout the conference. This finding is relevant both to topics of the book and to the running of lively conferences.

Pertinent to the Instructional Media and Creativity title of this volume, readers should notice that across the first three chapters they have experienced three different styles of media presentation of information. In the first chapter the discussion started immediately and was presented throughout the chapter as it actually occurred. In the second chapter of 28 pages, with only one exception, discussion was *not* presented. This chapter provided the typical type of presentation on which reader habits have usually been built and through which they have been extremely well practiced. In Guilford's (1966) third chapter, all the discussion has been presented at the end of the chapter after the formal presentation has been completed. The reader might ask himself which style he prefers. After answering, he might ponder to what degree his answer on his most preferred style is based upon his usual expectations and habitual reading responses and whether these habitual expectations may hinder his having a full creative experience while reading.

All the results above were quite different from our findings in one of our local school districts. Tape recordings made across several classes showed that teachers are talking an average of 80% or more of the time. Another fascinating classroom study focused on questioning in the classroom done at a large land grant State University in the East. The investigators wanted to know how many questions were asked in a typical classroom hour and how much time, on the average was spent working on answering each question. Quite surprisingly, across the several instructors observed, the average number of questions asked per hour was 40, a much larger number than anticipated in the study. From our measurements and from that result, it follows that the amount of time, on the average, spent answering each question was only a few seconds. All this clears up when one finds out who asked the questions—it was the teacher. And who answered the questions? Again it was the teacher. That's how curiosity and questioning by students is *not often encouraged* in classrooms. The instructor was by far the main person asking questions and then promptly answering his own questions. The students quickly realize that they should hardly ever enter into the questioning or discussion when the teacher is lecturing in front of the class.

For the first time at the end of the class period, the teacher may ask, "Are there any questions?" Even then, many and possibly the majority of the students have learned under both teacher and peer pressures, not to ask questions—and not to do so in order that the class will be dismissed as soon as possible.

Teaching for Multiple Creative Talents

The approach of developing multiple creative talents was built upon a great deal of underlying basic research on multiple talents and an empirically based theory of education (Taylor et al., 1964a). These were logically followed by the development of several projects with classroom implementations accompanied with evaluation by using new measuring devices constructed for this new approach. Over nearly two decades, many projects have been sparked in Utah and around the nation for developing and implementing this multiple creative talent approach in classrooms. Occasionally, this has occurred in entire demonstration schools and even in classrooms at all levels in some school districts.

In 1978 a conference was held in Utah with participants from 12 states which yielded a National Institute of Education (NIE) published volume titled *Teaching for Talents and Gifts: 1978 Status* with a subtitle of *Developing and Implementing Multiple Talent Teaching* (Taylor, 1978). Following that publication, Dr. Walter Talbot, then Utah's Superintendent of Schools, requested that a research report evaluating the results on several projects be produced to accompany the talent status volume. This research report on *Multiple Talent Teaching Results* was finally produced across 10 projects, the majority of which were outside of Utah. It was published soon thereafter in the *Congressional Record* (Taylor, 1980) including the following excerpts:

> *All the results on ten projects plus several replications scattered across the nation have almost uniformly been in favor of Multiple Talent Teaching over traditional academic-only-type of teaching.* **Practically all results were leaning positively with** *the large majority of these results being statistically significant differences.*
>
> *The probability would be essentially infinitesimal (about .000 . . .) that these strings of differences, practically all in one direction and across ten or more projects, could ever occur by chance.* **It is suspected that no new educational approach has ever attained such powerfully significant results on measured student performance across such a wide range of relevant classroom activities.**
>
> *In correspondence, Carol Schlichter (of Alabama) commented that "the fit of Multiple Talents in almost any area of educational programming is phenomenal." Rachel Morton (of North Carolina) has similarly written us that "the deeper I get into the multiple talent approach, the more it seems that it fits just about anywhere when people are looking for meaningful innovation in education.*

Project Implode at Bella Vista Elementary School in Utah's Jordan School District deserves high praise for its great accomplishments as the first school using multiple creative talents. That project also produced the first multi-talent printed manual for teachers called *Igniting Creative Potential.* The first totem pole picture of seven students across six totem poles was produced in October 1969 at Bella Vista by Beverly Lloyd. These first six talents as seen in Figure One were: (1) Academic; (2) Productive Thinking; (3) Communication; (4) Forecasting; (5) Decision-making; and (6) Planning. Later in 1984, three other totem poles were added to these six totem pole pictures to produce the present nine talents–(7) Implementing; (8) Human Relations; and (9) Discerning Opportunities. Because all of the other talents in the totem poles are high-tech, we have included the human relations talent in order to add high-touch to high-tech, as is usually required in high-tech fields.

Probably the greatest single gain for students is to unearth these new talents from "six feet underground" and get each talent actively functioning at some initial level on each totem pole. The second gain is to have students grow in their ability and effectiveness in using each talent.

Instead of processing for only the copper-like academic talents, we can also process for the uranium-like creative talents, the gold-like decision-making talents, and so forth in our schools. Like the mining specialists, we may realize that the waste products we have been dumping out in the streets for so long contain many precious talents–perhaps even more valuable than the one (or ones) we initially had solely extracted.

These high-tech creative talents are the high-level basic talents needed in high quality performances and accomplishments in careers and lifetime activities. There are therefore the high-level basic talents that need to be developed in school so that schooling will transfer over and prepare people for functioning effectively in their careers and lives.

A research-based theory of education produced for the U.S. Office of Education (Taylor et al., 1964a), stated as a first goal that education should be concerned with the identification and cultivation of all the nation's known human resources. The inborn potential brainpower resources are most certainly one of the most important of all the types of human resources. A mind is a terrible thing to waste, according to Sam Proctor (1978). It is also true that a large part of anyone's mind is a terrible thing to waste, because all students are potentially highly talented in at least one of the abundant variety of brainpower resources.

In the number of totem poles, we first moved into a diverging approach starting with two totem poles of academic and creative talents and then expanding from two to six and even more recently to nine. For flexibility, we now occasionally return to simplicity, as in the beginning. We only set up two totem poles: (1) the Academic (Learning) Totem Pole and (2) the broad Creative Talents Totem Pole consisting of all the Thinking, Producing, and Creating ways of Functioning, or ways of acquiring knowledge and functioning effectively.

The Talents Unlimited Project, developed for three financed years under Dr. Carol Schlichter's leadership applied successfully to be on the National Diffusion Network of the U.S. Department of Education. This project has been designated as the exemplary project for Gifted and Talented Programs for the nation. They have had adopters in practically every state in the nation. This decade of adoptions has occurred under the leadership of Sara Waldrop and Florence Replogle in Mobile, Alabama.

Recently Japan has taken a major step in creating a 26 man educational reform commission. The report they have produced is calling for greater flexibility in their educational structure and for creativity to be developed in all their students. They recommend having their students do such things as learn to think on their own, to judge on their own, etc. They also want students to search and think up all possible alternatives that might be relevant to the problem at hand. It appears that what they have in mind resembles very closely our model of teaching for creative talents which has proved to be very implementable and produces a better education than students have ever had before (Haberman, 1985).

Figure One.

Taylor's talent totem poles – 1984 extended version. Copyright © 1984, Calvin W. Taylor.

Some recent news articles have contained a variety of ideas relevant to this chapter. One headline stated that Japan's #1 resource is its people. This is similar to the statement by Utah's former State Superintendent, Walter Talbot. He said that our search for talents should have higher priority than our search for natural resources, because the discovery and development of the latter are fully dependent upon the former. Likewise, our search for talents should have higher priority than our search for knowledge because the acquisition of existing knowledge and the production of new knowledge are fully dependent upon the former. The above recommendations lead to the following two outcome statements: (1) When talents function creatively, people function effectively, and (2) When talents function effectively, people function creatively.

Teachers, parents, and supervisors should become *Talent Developers* as well as *Knowledge Dispensers*. Being Talent Developers is both possible and very important nowadays because computers and other devices can do some of the knowledge dispensing very well (Taylor, 1968, 1985).

This permits a *Simultaneous Double Curriculum* (Taylor, 1986) for developing more of the total creative-power resources. The inner talents function in the processing and acquiring of knowledge. That is, all talents can be used to acquire knowledge. Conversely, each type of knowledge can be used to activate and develop every talent. When this double curriculum system has knowledge and talents functioning together, students simultaneously grow in both knowledge and talents. The education costs are not increased. However, the yield is doubled by growth in both knowledge and talents. By this approach, students become more knowledgeable and function more effectively as multi-talented individuals while growing into adulthood. They will also become multi-talented adults who function more effectively for themselves and for society.

Earlier in our Utah studies, we administered our biographical inventory to high school students when they started a summer research participation program at a large research center. We learned that the Creativity score in our Biographical inventory would identify in advance the students who accomplished at high levels, even producing publishable research in a summer from those with lower creativity scores who, during the summer's experience, did not show as much promise in research work.

It was also found that the high school students, as a group, were more ready to do research during a summer's experience in large research centers than were medical students, graduate students, and high school teachers. In fact, the directors of the research projects said that if they could have only one of these groups to augment their regular staff in the summer, they definitely would want the high school students (Taylor et al., 1964b).

Also Jablonski (1964) found that some students who did not have high academic *nor* high 10 scores performed better and asked better research questions in summer projects than did the traditional academic types with higher academic school credentials. A local inventor gave a provocative speech about the process of inventing and marketing inventions. He believes that anyone can learn to become an inventor, because he says that he has never met anyone who didn't have an idea. He feels that his lack of formal education has helped him because he hasn't been "boxed in" by restrictive learning processes. He says that schools do not teach creativity and in that way people have put limitations on other people. To him, if one wants to be creative, "a person has to discard traditional thought systems, such as those taught in schools. Only by breaking away from those restraints, are people capable of linking the tangible solutions to an intangible problem."

Gabrielle Rico, Professor at San Jose State University, recently spoke to a huge audience of teachers at one of our large school districts. She recommended that one of the best ways for students to remember what they have learned is by "storying." That is, they either write or tell a story about what they are to learn (rather than memorizing it) so that both halves of the brain are used in telling or writing stories. Furthermore, such storying gives learning and meaning to life, noting that a mind without a story is devoid of meaning. She said that teachers must draw on both sides of a child's brain. The right hemisphere of the brain perceives the melody of life and the left hears the notes that compose the melody.

The same argument of using both halves of the brain by "storying" can be used for each of our multiple thinking-and-producing talents. In each case, these inner talent processes call for more fully processing the knowledge or concept being learned than mere memorization. Furthermore, these higher-level thinking talents call for producing a different type of product on their own, such as a plan, or a forecast, or a decision, etc. And each of these talents will call upon using subportions of both halves of the total brain. However, because of the brain's great complexity, as indicated both anatomically and by the findings from many factor analysis studies, different subportions in each half of the brain will be used by different high-level talents. Therefore, by using a multiple set of thinking-and-producing talents, a greater amount of each half of the brain will be activated and used than if only a single thinking talent were used.

An important point here is the evidence that schooling usually calls for students to use one side of the brain much more than the other. Typical schooling still has students use only a small portion of the total potential powers of the brain. Consequently, if we scientifically and systematically, in schooling, brought the less-used side of the brain up to the same use-level of the other side of the brain, the students would still be using far less than half of total potential powers of their brain. For example, let us estimate that schooling typically has 15% of the total brainpower being used on one side of the brain and only 3% on the other. Then if we brought both sides up to an equal level so that each one used 15% of the total brainpower, in combination, they would still be using only 30% of the total powers of the brain. The other 70% of the ofttimes more powerful parts of the brain would still be idle and untapped in school.

In summary, having students simultaneously work on knowledge-and-talents together will overcome both (1) *ignorance* of knowledge, and (2) *ignorance* of functioning effectively as individuals. It also stretches students' minds in two ways: (1) by working at a wider range and depth of knowledge, and (2) by activating more of their total brainpower potentials through using *thinking ways of learning knowledge.*

These are reasons why I am much more in favor of *lifelong thinking types of learning* rather than *lifelong learning* programs. I also favor "Thinking Centers" and "Talent Centers" and "Function Junctions" over "Learning Centers." The reader should also see the New York Times article by Goleman (1984) on *Styles of Thinking, Not IQ, Tied to Success* in careers and life.

The World Council for Gifted and Talented Children has selected Salt Lake City as the site for their 7th World Conference, from August 3-7, 1987. Starting in 1975, these biennial world conferences have been held in London, San Francisco, Jerusalem, Montreal, Manila, and Hamburg, typically with 40 or more nations participating in the conferences. To each of the several strands in the program we are adding an emphasis on creativity, leadership, and research along with a focus all-the-way-up from pre-school and elementary schools through secondary and higher education into adult careers and lives. To sharpen this emphasis, one type of key speaker will be those who have proven in their careers to be extremely gifted and creative adults. The special theme of the '87 Conference is *Expanding Awareness of Creative Potentials* throughout the world.

Some Last Comments

In general, schools do not have students deal with the unknown in a specific subject, nor do schools have students deal directly with the future. Yet the more that students are trained to look and focus backwards, the more that will become the main way they look at things.

In sharp contrast, however, creativity does not have these shortcomings. Working in the unknown is where creative talents can really sprout and blossom.

Those with a strong futuristic view have coined slogans such as "The future doesn't just happen. Each of us can help create it in one or more ways." Another version is "Creative talents make the future." To describe the importance of thinking about the future, on our Form U Biographical Inventory, one can search for those with high scores in both Creativity and Leadership. They are candidates with high potentials to be Creative Leaders—and perhaps even history-making leaders, according to Toynbee's (1967) descriptions. Some persons in the past have been such highly creative leaders that they appeared to have no followers—they were so far ahead of the crowd in their contribution(s). Such a person may not get the type of reward or support that comes from having followers. Consolidators may use the lack of followers as a club to keep him/her in stress and pain if she/he tries to move ahead on his work. Yet in the course of time, a few decades or even half a century or more later, much of the world could follow in the new path he had created. Such Creative Leaders could alternately be called Pathcreators. In *Widening Horizons In Creativity*—the first chapter by Arnold Toynbee (1964), the eminent British historian, titled "Is America Neglecting Her Creative Minority (Creative Talents)?" discussed this issue. In it he states that creativity is mankind's ultimate capital asset—a matter of life and death for any society. Later he says that America's need, and the world's need today, is a new burst of American style pioneering, and this time, not just within the confines of a single continent, but all around the globe. He concluded that if America is to fulfill her manifest destiny, she must treasure and foster all the creative potential that she has within her.

After corresponding with Toynbee, I met him in person, and he agreed to come to my 1967 summer creativity workshop. He spoke *On the Role of Creativity in History.* Throughout that speech, he illustrated his main point that *creative talents are the history-making talents.* If a nation wants to become more active in making history, it should move to identify and develop the creative talents in its people. If instead it turns its back on and neglects creativity, in effect, that country has abandoned and defaulted its history-making role, which will be picked up by some other nation(s) in the world (Toynbee, 1967).

A highly creative person in school or at work in an established organization can be surrounded by dilemmas and mixed signals. As Toynbee says, a creative person's presence raises the standards of endeavor and achievement, a useful source for society. But his providing this service will not appease his duller or lazier neighbors. The parent, teachers, or supervisor must protect and encourage each creative individual, not penalize him.

A creative person at any age is often difficult to understand. He or she tends to sense weaknesses or flaws in the established order. The creative person often becomes disenchanted with things as they are and may even "drop out" from customary ways of living and thinking. Such behavior does not endear him/her to those who are comfortable with the status quo.

Toynbee also said that suppression of creativity at any level can lead to explosions. "Establishments of the day" when faced with new, vital and creative elements in the society often do not handle wisely situations that put them in an awkward predicament.

When creative ability is thwarted, it is not extinguished; instead, it is likely to take an antisocial turn. This may have tragic results for the frustrated individual and the repressive society alike, according to Toynbee (1968).

These results were dealt with by Torrance and his team when they composed a song and made a recording of it on a cassette tape. We played it twice at our latest summer creativity workshop. It ends with a strong message, repeated and repeated, that "creation is a blessing and a curse"—or it could be "creativity is a blessing and a curse!"

One of the most memorable statements in our creativity research conference series came from Frank Barron. As he reflected upon individuals whose work had truly reshaped the world, he said that in their careers they often ended up in an organization that truly understood them. Guess how large that organization was? It had only one person in it. The person him/herself. Some artists, Pablo Picasso for example, manage to create a studio for themselves as part of their own living environment and work there the rest of their lives. The same is true for some writers, inventors, and scientists (like Barbara McClintock who late in her career won a lifetime Scot-free Prize Award the year before she won the Nobel Prize for the "jumping genes" work done in her backyard). Ansel Adams, the famous photographer, was quoted as saying that throughout his own career, he received all of his work assignments from only one person—himself.

A couple of years ago, I mentioned this to a person who had just won a five year, Scot-free Prize Award of high financial value. My impression was that he did not like that message, because he was seeking the security of a permanent tenured position at a large university.

Rather than remain as a full professor and researcher at one of the most eminent Universities of California, another person chose to resign. He said he would rather be outside working entirely on his own than continue to work inside at that university—and soon thereafter, he won a five-year Scot-free Prize Award.

Certain reports from the Carnegie Foundation for the Advancement of Teaching, whose President is Ernest L. Boyer, former U.S. Commissioner of Education, are noteworthy. Boyer stated that "the nation's colleges and universities are not as creative as they could be and are 'tired, living on the intellectual legacy of the past'." Many university leaders see themselves as cogs in a big machine, he says. "The truth is that when institutions lose integrity, people stop thinking freely. The time for imagining is lost. A sense of powerlessness sets in. New ideas are snuffed out. And universities become lifeless, uncreative, institutions—just another (bureaucratic) regulated industry" (Boyer, 1980).

At the end of last year Frank Newman released another report from the same Carnegie organization, in which he called for an "American Resurgence" in Higher Education. He said that what is lacking in our college graduates are the talents of being creative, taking risks, being innovative, seeing new solutions to problems, and having the capacity to be entrepreneurs, as well as having a sense of civic responsibility (Newman, 1985). Fortunately last year he became President of the Education Commission of the States. He is now in a position to influence the thinking and educational policy-making of all 50 governors, to bring out an "American Resurgence" through all levels of education, not just in higher education.

Let us summarize by citing two rules usually found for creative people in relation to organizations. At the same time, let us consider the case of a person who fortunately unlocks his mind and continues to learn better how to use his total set of high-level creative processes.

As he matures in his life and work career to become more creative, he will probably encounter *Rule #1* that "as individuals become increasingly creative, the organizational tendency is to organize creatives under administrative controls—or organize them out, i.e., ostracize them." (In other words, do them in, or do them out.) As he gains more seniority, along with his growing creativity, he may run into more and more obstacles because his organization has aged into the hands of Consolidators and has become more bureaucratic. Such Consolidators have been succeeding as they see it, by strengthening and perfecting the bureaucracy.

Yet Thomas Peters (1984) stated that once a person becomes highly productive (and creative), it is the manager's job to keep the bureaucracy off the backs of such productive people. Instead of that person and his creative ways being freed by a Consolidator from the company's bureaucracy, he would probably run into an organizational climate that increasingly stifles creativity. In this case, *Rule #2* found in creativity will be functioning, namely "the more creative his ideas become, the more likely he will become in trouble." This may be most true for those who stay in the organization faithfully, while trying to be most helpful to the organization by becoming more creative in new ideas, new methods, and new products. If the person has considerable seniority and even tenure, the official incentives for him are to remain in the organization—but to do so he must endure and fight or submit to the increasingly wet blanket against creativity.

To show that situations could be designed favorably for the creatives, let me describe an experience I had in a Del Mar organization. I was allowed, even encouraged to visit some of the workers doing their technical work. I asked one how he liked working there and he said, "Well, er, ah—it's heaven!" He then elaborated and showed, in his surroundings and facilities and equipment—and in his own fruitfulness—that he had truly earned such an ideal working situation. That life on-the-job could be like this for an increasing number of people all around the world!

Technical Appendix to the Chapter

Guilford's Functioning with the Simplicity and Complexity Issues

Guilford's recognition as an eminent scientist was well established before his major thrust, starting in the mid 1940's, into the analysis of the total intellect. His quantitative emphasis was shown in his books on psychometric methods and elementary statistical methods. His 1950 Presidential Address to the American Psychological Association is a definite landmark in research on creativity.

In each of the first three (1955, 1957, and 1959) reports of our Creativity Research Conference series, there are beautiful displays of the development of Guilford's three dimensional Structure-of-Intellect Model currently with 120 cells. His successive chapters across these reports display different stages in the unfolding of his own research. In 1955 he produced 3 two-dimensional tables. His Table One on *Discerning Thinking* shows 3 columns of *Content* (Figural, Structural, and Conceptual) and 5 rows of *Products* (Relations, Classes, Patterns-or-Systems, Problems, and Implications). His Table Two on *Productive Thinking* had the same 3 columns of *Content* and 7 different rows of *Products* (Names, Words, Ideas, Expressions, Correlates, Order, and Changes). Table Four on *Memory* had the same 3 columns of *Content* and 3 rows of *Products* (Associative Connections, Substance, and Span).

Finally, Table Three was different by *not* having columns and rows, but only sublists under three types of factors: *Divergent Thinking, Evaluation, and Symbolic.* Under each of these were lists of factors. These factors would be the entries within cells if he had been ready at that time to arrange each set of his findings into a two-dimensional matrix with columns and rows, as he had done in Tables One, Two, and Four described above. Under *Divergent Thinking,* his 4 factors listed were Adaptive Flexibility, Spontaneous Flexibility, Originality, and

Table Three.

Composite chart of the intellectual factors and representative tests.

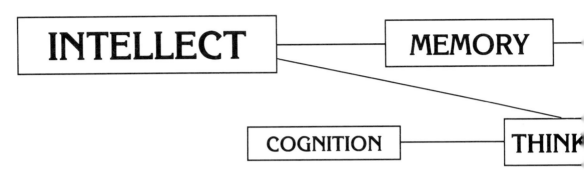

	Figural	Structural	Conceptual
Fundaments (units)	**Visual figural recognition** Street Gestalt Completion Mutilated Words **Auditory figural recognition** Haphazard Speech Ulogical Groupings		**Verbal comprehension** Vocabulary Reading Comprehension
Classes	**Figural classification** Figure Classification Picture Classification		**Conceptual classification** Word Classification Verbal Classification
Relations	**Education of figural relations** Figure Analogies Figure Matrix	**Education of structural relations** Seeing Trends II Correlate Completion II	**Education of conceptual relations** Verbal Analogies Word Matrix
Patterns or Systems	**Spatial orientation** G-Z Spatial Orientation Flags, Figures, Cards	**Education of structural patterns** Circle Reasoning Letter Triangle	**General reasoning** Arithmetic Reasoning Ship Destination
Implications	**Perceptual foresight** Competitive Planning Route Planning		**Conceptual foresight** Pertinent Questions Alternate Methods **Penetration** Social Institutions Similarities

Convergent ——————————— **PRODUC**

	Figural	Structural	Conceptual
Names	**Object naming** Form Naming Color Naming		**Concept naming** Picture-Group Naming Word-Group Naming
Correlates		**Education of Structural** Correlates Correlate Completion II Figure Analogies Completion	**Education of Conceptual** Correlates Vocabulary Completion Inventive Opposites
Orders			**Ordering** Picture Arrangement Sentence Order
Transfor-mations	**Visualization** G-Z Spatial Visualization Punched Holes	**Structural redefinition** Camouflaged Words Hidden Figures	**Conceptual redefinition** Gestalt Transformation Object Synthesis
Unique conclusions	**Symbol substitution** Sign Changes Form Reasoning	**Numerical facility** Numerical Operations	

*Appears at present to be one factor. Future results may show it to be two.

	Figural	Structural	Conceptual
Contents	**Visual memory** Reproduction of Designs Map Memory **Auditory Memory** Musical Memory Rhythm	**Memory span** Letter Span Digit Span	**Memory for ideas** Memory for Ideas Limericks
Associations		**Rote memory** Word - Number Color - Word	**Meaningful memory** Sentence Completion Related Words

NG — EVALUATION

	Figural	Structural	Conceptual
Identity of units	**Figural identification** G-Z Perceptual Speed Identical Forms	**Structural identification** Scattered X's Identical Numbers	
Differential	**Length estimation** Ratio Estimation Figure Estimation		
Logical		**Symbol manipulation** Symbol Manipulation Sign Changes II	**Logical evaluation** Logical Reasoning Puzzles
Experiential			**Experiential evaluation** Unusual Details Social Situations **Judgment** Practical Judgment Practical Estimation
Problem-atical			**Sensitivity to problems** Seeing Problems Seeing Deficiencies

ON — Divergent

	Figural	Structural	Conceptual
Words		**Word fluency** Prefixes Word Listing I	**Associational fluency** Controlled Associations II Simile Insertions
Ideas			**Ideational fluency** Thing Listing Brick Uses (fluency)
Expressions			**Expressional fluency** Four-Word Combinations FL Simile Interpretation
Adaptive shifts	**Figural adaptive flexibility** Hidden Pictures Gottschaldt Figures A	**Structural adaptive flexibility** Match Problems Planning Air Maneuvers	
Non-adaptive shifts			**Spontaneous flexibility** Brick Uses (flexibility) Unusual Uses
Novel responses			**Originality** Plot Titles (cleverness) Symbol Production
Details	**Elaboration*** Planning Elaboration Figure Production		**Elaboration*** Planning Elaboration Figure Production

Table Four.

	Total No. of Cells	No. of Filled in Cells	No. of Empty Cells	Gain Filled in
1955	59	42	17	0
1957	72	46	26	4
1959	120	53	67	7
1962	120	61	59	8
1977	120	98	22	37

Table Five.

	No. of Types of Content	No. of Mental Operations	No. of Operations
1955	3	6	15*
1957	3	5	24
1959	4	5	6
1962 & 1977	5	5	6

*Plus 12 factors later placed as entries within cells in his 3 dimensional SOI Model.

Elaboration. Under *Evaluation* his 5 factors were Perceptual Evaluation, Logical Evaluation, Experiential Evaluation, Judgement, and Speed of Judgement. Under *Symbolic,* Four factors were listed: Verbal Comprehension, Numeral Facility, Symbol Substitution, and Symbol Manipulation.

Guilford's 1957 Chart of the Intellect can be seen in Table Three. His 1959 Structure-of-Intellect can be seen in Guilford's chapter in this book.

Tables Four and Five summarize the sequence of filling in of his Structure Of Intellect (SOI) Model at 5 successive times: 1955, 1957, 1959, 1962, and 1977 (the publication year for *Way Beyond the IQ).*

Table Four shows that the main work on formulating his 120-cell Structure of Intellect occurred rapidly during the 1955-1959 period and then stabilized for two or more decades. Meanwhile, the location and placement of factors in his SOI model (including the crucial production of them), grew at almost a stable linear rate upwards for 22 years (from 1955-1977). Such predictable stabilized growth of newly discovered high-level factors was certainly worthy of continually sustained (stable) funding.

Table Five shows that great fluctuations and flexibility were occurring at each stage, most especially in the total number and the naming of products as the final 120 cell model was being shaped into a final form. Guilford's sustained productivity of new factors was accompanied by his repeated sharp insights into differences and his verbal versatility in naming factors, and also naming and renaming columns, rows, and slabs in both an increasing and decreasing number of categories (e.g., from 24 down to 6).

For his 1957 Total Intellect Chart (see his Table Three herein), he had 5 broad types of factors (Intellectual Operations), namely: *Cognition, Memory, Divergent Production, Convergent Production, and Evaluation.*

He had started earlier with multiple two-dimensional models, each with a different number of rows and columns. Gradually and by 1959 he had brilliantly created a standardized number of 4 rows *(Contents)* and 6 columns *(Products)* with uniform terminology and with 5 slabs representing each of the *Operations:* Cognition, Memory, Divergent Production, Convergent Production, and Evaluation. The latter three Operations are much more thinking styles of brain functioning, in contrast with the first two being learning and storing styles of Operations (see the SOI Model in Guilford's chapter in this book).

One of our frequently used descriptions is that Guilford's work kept unfolding and became increasingly complex (as displayed here in Table Three), so that it became less and less acceptable to the profession and to potential users. Then it folded up and became a simplified 3 dimensional block with standardized headings in each dimension. Yet, this block had hidden complexity within its 120 cells, most of which were empty at the time of its presentation at the 1959 conference when his 3-dimensional model emerged. It ended up with 4 input *Contents* plus 5 inner talent *Operations* plus 6 output *Products.*

In producing his 1959 folded-up model (i.e., his three dimensional block), his 24 products (the rows in the earlier Table One) had been reduced to the following six sequentially more difficult products:

Units	Systems
Classes	Transformations
Relations	Implications

There is also a meaningful sequence of the *Operations* from input of Content to the "inner talent operational processes" and then to the output of products. He says that their order is purely logical, beginning with the discovery of information (cognition) and ending with the testing of information (evaluation).

In Guilford's development of his model and of his filling in the cells in the model, it is obvious that his thinking was alternating between expanding (divergent) types to reducing (convergent) types. He went from 6 to 5 operations; he expanded from 3 to 4 contents; and he expanded tremendously into a 1957 list of 24 different products and then reduced greatly to yield a standardized list of 6 products.

As he was creating his 120-cell model, his thinking was flexibly fluctuating from divergent to convergent to divergent to convergent. Yet, each of his successive factorial research studies would have a convergently-produced single title with great divergence in the test scores covered in the expanded realm of the unknown, while his battery of scores were being reduced into *factors* which filled an increasing number of SOI cells. This total process ended up in an overall expansion of factors of the Intellect.

Footnote

1. The lack of validities for intellectual aptitude tests is one of the factors found in my study of fluency in writing (Taylor, 1947). This study was first to isolate and report Ideational Fluency and Expressional Fluency factors. The Ideational Fluency factor measures a *sheer quantity* of ideas a person produces (usually in writing). There is *no emphasis* on the creative quality of the ideas produced. It surprised me to find that Wallach (1985) focused nearly 40% of his chapter upon Ideational Fluency. The Ideational Fluency factor which is derived from the flow of ideas written *is not a major measure of creativity or giftedness.*

References

Boyer, E. L. (1980, November 21). Problem finders' needed: Boyer assails lack of creativity by 'tired' universities. *Higher Education & National Affairs, 29, (38),* 1-4.

Ellison, R. L., McDonald, B., James, L. R., Fox, D. G. & Taylor, C. W. (1968). *An investigation of organizational climate.* Salt Lake City, UT: Institute for Behavioral Research in Creativity.

Goleman, D. (1984, July 31). Successful executives rely on own kind of intelligence. *The New York Times,* pp. C1, C11.

Good scholars not always best. (1962, February 24) *Business Week,* pp. 77-78.

Guilford, J. P. (1964). Progress in the discovery of intellectual factors. In C. W. Taylor (Ed.), *Widening Horizons in Creativity* (pp. 261-297). New York: John Wiley & Sons.

Guilford, J. P. (1966). Basic problems in teaching for creativity. In C. W. Taylor (Ed.), *Instructional Media and Creativity* (pp. 71-103). New York: John Wiley and Sons.

Guilford, J. P. (1977). *Way beyond the I.Q.* Buffalo, NY: Creative Education Foundation/Bearly Limited.

Haberman, C. (1985, July 12) Japan schools, graded, get some hard knocks. *The New York Times,* A2.

Henry, E. R. (1966, June 10-11). *Autobiographical data as psychological predictors. Proceedings of Research Conference.* The Creativity Research Institute of the Smith-Richardson Foundation; Greensboro, NC.

IBRIC (1968). Alpha Biographical Inventory Manual. Salt Lake City, UT.

IBRIC (1978). Form U Biographical Inventory Manual. Salt Lake City, UT.

Jablonski, J. R. (1964). Developing creative research performance in public school children. In C. W. Taylor (Ed.), *Widening horizons in creativity* (pp. 203-219). New York: Wiley & Sons, Inc.

Lau, A. W., Taylor, C. W., Nelson, D. E. & Price, P. B. (1976). *Relationship of premedical and medical grades to physician performance measures.* (Mimeographed). Salt Lake City, UT: University of Utah.

McDonald, B. W. (1970). *Factored dimensions of organizational climate.* Unpublished doctoral dissertation, Salt Lake City, University of Utah.

Newman, F. (1985). *Higher education and the american resurgence.* The Carnegie Foundation for the Advancement of Teaching, Princeton, NJ.

NASA tries new recruiting tests. (1962, May 7). *Missiles and Rockets,* p. 17.

Nelson, D. E., Taylor, C. W. & Price, P. B. (1976). *Development of multiple measures of physician characteristic and performance.* Research Grant from the Public Health Service, DHEW, Contract No. HSM 110 71 171, mimeographed, 17 pps.

Peters, T. (1984, May/June). Author believes his own words. *Campus News Outlook,* Utah State University, 5.

Price, P. B., Taylor, C. W., Richards, J. M., Jr. & Jacobsen, T. L. (1964, February). Measurement of physician performance. *The Journal of Medical Education,* 39 *(2),* 203-211.

Price, P. B., Taylor, C. W., Nelson, D. E., Lewis, E. G., Loughmiller, G. C., Mathiesen, R., Murray, S. L. & Maxwell, J. G. (1971). *Measurement and predictors of physician performance: Two decades of intermittently sustained research.* Division of Health Manpower of the Department of Health, Education & Welfare, Grant No. PH 00017. Salt Lake City, UT: Aaron Press, 164 pps. (Remaining copies available in Taylor's office).

Proctor, S. D. (1978, November). A mind is a terrible thing to waste. *Phi Delta Kappan,* 60 (3), 201S-203S.

Taylor, C. W. (1947). A factoral study of fluency in writing. *Psychometrika, 12,* 239-262.

Taylor, C. W. (1958). Some variables functioning in productivity and creativity. *2nd research conference on the identification of creative scientific talent* (pp. 4-7). Supported by the National Science Foundation, Salt Lake City, UT: University of Utah Press.

Taylor, C. W. (1964). Process versus product in creativity: A spontaneous discussion of the conference participants. In C. W. Taylor (Ed.), *Widening horizons in creativity* (pp. 112-122). New York: John Wiley & Sons.

Taylor, C. W. (1966). Creativity through instructional media: A universe of challenges (Part I and Part II). In C. W. Taylor & F. W. Williams (Eds.), *Instructional media and creativity* (pp. 1-70). New York: John Wiley & Sons.

Taylor, C. W. (1968, December). Be talent developers . . . as well as knowledge dispensers. *Today's Education–NEA Journal,* 67-69..

Taylor, C. W. (1972a). *Climate for creativity.* Report of the Seventh National Research Conference on Creativity, Elmsford, NJ: Pergamon Press.

Taylor, C. W. (1972b). Can organizations be creative too? In C. W. Taylor (Ed.), *Climate for creativity* (pp. 1-23). Elmsford, NJ: Pergamon Press.

Taylor, C. W. (1973). Developing effectively functioning people, the accountable goal of multiple talent teaching. *Education,* 94 (2), 99-110.

Taylor, C. W. (1978). *Teaching for talents and gifts: 1978 Status. Developing and implementing multiple talent teaching* (NIE Report, Contract No. NIE-PO-77-0075). (Remaining copies available in Taylor's office).

Taylor, C. W. (1980, September 11). Multiple talent teaching results. *Congressional Record,* S12407-11.

Taylor, C. W. (1985). Cultivating multiple creative talents in students. *Journal for the Education of Gifted,* 3, 187-198.

Taylor, C. W. (1986). Cultivating simultaneous student growth in both multiple creative talents and knowledge. In J. Renzulli (Ed.), *Systems and Models in Gifted Education.* Mansfield Center, CT: Creative Learning Press.

Taylor, C. W., & Ellison, R. L. (1967, March 3). Biographical predictors of scientific performance. *Science,* 155 (3766), pp. 1075-1080.

Taylor, C. W., & Ellison, R. L. (1983, Summer). Search for student talent resources relevant to all USDE types of giftedness. *Gifted Child Quarterly,* 27 (3), 99-106.

Taylor, C. W., Ghiselin, B., Wolfer, Jr., Loy, L., & Bourne, L. E., Jr. (1964a). *Development of a theory of education from psychological and other basic research findings* (Final report, USDE Cooperative Research Project, No. 621). Salt Lake City: University of Utah, (mimeographed).

Taylor, C. W., Ghiselin, B. & Yagi, K. (1967). *Exploratory research on communication abilities and creative abilities.* Washington, D.C.: USGPO, 309 pps. (All remaining copies available in Taylor's office).

Taylor, C. W., Nelson, E., Gooley, G. M. & Ellison, R. L. (1964b). *Identifying research characteristics in high school students—a second study* (Mimeographed Report No. AFPSR-11-63). Supported by the Air Force Office of Scientific Research.

Taylor, C. W., Nelson, D. E. & Price, P. B. (1974). *Comprehensive analysis of physician and physician-in-training* (Vol. 1, Public Health Service Contract No. HSM 110 71 171). Salt Lake City: University of Utah.

Taylor, C. W., Smith, W. R., & Ghiselin, B. (1963). The creative and other contributions of one sample of research scientists: The inadequacy of undergraduate grade as substitute criteria for on-the-job research performance. In C. W. Taylor (Ed.), *Scientific creativity: Its recognition and development* (pp. 72-75). New York: Wiley & Sons.

Taylor, C. W. & Williams, F. E. (Eds.). (1966). *Instructional media and creativity.* New York: John Wiley & Sons.

Thurstone, L. L. (1935). *The vectors of mind.* Chicago: University of Chicago Press.

Thurstone, L. L. (1947). *Multiple factor analysis: A development and expansion of the vectors of mind.* Chicago: University of Chicago Press.

Thurstone, L. L. (1962). Creative talent. In L. L. Thurstone (Ed.), *Applications of psychology.* New York: Harper & Row.

Thurstone, L. L. (1964). Criterion of scientific success and the selection of scientific talent. In C. W. Taylor (Ed.), *Widening horizons in creativity* (pp. 10-16). New York: Wiley & Sons.

Toynbee, A. (1964). Is America neglecting her creative talents? In C. W. Taylor (Ed.), *Widening horizons in creativity* (pp. 3-9). New York: Wiley & Sons.

Toynbee, A. (1967). *On the role of creativity in history.* In C. W. Taylor (Ed.), 30 page booklet. Salt Lake City: University of Utah Press.

Toynbee, A. (1968, April). Creativity in our schools. Interviewed by Margaret Mason, in *The Instructor,* 21-22.

Wallach, M. A. (1985). Creativity, testing and giftedness. In Horowitz and O'Brien (Eds.), *The gifted and talented developmental perspectives* (pp. 99-123). Washington, D.C.: American Psychological Association.

7

The Creative Studies Project

Sidney J. Parnes
State University College at Buffalo

This article capsulizes my 30 years of continuing research into the deliberate development of creative ability. Large portions of material are drawn from a major report on the Creative Studies Project: *Toward Supersanity, Channeled Freedom* (now out of print), authored in 1973 by my colleague Dr. Ruth B. Noller and myself. It also draws from papers I have presented at national and international research conferences, as well as from a number of articles I wrote with various psychologists during these years of scientific evaluations of programs and methods for nurturing creative talent.[1]

The article contains five sections: (1) a brief overview of the international research on deliberate cultivation of creative abilities; (2) a concise review of the early creativity research at State University at Buffalo; (3) a brief summary of the findings of the Creative Studies Project which comprehensively evaluated a four-semester sequence of developmental courses at the college level; (4) a detailed "case study" of the Project, its research methods, results and implications; (5) further research questions suggested by the Project.

Overall Research on Deliberate Cultivation of Creativity

When I first embarked on the study of creativity in the mid 1950's, I searched far and wide for any scientific evidence that creativity could be developed and found nothing. By the end of that decade, researchers at the Third National Research Conference (Utah) on the Identification and Development of Creative Scientific Talent identified a total of six such studies (including our own first investigations at Buffalo), all of which showed significant positive results (Taylor, 1959).

Five Major Compilations

By now, in the mid-1980's, it is exciting to discover five major compilations in the U.S. literature of studies specifically covering the area of creativity development. Overwhelmingly, these show significant positive results when creative abilities are deliberately nurtured (Mansfield, et al., 1978; Parnes & Brunelle, 1967a & b; Rose & Lin, 1984; Taylor, C. W., 1959; Torrance, E. P., 1972). In addition to the five major summaries, there are numerous other compilations.

The general conclusions are the same: creative abilities *can* be developed by deliberate programs and methods. Since Alex F. Osborn's pioneering text, *Applied Imagination,* was first published in 1953, major summaries of research in creativity have appeared approximately every six years. This classic book spelled out deliberate methods for increasing creative abilities.

The largest single summary covered 142 individual research investigations on nurturing creative ability. That compilation contains 22 studies which evaluated the specific model used in the Creative Studies Project. Twenty of these showed significant positive effects (Torrance, 1972).

Real-Life Criteria

The most frequent limitation described by the first summary in 1959, and in scores of studies summarized since then in the literature, has been the lack of study of effects measured by ultimate or "real-life" criteria such as job performance. In 1984, however, it is most encouraging to note that a cluster of studies has evolved showing significant positive benefits for deliberate creative development in the "real-life" arena—in industry, academic achievement and personal adjustment areas. There are now a dozen studies demonstrating such positive results (Basadur, et al., 1982; Cohen, et al., 1960; Ekvall & Parnes, 1984; Heppner, et al., 1983; Heppner & Reeder, 1984; Jacobson, 1977; Jacobson, 1978; Karol & Richards, 1981; Parnes & Noller, 1973; Richards & Perri, 1978; Simberg & Shannon, 1959; Sommers, 1962). Half of these studies are discussed in a review of "Problem-Solving Training as Prevention with College Students" (Heppner, et al., 1984). The others (except Parnes & Noller, 1973, covered in this chapter) are discussed in Ekvall & Parnes, 1984. Only two studies using real-life criteria failed to show significant positive results. The first involved only one and one-half hour's training in brainstorming, as well as other limiting factors (Rickards, 1975), while the second showed significantly increased associational fluency, but did not appear to transfer this ability to real-life problems, probably due to the limiting experimental conditions described by the researchers (Korth, 1973).

In a research report to the U.S. Office of Education on "Development of New Criteria for the Evaluation of Creative Studies Programs" (Parnes & Treffinger, 1973) we demonstrated that complex problem situations can yield reliable and valid indices of creative problem-solving abilities. As indicated above, these real-life criteria seem to be appearing in more and more creativity development studies in addition to the more typical standardized tests of fluency, originality, etc. Furthermore, there has been a strong pattern of anecdotal evidence of gains on "real-life" criteria (Gordon, 1961; Osborn, 1963; Prince, 1970). Moreover, extensive surveys show the widespread industrial use of creative problem-solving processes in Europe and the United States (Geschka, 1975; Johansson, 1975); this should provide more potential for additional formal studies of the results of developmental programs with these processes.

Targeted Research

In addition to the need for more studies using "real-life" criteria to confirm and extend the pioneering ones mentioned, I see the need for more research targeted at specific methods and techniques of the creative development programs being studied. Heppner et al. (1984) likewise emphasized this need. Research by Bouchard (1972) and Ekvall and Parnes (1984) are examples. They provide data showing that brainstorming used together with deliberate analogy was much more effective than either process alone. Necka (1983), in Poland, has been scientifically studying some of these methodological differences. Many researchers are experimenting informally, but unfortunately, few scientific reports seem to be available in the literature. Many replications are needed with this and other method comparisons, using a variety of settings, subjects, problems, etc. until we learn enough to be much more focused with our training methods rather than using them in a kind of "shotgun approach" as we have in the past.

We now have convincing data showing that creativity-development programs work; what we need is similarly impressive data with "real-life" criteria showing which parts or combinations of what programs are optimum for what type of person or situation. To me, this is the challenge of the next 30 years!

Summary of Early Buffalo Research

The development of research in creativity at the State University of New York at Buffalo from 1949 to 1956 was concerned with pilot experimentation and the development of courses, programs and methods designed to stimulate creative behavior in students. Experimentation was first conducted in the evening division of the University and later, in the day division. Constant revision, adaptation, and improvement resulted from new insights gained through each experimental course and program.

After this period of preliminary exploration, we began an extensive research effort in 1957, to scientifically evaluate the results of these methods and programs. During the next ten years, as new knowledge was gained, intensive development activities paralleled the research efforts.

Research dealt with: (1) the effects of a semester's program in deliberate creativity-stimulation; (2) the relative effects on creative ability of a programmed course used alone or used with instructors and class interaction; (3) the effects of extended effort in creative problem-solving; and (4) the effectiveness of the specific problem-solving principle of deferred judgment.

Major findings were as follows: (1) The semester programs resulted in significant increments on the two measures of *quantity* of idea-production, and on three out of the five measures of *quality* of the ideas produced. In general, these increases in creative productivity remained evident in another group of students who were tested from one to four years *after* taking the course. A significant increment on the California Psychological Inventory's Dominance Scale also resulted from the program. (2) In the study regarding the programmed course, on almost every test the experimental students made greater gains than did the control students. On almost all the measures, the gains of the instructor-taught programmed groups were significantly superior to those of two control groups. Students in groups who took the program alone were significantly superior to control students in gains on most tests, and the instructor-taught groups tended to be consistently superior to the program-taught control groups who had no instructor. (3) Extended effort in idea-production results in a significantly greater proportion of good ideas among the later ideas produced. (4) Significantly more good quality ideas were produced by individuals under deferred-judgment instructions than under concurrent-judgment instructions. (Criteria included uniqueness and usefulness of ideas.) The subjects trained in a creative problem-solving course emphasizing the principle of deferred judgment produced a significantly greater number of good quality ideas when using the technique than did the untrained students. (The same criteria were employed.) Groups producing ideas on a creative problem-solving task produced significantly more good quality ideas when adhering to the deferred-judgment principle than when employing the more conventional discussion methods which entail concurrent evaluation of ideas. Groups which adhered to the deferred-judgment principle when generating ideas were likewise significantly more productive of good quality ideas than the same number of individuals working independently under conventional methods, with concurrent evaluation. It appears that the deferred judgment principle is equally applicable to individual idea-finding as well as to group collaboration.

Summary of Project Findings

What happens when you involve a group of incoming college freshmen in a unique sequence of semester-long, credit-bearing courses in Creative Studies?

Well, quite an impressive picture emerges, though not everything you might expect. If you are statistically oriented you can base your conclusion on some 200 research measurements made over the two-year period on the students and their comparable controls not taking the courses. If you are more interested in listening to the students you can hear their own interpretations of how the program affected them. The courses concentrated on awareness-development, creative problem-solving, synectics, and creative analysis (general semantics) processes.

First, to capsulize briefly the statistical picture, much of which will be spelled out later: (a) Students participating in the courses perform significantly better than comparable controls in coping with real-life situational tests, including not only the production of ideas, but also their evaluation and development. (b) They perform significantly better than comparable controls in applying their creative abilities in special tests given in English courses. (c) They perform significantly better than the comparable controls on the semantic and behavioral half of Guilford's Structure-of-Intellect (SOI) Model, including three of five of his mental operations— cognition, divergent production and convergent production; they show no significant accomplishment over the controls in the symbolic and figural half of Guilford's model, nor in his memory or evaluation operations. (d) Test results bear out their significant year-to-year improvement over comparable controls. (e) The data show consistent positive movement on personality measures by course students compared with their controls, although not significant on any single scale. One coping instrument, as well as the course students' own questionnaire responses, provided further significant evidence of gains in personality dimension. (f) Course students showed a growing tendency (not attaining statistical significance) to become more productive than comparable controls in their non-academic achievement in areas calling for creative performance. (g) Most course students reported large gains in their own productive, creative behavior; they rated the program as quite helpful in their other college courses and their everyday lives. In the second year, there was a significant increase in the percentage of students who reported large gains in ability to cope with problems and to participate actively in discussions. (h) As to the generalizability, it was concluded that, for a group comparable to our total sample of experimentals and controls who started such a two-year program of Creative Studies—and this would very likely include a portion of the student body at most colleges and universities—the gains in the study relative to time spent in courses would be expected for those continuing with the program.

Illustrative Summary

Perhaps the best way to illustrate the development of the students in this unique educational program is to graph results at the end of two years for eight of the nine measures that showed significant differences in favor of the students completing four semesters of courses over comparable controls who did not take the program. The ninth measure was analyzed in a different manner from the other eight. It involved a problem of current concern to professional researchers. The measure called for a plan of action to be developed by the subjects. These plans were presented anonymously to two experienced researchers who independently grouped them into seven quality-ranks. The research staff then compared the percentages of course students and controls whose plans were rated below average with those whose plans were rated average or above. Whereas only 37 per cent of controls' plans were average or above, 73 per cent of the course-students' plans were found to have been so ranked. This difference in percentages was statistically highly significant.

The eight measures plotted and explained in Figure One, plus the ninth just discussed but not graphed, represent 69 per cent of a total of thirteen in the cognition, divergent-production, and convergent-production operations of Guilford's SOI.[2] The significant gains occurred in the semantic and behavioral content-areas of the SOI. On three of the other four such measures, the two-year course students excelled the controls but not significantly; on the fourth, the two groups were equal.

The results are also graphed for the students who had dropped out after one, two, and three semesters but who were also tested at the end of the second year of college.[3] The differences are not necessarily significant between any two groups on the graph (indicated

Figure One.

Some results of the two-year program.

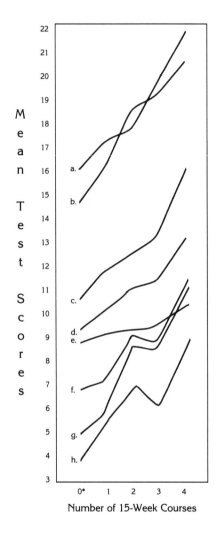

Number of 15-Week Courses

* Mean score for Control Group, who took no courses at all are shown as the starting points of the lines of this graph.

At the final testing session of the two-year program, students who took all four semester courses (E's) significantly outperformed comparable control students (C's) on all of the tests graphed on this page. Eight tests are shown. A ninth, where E's also significantly excelled C's, is not graphed.

The names of the eight graphed tests (described by number), beginning on page   are as follows:

a – Utility (Fluency), No. 13.

b – Problems in College, No. 15.

c – Utility (Flexibility), No. 13.

d – Problem Prevention, No. 16.

e – Multiple Social Problems, No. 12.

f – Evaluating Ideas, No. 14.

g – Improving Research Testing - Part I, No. 17.

h – Improving Research Testing - Part II: Making Decisions, No. 18.

by duration of stay in program) other than between the four-semester students and the controls. The consistency of the slopes in the graph is, however, quite suggestive. Examples of test items are provided later.

Detailed "Case Study" of the Creative Studies Project

Introduction

Dozens of individual research projects demonstrating the developability of creative talent culminated in the Carnegie Corporation financing a major effort in the 1960's to study the thinking processes of school children.

The study conducted by psychologists at the University of California at Berkley focused on programs for deliberately increasing thinking and problem-solving effectiveness of elementary school children. The results and their implications were striking. Richard Crutchfield, then president of the American Psychological Association, and Martin Covington summarized their results:

> *These data . . . suggest that the disposition, attitudes and skills which characterize the innovative thinker can be enhanced directly by methods and techniques which are presently available to educational planners.*
>
> *The nurturing of the cognitive skills of productive thinking should assume a central place in the curriculum, not a secondary or incidental one. Training of these skills should not be subordinated to the overriding demands of subject matter acquisition, as at present, but should be dealt with directly. What we need, in short, is a "cognitive curriculum" one which nurtures the process of productive thinking in its own right and yet in such a manner as to fully coordinated with the other more traditional content-centered curricula (Covington, 1967).*
>
> *It is a central purpose of education to train these cognitive skills of productive thinking, thus preparing the student for the effective and personally rewarding use of the mind with whatever subject matter and whatever problems he may have to deal (Crutchfield, 1969).*

Taking courage from these findings by nationally respected psychologists conducting major experimental research into the developability question, we launched, in 1969, our boldest venture: The Creative Studies Project. It was inaugurated at the State University College at Buffalo in 1969, under the ongoing sponsorship of the Creative Education Foundation and with occasional support from the Smith-Richardson Foundation of North Carolina and the U.S. Office of Education. This Project evaluated the impact of four consecutive semesters of a creative problem solving curriculum on various aspects of college students' behavior—in class, in college, in personal life, and in the community at large.

The Project provided for the development and evaluation of a longitudinal experimental program in creativity development. The entire curriculum was designed to interrelate the diverse knowledge students acquired so as to help them discover greater meaning in their coursework. The Creative Studies Program thus served as an intermediary between college curriculum and its impact on the personal and professional lives of the students.

Throughout the experimental program, students gained practice and leadership experience in applying a variety of creative problem-solving methods, using a range of practice problems representative of those they encounter in their academic studies, in their educational environment, and in the community that they were entering as concerned citizens. These diverse exercises were planned in consultation with faculty, counsellors, and administrators of the College, as well as members of professional, governmental, and other community groups.

National Advisory Committee for the Project

General preparation for the Project included the submission of the project plan to a broad, interdisciplinary group of national leaders who served as advisors for review and suggestions. This national advisory committee for the Project was comprised of 21 members drawn from prominent organizations and institutions all over the country.

An interdisciplinary college research committee also provided input. The committee included faculty from Education, Industrial Arts, Mathematics, Philosophy, the Child Study Center and Counseling and Guidance. Dr. Hayne Reese, of West Virginia University, served as overall consulting psychologist to the project.

Program Development[4]

In order to optimize the program, a "debugging" process was carried out with a pilot group of subjects. Students were recruited from the 1969-1970 freshman class for a pilot experimental program during the school year. They served as a pilot group throughout their freshman and sophomore years. The full-scale experimental group came from the following year's class (1970-1971), which was always a year behind the pilot group. In this way the research team had "debugged" each of the educational programs before testing it with the full-scale experimental group.

Detailed Research Information[5]

Some of the data were collected for both experimental and control subjects at the beginning of the experiment. Data from some of the same instruments, as well as from additional sources, were collected for all subjects over the Project's four-semester period.

Hypotheses

The hypotheses tested in the project were as follows: As a result of a four-semester sequence of Creative Studies courses, there will be significant differences, favoring those who have completed the sequence over those who have not, on: (1) selected tests of mental ability; (2) tests of creative application of academic subject matter; (3) non-academic achievement in areas calling for creative performance; (4) certain personality factors associated with creativity.

Experimental Design

The research sample was randomly selected from approximately 350 applicants for the Creative Studies program at the State University College at Buffalo. These applicants represented approximately 30 percent of the total incoming freshman group to whom the program had been offered.

From the total body of applicants, half were randomly placed in the experimental group—organized into six class sections of 25 each—to receive the four semesters (15 weeks each) of Creative Studies courses; the other half were randomly assigned to the control group (which was to receive no courses in Creative Studies until the conclusion of this two-year project). The purpose of the control group was to provide a base-line for differentiating between treatment effects and general growth and practice effects. All basic testing of experimentals and controls was done simultaneously on Saturdays or in late afternoons or evenings, when no classes were in session for any of the subjects. Some tests (of Hypothesis 2) were administered during class sessions in other courses (not Creative Studies). In these cases we used subsamples composed of all experimentals and controls who happened to be in the particular classes.

Scoring

Protocols were coded so that no rater knew whether he or she was rating the protocol of a control or an experimental subject. Reliability of raters was checked through applicable correlation coefficients between the scores of independent raters for all measures which required qualitative ratings. The reliabilities were acceptable: 39 were in the .90's; 9 were in the .80's; the remaining one was the only relatively low reliability, .65.

Analyses

As a principle, the random placement of subjects into experimental and control groups was expected to, and in fact did, eliminate group differences on the pre-tests. The efficiency of this randomization was checked by statistical tests. Since the differences on the pre-tests were nonsignificant, the semester-by-semester test scores of the experimental and control subjects were compared by analysis of variance.

Guilford's Structure-of-Intellect (SOI) Model

Our creative problem-solving process (Parnes et al., 1977) parallels Guilford's model very closely (Guilford, 1967, 1969a, 1969b). While we talk about "fact-finding" and "problem-finding," Guilford covers these processes in his first two operations, "cognition" and "memory;" our "idea-finding" parallels Guilford's operation of "divergent production." Hence, in our research design, we selected tests of each operation in Guilford's Structure-of-Intellect Model in order to determine which ones our courses were affecting. Most earlier research centered on divergent production, the operation most often associated with the word "creative." In our creative-studies model, however, "creative" is defined as a function of knowledge (cognition and memory), imagination (divergent production), and evaluation (convergent production and evaluation). Hence, our research examined possible changes in all of these operations.

All measures from Guilford's SOI tests were selected that seemed to have a relationship to the training. Following consultation with Guilford, parts of tests were used rather than entire tests, in order to allow a greater range of testing within reasonable time limitations. Many of the test items were questionably related to the training but were included in order to sample different aspects of the structure. In choosing one of several measures within a particular cell of Guilford's model, we generally used the most highly recommended tests (Sheridan Psychological Services, 1969); in the few exceptions, we consulted with Guilford as to the reasonableness of our choices. We designed several tests ourselves to measure everyday problem-solving abilities rather than to measure any specific SOI cell. We discussed these in conferences with Guilford who felt that it was possible to hypothesize that the specially developed tests were measuring certain SOI abilities. We have some support for this from correlations we obtained later among the tests (Parnes & Treffinger, 1973.[6]).

Preliminary tests were given from all five operations in Guilford's intellectual model. Inasmuch as our courses provide no "memory training," we hypothesized no changes in this one operation. Similarly, we did not hypothesize any changes in the type of evaluation processes measured by the SOI tests used, although we did hypothesize changes in the ability to develop evaluative criteria, an ability that Guilford hypothesized would fall under cognition or divergent production. We also hypothesized changes in ability to decide on a plan of action, an ability that Guilford hypothesized would come under convergent production.

Findings: Mental Ability and Related Measures[7]

Findings Pre-tests

On all 13 ability tests, there were no significant differences between subjects assigned to the experimental and control groups. Furthermore, the means for the experimental group were lower than for the control group on 9 of the 13 tests, indicating that, if anything, there was somewhat greater ability in the control subjects than in the experimental subjects.

Each successive semester, those experimentals and controls who remained in the experiment were also comparable on their pre-tests. There was only one instance out of 52 where a significant difference (.05 level) occurred in the pre-test comparability when analyzed at the end of each semester of the experiment.

Findings Post-tests

The findings that follow cover the results for all four of the major post-testing periods. On all but three of the 27 semantic tests used, the experimentals were superior to the controls, significantly so on 16. Two others were equal, with the third favoring the controls but nonsignificantly. In the behavioral area, the experimentals outperformed the controls on eight of nine tests, significantly on four. The one where controls excelled experimentals was again non significant. None of the eight figural tests showed significant differences, with six being slightly in favor of the experimentals and two slightly in favor of the controls. On seven symbolic tests, three differences favored the experimentals and four favored the controls, with no significance on any of the seven. One additional symbolic test was included among the special tests given to subsamples of experimentals and controls in English classes. On that test, experimentals significantly outperformed controls (See Figure Two).

Specially designed pilot-tests involving symbolic material have also been given in the math area. Preliminary examination of the responses was encouraging, as explained later under "Findings: Academic Achievement."

Ten tests of cognition were administered. Seven showed significant differences in favor of the experimental subjects, with the other three in the same direction. In the area of divergent production, 14 tests were administered. Nine of these tests showed significant differences in favor of the experimentals, with four of the other five favoring the same direction. The analysis of the test results where the controls scored better proved nonsignificant. Eight tests of convergent production were administered. The experimentals were significantly superior to the controls on four tests, ahead on three others and equal on one.

In the evaluation category, three tests were administered. Two of the tests showed nonsignificant differences in favor of the experimentals. On the third test, both groups were equal. Two other tests were given where experimentals significantly outperformed controls on the ability to generate multiple criteria for evaluating ideas. However, these two tests were included under the cognition and divergent-production areas because Guilford hypothesized, in informal conferences, that these two would fall under those operations rather than under evaluation. He pointed out that they measure the generation of products rather than the actual judging itself. In our own model, the criteria-generation stage is a vital part of the total evaluation process. The actual application of criteria is included, in our model, in the convergent-production processes where decisions are made and plans of action are produced by the subjects.

Only one memory test was given in the two years of the follow-up testing. No difference was hypothesized and no significant difference occurred.

Similarity of Test Results and Student Perceptions

Two of the three "operation" areas where the experimentals excelled most (cognition and divergent production) are the same as the two categories of highest perceived gain by the course students. On a questionnaire at the end of the second semester, course students were given 13 areas of possible gain from the course, with instructions to indicate their gain on a five-point scale: "not at all," "very little," "somewhat," "a good deal" and "a great deal." The students gave the highest ratings to "take more factors into consideration in making decisions" (88 per cent of students checking "good deal" or "great deal"), and "more prone to try different approaches" (83 per cent of students checking "good deal" or "great deal").

Figure Two.

SOI Intellectual operaitons where E's showed significant differences over C's in the four Post-Testing sessions . . . Guilford's (1969) definitions of terms provided.

"*Contents* are broad classes or types of information; information classified according to its substantive nature."

"*Operations* are the major kinds of intellectual activities or processes; things that the organism does with the raw materials of information. Information is defined as that which the organism discriminates."

Summary of 32 Tests: E > C on 30, 20 sig.; E = C on 1; C > E on 1, non-sig.

OPERATIONS

	COGNITION	DIVERGENT PRODUCTION	CONVERGENT PRODUCTION
	E > C 10 of 10; 7 sig. "Immediate discovery, awareness, rediscovery, or recognition of particular items of information; understanding or comprehension."	E > C 13 of 14; 9 sig. "Generation of information from given information, where the emphasis is upon variety and quantity of output from the same source; a search for logical alternatives."	E > C 7 of 8; 4 sig. (1 equal) "Generation of information from given information, where the needed information is fully determined by the given information; a search for logical imperatives."
SEMANTIC — "Information in the form of meanings to which words commonly become attached, hence most notable in verbal thinking and verbal communication, but not identical with words. Meaningful pictures also convey semantic information."	E > C on 10 of 10 7 sig.	E > C on 7 of 7 6 sig.	E > C on 5 of 6 3 sig. (i equal)
	Summary of 23 Semantic Tests: E > C on 22 of 23 16 sig. (1 equal)		
BEHAVIORAL — "Information, essentially non-verbal, involved in human interactions where the attitudes, needs, desires, moods, intentions, perceptions, thoughts, etc. of other people and of ourselves are involved."	Not Tested	E > C on 6 of 7 3 sig. (C > E on 1, non-sig.)	E > C on 2 of 2 1 sig.
	Summary of 9 Behavioral Tests: E > C on 8 of 9 4 sig. (C > E on 1, non. sig.)		

CONTENTS

These appeared to us to relate very closely to the Guilford processes of cognition and divergent production, respectively.

Students were apparently not indiscriminately high in their ratings on the questionnaire, for the percentages of students checking "good deal" or "great deal" for any particular item ranged from a high of 88 per cent, mentioned above, to a low of 15 per cent. The other areas where 60 per cent or more of the students indicated a good deal or great deal of gain from the course were as follows: exert more effort in mental tasks, not quitting so soon (71 per cent); better able to evaluate ideas (66 per cent); more open-minded to ideas of others (64 per cent); better able to develop ideas and put them to use (60 per cent).

Significant Growth in Perceived Gain

In the area of lowest perceived gain at the end of the first year, "participate more actively in discussions," 29 per cent more students indicated "a good deal" or "great deal" of gain at the end of two years than at the end of the first year. This was one of the largest growth-items in the second year. This item and "better able to cope with problems"—were the two largest gains from year one to year two, both significant. Improved problem coping went from 55 per cent checking "good deal" or "great deal" in the first year to 81 per cent the second year.

Further Evidence of Value of Second Year

A question which was raised repeatedly concerned whether or not the second year added anything to the benefit from a single year. Figure One on page 160 offers some answers to this question as do the students' written comments. A more definitive answer is provided by the following trends. Three tests (one in each of the three operations where significant differences were found) were repeated during the study, as pre-tests and as post-tests after each year: (1) divergent production of behavioral implications; (2) convergent production of semantic systems; (3) cognition of semantic implications. None showed any significant differences between experimentals and controls in pre-tests. In the first year, experimentals were greater than controls on the first two tests, but not significantly so on either. In the second year, however, experimentals surpassed controls significantly on both. In the third case, experimentals were slightly greater than controls on the pre-test, significantly greater in year one and again, significantly greater in year two. Moreover, the difference between the scores for year one and year two were also significant in favor of the second year.

Findings: Academic Achievement–English Subsample

Analyses were made of English test data for the subsample of experimentals and controls who were tested by their English instructors in English classes, using English-related creativity tests that were not associated with the Creative Studies project. Two out of five tests showed significant results, with the other three scoring in the same direction all favoring experimentals.

A sixth test involved the writing of an English theme on a topic allowing a good deal of creativity. These themes were graded in the usual way by each student's English instructor. No significant differences occurred on the grades. It is noteworthy, however, that the experimentals with their course emphasis on imagination did not suffer in their overall theme performance, as some feared, especially at the hands of an "unappreciative instructor." As a matter of fact, there was a slight tendency here again for experimentals to surpass the controls.

Regarding comparability of experimentals and controls who formed the subsample for this set of tests, there were no significant differences on: (1) the pre-tests of mental ability, (2) pre-entrance scores on English achievement in the New York State Regents Scholarship Examination, and (3) pre-entrance self-reports related to general academic achievement.

Compared with a second control group, those who did not volunteer for the experiment (not an equivalent population, but nonvolunteers who happened to be in English classes along with the subsample of experimental and control subjects of the overall experiment), the experimentals were significantly stronger than the nonvolunteers on five tests, all except the English theme. The volunteer controls were also superior to the nonvolunteers, but significantly only on one of the five tests.

Findings: Academic Achievement–Mathematics Pilot Study

An experimental math test was administered in math courses of experimentals and nonvolunteers of similar backgrounds, in math courses. Results in the test were not analyzed statistically; however, after making an analysis of the math test responses, the following comments were made by Harry M. Gehman, Professor Emeritus and retired Chairman of the Department of Mathematics at the State University of New York at Buffalo: "The students who were taking Creative Studies seemed to do better on the examination in the sense that they apparently could analyze the questions, some of which were word problems and some of which were purely geometrical. Regardless of the type of questions, they seemed to be better able to analyze what was given, what had to be found, and were then enabled to work better from that. Not only were they better able to define the problem but they were more citicial, too; where you gave them too much information, most of them spotted that. Obviously, you are teaching them to analyze things in ways that they have not been taught in other fields or other subjects."[8]

Findings: Imagery Production

Verbal imagery scores were also obtained from nonvolunteers in English classes and from the experimentals. On this test of ability to produce original verbal images, experimentals produced significantly higher mean scores than the nonvolunteer controls.[9] Unfortunately, data was not available from the volunteer controls.

Findings: Non-academic Achievement

Initially, we compared experimentals and controls using the Alpha Biographical Inventory (IBRIC, 1968), a measure of non-academic achievement. It is probably the most comprehensive and well-researched instrument for measuring this kind of achievement. The two-year course students and their controls were within less than half a per cent of one another in the pre-test on this measure—obviously nonsignificant.

The following areas from the American College Survey (Richards, Holland and Lutz, 1966) were surveyed by self-report: Leadership, social participation, art, social service, science, business, humanistic-cultural activities, religious service, music, writing, social science, and speech-drama. The majority of our subjects (experimentals and controls) did not attain even one-tenth of the total of 120 possible points on this scale. The accomplishments generally take considerable time or effort. Hence, growth on this measure is expected to be quite slow. At the end of two years of courses, experimentals showed a growing tendency, not yet significant, to surpass controls. Thirty-nine per cent of the experimentals made total scores of 15 and above, compared to only 23 per cent of the controls.

Career Competition

Not as a formal part of the experiment, but as a pilot study, all experimental and control students who had completed the five testing sessions (the pre-test and those at the end of each of the four semesters) were offered the following challenge:

> A number of volunteer consultants to the National Advisory Committee of our Creative Studies Project have expressed, in a concrete way, their deep interest in encouraging creative potential as fully as possible. These consultants, who are them-selves highly creative people established in their professional fields, have offered awards totaling $500 for a creative competition of an applied nature.

Size of Awards

Eight awards are offered as follows:

First Award	$150
Second Award	$100
Third Award	$ 75
Fourth and Fifth Awards	$ 50 each
Sixth, Seventh and Eighth	$ 25 each

Each award will be accompanied by a letter of commendation. Furthermore, each addi-tional outstanding entry will merit a letter of honorable mention.

Nature of Competition

The challenge for the competition is as follows:

> How would you go about entering the kind of career that is likely to tap most fully your creative potential? How would you go about convincing the appropriate decision-makers (employers, individuals or organizations) of your creative potential in that career?

There are no restrictions on the format of the entry.

The idea for the competition was conceived too late to be implemented as effectively as desired. It had to be given just before final exams—hardly the time to expect maximum attention or extended effort to a new challenge that was incidental to the pressures of the moment. Under the circumstances described, the number of entries was only 13 out of 158 eligible. Nevertheless, it is noteworthy that 12 were experimentals and one was a control. The contest was never mentioned or discussed during Creative Studies classes. All notifications and reminders were delivered to experimentals and controls alike, in writing. The first five winners were experimentals; one of the last three was the control subject. Obviously, the raters had only a code number of identification, thus insuring no bias.

Minimal Estimates

The results reported above would appear to represent minimal differences between course students and their comparable controls for the following reasons: (1) There was a large amount of interaction and discussion between experimentals and controls. Over two-thirds of the controls acknowledged having discussed the course materials with the experimental subjects, with a dozen indicating that they had actually studied course materials. This could be avoided only by using different universities for experimental and control groups, but this might mean a loss of comparability of backgrounds. Considering this, the significant differences in results obtained are even more impressive. The situation was unavoidable, since about half of the subjects lived in dormitories. (2) Experimental subjects reported frequently that they couldn't write fast enough to keep up with their ideas in timed fluency tests in the post-testing periods, but that they had not experienced this in the pre-tests.

Test Instruments

It is important to note that the tests used in the evaluation of the Creative Studies courses were not tests in the usual sense, constructed around the language of the course. Because of the wide variety of tests used, most of them required considerable transfer from the kinds of exercises and materials the students used in the classes. An examination of the material in the *Guide to Creative Action* (Parnes, Noller and Biondi, 1977), and *Creative Actionbook* (Noller, Parnes and Biondi, 1976), when compared with the tests given, will readily show that the training was not designed to "teach the tests." Fundamental principles of problem-solving were emphasized and practiced extensively throughout the course, and the results show that these principles may be applied in a variety of tests that require a particular type of thinking.

An example may make the point quite clearly: students, basically, are taught to be able to associate aspects of their knowledge and experience more readily in order to find meaningful relationships in that knowledge. They are not taught specifically, however, how to think of the multiple meanings in particular words. Yet in tests of this skill, experimental students did significantly better than control students in the first year of the program. Another example, along quite different lines from discovering alternate meanings of words, is the test called "Procedure Applications." In this test, students are given, for example, a chemical procedure, and asked to find applications of that procedure in other facets of life. Here, too, the experimental students significantly outperformed the controls by the second year of the Creative Studies courses.

To cite an example of a test that is closest to what is taught in the classes, we would name the Utility Test (listing other uses for a common object such as a rubber band). This test measures fluency and spontaneous flexibility. In this test, large gains would be expected and are typically found in students who have been exposed to courses in Creative Studies. Most of the tests used in the experiment, however, were a far cry from the kind of test that asks for "other uses for an object." None of the tests called for pure recall of knowledge. All of the tests called for utilization of knowledge in a wide variety of increasingly difficult mental tasks, none of which had been specifically presented anywhere in the courses.

Examples of Test Items

The following are examples of items from the tests on which experimental subjects significantly outperformed controls. Each example is excerpted from the cover (instruction) page of the test. "G" next to a test number indicates that the test was developed in Guilford's laboratories. Information on those tests and their availability may be obtained from Sheridan Psychological Services, Inc. A "B" next to a test number indicates that the test was developed in our Buffalo laboratories. Those tests are not available in published form. "S" next to test number 4 indicates that this test was developed in the psychological laboratories at State University of New York at Stony Brook by psychologists Marvin Goldfried and Thomas D'Zurilla.

1. (G) *Seeing Different Meanings*
   In this test each given word has a number of different possible meanings. Your task is to think of as many different meanings of each given word as you can. SAMPLE WORD: Scale

2. (B) *Rhyming Words*
   On the following pages you are to list words that rhyme with the words shown. SAMPLE WORD: Spoon. (This test is an adaptation of Guilford's test called "Rhymes.")

3. (G) *Possible Jobs*
   As the Inter-Planet Express prepared to land on Mars, the tourists were discussing

a new custom developed by Martians. Since the first settlers had arrived from earth, the Martians had taken to wearing emblems to show what each person's job is.

As the tourists looked through the videoscope, they saw one Martian wearing the emblem. (Line drawing of a shining light bulb within a circle.)

"Electrical engineer," said one of the tourists. "Light bulb manufacturer," said another. "Maybe a bright student," a third tourist suggested.

In this test you will see more of the emblems that the Martians wore. Imagine that you are one of the tourists. Think of as many possible jobs as you can which might be indicated by the emblems. If you are not sure whether one of your ideas is reasonable, write it down anyway and try to think of another idea.

4. (S) *Stony Brook Coping Problems*
As you read the situation, we would like you to imagine that you are now in this situation. When you have the situation clearly in mind, think of how you are most likely to react in such a situation. Then in the space below the situation, write down your total reaction in specific detail.

SAMPLE SITUATION:

It is about a month after the start of classes during your first semester, and several important examinations have been scheduled for the same week. The examination for your most difficult course has been scheduled for late Wednesday afternoon.

You are having breakfast on Wednesday morning, the day of your most difficult exam. You feel that you are inadequately prepared, and your full schedule of classes for Wednesday does not allow time for further study before the exam.

5. (G) *Alternate Uses*
In this test, you will be asked to consider some common objects. Each object has a common use, which will be stated. You are to list as many as six other uses for which the object or parts of the object could serve.

SAMPLE ITEM: A Newspaper (used for reading)

6. (G) *Apparatus Test*
In this test you will be given names of objects that are familiar to everyone. Your task is to suggest two improvements for each of the objects. Do not suggest an improvement that has already been made. You do not need to worry about your ideas being possible, so long as they are sensible.

It is not necessary to explain your reason for a suggested improvement. Your suggestions should be specific. A suggested improvement like 'The object should be made more efficient,' is too general to be acceptable.

You are to write two improvements for each object in this test. If you have difficulty with an item, do not spend too much time on it, but go on to the next item. Do not suggest similar improvements for two or more items, because duplication will not be counted.

SAMPLE ITEM: Telephone

7. (G) *Alternate Methods*
A house located near a stream is on fire. Twenty men, each carrying a bucket, arrive to help put out the fire. The house is about 20 yards from the stream. In how many ways could you organize this bucket brigade to deal with the fire?

8. (G) *Alternate Picture Meanings*
   Facial expressions and gestures can have many different meanings. Each item in this test is a picture of a facial expression or a gesture. You are to look at the picture and then write as many different things as you can that a person might say if he felt as the person in the picture does. (Line drawing of a person holding hand to face.)

9. (B) *Problems with Educational System*
   List below problems you see with our educational system. Do not discuss or solve these problems. Just list as many problems as you can think of.

10. (G) *Pertinent Questions*
    A student who has graduated from college is offered positions in the same occupation but in different parts of the country. What four questions have to be considered in making a choice?

11. (G) *Procedure Applications*
    In chemistry, one of the methods for getting a pure sample of some substance is by successive crystallizations. The substance is first put into solution then crystallized out. This removes some impurities. The process is repeated several times; each crystallization removes additional impurities until only the pure substance is left.
    If we think of this method in the general sense of refining or purifying by repeating a process, in what other instances might this method be used?

12. (G) *Multiple Social Problems*
    In each item of this test, two people of a typical family are described. You are to write as many different personal problems as you can that the two people can have with each other. The problem should involve the feelings, thoughts, and attitudes of the two people described. Look at the sample item: What personal problems can the BROTHER and SISTER have with each other?

13. (G) *Utility Test*
    List as many uses as you can think of for a rubberband.

14. (B) *Evaluating Ideas*
    List factors which you might take into consideration in evaluating the "uses" that you gave on the previous test, assuming that you were trying to decide which were the best ideas for actual use. Do not tell which idea you would select; simply list considerations which might enter into your decision, assuming you would make some use of the objects. If helpful, you may look back at the uses you gave on the previous test.

15. (B) *Problems in College*
    List problems which you think a student may face in college. Do not discuss or solve the problem; just list as many different ones as you can think of.

16. (B) *Problem Prevention*
    Regarding the problems you listed on the previous test, suggest briefly, ways that incoming freshmen might minimize those problems or prevent them entirely from occurring.

17. (B) *Improving Research Testing, Part I*
    Many educational experiments are conducted in which volunteer subjects like

yourselves are brought together for testing sessions such as this one. Researchers are extremely interested in ideas for improving such testing operations. Our Creative Studies staff and others in the College are anxious to obtain as many suggestions as possible from Project participants as to how these testing-sessions could be improved for the benefit of future subjects and researchers at our College. There are 3 parts to this test. You will be asked first for ideas, then for considerations for judging the ideas, and finally for a detailed plan based on your best ideas. List as many ideas as you can in which this overall testing operation (which consisted of 5 testing periods from September, 1970, until now) could be improved.

18. (B) *Improving Research Testing, Part II; Making Decisions*
     Regarding your ideas on the problem of improving this overall testing operation, list below as many factors as you can that might be taken into consideration in trying to decide which ideas are the best. You may look back at your ideas if you like. Do not decide here; simply list factors you might consider in deciding.

19. *Improving Research Testing Part III; Developing Plans*
     Based on the factors you listed in Part II, choose your best idea or combination of ideas from those you listed for improving this overall testing operation. State below; then develop the best plan you can for implementing the idea(s) for spelling out how it could be developed and used.

     Chosen Idea(s):
     Plan for implementation:

Some Student Reactions

Let me give a few examples of how students describe their accomplishments in the program. Each of the following reactions is from a different student.

The following is one of the most revealing statements, illustrative of the frustrations along with the overall effects:

> *Creative Studies always frustrates me every semester. In fact, I just feel like quitting the whole program. But when I look back I realize how much I have learned. The first year opened me up to thinking, exploring, creating, discussing—brought out in me an overall enthusiasm for learning. Already, I can see the difference from some of the sessions we've done this year. Synectics has helped me to see problems in many different ways—something that in September I never thought would happen. I think in a more organized, creative manner—I even record my ideas now—the thing I fought you the most on 1st semester. I never can really say until it's all over and I can look back and analyze the differences but I think that Creative Studies has helped me, more than any course I've ever had, to come up with more ideas and broaden my tolerance and appreciation for other ideas which at first glance I may have thought were of no value.*

Another insightful reaction follows:

> *Hi! It's funny how disillusioned I was with the course during the first semester. Then, near the end of it, I began to see the results of the course on me—definitely more awareness of challenges, problems, and a better attitude towards life—enjoying and taking more time to enjoy nature, objects, sensations, and media . . . This semester, I started writing poems which I never thought I could write. I wrote them*

when I was extra happy or extra depressed to express myself. I always felt good afterwards. Now I'm taking up photography. I intend to put poems and photos together in a scrapbook. I feel more confident and helpful when communicating with friends, etc. I can't see exactly how this course went about helping me to change for the better, but I know it has and I wouldn't drop the course. By my Junior year, I may transfer and lose 12 credits, but as my mother says—it may be the only REALLY worthwhile course I take. I agree. I wish there was a major offered in Creative Studies. I would definitely take it.

Many students discuss ways the courses help them in other subjects:

. . . for one thing—the original principles of CPS had more of a chance to "sink in." The second semester helped me a great deal with the business I'm involved with. It also helped me to see where the other classes were going. Coherency became easier. Since experimentation was encouraged—I used more and more integration with my other subjects. I found this doubly rewarding.

. . . before I never would have associated creativity with math, etc. It was really great the way we learned to use our creative abilities in a wide variety of situations, fields and problems.

Attitudes and self-confidence are frequently stressed:

. . . helped change my attitude to better regarding school, schoolmates, education as a whole—gives confidence to scared freshman.

Made me happier and a great deal less fearful of society . . . How can I tell you of my change to independency, of assurance in new fields, of ability to concentrate and solve a problem, of the friends that I have made—of the complete change in my family . . . It is unbelievable in the change in my family. My mother would have told you herself, but you had to dash off.

The concept of "value with enjoyment" is frequently stressed:

. . . the most exciting, challenging, hard, useful, course I shall ever take.

. . . a valuable and enjoyable experience—which in school is usually a rough combination to find.

Many do not at first see the immediate application in their lives.

At first I really didn't think I would actually use what I learned, out of class, but I was wrong.

And others mention strong implications for the future.

There are also many more things I have gained that I couldn't possibly evaluate at this point in my life. Someday, I'll tell you.

Some see it as a haven of relevance:

The reason I am probably flunking out of college today is because I can't find enough relevance in my courses to justify putting any effort into them. Same old bull shit. Your class sort of served to salvage the whole mess. I can now look upon my total college experience this far and feel that it had some value.

And many comments are made regarding expanded awareness:

This is just a sidelight but since taking this course I've taken an interest in other people. I find good things in everybody. I take interest in what they're doing whereas I used to not pay any attention.

. . . A lot of small things seem to have expanded lately–It's more apparent to me; things that I overlooked and took for granted before are things I would definitely be unhappy without; for example–a clear night in Buffalo. This seems to be very rare, but when it is clear I really get excited about it and go outside and look. I'm less afraid to let others know also. I guess I would have originally hesitated because I wouldn't want someone to think I was a nut. The other day J - - - - and H - - - - - - and I were walking and it had been raining–out there was this one little patch of blue sky sticking through the clouds. Without worrying about their reactions, I pointed it out and they both smiled and said that it looked "cool," and J - - - - said, "See, that's what that class does for you." He had noticed it also and was going to say something.

Not All React Positively

Do all students make these impressive gains and react positively to the program? The majority do; but definitely not all. For example, one student after three semesters exploded:

It has led to total frustration for me and I've come to dread class every week. I don't enjoy this class anymore and I don't plan on taking it next semester.

Others were more insightful:

As yet I have not realized that it has done anything for me. However, eventually I may realize that it has helped. Sometimes things are not obvious right away. Hopefully the light will dawn soon.

I really don't feel it has done much for me at all. I've enjoyed the course and it makes you feel wanted knowing that at least two professors really care about you. At best it has opened my eyes a little.

Generalizability of Results

What we have learned about the different types of students has been one of the most revealing aspects of the research project, and is discussed more fully later regarding the personality findings of the research and the generalizability of the results of the overall experiment. Suffice it to stress now that comparability of experimentals and controls who stayed with the program over the two full years remained the same, but that there was an attrition of almost 40 per cent at the end of each succeeding semester of the program and that many of these drop-outs are a different kind of student.

Of course, there are diverse reasons, beyond personality difference, why students do not complete the sequence; they leave the College, have scheduling problems, and so forth. The following is a revealing comment:

I used the Creative Studies method to solve my problem. The result I came up with was one I would never even think of before (due to what I was always told I should do). When I saw how this was the only answer that could make me happy and also would be worthwhile for me, it gave me the courage to make up my mind to act on my decision. And so I have decided to withdraw from school for awhile, until I decide what I want to do and then I will come back.

There are, however, significant and very interesting differences in personality between those who drop and those who stay through the sequence of courses. These will be discussed next.

Personality Questions

Let us now examine the personality findings with three questions in mind: (1) What differences are found between the personalities of experimental subjects and control students at the very beginning of the Project? (2) What differences are there between those students who stay with the Project vs. those who drop out after one or more semesters? (3) What changes associated with creativity occur in the personalities of the students during the two years of the Project?

Drop-Outs

Students who drop out of the study are, of course, classified as experimental or as control drop-outs. The experimental drop-outs are those who did not continue for all remaining courses after completing one or more courses in the series of four. Fortunately, all experimental drop-outs had taken the comprehensive battery of pre-tests; also, over 60 per cent of these students did continue taking the post-tests each semester as part of the overall study. (The majority of the others left the College before the end of the Project and were thus unavailable for post-tests.) This enabled many additional analyses comparing those who took all four courses with those taking fewer than four (Figure One). The control drop-outs are those controls who did not return for all further testing after completing one or more of the five testing sessions (including the pre-tests).

The Personality Tests

In the course of the two-year study, seven instruments were employed to measure personality traits of the subjects: (1) The Stony Brook Coping Problems. (SBCP) (Goldfried & D'Zurilla, 1972), (2) The Adjective Check List (ACL) (Gough and Heilbrun, 1965), (3) The Alpha Biographical Inventory (ABI) (IBRIC, 1968), (4) The Myers-Briggs Type Indicator (MBTI) (Myers, 1962), (5) The Minnesota Multiphasic Personality Inventory (MMPI) (Hathaway and McKinley, 1951), (6) The Strong Vocational Interest Blank (SVIB) (Strong, 1943), and (7) Specially-presented attitudinal questionnaires given to experimental students only (Parnes & Noller, 1974). The first two tests were administered during the formal testing periods of the study, along with the mental ability tests. The next two were provided as take-home tests at the conclusion of these formal testing-periods. The MMPI and SVIB were given to all incoming freshmen by the College Counseling Center whose Director at that time, Dr. Mazie Wagner, also provided the analyses and interpretations of the data from these two instruments. The attitudinal questionnaire was completed by experimentals (in class or at home) during the final week of classes in each school year.

Initial Comparability

Pre-test data were on hand for the ACL and ABI, as well as for the mental-ability tests discussed earlier; pre-test data were also in the files of the College Counseling Center for (1) MMPI, (2) SVIB, (3) the eight achievement scores (and total score) on the New York State Regents Scholarship Examination, (4) high-school grade averages, and (5) reading-ability scores.

Experimentals vs. Controls

Analyses of all of this pre-test data showed consistent comparability of the experimental and control groups. No significant differences occurred between the experimentals and the controls on any of the wide variety of measures except for one MMPI scale and one SVIB scale. Each of these two cases barely reached the .05 level. Out of 49 MMPI[10] comparisons and 106 SVIB[11] comparisons, this one difference for each instrument is, of course, far less than would be expected by chance alone.

For each semester's experimentals and controls who remained to be compared for treatment effect, their initial ACL and ABI scores were analyzed and found to be comparable throughout the study, as were their initial mental-ability scores. There was only one instance out of 116 ACL comparisons where a significant difference (.05 level) occurred in this pre-test comparability; on the ABI there were no significant differences found in any of the comparisons.

Subsequent analyses of the MMPI data were provided by the director of the Counseling Center at the end of the first year and of each semester of the second year. Of these 63 follow-up comparisons, there was only one where a significant difference (.05 level) occurred in the pre-tests.

Stay-ins vs. Drop-outs

However, when comparing pre-test data on the stay-ins vs. the drop-outs, significant and quite interesting differences were found in both experimentals and controls. Dr. Wagner of the Counseling Center reported (Wagner and Schubert, 1973a) that, according to analyses of the MMPI data, both experimental and control drop-outs as groups (not necessarily true for each individual) tended to be somewhat more depressive, hysterical, more directed toward deviancy, toward culturally disapproved behavior; appeared to be more impulsive, quicker to "take off" rather than stick with something, in closer contact with their "primary processes," "freer," more compulsive, obsessional, ruminative; showed less potential for "above-average achievement," less likely to succeed in college, more likely to drop out, to fail out or to get lower grades, and tended to be less responsible and more anxious. She reported that the above patterns were reinforced by the repeated instances of significant differences also found between the stay-in groups and drop-out groups on ACL scales as follows: Stay-ins significantly exceeded drop-outs on Total Adjectives Checked, Self-Control, Nurturance, Deference, and Welsh's Low Origence, High Intellectence[12]; drop-outs significantly exceeded stay-ins on Ability, Aggression and Change.

Not True for All Drop-outs

Obviously, the general personality characteristics described for the drop-outs do not hold true for each individual drop-out. The above picture is for the averages of all stay-ins vs. all drop-outs. There undoubtedly are drop-outs who score as less depressive, hysterical, etc. than the "average" stay-in, as well as stay-ins who score as more depressive, etc. than the "average" drop-out; the overlap of the distributions for the two groups for all scales is very considerable, and the mean differences, though significant, are not great.

Early Drop-outs Most Definitive

The most clear-cut picture of the group differences in personalities between "drop-outs" and "stay-ins" is seen when examining those who dropped after the first course, in the case of the experimentals or immediately after the pre-tests in the case of the controls. Here the reasons for dropping seem to be more frequently the result of disinterest or dissatisfaction—rather than because of scheduling difficulty or other problems which would not necessarily be associated with the personality syndrome of the "drop-out" (only 25 per cent were found to have dropped for these latter unrelated reasons); also, the numbers (dropping out) were the largest—57 experimentals and 44 controls. In later periods, the numbers possible for analysis in each "drop-out" group varied from a high of 34 to a low of 18 in experimentals and from 29 to 7 in controls. Even though the differences in scores between the "drop-out" and "stay-in" groups tended to remain in the same direction as for the initial "drop-outs," they did not always reach statistical significance, most likely because of the smaller numbers of subjects.

Volunteer Syndrome

The characteristics of the drop-outs described earlier closely resemble the personality-syndrome found in several published and unpublished studies of people who volunteer (unpaid) to be experimental subjects (Schubert, 1964; Rosenthal and Rosnow, 1969; MacDonald, 1972). In our own study, our total "volunteer" group would be considered to comprise all subjects who applied for the Project, whether they were assigned to the experimental or control group. When compared with the rest of the freshman class (all those who did not apply), our total volunteer group, like the drop-outs, appeared to lean strongly toward the personality syndrome described; however this was not true for the "stays" (both experimentals and controls) when analyzed without the "drops." The "stays" did not resemble the personality type of the volunteer but instead resembled the profile of the remainder of the freshmen class (the non-applicants or "non-volunteer"). The drop-outs, therefore, seem to be those who made the volunteer group as a whole appear to be different from the rest of the freshmen class in the above-described ways.

Artistic Preference

Looking at the "drops" vs. the "stays" in still another way—by scores on the SVIB—provides another interesting picture of differences between the two groups. Dr. Wagner's analyses (Wagner and Schubert, 1973a) showed that the female drops, as a group, were significantly higher on the following scales: Music, Entertainment, Model, Art Teacher, Artist, Interior Decorator, Newswoman; while the female stays, as a group, were significantly higher on Recreation Leadership, Office Practice, Mechanical, Social Service, Sports and Religious Activities. No significant differences were found among the males, perhaps due to the small sizes of the male groups. It thus appears that the female drops are more interested than the stays in artistic creativity as against broader applications of their creative potential. As a matter of fact, many who dropped because of their disappointment in the nature of the course had expected more emphasis on creative activities in the arts.

Implications of Findings re Drop-Outs

Many implications may be derived from the results obtained in our study of drop-outs. First of all, the data suggest that many of the drop-outs from the course tend to be like drop-outs in general. In fact, 45 per cent of the course drop-outs also left the College by the end of their sophomore year. The stay-ins turned out to be similar to the rest of the freshman class after many of those among the original applicants with the high "volunteer syndrome" dropped out. This suggests that those lower in self-control and higher on "manic" tendencies (impulsivity, spontaneity, etc.) seemed to seek the quick answer, the novel experience, and when it no longer appeared to be novel and exciting, they tended to drop out of the picture. This pattern seems consistent with our experience in class with many of the drop-outs. They would not work with the Creative Behavior Workbook (Parnes, 1967) and with the structure of the program—repeated practice in the total creative problem-solving process—but enjoyed greatly the ideation, the brainstorming, etc.

Theodore Levitt's contention that *Creativity Is Not Enough* (1963) seems relevant. His conception of "creativity" is one of idea-production alone. That is why he calls it "not enough"—

because he appreciates fully the necessity of evaluation and implementation of ideas. Whereas many writers define creativity the way Levitt does, it is important for us to emphasize that idea-production alone is not the conception we hold of creativity in our Creative Studies Project. As emphasized earlier, the processes we develop in our courses involve all phases, from sensing problems to the implementation and action stages themselves.

The drop-outs appear to be the people who are interested mainly in quick idea-production rather than viewing ideation in the context of a disciplined process. They seem to be the kind of persons that Levitt suggests have limited value in an organization. Although we do not feel that a person should have to be devoid of new ideas to get along in an organizational setting, we do think that he or she must be more than an idea-producer alone. In few instances can one enjoy that luxury, and rarely does such one-sided activity bring high-level results. That is why we concern ourselves with developing "channeled freedom" or self-disciplined freedom, rather than merely spontaneity as such. It seems that true creativity requires deep involvement and intense application.

MacKinnon reported a significant finding that is extremely relevant to the points we have been discussing regarding the stay-ins vs. the drop-outs.

> Both these studies, as well as others there is no time to review . . . show that when adolescents are identified as potentially creative scientists on the basis of manifest creative performance rather than on the basis of tests of divergent thinking and other so-called tests of creativity, they display the disciplined effectiveness of a well integrated person which does not match the widely held view of the creative adolescent as an undercontrolled, unconventional, non-conforming bohemian (MacKinnon, 1971).

In other words, when we look at the person in terms of what one *does* do with one's creative potential rather than in terms of what one *can* do (as measured by certain divergent traits shown in tests of creative behavior), we find the person who lives with "channeled freedom" rather than with undirected or irresponsible freedom.

In this regard, we have been conducting some pilot studies with ACL scores. We independently selected those adjectives (in the list of 300) that we thought might be expected to show growth as a result of the Creative Studies program. We discovered some adjectives that tended to the "self-disciplined" extreme (example, "planful") and others that suggested the "freedom" extreme (example, "spontaneous"). Others tended to be more "neutral." In all, we found 22 that Dr. Noller and I completely agreed on. We looked upon the qualities represented by those adjectives as contributing strongly to the likelihood of creative achievement. We then scored the protocols on this special scale of 22 adjectives. Some interesting findings resulted. First, we discovered that the experimental students who dropped out checked fewer adjectives on that scale in the post-tests than did those who stayed on; however, this only approached statistical significance (p. < .10) rather than reaching the required .05 level. Secondly, we isolated from all experimentals and controls combined, two special groups whose post-test scores we compared on this special scale. The two specially-selected groups were (1) high-scorers, and (2) low-scorers on the non-academic achievement inventory discussed earlier. High-scorers were those whose scores were one standard deviation or more above the mean; low-scorers were those whose scores were one standard deviation or more below the mean. We discovered that the high-scorers on the non-academic achievement inventory—which covers areas such as art, leadership, business, science, etc.—checked significantly (.01 level) more adjectives on our special scale than did the low-scorers. Since both measures were self-reports, it is possible that students who saw themselves in a particular way (on the ACL) tended to "exaggerate" their achievements on the other measure. However, it seems reasonable to suggest that the scale may represent the balance needed to accomplish creative achievements.

We feel that a closer look at this experimental scale must be taken because of the extremes represented within the single scale. For example, it is possible that someone might gain in "spontaneity" and lose in "rigidity," or vice versa, but maintain the same score from beginning to end. That is, someone might see oneself as becoming "spontaneous" and at the same time might feel no longer "planful." If in pre-tests one selected "planful" and omitted "spontaneous" and then reversed these in the post-tests, one's total score would remain the same. Yet some significant movement might have taken place (toward better or worse "balance"). Balance may actually be an inappropriate word. The "balanced" traits can complement one another rather than "off-setting" each other.

We say that people should learn to "stay loose" in their stance toward life and in their mental processes, but, of course, the question becomes, "How loose can one be before one falls apart?" And by the same token, "How tight can one remain before one freezes up?" This helps to portray the type of "balance" we feel is needed for one to be able to exercise creative potential productively in our society. Our hypothesis is that the "drop-out syndrome" represents a stance that is "too loose."

It is worth noting that we are using the word "balanced" in this sense in quite a different way than the word "balanced personality" is usually construed. We do not equate our term "balanced" with the term "normal," which more often implies the "conventional" type of individual in our society. Visualize instead a sling-shot. If one side of the elastic is weaker, it will not have full power and cannot be aimed for maximum accuracy. With two equally "balanced" elastic sides, the force and accuracy of propelling will be the greatest. So it is, we hypothesize, with the forces of our spontaneity and of our self-control as they mutually aid us in propelling ourselves toward our goals. If one force is weaker than the other, we may be weakened and/or misdirected. Utilizing these two complementary forces effectively is what Alex Osborn meant when he quipped, "Don't drive with your brakes on" (Osborn, 1963). Osborn's metaphor introduces the important elements of sequencing and timing that are not inherent in the sling-shot analogy. The gas pedal represents a tremendous force; when used by a skillful driver, it is "balanced" with appropriate sequencing and timing with the brake pedal, with its equally powerful capability. One can learn to develop and productively use these two forces in one's personality through effective sequencing and timing.

Supportive Evidence

There are several pieces of additional evidence supportive of the implications discussed above. The stay-in experimentals were significantly better than the drop-out experimentals at the end of the first year on one of Guilford's tests of ability to evaluate, ahead on a second and equal on the third. Furthermore, the control stay-ins were better than the experimental drop-outs on all three of these evaluation tests, although not significantly (only slight differences, but all three in the same direction). The same general pattern emerged on similar tests at the end of the second year. Taken together, these findings seem to indicate further support for the notion that the drop-outs tend to be less able on some of the detailed processes involved in evaluation and follow through.

Another indicator supportive of our hunches was the difference between the experimental drop-outs and stay-ins with respect to non-academic achievement in a variety of fields. Whereas the experimental stay-ins were stronger both years than control stay-ins, and also stronger than the experimental drop-outs, in 8 or 9 out of 12 areas of non-academic achievement (although non-significantly and only slightly in most instances), the control stay-ins were, surprisingly, stronger both years than experimental drop-outs to the same degree (not significantly) in 8 to 10 of the 12 areas. Pre-test scores on the ABI, which measured areas of pre-college non-academic achievement showed the same tendency (non-significant) for experimental stay-ins to surpass experimental drop-outs. These non-academic achievement areas tend to require initiative and imagination—but also the perseverance and follow-through which many of the drop-outs seemed to lack.

Another interesting difference between "volunteers" (experimentals and controls) and "non-volunteers" (non-applicants to the program) is found in the comparison of their test scores on a reading pre-test (Wagner & Schubert, 1973b). The "volunteers" (both experimentals and controls) had significantly higher numbers of items tried and a higher number of right answers, but showed no differences over "non-volunteers" in percentage of right answers on the reading test. In other words, the volunteers try more and get more right. This fact would seem to account for the findings reported earlier of both experimentals and controls being stronger in the English tests than the non-volunteers, but of the experimentals, moreover, being stronger than the controls because of the training effect. That is, both experimentals and controls appear to have tried more and attained more than did the more cautious non-volunteers—but the experimentals were even better able to do this. They had training to back up their efforts.

Personality Changes

In light of the above discussions, it is interesting to consider the two major results of comparisons between experimental stay-ins and their initially comparable control stay-ins on ACL post-tests: (1) On a group of pre-selected ACL scales, there was consistent positive movement by experimentals as compared with controls from pre-tests to the final tests at the end of the second year; (2) on no single ACL scale was there any significant difference between experimentals and controls on post-tests at the end of the first or second years.

Ten of Ten in Same Direction

Before any personality data had been seen, Dr. Noller and I studied the descriptions of all 24 scales of the ACL, examined the adjectives on the Domino Creativity scale (Domino, 1970) and on the four Welsh "Origence-Intellectence" scales, (Welsh, 1971) and made our predictions of which ones we expected to show differences in growth favoring experimental stays over controls stays. We agreed on nine scales in addition to our own special scale. These were: Achievement, Change, Dominance, Endurance, Intraception, Lability, Self-confidence, the Domino Creativity scale, and Welsh's Low Origence, High Intellectence scale. In all ten cases (including our own scale), the experimentals surpassed the controls in growth over the two years on these predicted measures; but individually they were not significant. However, with 10 out of 10 all in the same direction, the pattern of the scores, even though non-significant, suggests that additional study of the problem might well be warranted.

Coping Scale as Personality Measure

The SBCP "coping" instrument asks what one does, while the ACL asks how one sees oneself. On the SBCP, the experimentals, performance was significantly better than the controls, as discussed earlier.

The experimental students' own perceptions of growth through the program, moreover, provide important data, although it lacks a control comparison. In twelve of the thirteen items of perceived gain on a questionnaire given at the end of the second year, the majority of students checked the highest or next to highest rating on a 5-point scale (e.g.: "1" = not at all, "2" = very little, "3" = somewhat, "4" = a good deal, "5" = a great deal). The percentages of students checking "4" or "5" for each of the thirteen items is shown in Figure Three.

As reported earlier, two of the above items showed significant growth in students' perceived gains from the end of the first year to the end of the second. These were the items concerning coping with problems and participating in discussions.

Figure Three.

Summary analysis of student reactions at end of second year of Creative Studies—based on 94% of students who responded to questionnaire.

Description of Item	Percentage of Students Checking Two Top-Gain Categories
I find I tend to take more factors into consideration in making decisions than before the program.	91
I find that I am more prone to try different approaches to doing something or to attacking a problem than before the program.	84
I find I am better able to develop my ideas and put them to use than before the program.	84
I find I am better able to think up effective ideas than before the program.	81
I find myself better able to cope with problems than before the program.	81
I find myself more open-minded to ideas of others than before the program.	78
I find I am better able to evaluate my ideas than before the program.	74
I find myself more observant than before the program.	72
I find since taking the program that I tend to exert more effort in mental tasks rather than quitting so soon.	71
I find myself more aware of problems and challenges than before the program.	71
I find myself more self-confident than before the program.	58
I find myself more inquisitive than before the program.	52
I find myself a more active participant in discussions than before the program.	48

The MBTI was given as a take-home test at the end of the final testing period. The data from those who returned the instrument were not included in our computer analyses, but informal study of the data has indicated no reliable differences between experimentals and controls on scores on that test. We hope later to examine the data by items, as in the case of the ACL, in order to see if movement occurred toward balance.

Generalizations

We set out to answer three questions regarding the personality data in our study. Regarding the first, examining initial differences between personalities of experimentals and controls, the pre-test data provided strong, consistent evidence that the two total groups were indeed comparable, and that each subgroup of experimentals and controls who continued in each succeeding semester likewise remained comparable.

As to the second question, regarding stay-ins versus drop-outs, the data-analyses showed significant personality differences between the two groups. We also have evidence from the data on mental-ability tests that more of the high-scoring subjects and fewer of the low-scoring ones tended to stay on—although as pointed out earlier, experimentals and controls who stayed remained comparable throughout in both ability and personality. As a matter of fact, Dr. Wagner highlighted the strength of personality she found in the controls who stayed for the entire four semesters of testing; she claimed she would hire unseen any of these people, and that the "volunteer" characteristic seen so clearly in both groups at the onset of the study had been completely eliminated. She felt that the control stay-ins appeared to be even a stronger group than the experimental stay-ins. At any rate, the fact that the control stay-ins were initially at least as strong in personality and ability as the experimental stay-ins lends confidence that the effects attributed to the courses were truly treatment effects rather than possible differences in initial qualities.

The third question sought to examine personality changes during the two years of the project. The data show consistent positive movement by experimentals compared with controls, although not significant on any single scale. The SBCP as well as experimentals' questionnaire responses provided further statistically significant evidence of gains in personality dimensions.

From the findings regarding drop-outs vs. stay-ins, it appears, therefore, that there were other than merely chance factors that caused some students to drop and others to stay on. Hence we cannot conclude that the four semesters of courses would necessarily produce the same results with the entire experimental sample that began the program. However, we can repeat what we emphasized in our earlier summary of findings: for a group comparable to our total sample of experimentals and controls who started such a program, the gains shown in our study relative to time spent in courses would be expected from those continuing with the program. The first-semester findings alone, of course, tend to replicate and extend those of the earlier studies summarized at the beginning of the article.

Many More Can Benefit

Furthermore, considering the data showing the stay-ins (both experimentals and controls) to be similar in personality to the total freshman population from which they were drawn, we might infer that most of our incoming freshmen would profit from exposure to part or all of the program if they elected to take it.

Further Research Suggested

Every answer brings many more questions. Our study thus provides more questions than answers. The more we learn the more we realize how little we know. Ralph Sockman put it more poetically: "The larger the island of knowledge, the longer the shore line of wonder."

And so it has been with us as we amassed the large variety of data and observations during the years of our Creative Studies Project. Dr. Noller and I proposed the following questions as uppermost among countless that have arisen as we have proceeded with our studies. Some were raised by members of the National Advisory Committee concerned with the study throughout its duration.

* What percentages of students would apply for Creative Studies at other colleges and universities? What percentage would apply at the upper-class level?

* What type of person gains the most? Can we identify such people who would be most apt to profit from Creative Studies programs?

* What differences are there between those who dropped because they weren't interested in continuing and those who were simply not able to schedule the additional courses?

* How could the initial appeal for applicants to the program be designed so as to discourage the potential "drops" from applying? Should potential drop-outs be counselled on the results of preliminary tests? Could special courses be designed for those with the "drop-out syndrome?"

* Are there implications from our findings for admissions policy at our college or elsewhere?

* Why do larger numbers of females apply for the program than males? (About 25 per cent of our subjects were males, among both experimentals and controls, compared with about 40 per cent males among those available as applicants.) Would the same experimental results occur if the sexes were equally divided or if the opposite tendency occurred?

* Do art education programs tend to accomplish creativity-development for "art-oriented" people as ours do for the less "art-oriented" stay-ins in our program? Might art students be more inclined to stay with a series of courses that emphasized figural content? If so, why are some art-oriented students among the strongest in our courses? What can be discovered from these individuals to help structure programs for their drop-out counterparts?

* What modifications of the Creative Studies Project would be best suited to a program in an engineering school, a teacher's college, etc.

* What differences between experimentals and controls can be observed in their group processes in creative problem-solving?

* What physiological differences might we discover between experimentals and controls as they work on difficult problems alone or in groups?

* What differences are there between the results of incubation periods with experimentals and controls during problem-solving?

* What elements could be added to the program to facilitate the kinds of personality change that would in turn facilitate effectiveness in creative problem-solving?

* What would be learned by offering experimentals further courses after a period of time?

* What differences in effects would the program produce if offered during the final two years of college, or at other grade levels?

* How many and what kinds of questions do the experimentals vs. controls ask in other courses?

* How many experimentals and controls attempt independent study? Involving what types of activities? What is their relative success in same?

* How would experimentals compare with controls on Asch-type "conformity" tests?

* Would deliberate training in figural areas result in significant changes in the figural slab of Guilford's Structure of Intellect model? What training might affect performance on the Symbolic tests in his model?

* Some personality dispositions are desirable up to a point; beyond that maximum they may hinder rather than aid creative achievement. Would analysis of the personality data on selected scales show score ranges that correlate with success in Creative Studies, or score

ranges within which experimentals appear significantly more often than controls in the post-tests?

* What might be learned by analyzing all personality items (for example all of the individual 300 adjectives of the ACL) to see which discriminate significantly between the experimentals and controls or between the stay-ins and drop-outs? What new scales might be developed?

* Might our special ACL scale correlate with the "freedom" and "control" scales of Runner Studies of Attitude Patterns? What changes might the Creative Studies program produce on performance of the Runner instrument or on others such as the Omnibus Personality Inventory?

* To what extent might experimentals have distorted their responses on the self-report scales as a result of their wider reading about creativity and the creative personality? Might this have been true for controls also, with their ready access to the comprehensive Creative Studies Library and Reading Room in our College Library building?

* What kinds of situational tests might be used to observe creative process in action?

* Will important and measurable differences be found in the future between those who took the courses and those who did not? In the case of the experimental drop-out, with the different personality-type he or she seems to represent, will the impact of the number of courses taken make an ultimate difference in life? Will he or she attain more of the "balance" we have described than will the control drop-out counterpart?

* What changes have family members noticed in attitudes, behavior, etc.? Do changes persist without continued course-work?

* Would follow-up studies reveal above-average interest and participation by experimentals in service organizations, community projects, and other areas of positive social action?

* Will the experimental drop-outs show greater creative productivity and better mental health than their similar control drop-outs? What ultimate differences might be found between experimentals and controls, and between experimental drop-outs and control drop-outs—in style, creative productivity, mental health, professional success, etc.? Will there be differential numbers of drug addicts, alcoholics, individuals suffering nervous breakdowns, etc.?

* What would be indicated by a special follow-up of subjects known to be pursuing a career in education (including management training in industry, government, etc.)? Would they demonstrate specific applications of the principles of Creative Studies in the courses they teach?

* Will there be any evidence of more novel career-choices on the part of the experimentals?

* What differences may be discovered between experimentals and controls in their job performance?

* Will the program affect child-rearing practices of the experimentals, and resultant attitudes of off-spring toward an open-minded, creative approach?

Footnotes

1. See Meadow and Parnes, 1959a; Parnes & Meadow, 1959, 1960; Meadow, Parnes & Reese, 1959; Parnes, 1961; Meadow & Parnes, 1963; Parnes, 1964; Parnes, 1966; Parnes & Brunelle, 1967a and 1967b; Reese & Parnes, 1970 & 1972; Taylor & Parnes, 1970; Parnes, 1972; Parnes & Treffinger, 1973; Khatena & Parnes, 1974; Parnes, 1975; Reese, et al., 1976; Parnes, 1978; Ekvall & Parnes, 1984.
2. Definitions of these terms from Guilford's Structure-of-Intellect are provided in Figure 2.
3. For a detailed picture of the drop-out pattern, see Figure 1 in Reese et al., 1976.
4. For complete details on the two-year curriculum, see Parnes, Noller & Biondi, 1977; Noller, Parnes & Biondi, 1976; Noller & Parnes, 1972.
5. For greater details on research forms, memos, letters, enclosures, tests, and test sources, see Parnes and Noller, 1974.
6. For those familiar with the Guilford model, the selected measures sample: (1) all content-areas except behavioral for the "cognition" operation in his Structure model; (2) the semantic area of the "memory" operation; (3) 19 of the 23 cells of the "divergent production" operation (there was

nothing in Sheridan Psychological Services' summary report of recommended tests for the 24th cell–divergent production of figural relations); (4) the symbolic, semantic and behavioral areas of the "convergent production" operation, and (5) the symbolic and semantic areas of the "evaluation" operation.

7. For more detailed information on specific tests, SOI cells represented and statistical analyses, see Reese et al., 1976 and Parnes & Treffinger, 1973.
8. Personal letter.
9. See Khatena and Parnes, 1974 for details.
10. The MMPI scales consisted of the three validity scales, the nine Clinical scales, the Social-Introversion scale, and 36 new scales.
11. The SVIB scales were basic and occupational interest scales, analyzed separately for males and females.
12. High scorers on this scale tend to be individuals whose responses are intellectualized and who seldom act impulsively (Welsh, 1969).

References

Basadur, M., Graen, G. B. & Green, S. G. (1982). Training in creative problem solving: Effects on ideation and problem finding and solving in an industrial research organization. *Organizational Behavior and Human Performance, 30,* 41-70.

Bouchard, T. J. (1972). A comparison of two brainstorming procedures. *Journal of Applied Psychology, 56,* 418-421.

Cohen, D., Whitmeyer, J. W. & Funk, W. H. (1960). Effect of group cohesiveness and training upon creative thinking. *Journal of Applied Psychology, 44,* (5).

Covington, M. V. (1967, September). Productive thinking and a cognitive curriculum. Invited paper presented at symposium, *Studies of the inquiry process: Problems of theory, description and teaching.* American Psychological Convention, Washington, DC.

Crutchfield, R. S. (1969). Nurturing the cognitive skills of productive thinking. In Association for Supervision and Curriculum Development. National Education Association. *Yearbook.* Washington, DC: Author.

Domino, G. (1970) The identification of potentially creative persons from the adjective check list. *Journal of Consulting and Clinical Psychology, 35,* (1).

Ekvall, G. & Parnes, S. J. (1984). *Creative problem solving methods in product development: A second experiment.* Stockholm: FA Radet, Report No. 2.

Geschka, H. (1975). Introduction and use of idea-generating methods. In: *Creativity and motivation in industrial R. & D.* prepared by Working Group No. 14, European Industrial Research Management Association, through Battelle-Frankfort, Germany.

Goldfried, M. R. & D'Zurilla, T. J. (1972). *Assessment and facilitation of effective behavior in college freshman.* State University of New York at Stony Brook: Final Report Submitted to The National Institute of Mental Health, Research Grant No. MH15044.

Gordon, W. (1961). *Synectics.* New York: Harper.

Gough, H. G. & Heilbrun, A. B., Jr. (1965). *The adjective check list manual.* Palo Alto, CA: Consulting Psychologists Press.

Guilford, J. P. (1967). *The nature of human intelligence.* New York: McGraw-Hill.

Guilford, J. P. (1969a). *A general summary of twenty years of research on aptitudes of high-level personnel.* Los Angeles, CA: Aptitude Research Project, Department of Psychology, University of Southern California.

Guilford, J. P. (1969b). *Intelligence, creativity and their educational implications.* San Diego, CA: Robert R. Knapp.

Hathaway, S. R. & McKinley, J. C. (1951). *Manual for Minnesota Multiphasic Inventory.* New York: Psychological Corp.

Heppner, P. P., Baumgardner, A. H., Larson, L. M. & Petti, R. E. (1983). *Problem solving training for college students with problem solving deficits.* Paper presented at the annual meeting of the American Psychological Association, Anaheim, CA.

Heppner, P. P., Neal, G. W. & Larson, L. M. (1984, May). Problem solving training as prevention with college students. *Personnel and Guidance Journal,* 514-519.

Heppner, P. P. & Reeder, B. L. (1984). Training in problem solving for residence hall staff: Who is most satisfied? *Journal of College Student Personnel, 25,* 357-360.

Hertz, M. R. (1951). *Frequency tables for scoring responses to the Rorschach Inkblot Test* (3rd ed.). Cleveland, OH: The Press of Western Reserve University.

IBRIC, (1968) *Manual for alpha biographical inventory.* Greensboro, NC: Prediction Press.

Jacobson, N. S. (1977). Problem solving and contingency contracting–in the treatment of marital discord. *Journal of Consulting and Clinical Psychology, 45,* 92-100.

Jacobson, N. S. (1978). Specific and nonspecific factors in the effectiveness of a behavioral approach to the treatment of marital discord. *Journal of Consulting and Clinical Psychology, 46,* 442-452.

Johansson, B. (1975). *Creativity and creative problem-solving courses in United States industry.* Greensboro, NC: Center for Creative Leadership.

Karol, R. L. & Richards, C. S. (1981). Cognitive maintenance strategies for smoking reduction. *JSAS Catalog of Selected Documents in Psychology, 15* (Ms. No. 2204).

Khatena, J. & Parnes, S. J. (1974). Applied imagination and the production of original verbal images. *Perceptual and Motor Skills, 38,* 130.

Korth, W. L. (1973). Training in creative thinking: The effect on the individual of training in the "synectics" method of group problem solving. (Doctoral dissertation, University of N. Carolina at Chapel Hill.) *Dissertational Abstracts International, 33,* 3947B. (University Microfilms) No. 73-4849.

Levitt, T. (1963). *Creativity is not enough.* Harvard Business Review, 41 (3).

MacDonald, A. J. (1972). Characteristics of volunteer subjects under three recruiting methods: Pay, extra credit, love of science. *The Journal of Consulting and Clinical Psychology, 39,* (2).

MacKinnon, D. W. (1971), July 25-30). *The role of personality traits in the development of scientific abilities.* A paper prepared for the Symposium on Detection and Training of Scientific Abilities at the XVIIth International Congress of Applied Psychology, Liege, Belgium.

Mansfield, R. S., Busse, T. V. & Krepelka, E. J. (1978). The effectiveness of creativity training. *Review of Educational Research, 48,* (4), 517-536.

Meadow, A. & Parnes, S. J. (1959a). University of Buffalo research regarding development of creative talent. In C. W. Taylor (Ed.), *The Third (1959) University of Utah Research Conference on the Identification of Creative Scientific Talent.* Salt Lake City, Utah: University of Utah Press.

Meadow, A. & Parnes, S. J. (1959b, June). Evaluation of training in creative problem solving. *Journal of Applied Psychology, 43,* 189-194.

Meadow, A. & Parnes, S. J. (1963). Development of individual creative talent. In C. W. Taylor & F. Barron (Eds.), *Scientific creativity: Its recognition and development.* New York: Wiley.

Meadow, A., Parnes, S. J. & Reese, H. W. (1959). Influence of brainstorming instructions and problem sequence on a creative problem-solving test. *Journal of Applied Psychology, 43,* 413-416.

Myers, Isabel B. (1962). *Manual for the Myers-Briggs Type Indicator.* Princeton, NJ: Educational Testing Service.

Necka, E. (1983). On the efficiency of the techniques of creative thinking. *Zeszyty Naukowe U, 34,* 39-62.

Noller, R. B. & Parnes, S. J. (1972). Applied creativity: The creative studies project–Part III–The curriculum. *Journal of Creative Behavior, 6,* (4), 275-294.

Noller, R. B., Parnes, S. J. & Biondi, A. M. (1976). *Creative actionbook.* New York: Scribner's.

Osborn, A. F. (1963). *Applied imagination.* New York: Scribner's.

Parnes, S. J. (1959, April). This is brainstorming. *Adult leadership.*

Parnes, S. J. (1961, June). Effects of extended effort in creative problem solving. *Journal of Educational Psychology, 52,* 117-122.

Parnes, S. J. (1964). Research on developing creative behavior. In C. W. Taylor (Ed.), *Widening horizons in creativity.* New York: Wiley.

Parnes, S. J. (1966). Imagination: Developed and disciplined. In C. W. Taylor & F. E. Williams (Eds.), *Instructional Media & Creativity.* New York: Wiley.

Parnes, S. J. (1967). *Creative behavior workbook.* New York: Scribner's.

Parnes, S. J. (1972). *Creativity: Unlocking human potential.* Buffalo, NY: DOK.

Parnes, S. J. (1972). Programming creative behavior. In C. W. Taylor (Ed.), *Climate for Creativity.* New York: Pergamon.

Parnes, S. J. (1975). Aha! In I. Taylor & J. Getzels (Eds.), *Perspectives in creativity* (pp. 224-248). Chicago: Aldine.

Parnes, S. J. & Brunelle, E. A. (1967a). The literature of creativity (Part I). *Journal of Creative Behavior, 1* (1), 52-109.

Parnes, S. J. & Brunelle, E. A. (1967b). Literature of creativity (Part II). *Journal of Creative Behavior, 1* (2), 191-240.

Parnes, S. J. & Meadow, A. (1959, August). Effects of brainstorming instruction on creative problem solving of trained and untrained subjects. *Journal of Educational Psychology, 50,* 171-176.

Parnes, S. J. & Meadow, A. (1960). Evaluation of persistence of effects produced by a creative problem solving course. *Psychological Reports, 7,* 357-361.

Parnes, S. J. & Noller, R. B. (1973). *Toward supersanity: Channelled freedom.* Buffalo, NY: DOK.

Parnes, S. J. & Noller, R. B. (1974). *Toward supersanity: Channelled freedom-Research Supplement.* Buffalo, NY: DOK.

Parnes, S. J. & Noller, R. B. (1978). The creative studies project at S.U.C.B. In M. K. Raina (Ed.), *Creativity research: International perspectives* (pp. 272-274). National Council of Educational Research and Training. New Delhi, India.

Parnes, S. J., Noller, R. B. & Biondi, A. M. (1977). *Guide to creative action.* New York: Scribner's.

Parnes, S. J. & Treffinger, D. J. (1973). *Development of new criteria for the evaluation of creative studies programs.* U.S. Department of Health, Education and Welfare, Office of Education. Project No. 2B019, Grant No. OEG-2-2 B109.

Prince, G. (1970). *The practice of creativity.* New York: Harper.

Reese, H. W. & Parnes, S. J. (1970, June). Programming creative behavior. *Child Development Management, 41,* (2).

Reese, H. W., Parnes, S. J. (1972). Programming creative behavior. Reprinted in K. D. O'Leary & S. G. O'Leary (Eds.), *Classroom management: The successful use of behavior modification.* New York: Pergamon Press.

Reese, H. W., Parnes, S. J., Treffinger, D. J. & Kaltsounus, G. (1976). Effects of a creative studies program on structure-of-intellect factors. *Journal of Educational Psychology, 69* (4), 401-410.

Richards, C. S. & Perri, M. G. (1978). Do self-control treatments last? An evaluation of behavioral problem solving and faded counselor contact as treatment maintenance strategies. *Journal of Counseling Psychology, 25,* 376-383.

Richards, J. M., Jr., Holland, J. L. & Lutz, S. W. (1966). *The assessment of student accomplishment in college.* Research and Development Division. American College Testing Program. Iowa City, Iowa.

Rickards, T. (1975). Brainstorming: An examination of idea production rate and level of speculation in real managerial situations. *R&D Management, 6,* (1).

Rose, L. H. & Lin, H. T. (1984). A meta-analysis of long-term creativity training programs. *Journal of Creative Behavior, 18,* (1).

Rosenthal, R. & Rosnow, R. L. (1969). The volunteer project. In R. Rosenthal & R. L. Rosnow (Eds.), *Artifact in behavioral research.* New York: Academic Press.

Schubert, D. S. P. (1964). Arousal seeking as a motivation for volunteering: MMPI scores and central-nervous-system-stimulant use as suggestive of a trait. *Journal of Projective Techniques and Personality Assessment, 28,* (3).

Sheridan Psychological Services, (1969). *Tests selected to represent structure-of-intellect abilities.* Sheridan Psychological Services, Orange, CA.

Simberg, A. L. & Shannon, T. E. (1959, May 27). *The effect of AC creativity training on the AC suggestion program* (mimeographed report). Flint, MI: AC Spark Plug Division, General Motors Corporation.

Skinner, B. F. (1973). The free and happy student. *New York University Education Quarterly, 4,* (3).

Sommers, W. S. (1962). The influence of selected teaching methods on the development of creative thinking. *Dissertation Abstracts, 22* (11), 3954.

Strong, E. K. (1943). *Vocational interests of men and women.* Palo Alto, CA: University Press.

Taylor, C. W., (Ed.). (1959). *The Third University of Utah Research Conference on the Identification of Creative Scientific Talent.* Salt Lake City, Utah: University of Utah Press.

Taylor, C. W. & Parnes, S. J. (1970). Humanizing educational systems: A report of the eighth international creativity research conference. *Journal of Creative Behavior, 4,* (3), 169-182.

Torrance, E. P. (1972). Can we teach children to think creatively? *Journal of Creative Behavior, 6,* (2), 114-143.

Wagner, Mazie E. & Schubert, D. S. P. (1973a). *College drop-outs from a program for training in creativity.* Unpublished manuscript.

Wagner, Mazie E. & Schubert, D. S. P. (1973b). *Volunteers for psychological experiments.* Unpublished manuscript.

Wallach, M. A. & Wing, C. W., Jr. (1969). *The talented student,* New York: Holt.

Welsh, G. S. (1969, November). Relationship of personality and classroom performances in talented students. *Proceedings of the Twenty-First Annual Special Education Conference.* North Carolina Department of Public Instruction, Charlotte.

Welsh, G. S. (1971). Vocational interests and intelligence in gifted adolescents. *Educational and Psychological Measurement, 31,* (1).

8

Teaching for Creativity

E. Paul Torrance
The University of Georgia

PART ONE: Can We Teach Children to Think Creatively?*

It is difficult, if not impossible, for me to present an unbiased account of the status of knowledge about teaching children to think creatively.

I know that it is possible to teach children to think creatively and that it can be done in a variety of ways. I have done it. I have seen my wife do it; I have seen other excellent teachers do it. I have seen children who had seemed previously to be "non-thinkers" learn to think creatively, and I have seen them continuing for years thereafter to think creatively. I have seen, heard, and otherwise experienced their creativity. Their parents have told me that they saw it happening. Many of the children, now adults, say that it happened. I also know that these things would not have happened by chance because I have seen them "not happening" to multitudes of their peers.

My many years of experience in teaching children to think creatively make me prone to assume things that others question. For example, throughout my research on creativity I have assumed that children will not function very creatively if the testing or other activity interrupts or replaces highly interesting and valued activities. I have always guarded against using the physical education, art, or music periods for testing or conducting experiments. Whenever this was not avoided, it was always obvious to me that the children were not functioning at their highest level. Thus, when I began searching to find out if the *American Educational Research Journal* had ever published a study on creative thinking, I was surprised though pleased, to find that Elkind, Deblinger, and Adler (1970) had documented what I had long assumed to be true. These investigators tested 32 children ranging from five to 12 years on three creativity measures. Each child was tested twice, once when taken from an ongoing "interesting" task and once when taken from an ongoing "uninteresting" task. When the children expected to return to an "uninteresting" task, they were almost twice as "creative" as they were when they anticipated the resumption of an "interesting" activity. In my teaching and research I had observed this phenomenon hundreds of times. I "knew" that it was true. To me, it was so obvious that it required no documentation. Still, I was pleased to see such documentation.

I realize, too, that my deep involvement in creativity research and teaching may also make me unfit to evaluate the status of knowledge on teaching children to think creatively. I believe I have used as great a variety of devices as anyone to try to avoid deceiving myself. I cannot claim detachment. I try continually to move from involvement to detachment, for I believe that involvement is necessary to a genuine search for the truth. A part of my ongoing

*Reproduced with permisison from *The Journal of Creative Behavior*, (1972), (*6*), 114-143.

involvement is to teach a group of four and five year-olds once each week, and to teach in an elementary school at least two days each month. I believe that this kind of continuing involvement is necessary to keep me from deceiving myself and to make new discoveries possible.

I am particularly aware that many researchers are likely to discredit most of the 142 studies that I have surveyed for this paper, because 103 of them have used performance on the *Torrance Tests of Creative Thinking* as criteria. While I strongly favor and have used more "real life" criteria, I feel some responsibility for defending the validity of the instrument used in these 103 studies. It is unfortunate that the only study on the validity of these tests ever published in the *American Educational Research Journal* (Harvey, Hoffmeister & Coates, 1970) is filled with factual errors about the tests, and uses such irrelevant criteria as measures of supernaturalism, moral relativism, relativism of facts, concreteness-abstractness, and the like. I am unable to think of a logical rationale for expecting this type of validity. I prefer to place my confidence in the recently reported long-range predictive validity study (Torrance, 1971) using both publicly recognized and acknowledged adult creative achievements and self-reported peak creative achievements as criteria.

I realize that many educational psychologists (Cronbach, 1970; Elkind, Deblinger, and Adler, 1970) believe that the term "creativity" is too value laden and should not be used to designate the kinds of behavior involved in studies of teaching children to think creatively. On this score, I can only say that I believe the word describes the behavior investigated more adequately than any other word I know. Further, an effort has been made to stay within the limits of a definition I chose for my research in 1958. If one does not care to accept this definition, it is his privilege to use another label.

I must also acknowledge the criticism that "being able to think creatively" is not the same as "thinking creatively." All of us could probably think more creatively than we do. I am interested in the development of superstars, teachers who can equip children with the skills of creative thinking and with the motivations to continue thinking creatively throughout their lives. Even such superstars, however, cannot guarantee that their students will have a chance to behave creatively as adults.

In studying creative thinking and selecting studies for this survey I have not been bound by the constraint that Elkind places upon thinking even in its broadest sense, i.e. that it be logically determined. In creative thinking at its best there are strong elements of the emotional, the irrational. After this kind of thinking has occurred, however, it must be subjected to tests of logic. A part of the business of teaching children to think creatively is teaching them to understand and consciously to use these emotional, irrational processes and to formulate and apply criteria for evaluating alternative solutions.

It is becoming popular to maintain that "nobody can teach anybody anything" (Wees, 1971). When I teach children and see that creative thinking comes so naturally to most children, I vacillate on this issue myself. Yet when I find that children who are not being taught are so disabled as creative thinkers, I see how necessary teaching is. In my work I have characterized creativity as a natural human process motivated by strong human needs. Critics of efforts to teach children to think creatively have been quick to point out that if my definition is valid there is no need for teaching. Yet skills are involved, and skills of any kind have to be practiced to function very well. Ever present in all our experiments, however, is the question of just how much and what we are teaching and how much of the progress we observe is due to facilitating conditions that free natural processes to operate.

Procedure

Out of the studies of teaching children to think creatively that I have examined, 142 involve qualification and presentation of evidence and a still larger number are narrative reports. Studies with college students and adults have not been considered. The tables summarize the nature of these studies and their degree of success.

In most cases I have had access to the documentary reports. In some cases, however, I have had to rely upon journal articles and abstracts, and some of these lacked information necessary for analysis. I am familiar with a number of studies for which I have been unable to obtain reports and these have not been included. Although my survey is not complete, in my opinion the evidence from the 142 studies summarized in the tables gives useful guidance.

Ways of Teaching Children to Think Creatively

To help organize the data from the 142 studies I have examined, I have classified them into the following categories of ways of teaching children to think creatively:
1. Training programs emphasizing the Osborn-Parnes Creative Problem Solving procedures (Osborn, 1963; Parnes, 1967 a, b) or modification of it.
2. Other disciplined approaches such as training in general semantics, creative research, and the like.
3. Complex programs involving packages of materials, such as the Purdue Creativity Program; Covington, Crutchfield and Davies' (1972) Productive Thinking Program; and the Myers and Torrance (1964, 1966 a, b) and Torrance (1965 a, b) ideabooks.
4. The creative arts as vehicles for teaching and practicing creative thinking.
5. Media and reading programs designed to teach and give practice in creative thinking.
6. Curricular and administrative arrangements designed to create favorable conditions for learning and practicing creative thinking.
7. Teacher-classroom variables, indirect and direct control, classroom climate, and the like.
8. Motivation, reward, competition, and the like.
9. Testing conditions designed to facilitate a higher level of creative functioning or more valid and reliable test performance.

The frequency and estimate of success attained in the studies in each of these categories are summarized in Table One. In judging success, a score of 1 was awarded if all the measured objectives of the experiment were attained. If the experiment had a single objective, such as increasing the degree of originality of thinking, a score of 1 was still assigned. However, if data were presented for fluency, flexibility, originality, and elaboration and the only statistically significant gain over the control group was in originality, a score of .25 was awarded. If 10 of 20 tests of significance reached the .05 level of confidence, a score of .50 was awarded.

It will be noted from Table One that the most popular approch to teaching children to think creatively has been through complex programs involving packages of materials, the manipulation of teacher-classroom variables, and the use of modifications of the Osborn-Parnes Creative Problem Solving training program. Somewhat less popular have been the creative arts as vehicles, motivation techniques, and facilitating testing conditions.

The best batting averages have been compiled by those experiments using the various modifications of the Osborn-Parnes training program and other disciplined approaches—over 90 percent. Programs involving the creative arts, complex programs involving packages of materials, media and reading programs, motivation, and facilitating testing conditions have also been relatively successful—around 75 percent. The poorest batting averages have been compiled by studies involving curricular and administrative arrangements and teacher-classroom variables.

Let us look more carefully at the summaries for each of the nine categories.

Table One.

Summary of successes in teaching children to think creatively according to type of intervention.

Type of Intervention	Number Studies	Number Successes	Percentage Successes
Osborn-Parnes CPS and/or modifications	22	20.0	91
Other disciplined approaches	5	4.6	92
Complex programs involving packages of materials	25	18.0	72
Creative arts as vehicle	18	14.5	81
Media and reading programs	10	7.8	78
Curricular and administrative arrangements	8	4.0	50
Teacher-Classroom variables, climate	26	14.4	55
Motivation, reward, competition	12	8.0	67
Facilitating testing conditions	16	11.0	69
TOTAL	142	102.3	72

Osborn-Parnes Modifications

From Table Two it will be noted that all of the experiments using combinations of techniques based on the Osborn-Parnes training program achieved some degree of success. The Torrance (1961 a, b) study which produced impressive results for the second and third grades but failed to produce significant results in the first grade was quite brief (20 minutes) and was later replicated with first graders with successful results by Cartledge and Krauser (1963) and Cropley and Feuring (1971). Almost any regular practitioner of this approach to teaching children to think creatively could furnish dozens of unpublished studies with results equally as impressive as the ones cited in Table Two.

Other Disciplined Procedures

From Table Three, it will be noted that I have included under "other disciplined procedures" a method of teaching reading involving creative dramatics and remediation, programs for training children in creative research, and a program for training in general semantics. It will be noted that all of these projects seem to have been rather successful. Perhaps their success can be attributed to the fact that all of them involved both the cognitive and affective attributes of the subjects and gave practice in creative thinking.

Packages of Materials

The experimental studies involving complex programs with packages of materials, as will be noted in Table Four, have been concentrated upon three programs: (1) the Covington, Crutchfield and Davies (1972) *Productive Thinking Program,* (2) the Purdue Creative Thinking Program, and (3) the Myers and Torrance ideabooks. Each of these sets of materials scores fairly well, especially when there is class and teacher involvement in their use. Without this involvement, however, the battling average for this category is rather low.

Less frequently evaluated are the Wisconsin materials developed by Davis and his associates, the Montessori materials, and the Chicago Inservice Training Kit. Only in the case of the Purdue Creativity Program have separate components and combinations of components

Table Two.

Summary of experiments involving Osborn-Parnes Creative Problem-Solving training and/or modifications.*

Investigator	Grade Level	Nature of Treatment	Significant (.05) Differences
Beleff (1968)	9th	Exercises in brainstorming and questioning in social studies	TTCT fluency
Bond (1963)	4th	Osborn-Parnes training	TTCT variables
Cartledge & Krauser (1963)	1st	Osborn principles; Torrance materials	TTCT variables
Chung (1968)	5th	Osborn/Torrance materials	TTCT variables High and Low IQ
Cropley & Feuring (1971)	1st	Osborn/Torrance materials	TTCT flexibility originality, elab.
Eberle (1965)	JHS	Osborn-Parnes and Myers-Torrance exercises	TTCT and Guilford variables
Eberle (1967)	8th	Osborn-Parnes; Myers-Torrance	TTCT and Guilford variables
Eherts (1961)	5th	Brainstorming and exercises	TTCT variables
Goodrich (1969)	6th	Exercises, open-structure, etc.	TTCT originality
Hutchinson (1963, 1967)	JHS	Brainstorming and other productive thinking	4 of 10 Guilford variables
J. C. Jones (1970)	5th 6th	Strategies of divergent thinking	TTCT all verbal figural fluency
Khatena (1969, 1971)	Kg.	Strategies of divergent thinking	TTCT variables
Olkin (1967)	9th	Creative problem solving	TTCT variables
Parnes (1966)	12th	Osborn-Parnes, programmed and instructor taught	TTCT and Guilford variables
Perkins (1963)	5th 6th 7th	Creative Problem Solving training	TTCT variables except elabora.
Rains & Chaturvedi (1970)	HS	Creative Problem Solving training	TTCT variables
Reyburn (1963)	5th	Divergent thinking in speaking and writing	TTCT fluency and originality
Rouse (1963, 1965)	EMR Ages 7-17	Brainstorming and creative problem solving	TTCT variables
Rusch et al. (1967)	6th	Deliberate strategies	5 of 7 Guilford and Denny-Ives variables
Sullivan (1969)	9-14 yrs.	Brainstorming and creative problem solving	Verbal creative abilities
Torrance (1961)	1st-3rd	Training in idea production	TTCT in 2nd and 3rd
Yee (1964)	12th	Osborn-Parnes training	TTCT variables High and Low IQ

Table Three.

Summary of experiments involving disciplined procedures other than Osborn-Parnes training program.*

Investigator	Grade Level	Nature of Treatment	Significant (.05) Differences
Allen (1969)	5th	Reading instruction involving remediation and creative dramatics	Fluency for all treatment groups. Originality in creative dramatics plus remediation. Elaboration in all creative dramatics treatments.
Dunn (1968)	4th-8th	Techniques of survey and descriptive research	Creative research products
Schaefer	4th-5th	One hour/week on creative expression, sense perception, etc.	TTCT variables
Torrance & Myers (1962)	6th Gifted	Experiences in historical, descriptive, and experimental research	TTCT variables and research products
True (1966)	6th	General semantics training	TTCT, fluency and flexibility

Table Four.

Summary of experiments involving complex training programs with packages of materials.*

Investigator	Grade Level	Nature of Treatment	Significant (.05) Differences
Bahlke (1967), Bahlke et al. (1967)	3rd 5th	Purdue Creativity Program	Figural and verbal originality; verbal fluency; figural and verbal elaboration on TTCT
Bahlke (1969), Bahlke et al. (1967)	4th 6th	Purdue Creativity Program	4th: All TTCT var. 5th: 5 of 7 TTCT 6th: 3 of 7 TTCT Exercises most eff.
Britton (1968)	6th	Myers-Torrance materials	TTCT verbal fluency flexibility and all figural variables
Casey (1968)	6th	Myers-Torrance	TTCT fluency, flexibility and originality
Covington (1967)	5th	Productive Thinking Program	Success in problem solving and reflective reading
Covington & Crutchfield (1965)	5th 6th	Productive Thinking Program	Problem solving and TTCT fluency and originality
Crutchfield (1966)	6th	Productive Thinking Program	Problem solving and TTCT fluency and originality

Table Four (continued).

Investigator	Grade Level	Nature of Treatment	Significant (.05) Differences
Davis (1971) Davis et al. (1969)	6th-8th	10-week Wisconsin course	TTCT fluency
DeRoche (1965)	6th	Creativity exercises in science	TTCT variables and science achievement
Eberle (1965, 1967)	JHS	Myers-Torrance materials	TTCT and Guilford variables
Feldhusen et al. (1969)	4th-6th	Purdue Creativity Program	TTCT verbal fluency and originality; fig. originality and elab.
Feldhusen et al. (1970)	4th-6th	Purdue Creativity Program	4th: All TTCT var. 5th: 5 of 7 TTCT 6th: 3 of 7 TTCT
Feldhusen et al. (1971); Thomas et al. (1971)	4th-6th	Purdue Creativity Program	Exercises single most effective component; presentation least
Freyermuth (1968)	Kg.	Montessori Program	TTCT variables
Olton (1969)	5th-6th	Productive Thinking Program	No gains without teacher and class involvement
Olton, Waldrop et al. (1967)	5th	Productive Thinking Program	Problems and TTCT variables; high and low IQ
Provus (1970)	3rd-8th	Chicago Inservice Training Kit	Subjective evaluations
Robinson (1969)	4th	Purdue Creativity Program	TTCT variables
Shackel & Lawrence (1969)	6th	Scrambled textbook programmed exercises	TTCT and French measures
Speedie et al. (1971)	4th-6th	Purdue Creative Program; 7 mo. later	4th Exercises and stories TTCT still held; effects washed out for 5th & 6th
Sporburg (1971)	6th	Productive Thinking Program; little class and teacher involvement	No effects on Guilford tests
Torrance (1965b)	4th-6th	Myers-Torrance exercises	No growth in creative writing
Treffinger & Ripple (1969)	4th-7th	Productive Thinking Program; without class and teacher involvement	No differences on any TTCT variables
Waldrop et al. (1969)	5th	Productive Thinking Program	TTCT variables and problems; high and low IQ
Woodliffe (1970)	5th	Myers-Torrance exercises	Workbook plus inservice program, highest TTCT gains

been evaluated. The exercises seem to come out best in these evaluations, and the presentations of principles of creative thinking poorest. All three programs seem to have been effective with both the high and low Intelligence Quotient groups.

Creative Arts

The 18 experiments involving one or more of the creative arts as a vehicle for teaching children to think creatively seem to have been rather effective, as will be noted from Table Five. These experiments range from programs in which the curriculum is built upon the creative arts (Fortson, 1969; Torrance & Fortson, 1968) through those involving the creative arts as an extracurricular activity (Skipper, 1969; Even, 1906) to those involving such experiences in single courses and those involving special summer or other out-of-school programs. Most of these programs have a distinct out-of-school flavor.

Media and Reading Programs

The experiments involving various types of media and reading programs score a rather good batting average, as will be noted in Table Six. There are a number of reading programs that have built-in creativity components but the Reading 360 Program (Clymer, et al., 1969) probably represents the most thorough-going attempt in this direction. It is the only such program for which there is even a partial evaluation, insofar as I know. The Imagi/Craft Program is quite similar to the Purdue Creativity Program and might have been included in the same category. Its initial field test was a large one and produced impressive results; thus, its originators have not seen fit to run additional evaluations. Of the ideas represented by the list of experiments listed in Table Six, the Junior Great Books Club, the set of stimuli developed by Baker, and the use of typewriters in elementary school creative writing seem to offer promise. My guess is that in the hands of a skilled teacher who understands creative learning and teaching any one of these devices could be counted upon to produce significant results.

Curricular and Administrative Arrangements

The various curricular and administrative arrangement studies listed in Table Seven do not appear to be tremendously promising. I know that there have been creativity evaluations of other curricular and administrative arrangements that purport to foster creative development (such as the open classroom, the ungraded school, and the like) but I have been unable to obtain reports of these efforts.

The only really bright spot in this category is Seides' experiment in placing artistically and musically talented slow learners in a talent class and giving them opportunities for talent development. This impresses me as a potentially productive idea and what happened in this experiment seems to be similar to what has happened with older youngsters talented in the arts in the North Carolina School of the Arts (Giannini, 1968).

Teacher-Classroom and Climate Variables

While the number of studies involving teacher-classroom and climate variables is impressive, their success in teaching creative thinking has not been outstanding, as will be noted from Table Eight. Studies that have relied upon the creative thinking abilities of teachers have rather consistently failed to show significant results. The motivations of the teacher seem to be more powerful; the two studies using the Torrance Creative Motivation Scale for identifying high and low creative teachers (James, 1964; Torrance, 1965b) showed reasonably promising, though not really outstanding, results.

Table Five.

Summary of experiments involving the creative arts as vehicles for teaching children to think creatively.*

Investigator	Grade Level	Nature of Treatment	Significant (.05) Differences
Engle (1970)	HS	Creative writing	Marketable, publishable creative writing
Even (1964)	11th	Visual arts	TTCT flexibility and originality
Fortson (1969)	Kg.	Creative-Aesthetic Approach	TTCT variables Starkweather original
Frankston (1964)	8th	Visual arts	No difference in art or poetry ratings
Grossman (1969)	Kg.	Visual arts	TTCT variables
Hagander (1967)	5th	Creative writing	TTCT variables
P. M. Jones (1968, 1969)	6th	Mime, drama, visual arts, imaginative activity	TTCT variables
Karioth (1968)	4th Disad.	Creative dramatics	TTCT variables for post-test only cond.; not for pretested groups
Madeja (1965)	HS	Visual art; convergent-divergent thinking	TTCT higher for divergent; high divergents made higher gains
Skipper (1969)	7th-10th	Living Arts Program	No gains on originality females, fluency and aesthetic sensitivity; males sensitivity to probs.
Torrance (1965e)	1st-3rd	Creative movement	TTCT variables
Torrance (1965b)	4th-6th	Creative writing	3 of 3 measures of creative writing
Torrance (1965b)	10th-12th	Man, Nature & the Arts Seminar (Perception)	10 of 12 TTCT var.
Torrance (1968, 1969); Torrance & Fortson (1968)	Kg.	Creative-Aesthetic Approach	TTCT variables
Torrance (1972)	Kg.	Alternate Kg. approaches, including Creat-Aesthetic	Creat. Aesthetic superior on questioning
Torrance & Torrance (1972)	1st-7th	Creativity Workshop (Summer)	TTCT variables
Vaughan & Myers (1971)	4th-5th	Music improvisation	TTCT fluency; musical creativity
Witt (1971)	2nd-4th	6-year program emphasizing music, art, drama, dance, etc.	Recognized creative achievements in one or more of the arts.

Table Six.

Summary of experiments involving reading programs and media as vehicles for teaching children to think creatively.*

Investigator	Grade Level	Nature of Treatment	Significant (.05) Differences
Abbott (1972)	4th	Multimedia sensory exercises	TTCT fluency, flexibility, and elaboration
Baker (1963)	5th	Films, pictures, recordings, etc. for writing	More original stories
Casper (1964)	5th Gifted	Junior Great Books Program	Guilford operational fluency; not originality
Dallenbach & DeYong (1969)	5th-6th	TV process series	Generally no gains on TTCT except parochial students
Karnes (1963)	4th	Typing, creative writing	Creative thinking measures and creative writing
O'Brien et al. (1964)	Nurs.	Increased number of toys	Increase in observed imaginative activities
Thatcher (1965)	5th-6th	Basal Reading vs. Individual Reading	Ind. Read. higher on TTCT but not conclusive
Nash & Torrance (1970)	1st	Reading 360 Program	TTCT fluency, flexibility, originality; questioning
Torrance (1964), Torrance & Gupta (1964ab), Torrance (1965)	4th	Imagi/Craft Program	TTCT variables
Torrance (1970)	1st	Manipulation of toys	Question asking

Most of the studies that have focused on observation and analysis of classroom interaction have been unsuccessful. However, most of them have been doctoral studies lacking in strong commitment from the school systems involved. Where highly competent and seasoned persons have been involved—Soar (1968), Clark and Trowbridge (1971), Mitchell (1967, 1971), with an inservice trainer such as George I. Brown (1971)—the results have been much more promising. A number of promising sidelights worth noting emerge from this category of studies. There are indications that the verbal creative thinking abilities receive useful practice in expert indirect influence teaching while the figural creative thinking abilities, especially elaboration, receive such stimulation under the expert direct teacher. The results obtained by Torrance (1969 a, b, c, d) with dyadic interaction also suggests that experimentation with small group arrangements might be promising.

Motivation Studies

A number of critics of the studies reviewed in the previous section have argued that the results obtained in the studies summarized in the foregoing tables have resulted from increased

Table Seven.

Summary of experiments involving curricular and administrative arrangements for teaching children to think creatively.*

Investigator	Grade Level	Nature of Treatment	Significant (.05) Differences
Bennett et al. (1971)	HS Gifted	Independent study	Unique projects; high subjective evaluation
Gold (1965)	4th-6th Gifted	Self-directed study	No significant gains on TTCT
Paton (1965)	4-yr. olds	Language enrichment	No significant gains on TTCT
Phillips & Torrance (1972)	1st-3rd	Cognitive-structured curriculum	Superior growth in causal thinking
Seides (1967)	7th Slow	Placement in talent class (art, music)	TTCT variables
Torrance & Phillips (1969)	1st-2nd	Cognitive-structured curriculum	1st: Fig. & Verb. Flex. 2nd: Verbal Orig. & Fig. Elab.
Torrance & Phillips (1970)	1st-3rd	Cognitive-structured plus consultants in art, music creative writing, etc.	1st: 4 of 7 TTCT 2nd: 7 of 7 TTCT 3rd: 4 of 7 TTCT
Vreeland (1967)	Elem. JHS	Summer enrichment program	Some negative effects Generally no effect on TTCT

motivation rather than from anything that was taught. The results summarized in Table Nine certainly suggest that motivation alone is powerful enough to "make a difference." Most of these results, however, have been achieved through different kinds of extrinsic motivation and generally these kinds of motivation have to be reapplied each time the desired performance is required and cannot be counted upon for continued creative thinking.

Facilitating Testing Conditions

Throughout the history of the development of tests of creative thinking ability, there has been a recognition that children have to be motivated to think creatively, if one is to obtain a valid measure of their creative thinking ability. Early in my own work, I experimented with extended time limits, take-home tests, and variations in instructions. The elements finally packaged in 1966 as the research edition of the *Torrance Tests of Creative Thinking* represents a considerable compromise between what my associates and I considered reasonable and feasible for use in schools and what we considered ideal. We realize that our solution is not the best one possible, and we are still considering and evaluating other alternatives. The results summarized in Table Ten indicate that improved performance on tests of creative thinking can probably be obtained by appropriate warm-up just prior to the administration of the test, by a game-like atmosphere, and by providing a variety of visual materials in the testing room. Take-home administrations or extended time limits may produce more valid results, but introduce a variety of practical problems that seem difficult to solve. Some children's lives are so completely and rigidly scheduled that they are unable to find the time to write the responses that they think of with take-home tests. There are also the elements of control,

Table Eight.

Summary of experiments involving teacher-classroom and climate variables in teaching children to think creatively.*

Investigator	Grade Level	Nature of Treatment	Significant (.05) Differences
Broome (1967)	5th	Teacher creativity	No differences on TTCT
Castelli (1964)	3rd-6th	Teacher creativity	No differences in classroom behavior
Clark & Trowbridge (1971)	All Levels	Extensive inservice education	Increased divergent thinking in classroom (Aschner-Gallagher)
Crabtree (1967)	2nd	Jointly-determined vs. predetermined structure	In jointly-determined, more originality, flexibility, constructive play
Denny (1966)	6th	Observation, climate, structuring	No increase on Guilford tests
Enochs (1964)	5th	Teacher inservice; application of Torrance principles	TTCT originality and total
Haddon & Lytton (1968)	11-12 yr.	Informal progressive teaching in primary school	6 divergent thinking tests
Haddon & Lytton (1971)	Ditto	Follow up 4 yrs. later	Verbal tests held up
James (1964)	7th	High and low teachers on Torrance Creative Motivation Scale	Boys of high teachers, 4 of 8 TTCT var. Girls of high teachers 5 of 8 TTCT var.
Kaltsounis (1969)	4th-6th Deaf	Mutual language method vs. combined method	No difference on TTCT
Mann (1966)	1st	Climate for preconscious freedom	No differences on TTCT
Marburg (1965)	5th	Classroom climate; high and low MTAI	No differences on TTCT
Mitchell (1967, 1971)	3rd-6th	Sensitivity training (Brown)	14 of 23 subgroups showed changes on TTCT variables
Raina (1971)	8th-9th	Creative vs. noncreative school climate	TTCT variables
Rappel (1970)	2nd-5th	Direct vs. indirect influence (Flanders)	No differences on TTCT except figural flex
Soar (1968)	3rd-6th	Degree of indirectness (Flanders)	TTCT variables related to a degree of indirectness
Torrance (1965b)	1st-6th	Application of princ. (respectful of questions, ideas, etc.)	Critical incidents of creative classroom behavior
Torrance (1965b)	Kg.-6th	Inservice on rewarding creative beh.	12 of 44 TTCT in favor of Exp.
Torrance (1965b)	Kg.-6th	Torrance Creative Motivation Scale of teachers	TTCT variables for K-3; creative writing, 4-6
Torrance (1969ade, 1970d)	Kg.	Dyads and alone	TTCT originality

Table Eight (continued).

Investigator	Grade Level	Nature of Treatment	Significant (.05) Differences
Torrance (1969b)	Kg.	Dyads, alone, class	Greater willingness to try diff. in dyads
Weber (1967)	4th	Indirectness of control in first 3 years and 4th	TTCT verbal var. under indirect first 3 yrs.; TTCT figural elab. in 4th
Werner (1972)	1st-6th	Minicourse	No differences on TTCT
Wodtke (1963); Wodtke & Wallen (1965)	2nd-5th	High and low controlling teachers	Low controlling; TTCT verbal measures in 4; high controlling; TTCT elab. in 5th

Table Nine.

Summary of experiments involving motivation to facilitate creative thinking.*

Investigator	Grade Level	Nature of Treatment	Significant (.05) Differences
Chung (1968)	5th	Achievement-ego motiv. vs. task-reward motiv.	Task-reward raised TTCT fluency and flexibility
Raina (1968)	9th	Competition, prizes	TTCT variables
Raina & Chaturvedi (1968)	HS	Competition, prizes	TTCT variables
Torrance (1965b)	6th	Reward for originality vs. correctness	Reward for originality resulted in more original stories
Torrance (1965b)	6th	Reward for fluency vs. originality	Reward for originality resulted in more original ideas
Torrance (1965b)	1st-6th	Competition vs. practice	TTCT flu., 1, 3, 4 TTCT flx., 2, 4 TTCT orig., 2, 3, 6
Torrance (1965b)	1st-6th	Peer critical vs. peer creative evaluation	23 of 56 differences on TTCT figural
Torrance (1965b)	Kg.-6th	Unevaluated practice vs. evaluated practice	53 of 84 differences on TTCT figural
Torrance (1965b)	3rd-6th	Publication of creative writing in magazine	9 of 12 measures of creative writing
Turknett (1971)	Kg., 2nd, 4th	Group vs. individual reward	No differences, TTCT
Ward, Kogan, Pankove (1970)	5th	Reward for production of ideas immediate and delayed	Fluency higher on Wallach tasks

Table Ten.

Summary of experiments involving testing conditions.*

Investigator	Grade Level	Nature of Treatment	Significant (.05) Differences
Aliotti (1969)	1st Disad.	Movement and verbal warm up day prior to testing	TTCT differences not significant
Boersma & O'Bryan (1968)	4th	Standard vs. relaxed	Relaxed: TTCT
Elkind et al. (1970)	5-12 yrs.	Interruption of interesting vs. uninteresting task	Uninteresting Wallach-Kogan variables
Feldhusen et al. (1971)	5th, 8th	Standard, incubation take home, game-like	Highest TTCTr's with ach. on Standard and lowest on game-like
Harper & Powell (1971)	1st-3rd	Absolute music vs. program music	Absolute music, TTCT
Khatena (1971b)	10th 12th	Variations in time limits for response	Increased time for incubation, increased originality, TTCT
Kogan & Morgan (1969)	5th	Test-like and game-like (timed)	Game-like, higher fluency and unique responses Wallach tests
Mohan (1970)	4th	Cue rich and cue poor testing room	TTCT variables; helped high creatives more than lows
Nash (1971)	1st Disad.	Warm-up immediately prior to testing	TTCT figural
Norton (1971)	6th	Music	No significant differences TTCT
Roweton & Spencer (1972)	Intermediate	Practice	Significant effect only on Figural A, TTCT
Torrance (1969a)	6th Gifted	Take home after timed administration	Take home more valid for teacher curiosity nominations, TTCT
Towell (1972)	4th	Untimed	No significant increment, TTCT
Van Mondfrans et al. (1971)	5th 8th	Standard, incubation, take home, game-like	Standard, highest verbal means; take home, scores that fit best concept of creativity as unitary factor orthogonal to intell., TTCT
Ward (1969a)	Nurs.	Cul-poor, cue-rich environment	No significant environment effect Wallach-Kogan measures
Ward (1969b)	7-8 yrs.	Successive time periods	Increased uncommonness with time.

copying, getting unauthorized help, losing booklets, and the like. (Many schools will not even permit children to take home their textbooks.) Scoring problems are also compounded by the fact that some children produce such a large number of responses that the scoring task becomes quite time-consuming.

Summary

An effort has been made to summarize the results of 142 studies designed to test approaches to teaching children to think creatively. Though most of these studies use performances on tests of creative thinking and other creative school performances as criteria, it is contended that the evidence provided by these studies provides useful guidance to educators.

The most frequently reported types of experiments are those that emphasize teacher-classroom variables, complex programs involving packages of materials, and modifications of the Osborn-Parnes training program in creative problem solving. Those having the highest percentages of success in teaching children to think creatively are those that emphasize the Osborn-Parnes training program, other disciplined approaches, the creative arts, and media-oriented programs.

In answer to the question posed by the title of this paper, it does indeed seem possible to teach children to think creatively. The most successful approaches seem to be those that involve both cognitive and emotional functioning, provide adequate structure and motivation, and give opportunities for involvement, practice, and interaction with teachers and other children. Motivating and facilitating conditions certainly make a difference in creative functioning but differences seem to be greatest and most predictable when deliberate teaching is involved.

Footnote

*References for tables can be located in the original publication of this article, *The Journal of Creative Behavior (1972), (6),* 114-143.

References

Brown, G. I. (1971). *Human teaching for human learning.* New York: Viking.

Cartledge, C. J. & Krauser, E. L. (1963). Training first-grade children in creative thinking under quantitative and qualitative motivation. *Journal of Educational Psychology, 54,* 295-299.

Clark, B. M. & Trowbridge, N. (1971). Encouraging creativity through in-service teacher education. *Journal of Research and Development in Education, 4 (3),* 87-94.

Clymer, T. et. al. (1969). *Reading 360 Program.* Lexington, MA: Ginn.

Covington, M. V., Crutchfield, R. S. & Davies, L. B. (1972). *The productive thinking program.* Columbus, OH: Merrill.

Cronbach, L. J. (1970). Intelligence? Creativity? A parsimonious re-interpretation of the Wallach-Kogan data. *American Educational Research Journal, 7,* 351-357.

Cropley, A. J. & Feuring, E. (1971). Training creativity in young children. *Developmental Psychology, 4,* 105.

Elkind, D., Deblinger, Jr. & Adler, D. (1970). Motivation and creativity: The context effect. *American Educational Research Journal, 7,* 351-357.

Even, R. E. (1906). An experimental study of the comparative effect of selected art experiences on the creative performance and attitudes of academically superior students. Doctoral dissertation, University of Minnesota. (University Microfilms Order No. 64-4062; *Dissertation Abstracts* 24:4476).

Fortson, L. R. (1969). The creative-aesthetic approach to readiness and beginning reading and mathematics in the kindergarten. Doctoral disertation, University of Georgia. (University Microfilms Order No. 70-10, 187; *Dissertation Abstracts* 30: 5339-A).

Giannini, V. (1968). Nurturing talent and creativity in the arts. In P. Heist (Ed.), *The creative college student: An unmet challenge.* San Francisco: Jossey-Bass (pp. 73-83).

Harvey, O. J., Hoffmeister, J. K., Coates, C. & White, B. J. (1970). A partial evaluation of Torrance's test of creativity. *American Educational Research Journal, 7,* 359-372.

James G. R. (1964). The relationship of teacher characteristics and pupil creativity. Doctoral dissertation, University of North Carolina. (University Microfilms Order No. 64-9419; *Dissertation Abstracts* 25: 4544).

Mitchell, B. M. (1967). An assessment of changes in creativity factors of elementary school children involved in a creativity project. Doctoral dissertation, University of Denver. (University Microfilms Order No. 68-2399; *Dissertation Abstracts* 28: 3376).

Mitchell, B. M. (1971). The classroom pursuit of creativity: One strategy that worked. *Journal of Research and Development in Education, 4 (3),* 57-62.

Myers, R. E. & Torrance, E. P. (1964). *Invitations to thinking and doing.* Lexington, MA: Ginn.

Myers, R. E. & Torrance, E. P. (1966a). *For those who wonder.* Lexington, MA: Ginn.

Myers, R. E. & Torrance, E. P. (1966b). *Plots, puzzles and ploys.* Lexington, MA: Ginn.

Osborn, A. F. (1963). *Applied imagination.* (3rd Ed.) New York: Scribner's.

Parnes, S. J. (1967a). Methods and educational programs for stimulating creativity: A representative list. *Journal of Creative Behavior, 2,* 71-75.

Parnes, S. J. (1967b). *Creative behavior guidebook.* New York: Scribner's.

Skipper, C. E. (1969). A study of the development of creative abilities in adolescence. Dayton, OH: Living Arts Program.

Soar, R. S. (1968). Optimum teacher-pupil interaction for pupil growth. *Educational Leadership, 26,* 275-280.

Torrance, E. P. (1961a). Factors affecting creative thinking in children: an interim report. *Merrill-Palmer Quarterly, 7,* 171-180.

Torrance, E. P. (1961b). Priming creative thinking in the primary grades. *Elementary School Journal, 62,* 34-41.

Torrance, E. P. (1965a). Exploring the limits on the automation of guided, planned experiences in creative thinking. In Roucek, J. (Ed.), *Programmed Teaching* (pp. 57-70). New York: Philosophical Library.

Torrance, E. P. (1965b). *Rewarding creative behavior: Experiments in classroom creativity.* Englewood Cliffs, NJ: Prentice.

Torrance, E. P. (1969a). Curiosity of gifted children and performance on timed and untimed tests of creativity. *Gifted Child Quarterly, 13,* 155-158.

Torrance, E. P. (1969b). *Dimensions in early learning series: creativity.* Belmont, CA: Fearon.

Torrance, E. P. (1969c). Peer influences on preschool children's willingness to try difficult tasks. *Journal of Psychology, 72,* 189-194.

Torrance, E. P. (1969d). *A three-year study of the influence of a creative-aesthetic approach to school readiness and beginning reading and arithmetic on creative development.* Athens, GA: Research and Development Center in Educational Stimulation, University of Georgia.

Torrance, E. P. (1971, July). Long-range predictive studies of the Torrance tests of creative thinking and their international extensions. *Paper presented at the XVIIth International Congress of Applied Psychology,* Belgium.

Torrance, E. P. & Fortson, L. R. (1968). Creativity among young children and the creative-aesthetic approach. *Education, 89,* 27-30.

Wees, W. R. (1971). *Nobody can teach anyone anything.* New York: Doubleday.

PART TWO: Recent Trends in Teaching Children and Adults to Think Creatively

The foregoing paper (Torrance, 1972) was prepared in 1972. Mostly, I made an attempt to include all studies in which an attempt was made to teach children to think creatively. It will be noted that almost no study had been done before 1960. I (Torrance, 1986) conducted another study in which I attempted to locate all the studies with elementary and secondary children and also included 76 studies involving college students and adults. It was found that the pace of this type of research had continued unabated. However, some new trends emerged in the type of treatment and in the criteria used for evaluating the outcomes. This paper will emphasize these changes.

Training for Creativity Skills as Seen in 1983

In spite of massive evidence, there are continuous and vigorous oppositions to attempts to train children and adults in creativity skills (Keating, 1980; Mansfield & Busse, 1981; Stanley, 1980). There were still arguments that creative problem solving skills cannot be taught. The time devoted to the teaching of the skills tended to decline and there existed a failure to master the basics, and the hundreds of experiments demonstrated that the efforts lacked validity and had methodological flaws.

In 1983, I examined 166 experimental studies at the elementary and secondary level and 76 at the college and adult level conducted since the 1972 survey.

Table One presents a survey of successes in teaching students to think creatively according to the type of training procedure for the 166 elementary and secondary studies since the 1972 survey and compares these results with those revealed by the 1972 survey.

Although there are fewer studies in the 1983 survey than in the 1972 survey using the Osborn-Parnes Creative Problem Solving procedure, the percentage of successes continues to be higher than for other categories of experimental intervention. However, this is somewhat misleading as many of the other types of training programs rely upon the Osborn-Parnes procedures as a general system and combine it with other strategies. The difficulty may be that these procedures are not taught well enough and practiced, weakening the effects. In 1983, there was a big increase in the number of studies using other disciplined approaches (from 5 to 22). However, there seems to be little or no tendency in these experimental studies to embrace such disciplined procedures as Synectics, Edward deBono's Lateral Thinking, and the Japanese procedures such as the "KJ" and "NM" methods. Instead, the experimenters tend to devise their own disciplined procedures.

Table One.

Summary of successes in teaching students to think creatively according to type of intervention prior to and after 1972.

Type of Intervention	No. Studies 1972	No. Studies 1983	No. Success 1972	No. Success 1983	Percent Success 1972	Percent Success 1983
Osborn-Parnes CPS or modification	22	7	20.0	6.2	91	88
Other disciplined CPS procedures	5	22	4.6	16.2	92	73
Complex programs involving packages	25	31	18.0	18.7	72	60
Complex programs involving combination of strategies	—	15	—	11.5	—	77
Creative arts as vehicles	18	18	14.5	13.1	81	73
Media and reading programs	10	3	7.8	1.25	78	42
Curricular and administrative arr.	8	5	4.0	2.7	50	54
Teacher-classroom variables	26	14	14.4	8.8	55	63
Motivation, reward, competition	12	6	8.0	3.5	67	58
Facilitating testing conditions	16	20	11.0	14.1	69	70
Affective education programs	—	13	—	10.3	—	79
Altered awareness	—	6	—	4.0	—	67
Other conditions	—	6	—	2.8	—	47
Total	142	166	102.3	112.6	72	68

The popularity of complex programs involving packages of materials continued but the percentage of successes for these dropped somewhat (from 72 to 60%). However, a new category of complex programing involving a combination of strategies emerged and the record of successes of these experiments was fairly high (77% in 15 studies). The use of the arts (drama, music, visual arts, etc.) continued to be fairly common (18 both in 1972 and 1983). The use of media and reading programs to teach creative thinking skills declined both in number and percentage of successes (from 10 to 3 studies and from 78 to 42%). The use of curricular and administrative arrangements and teacher-classroom variables remained at about the same number and level of success, as did facilitating testing conditions and the use of motivation, reward, and competition. In addition to complex programs involving combination of strategies, two other categories emerged: affective education programs and altered awareness such as meditation, fantasy, and imagery training. The affective education programs showed a success rate of 70% and the altered awareness treatments showed one of 67%.

Table Two presents a comparison of all of the elementary and secondary studies (both the 1972 and 1983 surveys) with the college and adult studies in the present survey.

There are striking differences between the elementary/secondary and college/adult studies both in type of training and in percentage of successes. As a whole, the college/adult training was somewhat more successful than the elementary/secondary training (86% compared to 70%). Especially striking is the lack of college/adult studies using complex programs involving packages of curriculum materials; media and reading; curricular and administrative arrangements; teacher/classroom variables; motivation, reward, and competition. There were also few college/adult studies involving the creative arts, and effective education programs. The most frequently used intervention at the college/adult level was the use of complex programs involving several strategies. In many cases these were courses in creative thinking or regular subject matter courses taught by creative procedures. Also, there were proportionately more studies at the college/adult level using mediation, fantasy, and other altered awareness procedures than at the elementary/secondary level. Interestingly, however, there was an absence

Table Two.

Comparison of successes of different approaches to teaching creative thinking at the elementary/high school and college/adult levels.

Type of Intervention	No. Studies		No. Successes		Percentage	
	Elem/HS	Adults	Elem/HS	Adults	Elem/HS	Adults
Osborn-Parnes CPS & modifications	29	17	26.2	15.0	90	88
Other disciplined CPS procedures	27	11	20.8	10.9	77	99
Complex programs involving packages	56	2	36.7	1.7	66	85
Complex programs combining strategies	15	26	11.5	22.7	77	87
Creative arts as vehicles	36	4	27.6	2.9	77	72
Media and reading	13	0	10.1	—	78	—
Curricular and administrative arr.	13	0	6.7	—	52	—
Teacher-classroom variables	40	0	23.2	—	58	—
Motivation, reward, competition	18	0	11.5	—	64	—
Facilitating testing conditions	36	0	25.1	—	70	—
Affective educational programs	13	2	10.3	—	79	85
Altered awareness	6	7	4.0	5.2	67	74
Other conditions	6	7	2.8	6.8	47	97
Total	308	76	214.9	65.2	70	86

of discussion about the appropriateness of these methods at the elementary/secondary level. However, the author is personally aware of studies of this nature at the elementary school level that were aborted on account of agitation by community pressure groups.

Although, there seems to be a general trend for the emergence of affective and altered state procedures, most of the training methods are highly cognitive in their approach. For example, Robert Meeker (1979) used the Structure of Intellect (SOI) Model for a training program with gifted children in grades 3-6 with pre and posttesting and experimental and control groups. The experimental groups showed statistically significant gains greater than the controls on the SOI tests of creativity. This experimental design and the results characterize a majority of the studies reported during the past decade. A new trend that seems to be emerging is the possible superiority of well-planned training programs involving music and imagery (Lowery, 1982), creative writing (Coleman, 1982), consciousness raising (Gourley, Kelly, & Zucca, 1977), practice in environmental scanning (Friedman, Raymond, & Feldhusen, 1978) and other procedures for helping students tap into their higher levels of consciousness. From the results reported in recent years, there are indications that some of these technologies for tapping into higher levels of consciousness may be at least as effective as the teaching of deliberate, systematic procedures of creative problem solving.

There has been a continuing debate as to whether creative thinking skills should be taught directly and through courses separate from the rest of the curriculum. Edward deBono (1975, 1983) has been the leading advocate of the direct teaching of creative thinking skills (or "lateral thinking" as he calls it). His instructional materials have been rather widely adopted in England, Australia, Ireland, and Venezuela. In fact, he (deBono, 1978) reported that 106,000 teachers in Venezuela were trained to use his program and every school child takes a course in thinking skills (2 hours of direct instruction per week). He defended the reduction in time spent in teaching information in order to focus on the direct teaching of thinking.

For some time, deBono (1969, 1983) has attacked the fallacy that we do not need to do anything specific to help highly intelligent individuals learn how to think. He also contended that many highly intelligent people are rather ineffective thinkers. From time to time, research in gifted education has indicated that intellectually gifted students are actually poorer problem solvers than average ability students. With increased attention to the teaching of thinking skills in gifted education, it might be expected that these findings would be outdated. However, in 1982, Ludlow and Woodrum reported a study that indicates that the teaching of thinking skills in gifted education has not been very pervasive. With 20 gifted learners and 20 average learners matched for age and sex, they found that the average learners used significantly more advanced thinking strategies than the gifted learners when continued access to feedback was permitted. The gifted learners demonstrated superior performance on problems involving memory and attention but not on measures of performance efficiency and strategy selection. Gifted education literature is replete with suggestions for teaching creative problem-solving skills to gifted children and with descriptions of program materials that have been used successfully for this purpose. Some of the more promising suggestions have been offered by Brown (1983); Callahan (1978); Davis (1971); Dirkes (1977); Firestien and Treffinger (1983); Foster (1979); Khatena (1978); Kopelman, Galasso, and Strom (1977); Shibles (1979); Torrance (1979); Treffinger (1980a, b); and Wilson, Greer, and Johnson (1973). Much new material for facilitating creative thinking has emerged during the past decade (Callahan & Renzulli, 1977; deBono, 1975, 1976; Macaranas, 1982; Manning & Brown, 1979; Myers & Torrance, 1984; Renzulli, 1973).

Two national/international curriculum and interscholastic competition projects emerged during this decade and did much to introduce and give practice in creative thinking skills in gifted education, the Future Problem Solving Program (Crabbe, 1982; Torrance, 1980) and Olympics of the Mind (Gourley, 1981). Currently, it is estimated that over 150,000 gifted students participate each year in each of these programs in the United States alone. Considerable international interest has been aroused by both of these programs.

The Future Problem Solving Program was founded in 1974 by E. Paul and Pansy Torrance (Crabbe, 1982; Torrance & Torrance, 1978) with the goals of helping gifted students to:

1. Develop richer images of the future
2. Become more creative in their thinking
3. Develop and increase their communication skills, both oral and written
4. Develop and increase their teamwork skills
5. Integrate a problem solving model into their lives
6. Develop and increase their research skills

Each year, program participants suggest topics for the next year. These suggestions are then combined into a ballot which is submitted to all participants and the five topics receiving the largest number of votes are selected for study. Three of them become topics of the practice problems for which professional feedback is given; one is used for the state bowls, and the other is used for the national/international bowl. These five problems provide the solid substantive core for the year's program and changes each year. The Osborn-Parnes Creative Problem Solving Model was chosen for use in the program. The national organization also sponsors a scenario writing program each year, an advanced program in which teams study problems submitted by cooperating government and community agencies, corporations, and the like. Some states include community involvement and visual arts programs.

The Olympics of the Mind program was founded by Samuel Micklus and Theodore Gourley at Glassboro State College in New Jersey and had its debut in May 1978 with 28 New Jersey schools participating. This program was designed for highly creative students capable of developing unusual ideas and insights. Identification is based on the sport's tryout method and evaluation is based on the performances of the participants. The program appeals especially to students gifted in industrial design, but also has places for students gifted in creative writing, acting, leadership, and other creative expressive and problem-solving skills. Like the Future Problem Solving Program, this program spread rapidly to include students from all 50 states of the USA, many Canadian provinces, and several countries overseas. For the World Competition, both long-term and spontaneous problems are used. Long-term problems are given to participants (who work as a team) in advance of local, district, state or world competition. This affords teams time to prepare their own creative solutions to the problems. Spontaneous problems are given to the teams on the day of the competitions to challenge their ability to think "on their feet." The apparent success of this program demonstrated that the varsity sports model can be used to develop other types of gifted programs.

Throughout creativity research, various criteria have been used to judge, analyze, criticize and augment creativity behaviors. These behaviors can involve divergent thinking and/or ideational fluency.

Table Three gives an analysis of the kinds of criteria used in the 166 elementary/secondary and 76 college/adult studies examined. These data indicate that there is still a tendency to use psychometric measures such as divergent thinking or creative thinking scores to evaluate these studies. However, there is also considerable evidence of the use of more "real life" creativity indicators, such as the evaluation of creative products, creative behavior, and creative self-perceptions. This is especially true of the college/adult studies where earning money creatively, indicators of increased health and feelings of well-being, increased profits, and medical treatment techniques were among the criteria. Increased use of these more realistic criteria should help counteract common criticisms of creativity training research concerning the exclusive use of divergent thinking or creativity tests.

To get a better understanding of the nature of criteria other than scores on divergent thinking or creativity tests, the author examined the specific nature of the indicators used.

Table Three.

Frequencies and percentages of each type of criteria was used in the elementary/secondary and college/adult studies of effectiveness of creativity training.

Category or Subcategory of Criteria	Elem./Secondary		College/Adult	
	Number	Percent	Number	Percent
Psychometric Criteria:				
TTCT (Torrance Tests)	126	76	29	39
SOI (Guilford Tests)	9	5	11	15
Other tests, including author-developed	38	23	21	28
Non-psychometric Criteria:				
Creative Products	6	4	8	11
Creative Behavior	14	8	28	37
Creative self-perception (self evaluation, satisfaction, attitudes, etc.)	6	4	21	28

The following are examples of some of these indicators found in the elementary/secondary studies:

1. Various kinds of expressions of increased satisfaction.
2. Evidences that the promotion of creative performances does not detract from academic achievement.
3. Subjects produced more types of creative writing.
4. Personality growth and healthier self concepts.
5. Student wrote a novel.
6. Students showed better attitude toward mathematics.
7. Self questionnaires, blind judging of drawings for creativity, direct observations of behavior, and personal interviews.
8. Socio-emotional changes resulting from the creative curriculum of Developmental Therapy.
9. Making decisions to follow creative alternatives.

As might be expected, the types of non-psychometric criteria used in the college/adult studies are far more varied than those used in the elementary-secondary ones. The following are examples of what might be called "bottom line" criteria reported in the adult studies:

1. A 5-year followup revealed a $60 per man/hour profit on time spent on Creative Problem Solving training (10,000 hours).
2. A physician was trained in Creative Problem Solving and now uses the techniques with his patients.
3. The use of specific methods designed to increase certain creative abilities resulted in increases in knowledge of course subject matter.
4. A course required students to write a "creativity policy" for an organization, plan 50 staff meetings, and earn $100 in a creative way. These were used as the basis for evaluating the effectiveness of the training.

The following are examples of task outcomes used as criteria for evaluating the effectiveness of college/adult creativity training:

1. Observed improvements in the dynamics of groups in performing tasks.
2. Evaluation of product creativity for novelty, resolution, elaboration, and synthesis.

3. Aphasia patients were given "divergent thinking therapy" and observed for improvement in speech.
4. After a workshop, author observed indicators of increased humanization of a school and creative productivity of the teachers.
5. Creative art or handicraft, creative writing, ideas for two inventions, and ideas for creative teaching methods.
6. Subjects performed better in coping with "real life" situational tests and were generally more productive.

The following kinds of criteria resulted from questionnaires and interviews:

1. A sample of elderly people in a creative art project reported improved health, increased sociability, greater activity and participation in creative activities other than art, etc.
2. After a creativity workshop, participants expressed more positive attitudes about their creativity and their confidence in fostering creativity.
3. Workshop participants rated themselves on "creativity traits" and "leadership traits."
4. Assessment was made of creative problem solving problem programs of the creativity workshop participants.
5. Student logs and self-evaluation following a creativity course.

The following multi-level criteria were reported in college/adult studies:

1. Samples of autobiographical writing, observation of the subject's behavior, and self-evaluations.
2. A post-workshop evaluation was used to assess changes in the actual behavior of the participants.
3. Subjects engaged in meditation training were evaluated on a criterion reference basis for heightened consciousness, perceived changes, invention, unusual visualization, humor, and fantasy.
4. Graduates of a nursing program were evaluated by employers and self-evaluated.

The following are examples of non-psychometric instruments used in assessing the effectiveness of creativity training:

1. Projective style device used to see if students identified with creativity symbols.
2. Students' artistic drawings were evaluated by judges.
3. Writing assignments were rated for creativity.
4. A comparison of the number of alternatives the subjects were able to generate before and after the training.
5. Creative Life Line Curve, self-perceived creative production across the life span.

Trends in Creativity Training Since 1983

A more thorough survey has been made of the studies conducted since 1983 as well as a larger number of studies involving college students and adults before 1983. While I have not yet completed any detailed and systematic analysis of the changes reflected by these studies, certain trends are apparent. I shall summarize these briefly.

1. *Increased attention to specific creative problem solving skills.*

Although some attention has been given to the development of specific creativity thinking skills prior to 1983, there seems to be an increase of such. Guilford (1959) and Torrance (1966) identified problem finding as an important thinking ability and included tests of it in their batteries. Getzels and Csikzentmihalyi (1976) identified it as important to creative performance. However, it was not until later that studies involving training in problem finding appeared. A number of such studies have been conducted. For example: Basadur, Graen and Green (1982) conducted a study of effects ideation, problem finding and the solutions of problems of research in an industrial organization. They found that the problem finding and idea productions training resulted in significant systematic measures of effects both immediately after training and two weeks later. The results also suggest that the ideation trained and problem finding trained produced different results.

Another example is a study by Stratton and Brown (1972) who conducted a study emphasizing training in production and the judgment of solutions. They found that the production trained increased productivity but decreased quality.

All in all this line of research seems to indicate need for training and practice in each of the phases of the creative solving process.

2. *Cognitive theory emphasis*

For a considerable period of time cognitive theorists showed little interest in creative problem solving. However, in recent years we see quite a flurry of interest among cognitive theorists in creative problem solving. In a 1984 review, Norman Frederiksen reviewed quite a number of studies and theorists and their suggestions regarding how to teach creative problem solving. He shows how these suggestions are similar and different from the suggestions coming from creativity research itself. The cognitive theorists give attention to such concepts as information processing, the structure of problems, the elements in problem solving process, problem solving procedures, and pattern recognition. There has recently been a number of textbooks covering these concepts. For instance, Anderson (1982); Neves and Anderson (1981) describe in detail a theory about the acquisition of problem solving expertise. There also have appeared a number of courses on problem solving representing the cognitive approach. For instance, Rubenstein (1980); Larkin and Reif (1976); Elstein, Shulman and Sprafka (1978) work in this area. Frederiksen summarized these suggestions of cognitive psychology for instruction as follows:

1. Teach cognitive processes
2. Teach development of problem structure
3. Teach pattern recognition
4. Teach problem solving procedures
5. Teach knowledge base
6. Teach development of knowledge structures
7. Teach aptitude
8. Provide practice with feedback
9. Use models in instruction

3. *Guided fantasy and guided imagery*

Although guided fantasy and guided imagery have been mentioned as important in creative problem solving by numerous writers, it has only been recently that we have had any experiments on the efficacy on creative problem solving. Hershey and Kearns (1979) reported an experiment on the effects of guided fantasy on creative writing ability. They compared groups having guided fantasy sessions with groups having relaxation training. They found that the guided fantasy group achieved significantly better than the relaxation group on flexibility, fluency and originality of the Torrance Tests of creative training.

Khatena (1984) conducted a number of studies which demonstrated the positive effects of creative imagination imagery on creative problem solving. He also discusses the rationale training procedures and the measurement of creativity imagination imagery.

4. *Thematic fantasy play and the use of games*

There has been an increasing number of studies, mostly with preschool children, involving training for thematic fantasy play and games. Saltz and Johnson (1973) report a study of training in the fantasy play with disadvantaged children. They found a more frequent occurrence of dramatic play in their everyday activity and an increase in I.Q.

Robert D. Strom (1981) devised training programs in toy talk for use by parents, grand-parents, babysitters and preschool teachers. He and his students have shown rather consistently positive results in the development of creativity as a result of toy talk.

These two lines of investigations are examples of thematic fantasy play and the use of games.

5. *Training in creative writing to improve creative thinking*

There has also been an increase in studies in creative writing as a way of improving performance in creative problem solving. Flowers and Hayes (1977) report one such study. They taught problem solving strategies and practiced these strategies in the creative writing process. They see writing as a form of problem solving.

Harmon (1976) reported a study of the influences of exploratory writing experiences on creative thinking with third grade children using the verbal form of the Torrance Test of Creative Thinking. They found significant gains on fluency, flexibility and originality for the experimental groups over the control groups.

Hilgers (1980) reported an experiment involving training college composition students in the use of free writing and problem solving for the rhetorical invention. Significant differences were found on the writing proficiency, the observation of ideas and observance of writing conventions. Their results suggest that free writing deserves serious attention from researchers and the applicability of problem solving techniques in the teaching of composition at the college level.

6. *The influences of the Quality Circles Movement*

Although the Quality Circles idea in the United States is rather old, the Quality Circles Movement in industry and education in the United States is very recent. It became a national program in Japan and was imported from Japan by American industry. It has therefore introduced into creativity research some of the Japanese creative problem solving methods. While it resembles the Osborn-Parnes procedure it is somewhat more structured and designed to bring into play the intuitive abilities. They have also been able to bring into research creative problem solving with real problems and real criteria. They have refined the process and set measureable goals. They have been able in many instances to spell out the conditions for excellence. The work of the Quality Circles has also been characterized by the future orientation of problem solving and planning. The Quality Circles have made participative management meaningful. Examples of these studies are: Alexander (1984); Hodgetts and Fountain (1983); and Ryan (1983).

7. *Multiple Criteria*

Creativity research of the past has been rather consistently criticized for using artificial criteria. The Quality Circle Movement has introduced realistic criteria such as:
1. Amount of money saved
2. Amount of money made
3. Absentee rate
4. Amount of time saved

5. Number of accidents occurring
6. Quality of the product

Examples of these studies include Kleinberg (1981); Mroczkowski (1984); Pascarella (1981); and Shaw (1981).

With this impetus from Quality Circles in industry, researchers have been able to invent more realistic criteria, as seen in the foregoing section.

Conclusion

A thorough and detailed analysis of studies on creative problem solving training reflects the growing maturity of research and practice in the area. We shall still have studies as primitive as the early ones we had in the 1940's and 1950's, somewhat more mature ones as in the 1960's but we will have more of the diverse ones found in the 1970's and 1980's. The field will remain a challenge and one with many unanswered questions but greater enlightment.

References

Alexander, P. H. (1984, Feb.). A hidden benefit of quality circles. *Personnel Journal,* 54-58.

Anderson, J. R. (1982). Acquisition of cognitive skill. *Psychological Review, 89,* 369-406.

Basadur, M., Graen, G. B. & Green, S. G. (1980). Training in creative problem solving. *Organizational Behavior and Human Performance, 30,* 41-70.

Brown, M. (1983). *The inventive: Innovation to ingenuity.* LaHabra, CA: Foxtail Press.

Callahan, C. M. (1978). *Developing creativity in the gifted and talented.* Reston, VA: Council for Exceptional Children.

Callahan, C. M. & Renzulli, J. S. (1977). The effectiveness of a creativity training program in the language arts. *Gifted Child Quarterly, 21,* 538-546.

Coleman, D. R. (1982). The effects of pupil use of a creative writing scale as an evaluative and instructional tool by primary gifted students. (Doctoral dissertation. Kansas State University, 1981). *Dissertation Abstracts International, 42* (8), 3409-A. (University Microfilms Order Number 8127860).

Crabbe, A. B. (1982). Creating a brighter future: An update on the future problem solving program. *Journal for the Education of the Gifted, 5,* 2-11.

Davis, G. A. (1971). Teaching for creativity: Some guiding lights. *Journal of Research and Development in Education, 4* (3), 29-34.

deBono, E. (1969). *The mechanisms of mind.* London: Jonathan Cape.

deBono, E. (1975). *Think links.* Blandford Forum, Dorset, UK: Direct Education Services.

deBono, E. (1978). *CoRT thinking lesson series.* Blanford Forum, Dorset, UK: Direct Education Services.

deBono, E. (1983). The direct teaching of thinking as a skill. *Phi Delta Kappan, 64,* 703-708.

Dirkes, M. A. (1977). Learning through creative thinking. *Gifted Child Quarterly, 21,* 526-537.

Elstein, A. S., Shulman, L. S. & Sprafka, S. A. (1978). *Medical problem solving: An analysis of clinical reasoning.* Cambridge. MA: Harvard University Press.

Firestien, R. L. & Treffinger, D. J. (1983). Creative problem solving: Guidelines and resources for effective facilitation. *G/C/T Magazine,* Issue *26,* 2-10.

Flowers & Hayes (1977). Problem-solving strategies and the writing process. *College English, 39* (4), 449-461.

Foster, K. (1979). Creative problem solving. *Gifted Child Quarterly, 23,* 559-560.

Frederiksen, N. (1984). Implications of cognitive theory for instruction in problem solving. *Review of Educational Research, 54* (3), 363-407.

Friedman, F., Raymond, B. & Feldhusen, J. F. (1978). The effects of environmental scanning on creativity. *Gifted Child Quarterly, 22,* 248-257.

Getzels, J. W. & Csikszentmihalyi, M. (1976). *The creative vision.* New York: Wiley.

Gourley, T. J. (1981). Adapting the varsity sports model of non-psychomotor gifted students. *Gifted Child Quarterly, 25,* 164-166.

Gourley, T. J., Kelly, V. & Zucca, R. (1977). The application of a rational-psychedelic continuum concept of creativity to the classroom. *Gifted Child Quarterly, 21,* 103-108.

Guilford, J. P. (1959). *Personality.* New York: McGraw Hill.

Harmon, L. G. (1976). The influence of exploratory writing on the creativity of third grade children. (Doctoral dissertation, Mississippi State University, 1976). University Microfilms Order Number 76-20, 758, 153.

Hershey, M. & Kearns, P. (1979). The effect of guided fantasy on the creative thinking and writing ability of gifted students. *Gifted Child Quarterly, 23* (1), 71-77.

Hilgers, T. L. (1980). Training college composition students in the use of freewriting and problem-solving heuristics for rhetorical invention. *Research in the Teaching of English, 14* (4), 293-307.

Hodgetts, R. M. & Fountian, W. V. (1983, Nov.) The defense department evaluates a quality circle program. *Training and Development Journal,* 98-100.

Keating, D. P. (1980). Four faces of creativity: The continuing plight of the intellectually underserved. *Gifted Child Quarterly, 24,* 56-61.

Khatena, J. (1978). *The creatively gifted child: Suggestions for parents and teachers,* New York: Vantage Press.

Khatena, J. (1984). *Imagery and creative imagination.* Buffalo, NY: Bearly Limited.

Kleinberg, E. M. (1981, Nov.). How Westinghouse adapts quality circles to sales management. *Industrial Marketing,* 82-84.

Kopelman, M., Glasso, V. G. & Strom, P. (1977). A model program for the development of the creatively gifted in science. *Gifted Child Quarterly, 21,* 80-84.

Larkin, J. H. & Reif, F. (1976). Analysis and teaching of a general skill for studying scientific text. *Journal of Educational Psychology, 68,* 431-440.

Lowery, J. (1982). Developing creativity in gifted children. *Gifted Child Quarterly, 26,* 74-76.

Ludlow, B. L. & Woodrum, D. T. (1982). Problem solving strategies of gifted and average learners on a multiple discrimination task. *Gifted Child Quarterly, 26,* 99-104.

Macaranas, N. (1982). Fostering, experiencing, and developing creativity as a method of instruction in psychology. *Creative Child and Adult Quarterly, 7,* 15-29.

Manning, E. & Brown, M. (1979). East Whittier city schools gifted program project: Developing divergent modes of thinking in mentally gifted minor children. *Gifted Child Quarterly, 23,* 563-578.

Mansfield, R. S. & Busse, T. V. (1981). *The psychology of creativity and discovery.* Chicago: Nelson-Hall.

Meeker, R. (1979). Can creativity be developed in gifted? *Roeper Review, 2* (1), 17-18.

Mroczkowski, T. (1984, June). Quality circles, fine-what next? *Personnel Administrator,* 173-184.

Myers, R. E. & Torrance, E. P. (1984). *Wondering: Invitations to thinking about the future for primary grades.* Mansfield Center, CT: Creative Learning Press.

Neves, D. M. & Anderson, J. R. (1981). Knowledge compilation: Mechanisms for the automatization of cognitive skills. In J. R. Anderson (Ed.), *Cognitive skills and their acquisition.* Hillsdale, NJ: Erlbaum.

Pascarella, P. (1981, July). Humanagement at Honeywell. *Industry Week,* 33-36.

Renzulli, J. S. (1973). *New directions in creativity.* New York: Harper & Row.

Rubenstein, M. F. (1980). A decade of experience in teaching an interdisciplinary problem-solving course. In D. T. Tuma & F. Reif (Eds.), *Problem solving and education: Issues in teaching and research.* Hillsdale, NJ: Erlbaum.

Ryan, J. (1983, Dec.). The productivity/quality connection-plugging in at Westinghouse Electric. *Quality Progress,* 26-29.

Saltz, E. and Johnson, J. (1973). Training for thematic-fantasy play in culturally disadvantaged children: Preliminary results. *Studies in Intellectual development.* Center for the study of cognitive processes, Wayne State University, Detroit, Michigan.

Shaw, R. (1981, Sept.). Tapping the riches of creativity among working people. *Management Focus.* 25-29.

Shibles, W. (1979). How to teach creativity through humor and metaphor. *Creative Child and Adult Quarterly, 4,* 243-251.

Stanley, J. C. (1980). On educating the gifted. *Educational Researcher, 9,* 8-12.

Stratton, R. P. and Brown, R. (1972). Improving creative thinking by training in the production and/or judgment of solutions. *Journal of Educational Psychology, 63* (4), 390-397.

Strom, R. (1981). *Growing through play.* Monterey, CA: Brooks/Cole Publishing Co.

Torrance, E. P. (1966). *Torrance tests of creative thinking: Norms-technical manual.* Princeton, NJ: Personnel Press.

Torrance, E. P. (1972). Can we teach children to think creatively? *Journal of Creative Behavior, 6,* 114-143.

Torrance, E. P. (1979). *The search for satori and creativity.* Buffalo, NY: Bearly Limited.

Torrance, E. P. (1980). More than the ten rational processes. *Creative Child and Adult Quarterly, 5,* 9-19.

Torrance, E. P. (1986). *Recent training experiments in creativity training.* In preparation.

Torrance, E. P. & Torrance, J. P. (1978). Developing creativity instruction materials according to the Osborn-Parnes creative problem solving model. *Creative Child and Adult Quarterly, 3,* 80-90.

Treffinger, D. J. (1980a). Fostering independence and creativity. *Journal for the Education of the Gifted, 3,* 214-224.

Treffinger, D. J. (1980b). *Encouraging creative learning for the gifted and talented.* Ventura, CA: Ventura County School Superintendent Office.

Wilson, S. H., Greer, J. F. & Johnson, R. M. (1973). Synectics, a creative problem solving technique for the gifted. *Gifted Child Quarterly, 17,* 260-267.

9

An Analysis of Creativity*

Mel Rhodes
University of Arizona

Just as I finished writing the first draft of this paper I had an irrepressible urge to start over. I knew suddenly that I could reorganize and rewrite my material for greater clarity. Then I thought to myself, isn't this experience an example of the creative process? Isn't creativity, in simple language, the process of reorganizing knowledge (general or specific knowledge), and of articulating that synthesis so that other people can understand the meaning. Also, I thought, haven't I in this instance visualized the key to the secret nature of creativity? That secret being that original ideas are the by-products of (1) a human mind grasping the elements of a subject, (2) of prolonged thinking about the parts and their relationships to each other and to the whole, and (3) of sustained effort in working over the synthesis so that it can be embodied or articulated competently.

The United States Supreme Court has ruled in numerous cases that an invention is an idea rather than an object. If a man can prove that an idea was his by demonstrating or providing evidence that only he had the knowledge from which it was synthesized, he can claim patent to the invention. Collaborators who might have helped to embody the idea into object, provided it can be proved that they lacked the basic knowledge components in the idea—even though they do all of the crafting—are classified as technicians or craftsmen.

Likewise with art. Art was defined, after lengthy trials in the highest courts of our land, as concept rather than object. The shipping charges for a piece of metal are based on weight. But in the now-famous court trial of 1927, Roumanian-born Constantin Brancusi made art history when he contested the decision of United States customs officials concerning the proper charges for a curving brass column which he labeled *Bird in Space.* The customs officials contended the object was metal. Brancusi contended it was art. When sculptor Jacob Epstein was asked if a good mechanic could not polish up a brass rail and pass it off as art, he replied, "He can polish it up, but he cannot conceive of the object. That is the whole point." The court agreed. Its decision: "Objects which portray abstract ideas (in this case, "flight"), rather than imitate natural objects, may be classified as art."

My answer to the question, "What is creativity?", is this: The word creativity is a noun naming the phenomenon in which a person communicates a new concept (which is the product). Mental activity (or mental process) is implicit in the definition, and of course no one could conceive of a person living or operating in a vacuum, so the term *press* is also implicit. The definition begs the questions as to how new the concept must be and to whom it must be new.

Surge of Interest in Creativity

The big push of interest in the subject of creativity began in 1950 when J. P. Guilford of the University of Southern California was president of the American Psychological Association.

*Reproduced by permission of Phi Delta Kappan.

Guilford said in his presidential address to that organization that he found an appalling lack of research on creativity. He said he had searched *Psychological Abstracts* for a quarter of a century and found that only 186 out of 121,000 entries dealt in any way with creativity, imagination, or any topic closely related.

In the years since 1950 more than a dozen books have appeared on the subject, and I have approximately 300 reference cards to articles and monographs. The research undertaken since Guilford gave his speech has yielded results of basic significance to the field of education and to the archives of knowledge. These studies have rendered into baloney many former sacred cows. For instance, the idea that the IQ is a lump sum and that it is constant, the idea that "well-adjusted children" (often meaning conformers) will become the most useful citizens, the idea that people are born to be either creative or lacking in creative ability, the notion that creativity is more a way of feeling than a way of thinking, the idea that creativity is something mysterious and the notion that the word creativity applies to a simple, uncomplicated mental process that operates in unrestraint.

It is now clear that, instead, intellect is complex, that divergent thinkers and people of complex temperament have more original ideas than conformers and people of placid temperament, that environmental factors at all times in life form a psychological press that may be either constructive or destructive to creativity, that the technique of getting ideas can be learned and can be taught. It is also clear that whatsoever factors of personality or of intellect, of learning process or thinking process, or of environment are congruent with creativity, the same are congruent also with the educative process in general.

It would be difficult to describe the scope of the contributions to knowledge and to the field of education rendered during the last ten years by scholars on the trail of creativity. This is why I was perturbed when I read in the October, 1960, issue of *Harper's* magazine what Jacques Barzun, provost and dean of faculties at Columbia University, had written about "The Cults of 'Research' and 'Creativity'." Here is a quotation from the article:

> What "creative" means in common usage is hardly clear—it seems to correspond to the idea of fullness, to the completion of effort, a synthesis of parts, while it also conveys, like "research," the notion of something new and unexpectedly good . . . Use of the word creativity is a device by which we give ourselves easy satisfactions while avoiding necessary judgments. That the faculty of judgment is at stake can be shown from a simple enumeration:
>
> —Creative may mean the neglect of technical competence—witness a great deal of so-called new writing, new painting, and new art generally.
>
> —Creative may falsely dignify certain ordinary virtues—quickness of mind, sense of order and relevance and skill in using words—all of which can be subsumed under intelligence and intellectual training.
>
> —Creative may suggest modern, fresh, or unshackled by convention or tradition. In that sense it can be used to justify waste of time, as when students analyze contemporary writers and attribute to them as innovations literary devices that are found in Homer and Virgil.
>
> —Creative may also stand for a conscious or unconscious denial of the tremendous range of human ability. If a child in kindergarten is called creative for the finger-painting he produces, the distance between him and Rembrandt has somehow been shortened. Through a likening of potential and actual, a kind of democratic equality has been restored.
>
> . . . If small talents are creative, then since everyone has them, everyone has a Leonardo-like mind.

I understand what Barzun is saying. Indeed, the words creative and creativity have been loosely used and overused. In many examples "creative" means or implies nothing more than emotional freedom, relaxing of tensions, disinhibition, or freedom from censorship. Examples of such usage occur in expressions like "creative dancing" (when the activity referred to is shimmying), "creative art" (when the activity referred to is finger-painting), and "creative writing" (when the activity is "kitsch"–i.e., stories that follow a formula and are essentially the same, even though slightly different in details, as in pulp magazine trash).

What is happening here is that a word which should be reserved to name a complex, multifaceted phenomenon is misused to name only one part of a phenomenon. It is like explaining a hurricane by describing wind or explaining a bird's flight by describing its perchings. But creativity cannot be explained alone in terms of the emotional component of the process or in terms of any other single component, no matter how vital that component may be.

About five years ago I set out to find a definition of the word creativity, I was interested also in imagination, originality, and ingenuity. In time I had collected forty definitions of creativity and sixteen of imagination. The profusion was enough to give one the impression that creativity is a province for pseudo-intellectuals.

But as I inspected my collection I observed that the definitions are not mutually exclusive. They overlap and intertwine. When analyzed, as through a prism, the content of the definitions form four strands. Each strand has unique identity academically, but only in unity do the four strands operate functionally. It is this very fact of synthesis that causes fog in talk about creativity and this may be the basis for the semblance of a "cult."

One of these strands pertains essentially to the person as a human being. Another strand pertains to the mental processes that are operative in creating ideas. A third strand pertains to the influence of the ecological press on the person and upon his mental processes. And the fourth strand pertains to ideas. Ideas are usually expressed in the form of either language or craft and this is what we call product. Hereafter, I shall refer to these strands as the four P's of creativity, i.e., (1) person, (2) process, (3) press, (4) products.

Persons

The term *person,* as used here, covers information about personality, intellect, temperament, physique, traits, habits, attitudes, self-concept, value systems, defense mechanisms, and behavior. Basic questions in this department are: What is the coefficient of correlation between intelligence test scores and creativity? Is everyone potentially creative, to some extent? Is creativity a function of temperament as well as intelligence? More than intelligence? Do physique or physiological factors have any bearing on creativity? How important are attitudes, habits, and value systems? And what kinds of habits, attitudes, and values? In what way are they significant? What about neurotic personality–is neuroticism essential or is it detrimental to creativity?

Lewis Terman of Stanford made extensive psychological studies of approximately 1,000 gifted children over a period exceeding thirty years. He observed a difference between high intelligence and high creativity and said in one of his last papers that not more than one-third of his people with IQ's over 140 showed a marked degree of creativity. On the East Coast, Leta Hollingworth observed essentially the same thing with children of 180 IQ or better. In Chicago, Thurstone studied the Quiz Kids and remarked afterwards that they had phenomenal memories for details but that they were noticeably lacking in creativity.

Guilford hypothesized that intelligence tests were not measuring creative factors. Now he hypothesizes, on the basis of factorial studies, that intelligence is made up of 120 or more kinds of abilities and has devised tests to measure approximately fifty factors. In the future he hopes to build instruments to measure additional factors of intellect. Guilford's studies indicate that people who stand out (from their fellows) as creative thinkers, are characterized by sensitivity to problems, fluency of ideas, mental flexibility, divergent thinking, and ability to redefine familiar objects and concepts.

Getzels and Jackson note that children with quick humor are more creative.

Frank Barron found that people of complex temperament are more creative than people of simple temperament.

Mary Cover Jones submits the guess that late-maturers are more flexible thinkers than early-maturers, possibly because they have to be quick to keep up.

How Important are Attitudes and Habits?

Eric Fromm observes that a creative person has the capacity to be puzzled, the ability to concentrate, a genuine sense of self and confidence in self, the ability to accept conflict and tension. Fromm accepts the concept that equality does not mean sameness. A person who is truly creative is one who is willing to be born everyday. He is willing to let go of all "certainties" and illusions.

Tuska, in his book *Inventors and Inventions,* says, "If you would invent, acquire the good habit of observing. Observe and question! Ask yourself questions: Why did that happen? Why did not something happen? What started that? What stopped that? For example, why can a spider walk on its own web without getting tangled? To what can I attribute the wonderful characteristics of a spider's thread? Where might I use such a thread to advantage? Could a spider's thread be synthesized? How? In brief, daydream with a purpose."

Thomas Edison said that invention is 1 per cent inspiration and 99 per cent perspiration.

Can a Creative Person be Identified?

Almost any group of people, including school children, can name individuals among them who have off-beat ideas. Often the group will argue that so-and-so's ideas are crazy. But the question is, how crazy? Crazy enough to be useful? Crazy enough to change a trend? Crazy enough to revolutionize an industry—or a way of life?

Gilfillan, in his book *Sociology of Invention,* talks about the great lapses of time that have occurred between the time when ideas for great inventions were first merely mentioned and the development of the first working model or patent. Also, he discusses the time gap between patent and commercial use. The average time elapsed between first mention of the idea and commercial use of the same for nineteen inventions voted most useful (who voted was not stated) was 226 years. (These were inventions introduced between 1888 and 1913.) Studies regarding theories of government, philosophical insights, and scientific discoveries confirm the fact of time delay in communicating such ideas to the masses.

This fact of inability or reluctance on the part of the social group to accept new ideas, particularly unfamiliar concepts, complicates the task of identifying creative thinkers. But is not an individual who thinks differently from his associates and from sources of information doing his own thinking? And is he not the person who is likely to be creative?

Process

The term *process* applies to motivation, perception, learning, thinking, and communicating. Essential questions about process include: What causes some individuals to strive for original answers to questions while the majority are satisfied with conventional answers? What are the stages of the thinking process? Are the processes identical for problem solving and for creative thinking? If not, how do they differ? Can the creative thinking process be taught?

When the German physiologist and physicist Hermann Helmholtz was seventy years old, he was asked at his birthday party to analyze his thought processes. Later, Graham Wallas, in his book *The Art of Thought,* formulated Helmholtz's ideas into the familiar four stages: preparation, incubation, inspiration, and verification. The preparation step consists of observing, listening, asking, reading, collecting, comparing, contrasting, analyzing, and relating all kinds of objects and information. The incubation process is both conscious and unconscious. This step involves thinking about parts and relationships, reasoning, and often a fallow period. Inspirations very often appear during this fallow period. This probably accounts for the popular emphasis on releasing tensions in order to be creative. The step labeled verification is a period of hard work. This is the process of converting an idea into an object or into an articulated form.

In an address at M.I.T. in 1955, Alex Osborn, author of the popular book titled *Applied Imagination,* summed it up as follows: "I submit that creativity will never be a science—in fact, much of it will always remain a mystery—as much of a mystery as 'what makes our heart tick?' At the same time, I submit that creativity is an art—an applied art—a teachable art—a learnable art—an art in which all of us can make ourselves more and more proficient, if we will."

> "A large number of courses have been instituted in this country whose aim is to develop creativity . . . [but] no one knows at this stage what are the most effective ways of bringing about greater creative performance."—*J. P. Guilford, 1958*

Yes, the creative process can be taught. It is being taught in hundreds of classes across the nation—in colleges, universities, business organizations, military schools, and industries. Osborn's book has gone into twelve printings and over 100,000 copies have been sold. There is considerable research evidence to support the statement that the creative process can be taught. And in 1954 the Creative Education Foundation was formed solely for the purpose of encouraging a more creative trend in American education.

Press

The term *press* refers to the relationship between human beings and their environment. Creative production is the outcome of certain kinds of forces playing upon certain kinds of individuals as they grow up and as they function. A person forms ideas in response to tissue needs, sensations, perceptions, and imagination. A person receives sensations and perceptions from both internal and external sources. A person possesses multi-factorial intellect, including ability to store memories, to recall and to synthesize ideas. Each idea that emerges reflects uniquely upon the originator's self, his sensory equipment, his mentality, his value systems, and his conditioning to the everyday experiences of life. Each person perceives his environment in a unique way; one man's meat is another man's poison and vice versa. Studies of press attempt to measure congruence and dissonance in a person's ecology. Stern and Pace have introduced instruments designed to take two temperatures—(1) the climate of a particular environment, and (2) the reaction of a person to his environment. If and when these two scores can be obtained they can be coordinated to show the congruence and dissonance between individuals and their environment.

Liphshitz, writing for the *Journal of the Patent Office Society,* opened fire, a few years ago, on the authors of most histories and of biographical studies of inventors for treating the inventor as something apart from the world in general. He said that an intensive study of the history of inventions makes clear that they originate in a response to social needs and that there must be a sufficiently advanced stage of culture and a proper technical heritage to foster or allow an invention to be made. History proves that great inventions are never, and great discoveries seldom, the work of any one mind. Every great invention is either an aggregate of minor inventions or the final step of the progression.

Gilfillan said, "Inventions are not just accidents, nor the inscrutable products of sporadic genius, but have abundant and clear causes in prior scientific and technological development. And they have social causes and retarding factors, both new and constant, of changed needs and opportunities, growth of technical education, of buying power, of capital, patent and commercial systems, corporation laboratories and what not. All such basic factors causing invention give means of predicting the same.

"The existing and overwhelming influence of causes for invention is proved by the frequency of duplicate invention, where the same idea is hatched by different minds independently about the same time."

Products

The word *idea* refers to a thought which has been communicated to other people in the form of words, paint, clay, metal, stone, fabric, or other material. When we speak of an original idea, we imply a degree of newness in the concept. When an idea becomes embodied into tangible form it is called a *product.* Each product of a man's mind or hands presents a record of his thinking at some point in time. Thus an idea for a new machine reflects the inventor's specific thoughts at the moment when the concept was born. And by probing backward from the moment of inspiration it may be possible to trace the thoughts and the events leading up to the idea. Products are artifacts of thoughts. Through the study of artifacts, archeologists reconstruct the way of life of extinct peoples, officers of the law reconstruct the events leading up to a crime, and psychologists reconstruct the mental processes of inventing. Objective investigation into the nature of the creative process can proceed in only one direction, i.e., from product to person and thence to process and to press.

A system is needed for classifying products according to the scope of newness. For example, theories such as relativity or electromagnetic waves or mechanical flight are of tremendous scope. From any one of these theories, thousands of inventions may germinate. Therefore ideas in theory are of higher order in the scale of creativity than ideas for inventions. After inventions appear, numerous innovations or new twists in design or structure are suggested by users. Thus the idea for an invention is of higher order in the scale of creativity than an idea for an innovation to an existing invention. The significance of this suggestion to classify ideas by degree of newness is that it would place emphasis on higher mental processes rather than on dazzling objects.

In the history of the sciences, every branch floundered until facts were organized and classified. After a classification system was devised, the branch advanced rapidly. When astronomy grouped the heavenly bodies, outside of the sun and moon, into planets and fixed stars, it took a considerable step forward. When physics separated its phenomena into the broad categories of dynamics, sound, heat, light, electricity, and magnetism, the way was clear for more penetrating analyses. When Linneaus devised the system of binomial nomenclature, biology became a science. This bit of history seems to suggest that the mystery surrounding creativity could be dissipated by organizing artifacts into categories, first by kinds and then within each kind by degrees of newness. If this were to be done, data could be collected concerning the person responsible for a given idea, concerning the circumstances leading up to the idea, and concerning the mental activity producing the idea.

Ideas have been described in various ways for different purposes. One system distinguishes ideas by media of expression: for instance, music, art, poetry, and invention. Another system recognizes mood: for example, pastoral, satiric, and didactic moods in poetry, and allegro, andante, and adagio moods in music. Still another system recognizes values: in art, pictures are classified according to their utility or their associative or esthetic value; while in the realm of mechanics, machines are recognized according to the use to which they are to be put. There are other classification systems based on form, as for example sonatas, concertos, and symphonies in music; and ballads, sonnets, odes, and elegies in poetry.

Notwithstanding these several ways of classifying products, there is no standard system for organizing artifacts according to idea value or degree of originality. Consequently, any artifact is called "a creation" and mystery surrounds them all.

Above the entrance to Washington Station these words are carved in stone, "Man's imagination has conceived all numbers and letters—all tools, vessels, and shelters—every art and trade—all philosophy and poetry—and all politics."

Ralph Waldo Emerson said, "Every reform was once a private opinion."

Within a year of our nation's founding, the U.S. Patent Office was established—on the concept that the country would profit by protecting the right of individuals to profit by their ideas and inventions. Between 1776 and 1960 more than 3,000,000 patents were granted.

In the last decade, as a direct response to Guilford's speech to the APA about the need for research in the area of creativity, new and tremendously significant knowledge has been collected and put to use—and this knowledge, as fast as it is being disseminated, is causing fundamental changes throughout Academe.

Granted, the word creativity has been overworked. And it is used loosely. Also, the formal study of creativity has not yet reached the stage of advancement which botany reached when Linneaus organized flora into phyla and into classes. Students of creativity have not yet taken the time to distinguish the strands of the phenomenon and then carefully to classify new knowledge according to the pertinence thereof to either person, process, press, or product. I submit that the time has come for more precision in definition and usage, that only when the field is analyzed and organized—when the listener can be sure he knows what the speaker is talking about—will the pseudo aspect of the subject of creativity disappear.

My appeal is that as educators we recognize the importance of continuing our interest in the nature of creativity, that we be appreciative of the spade work that has been done in the decade just past, that we continue to identify the factors associated with the creative process, and above all that we do not throw out the baby with the bath water just because the water is cloudy.

The subject of creativity has interdisciplinary appeal. This is true because the phenomenon to which the term creativity applies is the phenomenon of synthesizing knowledge. Hope for greater unification of knowledge lies in the continuance of studies of creativity. There are adventures ahead in researching the four P's of creativity, in learning to identify the creative person, in teaching the creative process, in learning how to take the temperatures of a person and of his environment under changing circumstances and of arranging for congruence between the two, in developing a scale for classifying products by degrees of newness within a scheme of like kinds of products. And ultimately there will be a new perspective of education with a backdrop of unified knowledge.

Now is the time for every teacher to become more creative!

The Motivation to be Creative

Teresa M. Amabile
Brandeis University

People are gathered here in Buffalo at this conference, on this warm night in June of 1984, from all over the country. In fact, many have come from as far away as California. How was your trip? I imagine that it was simple, straightforward—and fast. And you can expect that it will be the same going home.

In 1950, if you wanted to travel from Buffalo to San Francisco, you had basically three options. There was no Buffalo International Airport but, if you were wealthy enough, you could travel to New York, perhaps, and from there take a series of slow plane rides over the next couple of days. Or you could try the train, planning to spend several days and nights chugging along through the countryside. Or, if you were the pioneer type, you could get in your car and, provided you were singleminded about it, you might reach your destination after a couple of weeks of two-lane roads and small-town rooming houses. All of which was fine, of course, if taking a leisurely trip was your goal. But if simply getting to California was the aim of your trip, the process of doing so presented major difficulty.

In 1984, if you want to travel from Buffalo to San Francisco, you can leave on a breakfast flight and get there in time for a lunch meeting. If the meeting is short enough, and you are jaded enough, you can even return in time to get a good night's sleep back in your own bed.

In 1950, space travel was the stuff of science fiction. In 1984, most of us barely notice when the space shuttle is making yet another trip.

In 1950, parents lived in dread of polio outbreaks. Patients suffering kidney failure were doomed to imminent death. And smallpox still took a terrible toll throughout much of the world.

By 1984, we no longer even think about the possibility of contracting polio. Kidney transplants have become highly effective and almost routine. And smallpox has been eradicated from the face of the earth.

In 1950, engineers were virtually inseparable from their slide rules; there was no more straightforward way of making computations. In 1984, most engineering students have never seen a slide rule, and it is not uncommon to see professionals casually unpacking their personal computers to get a little work done as they wait for airplanes.

In 1950, most people paid their bills by handing over the cash to the shopkeeper as soon as they made a purchase. And transcontinental telephone calls were an expensive ordeal, usually requiring a great deal of time for a connection. Now, in 1984, we can pick up our telephone and, without ever saying a word, use the pushbuttons to pay charges that we might have accumulated in dozens of stores over the past weeks. With that completed, we can listen to our day's phone messages and, within seconds, return a call made from the other side of the continent. If the number is busy, of course, we can simply tell our phone to keep redialing.

In these ways, and hundreds of other ways, life has changed dramatically since 1950—all because, in one way or another, somebody had an idea—all because somebody was creative. Certainly, the production of something creative involves much more than simply the having of wonderful ideas. But it is the having of wonderful ideas that distinguishes creativity from the other things that people do, and it is upon this that the progress of civilization rests.

Surely, it would be possible to list equally dramatic changes during any other period in recent history. I chose 1950 because it is particularly relevant. It is relevant in a personal sense because the 34 years since June of 1950 span my entire lifetime. All of these changes, and hundreds more just as incredible, have happened in my lifetime—and, I hope, that lifetime isn't yet half over! The year 1950 is also relevant to the theme of this symposium, since most creativity researchers date scientific inquirty into creativity from J. P. Guilford's address to the American Psychological Association that year. Most of what we know about creativity has been learned in the past 34 years. And we do know a great deal, especially about the personality characteristics of outstandingly creative people.

There is still a vast unexplored territory, though, and sometimes exploring that territory seems more difficult than cross-country travel used to be. For the past eight years, I have focused my research on how work environments affect creativity. How do social factors influence artistic, verbal, and problem-solving creativity? What is the mechanism by which they do so? Some answers to these questions have already emerged, although the research continues to generate even more questions. I will outline some of the strongest clues we have found, discuss some of the implications, and set some directions for future exploration.

The Difference Motivation Makes

The unifying theme in all my own research is that people will be most creative when they are motivated primarily by passionate interest in their work. This passionate interest is called intrinsic motivation—the motivation to work on something primarily for its own sake, because it is enjoyable, satisfying, challenging, or otherwise captivating. By contrast, extrinsic motivation is the motivation to work on something primarily because it is a means to an end; the work only represents a way to earn money, gain recognition, satisfy someone else's orders, or meet a deadline. According to the intrinsic motivation hypothesis of creativity, intrinsic motivation is conducive to creativity and extrinsic motivation is detrimental. Moreover, social factors in the work environment can influence intrinsic/extrinsic motivation and, as a consequence, can influence creativity as well.

This notion emerged from several sources. The first was my own experience. I was in kindergarten, I believe, when I first heard the word "creativity." My teacher had come to our home for the annual spring conference with my mother. Being a resourceful child, I was, of course, eavesdropping from the next room. I remember hearing Mrs. Bollier say, toward the end of the conference, "I think Teresa shows a lot of potential for artistic creativity. I hope that's something she can develop over the years." I was thrilled to hear this endorsement of my talent—although, to be honest, I had no idea what creativity meant. But it sounded like something that was good to have.

Unfortunately, that year represented the high point of my artistic career. The following fall, I entered a strictly regimented, traditional school where my experience with graphic art was limited to a couple of hours on Friday afternoon when the teachers were too exhausted to do anything else with us. Week after week, we were given small reproductions of masterworks in painting and asked to copy them on notepaper using the standard set of eight Crayola crayons. To make matters worse, we were strictly graded on the monstrosities we produced. Rather than developing my potential for artistic creativity, I developed a great deal of frustration. Somehow, Da Vinci's "Adoration of the Magi" looked wrong after I'd finished with it. I wondered where that promised creativity had gone.

Lessons from that early experience came to mind again when, several years ago, I encountered the second source of information leading to the intrinsic motivation hypothesis: the autobiographies, letters, and journals of outstandingly creative individuals. Albert Einstein, not known for his verbal fluency, was remarkably articulate about the undermining effects that a constraining educational system had on his creativity:

> In this field [Physics], I soon learned to scent out that which was able to lead to fundamentals and to turn aside from everything else, from the multitude of things which clutter up the mind and divert it from the essential. The hitch in this was, of course, the fact that one had to cram all this stuff into one's mind for the examinations, whether one liked it or not. This coercion had such a deterring effect upon me that, after I had passed the final examination, I found the consideration of any scientific problem distasteful to me for an entire year. (Einstein, 1949, p. 17)

Einstein seems to be saying that, although his level of intrinsic motivation for scientific problems was initially quite high, he was (temporarily) robbed of that motivation by the external constraints of the formal learning process. It is certainly fortunate that Einstein's induced distaste for science—and the attendant inhibition of his scientific creativity—lasted no more than one year. In fact, he devised a rather clever method for preserving his intrinsic motivation during his advanced study in Zurich:

> In justice I must add that in Switzerland we had to suffer far less under such coercion, which smothers every truly scientific impulse [. . .]. There were altogether only two examinations; aside from these, one could just about do as one pleased. This was especially the case if one had friend, as I did, who attended the lectures regularly and who worked over their content conscientiously. This gave one freedom in the choice of pursuits until a few months before the examination, a freedom which I enjoyed to a great extent and have gladly taken into the bargain the bad conscience connected with it as by far the lesser evil. (Einstein, 1949, pp. 18-19).

Einstein's final remarks on this point contain the essence of the intrinsic motivation hypothesis of creativity:

> It is, in fact, nothing short of a miracle that the modern methods of instruction have not yet entirely strangled the holy curiosity of inquiry; for this delicate little plant, aside from stimulation, stands mainly in need of freedom; without this it goes to wreck and ruin without fail. (Einstein, 1949, p. 19)

Repeatedly, this notion appears in the introspective writings of people well-known for their creativity. Feeling in some way controlled by extrinsic constraints undermines the capacity for creative thought. Feeling controlled mainly by the inner drive for discovery, by challenge, by the sheer enjoyment of work, however, can maintain and stimulate creativity. Arthur Schawlow, who recently won the Nobel prize in Physics, said this about his own creativity and the creativity of scientists with whom he has worked:

> The labor of love aspect is important. The successful scientists are often not the most talented, but the ones who are just impelled by curiosity—they've got to know what the answer is. (Going For The Gaps, 1982, p. 42)

From industry, there is considerable evidence that the most important advances in technology come not from the formal Research and Development process, but from what Thomas Peters calls "skunkworks"—small groups of renegade scientists or technicians who are left largely to their own devices. Often, they persist on a "bootleg" project that passionately interests them even when told not to do so. For example, General Electric has a strong transportation sector, and one of its most successful locomotives was developed by a small team of scientists and technicians who had been told four times to "cease and desist from building a locomotive." Clearly, it appears that organizations would do well to support such intrinsically motivated work, or at least benevolently look the other way. One manager at IBM says that he prowls the parking lot late at night to see how many cars are still there. He says, "It's a sure sign of bootlegging. And the amount of bootlegging is the key indicator of innovative health. (Peters, 1983, p. 18)

The intrinsic motivation hypothesis is not founded solely on introspective and anecdotal evidence, however. It is also derived from a third source that dovetails well with the others—social-psychological theories of motivation and empirical evidence relevant to those theories. Few theorists have discussed in detail the role of motivational variables in creativity. There are some, however, who have suggested that creativity is most likely to appear under intrinsic motivation. For example, Koestler (1964) speculated that the highest forms of creativity are generated under conditions of freedom from control, since it is under these conditions that a person may most easily reach back into the "intuitive regions" of the mind. Koestler saw this regression to unconscious, playful levels of thought as essential for creative production.

Carl Rogers (1954) also speculated on the importance of reliance upon self and freedom from external control in creativity. One of the three "inner conditions" that he saw as necessary for creativity is an internal locus of evaluation. With an internal locus, an individual is primarily concerned with self-evaluation; evaluation by others is only a secondary concern. In addition, Rogers proposed the absence of external evaluation as an environmental condition essential to fostering creativity.

A few other psychologists have proposed that self-perception of personal freedom is necessary for creative thought and expression. Crutchfield (1962) suggested a basic antipathy between conformity and creative thinking, asserting that "conformity pressures tend to elicit kinds of motivation in the individual that are incompatible with the creative process" (p. 121). According to Crutchfield, these conformity pressures can lead to extrinsic, "ego-involved" motivation, in which the work is only a means to an ulterior end. In his view, this contrasts sharply with intrinsic, "task-involved" motivation, in which the creative act is an end in itself. In describing the mechanism by which conformity pressure might be injurious to creative thinking, Crutchfield said:

> The outer pressure and inner compulsion to conform arouse extrinsic, ego-involved motives in the problem solver. His main efforts tend to become directed toward the goals of being accepted and rewarded by the group, of avoiding rejection and punishment. The solution of the problem itself becomes of secondary relevance, and his task-involved motivation diminishes. In being concerned with goals extrinsic to the task itself, and particularly as rendered anxious about potential threats in the situation, his cognitive processes become less flexible, his insights less sensitive. (p. 125)

In different ways, Koestler, Rogers, and Crutchfield all suggest that freedom from external control will enhance creative thinking. But the intrinsic motivation hypothesis of creativity derives more directly from social-psychological theories of motivation (deCharms, 1968; Deci, 1975; Lepper & Greene, 1978). According to these theories, people are intrinsically motivated if they see themselves as doing an activity primarily as an end in itself, and not as a means to some external goal. By contrast, people are considered extrinsically motivated if they see themselves as doing the activity primarily because of some extrinsic constraint. Extrinsic constraints are any social factors that people see as intended to control their task performance—factors such as offers of reward, commands to perform, imposed deadlines, or evaluation pressures.

Most recent intrinsic motivation research has been concerned with the "overjustification" hypothesis derived from the attribution theories of Bem (1972), Kelley (1967, 1973), and deCharms (1968). These theorists propose that when salient extrinsic constraints are imposed on a person's work, that person's intrinsic motivation for the work will decrease. Several studies have supported this hypothesis, using a variety of extrinsic constraints (including tangible reward for performance, surveillance, and externally imposed deadlines) (e.g., Amabile, De-

Jong, & Lepper, 1976; Condry, 1977; Deci, 1971, 1972a, 1972b; Kruglanski, 1975; Lepper & Greene, 1975; Ross, 1975).

For example, Lepper and his colleagues demonstrated this overjustification effect in a simple study with children (Lepper, Greene & Nisbett, 1973). These researchers chose children who had initially shown a high level of interest in playing with some magic markers that had been placed in their nursery-school classroom. Individually, each of these children was asked to draw some pictures with the markers. The experimenter promised some of them an attractive reward if they consented to draw the pictures; he did not mention reward to the other children. Later, when they were back in their classroom, those children who had contracted for reward spent much less time playing with the magic markers than the other children did. According to self-perception theory (Bem, 1972), during the experiment the rewarded children implicitly asked themselves, "Why am I doing this?" Since the reward was so obvious an explanation, the reward became, to them, their reason for drawing the pictures. As a result, they no longer saw themselves as interested in the activity for its own sake. And, back in their classroom, with no reward possible, they actually showed little interest. This undermining of intrinsic interest with extrinsic constraints has been demonstrated in a number of other studies with both children and adults.

Viewed in a larger perspective, the implications of these findings are rather startling. Parents, teachers, and business managers generally assume that a little reward is a good thing, and that a lot of reward is more of a good thing. How can it hurt to present children and adults with incentives for their work? This evidence suggests that it *can* hurt. Although rewards (and other constraints) can certainly motivate our performance in the short run, in the long run they may destroy our interest in our work.

It seemed a reasonable step from this empirical evidence on intrinsic motivation and the anecdotal evidence on creativity to the intrinsic motivation hypothesis of creativity. If creative people like Einstein complained that their creativity was undermined by social constraints, then perhaps the intrinsically motivated state (which is also undermined by social constraints) is necessary for, or at least conducive to, creativity.

How it Happens: Different Ways Out of the Maze

Any discussion of how creativity works and how it is affected by various factors depends, in part, on how creativity is defined. This in itself is enough to drive creativity researchers to despair; creativity is generally considered a slippery and even soft-headed concept. Nonetheless, there is some consensus: To be considered creative, something must be novel or different in some way (see Stein, 1974). But it cannot be merely bizarre. It must be correct, or valuable, or useful, or somehow appropriate to the task at hand. In addition, something should be said about the nature of the task. Some tasks or problems are completely straightforward; the path to the solution is clear and can be performed almost by rote. These tasks are called *algorithmic*. For example, there is only one correct solution for an arithmetic problem like 69-27 + 16. And there is only one way to bake a box cake according to the recipe—follow the steps outlined on the box. There is no room for creativity in the performance of these algorithmic tasks, so we must exclude such activities from the definition of creativity.

Other tasks are open-ended, such that the path to the solution is not completely clear and straightforward. These tasks are *heuristic;* some search is required. Heuristic forms of the problems mentioned earlier would be: "Find 3 numbers that can be added and subtracted to produce the sum of 58," and "Make a cake, choosing your own combination of ingredients." This open-endedness is what characterizes creativity tasks, such as the discovery of a new mathematical system or the invention of a new cake recipe.

The definition of creativity used in my own program of research includes all three elements: A product or response is creative if it is a novel and appropriate solution to an open-ended task.

Kenneth McGraw (1978) has suggested that algorithmic tasks and heuristic tasks are affected differently by different motivational states. Specifically, he says that extrinsic motivation enhances performance on straightforward, algorithmic tasks, but undermines performance on open-ended, heuristic tasks. McGraw has focused primarily on the effects of expected reward. He has shown that the expectation of reward can cause improvement on algorithmic tasks, but can interfere with heuristic tasks. For example, people usually do better on simple multiplication problems if they are working for reward. They usually perform more poorly, however, if they are expecting a reward for solving problems that require insight.

Several studies have demonstrated this effect. For example, Glucksberg (1962) gave subjects a deceptively simple problem. They were handed a candle, a box of thumbtacks, and a book of matches, and were told to use only these materials in mounting the candle on a vertical screen. The problem could only be solved by emptying the tacks out of the box and using it as a platform which could be tacked to the screen. Clearly, this problem is a heuristic one; the path to the solution is not at all obvious at the start. Subjects who were told that they could earn money for finding the solution quickly took much longer to solve the problem than subjects who worked without any mention of reward.

According to McGraw, then, social constraints such as offered reward should interfere with heuristic performances because they induce an extrinsic motivation. Clearly, different types of social constraints have different properties. Things people normally view negatively, such as deadlines, surveillance, and constrained choice, can operate as extrinsic constraints just as surely as things that are viewed quite positively, such as working for a promised reward, or expecting a favorable evaluation. I believe that all social constraints can have the same effects that McGraw found with reward, the same facilitative effects on algorithmic tasks and the same inhibitory effects on heuristic tasks.

The important point is this: since creativity tasks are, by definition, heuristic, performance on these tasks should be enhanced by anything that enhances intrinsic motivation, and undermined by anything that undermines intrinsic motivation. Certainly, intrinsic/extrinsic motivational states are affected by more than just the presence or absence of extrinsic constraints in the social environment. In fact, we can think of motivational orientation toward a task as both a trait and a state. The trait part of motivation consists of a person's individual and relatively enduring preferences for certain kinds of activities (see Holland, 1973). Whether because of innate temperament, acquired personality characteristics, natural abilities, or previous learning experiences, each of us likes certain kinds of activities and dislikes others. Quite apart from any particular social context, then, we should expect that people will be more creative on things that they personally enjoy.

But, clearly, social contexts also affect motivational orientation. Starting from whatever baseline level of interest they may have in a certain task, people can be strongly affected by the social environment. If they are working in the presence of strong extrinsic constraints, they will be likely to see themselves as motivated by those constraints. In other words, they will be likely to see themselves as extrinsically motivated, and whatever interest they had in the task will be likely to decrease.

How might motivational state, whether intrinsic or extrinsic, influence creativity? In considering this question, think of a creativity problem as a maze that you must wander through. I mean "problem" in a very general sense here, such that an artist sitting down to do a painting faces a creativity problem just as surely as a scientist sitting down to contemplate a surprising result. Each is at the starting point of a maze; the problem is to somehow find a satisfactory way out of that maze.

Say there is only one starting point for the maze, that there may be more than one way of getting out, and that some ending points (exits) are more satisfactory than others. Moreover, there is one sure-fire exit. To get there, you simply apply an algorithm that you know very well; the path to the endpoint is completely clear and straightforward. If you are the artist, the

Figure One.

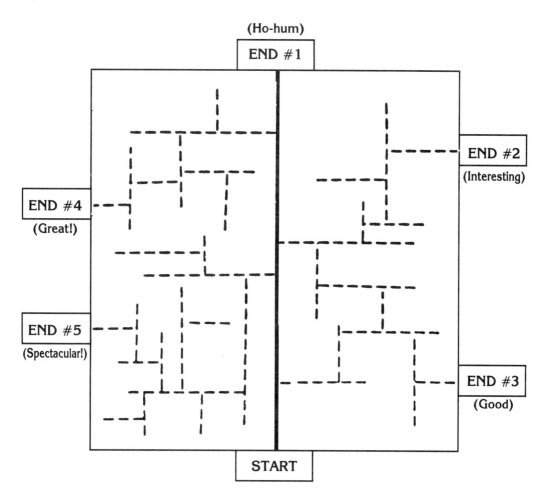

straightforward solution might be to simply paint whatever object is in front of you, using realistic colors and perspectives, in precisely the technique you were taught in art school. If you are the scientist, the straightforward solution might be to simply apply the familiar experiments for identifying a new chemical compound.

Most likely, the straightforward solution, while acceptable, will be quite uninspired and uninspiring. It will, in short, be quite low in creativity. The other ways out of the maze, however, might lead to quite innovative results. In Figure One, which illustrates this maze metaphor, there are at least four other end points besides the obvious one. Each of them is more creative than the first one, and some are downright brilliant. The catch, of course, is that these endpoints cannot be reached by taking the straightforward pathway. You have to do some exploration, and you have to take some risks. Departing from the beaten path is risky because some of the pathways lead to dead ends. A great deal of psychological research has shown that risk-taking plays a crucial role in creativity. In the maze metaphor, risk-taking through exploration is the only way to avoid a hum-drum solution.

If you are extrinsically motivated, your primary motive is to achieve the extrinsic goal. You are working for something that is external to the maze: You have to earn the reward, or win the competition, or get the promotion, or please those who are watching you. You are so singleminded about the goal that you don't take the time to think much about the maze itself. Since you're only interested in getting out as quickly as possible (reaching the goal as easily as possible), you will be likely to take only the most obvious, well-traveled route. In other words, you are unlikely to be creative.

By contrast, if you are intrinsically motivated, you *enjoy being in the maze*. You enjoy playing in it, nosing around, trying out different pathways, exploring, thinking things through before blindly plunging ahead. You're not really concentrating on anything else but how much you enjoy the problem itself, how much you like the challenge and the intrigue. Since you enjoy the activity of exploring the maze, you will be likely to take full advantage of its possibilities. In other words, you are likely to be creative.

Because they result in radically different approaches to work, intrinsic and extrinsic motivational orientations can lead to outcomes that are qualitatively quite different. Edward Deci describes one vivid example of this difference:

> For centuries artists of the Middle and Far East have been hand-weaving oriental rugs. They have done this in traditional ways that reflect the beauty of their heritage and of themselves as individuals. In the late 19th century and increasingly up to the present, Western consumers and business people have used money and other controls to exert influence on the rug weavers. Wool is now being spun by machine rather than by hand; rugs are more uniform in color, design, and size; chemical processes are used to treat the color and sheen of rugs. Weavers have become more extrinsically oriented, and the rugs are very different. It has been said that modern rugs seem to come from the hands of the weavers, whereas the older rugs seem to have come from the hearts of the weavers. (1978, p. 195)

Intrinsically motivated work, work that comes from the heart and not from the most straightforward, mechanical method, is most likely to produce true creativity.

The Evidence

Over the past eight years, my colleagues and I have gathered a great deal of evidence on the intrinsic motivation hypothesis of creativity. In all of it, our aim has been the same: To determine if social factors in the work environment, by influencing intrinsic/extrinsic motivational orientation, affect creativity. With few exceptions, our evidence tells us that the answer to this question is Yes, whether we are studying adults or children, whether we are examining problem-solving, verbal creativity, or artistic creativity.

The evidence comes from four sources. The first, which I described earlier, is based on the retrospective reports of people who have been widely recognized for their creativity. My students and I have combed through the autobiographies, letters, and journals of such people, looking for remarks on the effects of various social factors on their motivation for creative work and the creativity of the work they did produce under various work environments.

The second source is experimental research that I have conducted in collaboration with colleagues and students. All of these studies use the same basic paradigm: Subjects participate in individual sessions in a laboratory. They are each given an open-ended activity (a heuristic, creativity task) that results in some product. We manipulate the conditions under which subjects work. Some of them are placed under a strong extrinsic constraint and others are placed under a lower level of constraint, or no constraint at all. After they have finished working, we try in some way to assess their intrinsic interest in the work they have just done. Finally, when the study is completed, we obtain ratings of the creativity of each subject's work.

The creativity measures we use in these studies are all based on consensual assessment (Amabile, 1982b). This technique rests on an operational definition of creativity:

> A product or response is creative to the extent that appropriate observers indepen-

dently agree it is creative. Appropriate observers are those familiar with the domain in which the product was created or the response articulated.

Earlier, I presented a conceptual definition of creativity: A product or response is creative if it is a novel and appropriate solution to an open-ended task. As reasonable as this definition may be, it is difficult to translate into useful measurement operations. We have no objective yardsticks of novelty that we can apply to a wide variety of domains, and it is even difficult to measure appropriateness (or how heuristic a task is, for that matter).

But people seem to know what they mean when they call something creative. Although it is difficult to describe what features of products or ideas lead people to say that something is more or less creative, creativity seems to be something that people can recognize when they see it. Thus, it is reasonable to rely on subjective judgments of creativity by experts in a particular field. If, using their own individual subjective definitions of creativity, those experts agree on the creativity of products obtained in our studies, then we accept their judgments as valid measures of creativity.

One creativity task we have used in this research involves artistic production. Subjects are given a wide variety of colored pieces of paper and other materials, cardboard and glue, and are asked to make a collage. The instructions are deliberately open-ended, since the definition of creativity requires a heuristic task. And the task is deliberately chosen as a relatively easy one, since we want to look at the effects of social environments and not the effects of special skills such as drawing ability. Everyone is given a fairly liberal time period in which to complete the collage. After all the subject-sessions have been completed, we find approximately ten people who have had at least three years of experience doing studio art, and have them come into the laboratory individually to rate the collages on creativity. We ask them to rate each collage relative to the others, using their own subjective definitions of creativity. Typically, this method yields interjudge reliability over .75. In other words, working independently, without being trained to agree, and without being told what to look for, these judges agree with each other quite well on the degree of creativity demonstrated in each collage.

We have designed similar measures of verbal creativity—similar in the sense that the tasks and instructions are relatively open-ended, the tasks do not depend heavily on special skills, and the experts used as judges show high degrees of interjudge reliability in their assessments of the creativity of the products. For adults, we present instructions for writing a haiku-style poem or a free-verse poem on a particular theme. The judges for this task are people who have been involved in reading and writing poetry for at least three years. For children, we present a storybook that has no words and ask them to tell the story aloud by saying one sentence for each page in the book. Later, elementary-school teachers read transcripts of the children's stories and rate them on creativity.

A measure of problem-solving is in the preliminary development stages. For this task, we present subjects with several identical regular geometric outlines and ask them to fill in the outline in as many different ways as they can with smaller regular geometric shapes. The judges are mathematicians.

These measures, or variants on them, have been used in our laboratory studies of adults' creativity and in the third kind of evidence we have gathered on the intrinsic motivation hypothesis: school-based studies of children's creativity. Most of the research we have done with children follows a paradigm similar to that used for adults. Each child participates in an individual session outside of the classroom. During these sessions, the children are all given the same creativity task or tasks (such as making a collage and telling a story). Each child is presented with these activities under one of the experimental conditions of the particular study—for example, a strong social constraint, or a weak social constraint, or no constraint. After all of the sessions have been completed, appropriate judges assess the creativity of each of the products made by the children.

The fourth kind of evidence comes from a radically different methodology used with a radically different subject population. In collaboration with Stan Gryskiewicz of the Center for Creative Leadership, I have interviewed 120 scientists working in Research and Development laboratories within a wide variety of corporations from around the world (Amabile & Gryskiewicz, 1985). Using this non-experimental technique, we have attempted to discover how the social/environmental factors that we study experimentally affect motivation and creativity in this real-world arena for creativity. Because we wanted to discover the specific stimulants and obstacles to creativity in the corporate environment (and, particularly, within the R & D environment), we asked a very specific question. We asked each scientist to tell us about two events from his or her work experience—one that stood out as an example of high creativity and one that stood out as an example of low creativity (defining creativity in whatever manner they wished). We told them to describe the problem or task, the context, and anything about the persons involved or the work environment that distinguished that event from others.

Overall, there is remarkable concordance between these four quite different sources of evidence: Retrospective reports of outstandingly creative people, laboratory experiments on the effects of social factors on adults' creativity, experimental studies of the effects of these same social factors on children's creativity, and detailed anecdotal reports of the influence of social factors on creativity in Research and Development. These sources yield information on six specific social factors in the work environment: evaluation, surveillance, reward, competition, restriction of choice, and time pressures.

Going for the Perfect 10: Evaluation

It is clear, from the introspective writings of well-known creative people, that, perhaps more than anything else, an excessive concern with external evaluation undermines their creativity. A prime example is the poet Sylvia Plath, whose obsession with favorable reaction to her work precipitated a severe writer's block that persisted for years. Her journals are full of explicit and implicit concern about external evaluation of her writing:

> I have been spoiled, so spoiled by my early success with Seventeen, with Harper's, and Mademoiselle. I figured if I ever worked over a story and it didn't sell, or wrote a piece for practice and couldn't market it, something was wrong. I was gifted, talented—oh, all the editors said so—so why couldn't I expect big returns for every minute of writing? (Hughes &McCullough, 1982, p. 250)
>
> I dream too much of fame, posturings, a novel published, not people gesturing, speaking, growing and cracking into print. (p. 180)
>
> Editors and publishers and critics and the world . . . I want acceptance there, to feel my work good and well-taken. Which ironically freezes me at my work, corrupts my nunnish labor of work-for-itself-as-its-own-reward. (p. 305)

The notion that excessive or inappropriate concern with evaluation can undermine creativity has long been part of the tradition of creativity research. Three decades ago, the brainstorming principles articulated by Osborn (1953) and developed into the Creative Problem Solving Program (Parnes, 1967) rested on the assumption that evaluation can be detrimental to creativity. Indeed, the "deferment of judgment" principle gives rise to the first rule of brainstorming: "Criticism is ruled out."

Because external evaluation of work is so pervasive in educational and industrial settings, we have conducted a number of studies to examine its possible impact on creativity. The initial study of evaluation expectation (Amabile, 1979) was designed to test the hypothesis that such constraint will undermine creativity performance on heuristic tasks. The task used was collage-making—a task for which the path to a "creative solution" is not clear and straightforward. For some subjects in constraint conditions, however, this task was rendered algorithmic: They were given specific instructions on how to make a collage that would be judged as creative. In this way, it was possible to test the hypothesized differential effects of constraint on heuristic and algorithmic tasks.

In accord with McGraw's (1978) theory, I predicted that subjects placed under constraint (evaluation expectation) for the heuristic collage-making task would show lower levels of both creativity and intrinsic interest in the task than would no-constraint controls. In addition, since McGraw suggests that extrinsic motivation will enhance performance on algorithmic tasks, I expected that the group placed under constraint but given explicit instructions on "being creative" would show higher levels of creativity than controls, but would show lower levels of intrinsic interest.

In addition to the constraint and instructions variables, a "focus" variable was included in this design. Some subjects within each level of evaluation expectation were asked to focus on the creativity of their art works. Some were asked to focus on the technical aspects; others were not given any particular focus. This variable was included to determine whether, in some unexpected way, subjects could generate algorithms for producing creative collages simply by knowing that the task called for creativity.

The subjects in this study were 95 women enrolled in an introductory psychology course at Stanford University. Subjects in the control conditions (nonevaluation-no focus, nonevaluation-technical focus, and nonevaluation-creativity focus) were told:

> There is one important point that I should make clear before you begin. We won't be using your design as source of data. We are not interested at all in the activity itself or what you do with the activity. We are only interested in the mood you report on the questionnaire. So we do not care about the design itself at all—its only purpose is to provide you with this experience so we can see how it affects your mood.

In addition, the subjects in the nonevaluation-technical focus condition were asked to concentrate on the technical aspects of the activity "for this particular mood induction," and subjects in the nonevaluation-creativity focus condition were asked to focus on the creative aspects.

The basic instructions for the five experimental groups (evaluation-no focus, evaluation-technical focus, evaluation-creativity focus, evaluation-specific technical focus, evaluation-specific creativity focus) were:

> There is one more important point that I should make clear before you begin. In addition to your questionnaire, we will be looking at your finished design as an important source of data. We have five graduate artists from the Stanford Art Department working with us, and when this experiment is over, we will have them come in to judge each art work. They will make a detailed evaluation of your design, noting the good points and criticizing the weaknesses. And since we know that our subjects are interested in how they were evaluated, we will send you a copy of each judge's evaluation of your design in about two weeks.

In addition, subjects in the evaluation-technical focus condition were told that the judges would base their evaluation on how technically good the designs were. Subjects in the evaluation-creativity focus condition were told that the judges would base their evaluation on how creative the designs were. Those in the evaluation-specific technical focus condition were told that the judges would make their technical evaluation on the basis of six elements: (1) the neatness of the design; (2) the balance of the design; (3) the amount of planning evident; (4) the level of organization in the design; (5) the presence of actual recognizable figures or objects in the design; and (6) the degree to which the design expresses something to them. Finally, subjects in the evaluation-specific creativity focus condition were told that judges would base their creativity evaluation on seven elements: (1) the novelty of the idea; (2) the novelty shown in the use of the materials; (3) the amount of variation in the shapes used; (4) the asymmetry in the design; (5) the amount of detail in the design; (6) the complexity of the design; and (7) the amount of effort evident. These components had, in fact, correlated closely with pretest judges' ratings of technical goodness and creativity, respectively.

The 95 collages were judged on 16 artistic dimensions by 15 artists. Judges' ratings on the creativity of these collages strongly support the hypothesis that evaluation expectation is detrimental to creativity. With one exception, the nonevaluation groups were higher on creativity than the corresponding evaluation groups. That is, the nonevaluation-no focus group was higher than the evaluation-no focus group; the nonevaluation-technical focus group was higher than both the evaluation-technical focus group and the evaluation-specific technical focus group; and the nonevaluation-creativity focus group was higher than the evaluation-creativity focus group. As predicted from McGraw's theory, the only evaluation group that was higher on creativity than the corresponding nonevaluation group was that which received specific, detailed instructions (an *algorithm*) for producing a collage that would be judged as creative. This one group, the evaluation-specific creativity focus group, was higher on creativity than the nonevaluation-creativity focus group.

In this study, I assessed subjects' intrinsic interest in the collage activity with a questionnaire administered after they had finished their collages. One item on this questionnaire, for example, asked, "Did you view your engagement in the art activity as motivated more by intrinsic factors, like your own interest, or by extrinsic factors, like the experimenter's instructions?" I had predicted that, overall, the nonevaluation groups would be higher in self-rated interest than the experimental groups. In particular, I expected that even though the specific creativity focus subjects might exhibit superior creativity as a result of their task instruction, their intrinsic interest would still be undermined by evaluation expectation. This overall pattern was, in fact, obtained.

This study, then, demonstrates a negative effect of evaluation expectation on creativity. On the face of it, however, it also appears to demonstrate a positive effect of evaluation expectation if people are given specific instructions on how to "be creative." For two reasons, this high creativity of the specific creativity instructions group must be interpreted cautiously. On a practical level, it is unlikely that creativity in everyday performance could be enhanced by telling people exactly what constitutes a creative performance. The reason we value creative work so highly is that we cannot know beforehand just how to achieve a novel and appropriate response. On a theoretical level, the conceptual definition of creativity clearly disallows the consideration of the specific instruction task as "creative." According to that definition, the task must be heuristic for the product of task engagement to be considered creative. In this study, specific instructions on how to make a collage that would be judged as "creative" rendered the task algorithmic. Thus, according to the conceptual definition, it is simply inappropriate to assign the label "creative" to the performance of the specific creativity instructions group. It is appropriate, though, to assign that label to the performance of the nonevaluation groups since, for them, the task remained a heuristic one.

In order to firmly establish the finding that evaluation expectation has negative effects on adults' creativity, we did two replications. In both, a simple design was used: (1) subjects expected or did not expect evaluation of their work, and (2) they worked either alone or in the presence of others. One of these studies examined verbal creativity and the other, artistic creativity. Since the latter also included surveillance as a factor, I will discuss it in the next section. That study's results on the evaluation factor, however, were strongly supportive of the conclusion that expected evaluation undermines creativity.

In the study of verbal creativity (Amabile, Goldfarb, & Brackfield, 1982, Study One), there were four experimental conditions. Subjects either expected that their written work would be evaluated by experts, or they expected no evaluation. In addition, they either worked alone or in a group of others where each person wrote individually. Subjects in this study were 48 female undergraduates enrolled in an introductory psychology course at Brandeis University. So that subjects would remain ignorant of the study's focus on creativity, they were all told that this was an experiment on handwriting analysis. They were each to write a haiku-style poem as a handwriting sample with "original content" (which presumably would yield a better sample than copied material).

Subjects in the evaluation conditions were told that the experimenter intended to relate handwriting features to poem content, and that both would be evaluated by expert judges. In addition, these subjects expected that they would receive a copy of the judges' evaluations of their poems. Those in the nonevaluation conditions were told that the experimenter was simply interested in the handwriting of an original work and was not at all concerned with the content of their poems. Evaluation of poem content was not mentioned. As a cross variable, either subjects were alone as they worked on their poems, or they worked in a room with three others (the "coaction" condition).

Creativity of the poems was assessed according to the consensual assessment technique. In strong support of the intrinsic motivation hypothesis, and in good agreement with the earlier study, there was a significant main effect of evaluation expectation on the creativity ratings. Nonevaluation subjects wrote poems that were significantly more creative than those written by evaluation subjects. There was no main effect of the coaction variable, and no interaction between the two.

Evaluation was one of the most important environmental obstacles to creativity that appeared in the interviews with R&D scientists (Amabile & Gryskiewicz, 1985). In their descriptions of low creativity events, these scientists repeatedly mentioned oppressive or overly salient evaluation procedures. In fact, evaluation was ranked as the fifth most frequently-mentioned obstacle, appearing in fully one-third of the interviews.

These studies demonstrate that expected evaluation can undermine adults' artistic, verbal, and problem-solving creativity. Do the same effects hold for young children? The evidence is not yet clear. In two attempts to demonstrate this effect with children, we failed. In a third attempt, we partially succeeded. In the first study (Mukai, 1983), 121 boys and girls in Grades 1-5 made collages under one of four conditions: (1) adult evaluation, where they expected that a principal from another school would give them a report card on their artwork; (2) peer evaluation, where they expected that a child from another school would give them a report card on their artwork; (3) self-evaluation, where they expected that they would later anonymously fill out a report card for themselves on their artwork; and (4) no evaluation, where report cards were never mentioned. Judges' subsequent ratings of the creativity of the children's collages revealed no significant differences between the groups.

In the second evaluation-expectation study with children, we increased the salience of the evaluation manipulation, and we had children both make collages and tell stories. Here, in addition to a no-evaluation condition, there was an adult evaluation condition, in which children expected that the experimenter herself would immediately give them report cards on their work and would later show those report cards to the teacher. In a third condition, children again expected to fill out self-evaluative report cards. There were no significant differences between conditions on either of the measures of creativity.

The reasons for these negative results are puzzling. Perhaps children in this age range are too young to be affected by the promise of future evaluation of their work. We now have some evidence that this may be the case. In a recent dissertation (Hennessey, 1985), children (ages 7-12) made designs using a computer under conditions of no expected evaluation, expected evaluation from the experimenter, or expected evaluation from the computer. For the younger children, there was no significant effect of the evaluation variable—the same finding we obtained previously. However, for the older children (ages 10-12), there was a significant negative effect of expected evaluation. Children in the nonevaluation group produced designs rated as significantly more creative than those produced by children in the experimenter-evaluation condition. The superiority of the nonevaluation group over the computer-evaluation group was nearly statistically significant. It appears, then, that expected evaluation may only have a negative impact on children who are older than elementary-school age.

What about *actual* evaluation, in contrast to mere promised evaluation? Perhaps this might have more of an impact on young children. My colleagues and I (Berglas et al., 1981) set out to examine the effects of actual prior evaluation on children's subsequent creativity. In an attempt to study the impact of increasing the external-control aspects of the evaluation, we included a condition designed to raise its salience (the "size of the stakes"). Thus, some children were told that their doing well determined the potential job status of the experimenter. For others, no external event was contingent on their performance. It was expected that increasing the salience of evaluation would lead to greater creativity decrements. In addition, we decided to examine possible differential effects of types of positive evaluation. Based on earlier theorizing (Deci, 1975), it seemed likely that evaluation directed at specific aspects of task performance (task-based evaluation) would convey more clear and salient competence information than would evaluation vaguely praising the performer (person-based evaluation). Thus, task-based evaluation should have a less detrimental effect on creativity than person-based evaluation.

This study employed a 2 X 2 factorial design with a separate control group. The subjects were 97 boys and girls in grades 2-6 at a private elementary school in eastern Massachusetts. All children made two art works. Experimental-group subjects received positive evaluations on their first art work, with half receiving task-based evaluation, and half receiving person-based. As a cross dimension, half of these subjects believed that the experimenter's welfare was in some way contingent on their performance, and half did not. After receiving their evaluations, the experimental-group subjects made the second art work—a collage that was subsequently rated on creativity. Control-group subjects simply made the two art works, with no evaluation and no information about external contingencies for their performance.

Feedback based on specific information about task performance led to somewhat higher levels of creativity. In addition, there was some tendency for children who believed the experimenter was dependent on their performance to produce less creative collages. Neither of these main effects was significant by an analysis of variance, however, nor was their interaction.

The most striking pattern in the creativity results is the clear superiority of the control group over all four experimental groups. Thus, although there might be some differences between types of positive evaluation in their effect on subsequent creativity, this study suggests that the overall negative effects of prior evaluation may be much more important. Certainly, all of the experimental-group children had received competence information about their artistic ability. At the same time, they most likely expected that their performance on the second activity—collage-making—would also be evaluated by the experimenter. This controlling aspect might have been more salient than the informational aspect of the feedback, regardless of whether it was person- or task-based.

It appears, then, that concern about external evaluation can definitely undermine the creativity of adults. For young children, however, the promise of external evaluation may not be concrete or salient enough unless they have actually experienced prior evaluation from the source in question.

Big Brother is Watching You: Surveillance

Many people feel that the presence of others while they are working can interfere with their creativity, particularly if those others are watching their work. Why might we expect surveillance to undermine creativity? Whoever the members of the audience might be, there is almost always some possibility for evaluative reactions on the part of that audience. Thus, since expected evaluation appears to have negative effects on creativity, we might predict that surveillance of work would have the same negative effects.

Subjects in the study designed to examine this phenomenon (Amabile, Goldfarb, & Brackfield, 1982, Study 2) were 40 undergraduate women enrolled in an introductory psychology course at Brandeis University. They participated in individual sessions. Equal numbers of subjects were assigned randomly to one of four conditions: nonevaluation-no audience, nonevaluation-audience, evaluation-no audience, evaluation-audience. In this study, no subjects were told to focus on particular aspects of the collages. As in the previous study (Amabile, 1979), women with extremely high levels of art experience were excluded, and subjects were told that the experiment examined the effects of various activities on mood.

The experimenter introduced the crucial manipulations as she presented the task. She told subjects in the evaluation-audience condition that their art works would be used as an important source of data in the experiment. She told them that, on the other side of a one-way mirror in the experimental room, four student-artists were waiting to watch subjects making their collages. These artists had supposedly been hired to make expert evaluations of their collage-making and their finished products, "noting the good points and criticizing the weaknesses." In addition, the experimenter told the subjects that they would see these evaluations before they left the experimental session.

Subjects in the evaluation-no audience condition received similar instructions. For them, however, a heavy curtain was drawn across the one-way mirror. They were informed that four student-artists waited in a conference room down the hall to view and inspect the finished collages. As in the evaluation-audience condition, subjects were told that the judges' expert evaluations would note the good points and criticize the weaknesses, and that they would see these evaluations before leaving.

Evaluation was not mentioned to subjects in the two nonevaluation conditions and, indeed, they believed that the collage would not be used as a source of data. Subjects in the nonevaluation-audience condition were told that other subjects waited for a different experiment in the room on the other side of the one-way mirror. These other undergraduates were supposedly waiting in the dark for a vision experiment. Thus, although subjects in this condition believed that they would be seen while working on their collages, the audience would be relatively nonevaluative. Subjects in the nonevaluation-no audience condition were told nothing about an audience; for them, the one-way mirror was covered.

In support of the intrinsic motivation hypothesis of creativity, and in replication of the earlier study on adults' artistic creativity, the results revealed a significant effect of evaluation expectation on creativity. In addition, there was a nearly significant negative effect of surveillance on creativity: Those subjects who believed they were being watched made less creative collages than those for whom the mirror was covered, regardless of the nature of the expected audience.

Subjects' post-experimental questionnaire responses in this study yielded some intriguing results. Apparently, evaluation was quite salient to subjects in those conditions. When asked to rate the extent to which they felt anxious, evaluation subjects gave significantly higher self-ratings than did nonevaluation subjects. A similar main effect of evaluation held for subjects' responses to a question asking how concerned they were with possible evaluations of their work. In light of the possibility that attention might mediate detrimental effects of constraint on creativity, one result from this questionnaire is of primary importance: Evaluation subjects reported significantly more distraction while working than did nonevaluation subjects. As might be expected, there was a significant negative correlation ($r = -.41$) between subjects' rated concern with evaluation and the creativity of their collages.

Apparently, then, surveillance might have the same sort of undermining effect on creativity that expected external evaluation does. If, as discussed earlier, it is harmful to creativity to believe that someone will be critically viewing our work in the future, it may also be harmful to believe that someone is watching our work in the present.

An Offer You Can't Refuse: Reward

In one of my interviews with Research and Development managers, the interviewee was telling a particularly engrossing study. A small team of researchers had made an important break-through in the development of a new product. At the end of his story, as he was trying to find reasons for their success, he said, "There was no defined reward; people were working for the challenge and the potential that a new business would be established that they could benefit from."

This was a fairly common theme in the creativity interviews: Although researchers must feel that their efforts will be properly compensated by good salary and benefits, promotions, favorable working conditions, and so on, they find it easier to be creative when there is no specific, well-defined, large reward riding on the success of a particular project.

A concentration on reward seems to be detrimental to other types of creative endeavors, as well. It is startling that T. S. Eliot became depressed after he won the Nobel prize in literature. When a friend approached him with congratulations, saying, "It's high time, I would say!" Eliot replied, "Rather too soon, I would say. The Nobel is a ticket to one's own funeral. No one has ever done anything after he got it." (Simpson, 1982, p. 11). Wherever Eliot had collected his data on that point, he firmly believed that the receipt of this "ultimate" prize somehow depleted an author's productivity and creativity.

The poet Anne Sexton, too, seemed wary of the detrimental effects that excessive concern with reward could have on creativity. In a letter to her agent, she said, "I am in love with money, so don't be mistaken, but first I want to write good poems. After that I am anxious as hell to make money and fame and bring the stars all down." (Sexton & Ames, 1977, pp. 287-288). And when her friend W. D. Snodgrass won the Pulitzer Prize for poetry, she cautioned him against losing his original intrinsic motivation for writing:

> So okay. "Heart's Needle" is a great poem. But you have got better than that inside you. To hell with their prize and their fame. You've got to sit down now and write some more "real" . . . write me some blood. That is why you were great in the first place. Don't let prizes stop you from your original courage. (Sexton & Ames, 1977, pp. 109-110)

And contracting for reward, even receiving some of the reward in advance, might have similar negative effects. Dostoevsky appears to have been virtually paralyzed by a large monetary advance for writing a novel which he had not yet even conceived:

> And as for me, this is my story: I worked and was tortured. You know what it means to compose? No, thank God, you do not! I believe you have never written to order, by the yard, and have never experienced that hellish torture. Having received in advance from the Russy Viestnik so much money (Horror! 4,500 rubles). I fully hoped in the beginning of the year that poesy would not desert me, that the poetical idea would flash out and develop artistically towards the end of the year, and that I should succeed in satisfying everyone . . . but on the 4th of December . . . I threw it all to the devil. I assure you that the novel might have been tolerable; but I got incredibly sick of it just because it was tolerable, and not positively good—I did not want that. (Allen, 1948, p. 231)

Because reward is such a widely-studied variable in psychology, there has been some interest among researchers in the effects of reward on creativity. One experimental study of this question (McGraw & McCullers, 1979) used a measure that is quite different from those used in my program of research: Luchins' (1942) water jar problems. Each problem presents subjects with drawings of three water jars (A, B, and C) of different sizes. For each problem, subjects are to write an equation for using the three jars to measure out an exact amount of water. Each of the first nine problems in the series can be solved with the same equation, B

- A - 2C. Problem #10, the "set-breaking" problem, can only be solved with a different, simpler equation: A - C. Breaking out of a mental set can be considered an important aspect of creative thinking; indeed, it can be thought of as breaking out of familiar algorithms and attacking a problem heuristically. The water jar series first establishes a mental set and then tests whether people can break out of that set. In this particular study, half of the subjects were offered rewards for solving the water jar problems, and half were not. Although there were no differences in solution time or error rates on the first nine problems, subjects who had been offered rewards took significantly longer to solve the tenth problem than did non-rewarded subjects, and they made more errors on that problem. It appears that, because they were extrinsically motivated, they persisted in attempting to use their familiar algorithm, even when it was inappropriate.

Another study found effects for both performance and expressed interest. Most studies that examine the effects of reward on intrinsic motivation use a paradigm in which subjects are promised some tangible reward before engaging in an activity, but the reward itself is delivered after the activity has been completed. Critics of overjustification research (e.g., Reiss & Sushinsky, 1975) have suggested that this methodology allows for alternative explanations of subsequent declines in task engagement. For example, they suggest that subjects are so distracted by anticipation of reward during the initial task engagement that their enjoyment of the activity is hampered. Thus, according to this explanation, later lack of interest in the activity occurs not because subjects came to see it only as a means to some external goal, but because their intrinsic enjoyment of the activity was directly blocked by the "competing response" of reward anticipation.

In this study of reward effects on children's creativity, Beth Hennessey and I (Amabile, Hennessey, & Grossman, 1986, Study One) used a paradigm that renders the competing response hypothesis untenable. The reward offered to children before task engagement was not a tangible gift to be delivered afterwards. Rather, it was an enjoyable activity—using a Polaroid camera—that children were allowed to do before the target activity. In other words, children in the reward condition promised to do the target activity in order to first have a chance to use the camera. Children in the no-reward condition were simply allowed to use the camera and then given the target activity; there was no contingency between the two. Since children in both conditions had already enjoyed the "reward" before the activity began, then, it is unlikely that any reward-related "competing responses" were operating.

In addition to the offer of reward, task labeling was introduced as a second independent variable in this study. This was done to test the possibility that simply viewing activities as "work" can lead to the same undermining effects on intrinsic motivation and creativity as being placed under extrinsic constraints. That is, rather than cognitively discounting their own interest in an activity when some salient external goal is present, people (particularly children) might simply come to see such activity as "work"—as something that is done only under external constraint. Thus, introducing a task to children as "work" might directly instantiate the task attitude that they are presumed to develop under conditions of social constraint.

The 58 boys and 57 girls who participated in this study were enrolled in Grades 1-5. Within each grade, children were randomly assigned to experimental condition according to a 2 x 3 factorial design: Two levels of reward (reward or no reward) were crossed with three levels of task label ("work" or "play" or no label). The children participated in individual sessions with a female experimenter who told them that she had different activities for them to do. The target activity for all children was the same—telling a story to a book without words.

The experimenter began by telling children in the reward conditions that she would let them take two pictures with a Polaroid camera if they would promise to then tell her a story from the book. All children expressed enthusiasm for playing with the camera, and all did promise to do the target activity later. At this point, the experimenter asked children in the reward conditions to sign a contract stating their promise. Children in the no-reward conditions were simply told that the experimenter had two different things for them to do–taking pictures with a Polaroid camera, and telling a story from a book. No promise was requested and no contract was presented. All children were then allowed to use the camera to take two photographs of interesting objects the experimenter had brought. These photographs were than labeled with the child's name and placed in a large album.

After the picture-taking session had ended, the experimenter reminded children in the reward conditions of their promise to tell a story. She then presented the storytelling task according to the appropriate label condition. To children in the "work" conditions, she presented the task as "something for you to work on." To those in the "play" conditions, she presented it as "something for you to play with." She used neither a work label nor a play label in presenting the task to children in the "no label" conditions.

Overall, children in the no-reward conditions told stories that were significantly more creative than those told by children in the reward conditions. There was, however, no significant effect of the task label variable. Although it is possible that overjustification effects are not mediated by an adoption of the view that a task is "work," it is also possible that the task label manipulation in this study was too weak to produce any reliable effects. We are conducting new research to address this question.

This study, then, provides clear evidence that, at least under some circumstances, undertaking an activity as a means to an end can undermine creativity. It is important that this effect occurs even when nonrewarded subjects also experience the "reward," and even when the reward is delivered before the target activity. The only difference in the experiences of rewarded and nonrewarded children in this study was their perception of the reward as contingent or not contingent upon the target activity. Thus, it appears that the perception of a task as the means to an end is crucial to creativity decrements in task engagement.

A number of theorists have proposed that, in order to undermine intrinsic interest, rewards must be perceived as a means to an extrinsic end (Calder & Staw, 1975; Deci, 1975; Kruglanski et al., 1971; Lepper & Greene, 1978; Ross, 1977; Staw, 1976). One clear way to demonstrate the crucial role of perceiving a task as a means to a reward is to offer people a *choice* concerning task engagement. If people perceive themselves as freely choosing to do an activity for which a reward is offered, they might well adopt an extrinsic motivational orientation toward that activity. They should come to view the task as work, and their own engagement in the activity as motivated by that external reward. On the other hand, if people are simply presented with a task to do and told that they will be paid, with no choice in the matter, reward should not have this detrimental effect.

In a recent study (Amabile, Hennessey, & Grossman, 1986, Study Three), my students and I examined the interactive effects of reward and choice on adults' artistic creativity. All subjects were brought to the laboratory expecting to take part in a person perception experiment to partially fulfill a course requirement. About 10 minutes into the person perception task, the experimenter pretended that a videotape player was operating incorrectly, forcing her to terminate the experiment for which the subjects had come to the laboratory. She then presented the target activity (collage-making) as an alternative experiment the subject could do. The person perception task was used to ensure that reward subjects would perceive themselves as being rewarded for the target activity itself, and not simply for experiment participation.

In presenting the collage task, the experimenter delivered the independent-variable manipulation according to a 2 x 2 factorial design which crossed two levels of choice with two levels of reward. In the no-choice, no-reward condition, subjects were told:

Well, I'm doing another study and I guess I can have you do that instead for the rest of the time. It involves spending about 15 minutes making a paper collage.

In addition to this, subjects in the no choice, reward condition were told, "I'm paying subjects $2 in that study, so what I'll do is give you credit for the part you just did and you'll earn $2 for doing the second study." By contrast, instructions to the subjects in the choice, no-reward condition stressed the voluntary nature of further participation:

> Well, I'm doing another study and I guess I could have you do that instead for the rest of the time. It involves spending about 15 minutes making a paper collage. Would you be willing to do that?

Additionally, subjects in the choice, reward condition were told, "I can give you credit for the part you just did, and since I'm paying subjects for the second study, you can earn $2 if you'll agree to do the collage. Would you be willing to do that for $2?" All subjects in the choice conditions agreed to participate in the collage-making activity. After presenting the standard collage materials, the experimenter placed $2 on the table in front of subjects in the reward conditions, in order to increase the salience of the reward. Subjects were left alone for 15 minutes to work on their collages.

The expected interaction between reward and choice was obtained. Subjects who chose to engage in the activity in order to obtain a reward exhibited the lowest creativity. On the other hand, those who earned a reward for doing the art activity with no choice in the matter exhibited the highest creativity. The two nonrewarded groups were intermediate.

Thus, choice can be an important mediator of the effects of reward on creativity. As noted earlier, previous theories of intrinsic motivation suggest that subjects who perceive themselves as contracting to do a task in order to receive a reward will experience decrements in intrinsic motivation. By extension of the intrinsic motivation hypothesis of creativity, this effect should obtain for the creativity of the performance as well. This notion, however, can only explain the relatively low creativity of the choice-reward group. It cannot explain the extremely high creativity of the no choice-reward group.

In their discussion of the interaction between reward and choice, some theorists (Folger et al., 1978; Kruglanski, 1978) suggest that high levels of intrinsic interest might be obtained under no choice-reward conditions because subjects in those conditions experience positive affect. The same phenomenon could be operating in this study. Subjects in the no choice-reward condition would not be extrinsically motivated, because they would have no reason to perceive the art activity as a means they chose to achieve some external end. They would, however, be expected to feel rather happy about making an unexpected $2 for 15 minutes' work, in addition to the experimental credit they expected to receive. This positive affect could be expected to add to the intrinsic interest that subjects already had in the collage-making activity, thus enhancing their creativity. By contrast, subjects in the reward-choice condition might have perceived themselves as extrinsically motivated, as having contracted to do the task in order to obtain a reward. Their feelings of being pressured while working support this explanation. This negative affect, this feeling of being pressured, could well have undermined their creativity.

Recently, we replicated this interaction between reward and choice with children (Amabile, Hennessey, & Grossman, 1986, Study Two). The subjects in this study were 80 boys and girls in Grades 3-5. Children were randomly assigned to one of four conditions: choice-reward, choice-no reward, no choice-reward, and no choice-no reward. The two target activities were collage-making and storytelling. The reward consisted of being allowed to take two pictures with a Polaroid camera, which was the first activity introduced either as a reward (in the reward conditions) or as simply one of the activities (in the no reward conditions).

Children participated in the experimental sessions individually. Children in the choice-reward condition, after a brief explanation of the tasks, were told:

> You can do these things or you can go back to your classroom if you want, but if you promise to work on these things for me, I will let you, as a reward, first take two photographs with this camera. Some kids decide to stay and work on the activities for some reward, and some kids decide to leave. What would you like to do? If the

child agreed to stay, he was then asked to sign a contract stating his promise to do the activities if given the reward. In the choice-no reward condition, children were told: "You can do these things or you can go back to your classroom if you want. Some kids decide to stay and work on the activities and some kids decide to leave. What would you like to do?" Children in the no choice-reward condition were told: "Because you are going to work on these things for me, as a reward, I am first going to let you take two photographs with this camera." And in the no choice-no reward condition, the three tasks were introduced and then the session began.

Creativity of the collages and stories was assessed according to the consensual assessment technique. As with the adults, a significant interaction between reward and choice was obtained. For both the stories and the collages, children who chose to engage in the activity in order to obtain a reward (choice-reward condition) exhibited the lowest creativity of all four groups.

These studies on the effects of reward on creativity agree well with the observations of the R&D managers in the interview study described earlier. Among the organizational factors most inhibiting to creativity, overly-salient or inequitable reward systems were mentioned often. As one interviewee put it, "Rewards have an effect on creativity. I would not like to be put in a situation where you are told that you will get this reward if you get this particular job done" (Amabile, & Gryskiewicz, 1985, p. 22). The conclusion seems clear: contracting to receive a salient reward for doing some activity, seeing oneself as doing the activity in order to obtain the reward, can decrease intrinsic motivation in the work itself and undermine the creativity of the outcome.

Winning Isn't Everything, But Losing Is Nothing: Competition

One of the R&D managers I interviewed made a startling statement. He said, "Productivity has stifled creativity." He did not mean that creative people cannot be productive, or that productive work cannot also be creative. He elaborated: "Productivity has stifled creativity. Someone in our group has a great idea: the problem is there's not enough time to explore it fully. Because of the competition we face, there's too much emphasis on immediate productivity."

This quote reveals what may be considered the perverse nature of the creative process: The more desperately we want (or need) to be creative, the more difficult it becomes. We cannot win for trying, it seems. Competition seems capable of eliciting precisely the wrong kind of trying–wanting only to produce something faster than everyone else or better than everyone else by external standards. This, too, was a factor that trapped Sylvia Plath in her longstanding writer's block. She often fell into fits of jealousy and competitive rage, saying, for example, "Yes, I want the world's praise, money, and love, and am furious with anyone, especially with anyone I know or who has had a similar experience, getting ahead of me" (Hughes & McCullough, 1982). On many occasions, these concerns clearly interfered with Plath's ability to work:

> All I need now is to hear that G. S. [George Starbuck] or M. K. [Maxine Kumin] has won the Yale and get a rejection of my children's book. A. S. [Anne Sexton] has her book accepted at Houghton Mifflin and this afternoon will be drinking champagne. Also an essay accepted by PJHH, the copycat. But who's to criticize a more successful copycat. Not to mention a poetry reading at McLean . . . And now my essay, on Withens, will come back from PJHH, and my green-eyed fury prevents me from working. (Hughes & McCullough, 1982, p. 304)

A group of 49 corporate executives, lower-level managers, educators, and researchers participating in a creativity conference served as subjects in a simple study I conducted on the effects of competition on creativity. All of the participants received a booklet containing Luchins' (1942) water jar problems that I described earlier; there were 5 set-making problems and one set-breaking problem at the end. In contrast to the set-breaking problem used by McGraw and McCullers (1979), however, the set-breaking problem could be solved either by the familiar algorithmic 3-jar solution or by the more elegant set-breaking 2-jar solution. At the end of the booklet, there were a few riddles to occupy people who finished before the others.

Half of the participants read noncompetitive instructions at the front of their booklets:

We are giving these problems to illustrate the stages of problem-solving. You'll find that, for each problem, you need to take given elements and figure out how to combine them to get the answer. Before you start on the problems themselves, you will find some instructions at the beginning of the "Water Jar" booklet.

The rest of the participants read competitive instructions:

In the spirit of friendly competition, we're going to have a contest for the best job on these problems. If more than one person gets all the problems correct, we will judge the winner on the basis of the fastest solution time. So, before you start, print your name clearly on the front of your "Water Jar" booklet. And, write the time you finished the last water-jar problem under your name.

On a number of measures the noncompetition group did better. More subjects in this group broke set at least once and solved all six problems correctly. Most importantly, for the last problem, the set-breaking problem, subjects in the noncompetition group used a 2-jar solution instead of the standard 3-jar solution significantly more than subjects in the competition group. Interestingly, although we had intended the riddles to serve simply as a filler task, we found that there were differences between the two groups on that task too. The noncompetition participants were much more likely to try the riddles, suggesting that they were indeed more intrinsically motivated toward this activity than the competition group. Using the maze analogy, we can say that the noncompetition people simply enjoyed being in the maze (working on the problems and riddles in the booklet); they were more willing to explore, to take risks, and they ended up producing more non-standard solutions. By contrast, the extrinsically motivated competition people were more singleminded about getting the goal (winning the competition) by just getting through the maze. They approached the problems in the booklet algorithmically, and as a result were more likely to produce very standard solutions.

Using a very different kind of task, we looked at the effects of competition on children's creativity (Amabile, 1982a). These children were 22 girls, ages 7-12, who participated in one of two "Art Parties." At one party, the girls were asked to make a collage as one of several art activities. At the other party, the girls were told that, as soon as they finished their collages, the artworks would be judged by 3 adults who would then award prizes to the three best. (The same three prizes, incidentally, were present for the noncompetition group, but those girls were told that the prizes would be raffled off.) Not only did the competing girls make collages that were judged as less creative than the noncompetitive girls, but they were also much more restrictive in their approach to the materials. There was much less variability in use of the materials (number of colors used, for example) among girls in the competition group.

As with the other "creativity killers," competition also appears in the list of environmental obstacles to creativity in the stories told to us by R&D scientists: "We had two groups trying to achieve the same thing. It became a win-lose situation, and we all ended up losing," (Amabile & Gryskiewicz, 1985, p. 31).

These results, with both adults and children, suggest that competition can act as a negative influence on creativity in much the same way as the other constraints (such as evaluation, surveillance, and reward). The picture may be more complex than it seems, however. The interviews with R&D managers provide evidence that, while competition can undermine creativity under some circumstances, it can enhance creativity under others. Specifically, competition may be most damaging if an individual feels that he or she must compete with others for rewards or praise. However, if people are working as a team that competes with other teams (either within or outside of a given organizaiton), creativity within the group may actually be enhanced. Experimental research will be needed before we can determine whether this is, in fact, the case and, if it is, what the mechanism might be.

Do it My Way or Do it the Wrong Way: Restricted Choice

Perhaps more than any other single factor, freedom of choice in how to approach problems seems crucial in the creativity of Research and Development personnel. Again and again, my interviewees said that they and their teams are most creative when allowed control over specific plans for how to attack a problem, the specific techniques to use, the pacing of the project, and the use of available resources. One manager claimed that creativity was simply not possible without that freedom of choice: "The boss said, 'If you have free time, work on whatever you like.' That's when I came up with my best idea." Another said that a lack of controlling structure allowed him the freedom to be creative: "I think I came up with this solution to the problem because management didn't believe there *was* a solution to the problem. They gave it to me because I was new, and then they just left me alone. The lack of structure made a big difference."

A sense of internal control and freedom appears also in the writings of more artistically creative individuals. In describing one of the breakthrough periods of modern art, Picasso said, "When we invented cubism, we had no intention of inventing cubism, but simply of expressing what was in us. Nobody drew up a program of action, and though our friends the poets followed our efforts attentively, they never dictated to us" (Zervos, 1952, p. 51).

We conducted a simple study to examine the role of restrictive choice and free choice in children's creativity (Amabile & Gitomer, 1984). These preschool-age boys and girls participated in individual sessions with the experimenter. Materials for making paper collages were divided into ten bins that were displayed to the children as they entered the experimental room. The experimenter told children in the free choice condition that they should choose whichever five boxes they wished to use in making their collage. She told the others that she would make the choice for them. (The specific materials chosen here depended on those used by children in the free choice condition; in other words, a yoked design was used.) For all children, the five boxes not to be used were removed. When the collages made by the children were later judged on creativity, there were significant differences. The collages from the free choice condition were more creative than those from children whose materials were chosen by the experimenter.

Of all the environmental obstacles to creativity that appeared in the low creativity stories told to us by R&D scientists, constrained choice was the most important single factor. It was mentioned by fully half of the people we interviewed. An example: "That was a low creativity situation because they wanted me to follow a particular path without adding any of my input into it. If you want to use your creativity, you can't be told the exact way something should be done." (Amabile & Gryskiewicz, 1985, p. 26)

We Need it Yesterday: Time Pressure

The pressure created by time restrictions may be more immediate in its effects on creativity than any other extrinsic constraint. With strong implicit or explicit deadlines, people may be paralyzed from working at all. Although we do not have experimental data on this point, there is some suggestive evidence. The novelist Thomas Wolfe serves as a good example. After the success of his first novel, he became burdened by the expectations he felt others had for him to produce another masterwork quickly. Although no publisher had given him a deadline for completion of this second manuscript, he had a clear sense of the implicit expectations.

> *At any rate, while my life and energy were absorbed in the emotional vortex which my first book had created, I was getting almost no work done on the second . . . A young writer without a public does not feel the sense of necessity, the pressure of time, as does a writer who has been published and who must now begin to think of time schedules, publishing seasons, the completion of his next book. I realized with a sense of definite shock that I had let six months go by since the publication of my first book and that, save for a great many notes and fragments, I had done nothing. (Wolfe, 1936, p. 26)*

Once the time pressure became explicit, Wolfe's despair and distraction only intensified:

> *Almost a year and a half had elapsed since the publication of my first book and already people had begun to ask that question which is so well meant, but which as year followed year was to become more intolerable to my ears than the most deliberate mockery: "Have you finished your next book yet?" "When is it going to be published?" . . . now, for the first time, I was irrevocably committed so far as the publication of my book was concerned. I began to feel the sensation of pressure, and of naked desperation, which was to become almost maddeningly intolerable in the next three years. (pp. 49-50)*

For members of Research and Development laboratories, too, time pressure is an extrinsic constraint mentioned frequently as a killer of creativity. Indeed, fully one-third mentioned time pressure in their low creativity stories, and one-third mentioned sufficient time as a positive factor in their high creativity stories. Consider these two contrasting quotes: "There was pressure to get the product produced quickly. It was a long-range product, but this is a short-range company"; "He was insulated from day-to-day firefighting, so that he was able to step back and take the time to think of this process and develop it over several months". (Amabile & Gryskiewicz, 1985, pp. 20 & 29).

We will need experimental research to say for sure, but it appears that stringent time limits for work also may operate as an extrinsic constraint undermining intrinsic motivation and creativity.

A Direct Test of the Intrinsic Motivation Hypothesis

Despite obvious differences in the constraints of reward, evaluation, surveillance, competition, restriction of choice, and time pressures, self-perception theory suggests that they should all induce an extrinsic motivational orientation toward the task in question. And, according to the intrinsic motivation hypothesis of creativity, this extrinsic orientation should be detrimental to creativity. Thus, motivational orientation may be the mechanism by which a variety of social factors influence creativity. In addition, motivational orientation toward a task may be an important variable in its own right. People who generally approach their work with an intrinsic orientation may be more consistently creative than people who adopt an extrinsic orientation. Despite its potential importance, the effect of motivational orientation on creativity was not directly studied in any of the experiments I have presented. Instead, in each of those studies, we manipulated some social factor that we assumed would influence motivational state (sometimes attempting to measure motivational state after the fact), and then attributed any differences in creativity to differences in motivation. In order to obtain direct evidence on the intrinsic motivation hypothesis, we did a study (Amabile, 1985) designed to directly create an extrinsic motivational state in some subjects, without going through the intermediate step of imposing an extrinsic constraint. The same method was used to directly create an intrinsically motivated state in other subjects.

For this purpose, we borrowed a technique from Gerald Salancik (1975). Subjects were asked to complete a questionnaire about their attitudes toward something (in this case, attitudes toward the creativity task). Some are given an "intrinsic questionnaire"; all of the items deal with the intrinsically interesting aspects of the activity. Other subjects complete an "extrinsic questionnaire", which deals with only extrinsic reasons for doing the activity. The purpose of the questionnaire is simply to lead subjects to think about the activity in intrinsic terms or in extrinsic terms. Then, immediate effects of this intrinsic or extrinsic orientation can be directly observed.

It was important in this study to find subjects who were already involved in some creative activity on a regular basis so that we might temporarily influence their orientation toward that activity. To this end, we recruited creative writers, using advertisements such as this: "Writers: if you are involved in writing, especially poetry, fiction, or drama, you can make three dollars for about an hour of your time. We are studying people's reasons for writing." Most of those who responded to the ad were undergraduate or graduate students in English or creative writing at Brandeis University or Boston University, although a few were not affiliated with any university. The most important characteristics of these participants, for our purposes, is that they identified themselves as *writers*–they came to us with a high level of involvement in writing.

We had some additional criteria for choosing participants from those answering our ad; subjects had to answer "yes" to one or more of the following:

1. *Completion of one or more advanced creative writing courses.*
2. *Publication of one or more works of poetry.*
3. *Publication of one or more works of fiction or drama.*
4. *Spending an average of four or more hours of their own time per week in writing poetry or fiction.*

The average response to the last question was 6.3 hours, with a range of 3 to 18. Obviously, this group did consist of people who were committed to creative writing.

The basic idea of this study was to have each writer come to the laboratory individually and, once there, to complete a questionnaire on "Reasons for Writing"–reasons for being involved in writing. (Some subjects, in a control condition, did not complete any questionnaire.) The questionnaire would either present only intrinsic reasons for writing or only extrinsic reasons, leading the writer to concentrate on either intrinsic or extrinsic motives for writing. Then, all of the writers would be asked to write a brief poem, which could later be judged by our expert-assessment technique. In this way, we could look at the effects of temporary motivational orientation on creativity.

We wanted to present our subjects with items about writing that were as purely intrinsic or as purely extrinsic as possible. To get such items, we generated an initial list of 30 reasons for writing and asked a group of undergraduates at Brandeis to identify each reason as intrinsic, extrinsic, or neither/both, according to these definitions:

> An **intrinsic** reason is one that focuses on the person's interest in and enjoyment of writing for its own sake, for the pleasure of the actual writing. An **extrinsic** reason is one that focuses on the external things a person can get by writing, the tangible and intangible rewards from other people. An **intrinsically** motivated person is self-motivated, and would write even in the absence of external goals or pressures. An **extrinsically** motivated person is motivated by other sources, by external goals and pressures.

Seven of the reasons were consistently identified as intrinsic:

1. You get a lot of pleasure out of reading something good that you have written.
2. You enjoy the opportunity for self-expression.
3. You achieve new insights through your writing.

4. You derive satisfaction from expressing yourself clearly and eloquently.
5. You feel relaxed when writing.
6. You like to play with words.
7. You enjoy becoming involved with ideas, characters, events, and images in your writing.

Seven other reasons were consistently rated as extrinsic:

1. You realize that, with the introduction of dozens of magazines every year, the market for freelance writing is constantly expanding.
2. You want your writing teachers to be favorably impressed with your writing talent.
3. You have heard of cases where one bestselling novel or collection of poems has made the author financially secure.
4. You enjoy public recognition of your work.
5. You know that many of the best jobs available require good writing skills.
6. You know that writing ability is one of the major criteria for acceptance into graduate school.
7. Your teachers and parents have encouraged you to go into writing.

The introductory paragraph on the two questionnaires was identical. This introduction informed the writers that, in order to study their reasons for being involved in writing, we wanted them to rank-order the seven reasons in order of importance to them. After rank-ordering either the intrinsic reasons or the extrinsic reasons (depending on their condition), the writers were asked to write a short poem where the first and last lines consisted of the single word "Laughter". (Those in the control group were simply asked to write the poem, without completing any questionnaire at all.)

After the study was complete, we asked several poets to judge these haiku-like poems on creativity. The results were quite dramatic. As you might expect, the writers in the control group wrote poems that were judged fairly high on creativity; these were, after all, creative writers. Here is an example of a poem from this group, judged high in creativity:

Laughter
Immortal, true
Blooms, inspires, sings
The song of all smiles
Laughter

The writers in the intrinsic group wrote poems that were judged as somewhat higher in creativity than those in the control group, but the difference was not large. Here is an example from this group, also judged high in creativity:

Laughter
Edgy, breathless
Fracturing, punctuating, breaks
Bullet-like gasps uncontrolled
Laughter

The most important result comes from the extrinsic group. Those writers produced poems that were judged as much lower in creativity than the poems produced by either of the other groups. An example:

Laughter
Cheerful, excited
Sharing, Opening, Expressing
A clear moment of peace
Laughter

Consider the implications of this study. These writers entered our laboratory with an intrinsic motivational orientation toward writing. Apparently, we were not able to increase that intrinsic orientation much; the creativity of the intrinsic group isn't notably higher than the creativity of the control group. But with a terribly brief and simple manipulation, we significantly reduced the creativity of writers in the extrinsic group. People who had been writing creatively for years, who had long-standing interests in creative writing, suddenly found their creativity blocked after spending barely five minutes thinking about the extrinsic reasons for doing what they do.

(Lest it seem we took creative writers, stripped them of their creativity, and then turned them loose, let me say that we fully debriefed all of our participants before they left the lab, and we had all of the extrinsic subjects fill out the intrinsic questionnaire at the end of their experimental sessions.)

Intrinsic motivation, then, does seem to be more conducive to creativity than extrinsic motivation. Creativity can be undermined by evaluation expectation, surveillance, reward expectation, competition, or restriction of choice, and it can also be undermined by simply thinking about all the external constraints that might be placed on one's work.

How It Fits Together

I do not mean to suggest that intrinsic motivation is *all* we need to be creative. Certainly, we cannot just leave children alone, in their natural state, and watch their creativity blossom. And we cannot expect to just leave adults to their own devices and watch them produce creative work on any task they undertake. In my theory of creativity (Amabile, 1983), I outline three components that are necessary for creative work in any domain (Figure Two illustrates how I believe these components enter into the creative process):

1. *Domain-relevant skills.* This component includes knowledge about the domain in question (for example, knowledge about chemistry), technical skills required for work within the domain (such as laboratory skills), and special domain-relevant talent (such as talent for visualizing molecules and their interaction). Domain-relevant skills depend on cognitive abilities, perceptual and motor skills, and formal and informal education. As another example, domain-relevant skills for musical creativity in our culture might include a familiarity with western music forms and instruments, the ability to play an instrument and to transfer ideas into musical notation, and a special talent for hearing in imagination several instruments playing together. Domain-relevant skills can influence creativity on any task within the domain of endeavor—any research in chemistry, for example, or any musical composition.

2. *Creativity-relevant skills.* This component includes a cognitive style marked by an ability to break mental habits and an appreciation of complexity. It also includes a work style characterized by an ability to concentrate effort for long periods of time, a sense about when to leave a stubborn problem for a while, and a generally high energy level. Finally, it includes an implicit or explicit knowledge of creativity heuristics. These are simply rules of thumb for generating ideas—for example, "Try something counter-intuitive."

   Creativity-relevant skills can be influenced by training, by experience in generating ideas, and by personality characteristics.

   Creativity-relevant skills operate at the most general level; they can influence performance in any domain.

3. *Task motivation.* Task motivation can be very specific to particular tasks within domains, and may even vary over time for a particular task. As I have suggested,

Figure Two.

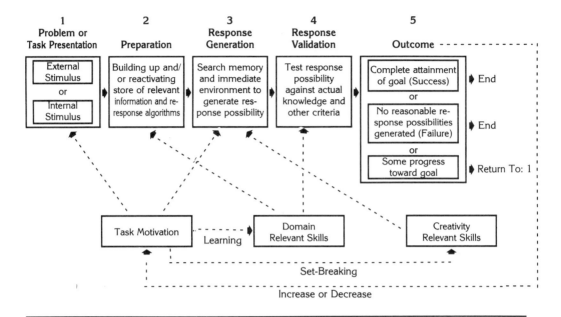

an intrinsic task motivation (doing the task for its own sake) should be more conducive to creativity than an extrinsic task motivation (doing the task as a means to some extrinsic goal). Overall task motivation will depend on both the individual's initial attitude toward the task (we all have our somewhat idiosyncratic preferences for activities) and the presence or absence of salient constraints in the social environment. If such constraints are present, motivation should become extrinsic. There is a third factor that can influence overall task motivation: the individual's own ability to diminish the importance of extrinsic constraints. This last point can be an important one, and I will return to it later.

Each of the three components must be present for creativity to emerge. The higher the level of the three components, the higher the overall creativity. Clearly, then, much more is required than an intrinsic task motivation. But, in trying to maximize a person's creativity in the workplace or the classroom, it might be best to focus on the task motivation component. Unlike creativity-relevant skills and domain-relevant skills, task motivation can be influenced quickly, easily, and inexpensively by relatively small changes in the social environment. At the same time, though, these changes can be very powerful. According to my theory, task motivation makes the difference between what a person *can* do (based on domain-relevant and creativity-relevant skills) and what that person *will* do.

Now What?

Just as it is exciting to contemplate what the past 30 years have brought to both technological advances in everyday life and progress in creativity research, it is exciting to consider what the next 30 years might bring. Though it is impossible to predict with any certainty what questions creativity researchers will be tackling, we can at least engage in some wishful thinking: What seem to be the most important questions to answer next?

I have just briefly outlined my theory of creativity. There is a good deal of research on a few elements of the theory, such as the impact of social factors on task motivation and the generation of creative ideas, and the particular personality characteristics and work styles that show up most often in people who produce creative work. There are large gaps in the evidence needed to uphold this theory, though, as is the case for all other proposed comprehensive theories of creativity. For example, we need data on the particular elements that fall within each of the three components, the interaction and feedback between the components, and the point or points in the creative process where each component enters in most significantly. It is obviously important, then, to look at the creative process as a whole and to continue development on a comprehensive theory of creativity.

More specifically, however, there are a number of questions relevant to creativity motivation in particular. First, we need more evidence on the precise mechanism by which social constraints kill creativity. I reported some data suggesting that, in fact, the undermining is mediated by the change from intrinsic to extrinsic motivational orientation. However, the motivational measures do not always show the predicted differences. While there is no evidence whatsoever that extrinsic motivation might be more conducive to creativity than intrinsic, we need to find better ways of demonstrating that, in fact, the mechanism is precisely what we say it is. Once this issue has been settled, the next step will be to uncover the cognitive or affective processes through which motivational orientation influences creative behavior.

Second, we will need to examine any possible interactions between intrinsic and extrinsic motivation. This is, of course, a more general issue that goes beyond the psychology of creativity. I have been implicitly assuming a hydraulic model: as extrinsic motivation goes up, intrinsic motivation goes down, and vice versa. But my interviews with R&D managers, and my examination of some literature on motivation, suggest that the picture may be much more complex than that. There may, in fact, be circumstances under which the two types of motivation are additive, or there may be some types of individuals for whom this would be the case.

Third, we must, overall, pay more attention to the role of the individual in the processes I have described. In taking a social-psychological approach to creativity and, particularly, creativity motivation, I have neglected the possible influence of individual differences in traits, temperaments, abilities, and interests. Surely, I have included these individual-difference factors in my theory, but I have excluded them from my experimental studies by controlling for them or allowing them to operate as random effects that only contribute to background noise. It is time to take these factors out of the background and integrate social-psychological studies of creativity with personality concepts and methods.

Fourth, although we have examined a good number of social/environmental variables that might influence motivation and creativity, there are many more that lie relatively untouched. For example, there is virtually no data on the effects of time pressure on creativity, and, as I mentioned earlier, possible differential effects of competition need to be studied in careful detail.

Fifth, while we are looking at other social/environmental variables, we also need to look at other social environments. To date, most of the solid data we have on creativity motivation have come from tightly controlled experiments in psychological laboratories or school settings. The effect of work environment on motivation and creativity in industry is a vital issue, but good data on that issue is quite scarce. The interviews with R&D managers represent a first step in that direction, but a true parade of progress will require a great deal of concentrated effort. So, too, will progress on questions of creativity in other real-world settings, such as classrooms and homes.

Finally, I realize that, as far as practical implications are concerned, my research to this point is capable of quite effectively telling people how to destroy creativity. Some managers, teachers, and parents might find this somewhat limited in utility. I have shown that creativity can be undermined by evaluation expectation, surveillance, reward expectation, competition, and, perhaps, time pressures, and that it can also be undermined by simply thinking about all the external constraints placed on one's work. We need to find out whether, if this is so, anything can be done about it. Are we always at the mercy of our social environments? Is it possible to be creative in the face of extrinsic constraints? How can managers and teachers and parents possibly avoid the potentially disastrous consequences of evaluation, reward, and competition? There are several possibilities to be pursued.

The first solution might be to focus on the social environment. As much as possible, those who oversee (or have impact on) the performance of other people should try to take the emphasis off extrinsic constraints. Obviously, it would be impossible to eliminate the evaluation of performance or the use of reward systems or any of the other factors I've mentioned. It is possible to reduce their salience, to place the focus more on the work itself and less on the external controls. For example, rather than constantly reminding workers about performance reviews, it might be more effective to encourage them to do *self-evaluations* of their own work. This could well result in work that is quite acceptable, because people can be very stringent self-evaluators. Simultaneously, creativity would be maintained, because people could concentrate on the work for its own sake, rather than focusing on external pressures.

The point is that anything reducing the salience of extrinsic constraints should enhance creativity. It might even be possible for workers themselves to do "mind tricks" that will make extrinsic constraints seem distant and unimportant. James Watson and Francis Crick felt a fierce competition with Linus Pauling during their search for the structure of DNA. In Watson's account (Watson, 1968), barely a page goes by without mention of Watson and Crick's obsession with trying to assess Pauling's progress and their chances of beating him to the Nobel Prize. Obviously, their creativity was not completely undermined by this extrinsic constraint; they did reach their goal. But a close examination of Watson's story suggests something very interesting. While they were actually in their laboratory, doing their best work, or pondering the problem during a quiet moment, they became so totally absorbed in the scientific puzzle that everything else receded in importance—including the competition with Pauling.

The second method for keeping creativity alive might focus not on the social environment but on the individual. If knowledge, technical skills, creativity techniques, and talents can be developed to high levels, it might still be possible under extrinsic motivation to produce work that is recognized as creative. Recall the three factors that contribute to creativity: domain-relevant skills, creativity-relevant skills, and task motivation. Even if task motivation is largely extrinsic, some levels of creativity might be achieved as long as domain-relevant and creativity-relevant skills remain at a high level.

There is some evidence that this happened with Picasso in the last years of his life. Some critics suggest that, during those last years, Picasso became so obsessed with the outrageously high prices his paintings commanded that he lost his "creative spark." We might say that he lost his intrinsic motivation. Yet, during those years, Picasso still succeeded in producing work that many people regarded as creative. It might be that he had actually developed an algorithm for producing a "creative" painting. Picasso might have had such an extraordinarily high level of talent and skill and knowledge that, almost by rote—without any particular spark of intrinsic motivation—he could produce work others would see as creative.

A third possible method for keeping creativity alive also focuses on the individual. If a person can start out with a very high level of intrinsic motivation, it might be virtually impossible to wipe it out with the imposition of extrinsic constraints. For ourselves, we can try as much as possible to concentrate on and appreciate the intrinsically rewarding aspects of our work. For those under our influence, we can try to emphasize those aspects of work and increase the intrinsic satisfaction of the work process itself. It might be a good idea, for example, to simply ask people what they most enjoy about their work and then allow them more time, freedom, and resources to build on those areas.

Woody Allen seems to present an ideal example of unshakeable intrinsic motivation. Few professions are as loaded with salient extrinsic constraints as moviemaking. Not only do millions of dollars rest on the success of each individual project, but the product will be evaluated by millions of people. Not only that, but expert evaluation of the movie by critics is available for hundreds of millions of people to see. Yet, in the face of all this constraint, Allen seems to continue along, quietly taking one risk after another with new forms and styles. In his interviews, he sounds highly intrinsically motivated. Certainly, he wants his projects to succeed financially. But he's not working primarily for the money; he's working to please and challenge himself. And he hardly seems concerned about evaluation of his work. He avoids reading reviews of his movies. On the night his *Annie Hall* received the most positive evaluation given to movies, the Oscar, Allen preferred to do something he *really* enjoyed—playing clarinet with his jazz band in Manhattan.

We have just collected some exciting new data on two of these methods for keeping creativity alive: take the focus off extrinsic goals and constraints, and concentrate on intrinsic motives. Beth Hennessey, Barbara Grossman, and I tried to train children to focus on their intrinsic motives for doing various types of schoolwork and to minimize the importance of extrinsic constraints. We used a simple modeling procedure. The children in the study watched videotapes in which other children served as models of intrinsically motivated individuals. When the adult on the videotape asked the child-models what they liked to do in school and why, the models replied (according to a script we had written) with statements of interest, excitement and deep involvement in some aspect of their studies. When the adult asked how they felt about teacher approval and getting high marks, the models said that, although such things were nice, they were not as important as really trying to enjoy your work. There was one dominant message throughout the training videotape and the accompanying discussion we had with the children in this study: it's nice to get rewards, approval, and so on, but the most important factor is to be aware of the intrinsically interesting, satisfying, and challenging aspects of whatever you are doing.

The training succeeded; those children who had been trained showed higher levels of intrinsic motivation than children who had not gone through the training. More importantly, the trained children showed no decrement of creativity under extrinsic constraint. In effect, what we have done is to show that children—and, we hypothesize, adults, too—can be *immunized* against the negative effects of extrinsic constraints on their intrinsic motivation and creativity.

A person's creativity can be killed in an atmosphere fraught with evaluation pressures, reward systems, competition, restriction of choice, and anything else that takes the focus off the intrinsic properties of the work itself. But a person's creativity may be kept alive in an atmosphere with minimal extrinsic constraint and maximal support of skill training, talent development, and intrinsic enjoyment of the work. And, then, as much as possible, perhaps it is best to simply be left alone.

References

Allen, W. (1948). *Writers on writing.* London: Phoenix House.

Amabile, T. M. (1979). Effects of external evaluation on artistic creativity. *Journal of Personality and Social Psychology, 37,* 221-233.

Amabile, T. M. (1982a). Children's artistic creativity: Detrimental effects of competition in a field setting. *Personality and Social Psychology Bulletin, 8,* 573-578.

Amabile, T. M. (1982b). Social psychology of creativity: A consensual assessment technique. *Journal of Personality and Social Psychology, 43,* 997-1013.

Amabile, T. M. (1983). The social psychology of creativity: A componential conceptualization. *Journal of Personality and Social Psychology, 45,* 357-376.

Amabile, T. M. (1985). Motivation and creativity: Effects of motivational orientation on creative writers. *Journal of Personality and Social Psychology, 48,* 393-399.

Amabile, T. M., DeJong, W., & Lepper, M. (1976). Effects of externally imposed deadlines on subsequent intrinsic motivation. *Journal of Personality and Social Psychology, 34,* 92-98.

Amabile, T. M. & Gitomer, J. (1984). Children's artistic creativity: Effects of choice in task materials. *Personality and Social Psychology Bulletin, 10,* 209-215.

Amabile, T. M., Goldfarb, P., & Brackfield, S. C. (1982). *Effects of social facilitation and evaluation on creativity.* Unpublished manuscript, Brandeis University.

Amabile, T. M. & Gryskiewicz, S. S. (1985). *Creativity in the R&D laboratory.* Technical report, Center for Creative Leadership, Greensboro, NC.

Amabile, T. M., Hennessey, B. A., & Grossman, B. S. (1986). Social influences on creativity: Effects of contracted-for reward. *Journal of Personality and Social Psychology, 50,* 14-23.

Bem, D. (1972). Self-perception theory. In L. Berkowitz (Ed.), *Advances in experimental social psychology: Vol. 6* (pp. 1-62). New York: Academic Press.

Berglas, S., Amabile, T. M., & Handel, M. (1981). *Effects of evaluation on children's artistic creativity.* Unpublished manuscript, Brandeis University.

Calder, B. & Staw, B. (1975). Self-perception of intrinsic and extrinsic motivation. *Journal of Personality and Social Psychology, 31,* 599-605.

Condry, Jr. (1977). Enemies of exploration: Self-initiated versus other-initiated learning. *Journal of Personality and Social Psychology, 35,* 459-477.

Crutchfield, R. (1962). Conformity and creative thinking. In H. Gruber, G. Terrell, & M. Wertheimer (Eds.), *Contemporary approaches to creative thinking* (pp. 120-143). New York: Atherton Press.

deCharms, R. (1968). *Personal causation.* New York: Academic Press.

Deci, E. (1971). Effects of externally mediated rewards on intrinsic motivation. *Journal of Personality and Social Psychology, 18,* 105-115.

Deci, E. (1972a). Intrinsic motivation, extrinsic reinforcement, and inequity. *Journal of Personality and Social Psychology, 22,* 113-120.

Deci, E. (1972b). The effects of contingent and noncontingent rewards and controls on intrinsic motivation. *Organizational Behavior and Human Performance, 8,* 217-229.

Dec, E. (1975). *Intrinsic motivation.* New York: Plenum.

Deci, E. (1978). Applications of research on the effects of rewards. In M. Lepper & D. Greene (Eds.), *The hidden costs of reward* (pp. 193-204). New Jersey: Lawrence Erlbaum.

Einstein, A. (1949). Autobiography. In P. Schilpp, *Albert Einstein: Philosopher-scientist.* Evanston, IL: Library of Living Philosophers Inc.

Folger, R., Rosenfield, D., & Hays, R. P. (1978). Equity and intrinsic motivation: The role of choice. *Journal of Personality and Social Psychology, 36,* 557-564.

Glucksberg, S. (1962). The influence of strength of drive on functional fixedness and perceptual recognition. *Journal of Experimental Psychology, 63,* 36-41.

Going for the gaps. (1982, Fall). *The Stanford Magazine,* pp. 38-41.

Hennessey, B. A. (1985). *The effect of extrinsic constraints on children's creativity while using a computer.* Doctoral dissertation, Brandeis University, Waltham, MA.

Holland, J. L. (1973). *Making vocational choices: A theory of careers.* Englewood Cliffs, NJ: Prentice-Hall.

Hughes, T. & McCullough, F. (Eds.). (1982). *The journals of Sylvia Plath.* New York: Dial.

Kelley, H. (1967). Attribution theory in social psychology. In D. Levine (Ed.), *Nebraska symposium on motivation: Vol. 15* (pp. 192-238). Lincoln: University of Nebraska.

Kelley, H. (1973). The processes of causal attribution. *American Psychologist, 28,* 107-128.

Koestler, A. (1964). *The act of creation.* New York: Dell.

Kruglanski, A. W. (1975). The endogenous-exogenous partition in attribution theory. *Psychological Review, 82,* 387-406.

Kruglanski, A. W. (1978). Endogenous attribution and intrinsic motivation. In M. Lepper & D. Greene (Eds.), *The hidden costs of reward* (pp. 85-108). Hillsdale, NJ: Erlbaum.

Kruglanski, A. W., Friedman, I., & Zeevi, G. (1971). The effects of extrinsic incentive on some qualitative aspects of task performance. *Journal of Personality, 39,* 606-617.

Lepper, M. & Greene, D. (1975). Turning play into work: Effects of adult surveillance and extrinsic rewards on children's intrinsic motivation. *Journal of Personality and Social Psychology, 31,* 479-486.

Lepper, M. & Greene, D. (1978). Overjustification research and beyond: Toward a means-end analysis of intrinsic and extrinsic motivation. In M. Lepper & D. Greene (Eds.), *The hidden costs of reward* (pp. 109-148). Hillsdale, NJ: Erlbaum.

Lepper, M., Greene, D., & Nisbett, R. (1973). Undermining children's intrinsic interest with extrinsic rewards: A test of the "overjustification" hypothesis. *Journal of Personality and Social Psychology, 28,* 129-137.

Luchins, A. (1942). Mechanization in problem solving: The effect of Einstellung. *Psychological Monographs, 54* (6, Whole No. 248).

McGraw, K. (1978). The detrimental effects of reward on performance: A literature review and a prediction model. In M. Lepper & D. Greene (Eds.), *The hidden costs of reward* (pp. 33-60). Hillsdale, NJ: Erlbaum.

McGraw, K. & McCullers, J. (1979). Evidence of a detrimental effect of extrinsic incentives on breaking a mental set. *Journal of Experimental Social Psychology, 15,* 285-294.

Mukai, C. (1983). *Effects of anticipated evaluation on artistic creativity in children.* Unpublished manuscript, Brandeis University.

Osborn, A. F. (1953). *Applied imagination.* New York: Scribner's.

Parnes, S. J. (1967). *Creative behavior guidebook.* New York: Scribner's.

Peters, T. J. (1983, summer). The mythology of innovation, or a skunkworks tale, part I. *The Stanford Magazine,* pp. 13-21.

Reiss, S. & Sushinsky, L. W. (1975). Overjustification, competing responses, and the acquisition of intrinsic interest. *Journal of Personality and Social Psychology, 31,* 1116-1125.

Rogers, C. (1954). Towards a theory of creativity. *ETC: A review of general semantics, 11,* 249-260.

Ross, M. (1975). Salience of reward and intrinsic motivation. *Journal of Personality and Social Psychology, 32,* 245-254.

Ross, M. (1976). The self-perception of intrinsic motivation. In J. H. Harvey, W. J. Ickes, & R. F. Kidd (Eds.). *New directions in attribution research: Vol. 1* (pp. 121-141). Hillsdale, NJ: Erlbaum.

Salancik, G. (1975). *Retrospective attribution of past behavior and commitment to future behavior.* Unpublished manuscript, University of Illinois.

Sexton, L. G. & Ames, L. (1977). *Anne Sexton: A self-portrait in letters.* Boston: Houghton Mifflin.

Simpson, E. (1982). Eliot and friends. *The New York Times Book Review,* January 24, pp. 11-27.

Staw, B. M. (1976). *Intrinsic and extrinsic motivation.* Morristown, NJ: General Learning Press.

Stein, M. I. (1974). *Stimulating creativity.* Vol. 1. New York: Academic Press.

Watson, J. D. (1968). *The double helix.* New York: Atheneum.

Wolfe, T. (1936). *The story of a novel.* New York: Scribner's.

Zervos, C. (1952). Conversation with Picasso. In B. Ghiselin (Ed.), *The creative process* (pp. 55-60). Berkeley: University of California Press.

11

Some Needed Research on the Cognitive Limits of Creativity

Conrad F. Toepfer, Jr.
State University of New York at Buffalo

The contemporary knowledge explosions in both psychology and neurology are providing bases for rethinking all areas of human behavior. These data offer fascinating possibilities for considering new dimensions on the frontiers of creativity research. This chapter shall consider some of these questions and pursue some research possibilities which may add to the sum of what is presently known about creative thinking, problem solving and learning. The writer's objectives in developing this chapter are: (1) to provide a knowledge base of current information about major concerns in cognitive development in psychological and neurological areas; and, (2) to frame major research areas and questions linking those data with creativity concerns. As a curriculum theorist, this writer's interests are in defining ways in which teaching and learning can respond to these validated neurological and psychological findings. Gordon (1984) discusses issues involved in efforts to broaden present information relating to the limits of cognition. Scholars concerned with the creativity field likewise need to consider the directions which such investigations bring to confirming present knowledge in their field as well as suggesting needed areas of investigation.

The different ways in which people demonstrate their individual ways of creative thinking need to be studied in terms of how humans actually do learn. Guilford's concerns (1967) about the structures of intellect established a frontier which assisted scholars and researchers in the creativity field. Kirton (1977) extended this by considering learning style differences among adaptors and innovators. Torrance's development and refinement of a test of thinking style (Torrance et al. 1977, 1978, 1980) provided data from which Torrance and Yun Horng (1980a) were able to further reinforce Kirton's earlier data on adaptors and innovators. These data need to be further considered from the perspective of how human neurological development, as part of one's total growth, may indicate stages at which creativity itself may progressively appear and mature. This chapter will take its focus in examining these and other creativity issues as they relate to learning in light of neurological and psychological findings.

The Readiness Issue and Creativity

The essential information presented by the authors of the chapters in Part I of this volume points to the need to consider readiness and the creativity field. Dissecting the whole of creativity may seem somewhat strange to those who hold a more-or-less gestalt philosophy about creativity. Yet, there is an "incredible journey" which must be pursued in light of current and emerging scientific information. MacLean's (1984) description of the development of the brain points to a number of directions about the educational implications of this neurological development. The knowledge explosion in neurology increases possibilities for researching the readiness of learners to deal with different levels of cognition. William James (1890) observed, "to detect the moment of instinctive readiness for the subject is then, the first duty of every educator" (p. 16). In what ways can neurological and psychological findings provide avenues for studying the relationship of creativity to readiness for learning? It is also possible that beyond IQ (Piaget, 1969; Reynolds, 1981), there are kinds of perceptual and other information processing readiness which may help us understand creativity in dimensions not yet identified. Let us consider some of these areas suggesting further investigation.

The Living, Growing Brain and Mind

There is a major need to screen neurological findings about how the brain actually functions against current developments about learning from the area of psychology. This would develop a neuropsychology of learning (Hynd & Obrzut, 1981; Reynolds, 1981, 1982) and provides an on-going basis to syncretize these findings as they emerge. This writer (1982) contends there are important possible implications, for instance, of brain growth periodization and hemispheric dominance for rethinking curriculum design of school experiences for children. This also suggests the need to consider how children's creative abilities may relate to their stages of individual intellectual growth and development. However, educators have more or less assumed that there is a constant continuum in the growth of the mind and thinking capacities of children. With the exception of the past two decades, there has been relatively little consideration of the implications of stage-wise growth of thinking levels and of the brain during childhood and adolescence. The area of learning psychology was first to develop data leading to such considerations.

Piaget's Stages of Learning

Psychologist Jean Piaget posited that learning stages appear as youngsters grow chronologically. This was based upon years of study of young children at the Rousseau Institute in Geneva, Switzerland. Piaget (1969) identified the exhibition of new and higher level intellectual skills in children at common age-linked periods. While these data have been studied extensively over the past two decades, there has not been definitive research of the relationship of creativity to learning skills which appear at these stages.

Piaget discovered that children learn primarily through their senses from birth through one-and-a-half and sometimes to two years of age. For that reason this period was called the *sensorimotor learning stage*. The characteristics of the infant's intellectual development during this sensorimotor learning stage are shown in Figure One.

Consider how cognitive development may be limited as an infant is either slow, average or precocious in developing and using these sensorimotor means. Piaget saw that readiness for moving on to the next learning stage depends on the consolidation and maturation of the skills appropriate to each particular learning stage. The period of sensorimotor development is the first opportunity to influence the infant's environment and study an individual's progress through this initial stage.

The study of cognition, such as it is during this stage, must identify the degree to which the infant masters and consolidates her/his sensorimotor tasks. While creativity research needs to deal with several major concerns at each stage in a child's cognitive development, mastery and consolidation are most important during this initial stage.

First, the degree to which different kinds of interaction and intervention with infants impacts on achievement, mastery and consolidation of sensorimotor tasks requires careful study. Consideration of those tasks in which difficulty is experienced, or others in which precocity toward beginning symbolic activity is demonstrated, require careful attention. Precocity is a major characteristic of many creative individuals. This includes early abilities in art, cognition, communication skills, music, perception, and abilities to perceive and process information. Precocity also entails earlier demonstration of creative thinking and problem

Figure One.

Piaget's Sensorimotor Learning Stage.

The Child:

- exercises her/his given sensorimotor mechanisms in this basically pre-verbal period.
- learns basically through sight, touch, smell, hearing and tasting objects as hand-eye coordination develops to get them to the mouth.
- is unable to follow object displacements unless the object is visible—no permanence of objects.
- finds hidden objects through a random physical searching process.
- imitates overtly by trial and error and gradually internalizes her/his own behavior.
- changes play from motor games to make believe representations.
- experiences difficulty in means-ends separation.
- seems to use action to represent an object and shifts slowly from action to its effects.
- is action-centered in her/his behavior.
- develops the foundation for symbolic activity during this stage.

---

solving as the individual develops and matures her/his cognitive capacities. Creativity research also needs to identify and isolate both degree and the ways in which earlier mastery and consolidation of sensorimotor tasks may be influenced. The following creativity frontier issues will require the interaction of creativity and early childhood researchers to attempt to answer the following concerns:

1. Can precocity and earlier readiness for developing the capacity to manipulate symbols common to the concrete preoperational learning stage be facilitated?
2. Can precocity and earlier readiness for the skills of later learning stages be facilitated?
3. Can creative behaviors in which infants can develop readiness for sensorimotor tasks be identified?
4. Can creative behaviors appropriate with sensorimotor cognitive levels be identified and enhanced?
5. What kinds of activities could be developed and/or utilized to ascertain these possibilities?

The second Piagetian learning stage occurs for most children between age 2 and 7 years. Known as the *concrete preoperational learning stage,* this period coincides with the time when the child greatly expands her/his interactions with peers beyond the previous limits of the home. Day-care, nursery school programs, exploration of areas outside the home and elementary school provide a range of new settings and persons that serve as major means for transition from the sensorimotor stage. These new experiences are also important in dealing with those intellectual tasks which are common to concrete preoperational development. The characteristics of the child's intellectual development during her/his concrete preoperational learning stage are shown in Figure Two.

As consolidation and refinement of sensorimotor tasks provide necessary readiness, children expand oral language and develop reading and other language arts skills (Geshwind 1972; Pappas 1984). However, readiness to develop these critically important skills must be identified and not assumed. Piaget (1955) was first to consider insights on language development from the child's perspective. Many famous creative figures, including Leonard Bernstein, T. S. Eliot, Alfred Hitchcock, Wolfgang Amadeus Mozart, and Charles Steinmetz displayed remarkable precocity with language before the years typical of the concrete preoperational

Figure Two.

Piaget's Concrete Preoperational Learning Stage.

The Child:

- develops the capacity for manipulating symbols that represent the environment.
- develops abilities to use alphabet, numbers (linear, sequential processing), images, pictures and shapes (holistic, visual-spatial processing).
- is perceptually oriented and does not use logical thought as reasoning by implication.
- develops a system of codified symbols for manipulations and communications.
- shifts her/his interests from action to explanation.
- can internalize her/his imitations.
- is very concrete-minded and highly egocentric in her/his thinking.
- lacks operational reversibility in her/his thinking activities.
- is unable to integrate a series of conditions into a coherent whole.
- is unable to reason inductively or deductively and proceeds from particular to particular.
- cannot conserve but can perform the rudiments of classification and serial ordering.

---

age-frame. However, other equally creative personages, including Johannes Brahms, Albert Einstein, Thomas Edison, Harvey Firestone and Eleanor Roosevelt delayed significantly beyond that age-frame before demonstrating similar communication skills. One's personal achievement of the intellectual characteristics Piaget attributes to each learning stage may vary among individuals, although most children do so during the approximate intervals identified by Piaget. Because of this, the times at which any two creative individuals might experience the same learning stage could vary considerably. For instance, the lives of both individuals give cause to speculate that Einstein went through concrete preoperational development between age 4 and 9 years while the precocious Mozart may have experienced the same maturation between 1 to 4 years of age. Yet, no one would deny that both individuals were among the major creative geniuses known to human history. This also raises the need to identify and research the differences between so-called "innate" creative ability and the degree to which creative behavior may be influenced, assisted or enhanced by intervention activities which meet specific readiness needs.

It is important not to fall into generalizations about exact relationships of either precocious or delayed abilities to one's ultimate creative abilities. Educational systems also must be careful that learners who delay in particular readiness are not locked out of later opportunities by expectations because certain abilities do not appear at the norm of expectations. In addition to being punitive, such practices can cause learners to develop lower self esteem which will handicap their subsequent intellectual and emotional development. Programs for gifted/talented and creative learners which have fixed regulations for early identification and continuation in those programs need to carefully consider such practices. It has been established (Pappas 1984) that learning to read fully requires developed reading readiness. When children without developed readiness are placed in learning situations which "force" reading, they often develop reading problems which are extremely difficult to overcome. These children also evidence a high incidence of dislike for reading. The nurture and development of creativity in children is not well served when this occurs. The readiness issue for concrete preoperational tasks is another primary concern with regards to developing intellectual skills normally associated with this Piagetian learning stage. Language development, early childhood and creativity researchers will need to collaborate in designing means to identify answers to these important questions:

    1. Can precocity and earlier readiness for elementary logical operations and cogni-

tive operations common to later learning stages be facilitated?

2. Can precocity and earlier readiness for the skills of the formal operations learning stage be facilitated?
3. Can creative behaviors in which concrete preoperational children deal with mastering and consolidating sensorimotor tasks be identified?
4. Can creative behaviors appropriate with concrete preoperational cognitive levels be identified and enhanced?
5. What kinds of activities could be developed and/or utilized to ascertain these possibilities?

The third Piagetian learning stage occurs for most children between 7 and 11 years of age. During age 9 to 11 years, many children are approaching and achieving their transition from childhood to beginning adolescence. The physical, social and emotional demands upon children during this metamorphosis are extremely stressful. The fact that some children are well into their pubescent metamorphosis by age 11, while others have not yet begun it, creates adjustment problems to beginning adolescence. This concern can also distract them from dealing specifically with the changes in intellectual capacities experienced during the consolidation of their concrete operational processing skills. This marks the first time in their lives in which differences in body size, shape and sexuality have major impact upon individual and peer relationships. Concerns over one's own precocious, average, or delayed beginning of the pubescent transformation brings concerns to concrete operational thinking children which disrupt earlier commonality of development formerly experienced with the majority of their agemates. These differences will continue to intensify during the next (formal operational, age 11-14 years) developmental period. The years of concrete operational development must also cope with school environmental changes as students move from self-contained, elementary school classrooms to junior high and middle school buildings. In the latter, they will begin to deal with as many as 6 individual teachers during the school day. They also are now the youngest and among the smaller students in the school, whereas, they were the oldest and the student leaders in the elementary school. The characteristics of the maturing child's intellectual development during her/his *concrete operational learning stage* are shown in Figure Three.

During the final two years of this stage, educators need to pay attention to children's intellectual needs as well as assist youngsters in dealing with the beginnings of the physical,

---

Figure Three.

Piaget's Concrete Operational Learning Stage.

The Maturing Child:

- can perform elementary logical operations on concrete objects as she/he liberates her/himself from largely perceptual judgments.
- performs operations such as serial ordering, classification, numbering, space and time, associativity, transitivity, identity and negation.
- begins to be troubled by inconsistencies in thought and action.
- becomes logical and develops reversible thinking.
- is aware of variables.
- becomes aware of part and whole relationships.
- develops conservation skills with numbers, mass, weight and sometimes volume.
- understands and uses logic of classes and demonstrates class inclusion, ascending and descending hierarchies.
- can deal with simple word problems but still has difficulty with somewhat complex ones.
- becomes less egocentric in representing objects in her/his social relationships.

social and emotional developmental variance previously described. This poses a range of complicating factors as readiness for development of these skills is assessed and learning activities initiated. Early physical development may or may not be linked with earlier readiness either for creativity development or readiness to initiate concrete operational tasks during this period. Problems of self-concept and esteem caused by individual child differences in pubescent development from her/his peers may interfere with the ability to concentrate on cognitive and creative activities even though that child does have the necessary readiness. Teachers dealing with this age group must maintain flexibility in their expectations about consistency of student reactions. Their individual behavior and mood will fluctuate greatly because of episodes over which there is virtually no control. The use of creative approaches by adults in planning activities for his age group will be important in developing effective and appropriate concrete operational learning activities. This can assist in dealing with readiness issues which become increasingly more difficult to identify. The difficulties of beginning pubescent tasks which emerge during the age 10 and 11 years of this learning stage should not be underestimated. Creativity-learning issues take on an additional concern during this learning stage. The following questions need to be considered:

1. Can precocity and earlier readiness for hypothetical deductive reasoning skills associated with the formal operations learning stage be facilitated?
2. What issues of early onset of pubescent development pose the greatest difficulties in dealing with concrete operational development?
3. Can creative behaviors in which concrete operational children deal with mastering and consolidating concrete preoperational tasks be identified?
4. Can creative behaviors for dealing with individual and small group concerns about pubescent development issues be utilized to clarify concrete operational learning needs?
5. What kinds of activities could be developed and/or utilized to ascertain these possibilities?

The final Piagetian stage occurs for emerging adolescents between 11 and 14 years of age. The social and emotional emancipation begun among most maturing children during the concrete operational timeframe continues. The 11 to 14 years age-frame extends the complications of pubescent adjustment, development of sexuality, and sex role identification. This is accompanied by heavy increases in peer pressure and expectations and further complicated by the fact that individual pubescent transformation differs not only between, but within the sexes. Females generally experience this transformation from 14 to 18 months earlier than males. There also may be a variance as great as 3 years between two members of the same sex who demonstrate the same level of pubescent development, one of whom is very precocious and the other who is delaying significantly in physical, pubescent arrival. These physiological phenomena create major social and emotional concerns during the age-frame in which the transition to begin formal operations usually begins. This often creates serious distractions which hinder young adolescents from attending fully to the intellectual tasks they face in initiating formal operational skills and meeting the tasks of this learning stage. The characteristics of the maturing adolescent's intellectual development during her/his *formal operational learning stage* are shown in Figure Four.

During the formal operational learning stage the adolescent develops intellectual characteristics which shall mature into her/his adult information cognition skills (Martorano, 1972). Arlin (1975) posits the possibility of an additional stage of problem defining skills for some. However, the great percentage of humans appear to achieve their full range of information processing skills and the cognitive capacities which will influence their creative thinking abilities during this period.

Creativity research needs to identify the degree to which intervention strategies could either assist adolescents to develop or further mature creative skills or tendencies during this

Figure Four.

Piaget's Formal Operational Learning Stage.

The Adolescent:

- approaches and gradually begins hypothetical-deductive thinking as reasoning becomes more abstract.
- begins to perform operations of formal logic.
- can use mathematical operations associated with groups and lattices in complex combinations.
- can do reasoning with proportions and ratios.
- can begin to think reflectively and accept assumptions which are contrary to facts.
- can perform controlled experimentation.
- becomes concerned about reality and introduces idealized schemes to bring reality in line with her/his own thinking.
- becomes relatively freed from dependence on concrete reality.
- can subordinate the content of a problem to the form of relations within it and is impressed by the form of an argument over its content.
- can reverse directions between reality and possibility and check the viability of the latter by experimentation.
- can reason conjunctively, disjunctively, by negation or implication.

---

last Piagetian cognitive stage. The investigation of latency issues could provide new information as to why some individuals delay in developing and manifesting creative abilities until well into their adult years. Creativity and adolescent psychology researchers need to collaborate in dealing with other research questions involving this final Piagetian learning stage:

1. Which pubescent development issues pose the greatest difficulties in dealing with the development of creative thinking skills during the formal operational learning stage?
2. Can creative behaviors in which formal operational adolescents deal with mastering and consolidating those tasks be identified?
3. Can creative behaviors for dealing with individual and small group concerns about pubescent development issues be utilized to clarify formal operational learning needs?
4. What kinds of activities could be developed and/or utilized to ascertain these possibilities?

Recent Psychological Findings on Readiness Concerns and Creativity Issues

Elkind (1980) observes that it is extremely difficult to really understand children's thinking levels when an adult can function at cognitive levels above those of the child. He describes this ability of adults to process information using their personal, full range of thinking skills as "automatization." It is, he states, almost impossible for adults to understand how a child processes information when the adult is automatically functioning above the child's maximum cognitive level. Elkind describes the state of a child who has not yet reached the adult's thinking levels as *the intellectual unconscious.* He notes that "Getting at the intellectual unconscious, however, presents a very special problem. Once a person becomes truly skilled in a particular action, there is no way to get back to the intellectual unconscious" (p. 19). Piaget identified (1958, 1967) that a child must construct the environment in which she/he develops new skills and then use them to learn new information. The implications of Piaget's ideas on constructivism will be discussed further in a later section of this chapter. To deal with how children can and do think at a particular age, adults must likewise identify the components of the stages and levels of learning which the child has achieved. Without this knowledge, the teacher may plan new instruction which is beyond the child's actual readiness and create problems as that child attempts to understand things which are beyond her/his readiness at that time. Adelson's (1983) reflection on James' 1890 observation that "to identify the moment of the instinctive readiness for the subject is, then, the first duty of educators" was that James was "discussing that which we now call cognitive readiness—the level of intellectual growth that allows the student to grasp the knowledge offered by the teacher" (p. 157). Piaget's personal interests were in working with younger children. Consequently, his data provide far less information about students of age 11 years and older (the formal operational learning stage) and offers less help to those who work with learners at that learning stage.

Adelson is concerned with identifying how soon young adolescents (ages 11-14 years) really develop full formal reasoning skills. Data from his work identify that the 12 year old normally "does not have the conceptual framework by which to organize and order the information that the educator provides." On the basis of his investigations with both younger and older adolescents, Adelson (1983) concluded that "the major difference between younger and older adolescents was the capacity of the latter to think abstractly when the occasion demanded it" (p. 157). Figure Five presents four of Adelson's tables which display these data.

Adelson's findings identify that young adolescents do not move as rapidly into formal operations as Piaget's original data might suggest. Recall the comments made earlier in this chapter when introducing the section on the Piagetian learning stages. They were to the effect that Piaget's primary interests were in young children. The majority of his work was done with children of ten years of age and younger. His detailed investigations of children's intellectual skill development during the first three learning stage age-frames developed accurate estimates of the age-frames at which most children could be expected to manifest progressively higher intellectual abilities during each learning stage age-frame.

Piaget did correctly report that children demonstrate the capacity to develop formal operational thinking in the 11-15 years frame. However, because of his lesser interst in this older age group, he did not study them in the detail he did with younger children. This lack of such detailed study also meant there was not a similar establishment of the pace at which progression into formal operational skills could be expected during this final learning stage age-frame. The work of Elkind (1980) and Adelson (1983) helps to establish that most adolescents do not move rapidly into formal operations at the beginning of this fourth learning stage. It also appears that consolidation of concrete skills initiated in the prior concrete operational stage continues and establishes the basis for gradual development of beginning formal operational capabilities by young adolescents. The data presented in Figure Five offer educators who work with the age 11-14 years age-frame compelling reasons to rethink notions about how rapidly young adolescents can be expected to develop formal thinking skills.

Adelson's work further suggests major frontier issues for creativity research. This deals with the study of populations in the formal operational age-frame to build upon Adelson's investigations. Comparative study of this population on both learning stage and creativity tests and measures needs to be developed. Resulting data would help define and establish the relationship between learning stage readiness and creativity readiness issues during the age-frame in which most humans develop their abstract learning skills. It would also provide bases for identifying and describing which readiness indicators are related to particular levels and degrees of creative capacities. The learning psychology areas discussed here provide an important data base to investigate persisting creativity readiness questions. Careful consideration of the frontier issues which have been raised here is essential to identify ways in which humans may be assisted to fully develop their creative abilities at each intellectual development stage. These data identified the age-frames during which the majority of youngsters could be expected to approach and develop intellectual abilities at the next higher learning stage.

Figure Five.

Differences in abstraction between young and older adolescents.

Table 1. Percent demonstrating different levels of abstraction in the conceptualization of government (N = 326)

By Age	11	13	15	18
Concrete	57	27	07	00
Low Level Abstraction	28	64	51	16
High Level Abstraction	00	07	42	71
Don't Know or Not Ascertained	15	05	00	13

Table 2. Percent mentioning community survival in describing purpose of mandatory vaccination (N = 434)

By Age	12	14	16	18
Survival of Community	07	14	23	45

Table 3. Percent offering different opinions on the purpose of laws (N = 433)

By Age	12	14	16	18
Restriction	37	35	29	19
Setting Standards	16	22	34	34
Sense of Community	02	09	14	18
Other	45	34	23	19

Table 4. Percent offering different opinions on the purpose of government (N = 336)

By Age	11	13	15	18
Restriction	73	68	44	20
Restriction and Benefit	12	18	33	38
Benefit	07	08	20	41
Other	08	05	03	01

(Tables from Adelson, pp. 157-159)

Piaget's investigations with youngsters 10 years-old and younger identified the rates which initiation and maturation of intellectual skills could be anticipated in the sensorimotor, concrete preoperational, and concrete operational learning stages. The respective works of Elkind and Adelson provide information suggesting that adolescents do not approach and achieve formal operations as early as was assumed. Earlier assumptions about the onset of formal operations skills were made lacking detailed studies by Piaget of adolescents during their 11-14 years age-frame to the degree he had studied children during their earlier learning stage timeframes. This area of information did not deal with psychobiological development of the brain or neurological studies of the chronology of physiological development in the brain.

Brain Growth Periodization

Herman Epstein (1974, 1978, 1979, 1979a, 1981) related the physiological growth of the brain to previously known information about the mind's capacity to grow in its ability to process information at progressively more difficult stages. His data and notions about brain growth periodization brought such information to the attention of educators. Developed from Epstein's biophysicist perspective, they deal with developing aneurobiological consideration of learning issues. These data deserve careful consideration as another significant frontier area for studying how individuals develop and mature creatively. Called *phrenoblysis,* this was described by Epstein as special mind and brain growth periods. These were determined on the basis of his study of human brain development, skull development and human mental development (1974). He subsequently described these as growth spurts during brain development (1978) and discovered that the physiological growth of the brain in humans also fell into a stage-wise pattern. These growth periods were identified as from 3 to 10 months, 2 to 4 years, 6 to 8 years, 10 to 12 + years and 14 to 16 + years. As a corollary, he also identified age periods of slower brain growth at ages 4 to 6, 8 to 10 and 12 to 14 years.

Epstein's concern was to identify the implications of such scientific data for developing educational strategies which might enhance teaching and learning for children and adolescents. He estimated that as many as 85% of children may experience this pattern of physiological brain growth. Epstein posited the relationship between brain and intelligence development in humans might well explain the developmental learning stages established by Piaget. He further observed:

> It can be seen that there is a brain growth stage on the onsets of the Piaget stages whose ages are classically given by Piagetians. Although many investigations challenge the stage linkage of these Piaget stages, recent evidence shows that Piaget stages are more firmly linked to age than supposed even by the Piagetians themselves. It is important to note that the presumptive correlation of brain growth stages and the Piaget stages requires a prediction that a new Piaget stage will be found corresponding to the fifth and last brain growth stage around age 15 years. Beginning in 1975, Arlin has shown appreciable evidence for a fifth Piaget stage, and her most recent data place the onset age as between 14 and 16 years, precisely as predicted.

> The natures of the Piaget stages are such that there is a qualitative change in mental functioning at each of the onset stages, as would be expected, if there is a very significant increase in neural complexity (Epstein, 1979a; pp. 3-4).

Epstein's data suggest that the brain, like other organs, does grow in a stage-wise fashion. Sylwester's data (et al. 1981, 1982a, b, c, 1984), further identify ways in which the brain grows during the stages of human development. Elkind's and Adelson's respective concerns discussed earlier also support Epstein's foregoing statement which was made prior to formulation of their conclusions. Epstein cites Shayer's data on the distribution of learners among the Piagetian learning stages which interfaced with Epstein's developmental brain growth timeframes. Adelson's data (1983) further substantiates Shayer's and Epstein's contentions that most adolescents do not initiate higher formal operational thinking abilities early in that time-frame. Figure Six presents these data by Shayer et al. (1976, 1978).

Shayer's data identify average ages at which the percentages of children shown are at particular developmental stage levels. The breakdown indicates whether children are at the

Figure Six.

Distribution of thinking abilities by Piagetian developmental stages.

Age (Years)	Pre Operational	Concrete Onset	Concrete Mature	Formal Onset	Formal Mature
5	85	15			
6	60	35	5		
7	35	55	10		
8	25	55	20		
9	15	55	30		
10	12	52	35	1	
11	6	49	40	5	
12	5	32	51	12	
13	2	34	44	14	6
14	1	32	43	15	9
15	1	14	53	19	13
16	1	15	54	17	13
17	3	19	47	19	12
18	1	15	50	15	19

(Shayer's Data [other than age are %] as Cited by Epstein 1979a)

onset or maturation of the skills at that particular developmental stage. Arlin's test (1984a) now allows teachers to identify similar information about each student's learning stage skills in their own classrooms. This will be discussed further in the later section on Cognitive Levels Matching.

Achievement and learning of facts and skills decreases during those segments of the classical Piagetian learning stages which Epstein identifies as lower brain growth or plateau periods. Figure Seven identifies that relationship with the last three Piagetian learning stages.

Figure Seven relates the brain spurt and slow growth intervals within each of the classic Piagetian learning stages. This writer (1981) reviewed the postulation of possible relationships in the growth of the brain to the times at which learning stages appear and signify progressive changes in children's intellectual skills. The possibilities of such correlations of the biological growth of the brain with the Piagetian learning stages are all the more interesting in light of data about children's mental age growth.

Figure Seven.

Brain spurt and slow growth periods in Piagetian learning stages.

Piagetian Stage Age Frames	Epstein Growth Spurt Periods	Epstein Slower Growth Periods
Sensorimotor Birth to 18 months	3 - 10 months	
Concrete Preoperational 2 - 7 years	2 - 4 years	4 - 6 years
Concrete Operational 7 - 11 years	6 - 8 years	8 - 10 years
Formal Operational 11 - 14 years	10 - 12 years	12 - 14 years
Arlin's Postulated Fifth Piagetian Stage	14 - 16 years	

Shuttleworth's study (1939) shows that children demonstrate great differences in average mental age growth during particular time intervals in their lives. Epstein (1978) interpreted Shuttleworth's data in light of the slow growth and spurt intervals shown in Figure Seven. During some sequences of these two year intervals, this difference can be as wide as a 40 month increase followed by only 7 months increase in mental age during the next one. Epstein observed this in Shuttleworth's data on the age 10-12 years interval followed by that drop in mental age growth during the subsequent age 12-14 years age-frame.

It is important that research be continued into the different ways children can and do learn during the proposed slow and spurt growth periods which Epstein identifies within the Piagetian learning stages. Work underway in the Shoreham-Wading River Schools (Brooks and Fusco, 1984, and Brooks, Fusco & Grennon, 1983) will be discussed later in this chapter. Recall the earlier discussion of Adelson's findings regarding differences in how 12 to 14 year-olds develop formal operational thinking skills from 14 to 16 year-olds as you read the information Figure Six presents on this learning stage.

It is necessary to consider carefully Adelson's findings on the ages at which adolescents demonstrated the ability to initiate and develop mature formal operations during the years of the Piagetian formal operational learning stage. The planning and sequencing of intellectual challenges which young adolescents can be expected to master need to be considered in light of those data. Studies of achievement during the age 10 to 14 age range historically show the following patterns. Achievement during the age 10-12 year interval (which includes most 5th and 6th grade youngsters) is very high. However, it is also clear that increases in school achievement during the subsequent 12 to 14 years age interval (which includes most 7th and 8th grade youngsters) is the lowest experienced by children during any interval in their schooling years. Achievement during the 14 to 16 year (which includes most 9th and 10th grade adolescents) interval increases to about the same level found in the 10 to 12 year period.

These findings enhance the possibility that Epstein may have identified a biological base for the Piagetian learning stages. Research on the nature of the neurological development occurring in the brain during these intervals identified by Epstein shows the brain is developing or shifting and maturing synapses accompanied by significant increases in dendritic growth (Huttenlocher, 1979) during these intervals. This development and maturation of synaptic and dendritic growth provides neural networks which allow the child to accommodate progressively more difficult learning and information processing demands. Yakovlev and Lecours (1967) discuss the times at which this growth has been identified. Chiaia and Teyler (1984) further synthesize such information for laypersons.

Fagan and Szymanski (1983) are doing longitudinal studies of groups of primary grades children using both brain and intellectual measurements. Their initial findings further build the possibilities that children do initiate new and higher level thinking skills after, rather than before or independent of, noted increases in the sizes of the brains. As Strahan and this writer (1984) identify, educators need to study these implications in examining the existing scope and sequences of learning challenges in school programs. These data further indicate that planning learning experiences for all children on a constant continuum is an error. The profile of a child's learning achievement across the school years, as was cited earlier, is episodic rather than continuous. Brooks, Fusco, & Grennon (1983) show this relation in Figure Eight.

The combination of the Piaget and Epstein data provide a powerful reason to consider differences of degree and emphasis which may be expected during particular intervals in a child's school experience. This should not be construed as meaning there are intervals during which learning cannot take place. Rather, these data can assist in identifying how differences in which children acquire new intellectual skills can be used to plan more efficient ways they can deal with facts and information during specific intervals. Educators should study the degree to which children initiate and develop new intellectual skills during brain growth spurt

Figure Eight.

Parallel between Epstein's Brain Growth Stages and Piaget's Stages of Cognitive Development.

Brain Growth Spurts (Epstein)		Cognitive Stages		
14-16+ yrs. — 5	**Fifth Stage** Current research indicates that a fifth stage, creative problem finding, may be distinguishable from formal operational thought.	15 + years	(Arlin)	
10-12 + yrs. — 4	**Formal Operational** Child is capable of hypothetic-deductive reasoning and abstract thought.	11 + years	(Piaget)	
6-8 years — 3	**Concrete Operational** Child develops logical structures to deal with changing objects in the physical world.	7 to 11 yrs.		
2-4 years — 2	**Pre-Operational** Child is able to represent objects and relate them to one another through use of language and other symbols.	2 to 7 yrs.		Cognitive Stages
3-10 mos. — 1	**Sensorimotor** Child deals with environment at perceptual level.	0 to 2 yrs.		

(From Brooks, Fusco & Grennon, 1983)

and slow growth periods. The planning of how a child can best learn new facts and information must be considered in light of her/his skill development profile at that given time. If, for instance, she/he is in an interval of slow growth and not initiating higher level skills to a great degree, new facts and information might be more effectively assimilated by offering them at levels which use and allow the child to consolidate her/his present intellectual skills. As the child demonstrates readiness to initiate new and higher level skills, the facts and information to be learned can be presented in progressively higher challenges appropriate to the child's increased ability to initiate and develop those skills.

The Epstein rubric is an important means to help define the readiness for a child to move on to higher level processing challenges with maximum success at each level. As one does not drive a high performance automobile in high gear at all times, the child does not think continually at the highest cognitive level she/he has achieved. Children *shift gears* as they demonstrate their increasing ability to use different learned cognitive level skills in different learning settings. As the learner *adds more gears to her/his personal gearbox,* she/he will *shift* up and down through those abilities as necessary.

It would be erroneous to assume, for instance, that on the dawn of her/his 10th birthday, every child shifts into 24 months of unbridled brain growth which then comes to a screeching halt on birthday 12 for the next 24 months. In actuality, Epstein's data indicate that the majority of children will experience their individual brain growth spurt or slow growth period somewhere in the two year interval identified. One child might experience a particular spurt during a short and rapid 3 month burst within her/his 10 to 12 years lifeframe. Another might experience the same growth over a more even 20 month period during the same two year interval. The same variance is possible for slow growth episodes. Thus, the Epstein stage intervals are times during which educators can anticipate changes in children's learning skills. However, they should not be considered as univeral expectations for the exact times at which each child will experience this phenomenon. Identification of changes in thinking levels among young children through Piagetian interviews and testing have been available since Piaget's work (Sund, 1977). Development of similar measures for older children and adolescents has been a more recent undertaking. Arlin's test of formal reasoning (1984a) developed upon earlier measures by Ankney and Joyce (1976), Burney (1976), and Lawson (1978). Arlin's test identifies whether a child is at low or high concrete operational or formal operational levels. This information can be used to plan learning experiences which appropriately help learners consolidate present skills and initiate new ones for which they possess readiness.

Cognitive Levels Matching

The development of cognitive levels matching has helped educators to respond to the issues suggested by the interface of the Piagetian and Epstein stages. Hunt (1961) described the major problem facing education as "the problem of the match." Epstein (1981) described cognitive levels matching as the need to provide teachers with the ability: (1) to identify and diagnose student cognitive levels; and, (2) to then organize learning activities which match the learner's readiness to learn information by consolidating existing skills and initiating new ones as her/his readiness indicates. Cognitive levels matching is seen by this writer as dealing with James' concern that "to detect the moment of instinctive readiness for the subject is then, the first duty of every educator" (James, 1890; p. 16). In providing teachers with these capacities, the ultimate purpose of cognitive levels matching is to minimize both the over and under challenge in learning and identify the most appropriate levels to challenge child and adolescent variance in cognitive abilities during her/his journey through the years of schooling.

The Shoreham-Wading River, New York Schools (Brooks, Fusco & Grennon, 1983) are now in the sixth year of developing such an approach on a district-wide basis. This program provides teachers with continuing staff development and inservice experiences. Brooks (1984) notes that the cognitive levels matching project sought to facilitate cognitive development by appropriate educational intervention. Teachers involved in the project have gained the skills to identify individual learner's cognitive levels and develop learning activities which match and respond to learner's changing cognitive levels. Along with Epstein, Shayer and others, Arlin (1984b) is working with the Shoreham district in the continuing development of this approach. Independent testing of its results are being done by Educational Testing Service.

Brooks and Fusco (1984) describe how the Piagetian principle of constructivism is necessary to develop learning activities which respond to children's differing capabilities as their cognitive levels change. Again, Elkind's (1980) notions on "automatization" and "the intellectual unconscious" need to be understood by educators in constructing learning activities and an environment which does not assume that youngsters think as adults do. Brooks and Fusco (1984) provide specific examples of how the child's point of view must be central in professional decisions regarding curricular adaptations questioning techniques, testing, and administration of school programs. Brooks (1984) discusses the importance of the relationship between the "knower and the known" in cognitive levels matching. Smock (1981) described this as the subject-object unity. Brooks (1984) further observes that "the notion that knowledge can be acquired via incremental skill or subskill acquisition, the sequence of which is pre-identified and imposed through adult logic applied to children's constrictions, ignores the primacy of the child's point of view. Yet it remains a preeminent foundation of our educational system" (p. 24).

By using the constructivist principle in cognitive levels matching, teachers learn how to format learning so that children can construct the means for their own learning. Sigel (1984) maintains that all humans understand the world through representations of it. Constructivism can use "distancing strategies" as a means to allow the learner to construct this relationship from her/his own experience of the world in relationship to what is to be learned. Sigel and Cocking (1977) make the important point that distancing is not detachment of adults/teachers from the child, but facilitating and working with the child as she/he constructs an understanding of that situation. Cognitive levels matching substantiates that children can neither accelerate content acquisition nor accelerate incremental sub-skill development beyond their cognitive skill levels at a particular developmental stage. Constructivism helps the child to construct ways to process information rather than *parrot* content which is beyond her/his ability to understand. For example, it does not benefit a child to impose formal learning expectations prematurely when that child can learn facts and information effectively in a different way by using lower level skills which are already in place.

In writing of her experiences in designing and teaching cognitive levels matching activities, Grennon (1984) observes, "the delicate factor in bringing students to the leading edge of their intellectual abilities lies in the teacher's understanding of the inextricable tie between affect and cognition" and further, that "Teachers need to attend not only to the cognitive development of students, but to the vulnerable emotional states that various teaching practices can generate" (p. 15). While longitudinal evaluation of the cognitive levels matching (CLM) project at Shoreham-Wading River is still in process, Brooks (1984) reports three findings from preliminary data:

1. The CLM experience has significantly touched most participants: "I never realized that my questions were so closed;" "I finally understand why my students never understand this concept;" "The problem I presented to the class was not the same problem most of the children perceived."
2. It gives teachers a common focus for communicating about children: "Missing addends is a tough concept for John because he is unable to conserve numbers."
3. It gives teachers a way to assess the appropriateness of curriculum materials: "The metaphors in this book may be too complex for my class" (p. 27).

Even from this preliminary data, cognitive levels matching has demonstrated its capacity to increase teacher understanding of the dynamic interaction of teaching and learning within a constructivist framework. It would appear that cognitive levels matching provides an effective strategy for planning instruction to deal with the match of readiness and task which both James (1890) and Hunt (1961) observed as the major challenge facing educators.

Brain Growth Periodization-Cognitive Levels Matching and Creativity Issues

The implications of the Piagetian stages for creativity were presented earlier in this chapter. They heighten the creativity issues raised about readiness to learn during the progressing chronological epochs in children's lives. Figure Nine adapts information from Arlin's chart (1984a) and presents the interface of data on brain growth stages with both cognitive levels and the Piagetian learning stages.

Let us now consider those creativity issues in terms of what brain growth periodization and cognitive levels matching suggest. The focus of concern is, of course, to relate these data to questions which will help ascertain the reality of cognitive limits to creativity.

The sensorimotor period contains the Epstein age 3 to 10 months growth spurt. Studying this epoch will require the careful collaboration of researchers from creativity, early childhood and parenting backgrounds. The implications for educating parents to understand cognitive level matching needs in this first and most critical period of brain growth are staggering. Infants complete the major portion of neuron development during the 3 to 10 months period and DNA synthesis is completed before 18 months of age. Such collaborative study and investigation of the following creativity-learning issues during the sensorimotor developmental stage requires very high priority:

1. Can precocity and earlier readiness for developing the capacity to manipulate symbols common to the concrete preoperational learning stage be facilitated?

Figure Nine.

Relation of brain growth, cognitive and Piagetian data.

Brain Growth Stage	Cognitive Levels	Piaget Stages
3 - 10 months Motor Neuron Development Cerebellum		1. Sensorimotor (0 - 18 months)
2 - 4 years angular gyrus years Hearing/binocular vision language development	IA - Play IB - Trial/Error	2. Preoperational (2-5-7)

6 - 8 years
angular gyrus reading/writing
	IIA - Some attempt at system	3. Concrete Operations
		   (5-7) - (11-14) or
		   (15-17) or ?

10 - 12 years rear right hemisphere abstract thought	IIIA - Systematic, generalizes but doesn't exhaust	4. Formal Operations (11-14 years or ?)
14 - 16 years angular gyrus (?) rear left hemisphere problem finding and self-awareness	IIIB - Fully formal, considers rival hypotheses, etc.	5. Post Formal (Arlin) (15-17)

(Arlin's sources in developing the information in Figure Eight were Epstein [1978], Sylwester [1982], and Elkind [1969]).

---

2. Can precocity and earlier readiness for the skills of later learning stages be facilitated?
3. Can creative behaviors in which infants can develop readiness for sensorimotor tasks be identified?
4. Can creative behaviors appropriate with sensorimotor cognitive levels be identified and enhanced?
5. What kinds of activities could be developed and/or utilized to ascertain these possibilities?

The brain growth spurt and slow growth intervals Epstein identified within the Piagetian concrete preoperational learning stage raise important concerns. As children complete their sensorimotor development, the issue of the possibilities of how there may be cognitive limits for creativity development takes on increasing importance. These consequences deal with a child's readiness to initiate successfully such critical skill tasks as reading and language processing skills. In addition, continuing attention needs to be given to identifying readiness to initiate holistic and visual-spatial learning. When children lacking necessary readiness for reading, for example, are placed in learning situations which "force" reading, they often experience developmental problems which are extremely difficult to overcome. The most critical issue in this developmental stage may well be avoiding overchallenge or challenges which go beyond the child's readiness to initiate and mature these fundamental skills. The nurture and development of creativity in children is not well served when this inappropriate kind of action occurs. Again, James' (1890) concern "to identify the moment of the instinctive readiness for the subject is, then, the first duty of every educator" is a fundamental issue. This is central to identifying the appropriate times at which a child can initiate development of her/his creative potential during particular age frames. Identifying the relation of information gathering and processing skills to creativity issues during the subsequent concrete preoperational learning stage will require answers to the following questions:

1. Can precocity and earlier readiness for elementary logical operations and cognitive operations common to later learning stages be facilitated?
2. Can precocity and earlier readiness for the skills of the formal operations learning stage be facilitated?
3. Can creative behaviors in which concrete preoperational children deal with mastering and consolidating sensorimotor tasks be identified?
4. Can creative behaviors appropriate with concrete preoperational cognitive levels be identified and enhanced?
5. What kinds of activities could be developed and/or utilized to ascertain these possibilities?

The concrete operational learning stage brings the maturing of concrete operational processing skills as well as transition to initiation of beginning formal operational skills by a few precocious children. The study of creative approaches with this age group should focus on identifying effective and appropriate ways to mature concrete operational learning abilities. This is important because readiness issues become increasingly more complex for this age group. The definition of creativity-learning issues must also deal with the social-emotional aspects of beginning pubescent tasks which appear during this developmental stage.

Denmark (1981) researched the relationship among creative thinking, problem solving, and specific elements of classroom climate in a sample of fourth, fifth, and sixth grade students. Sherwood and Strahan (1984) discuss the implications of Denmark's findings about creativity concerns related to the cognitive level characteristics of middle grades youngsters. Denmark's findings dealt with the fourth grade slump described earlier by Torrance (1974). Denmark's data on fourth graders showed that they scored significantly lower than third and fifth graders for elaboration and total creativity scores in the sample he studied. Denmark considered the most significant results of this research to be the inverse relationship between creativity and developmental logical thinking tasks. Sherwood and Strahan discuss the need to integrate creative education activities with generalized autonomy as school programs attempt to better meet creative learning needs of this population. Denmark's findings support Torrance's (1974) concerns and raise important issues which will require careful investigation.

The use of creative problem solving activities appropriate to cognitive levels of individual children during their concrete operational developmental stage could become very helpful as means to deal with their pubescent transition problems. Creativity researchers need to deal with and help children resolve the following issues during their concrete operational developmental stage:

1. Can precocity and earlier readiness for hypothetical deductive reasoning skills associated with the formal operations learning stage be facilitated?
2. What issues of early onset of pubescent development pose the greatest difficulties in dealing with concrete operational development?
3. Can creative behaviors in which concrete operational children deal with mastering and consolidating concrete preoperational tasks be identified?
4. Can creative behaviors for dealing with individual and small group concerns

about pubescent development issues be utilized to clarify concrete operational learning needs?

5. What kinds of activities could be developed and/or utilized to ascertain these possibilities?

Creativity research about the formal operational stage needs to identify the degree to which intervention strategies can either develop or further mature creative skills or tendencies during this stage. Since adolescents initiate and mature their individual pubescent development at widely varying times and rates during their own 9 to 17 years age-frame, creative problem solving activities again offer promising means for dealing with and resolving personal pubescent transition problems. The adolescent's personal-social development during her/his formal operational developmental stage could provide the most meaningful set for initiating and refining creative problem solving approaches. This could contribute both to the development and refinement of creative thinking for use in other aspects of her/his life as well as a creativity skill for use in adult life. Again, the collaboration of researchers in creativity and adolescent psychology are essential in dealing with these specific research questions involving learning issues characteristic of the formal operational learning stage:

1. Which pubescent development issues pose the greatest difficulties in dealing with the development of creative thinking skills during the formal operational learning stage?

2. Can creative behaviors in which formal operational adolescents deal with mastering and consolidating those tasks be identified?

3. Can creative behaviors for dealing with individual and small group concerns about pubescent development issues be utilized to clarify formal operational learning needs?

4. What kinds of activities could be developed and/or utilized to ascertain these possibilities?

Johnson (1980a, b) has broken important ground in his investigation of the degree to which there are significant differences in the creative thinking potential of children in different Piagetian cognitive developmental stages. His study pursued the degree to which there are differences in creative thinking potential of children when the interaction of their Piagetian stage, cognitive development, and IQ is considered. This offers an interesting potential for studying cognitive-matching level programs as well. Johnson tested subjects with the Otis-Lennon Mental Abilities and Torrance Test of Creative Thinking (TTCT). Sherwood and Strahan (1984) discuss Johnson's conclusions and their importance for further consideration.

While children did not demonstrate significant stage-wise score increases for any of the TTCT scores, they did demonstrate sequential stage-wise TTCT increases but in figural originality and elaboration only. While average concrete operational learners scored highest on all TTCT indicators, except elaboration, Johnson also found that early formal operational students demonstrated the potential for scoring the best. Those interested in the questions raised earlier on researching creativity concerns in the range of cognitive levels will find Johnson's research of great interest.

Arlin's (1975) positing of a possible fifth Piagetian growth stage requires continuing study. Her research is building evidence as to the possibilities of a fifth Piagetian stage which corresponds to the brain growth stage Epstein identifies during the age 14 to 16 years interval. Creativity research needs to investigate the relation of these findings to particular creative behaviors most often demonstrated by maturing adolescents and young adults during this timeframe. Study of how learners at this stage utilize creative thinking and problem solving approaches is an important creativity learning issue. Studying the problems surrounding the incidence and degree of latency issues might assist in identifying why some individuals delay in developing and manifesting creative abilities until well into their adult years.

There is also a need to study the Creative Problem Solving Process (Isaksen & Treffinger 1985; Noller, Parnes & Biondi 1976; and Parnes, Noller & Biondi 1977) in terms of questions about its relation to possible cognitive limits of creativity. The steps in the Creative Problem Solving process (CPS) need to be considered in terms of the ages at which children demonstrate readiness and the ability to perform the tasks inherent in each step of that model. Furthermore, the difficulty of problems which a child is asked to solve needs to be assessed against her/his readiness to function at the cognitive levels which she/he has achieved at that particular time. Even if the child can comprehend the component steps in CPS itself, the nature of the cognitive level of the problem to be solved cannot be overlooked.

For this reason alone, studies must be made of how the kinds of creative behaviors children demonstrate do relate to their personal cognitive developmental levels. This is central to organizing a data base on norms and variations in the relation of creativity skills to intellectual developmental stages and cognitive levels. In regard to concerns about the characteristics of children in each of the cognitive levels discussed, the child's readiness to move from concrete to formal operational abilities is crucial. This is so because achievement of readiness to function at particular cognitive levels may be prerequisite to fully understanding and performing several of the steps in the CPS. Problem Finding, Idea Finding, Solution-Finding, and Acceptance-Finding are the CPS steps which seem to be most critically involved with cognitive levels. The level of abstraction and formal operations ability required in each of these steps needs to be researched and identified. In the section "How Do We Overcome the Blocks?", Parnes (1981, Chapter 5) anticipates these concerns in considering the blocks persons may experience learning how to use the CPS.

What are the readiness and ability issues involved in deferring judgment in the various diverging phases of CPS? Deferring judgment seems to approximate closely the Piagetian concept of suspending judgment. Experiences with cognitive levels matching conclude that the ability to suspend judgment fully is a formal operational skill. Work with students identifies that in dealing with reasons for events, including activities such as a story line and examining historical issues, the following cognitive limits prevail. Preoperational learners can only interpret phenomena egocentrically; concrete operational learners can order relationships of the events; and, formal operational learners can suspend judgment and make an abstract formulation of a relationship which covers all cases in the range of events involved in that situation.

This makes it imperative that the nature of deferring judgment also be examined to identify the degree to which it is related to cognitive level abilities. This should investigate the skills and degree of deferring judgment found in children at different ages who attempt to use the CPS. This should investigate matching their abilities to defer judgment with the cognitive level skills discussed here. Since deferring judgment is essential to Idea Finding, the possibilities for children effectively utilizing the remaining steps of CPS could be negated if they do not have the capacity to defer judgment before moving to the Solution-Finding and Acceptance-Finding steps.

The study of differences in the ability of children at different cognitive level age-frames to defer judgment could provide data to address another concern. Such data might support a hypothesis to the effect that the reason most preadolescents, fewer adolescents and some adults tend to move to what Parnes (1981) identifies as "automatic reactions" (pp. 87-89), is rooted in their inability to defer judgment fully. Research is also needed to identify the degree to which one's inability to use all her/his senses (Parnes, pp. 99-101) in deferring judgment may deal with the lack of readiness to defer judgment.

The final steps of Solution-Finding and Acceptance-Finding in CPS similarly need study in terms of how their successful use relates to those skills and readinesses which children demonstrate at each cognitive level and Piagetian stage. It seems clear that a major area of research needs to be established which studies the relationship of creativity, creative learning and problem solving to the neuropsychological readiness issues discussed here.

Readiness Issues Relating to Hemispheric Specialization of the Brain

Creativity scholars are aware of brain hemisphericity-creativity issues to a far greater degree than the cognitive levels issues just considered. Torrance (1982) synthesizes the major pedagogic concerns about creativity issues. For this reason, this section will not summarize that information but shall deal only with issues suggested by neurological findings.

There is a need to study ways in which Electoencephalograms (EEG) can corroborate information on brain hemisphericity or lateralization from the Torrance Style of Learning and Thinking (SOLAT) tests (Torrance et al. 1977, 1978, 1980, Reynolds, et al. 1979). Furst (1976) has examined implications of what EEG patterns suggest about right hemispheric visual-spatial functions. Galin, Johnstone, Nakell & Herron (1979) further identify information about how normal children develop the capacity to transfer tactile information between hemispheres. The creativity field must give attention to relating its research data on pedagogic concerns about hemisphericity with the growing body of EEG and other data on patterns of brain function. Sinatra's (1983) findings on hemispheristic influences on language development also require investigation by creativity researchers. The left hemisphere contains the major language and speech processing centers in the brain. However, the right hemisphere also contains minor centers for language and speech processing (Glassner 1980, Searleman 1977). Cultural differences between occidentals and orientals reflect the latter's advantage in right hemisphere language and speech processing (Merrill 1981). Oriental cultures concentrate on facilitating young children's development of right hemispheric readiness to support language skill development. Children are assisted in gaining a *picture/image vocabulary* before turning to typical left hemisphere linear processing skills which deal in grammar, word patterns, syntax, and the like. Occidental cultures, on the other hand, move youngsters to linear language skills as soon as reading readiness (a left hemisphere linear function in our culture) is established. Occidentals appear never to catch up with orientals in these right hemisphere capabilities. Creativity research needs to examine whether earlier development of right hemisphere and lateralized language processing skills could alter this skill development pattern among children in our culture.

Khatena's recent work (1984) offers a range of powerful issues in imagery and creative imagination which need to be considered in this investigation. His multidimensional interactive creative imagination imagery model (pp. 37-42) provides a construct which could assist in defining creativity studies of bilateralized language development as children grow and develop. His fifth chapter further provides a model as to how individuals may process both psychological and physiological inputs in developing such skills. His later chapters on measurement and research of creative imagination further provide creativity researchers with exciting possibilities for formulating research of the areas suggested in this section. The discussion begun here cannot be deliberated further until that information is carefully reviewed. It is anticipated that this information will prove to be an exciting future agenda area.

Left hemisphere skills dominate in our culture to the point that school experiences and curricula are also strongly biased toward linear processing skills. The issue could rest in the fact that this "left hemisphere curriculum" is also taught by adults who largely are left brain dominant themselves. One means to research and determine alternate approaches would require that pre-school, kindergarten, and first grade learners be taught by two person teaching teams. For experimental purposes, one of the two teachers on each team should be right brain dominant. This would establish a favorable placement for youngsters who come to school as either right brain preferred or dominant learning styles. Every child would then have a teacher who could match her/his dominance as well as a model to nurture subordinate skills residing in their subordinate hemisphere.

Research with such a model could further identify information about the actual cognitive limits and capacities of young children to respond to early learning of skills attributed to each hemisphere. This would also place them in a setting which provides daily access to teachers who can respond specifically to both their dominant and subordinate skills and processing centers. This could identify possibilities for lateralizing skills in each hemisphere and bilateralizing abilities in both hemispheres which could help children learn to process information in both linear and visual spatial ways. Cohen and Gainer (1976), and Edwards (1979) both consider how visual spatial learning approaches normally associated with art and drawing might be learned by more persons than is possible in today's predominantly linear organization of the majority of cognitive processing skills in our culture.

Neural Plasticity

The last situation addressed raises the issue of the degree to which children have ability to process information with centers which reside in different areas of the brain. This deals with the neurological phenomenon known as neural plasticity. Levine (1984) presents the issues of neural plasticity which are central to the child's ability to redirect hemispheric and other neurological skills. Complementary specialization of the brain is possible only as this plasticity or, the ability to re-direct development of neural networks exists. Changes in an individual's handedness, dominance of eye and the like, can best be reorganized during the neural plasticity period. As the brain matures, the myelinization process gradually ends one's neural plasticity (Johnson 1980b). When a neural circuit matures, it is encased in a sheath of fatty myelin. While this intensifies the strength and the speed of that circuit to transmit its neural function, it also restricts and largely limits the circuit's ability to redirect its functions. As Gazzaniga (1974) comments, cerebral dominance as a decision system is largely determined by the development of neurological networking before myelinization is complete. Torrance (1982) raises the point that the profiles of the most creative persons reveal a high degree of bilateralization or development of skills in both hemispheres. Bilateralization has to be initiated before mylelinization of the brain is complete. For this reason the neural plasticity issue poses a major concern in considering cognitive limits to development of creativity.

Myelinization of the corpus callosum is a critical episode. The corpus callosum (Sperry, 1964) is the massive fiber system connecting the two hemispheres and through which the adult brain must interact. His continuing investigation of the corpus callosum's interface of hemispheric functions (1982) eventually resulted in his selection as a Nobel Laureate. Lenneberg (1967); Yakoviev & Lecours (1967); and Levine (1984), each claim that the full myelinization and maturation of the corpus callosum is not complete until somewhere during the age 10 to 13 year interval. Initiation of the processing skills residing in each hemisphere prior to completion of the corpus callosum's myelinization are critical events in this episode. There is reason to believe that if these abilities of each hemisphere are not initiated prior to completion of the myelinization of the corpus callosum that further development of these abilities is severely curtailed.

Case histories show that many persons suffering a severe cerebral stroke in their left hemisphere (site of the major language processing centers) do not regain speech or language facility. However, a minority of such victims with this specific trauma do regain speech and language facility. Since neural tissue is so fragile that it normally infarcts after such trauma, it is felt that those individuals who do regain speech and language facility actually did not rehabilitate their left hemisphere. Patricia Neal, the actress, was such a case. It is contended that such individuals had developed enough of the minor speech and language processing systems in the right hemisphere of the brain prior to complete myelinization of their corpus callosum. This is given as the reason they could process through the corpus callosum and relearn speech and language facility by using these minor centers following the stroke in their left hemisphere. It is further assumed that the majority of victims of left hemisphere strokes who fail to regain speech and language facility had experienced insufficient development of their right hemisphere minor speech and language centers prior to complete myelinization of their corpus callosum. Thus they could not process through the corpus callosum to initiate speech and language facility in the minor processing centers in the right hemisphere following the stroke in the left hemisphere of their brain. There is a need to examine the degree to which known bilateralized thinkers do and do not experience this phenomenon following massive cerebral strokes in the left hemisphere of their brains.

In the matter of dominance in handedness, the following has also been observed. Cross dominance means that one side of the body is controlled by the opposite hemisphere of the brain. If a person's right arm is dominant, she/he is almost always a left brain dominant individual. Children who break their dominant arm prior to myelinization of their corpus callosum usually demonstrate the ability to develop particular skills in their subordinate arm while incapacitated. This includes skills such as writing, throwing a ball and applying make-up or grooming. This adaptability is a prime example of neural plasticity. Before neural circuits have fully matured and myelinized, a trauma, such as a broken dominant arm, can stimulate still immature circuits to redirect their functions. Such episodes may facilitate increases in cross and mixed dominance as well as increase bilateralization of functions in both hemispheres. This happens far less frequently to adults who experience similar accidents. Limited data suggest that those few adults who can make such adjustments after an injury, such as a broken dominant arm, have achieved varying degrees of bilateralized capabilities in their brain prior to myelinization of the corpus callosum.

Recent Data on Sex Differences and Hemisphericity

Wittelson (1976) discusses several areas of sex difference which impact on learning and expectations of typical school programs. The corpus callosum in females is 40% thicker than in males. Consequently, females have considerably more interconnecting possibilities between hemispheres. Males usually have larger right hemispheres while the reverse is true of most females. Michalak (1984) has made some fascinating observations on these differences. Because of cross dominance, the right hemisphere has dominant input from the left ear while the left hemisphere responds more directly to the right ear. This establishes some interesting advantages and disadvantages for females and males.

The left hemisphere contains the major language centers. Females typically have a larger left hemisphere and tend to be stronger processors of language. This gives females an added advantage because normally they have direct input of language from the right ear directly to the left hemisphere where the dominant language processing centers reside. This is offered as a biological reason why females typically respond to language better than males. This means they directly input from their dominant right ear to the major language processing centers in the left hemisphere without having to cross over through the corpus callosum. They dominantly focus on language sounds and tend to be distracted by environmental sounds processed by their subordinate left ear to the right hemisphere.

Males, on the other hand, have larger right hemispheres and their left ear sends environmental sounds directly to their right hemisphere which deals primarily with holistic visual-spatial inputs. Contrary to females, they dominantly focus on environmental sounds and often tend to be distracted by language sounds processed by their subordinate right ear to their left hemisphere. As their left dominant ear attempts to support the right in dealing with language inputs, males experience a disadvantage from females. Their left ear transmits language to the right hemisphere where it then must process that input through the corpus callosum to reach the major speech centers in that left hemisphere. With a 40% thinner corpus callosum and less interconnecting fibers in that fiber system, males experience an approximate 20 to

40 millisecond delay over females in transmitting language/speech signals to the language processing centers in their left hemisphere. Michalak's investigations indicate that cognitive development of males and females is strongly influenced by sex related variables such as these auditory input differences. This supports Kinsbourne and Hiscock's (1978) earlier positions on the influences of cerebral lateralization on cognitive development. Females are more lateralized in the left and males in the right hemispheres. This also reinforces Riegle's (1979, 1980) findings about differences in lateralized brain development of adolescent females from males.

Brain Hemisphericity and Creativity Issues

Despite the growing data supporting hemispheric specialization, it is important to consider Levy's contentions (1982) that children do think with whole brains. The ways in which children can integrate their hemispheric abilities are important as researchers consider the holistic implications of creative behavior in children. Hemisphericity research should help us identify both the holistic and hemispheric ways in which the brain facilitates learning and creative activity. Careful investigation of the relationship of creativity to the bilateralized abilities of individuals needs to pursue two major questions:

1. To what degree does one's creativity relate to the way that individual can deal with a particular learning situation from both linear-sequential and visual-spatial points of view?
2. Does a major criterion of creativity actually lie in one's ability to examine or dissect a situation in a linear, deductive sense and then re-assemble it in an inductive, holistic manner?

A sub-investigation of this second question should also pursue the degree which individuals demonstrate an ability to comprehend a situation in a holistic manner and then re-assemble it in a linear manner. As information relating to these questions is gathered, the importance of helping all children optimally develop the processing centers in each hemisphere of the brain may gain higher priority. Likewise, learning activities may also give increased priority to helping children solve learning tasks by using skills and capabilities which integrate their hemispheric abilities as they progress through their school years. The growing data base regarding neural plasticity and myelinization of neural circuitry generally, and of the corpus callosum in particular, needs particular study in light of data from both holistic and hemispheric investigations of how children do learn and think. As studies identify how and when children demonstrate progressive creative thinking abilities, further research must also identify how creative thinking may be used to maximize what children can and do learn as they grow through adolescence (Levin 1976).

Additional work needs to be done in spelling out further broad and specific definitions of creative thinking. Torrance's work (1974) in developing tests of creative thinking needs to be taken further to establish greater areas of common agreement on the nature and definition of creativity and creative thinking. The goal here is not to arrive at a central or monolithic definition of these terms but to research more predictable traits of these areas as they relate to the growth and development of children's cognitive abilities. Dr. Torrance's chapter in this volume should provide further direction for charting directions and possibilities in teaching for creativity. The actual limits of cognition and creativity require the development of these benchmark areas of agreement to pursue the specific implications of the interface of the growth of these capacities in children.

The other major area of hemispheristic questions about the cognitive limits of creativity deals with the entire learning styles issue. This author feels that area is too broad to include as part of this chapter. Also, the work of Kirton (1977, 1980) needs to be carefully related to research of other learning styles scholars as a precurser to fully considering cognitive limits issues.

Summary

Hopefully this chapter has provided some helpful information for the reader. You will recall that the writer's objectives in developing this chapter were:

1. To provide a knowledge base of current information about major concerns in cognitive development in psychological and neurological areas; and,
2. To frame major research areas and questions linking those data with creativity concerns.

The second objective was subject to the writer's interpretation of both the psychological and neurological data bases from his perspective of a curriculum theorist with interests in the creativity field. As such, and because of the limits of length of this chapter, the results should not be taken as not an inclusive listing of such concerns. It is intended, rather, to serve as a list of major creativity concerns developed from that perspective. Lastly, it is hoped that creativity scholars will find this information of help as they utilize their own expertise in the creativity field to raise major issues and questions specific to their own research interests.

Footnotes

1. Editor's note: See Dr. Khatena's chapter in this volume for additional information.
2. Editor's note: See Dr. Khatena's chapter in this volume for additional information.

References

Adelson, J. (1983, Summer). The growth of thought in adolescence. *Educational Horizons,* 156-162.

Ankney, P. & Joyce, L. (1976). The development of a piagetian pencil and paper test for assessing concrete operational reasoning. In R. Sund (Ed.), *Piaget for Educators* (pp. 154-164). Columbus, OH: Charles E. Merrill Publishing Co.

Arlin, P. (1975). Cognitive development in adulthood: A fifth stage? *Developmental Psychology, 2,* 602-606.

Arlin, P. (1984a). *The Arlin test of formal reasoning.* East Aurora, NY: Slosson Educational Publications.

Arlin, P. (1984b). Cognitive levels matching: An instructional model and a model of teacher change. In M. Frank (Ed.), *A child's brain* (pp. 99-110). New York: Haworth Press.

Brooks, M. (1984, November). A constructivist approach to staff development, *Educational Leadership, 42* (3), 23-27.

Brooks, M. & Fusco, E. (1984). Constructivism and education: The child's point of view. In M. Frank (Ed.), *A child's brain* (pp. 111-132). New York: Haworth Press.

Brooks, M., Fusco, E. & Grennon, J. (1983, May). Cognitive levels matching. *Educational Leadership, 40* (8), 4-8.

Burney, D. (1976). Construction and validation of an object formal reasoning test. In R. Sund, (Ed). *Piaget for Educators* (pp. 165-172). Columbus, OH: Charles E. Merrill Publishing Co.

Chiaia, N. & Teyler, T. (1984). Higher brain function. In M. Frank (Ed.), *A child's brain* (pp. 45-76). New York: Haworth Press.

Cohen, R. & Gainer, E. (1976). *Art, another language for learning.* New York: Citation Press.

Denemark, R. (1981). *Creative thinking, problem-solving and cognitive classroom structure.* Unpublished doctoral dissertation, Fordham University.

Edwards, B. (1979). *Drawing on the right side of the brain.* Los Angeles: J. P. Tarcher, Inc.

Elkind, D. (1969). Egocenticism in adolescence. *Child Development, 38,* 1025-1034.

Elkind, D. (1980, Fall). Adolescent thinking and the curriculum. *New York University Education Quarterly,* 18-24.

Epstein, H. (1974). Phrenoblysis: Special brain and mind growth spurts. *Developmental Psychobiology, 3,* 207-224.

Epstein, H. (1978). Growth spurts during brain development: Implications for educational policy. In J. Chall & A. Mirsky (Eds.), *Education and the brain* (pp. 343-370). Seventy-seventh yearbook of the National Society for the Study of Education, II. Chicago: University of Chicago Press.

Epstein, H. (1979). Correlated brain and intelligence development in humans. In M. Hagn, D. Jensen & B. Dudek (Eds.), *Development and evolution of brain size* (pp. 157-182). New York: Academic Press.

Epstein, H. (1979a, Fall). Brain growth and cognitive functioning, *Colorado Journal of Educational Research, 19,* 3-4.

Epstein, H. (1981, May). Learning how to learn: Matching instructional levels. *The Principal,* 25-30.

Fagan, T. & Szymanski, M. (1983). Can educators determine children's mind and growth stages? *Transescence: The Journal on Emerging Adolescent Education, 11* (2), 32-35.

Furst, C. (1976). EEG asymmetry and visual-spatial performance. *Nature, 200,* 254-255.

Galin, D., Johnstone, J., Nakell, L. & Herron, J. (1979). Development of the capacity for tactile transfer of information between hemispheres in normal children. *Science 204,* 1330-1331.

Gazzaniga, M. (1974). Cerebral dominance viewed as a decision system. In S. Dimons & J. Beaumont (Eds.), *Hemispheric functions in the human brain* (pp. 223-234). London: Halstead Press.

Geshwind, N. (1972, April). Language and the brain. *Scientific American, 226,* 76-83.

Glassner, B. (1980, Spring). Preliminary report: Hemispheric relation in composing. *Journal of Education, 162,* 74-95.

Grennon, J. (1984, November). Making sense of student thinking, *Educational Leadership, 42* (3), 11-16.

Gordon, H. (1984). The assessment of cognitive function for use in education. In M. Frank (Ed.), *A child's brain* (pp. 207-218). New York: Haworth Press.

Guilford, J. P. (1967). *The nature of human intelligence.* New York: McGraw-Hill.

Hunt, J. (1961). *Intelligence and experience.* New York: Ronald Press.

Huttenlocher, P. (1979). Synaptic density in the human frontal cortex—developmental changes and effects of aging. *Brain Research, 163,* 195-205.

Hynd, G., & Obrzut, J. (Eds.). (1981). *Neuropsychological assessment and the school-age child:* Issues and procedures. New York: Grune and Stratton, Inc.

Isaksen, S. G., & Treffinger, D. J. (1985). *Creative problem solving: The basic course.* Buffalo, NY: Bearly Limited.

James, W. (1890). *The principles of psychology.* New York: Henry Holt & Company.

Johnson, L. (1980a). *A study to investigate the relationship of Piagetian stage of cognitive development and I.Q. to creative thinking potential.* Unpublished doctoral dissertation, Indiana State University.

Johnson, V. (1980b). Myelin and maturation: A fresh look at Piaget. *Science Teacher, 49* (3), 41-49.

Khatena, J. (1984). *Imagery and creative imagination.* Buffalo, NY: Bearly Limited.

Kirton, M. (1977). *Research edition: Kirton adaption-innovation inventory.* Windsor, Berks., England: NFER Publishing Co., Ltd.

Kirton M. (1980). Adaptors and innovators: The way people approach problems. *Planned Innovation, 3,* 51-57.

Kinsbourne, M., & Hiscock, M. (1978). Cerebral lateralization and cognitive development. In J. Chall & A. Mirsky (Eds.), *Education and the Brain,* Seventy-Seventh yearbook of the National Society for the Study of Education, II. Chicago: University of Chicago Press.

Lawson, A. (1978). The development and validation of a classroom test of formal operations. *Journal of Research in Science Teaching. 15,* 11-24.

Lenneberg, E. (1967). *Biological foundations of language.* New York: Wiley.

Levin, J. (1976). What have we learned about maximizing what children learn? In J. Levin & V. Allen (Eds.). *Cognitive learning in children: Theories and strategies* (pp. 105-134). New York: Academic Press.

Levine, S. (1984). Hemispheric specialization and functional plasticity during development. In M. Frank (Ed.), *A child's brain* (pp. 77-98). New York: Haworth Press.

Levy, J. (1982). Children think with whole brains: Myth and reality. In J. Keefe (Ed.), *Student learning styles and brain behavior* (pp. 173-184). Reston, VA: National Association of Secondary School Principals.

MacLean, P. (1984). Brain evolution: The origins of social and cognitive behaviors. In M. Frank (Ed.), *A child's brain* (pp. 9-22). New York: Haworth Press.

Merrill, S. (1981, November). The Japanese brain. *Science Digest,* 74-75.

Martorano, S. (1972). A developmental analysis of performance on Piaget's formal operations tasks. *Developmental Psychology, 13* (6), 666-672.

Michalak, G. (1984). *Educating the whole brain.* Unpublished paper (copyrighted). Getzville, NY: G. Michalak.

Noller, R., Parnes, S., & Biondi, A. (1976). *Creative Actionbook.* New York: Charles Scribners.

Pappas, C. (1984). The relationship between language development and brain development. In M. Frank (Ed.), *A child's brain,* (pp. 133-170). New York: Haworth Press.

Parnes, S. (1981). *The magic of your mind.* Buffalo, NY: The Creative Education Foundation in association with Bearly Limited.

Parnes, S., Noller, R. & Biondi, A. (1977). *Guide to creative action.* New York: Charles Scribners.

Piaget, J. (1955). *The language and thought of a child.* New York: Meridian Books.

Piaget, J. & Inhelder, B. (1958). *The growth of logical thinking from childhood to adolescence.* New York: Basic Books.

Piaget, J. (1967). *The child's conception of the world.* Towota, NJ: Littlefield, Adams & Co.

Piaget, J. (1969). *The psychology of intelligence.* (Trans. M. Piercy and D. Berlyna) Towota, NJ: Littlefield, Adams and Company.

Reynolds, C. (1981). The neuropsychological basis of intelligence. In G. Hynd and J. Obrzut, (Eds.), *Neuropsychological assessment and the school age child* (pp. 87-124). New York: Grune and Stratton, Inc.

Reynolds, C. (1982, Spring). Neurological assessment in education: A caution. *The Journal of Research and Development in Education, 15* (3), 76-79.

Reynolds, C., Kaltsounis, B., & Torrance, E. P. (1979). A child's form of your style of learning and thinking: Preliminary norms and technical data. *Gifted Child Quarterly, 23,* 757-766.

Riegel, T., Jr. (1979, April). A lateralization study with high school students and unanswered questions underlying the emerging left-right model. Paper presented at the Conference on the Relationship of Cerebral Lateralization in Education, Atlanta, GA.

Riegel, T., Jr. (1980). Laterality of high school students and its relation to convergent and divergent abilities. *Dissertation Abstracts International, 40* (11). (University Microfilms Order No. 801062.)

Searleman, A. (1977). A review of right hemispheric linguistic abilities. *Psychological Bulletin, 34,* 503-528.

Shayer, M., Kuchemenn, D., & Wylam, (1978). The distribution of Piagetian stages of thinking in British middle and secondary school children 11, 14, to 16 year-olds and sex differences. *The British Journal of Educational Psychology, 48,* 62-70.

Sherwood, L., & Strahan, D. (1984). Research on creativity in the middle school. *Transescence: The Journal of Emerging Adolescent Education, 12,* (2), 7-12.

Shuttleworth, F. K. (1939). The physical and mental growth of girls and boys, age six to nineteen in relation to age at maximum growth. *Monographs of the Society for Research in Child Development, 14* (3).

Sigel, I. (1984, November). A constructivist perspective for teaching thinking. *Educational Leadership, 42* (3), 18-21.

Sigel, I., & Cocking, R. (1977). *Cognitive development from childhood to adolescence: A constructivist perspective.* New York: Holt, Rinehart & Winston.

Sinatra, R. (1983, May). Brain research sheds light on language learning. *Educational Leadership, 40* (8), 9-12.

Smock, C. (1981). Constructivism and educational practices. In I. Sigel, D. Brodzinski, & R. Golinkiff (Eds.), *New directions in Piagetian theory and practice,* (pp. 51-69). Hillsdale, NJ: Lawrence Erbaum Associates.

Sperry, R. (1964, January). The great cerebral commissure. *Scientific American, 210,* 42-52.

Sperry, R. (1982). Some effects of disconnecting the cerebral hemispheres. (Nobel prize presentation) *Science, 217,* 1223-1226.

Strahan, D. & Toepfer, C., Jr. (1984). The impact of brain research on education: Agents of change. In M. Frank (Ed.), *A child's brain* (pp. 219-234). New York: Haworth Press.

Sund, R. (1977). *Piaget for educators.* Columbus, OH: Charles E. Merrill Publishing Co.

Sylwester, R., Chall, Jr., Wittrock, M., & Hart, L. (1981, October). Symposium: Educational implications of recent brain research. *Educational Leadership, 39* (1), 6-17.

Sylwester, R. (1982a, September). A child's brain part I, now thanks to recent brain research you can understand it. *Instructor,* 90-93.

Sylwester, R. (1982b, October). A child's brain part II, the human brain: How every single cell is organized for action. *Instructor,* 64-67.

Sylwester, R. (1982c, November). A child's brain part III, what you should know about skin: The outside layer of the brain. *Instructor,* 44-46.

Sylwester, R. (1984). The neurosciences and the education profession: Inserting new knowledge of a child's developing brain into an already well-developed school. In M. Frank (Ed.), *A child's brain* (pp. 1-8). New York: Haworth Press.

Toepfer, C., Jr. (1981). Brain growth periodization research: Curricular implications for nursery through grade 12 learning. ERIC Document Reproduction Service No. ED. 204 835 EA 031 727.

Toepfer, C., Jr. (1982, Spring). Curriculum design and neuropsychological development. *The Journal of Research and Development in Education,* 15 (3), 1-11.

Torrance, E. P. (1974). *Norms-technical manual: Torrance tests of creative thinking.* Bensenville, IL: Scholastic Testing Service.

Torrance, E. P. (1982, Spring). Hemisphericity and creative functioning. *The Journal of Research and Development in Education,* 15 (3), 29-37.

Torrance, E. P., Reynolds, C., Reigel, T., Jr., & Ball, O. (1977). Your style of learning and thinking, forms A and B: Preliminary norms, abbreviated technical notes, scoring keys, and selected references. *Gifted Child Quarterly, 21,* 563-573.

Torrance, E. P., Reynolds, C., Ball, O., & Riegel, T., Jr. (1978). *Revised norms-technical manual for your style of thinking.* Athens, GA: Georgia Studies of Creative Behavior.

Torrance, E. P. & Reynolds, C. (1980). *Preliminary norms-technical manual for your style of learning and thinking, Form C.* Athens, GA: Georgia Studies of Creative Behavior, University of Georgia.

Torrance, E. P., & Yun Horng, R. (1980a). Creativity and style of learning and thinking characteristics of adaptors and innovators. *The Creative Child Quarterly, 5* (2), 80-85.

Wittelson, S. (1976, July). Sex and the single hemisphere. *Science Education, 193,* 425-426.

Yakovlev, P., & Lecours, A. (1967). The meylogenetic cycle of regional maturation of the brain. In A. Minkowski (Ed.), *Regional development of the brain in early life.* Oxford: Blackwell Scientific Publications.

12

Adaptors and Innovators:
Cognitive Style and Personality

Michael J. Kirton
The Hatfield Polytechnic Institute

Level or Style?

Previous studies in the fields of decision-making and creative thinking have been dominated by concern with efficiency in solving problems and with the frequency with which effective ideas are produced: in other words, with the *level* of the intellectual process. Less attention has been paid to the different ways in which individuals approach problems or the strategies which consciously or unconsciously are adopted: in other words to the *style* of problem-solving. It may be that a main reason for the continued domination of level over style has been that the two concepts have not been sufficiently separated and fit into an adequate theoretical framework. This accounts for, among other things, a plethora of terms but a lack of consistent, expected relationships between measures, and between measures and correlates.

A recent attempt to differentiate between level and style (Stamp, 1984) uses as axes Simple-Complex vs. Holistic-Analytic, and examines seven studies: Hudson, 1966; Mitroff 1974; Mitroff & Kilmann, 1981; Driver & Mock, 1975; McKenny & Keen, 1974; Morse & Gordon, 1974; Kolb & Fry, 1975 (See Figure One). Stamp (1984) notes that one study (Mitroff's) uses only three categories (Holistic-Simple is missing); another has two (Mitroff & Kilmann) falling into the quadrants Holistic-Complex vs. Analytic-Complex, the former being in practice, if not in theory, what most theorists concentrate on. Just as illustrative of the present confusion, Hudson's study is made to stretch into each quadrant by splitting the convergent-divergent dimension, which in much of his theory clearly relates to style alone. It is divided into extreme and moderate convergers (simple-complex) and diverger and extreme diverger *and converger* (my italics). This conflation is replicated in other works which are more difficult to include into Stamp's schema. Two of the Myers-Briggs Type Indicator's (Myers, 1962) supposedly *unrelated* dimensions, Sensing-Intuition and Judgement-Perception, appear clearly to relate to style and show fairly high correlations with at least one inventory of it (Gryskiewicz, 1982; Carne & Kirton, 1982), yet the Myers Briggs manual clearly states that respondents high on *both* measures are *highly creative;* a term that equally clearly relates to level. Just to make matters a little more complicated, we can also read that: "However important a preference for intuition may be, it is certainly not a sufficient condition for creativity (p.34)."

For Cattell in his 16 Personality Factors (PF) (Cattel, Eber & Tatsouka, 1970), "creativity" (unspecified as to level or style) is a higher order factor, made up of a number of factors which relate to and correlate with style (Kirton & DeCiantis, 1986); however, he also includes an estimate of intelligence (Factor B) with double weighting for good measure. Surely IQ should be regarded as a correlate of level. His creativity factor correlates poorly with the adaption-innovation inventory, and so, to almost exactly the same degree, does Jackson's Personality Inventory (1976) measure of Creativity (Goldsmith, 1984). Torrance's (Torrance & Horng, 1980; Torrance, 1982) Right-Left Brain Hemispheric Preference conversely correlates

Figure One.

Stamp's Level vs. Style Schema.

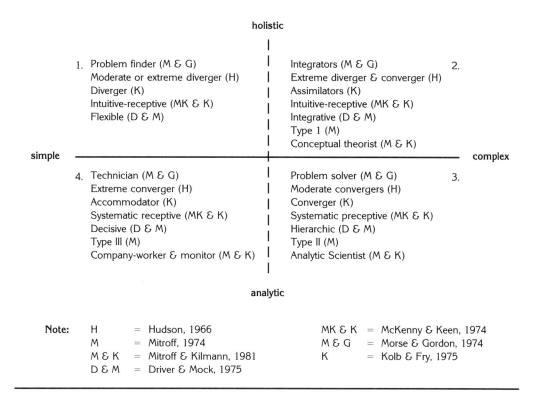

<table>
<tr><td colspan="3" align="center">holistic</td></tr>
</table>

1. Problem finder (M & G) Moderate or extreme diverger (H) Diverger (K) Intuitive-receptive (MK & K) Flexible (D & M)	Integrators (M & G) 2. Extreme diverger & converger (H) Assimilators (K) Intuitive-receptive (MK & K) Integrative (D & M) Type 1 (M) Conceptual theorist (M & K)

simple ———————————————————————— complex

4. Technician (M & G) Extreme converger (H) Accommodator (K) Systematic receptive (MK & K) Decisive (D & M) Type III (M) Company-worker & monitor (M & K)	Problem solver (M & G) 3. Moderate convergers (H) Converger (K) Systematic preceptive (MK & K) Hierarchic (D & M) Type II (M) Analytic Scientist (M & K)

analytic

Note:	H	= Hudson, 1966	MK & K	= McKenny & Keen, 1974
	M	= Mitroff, 1974	M & G	= Morse & Gordon, 1974
	M & K	= Mitroff & Kilmann, 1981	K	= Kolb & Fry, 1975
	D & M	= Driver & Mock, 1975		

highly with adaption-innovation (nearly as highly as Myers-Briggs S-N and J-P combined) but there seems no good reason why Hemispheric Preference should relate to IQ.

The adaption-innovation theory (Kirton, 1976) does distinguish between level and style, if only by purporting to be solely concerned with style and unrelated to level. The Kirton Adaption-Innovation Inventory (Kirton, 1977a) which is the measure of the theory supports the distinction operationally not only, as has been stated, by relating significantly to Hemispheric Preference and other measures largely related to style, but also as will be seen later (pp. 290-295) its lack of relationship with IQ, or with measures of creativity dominated by the level concept, i.e. Guilford type measures (Kirton, 1978a). This operational cleavage has another useful advantage. Whereas measures of level were heavily affected by such factors as intelligence and previous experience, and thus could be criticized in terms of their reliability and validity, the measure of style here described is not contaminated in this way. And, as will be shown, the measure of adaption-innovation has useful applications in the world of business, commerce and administration.

Terminology

Adaption

Adaption is the characteristic behavior of individuals who, when confronted with a problem, turn to the conventional rules, practices and perceptions of the group to which they belong (which, may be a working group, a cultural group or a professional or other occupational group), and derive their ideas towards the solution of the problem from these established procedures. When there is no ready made answer provided by the repertoire of conventional responses, then the adaptor will seek to adapt or stretch a conventional response until it can be used in the solution of the problem. Thus much of the behavior under this heading is seen as making improvements on existing methods, or as Drucker (1969) puts it "doing better" what is done already—a strategy which tends to dominate management.

Innovation

Innovation is the characteristic behavior of individuals who, when confronted with a problem, attempt to reorganize or restructure the problem, and to approach it in a new light, free from any of the customary perceptions or presuppositions which would be the conventional starting-point for its solution. Innovators thus produce answers which are less predictable and thereby sometimes less acceptable to the group (see Figure Two). This approach can be described as "doing things differently" in contrast to the Adaptor's "doing things better."

Innovators and Adaptors in Organizations

Organizations in general (Whyte, 1957; Bakke, 1965; Weber, 1970; Mulkay, 1972) and especially organizations which are large in size and budget (Veblen, 1928; Swatez, 1970) have a tendency to encourage bureaucracy and adaption in order to minimize risk. It has been said by Weber (1970), Merton (1957) and Parsons (1951) that the aims of a bureaucratic structure are precision, reliability and efficiency and that the bureaucratic structure exerts constant pressure on officials to be methodical, prudent and disciplined, and to attain an unusual degree of conformity. These are the qualities that the adaption-innovation theory attributes to the 'adaptor' personality. For the marked adaptor, the longer an institutional practice has existed, the more he feels it can be taken for granted. So when confronted by a problem, he does not see it as a stimulus to question or change the structure in which the problem is embedded, but seeks a solution within that structure, in ways already tried and understood—ways which are safe, sure and predictable. He can be relied upon to carry out a thorough, disciplined search for ways to eliminate problems by 'doing things better' with a minimum of risk and a maximum of continuity and stability. This behavior contrasts strongly with that of the marked innovator. The latter's solution, because it is less understood, and its assumptions untested, appears more risky, less sound, involves more 'ripple-effect' changes in areas less obviously needing to be affected; in short, it brings about changes with outcomes that cannot be envisaged so precisely. This diminution of predictive certainty is unsettling and not to be undertaken lightly, if at all, by most people—but particularly by adaptors, who feel not only more loyal to consensus policy but less willing to jeopardize the integrity of the system, or even the institution. The innovator, in contrast to the adaptor, is liable to be less concerned with the views of others, more abrasive in the presentation of his solution, and more at home in a turbulent environment. He is liable to be seen as less oriented towards company needs (since his perception of what is needed may differ from that of the adaptors) and less concerned with the effect on other people of the methods by which he pursues his goals than adaptors find tolerable. Tolerance of the innovator is at its lowest ebb when adaptors feel pressure from the need for quick and radical change. Yet it is the innovators' least acceptable features which make them as necessary to healthy institutions as the adaptors' more easily recognized virtues make them necessary.

Relationships between Innovators and Adaptors

Problems of fruitful collaboration between innovators and adaptors are not infrequently based on the colored and often inaccurate perceptions which each group has of the other. Innovators tend to be seen by adaptors as abrasive, insensitive and disruptive, unaware of the

Figure Two.

Behaviour Descriptions of Adaptors and Innovators.

Adaptor	Innovator
Characterized by precision, reliability, efficiency, methodicalness, prudence, discipline, conformity.	Seen as undisciplined, thinking tangentially, approaching tasks from unsuspected angles.
Concerned with resolving problems rather than finding them.	Could be said to discover problems and discover avenues of solution.
Seeks solutions to problems in tried and understood ways.	Queries problems' concomitant assumptions; manipulates problems.
Reduces problems by improvement and greater efficiency, with maximum of continuity and stability	Is catalyst to settled groups, irreverent of their consensual views; seen as abrasive, creating dissenance.
Seen as sound, conforming, safe, dependable.	Seen as unsound, impractical; often shocks his opposite.
Liable to make goals of means.	In pursuit of goals treats accepted means with little regard.
Seems imperious to boredom, seems able to maintain high accuracy in long spells of detailed work.	Capable of detailed routine (system maintenance) work for only short bursts. Quick to delegate routine tasks.
Is an authority within given structures.	Tends to take control in unstructured situations.
Challenges rules rarely; cautiously, when assured of strong support.	Often challenges rules, has little respect for past custom.
Tends to high self-doubt. Reacts to criticism by closer outward conformity. Vulnerable to social pressure and authority; compliant.	Appears to have low self-doubt when generating ideas, not needing consensus to maintain certitude in face of opposition.
Is essential to the functioning of the institution all the time, but occasionally needs to be "dug out" of his systems.	In the institution is ideal in unscheduled crises, or better still to help to avoid them, if he can be controlled.
When collaborating with innovators: supplies stability, order and continuity to the partnership.	*When collaborating with adaptors:* supplies the task orientations, the break with the past and accepted theory.
Sensitive to people, maintains group cohesion and cooperation.	Insensitive to people, often threatens group cohesion and cooperation.
Provides a safe base for the innovator's riskier operations.	Provides the dynamics to bring about periodic radical change, without which institutions tend to ossify.

Originally printed in the *Journal of Applied Psychology*, 1976, 61, 5, 622-629.

havoc they are causing. Adaptors are seen by innovators, on the other hand, as stuffy and unenterprising, wedded to systems, rules and norms of behavior which (in the opinion of the innovators) are restrictive and ineffectual. Consequently, disagreement and conflict are likely to arise when the more extreme types of innovator and adaptor come into working contact. Innovators are prone to overlook the extent to which the smooth running of any operation depends on a high degree of adaptiveness in the group but will be intensely aware of, and critical of, the features of adaptiveness which limit long-term effectiveness: lack of enterprise, inflexibility of the system and preoccupation with detail.

Innovators may become isolated in two ways: from each other, since one innovator is not likely to show much respect for the theories of another, and can thus appear to him as abrasive and uncompromising as he would to an adaptor. And as will be readily understood, innovators tend to become isolated from adaptors, either because of their disregard for accepted conventions and standards of procedure, or because they apply unacceptable pressure on adaptors to change their ways. A similar process of isolation was seen by Rogers (1959) in his account of the creative loner.

Measure

According to the A-I theory every individual can be located on a continuum on which the habitual Adaptor and the habitual Innovator are at the extreme ends. The theory further postulates that the position of each individual on the continuum is relatively stable, and that

---

Figure Three.

Distribution: Adaptors and Innovators.

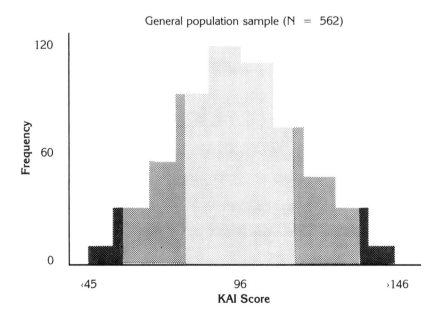

General population sample (N = 562)

Note: Shadings represent standard deviations.
         Main and replication general population samples (Kirton, 1977a).

the distribution of these positions in the general population approximates the normal curve. The Kirton Adaption-Innovation Inventory (Kirton, 1976, 1977a) produces a score which indicates the position of the individual on this dimension. The Inventory consists of 32 items, each of which is scored by the subject on a scale from 1 to 5, giving a theoretical range of total scores from 32 to 160, with a mean of 96. The observed range in the general population, based on a sample of over 1,000 subjects, is slightly more restricted, running from 46 to 146, with a mean value of 95. Two further general population samples (U.S.A., Goldsmith, 1985; N = 214; Italy, Prato Previde, 1985; N = 850) yield means within one point of the British means. The distribution conforms almost exactly to the normal curve (see Figure Three). The internal reliability coefficient has been variously estimated, 0.88 for each of two general population (N = 286; 276) U.K. samples (Kirton, 1976); 0.85 for New Zealand students (17-18 years old, N = 412 Kirton, 1978a); 0.88 for a 256 sample of managers (Keller & Holland, 1978a); .86 for a U.S. general population sample (N = 214) (Goldsmith, 1985); a recently translated Italian version yields a coefficient of 0.87 from a general population sample of circa 850. A test-retest coefficient of 0.82 was obtained (Kirton, 1976) from 64 New Zealand students after an interval of 7 months. Gryskiewicz et al. (1986) reported a coefficient of 0.84 for 106 U.S. managers on courses, with intervals of between five and 17 months. Social desirability influence has also been found to be of negligible amount (Kirton, 1977a; Goldsmith & Matherly, 1986).

Development of the Theory

One main strand in the development of the A-I theory was the residual puzzles left over from a study of change in industry (Kirton, 1961) in which, for example, a new product or a new accounting procedure had been proposed, and where this initiative had met with varying degrees of success. The aim of the study was to follow the process through which a new idea advanced from its original conception to eventual full acceptance and implementation. In each of the examples studied, this process would involve the collaboration of many managers and of more than one department in the firm concerned. The stages which were identified were: perception of the problem; analysis of the problem; proposal of a solution; analysis of the proposed solution; agreement to change; acceptance of change; delegation of the actions required to produce change; and implementation. The study was particularly concerned with the breakdown of this process at various stages and the consequent fate of the original proposal. Application of the A-I theory was able to throw some light on elements of such breakdowns which were otherwise not explicable.

Four observations were made and these became bases for the new theory. They were:

(1) *Delays in introducing change:* Despite the assertion of managers that they were collectively both sensitivie to the need for change, and willing to embark on programs of change, there was a considerable lapse of time—commonly two or three years—between the first formulation of a new idea and the date on which it was definitely accepted as a workable course of action. On the other hand, a few proposals were accepted almost immediately, with a bare minimum of critical analysis. In this there was no relationship between the magnitude of the proposed change and the length of the delay in implementation.

(2) *Objections to new ideas:* In many cases ideas were originally blocked by well-argued objections which continued to hold sway until some occurrence which can usefully be termed a "precipitating event," after which the proposal went forward as if the objections had never existed, and all arguments based on lack of real need, lack of sufficient resources and so on, were never heard again.

(3) *Originator and the group:* It was frequently observed that those ideas which encountered the opposition or delay had been put forward by a group of managers who were in one way or another regarded as *personae non gratae,* or regarded as outsiders by the acknowledged "establishment" group of managers, even after the ideas they advocated had not only been accepted but had proved to be and were recognized to be highly successful. Similarly, when proposals put forward were on the face of it palatable to the "establishment," the managers responsible for these suggestions were accepted and approved by the "establishment," and remained so even after those proposals were later rejected or were tried out and proved to be unsuccessful.

(4) *Paradigm supporting and paradigm breaking ideas:* Ideas that seemed to be closely related to, supportive of, and applications of generally agreed paradigms, policies, mores and customs, were the ones more easily accepted; those that had elements which challenged this consensus were more difficult to get accepted. The paradigm-related ideas were those where the precipitating events that triggered them were more readily foreseen or when seen, acted upon early; the other solutions were for precipitating events that were not so readily seen as such. The ideas or solutions based on consensually agreed problems were more often put forward by the members of the "establishment" group; conversely, the paradigm-breakers tended to be thought up and advocated by those in a more peripheral locus via à vis the "establishment."

Acceptability of Adaptive and Innovative Ideas

Adaptive solutions are those which derive directly from the agreed values and strategies of the group, and are thus more readily understood and approved by the group, not only by colleagues who are themselves adaptors, but also by those who are by nature innovators, but who are not directly concerned with the problem which is being handled. Such solutions offer no threat to what might be termed as "received ideas" and produce no intellectual discomfort. As a result they reflect favorably on the people who put them forward, even if, as in some cases, the proposed solutions are seen to fail. The authors of these (adaptive) ideas, being themselves in most cases adaptors, are in a relationship of mutual admiration with the establishment; this has led those managers of the opposite turn of mind–the innovators–to assert that adaptors owe their success to and maintain their position simply by agreeing with their superiors. However, in a study carried out by Kirton (1977b) in which KAI scores of 93 middle managers were compared with a measure of superior-subordinate identification, no relationship was found to exist. It appears more likely that managers in the "establishment group" in the upper reaches of a hierarchy share the same basic values as those of their subordinates who are adaptors, and that there is, therefore a greater chance of agreement between them on broad issues and courses of action. When they find themselves disagreeing on points of detail, they are inclined to see this as useful rather than serious and continue to perceive themselves and their subordinates as being in general harmony.

When ideas fail, those original authors who are adaptors are less likely to be blamed than those who are innovators, since the former share with the establishment, and in some cases with a wider circle of influential people, the same set of basic assumptions, and even when these are subsequently shown to be erroneous, the tendency is to explain failure away as misfortune, or as attributable to unforeseen events, and to direct blame away from the authors themselves. To condemn them would be, in the eyes of the establishment, to condemn themselves.

The authors of innovative ideas, which depart from and may even challenge the beliefs, values and practices of the group, tend to be viewed with suspicion, and may be subjected to derision. This rejection or virtual hostility may persist even when those innovative ideas are shown to be successful. Non-conformists are not forgiven for being right.

Personality and Cognitive Style

As might well be expected, evidence is now accumulating that various aspects of personality are related to the characteristic differences in thinking displayed by innovators and adaptors. There is a significant correlation between hemispheric preference and KAI scores; the more methodical, planned approach of the left-brain dominated being related to adaption, and the more intuitive style of the right-brain dominated being related to innovation. In the field of social psychological behavior, innovators find it difficult to collaborate with others, while adaptors find it easier. The latter more rapidly establish common ground with other people and can share assumptions, guidelines and accepted practices to form a solid basis for collaboration. Innovators, who have the same need to form associations in this way, are less capable of doing so. They are less concerned with ironing out differences in standpoint, and less likely to remain in conformity with accepted patterns of procedure, even in those cases where they have themselves contributed to the development of those patterns.

These notions and observations make it plain that there must be a relationship between cognitive style and personality, or to be even bolder, that cognitive style is part of personality. This statement, at least the first part of this statement, is not new and is often implied in the current literature. It has not been sufficiently theoretically developed because of the current conflation of level and style among creativity, problem-solving and decision making. Some of the confounding elements need to be separated before they can usefully be combined. Before embarking on the exposition of whether "high creativity" is related to intelligence, risk taking, stimulation-seeking, etc., it must be made clear whether "high creativity" relates to level or style; in the test of such correlates, measures of the concepts involved must have sound, reliable psychometric foundation, and be relatively pure measures of such concepts.

To be able to undertake creative problem solving, a person needs to have appropriate amounts (i.e. not some minimum absolute amounts) of intelligence, knowledge, experience and scope. ("Appropriate" means in this context amounts relevant to the milieu in which the person operates and relevant to the difficulty of the problem requiring solution). Some of these concepts relate to level, more of them to style. Three large studies (Kirton, 1978a; Gryskiewicz, 1982; Flegg unpub.) show that KAI is not likely to be related to IQ (see Table One). But to what else is it related that is relevant to style? Numerous data are now available which fit the literature well.

Factor Traits of the KAI

Repeated factor analyses of the KAI (Goldsmith, 1985; Keller & Holland, 1978a; Kirton, 1976, Kirton, 1977a; Mulligan & Martin, 1980; Prato Previde, 1985) using large samples drawn from different populations in four countries—U.K., U.S.A., New Zealand and Italy—show that in addition to the adaptor-innovator concept being unidimensional, it is composed of three stable, reliable factor traits.

The first of these is labelled Sufficiency vs. Proliferation of Originality. It shares many elements of Rogers' (1959) concept of the "creative loner". Adaptors prefer to produce (as distinct from being capable of producing) fewer original ideas which are seen by them as sound, useful and relevant to the situation as they perceive it. By contrast, innovators proliferate ideas, also by preference—Rogers suggests that his creative loner compulsively toys with ideas. When extreme types view each other pejoratively (as they tend to do—see also Myers 1962, p. 76) the innovator claims that the adaptor originates with a finger on the stop button; the adaptor sees the innovator as an originator who cannot find such a button. A possible consequ-

Table One.

Correlations between KAI (style) and measures of creativity (level), IQ and English exam.

From Kirton (1978) Creativity	r	From Flegg (1983, unpub.) IQ	r	From Gryskiewicz (1982) IQ[e]	r
Word Fluency[a]	.07	AH2 General[c]	.12	N = 95 managers	-.01
Alternate Uses[b]	.08	CT82 Shapes[d]	-.01	N = 83 managers	-.14
Utilities[b]	.07	GT90B Verbal[d]	.12	N = 161 managers	-.04
IQ		GT70B Non-verbal[d]	-.01	N = 99 managers	-.11
Otis Higher (Form A)	.00	EA2A Arithmetic[d]	.09		
English Exam	-.03	VMD Diagrams[d]	.04		

N = 412	N = 437		N = 438
New Zealand Students (17-18 years)	U.K. apprentices (mean age 16½ years)		

KAI mean: 104, s.d. 11.5

KAI mean: 84.12. s.d. 10.25
(Compared to Flegg's pilot
published (Kirton & Pender,
1982) mean of 88.4, s.d. 10.6
for 50 apprentices)

References to Tests:
(a) Thurstone & Thurstone, 1947; (b) French et al, 1963; (c) Heim, Watts & Simmonds, 1975; (d) From National Institute of Industrial Psychology Battery: Nelson/NFER, 1964 - 1979; (e) Shipley, 1949; Dennis 1973

ence of these (admittedly extreme) differences is that the adaptor tends to produce too few original ideas to ensure that at least some offer truly radical, paradigm-cracking, solutions; the innovator produces so many that it is difficult to select a "good," appropriate, useful and immediately acceptable solution. Most will be discarded or even fail, a few will be spectacularly successful.

The second factor has a parallel with Weber's (1948, cited in 1970) analysis of the aims of bureaucratic structure which he posits are precision, reliability and efficiency. Innovation, being in some measure a discontinuity, can rarely be expected initially to be efficient; efficiency can usually only be achieved by development, which is an adaptive process. (Compare, for instance, the first paddle steamers with the then current, efficiently elegant productions of the Boston shipyards).

The third factor relates to group/rule conformity (formal or informal, as appropriate). This factor relates to Merton's (1957) analysis of bureaucratic structure which " . . . exerts a constant pressure on officials to be methodical, prudent, disciplined . . . (and to attain) . . . an unusual degree of conformity" (p. 198).[1] These qualities will yield high quality adaption but not innovation.

Personality Correlates

Numerous studies have been published or are in progress which explore the correlates of KAI. It has already been noted that two of the Myers-Briggs dimensions, viz: Sensing-Intuition $(r = .44)$ and Judgement-Perception $(r = .53)$ are well related; in combination more so $(r$

Table Two.

Creativity and Style of Thinking Correlates of Adaption-Innovation (Kirton Adaption-Innovation-Inventory).

Measure	Number	Coefficient Correlation	Level of Significance
Creative Personality (Torrance WKPAY)[a]	33	.59	‹.001
Cue Test (Stein)[b]	33	.35	‹.05
Similes (Schaeffer)[c]	33	.16	NS
Possible Jobs (Gershon & Guilford)[d]	33	.06	NS
Seeing Problems (Guilford)[e]	33	.17	NS
Creative Motivation (Torrance)[f]	33	.46	‹.01
Creative Self Perception (SAM, Khatena)[a]	33	.41	‹.01
Rorschach Movement[g]	33	.32	‹.06
Rorschach Originality[g]	33	.29	‹.10
TTCT Fluency[h]	33	.36	‹.04
TTCT Flexibility[h]	33	.34	‹.05
TTCT Originality[h]	33	.43	‹.01
TTCT Elaboration[h]	33	.26	NS
TTCT Creative Strengths Checklist[h]	33	.36	‹.05
Right Hemisphere Style of Thinking (A)[i]	33	.52	‹.001
Right Hemisphere Style of Thinking (C)[i]	33	.53	‹.001
Left Hemisphere Style of Thinking (A)[i]	33	-.40	‹.02
Left Hemisphere Style of Thinking (C)[i]	33	-.49	‹.01
Integrated Style of Thinking (A)[i]	33	-.03	NS
Integrated Style of Thinking (C)[i]	33	-.06	NS

References to tests:
(a) Khatena & Torrance (1976); (b) Stein (1975); (c) Schaeffer (1971); (d) Gershon & Guilford (1963); (e) Guilford (1969); (f) Torrance (1971); (g) Hertz (1946); (h) Torrance (1974); (i) Torrance, Reynolds, Ball & Riegel (1978)

Reprinted from *The Creative Child and Adult Quarterly*, Vol. V, No. 2, 1980

= .62). Gryskiewicz's (1982) work confirms these findings. Torrance's Left-Right brain hemispheric preference test also correlates highly (r = Right A . 52; Right C .53; Left A -.40; Left C -.44). These measures may, however, be regarded less as correlates than as other measures of style. So too may be Torrance's WKPAY (Torrance & Horng, 1980; Ettlie & O'Keefe, 1982; both r = .59; Farese, 1982, r = .41), Torrance's (1971) Creative Motivation (Torrance & Horng, 1980 r = .46), Khatena & Torrance's (1976) Creative Self-Perception (Torrance & Horng, 1980, r = .41, Ettlie & O'Keefe, 1982, r = .35) (see Table Two).

Conversely (see Table Four), Guilford type measures (originality, flexibility, etc.) relate poorly, since they seem to have been conceived as measures of level (Kirton, 1978a; Torrance & Horng, 1980; Torrance, 1982). To fit this pattern IQ and attainment, scores should also have an insignificant relationship with KAI (which they do—see Table One on pg. 290). Theoretically there seems no good reason why age and education should be significantly related to KAI and they too have been found negligibly so (Kirton, 1976; Keller & Holland, 1978a; Ettlie & O'Keefe, 1982).[2] Socio-economic status, and sex (Kirton, 1976) also have very slight relationships (none accounting for as much as 4% of the variance) although the latter is persistent over a number of studies, and countries.

The more obvious correlates have been more extensively researched. Most theorists suppose that a package of concepts, all themselves highly related and here dubbed collectively the "Adorno concepts" are inimical to "high creativity"—now identified as style not level. They are Rokeach's (1960) and Troldahl & Powell's (1965) Dogmatism (Kirton, 1976; Goldsmith, 1984) Budner's (1962) (Kirton, 1976; Keller & Holland, 1978a) and MacDonald's (1970) revision of Rydell & Rosen's (1966) Intolerance of Ambiguity, Wilson & Patterson's (1968) Conservatism (Kirton, 1976), and Gough's (1956) Inflexibility (Kirton, 1976; Gryskiewicz, 1982). The correlations vary somewhat as might be expected but the various estimates are closely clustered in the area of (r = .3s to .5). The same magnitude of relationship has been found with Extraversion (both EPI, Eysenck & Eysenck, 1964 and Campbell, 1974), supporting Rogers' (1959) creative loner description (Kirton, 1976; Gryskiewicz, 1982). Some of Cattell's (16PF) factors are also correlates, viz: E (humble/assertive) .42; G (Expedient/Conscientious) -.44; Q (Conservative/Experimenting) .60 and Q3 (Undisciplined/Controlled) -.35. Of the higher order factors IV (Subduedness/Independence) .55 and, less well, III (Tender Emotionality/Alert Poise) .26; X (Low/High Creativity—already mentioned) .28[3] (Kirton & DeCiantis, 1986), N = 83). What is of significance is not just the way the correlations cluster in the expected magnitude range but the fact that they are all in the expected direction—expected not only by the adaption-innovation theory but by the literature also.

Other correlations, both in terms of magnitude and direction, also fit the pattern that is steadily emerging. Goldsmith (1985) has now replicated Keller & Holland's (1978a) finding of a modest relationship between KAI and Rosenberg's (1965) Self Esteem scale (r = .32; r = .27) but with a more substantial connection with the Sufficiency of Originality Factor Trait (r = .37; r = .56). Further relationships found by Gryskiewicz (1982) are also of interest: Tellegan's (1982) Control-Impulse Scale (TCI) r = .43 to .56 (note that Gryskiewicz uses four management samples of between N = 83 to N = 161); Wesley's (1953) Rigidity or need for structure, r = -.42 to -.56; Gough's (1956) Capacity for Status, r = .19; .36 and .39; Gough's (1956) Social Presence or Spontaneity, self confidence scale, r = .26; .37; .38[4]; Goldsmith (1984) has two more results using the Jackson Personality Inventory (1976): Risk taking, r = .48 and Sensation seeking, r = .47. Keller & Holland (1978a) also report a significant relationship with Need for Clarity (Ivancevich & Donnelly, 1974) r = .36. Both Kirton (1976) and Gryskiewicz (1982) report significant relationships with extraversion-introversion: Kirton's two samples (using Eysenck & Eysenck's 1964 EPI) r = .46; r = .45; Gryskiewicz's four samples (using Strong Campbell [Campbell, 1974]) r's = .34; .34; .25; .30 supporting Rogers' contention that innovators tend to be extravertive.

It is apparent that many of these concepts that relate to adaption-innovation can be deemed a "package," borrowing a term from gene theory, being themselves interrelated. For instance, Extraversion and sensation-seeking are generally thought and often found to be related, along with (Feij, 1979) such other traits as, experience seeking (see also Loy, 1969) disinhibition and boredom susceptibility. Intuitively most people suspect that these relationships exist and most work done tends to confirm them. Unfortunately not all the tests have good psychometric attributes and occasionally this leads to some disarray in the published findings. Walk's intolerance of ambiguity scale was considered for inclusion in Kirton's (1976) battery but was dropped because it was revealed (Ehrlich, 1965) to have insignificant (0.06) internal reliability. Ray's (1970) revision of Rokeach's (1960) Dogmatism Scale was included but had to be discarded (Kirton, 1977c). The other scales used in the Adorno battery (see Kirton

Table Three.

Intercorrelations between "Adorno" type tests and KAI.

Dogmatism (Rokeach)	X	.49	.43	.49	.38	—
Intolerance of Ambiguity (Budner)	.56	X	.27	.27	-.06	—
Intolerance of Ambiguity (MacDonald)	.48	.56	X	.53	.38	-.44
Inflexibility (Gough)	.52	.51	.60	X	.53	-.46
Conservatism (Wilson & Patterson)	.44	.36	.59	.59	X	-.34
KAI	-.25	-.30	-.45	-.46	-.37	X

Note:
N = 286
Correlations in upper triangular matrix for tests in original form; in lower triangular matrix for tests reduced by item analyses.
Only correlations ≥ .20 are entered.

Table Four.

Factor Analyses Torrance Matrix.

Scales		Factors	
		One	Two
Left Hemisphere Style of Thinking (C)	Torrance, Reynolds, Ball & Riegel, 1978	.84	—
Right Hemisphere Style of Thinking (C)	Torrance, Reynolds, Ball & Riegel, 1978	.76	—
Creative Personality (WKPAY)	Khatena & Torrance, 1976	.72	—
KAI	Kirton, 1976	.66	—
Creative Self Perception (SAM)	Khatena & Torrance, 1976	.57	—
Creative Motivation	Torrance, 1971	.56	.33
Cue Test	Stein, 1975	.42	—
Originality (Rorschach)	Hertz, 1946	.35	—
TTCT Fluency	Torrance, 1974	—	.87
TTCT Originality	Torrance, 1974	.35	.84
TTCT Flexibility	Torrance, 1974	.33	.69
TTCT Elaboration	Torrance, 1974	.35	.67
Possible Jobs	Gershon & Guilford, 1963	—	.41
Similies	Shaefer, 1971	—	.36
Movement (Rorschach)	Hertz, 1946	—	.31
	(Cumulative %)	(50.5)	(67.7)

Note:
Only loadings ≥ .30 entered.
Analysis on data provided by kind permission of Professor E. Torrance (see: Torrance & Horng, 1980).
Tests not loading .30 on either factor: Integrated Hem. S. T. (heaviest loading on Factor 3); Seeing Problems – Guilford 1969 (Factor 4); TTCT Creative Strengths Checklist (Factor 5).

1977a) when first set into a correlation matrix produced encouraging but patchy results. Following an item analysis, many items were dropped and the revised matrix (see Table Three) showed more consistent results along intuitive expectations. Subsequent repeated factor analyses (Kirton, 1977a p. 49) showed the five tests as five items in a super scale, their internal reliability (KR 20) being .86[5].

Wallach & Kogan (1965) likewise complain that creativity scales also produce patchy results which they attribute wholly to the poor psychometric properties of at least some tests. However, they overlooked the distinction between level and style. Factor analysis should reveal (see Table Four) two factors containing the bulk of the scales with the less related scales scattering largely in isolation over lesser factors. The concepts of cognitive complexity (preference vs. capacity) and also modes of imagery and their varied, not always easily recognizable effects on problem solving (Gryskiewicz, 1980; Ekvall, 1981; Casbolt, 1984) also need sorting out in much the same way.

What is emerging then is a fuller picture of the personality characteristics of the adaptor-innovator styles of cognitive process. The innovator tends to be more extravert, less dogmatic, more tolerant of ambiguity, more radical, more flexible, more creatively motivated, more creatively self-perceptive, more assertive, expedient, self-assured, undisciplined, independent and sensation-seeking than the adaptor; with more self-esteem, liable to risk-taking, needing (and linking) less structure, and is more spontaneous. The adaptor is more controlled, less stimulating, more steady, reliable, prudent and probably more often seen as right and dependable, better able to fit into teams, get on with authority, be sensitive to policy and mores; be more realistic, efficient and orderly. Neither type (extreme) is likely to be any more or less neurotic, more or less likely to reach high position (except in conditions unfavorable to type), be more or less intelligent, resourceful, original, creative and generally regarded in worldly terms as successful.

Two sorts of anomalies need to be sorted out, one arising from a confusion of terms and the other from results emanating from complex settings where orthogonal variables are undifferentiated in practice. For instance, Keller & Holland (1978b) report that innovators tend to reach higher organizational levels (r = .22) than adaptors. The setting of this study is, however, an R&D establishment where, *in this case,* they have advantages over at least some of the adaptors who are there for *administrative skills;* skills that may be less rewarded, if just as needed, than elsewhere. Similar confusions can be detected for similar reasons in Loy's (1969) work already quoted. This work's criterion is the early-late *adoption* of ideas without regard to the style of the notion or the style of the adopter but taking into account, however, concepts such as professional status, occupational status and peer status as well as education and intelligence. As has already been stated here the KAI does not correlate with any of these variables, though they must be taken into account when examining success in its broadest meaning.

Ettlie & O'Keefe (1982) have two results that give rise to some of those residual problems of research that are either intriguing or infuriating according to the researcher's taste and circumstance. They find a correlation between KAI and Hardin's (1967) Readiness to Change Scale of .38 and Hage & Dewar's (1973) Change Scale of .30. If one takes the current literature position that "innovators" welcome change—any change, any time—and the rest of us have greater or lesser degrees of "resistance to change," then these correlations, although significant, seem too low, accounting as they do for merely around 10% of the variance. The concept of "resistance to change" begs a number of important issues. As measured by Trumbo (1961) for instance, it ignores the obvious fact that homo sapiens is *inter alia* a problem solving animal and so constantly liable to be change-inducing. In addition, cognitive style notwithstanding, a human being is quite likely to embrace with enthusiasm any changes affecting him/her favorably and resist any that do not, or that are difficult to estimate in terms of outcome (Kirton & Mulligan, 1973). Within these contexts the type of change and its relationship to style of changes are also to be taken into account as this paper argues. Given these factors Ettlie & O'Keefe's correlations may seem too large.

One approach not to be ignored is that currently the terms of our theories are too imprecise and our measures too inaccurate to bear the weight of useful exploration. Another line of speculation is that although adaptors may have a marked preference for adaptive changes and innovators an equally marked preference for innovative type changes, there are differences elsewhere to account for middling, if significant, results: innovators may be slightly more tolerant of adaptive changes than adaptors are of innovative changes. It may also be that researchers tend to be innovative and harp on innovative change whilst overlooking the importance of adaptive change, so weighting and biasing their theories, results and conclusions.

Clearly there is much left to be known in this field; researchers are handicapped by having a brain no better, no more subtle or penetrative than the brains of their subjects: nor can they be more detached from their own strengths, weaknesses and predilections.

Perhaps, however, the layman is more perceptive than he is usually given credit for. Keller & Holland (1979) report that peer and superior ratings of individual colleagues' innovativeness correlate .40 with KAI scores. Kirton & McCarthy (1985) had a different approach. They obtained KAI scores from course members, gave a short lecture describing the theory and some notion of the way KAI scores distributed in general. Where the course members had little experience of working with each other, group estimates of individuals correlated .37 with actual scores. Where their experience was greater the correlation rose to .84. Individual estimates of their own scores correlated .79 with actual KAI scores. These may be useful findings in the practical task of getting people to tolerate each other in mixed teams. At least they can grasp the main issues and make good working estimates of each other—a foundation to an understanding that needs to underlie tolerance.

Group Differences in Adaption-Innovation

Earlier work on the adaption-innovation theory was directed towards the description and classification of the two cognitive styles. More recent studies have been concerned with variations in A-I score between one group and another, and with confirming that these variations correspond to what could be deduced from the A-I theory. A number of studies have investigated the extent to which some clearly identifiable groups differ in their mean scores from the population mean, and the extent to which they differ from each other. The hypothesis being tested in each case was that the observed differences in mean score would be in the direction which would be predicted by the A-I theory. The groups studied were defined by various criteria, which included cultural background, occupation and sex. Before examining the results of these enquiries, which deal only with the mean scores of the groups being studied, it is important to point out that there was commonly a wide variation between the scores of individuals within even relatively homogeneous groups, often of the order of a minimum of 70 to a maximum of 120.[6] This finding has important implications for the understanding of change, against the background of group differences at different levels in an organization, or between departments, or between specific occupational roles.

It has been shown that when groups of different nationalities share a broadly similar culture their A-I mean scores show very little variation. Samples from Britain (Kirton, 1976; 1977a; 1980), the U.S.A. (Keller & Holland, 1978a; Goldsmith, 1985), Canada (Kirton, 1980), New Zealand (Kirton, 1977a), Italy (Prato Previde, 1985) and Mexico (Keller, 1983) and Belgium (Peeters, unpub.) have produced remarkably similar mean scores. A sample of occidental managers from Singapore and Malaysia (Thomson, 1980) produced a mean of 95.0 which is very close to that of their Western counterparts; a sample of U.K. managers showed a mean of 97, while the male subset of the general population sample for the U.K. had a mean of

98.[7] However, samples of Indian and Iranian managers (Hossaini, 1981; Dewan, 1982; Khaneja, 1982) produced more adaptive means (ca. 91) than similar samples from other countries mentioned above. A study still in progress (Pottas, unpub.) will show that black South African business students also show more adaptive means. These differences may not simply reflect a dichotomy between Western, Chinese western groups, and others.

Crossing Conventional Boundaries

A further hypothesis put forward by Kirton (1978b) is that where certain boundaries exist in a culture-pattern, in the form of expectations which impose a limit on the behavior of the individuals in that culture, those people who show by their actions that they are prepared to cross those boundaries are more likely to be shown to be innovative; and the more boundaries involved, and the more rigidly they are held in the society concerned, the higher the innovative score of those who cross. In one of the studies referred to above (Thomson, 1980) managers in Western-owned companies in Singapore were higher in innovativeness than those working in locally owned companies, and the latter scored higher than comparable people working in the middle ranks of the Civil Service, who were the most adaptive of the three groups. In an extremely interesting series of investigations inspired by Professor P. Mathur on Indian and Iranian managers by her post graduates, Hossaini (1981), Dewan (1982), and Khaneja (1982), it was shown that entrepreneurs had more innovative scores than others (means of 97.9 compared with 90.5) and that both groups scored much higher than Government Officers, whose mean KAI score was as low as 77.2. Indian women entrepreneurial managers were found to be even more innovative than their male counterparts; they had had to cross two boundaries: first by breaking with tradition in adopting a role conventionally reserved for the male, and second by moving even further into the world of risk-taking in which only the more adventurous males would be expected to operate.

From among the general population samples used in the original main KAI study 88 managers were identified. The mean score of this group was 97.1 s.d. 16.9 (Kirton, 1977a). This is almost identical to the mean of the 207 Italian managers (Prato Previde, 1985) 99 s.d. 17. Different occupation groups yield means on either side of this score if they are both select and homogeneous but remain close to this score if they are non-select and heterogeneous. For instance, three samples of apprentices and their teachers yielded: 82.4 s.d. 7.1 N = 22 (Mathews, unpub.); 88.4 s.d. 10.6 = 50 (Flegg, unpub.); and 84.12 s.d. 10.25 N = 437 (Flegg, unpub.). This compares with R&D personnel with a mean of 100.9 s.d. 14.3 N = 256 (Keller & Holland, 1978a) and 104.2 s.d. 13.2 N = 90 (Davies, unpub.). All the results are reported in Kirton & Pender, 1982. A more heterogeneous group (Ettlie & O'Keefe, 1982) of 123 U.S. undergraduate business students yielded a socre of 98.1 s.d. 14.21. A further British sample of 79 managers (Kirton, 1980) yielded a mean of 96.9 s.d. 15.27. A tiny group of engineers (otherwise unspecified as to specialism) in a British pharmaceutical company yielded a mean of 97.3 covering a wide range of individual scores (ibid). Three samples of U.S. teachers totalling 834 (Dershimer, 1980; Jorde, 1984; Pulvino, 1979) also gave a mean in the same area of magnitude: 95.9. In all these results the pattern to be looked for is that general samples should have mean scores approximate to that of the general population where the group has an occupation or tasks in which adaptors and innovators can do equally well. Where its tasks are more structured (e.g. apprentices, most production or accounting) it should veer towards a more adaptive mean; where less structured (e.g. most marketing, personnel or finance) it will veer towards the other pole. Other factors will also operate (cumulatively or subtractively), e.g. whether the company as a whole is orientated in a particular direction (e.g. Miles & Snow's defender vs. prospector companies—unpublished correspondence with Snow); whether or not a group has selected itself for general management courses or been sent.

Further evidence of the relationship between professional categories and adaption-innovation comes from a dissertation by Holland (1982) which suggests that bank employees are inclined to be adaptors; Hayward & Everett (1983) showed the same to be true of Local Government employees. By contrast, employees of companies where research and development is a major orientation tend to be innovative (Keller & Holland, 1978b). The first two of these studies illustrate also the hypothesis that with the passage of time the mean KAI score of the members of a working organization will change in such a way as to reflect the climate of the organization. Both Holland and Hayward & Everett showed that when groups of new recruits had mean scores which differed from the mean of the established group they were joining, a lapse of time (3 years and 5 years respectively) produced a considerable narrowing of the gap between the means (as a result of turnover, not individual change.)

Further light on the relationship between individuals and organizations in terms of KAI scores was provided by the hypothesis (Kirton, 1977a; 1980) that managers who work in a particularly stable environment will tend to be adaptive, while the mean scores of those whose environment could be described as turbulent tend towards innovation. This hypothesis was supported by the work of Thomson already referred to, which showed that a sample of middle-ranking Civil Servants in Singapore was markedly oriented towards adaption, with a mean of 89.0, whereas a sample of managers in multinational companies in the same country was just as markedly inclined to innovation, with a mean of 107.0.

Differences Within Organizations

It is unlikely, as well as undesirable, that any organization is so monolithic in its structure, and so undifferentiated in the demands it makes on its personnel, that it produces a total uniformity of cognitive style.

This was illustrated by a study (Kirton, 1980) which showed that adaptors were more at home in those departments of a company which needed to concentrate on problems emanating from within their own department (e.g. production). Innovators, on the other hand, tended to be found in greater numbers in departments whose problems arose from outside the department (e.g. sales, progress chasing). A study by Keller & Holland (1978b) in American research and development departments found that adaptors and innovators had different roles in the sphere of internal communications: adaptors being more valued for their knowledge of company procedures and innovators being more valued when the information to be communicated was of an advanced technological nature.

Kirton (1980) made a study of members of management training courses, differentiating between those who had selected themselves to go on the course concerned, and those who had been sent in pursuance of the company's training policy. Members of three different courses were tested: one self-selected group of British managers, one company-selected group of British managers, and one self-selected group of Canadian managers. The results showed that the company-selected managers were higher on adaption than the self-selected managers: managers who had nominated themselves to go on the course were, as the KAI theory would predict, more inclined to be innovators. The Canadian (innovatively inclined) group could be divided, according to their job titles into those who worked in adaptor-oriented departments (e.g. line management) and those from the more innovator-oriented departments (e.g. personnel). The latter group were found to be significantly more innovative than the former, with a mean of 116.4 compared with a mean of 100.1.[8] These findings led to a much larger study (Kirton & Pender, 1982) in which the scores of 2,375 subjects collected in various investigations were analyzed with reference to the different occupational types represented and the varying degrees of self-selection to courses. Occupations involving a narrow range of acceptable procedures, rigid training and a closely structured working environment included engineering instructors and engineering apprentices; those with more flexible and widely-ranging procedures were represented by research and development personnel. The differences were large, statistically significant, and in the expected direction.

Even within the narrow boundaries of a single job there can be found differences in cognitive style between sub-groups of employees whose functions are specialized. For example, a study now in progress suggests that such a difference exists among quality control workers in a Local Government body. One sub-group was engaged in the vital task of monitoring (an essentially in-unit activity), while another had the task of solving anomalies which were thrown up in the system from time to time (involving in the process several units in the organization). The first of these quality control sub-groups showed a clear inclination towards adaption; the second were grouped towards the innovative end of the scale. Gul (1986) supports the findings. Gul's sample of 63 final year undergraduates in accountancy at Wollongong, Australia (mean age 21; range 20-45) showed a more adaptive mean than that expected from a general population; 24 scoring over 96 (innovative) and 39 below (adaptive). Although a small total sample, the innovators differed significantly from the adaptors in that they preferred financial management topics rather than accounting and auditing (and vice versa—see also Kirton, 1980); preferred as career choices industry and commerce rather than Chartered Accountancy and Government; and were more interested in the broader general subjects in their course. There was no difference in their interest in computers, unlike the U.S. teacher sample reported by Dershimer (1980) where innovators were more likely to be interested.

Findings of the kind reported in this section show that different roles in a working organization, and even differences of function within one identifiable job, can be more appropriately carried out by innovators or adaptors. Use of evidence along these lines could lead to the better matching of man to job; more controlled balance within teams; and in the long term to better integration of the specific assets of innovators and adaptors within a company.

Who are the Agents for Change?

Every organization has its own particular climate or microculture, and at any given time most of the key individuals reflect this general outlook. The climate is in turn communicated to others in the organization, and in time the movement of individuals out of and into the organization will strengthen the general organizational ethos. However, the range of differences within groups, almost irrespective of a group's mean, seems to remain unaffected, i.e. not narrowed; standard distribution also is affected very little; these observations are of critical importance in the understanding of how it is that potential agents for change exist within the group.

It has already been noted that while the mean adaptor-innovator score may vary considerably from one group to another, there remain wide variations between individuals within a group. This must mean that many individuals will find themselves part of a group whose mean score differs markedly from their own. This situation could occur because they are temporary members of the group, in transit; for example, for the duration of a training scheme. However, it may be that they are trapped and unhappy, and will strive to move out of the group (Holland, 1982; Hayward & Everett, 1983) or that they have developed for themselves a specific role within the group which they find satisfying and which the group finds acceptable. Changes in the group's precise function, or climate of opinion, or a change of boss, may mean that an individual will find himself moving from one of these categories to another.

The situation in which the individual has developed a satisfying role in the group deserves closer examination, since it has important implications and practical applications in the field of A-I theory. (This analysis will need to be in speculative terms until the completion of research which is being carried out at the present time).

All people are capable of being agents for change, and could effect changes as individuals unrelated to any other person. Within groups such agents may operate in accordance with that group's prevailing cognitive style mode or in contrast to it. These classifications can be dubbed AC1, AC2, AC3; such that every person (in a group) will be both an AC1 and either an AC2 or AC3 depending on group orientation. Shifts of individuals or groups will not affect AC1 classification but will shift the individual from AC2 to AC3 or vice versa (see Figure Four).

The individual in the AC3 mode who can successfully accept and be accepted by a working environment whose cognitive style is markedly different from his own must have particular characteristics which enable him to survive, and it is those characteristics which make him a potential agent for change within the group; an agent for change in the contrasting orientation of that group.

In the first place he must have the professional or technical knowledge and skills which will enable him to be recognized by others as a valuable group member at times when major changes are not envisaged. He must also be able to gain and maintain the respect of his colleagues and his superiors, and thus to have the necessary status for his ideas to be recognized and taken seriously. Thirdly, he will need the capacity and the techniques for influencing others, whether by dominance of personality, or persuasiveness or other aspects of leadership to be able to see that his proposals are carried through. In this his different cognitive style will give him a powerful advantage over his colleagues, because he will be able to anticipate events which others may well not foresee, since their particular cognitive style may mean that they are not directing their thoughts in that direction. Like any member of a minority (temporary or permanent) he may have to have more skills etc. than an equivalent in the majority group (AC2). The agent for change must therefore be competent, respected and influential. His success in achieving these assets may be made more easy for him by

Figure Four.
Location of Agents for Change.

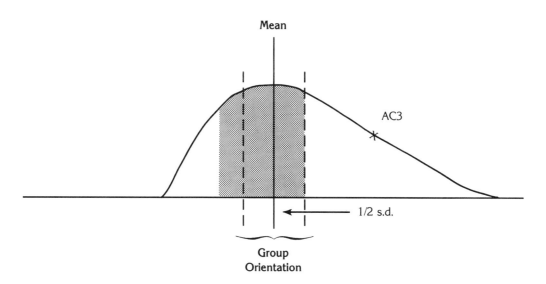

Mean of group displaced from that of general population in direction of either adaption or innovation. Range largely unaffected. X marks likely position of *successful* (AC3) agent for change involving contrasting orientation. Shaded area contains those who are all likely to be successful agents for change (AC2) within prevailing mores. Outside these limits lie those who are more likely to be unsuccessful agents for change (without special help and tolerance from those within the limits). Note: everyone is a *potential* agent for change (ACI).

being selected for, or selecting for himself, a working role within the unit which is more compatible with his own cognitive style than some other tasks. In the normal way he will be seen as supportive to the main function of the group. At a point of crisis, or, otherwise expressed, upon the occurrence of some "precipitating event," this individual becomes at once a potential leader towards change, particularly if he has foreseen and prepared for the critical event. In taking advantage of the position his personal qualities will come into play, and for full capitalization of the new possibilities, management will need to be aware of the situation, and to understand the processes of change which have occurred and could continue to develop. In this both individual and group counselling, based on adaption-innovation theory, can play a positive part (Lindsay, 1985).

It must be emphasized that the agent for change may be either an innovator or an adaptor. In a predominantly innovator group the agent of change will be an adaptor, and vice versa. This discovery overthrows traditional assumptions that heralding and initiating change is the prerogative of the type of person to whom the term innovator is now applied. A precipitating event may require either an innovative or an adaptive solution; whether it is generally expected or not depends on the original orientation of the group and the nature of its task. An example in which an adaptor is an agent for change in a team of innovators is provided by the case in which the precipitating event takes the form of a bank's refusal to extend credit as support to further new enterprise in a company that has cash flow problems. At this point the adaptor, who has been anticipating the event for months, is at hand with facts, figures and a contingency plan neatly worked out, and becomes a potential agent for change. This can be transformed into action if the change-agent has the personal qualities of competence, status and ability to influence others.

The foregoing discussion has dealt with groups whose mean A-I scores diverge to some extent from the population mean. It seems likely that the greater the extent of this divergence, the more dramatic the precipitating event would have to be to move the group's orientation back towards the center. The effects on the group and the agent for change may be drastic. However, a team in which there is temporary disequilibrium may be precisely what is required to meet the demands of sudden change and movement forwards from that crisis. Recognition of the factors involved and appreciation of the value of flexibility in such a situation is a key task of management to which this theory may make a contribution. In a wider context, it is hoped that the adaption-innovation theory will offer an insight into the interactions between the individual, the organization and the processes of change. By using the theory as an additional resource when forward planning, it may be possible to foresee the effect of changes brought about by extraneous factors, and to control the actual process of change and its ramifications within the organization. To the extent that imbalance and confusion can be minimized, the beneficial and progressive aspects of change can be enhanced.

Footnotes

1. Russell assumes that " . . . there is a strong similarity between [Kirton's adaptors and innovators] and Merton's acceptance-ritualistic and innovation-retreatism individual response forms, respectively" (Russell, 1980).
2. On education Keller & Holland do not agree (r = .34), but their sample is made up of a mixture of R&D practitioners and administrators all in R&D establishments. The administrators are more adaptive and probably less well educated.
3. Jackson's (1976) measure of creativity correlates .28 (Goldsmith, 1984).
4. Three samples only.
5. Incorrectly listed as .71 in the unrevised manual.
6. The widest ranges obtained from large general population samples are 45 to 146.

7. Males predominate in all the manager samples quoted here.
8. Since the members of the group were self-selected, it is to be expected that the mean for the whole group would be higher than for the general population, i.e. more innovative.

References

Bakke, E. W. (1965). *Concept of the social organization.* In M. Haire (Ed.), *Modern organization theory,* New York: Wiley.

Budner, S. (1962). Intolerance of ambiguity as a personality variable. *Journal of Personality, 30,* 29-50.

Campbell, D. P. (1974). *Introversion extraversion scale.* Strong Campbell interest inventory, CA: Stanford University.

Carne, J. C. & Kirton, M. J. (1982). Styles of creativity: Test score correlations between the Kirton adaption-innovation inventory and the Myers-Briggs type indicator. *Psychological Reports, 50,* 31-36.

Casbolt, D. M. (1984). *The effects of idea generation technique, problem type and creative thinking style on individual problem solving performance.* Unpublished doctoral dissertation, University of Ohio, Athens.

Cattell, R. B., Eber, H. W. & Tatsouka, M. M. (1970). *The Sixteen Personality Factor Questionnaire* (16PF). Institute for Personality and Ability Testing, Inc. (IPAT), Champaign, IL.

Dennis, D. M. 1973, Predicting full scale WAIS IQ's with the Shipley. *Journal of Clinical Psychology, 29,* 366-368.

Dershimer, E. L. (1980). *Study to identify the characteristics of teachers willing to implement computer based instruction using microcomputers in the classroom.* Unpublished doctoral dissertation, Memphis State University, Memphis, Tennessee.

Dewan, S. (1982). *Personality characteristics of entrepreneurs.* Unpublished doctoral dissertation, Institute of Technology, Delhi.

Driver, M. J. & Mock, T. J. (1975, July). Human information processing, decision style theory and accounting information systems. *The Accounting Review,* 490-509.

Drucker, P. F. (1969). Management's new role. *Harvard Business Review, 47,* 49-54.

Ehrlich, D. (1965). Intolerance of ambiguity: Walk's A scale. *Psychological Reports, 17,* 591-594.

Ekvall, G. (1981). *Creative problem solving methods in product development: A comparative study.* Report No. 1 to The Swedish Council for Management and Organizational Behavior.

Ettlie, J. E. & O'Keefe, R. D. (1982). Innovative attitudes, values and intensions in organizations. *Journal of Management Studies, 19,* 193-182.

Eysenck, H. J. & Eysenck, S. B. G. (1964). *Manual of the Eysenck personality inventory.* London: University of London Press.

Farese, L. A. (1982). *Matched learning styles of adaptors and innovators to the creativity training techniques of the psychoanalytic approach.* Masters Thesis, Montclair State College, New Jersey.

Feij, J. A. (1979). *Sensation-seeking: Measurement and psychophysiological correlates.* Presented paper at International Conference on Temperament, Grogegorzewice, Poland.

French, J. W., Ekstrom, R. B. & Price, L. A. 1963, *Manual for kit of reference tests for cognitive factors.* Princeton, NJ: Educational Testing Service.

Gershon, A. & Guilford, J. P. (1963). *Possible jobs: Scoring guide.* Orange, CA: Sheridan Psychological Services.

Goldsmith, R. E. (1984). Personality characteristics: Association with adaption-innovation. *Journal of Psychology, 117,* 159-165.

Goldsmith, R. E. (1985). A factorial composition of the KAI inventory. *Educational & Psychological Measurement, 45,* 245-250.

Goldsmith, R. E. (1986). Personality and adaptive-innovative problem solving. *Journal of Social Behavior and Personality,* 95-106.

Goldsmith, R. E. & Matherly, T. A. (1986). The Kirton adaption-innovation inventory, faking and social desirability: A replication and extension. *Psychological Reports, 58,* 269-270.

Gough, H. G. (1956). *California psychological inventory.* Palo Alto, CA: Consulting Psychologists' Press.

Gul, F. A. (1986). Adaptors and innovators: An empirical study of academic and career preferences of accounting undergraduates. *Journal of Accounting Education,* (In press).

Gryskiewicz, S. S. (1980). *A study of creative problem solving techniques in group settings.* Unpublished doctoral dissertation, Birkbeck College, University of London.

Gryskiewicz, S. S. (1982). *The Kirton adaption-innovation inventory in creative leadership development.* Invited paper for the Occupational Psychology Conference of the British Psychological Society, Sussex University.

Gryskiewicz, S. S., Hills, D. W., Holt, K. & Hills, K. (1986). *Understanding managerial creativity: The Kirton adaption-innovation inventory and other assessment measures.* Technical Report. Greensboro, NC: Center for Creative Leadership.

Guilford, J. P. (1969). *Seeing problems: Manual for administration and interpretation.* Orange, CA: Sheridan Psychological Services.

Hage, J. & Dewar, R. (1973). Elite values versus organizational structure in predicting innovation. *Administrative Science Quarterly, 18,* 279-290.

Hardin, E. (1967). Job satisfaction and desire for change. *Journal of Applied Psychology, 51,* 20-27.

Hayward, G. & Everett, C. (1983). Adaptors and innovators: Data from the Kirton adaption-innovation inventory in a local authority setting. *Journal Occupation Psychology, 56,* 339-342.

Hertz, M. R. (1946). *Frequency tables to be used in scoring responses to the Rorschach ink blot test.* (3rd ed.) Cleveland, OH: Western Reserve University.

Holland, P. A. (1982). *Creative thinking: An asset or liability in employment.* Unpublished masters thesis, University of Manchester, Manchester, England.

Hossaini, H. R. (1981). *Leadership effectiveness and cognitive style among Iranian and Indian middle managers.* Unpublished doctoral dissertation, Institute of Technology, Delhi.

Hudson, L. (1966). *Contrary imaginations: A psychological study of the English schoolboy.* London: Methuen.

Ivancevich, J. M. & Donnelly, J. H. (1974). A study of role clarity and need for clarity for three occupational groups. *Academy of Management Journal, 17,*28-36.

Jackson, D. N. (1976). *Jackson personality inventory manual.* Goshen, NY: Research Psychologists' Press.

Jorde, P. (1984). *The relationship between selected personal characteristics of administrators and willingness to adopt computer technology.* Unpublished doctoral dissertation, Stanford University, Stanford.

Keller, R. T. (1983). *A cross-national validation study for research and development professional employees.* Invited paper to Academy of Management Annual Meeting, Dallas, TX.

Keller, R. T. & Holland, W. E. (1978a). A cross-validation study of the Kirton adaption-innovation inventory in three research and development organizations. *Applied Psychological Measurement, 2,* 563-570.

Keller, R. T. & Holland, W. E. (1978b). Individual characteristics of innovativeness and communication in research and development organizations. *Journal of Applied Psychology, 63,* 759-762.

Keller, R. T. & Holland, W. E. (1979). Towards a selection battery for research and development professional employees. *IEEE Transactions on Engineering Management,* Vol. EM-26, 4.

Khaneja, D. (1982). *Relationship of the adaption-innovation continuum top achievement orientation in entrepreneurs and non-entrepreneurs.* Unpublished doctoral dissertation, Institute of Technology, Delhi.

Khatena, J. & Torrance, E. P. (1976). *Manual for Khatena-Torrance creative perception inventory.* Chicago: Steolting Co.

Kirton, M. J. (1961). *Management initiative.* London: Acton Society Trust.

Kirton, M. J. (1976). Adaptors and innovators: A description and measure. *Journal of Applied Psychology, 61,* 622-629.

Kirton, M. J. (1977a). *Manual of the Kirton adaption-innovation inventory.* London: National Foundation for Educational Research.

Kirton, M. J. (1977b). Adaptors and innovators and superior-subordinate identification. *Psychological Reports, 41,* 289-290.

Kirton, M. J. (1977c). Ray's balanced dogmatism scale re-examined. *British Journal of Social & Clinical Psychology, 16,* 97-98.

Kirton, M. J. (1978a). Have adaptors and innovators equal levels of creativity?, *Psychological Reports, 42,* 695-698.

Kirton, M. J. (1978b). Adaptors and innovators in culture clash. *Current Anthropology, 19,* 611-612.

Kirton, M. J. (1980). Adaptors and innovators in organizations. *Human Relations, 3,* 213-224.

Kirton, M. J. & DeCiantis, S. M. (1986). Cognitive style and personality: The Kirton adaption-innovation and Cattell's sixteen personality factor inventories. *Personality and Individual Differences, 7*, (in press).

Kirton, M. J., & McCarthy, Rosalyn M. (1985). Personal and group estimates of the Kirton inventory scores. *Psychological Reports, 57*, 1067-1070.

Kirton, M. J. & Mulligan, G. (1973). Correlates of managers' attitudes towards change. *Journal of Applied Psychology, 58*, 101-107.

Kirton, M. J. & Pender, S. R. (1982). The adaption-innovation continuum: Occupational type and course selection. *Psychological Reports, 51*, 883-886.

Kolb, D. A. & Fry, R. (1975). Towards an applied theory of experimental learning. *In C. L. Cooper (Ed.), Theories of Group Processes,* (pp. 33-57). New York: Wiley.

Lindsay, P. R. (1985). Counseling to resolve a clash of cognitive styles. *Technovation, 3*, 57-67.

Loy, J. W. Jr. (1969). Social psychological characteristics of innovators. *Americal Sociological Review, 34*, 73-82.

Mehrabian, A. & Russell, J. A. (1974). *An approach to environmental psychology.* Cambridge, MA: The Massachusetts Institute of Technology (M.I.T.) Press.

MacDonald, A. P. Jr. (1970). Revised scale for ambiguity tolerance. *Psychological Reports, 26*, 791-798.

McKenny, J. L. & Keen, P. G. W. (1974, May/June). How managers' minds work. *Harvard Business Review,* 79-90.

Merton, R. K. (Ed.) (1957). Bureaucratic structure and personality. *Social Theory and Social Structure.* New York: Free Press of Glencoe.

Miles, R. E. & Snow, C. C. (1978). *Organizational strategy, structure & process,* New York: McGraw Hill.

Mitroff, I. I. (1974). The subjective side of science: An inquiry into the psychology of the Apollo moon scientists. *Elsevier.*

Mitroff, I. I. & Kilmann, R. H. (1981). A four-fold way of knowing: The varieties of social science experience. *Theory and Society, 2*, 227-248.

Morse, E. V. & Gordon, G. (1974). Cognitive skills: A determinant of scientists' local-cosmopolitan orientation. *Academy of Management Journal,* 709-723.

Mulkay, M. S. (1972). *The Social Process of Innovation.* London: Macmillan.

Mulligan, G. & Martin, W. (1980). Adaptors, innovators and the KAI. *Psychological Reports, 46*, 883-892.

Myers, I. B. (1962). *The Myers Briggs type indicator.* Palo Alto, CA: Consulting Psychologists Press.

Parsons, T. (1951). *The Social System.* New York: Free Press of Glencoe.

Prato Previde, G. (1985). Adattotori ed innovatori: I risultati della standardizzazione italiana del KAI, *Ricerche di Psicologia,* (in press).

Pulvino, C. A. (1979). *Teacher motivation and innovation and its relation to principal leader behaviour and organization structure.* Unpublished doctoral dissertation, University of Wisconsin, Madison.

Ray, J. J. (1970). The development and validation of a balanced dogmatism scale. *Australian Journal of Psychology, 22*, 253-260.

Rokeach, M. (1960). *The open and closed mind.* New York: Basic Books.

Rosenberg, M. (1965). *Society and the adolescent self-image.* Princeton, NJ: Princeton University Press.

Rogers, C. R. (1959). *Towards a theory of creativity.* In H. H. Anderson (Ed.), *Creativity and its cultivation.* New York: Harper.

Russell, K. J. (1980). The orientation to work controversy and the social construction of work value systems. *Journal of Management Studies,* 164-184.

Rydell, S. T. & Rosen, E. (1966). Measurement and some correlates of need cognition. *Psychological Reports, 90*, 139-165.

Schaefer, C. E. (1971). *Similes test manual.* Goshen, NY: Research Psychologists Press.

Shipley, W. C. (1940). A self-administering scale for measuring intellectual deterioration. *Journal of Psychology, 9*, 371-377.

Stamp, G. (1984). Management styles. *Leadership & Organizational Development Journal,* (in press).

Stein, M. I. (1975). *Manual: Physiognomic cue test.* New York: Behavioral Publications.

Swatez, G. M. (1970). The social organization of a university laboratory. *Minerva: A review of science learning & policy,* VIII, 36-58.

Tellegan, A. (1982). Cited in S. S. Gryskiewicz, The Kirton adaption-innovation inventory in creative leadership development. Invited paper for the Occupational Psychology Conference of the British Psychological Society, Sussex University.

Thomson, D. (1980). Adaptors and innovators: A replication study on managers in Singapore and Malaysia. *Psychological Reports, 47,* 383-387.

Thurstone, L. L. & Thurstone, G. W. (1947). *Primary mental abilities.* Chicago: Science Research Associates.

Torrance, E. P. (1971). *Technical norms manual for the creative motivation scale.* Athens, GA: Georgia Studies of Creative Behavior, University of Georgia.

Torrance, E. P. (1974). *Norms technical manual: Torrance tests of creative thinking.* Bensenville, IL: Scholastic Testing Service.

Torrance, E. P. (1982). Hemisphericity and creative functioning. *Journal of Research & Development in Education, 15,* 29-37.

Torrance, E. P. & Horng, Ruey Yun. (1980). Creativity, style of learning and thinking characteristics of adaptors and innovators. *The Creative Child & Adult Quarterly, V,* 80-85.

Torrance, E. P., Reynolds, C. R., Ball, O. E. & Riegel, T. R. (1978). *Revised norms-technical manual for your style of learning and thinking.* Athens, GA: Georgia Studies of Creative Behavior, University of Georgia.

Troldahl, V. & Powell, F. (1965). A short form dogmatism scale for use in field studies. *Social Forces, 44,* 211-214.

Trumbo, D. A. (1961). Individual and group correlates of attitudes to work-related change. *Journal of Applied Psychology, 45,* 338-344.

Veblen, T. (1928). *The theory of the leisure class.* New York: Vanguard Press.

Wallach, M. A. & Kogan, N. (1965). *Modes of thinking in young children: A study of the creativity - intelligence distinction.* New York: Holt, Reinhart & Winston.

Weber, M. (1970). In H. H. Gerth & C. W. Mills (Eds. & trans.) *Essays in Sociology,* London: Routledge & Kegan Paul.

Wesley, E. L. (1953). Preservative behavior in a concept-formation task. *Journal of Abnormal and Social Psychology, 8,* 129-134.

Whyte, W. H. (1957). *The Organization Man.* London: Cape.

Wilson, G. D. & Patterson, J. R. (1968). A new measure of conservatism. *British Journal of Social and Clinical Psychology, 7,* 274-279.

Zuckerman, M. (1974). The sensation seeking motive. In B. A. Maher (Ed.), *Progress in Experimental Personality Research.* Vol. 7, New York, Academic Press.

Unpublished References

Thanks are due for the use of their unpublished data to:

Davies, G. B., Cambridge Management Centre, UK.

Flegg, D., Industrial Training Research Unit, Cambridge, UK.

Mathews, D., Engineering Industry Training Board, UK.

Peeters, L., Janssen Pharmaceutical, Belgium.

Pottas, C. D., University of Pretoria, South Africa.

Snow, C. C., Pennsylvania State University, U.S.A.

13

Predictable Creativity

Stanley S. Gryskiewicz
Center for Creative Leadership

Predictable creativity—an oxymoron which suggests that there can be some control of the creative process.

Like it or not, "bottom line" is the standard used to assess the efficacy of management development experiences. This is especially true when training or when human resource departments seek to introduce the "light weight" sounding courses like "creativity" or "incubation" or even "creative problem-solving." Acceptable course content areas include decision making, leadership, planning, evaluation—these have won acceptance and have demonstrated their usefulness. Now we must seek the same acceptance for creative problem-solving procedures that we know to be viable and research-based.

We must find ways to make our terminology and outcomes compatible with the standards used to measure "bottom line." The amount of published research and years of practical experience have produced converts who believe in the validity of idea generation techniques. These supporters now must solve the problem of acceptance.

It is with this concern in mind that we offer for your consideration the Targeted Innovation Model of creative problem solving. (1) The model suggests that creative problem-solving technology can impact in a predictable manner upon both the quality and the quantity of ideas generated for a given problem. Ultimately, it will be this element of predictability that contributes to technique acceptance in an industrial setting.

Our bias is that there is no one best creative problem-solving technique. Any one of a large number can be used for idea generation (Geschka, 1980; Geschka, Schaude, Schlicksupp, 1973; Schaude, 1979; Van Gundy, 1981). Traditionally, a skilled and successful facilitator uses the technique he/she feels most comfortable with, or one with which the group is comfortable.

I would like to suggest that there may be an additional factor which impacts upon the technology used to generate ideas. This factor is based upon our research findings which compared several creative problem-solving techniques in industrial settings. We found that the type of solution desired could determine the technology selected.

Our data suggests that the desired end product determines the choice of technology. The procedure permits the creative problem-solving user to say, "We need A solutions, therefore, we will use technique X," or "The situation is crying for type B solutions, thus I will increase the probability of obtaining these by using technique Y." Creative problem-solving facilitators carry a tool kit. The kit contains several idea generation techniques that the facilitator can choose from, depending upon his/her expertise, the comfort level of the group, and the end product desired. What we propose is a goal referenced model for creative problem solving.

Creativity Style

The underlying construct used to define solution types is attributed to Michael Kirton (1976).

He proposed a personality construct which suggests that people vary in their approach to defining problems. This construct is a continuum which is anchored at one end by an adaptive approach to problem definition and at the other by an innovative approach. The adaptive mode is characterized by ideas responding directly to the problem seen within the current known setting. The innovative mode treats the problem definition as the problem. Within this mode ideas often go outside the problem as initially defined. Given these individual differences, different people (adaptors and innovators) have different problem perspectives.

Kirton's construct, for our purposes at the Center for Creative Leadership, has been used to better understand and demystify creativity. The adaptor type requires ideas which recognize environmental constraints and is aimed at doing things *better*. The focus of the innovative type of creativity is on testing the definition of the problem—stretching environmental constraints and is aimed at doing things *differently*.

Kirton (1982) has argued that the KAI (the instrument designed to measure the adaptive-innovative distinction) measures *style* rather than *level* of creativity. Historically, creative problem-solving research has failed to make this distinction. The divergent/convergent thinking discussions, for instance, have associated the ability to produce a high quantity of ideas with an individual's level of creativity, rather than with one's style (Gryskiewicz, 1980a).

What are the factors that help managers determine the products they need? Speaking generically, what type solutions do they need and what contingencies must be considered when deciding? Once managers can articulate the solution parameters needed, techniques can be chosen which are designed to obtain these products. In other words: You know where you are going; why not use a technique that will help you get there? What follows are ways of determining the products needed and the procedures for generating them.

Missing Key: Workable Creativity

Within management also, the difference between creativity level and creativity style has been muddled; however, managers have made the confusion on qualitative rather than quantitative grounds.

Necessary here is an interpretation that recognizes the quantitative and qualitative differences in creativity, and casts these differences in the light of style rather than that of level. Kirton's theory offers people concerned with creativity just such an interpretation, one which allows the practitioner to measure differences in style and also helps people understand their predisposed strengths and weaknesses.

Our research and its application within managerial populations in the United States has found value in this approach. The way in which leaders define problems has implications for the products they produce. Kirton (1980) reports that these differences impact upon organizational development. He suggests that both adaptors and innovators are needed for the organization as a whole and also within departments. Both styles of creativity are valuable to an organization, and our research suggests that an organization with the flexibility to use both approaches appropriately has the advantage.

Using the Kirton construct, the author generated four categories of solutions along the Adaptive-Innovative continuum (Table One). While this schema represents a packaging problem we researched, it also has been modified for a variety of industrial clients to include uses for new products.

Our data indicate that it is possible to match creative problem-solving technologies with these categories. It was found that:

1. Technology One, Brainwriting, was most likely to produce Category One products.
2. Technology Two, Brainstorming, tended to produce products that fit within Category Two or Three.

Table One.

Packaging Problem: How else can we use our spare packaging capacity?

ADAPTIVE	Category One:	**Direct** – Solution answers the question – what else can we put in the package without modifying it?
	Category Two:	**Supplementary** – Solution involves a new use for the package.
	Category Three:	**Modify** – Solution involves a structural change in the package such as modifying its shape.
INNOVATIVE	Category Four:	**Tangential** – Solution involves different uses for the materials with which the package is constructed.

3. Technology Three, Excursion, was most likely to generate Category Four responses.

Such structural reproduction of the KAI construct can provide managers with more cost effective technology choices depending on the type of products to be generated (Gryskiewicz, 1980b, 1981).

The Targeted Innovation Model

Figure One represents a generalization from the above small group research findings and is offered as a targeted, cost effective model for product development. It represents a predictable goal referenced model for targeted creative problem solving.

Figure One.

Goal Reference Model for Targeted Innovation.

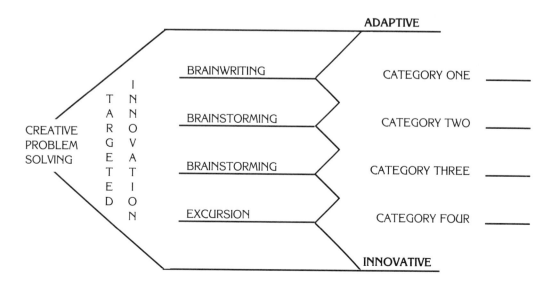

The model begins to address that bottom line which constantly confronts the practitioner/manager. It is important to use creative problem-solving technologies that are accurate, generate user satisfaction, and increase efficiency. As problem-solving groups are expensive and often are questioned on cost-effectiveness, Targeted Innovation presents a focused, time-saving approach.

As the model is presented, it represents a move away from the traditional shotgun approach of creative problem to a rifled approach using the type of solution needed as the target. Such an approach has removed the looseness and lack of "real life" application often associated with creative problem solving as reported in more traditional settings (Mansfield, Busse, & Krepelka, 1978).

What becomes most critical now is for the practitioner to state the outcome need clearly. Once the social scientist becomes aware of the more practical concerns such as user reaction, product quality, and product requirement, both the social scientist and practitioner can begin to understand each other's concerns and constraints. Managers can be more efficient when outcomes determine technology selection.

The factors used to decide the category of product quality needed were established by R&D managers attending courses at the Center for Creative Leadership. Table Two lists these contingencies.

Additional Findings

Quantity Data

The major theory reviewed by the following research was the role of oral behavior as a contributor to uniformity pressure's influence upon the quantity of ideas in problem-solving groups. Such an impact was assessed by comparing the performances of real and nominal groups using the following four technologies:

Brainstorming: Oral problem solving using Osborn's four brainstorming rules.

Brainwriting I: Non-oral problem solving using Osborn's four rules.

Brainwriting II: Non-oral problem solving *without* using Osborn's four rules.

Excursion: Oral problem solving using novel scenarios as a means to stimulate idea generation.

Real groups were defined as people working together to solve a problem. Nominal group members worked individually generating problem solutions. For analysis purposes, the same number of individuals were randomly assigned to nominal groups as had worked together in real groups. With time for problem solving held constant, the combined products of individuals working alone (in nominal groups) were compared with the products of real groups. This real group/nominal group paradigm was first reported in Taylor and McNemar (1955) and used to answer the research questions: Did group participation facilitate or inhibit creative thinking? Taylor, Berry, and Block (1958) published the first study designed to answer this question.

Based upon almost 25 years of research using Taylor's paradigm, this author put forward the following hypotheses.

- Hypothesis 1—Nominal group brainstorming (NBS) will produce a higher quantity of ideas than real group brainstorming (RBS). This would replicate past research findings.
- Hypothesis 2—If oral behavior is removed, real brainwriting groups will produce a higher quantity of ideas than the nominal group. This will be true of Brainwriting I (participants were supplied with Osborn's four rules of brainstorming) and Brainwriting II (participants were not given Osborn's four rules).
- Hypothesis 3—Brainwriting I (BWI) will generate more ideas than Brainwriting II

Table Two.

Ten Contingencies for Targeted Innovation in an R&D Setting.

1. **Team Experience** — The longer team members remain together the more adaptive their products will become.

2. **Destination of Output** — If the product is requested by the organization's hierarchy, the products will tend to be more adaptive. If the output is to go laterally or down in the organization, more innovative output can be expected.

3. **Nature of the Client** — History of the kind of products found acceptable by the client determines whether to pursue adaptive or innovative type solutions.

4. **The Recurring Problem** — The reappearing generic problem signals the need for an innovative approach.

5. **Degree of Crisis** — The greater the crisis the more likely an innovative idea will be accepted.

6. **Project Phase** — During early stages of a project innovative products are more likely to be acceptable. As the project matures, adaptive responses are advised.

7. **Insurance** — If you have a product line that is a market leader, it is desirable to have alternatives ready should this position be threatened either by patents expiring or by new entries from competitors. This need for "insurance" products suggests the need for long-term innovative choices.

8. **Diversification** — The need for additional markets is opportune for innovative products.

9. **Time** — Time requirements are more likely to be longer for an innovative rather than an adaptive change.

10. **Project Budget** — Adaptive ideas are more amenable when project funds are limited. Large budgets may provide resources necessary for more innovative solutions.

(BWII) in both nominal and real groups because the latter technology does not employ the four brainstorming rules.
- Hypothesis 4–Excursion will produce fewer ideas than the other three technologies because it is oral and the brainstorming rules are not used.

Figure Two represents the average of group mean data points found using the four idea-generating technologies described above.

As predicted, Hypothesis 1 and 2 were confirmed. Hypothesis 3 was confirmed when comparing Brainwriting I and II in the real group setting. In the nominal group comparisons, the trend was evident but the difference was not significant.

Figure Two.

Mean U.S. Quantity Data for Number of Ideas by Treatment.

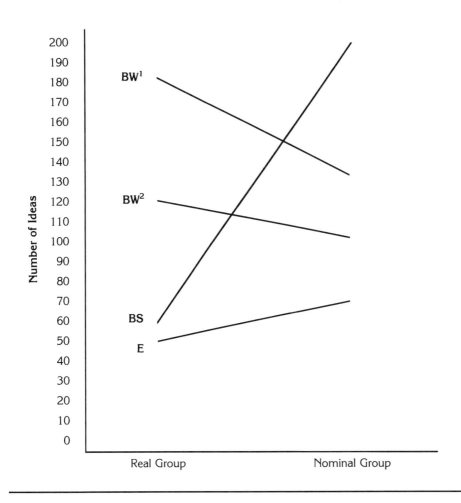

Hypothesis 4 was confirmed for all comparisons except Real Excursion with Real Brainstorming and Nominal Excursion with Nominal Brainwriting II. These differences are reported in Table Three.

Expert Data

The most surprising results occur when you cross reference quantity data with qualitative rating by experts in the field. When 30 ideas from each condition were randomly selected and rated by experts from the industry that generated the problem, those ideas produced by the excursion technology resulted in higher total feasibility scores (2) for the United Kingdom study (comparing Brainstorming, Brainwriting I and Excursion) and the second highest feasibility score in the U.S. study. If the quantity criteria exposed by past researchers had been adhered to, Excursion as a productive creative problem-solving technique would have been eliminated. Such results caution against a premature discarding of creative problem-solving technologies based on quantity data alone.

Table Three.

Duncan's Multiple Range Test: Comparison of Eight Treatment Means for Number of Ideas Generated

	Means	R 61.4	RBS 63.8	E 67.4	NBWII 95.6	RBWII 121.4	NBWI 131.8	RBWI 179	NBS 223	Shortest Significant Ranges
RE	61.4		2.4	6.0	34.2	60.0*	70.4*	117.6*	161.6*	$R_2 = 47.1$
RBS	63.8			3.6	31.8	57.6*	68.0*	115.2*	159.2*	$R_3 = 49.57$
E	67.4				28.2	54.0*	64.4*	111.6*	155.6*	$R_4 = 51.06$
NBWII	95.6					25.8*	36.2	83.4*	127.4*	$R_5 = 52.21$
RBWII	121.4						10.4	57.6*	101.6*	$R_6 = 53.03$
NBWI	131.8							47.2	91.2*	$R_7 = 53.86$
RBWI	179.0								44.0	$R_8 = 54.35$

* Significant at .05

Finally, how do the experts' evaluations help the practitioner? The results are mixed, but it is quite clear that qualitative dependent measures can no longer be excluded when evaluating creative problem-solving technologies, especially when quality can be controlled and can become predictable as suggested by the Targeted Innovation Model.

Implications

The above model and others that are research based facilitate greatly the overall acceptance of creativity as a useful construct. The application of creativity to problem solving, however, is only one part of a total organizational innovation program. Creative problem solving has received much negative press because of misinterpreted research findings, unskilled group facilitators, lack of attention to idea evaluation (the meticulous, unexciting stage) and missed opportunities to work directly in industrial settings evaluating the various idea-generation technologies with meaningful measures.

Predictably, this author believes that the Targeted Innovation Model takes into account the above detractors and seeks to champion the cause of creativity. Creativity in organizations ought to be as common, useful and accepted as the accounting and marketing principles used widely today—especially if we consider and target our audience.

Some Future Research Directions

It became clear when I began to answer for myself the "so what" question about the Targeted Innovation model that any creative problem solving model does not exist in a vacuum. The organization and its climate, the external factors, such as cost, time, financial indicators, innovation history, and potential, must all be considered when model application is discussed. Therefore, my recommendations for future research directions will stress a more complete understanding of the work climate which surrounds the creative problem solving tools we have previously researched.

Future directions should include:

1. Inductive research designs to ascertain the work group dynamics that may either inhibit or facilitate the use of creative problem solving models. These research designs should include observational and interview data to supply direction. Questionnaire data is needed to focus the question, and provide the data for a higher quality of analyses for purposes of reliability and validity.
2. Cross functional and cross organizational research to see if functionally derived cultures (e.g., manufacturing, research and development, and marketing) or organizationally derived cultures (hi-tech, manufacturing, and service) differ on their receptivity to innovation and how they use creative problem solving models. As researchers, we should be sensitive to the culture of the organization in which these models will either survive and grow or die.
3. Sensitivity to cross cultural differences and related implications. There are many of us working around the world in this creative problem solving field who have a common purpose. Perhaps an attempt to pool our experiences in a systematic way could provide a vehicle for course design changes or intervention changes which take into account the culture of the nationalities represented. A similar schema was produced by Geert Hofstede (1980) and was used by the IBM Corporation to design culturally relevant management development programs.

As my three suggestions indicate, I have a bias which developed outside the laboratory during my role as an interventionist. What is discovered in the lab must also be true in the context of the work group, the organization, and the culture. It is my belief that with a better understanding of these contexts and their relevant contingencies, we can bring our future research into sharper focus.

Footnotes

1. The Targeted Innovation creative problem-solving model was first reported in the Proceedings of Creativity Week III, 1980, in a chapter by this author entitled "Targeted Innovation: A Situational Approach." It reports a portion of the writer's doctoral thesis from London University.
2. Feasibility reflects an internal industry rating made up of four factors which include marketability, cost effectiveness, technical considerations, and production.

References

Geschka, H. (1980). Perspectives on using various creativity techniques. In S. S. Gryskiewicz (Ed.), *Creativity Week II, 1979 Proceedings (pp. 49-61).* Greensboro, NC: Center for Creative Leadership.

Geschka, H., Schaude, G. R. & Schlicksupp, H. (1973, August 6). Modern techniques for solving problems. *Chemical Engineering,* 91-97.

Gryskiewicz, S. S. (1980a). Creative Problem Solving: Are individuals still superior to groups? *Planned Innovation, 3,* 3-5.

Gryskiewicz, S. S. (1980b). A study of creative problem-solving techniques in group settings. A thesis submitted in fulfillment of the degree of Doctor of Philosophy in The University of London. October.

Gryskiewicz, S. S. (1981). Targeted innovation: A situational approach. In S. S. Gryskiewicz (Ed.), *Creativity Week III, 1980 Proceedings* (pp. 77-103). Greensboro, NC: Center for Creative Leadership.

Hofstede, G. (1980). *Culture's Consequences: International differences in work-related values.* Beverly Hills, CA: Sage Publications.

Kirton, M. J. (1976). Adaptors and innovators: A description and measure. *Journal of Applied Psychology, 61,* 622-629.

Kirton, M. J. (1980). Adaptors and innovators in organizations. *Human Relations, 33,* No. 4, 213-224.

Kirton, M. J. (1982). Adaption-innovation: A theory of organizational creativity. In S. S. Gryskiewicz & J. Shields (Eds.), *Creativity Week IV, 1981 Proceedings* (pp. 90-104). Greensboro, NC: Center for Creative Leadership.

Mansfield, R. S., Busse, T. V., & Krepelka, E. J. (1978). The effectiveness of creativity training. *Review of Educational Research, 48,* 517-536.

Schaude, G. R. (1979). Methods of idea generation. In S. S. Gryskiewicz (Ed.), *Creativity Week I, 1978 Proceedings* (pp. 54-76). Greensboro, NC: Center for Creative Leadership.

Taylor, D. W., Berry, P. D. & Block, C. H. (1958). Does group participation when using brainstorming facilitate or inhibit creative thinking? *Administrative Sciences Quarterly, 3,* 23-47.

Taylor, D. W. & McNemar, O. W. (1955). Problem solving and thinking. In C. P. Stone (Ed.), *Annual Review of Psychology, 6,* 455-482.

Van Gundy, A. (1981). Comparing "little known" creative problem solving techniques. In S. S. Gryskiewicz (Ed.), *Creativity Week III, 1980 Proceedings* (pp. 58-76). Greensboro, NC: Center for Creative Leadership.

14

Research Potential of Imagery and Creative Imagination

Joe Khatena
Mississippi State University

Many of us have been interested in the fascinating subject of creativity, but it was not until the 1950's that a disciplined approach to the study of creativity became a fact. Although Galton's work on hereditary genius may have indirectly opened the door to the more formal study of imagery, it was not until Guilford (1967) proposed the Structure-of-Intellect model which included divergent thinking abilities (a narrower definition of creative mental functioning) as a major dimension of intellectual operations as well as transformation and redefinition abilities, that exploration of creativity began in earnest. As a result of the innumerable contributions by many scholars in the field, creativity has not only become legitimized but also recognized as a significant and key factor in our endeavors and achievements.

It should come as no surprise to find that most attempts to study the human mind and its relatively intangible, and unverifiable functions have stirred up many disagreements. The lack of sympathy for developing new ideas in this field has retarded rather than facilitated discovery. The study of imagery is one instance of this. I cannot help wondering what great progress could have been made to this important field of inquiry had not the narrow vision of Watson and Behaviorism obstructed its growth. Imagery, readmitted in the 1960s as a legitimate area of study in psychology, was aptly described by Holt (1964) as the "return of the ostracised." Its revival coincided with the growth of cognitive psychology (Holt, 1972), the resurgence of humanistic psychology and, the entire humanistic movement (Gowan, 1978a). Today, the significance of imagery has been established beyond a doubt (Sheikh, 1977), so that it is no longer necessary to question the existence of imagery, but to ask questions about the significance of image properties and representations (Ahsen, 1981). To go a step further, it is appropriate to consider imagery not so much as an esoteric mind function but as the totality of humankind's relationship with the environment and cosmic interactive forces.

Creativity and Imagination

Creativity is a very complex near elusive phenomenon. Its description at best remains incomplete, its measurement a baffling challenge. Through wide usage, the term has become associated with various aspects of creative behavior and mental processes that range among a cognitive-emotive continuum, complicated by various definitions about its energy source. Theoretical classifications of creativity are not found wanting (e.g. Gowan, 1972; Roweton, 1973; Treffinger, Isaksen & Firestien, 1983), and generally include creativity as one or more of the following: cognitive, rational and semantic; as personal and environmental relative to child-rearing practices; as a high degree of mental health; as Freudian; as psychedelic; as definitional; as behavioristic; and as dispositional. The best definitions of creativity arise from theoretical frameworks. That is, they operationalize constructs that become verifiable hypotheses.

Some examples of earlier definitions of creativity as mental processes are thinking by analogy (Ribot, 1906), seeing relations with both conscious and subconscious processes operating for the education of relations and correlates (Spearman, 1930), and more recently as the intellectual operation of divergent thinking, redefinition, and transformation abilities set in motion by sensitivity to problems (Guilford, 1967), the process of sensing gaps or disturbing missing elements, forming hypotheses concerning them, testing these hypotheses (Torrance, 1962), and the power of the imagination to break way from perceptual set so as to restructure new ideas, thoughts, and feelings into novel and meaningful associative bonds (Khatena & Torrance, 1973), with the latter three directly connected to the development of published measures of creativity. Many poets regard imagination as some force outside of themselves that is responsible for their creative experiences and works. Imagination has been described by William Blake as "Spiritual energy" in whose exercise we experience in some way the activity of God. Samuel T. Coleridge has called it "an ability of prime importance because human beings in their creative activity simulate the creative act of God" (1954, p. 167). He differentiates imagination as primary and secondary, such that primary imagination derives from God's creative being and acts, and secondary imagination manifests humankind's creativity in microcosmic form of the latter?

> The primary imagination I hold to be the living power and prime agent of all human perception, and as a repetition in the finite mind of the infinite mind of the eternal act of creation in the infinite I AM. The secondary I consider as an echo of the former, co-existing with the conscious will, yet still as identical with the primary in the kind of its agency, and differing only in degree, and in the mode of its operation. It dissolves, diffuses, dissipates, in order to recreate; or where this process is rendered impossible, yet still, at all events, it struggles to idealize and to unify. It is essentially vital, even as all objects (as objects) are essentially fixed and dead. (Coleridge, 1817/1954, p. 167).

Coleridge further distinguishes between imagination and fancy, explaining that the former is concerned with the creative, whereas the latter with memory functions.

> Fancy . . . has no other counters to play with but fixities and definites. The fancy is indeed no other than a mode of memory emancipated from the order of time and space; and blended with, and modified by that empirical phenomenon of the will which we express by the word choice. But equally with the ordinary memory it must receive all its materials ready made from the law of association. (Coleridge, 1817/1954, p. 167)

Imagination when energized by creativity articulates the world of reality not in the province of Fancy that operates within the parameters of memory but in the province of the secondary imagination which is an active operation of mind that produces transformations and newness. The distinction that Coleridge makes between primary and secondary imagination is important in that it distinguishes God or Cosmically (to use a more neutral, universal term) inspired vision from faculties more under the control of the individual and therefore educationally malleable.

According to Peter McKellar (1957), A-thinking relates to dreaming, waking, fantasy, and events that sometimes accompanies phenomena prominent in psychosis which he likens to authorship and its raw materials; whereas R-thinking relates to processes of reasoning, logic, and reality-adjustment which he likens to editorship. Imagination involves the fine interplay of both A-thinking and R-thinking for the occurrence of socially useful thought products or works of art and science. John Eccles (1972) speculates on the characteristics of a brain exhibiting creative imagination as processing information received via neuro-physiological pathways as follows:

> The creative brain must first of all possess an adequate number of neurons,

having a wealth of synaptic connections between them. It must have, as it were, the structured basis for an immense range of patterns of activity. The synapses of the brain should also have a sensitive tendency to increase their function with usage, so that they may readily form and maintain memory patterns. Such a brain will accumulate an immense wealth of engrams of highly specific character. In addition, this brain possesses a peculiar potency for unresting activity, weaving the spatio-temporal patterns of its engrams in continually novel and interacting forms, the stage is set for the deliverance of a 'brain child' that is sired, as we say, by creative imagination. (p. 40)

Much activity of the brain that relates to creative imagination has to do with imagery or the reexperiencing of images and their language correlates. Eccles suggests that, by association, one image is evocative of other images. When images of beauty and subtlety blend in harmony and are expressed in language (verbal, musical, or pictorial) they evoke transcendent experiences in one's self or others leading to artistic creation of a simple or lyrical kind. Eccles adds an entirely different order of image making when he links it to illumination that brings about new insight or understanding. In science, this may take the form of a new hypothesis that embraces and transcends an older hypothesis, Harold Rugg (1963) views creative imagination as problem solving activity that involves the whole conscious and nonconscious regions of the mind connected by the transliminal mind which is where the creative flash or illumination occurs.

R. W. Gerard (cited in Ghiselin, 1952) in the manner Gestalt psychologists emphasized the importance of closure and insight where in the act of creative thinking one gestalt is destroyed in favor of a better one. Creative imagination is described by Gerard as "an action of mind that produces a new insight" (p. 226) or "as the heat of mental work transforming the soft ingot of fancy into the hard steel of finished creations" (p. 227).

The problem solving functions of the creative imagination are observed by C. M. Bowra (1969) as a mysterious activity of the mind:

When we use our imagination we are first stirred by some alluring puzzle which calls for a solution, and then by our own creations in the mind, we are able to see much that was before dark or unintelligible. (p. 7)

Imagination as manifested in creative problem solving activity may be viewed as the activity of creative energy fields that are both mental and emotive (Vargiu, 1977) with a large number of simple "mental elements" within the boundary of a "creative energy field" such that:

1) Each element will respond to the influence of the creative field, and
2) All mental elements can interact with one another.

To illustrate this he describes the well known behavior of a thin layer of iron filing in the presence of a magnet:

At first, the field is too weak to set the iron particles in motion. They are held in position by friction. As the intensity of the magnetic field increases, some of the iron particles overcome friction and begin to move, interacting with the nearby granules in a way that increases the overall magnetization. This in turn sets other particles in motion, accelerating the process and starting an "avalanche effect" or "chain reaction" which causes the pattern to suddenly form itself, independently of any further approach of the magnet. (p. 23)

Using this analogy he suggests that mental elements must pass through the stages of preparation, frustration, incubation, illumination, and elaboration with the suddenness of illumination compared to an "avalanche effect." The interaction between mental elements and emotional field constitutes the very essence of imagination and causes images energized by feelings to be formed in the mind.

Figure One.

Intellectual Abilities Activated by Energy Fields.

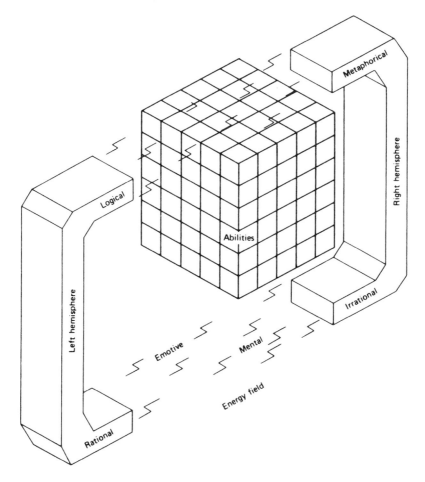

Incubation is an important activity of the brain involved in creative imagination: it is the precursor to illumination. For instance, Coleridge tells us of his incubation-illumination experience in which "images rose up before him as things" to become the content of his famous poem Kubla Khan. Fredrich Kekulé von Stradonitz's experience of imagery just prior to, and contingent on illumination led to the structure of the benzene ring, which became the foundation of organic chemistry.

Intellectual abilities as well as emotive energy fields are involved in the function of creative imagination: they operate in various ways to lead to incubation, creative imagery, and illumination in the creative process (Khatena, 1982). The structure of intellect abilities when synthesized with Vargiu's thoughts on creativity and placed in the context of energizing magnetic fields of forces, mental and emotive, become central to the function of creative imagination. Activity set in motion by imagination causes these dimensions to act and interact with one another such that if a problem is presented for processing, incubation is set in motion to produce imagery for illumination and problem solution (Figure One).

Creative Imagination Imagery
as Multidimensional and Interactive

In psychology, an image has been defined as a perception in the absence of an external stimulus. Rosemary Gordon (1972) speaks of an image as:

> The perception of forms, or colors, or sounds, or smells, or movements, or tastes in the absence of an actual external stimulus which could have caused such perception. This does not mean that such external stimuli did not present themselves in the past nor that the image is independent of such past experiences. But it does mean that at the time of the perception of the image no such stimulus is present. (p.63)

Ahsen (1982) considers the image as a centrally aroused sensation which extends from the perception of an external object to its mental reproduction of imaginative reconstruction with such a degree of sensory realism that the subject can interact with the image as he would interact with a real object. Specific somatic or neurophysiological experience and change transmits received sensory stimulation of the real object to its mental image referent. Further, an image as a centrally aroused sensation is seen as having a certain definite significance or many layers of meaning whose sources are the conscious, nonconscious, past, present, and future. This represents Ahsen's holistic model of image, soma, and meaning or ISM.

Multidimensional Interactive Creative Imagination Imagery Model

The ISM model may be said to be the precursor of a holistic imagery system that includes primary and secondary imagination, additional multivariate interactive components of mental set, emotive-motivational influences, hereditary based intellectual operations, and communication of emergent images tied to a feedback-feedforward system. I have called this holistic model the Multidimensional Interactive Creative Imagination Imaging Model or MICIIM (Khatena, 1983a), a model in keeping with a general systems approach to the study of the subject (Figure Two).

The MICIIM consists of three main dimensions, namely, Environment, Individual and Cosmic.

1. Environment

The dimension of Environment refers to everything external to the individual, this includes the physical universe, other persons (both as single individuals and as constituents of socio-cultural groups) and events. Together these comprise the individual's external reality which is internalized to become the inner and private reality of self and the controls of the individual's mental life and experience. By its nature the Environment dimension is developmental—that is, its shaping influences are spread over time, and its effects are gradual for the most part, although they may be contemporaneous if not immediate. Of particular interest here is the development of intellect and creativity that cannot be treated as isolated from its socio-cultural origins, but rather as conditions which hinder or facilitate the development of genius and determine the frequency of its occurrence (Arieti, 1976; Simonton, 1978).

2. Individual

This dimension relates to everything that constitutes the Individual, namely, the soma or neurophysiological aspects and psychological aspect whose center is the individual. Structures and functions of both the neurophysiological and psychological aspects are complementary. Focus here will be on the psychological generally and the intellect specifically; the physiological will find inclusion to the extent that the senses receive and transmit information in images or

Figure Two.
Multidimensional Interactive Creative Imagination Imagery Model.

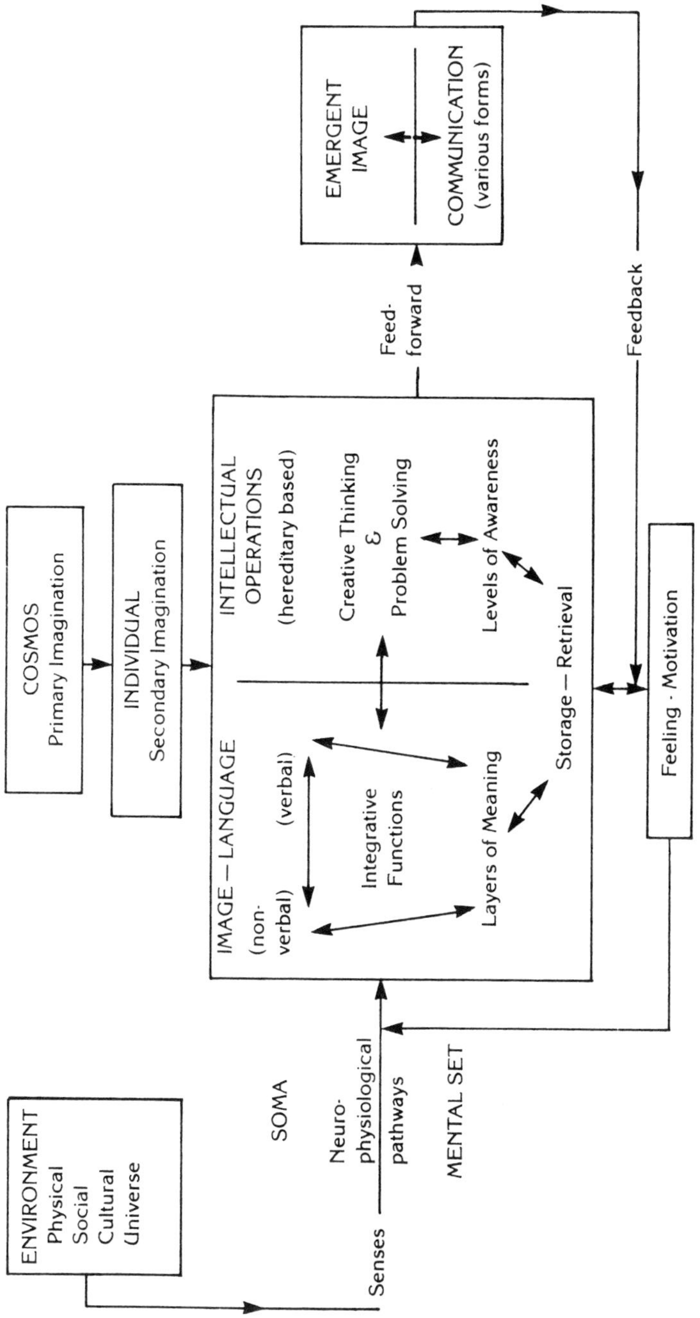

ENVIRONMENT
Physical
Social
Cultural
Universe

COSMOS
Primary Imagination

INDIVIDUAL
Secondary Imagination

SOMA

Neuro-
physiological
pathways

Senses

MENTAL SET

IMAGE — LANGUAGE
(non-
verbal)   (verbal)

Integrative
Functions

Layers of Meaning

INTELLECTUAL
OPERATIONS
(hereditary based)

Creative Thinking
&
Problem Solving

Levels of Awareness

Storage — Retrieval

Feeling - Motivation

Feed-
forward

Feedback

EMERGENT
IMAGE

COMMUNICATION
(various forms)

in their coded forms from the external world to brain centers activating intellectual functions and various levels of awareness towards emergent image-language production for output and communication. Other aspects of the individual include feeling-motivation which energizes mental processing, the mental set of past experiences which screens and filters input information, a feedback system which controls mental processing and communication which is used for feedforward, and secondary imagination functions closely linked to the creative springs of mental functioning. Another facet of the Individual dimension relates to intellectual and creative development both as changes in terms of chronology relative to continuous or discontinuous growth, and transformative leaps relative to developmental stage (Gowan, 1972) and general systems (Land, 1973) and theories (Khatena, 1982).

3. Cosmic

Of the three dimensions, the Cosmic invites the most controversy, but its relationship to the Individual and Environment dimensions cannot be ruled out or denied although objective verification may not at present appear feasible. In fact, the Cosmic has been considered by numerous thinkers of the world as essential to the unity of humankind and the Universe. The Cosmic may be thought of as the original creative life force whose power and action are manifest in all that is. Creative products are but specific instances of it. The parent of inspiration in the highest sense, the Cosmic has been perceived by geniuses in the arts and sciences as necessary to the creation of their great works—awe inspiring experiences when they are one with the Creator. The creative energy in humankind is merely a projection in microcosm of the macrocosm, "secondary imagination" impelled to motion by "primary imagination."

Among the speculative discussions in recent years about Man's relationship with the Cosmic, the Pribram-Bohm hologram model of ultimate reality is the most provocative. Their model suggests that the brain is a hologram interpreting a holographic universe: it mathematically constructs "hard reality" by interpreting frequencies from a dimension transcending time and space. As any piece of a hologram reconstructs the entire image, so too the brain, a bit of the greater hologram, reconstructs the whole (Ferguson, 1978; Pribram, 1978).

In a recent paper on principles of imagery in literature, Ahsen (1982) discusses Janusian perception as involving the historical and primordial, where one face of perception emphasizes historical input, while the other funnels in the eternal, which is firmly embedded in the genetic structure and its parallel holographic relationships with the whole cosmos. In terms of the "psi" phenomenon the interactions of the Individual, Environment and Cosmos have been described by psychologists as the emergent psychic energy of the individual and/or group appearing and transcending the constraints of ordinary time, space and force.

To explain the model from its image perspective, let us say that a real object is encountered and received by the various senses as a centrally evoked image which is transmitted to the brain via neurophysiological pathways. The quality and kind of sensory reaction and its transmission to the brain by the senses and neurophysiological system are governed by mental sets based on previous somatic and mental experiences and meanings. Images in the brain are then encoded in some language form, predominantly factual in meaning at first, but developing more dimensions as these relate and interact with other image and language experiences in the storage-retrieval system. Hereditary intellectual abilities (cognition, memory, convergent thinking, divergent thinking, and evaluation) based upon an information psychology model (Guilford, 1967), operates on the images and/or their language referents. These several areas of mental functioning associate and interact with the storage-retrieval dimension, influence and are influenced by the emotive-motivational system. Mental activity involves various levels of awareness which lie on a continuum from full consciousness to full nonconsciousness and have association with altered states of consciousness and nonordinary reality. Outcomes of interrelated and interactive brain activity are emergent images that for purposes of communication take one of another of available language forms such that more direct communication, for instance, lies in artistic representation. Finally, communication is tied to total brain activity in a feedback loop that includes feedforward towards the emergent image functions and their communication correlates. Then there is the function of the secondary imagination which draws life from primary imagination in moments of heightened experience, vision or inspiration. This energizes mental resources to high creative output, or in less ecstatic moments, sets mental functions to working at more ordinary levels of creative output.

Cosmic Illumination of Genius

The three interactive dimensions, the Environmental, Individual and Cosmic, are significant to human functioning generally and imagery specifically. Continua of abilities ranging from very low to very high, of emotionality from very low to very high sensitivity, of states of consciousness from full awareness to complete unawareness, and the like, are of the Individual dimension. The same may be said of the Environment dimension relating exposure and

---

Figure Three.

Relationship of Individual-Environment Dimensions Illumed by the Cosmic.

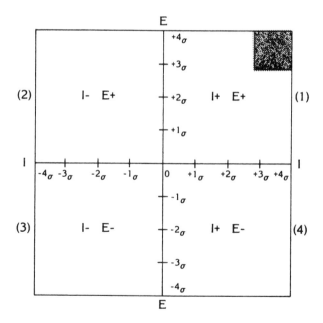

QUADRANT 1:	Optimum situation; both the individual & environment dimensions are in positive interaction.
QUADRANT 2:	Positive interactions of the environment dimension with the negative of the individual dimension.
QUADRANT 3:	Negative interactions of both dimensions.
QUADRANT 4:	Negative interaction of the environment dimension with positive of the individual dimension.

influence to a variety of environmental variables ranging from least to most effective. Together, these form the Individual-Environment planes of possible interactions. Cosmic influences do appear to range along continua but appear to act in an all or nothing way so that one is or is not illuminated. If we were to draw the Individual and Environment planes of variability as two axes, X and Y intersecting at right angles such that each ranges from -4 to +4 standard deviations through a mean of zero, four quadrants are set up (Figure Three). It is quadrant 1 that represents an optimum situation where both the Individual and Environment dimensions are in positive interaction with the greatest potential to receive cosmic influences especially in the area of interactions marked off by the coordinates that are 3-4 above the mean (shaded area in Figure Three).

Persons occupying positions in the shared area are those who possess not only a creative intellect in the upper regions of genius but also unique striking power to make contact with an impersonal universal source of knowledge identified as the 'collective consciousness'. Such persons possess what Gowan (1980) calls 'exotic abilities' meaning extensions of more ordinary abilities, available yet held ephemerally and tenuously and not under the possessor's full control. These abilities are most dependent on careful tuning and attention to small vibrations, and have the power to amplify what comes to the mind. They are creative in the sense of being able to extend the incubation processes from an unconscious to an intuitive practice but whose mechanism of practice and production is never well understood by the possessor. Exotic abilities represent in wild form a mutant ability which practice and education can domesticate into an enhanced power. Such geniuses leave behind a rich cultural legacy of ideas, thoughts and feelings that has manifested itself in great contributions to art, music, literature, drama, poetry, philosophy, religion, science and politics. Both Arieti (1976) and Simonton (1978) have pointed to the fact that the efflorescence of great geniuses is not a frequent occurrence, but they have made a difference to our lives, and somehow our minds are made up of their stuff with potentials and capacities for germination and creativity.

Research on Creative Imagination and Imagery

The Multidimensional Interactive Creative Imagination Imagery Model proposed should give perspective to the study of imagery though the element of cosmic influence in itself is rare and at present difficult to verify objectively. However, this ought not to preclude its inclusion as an important dimension of imagery. Recently, Torrance and Hall (1980), in considering the status of measures of creativity, suggested directions that may be taken to assess "the further reaches of creative potential." The day may come when increased sophistication of our technology will make the objective verification of cosmic influence on the individual engaged in creative activity possible. Gowan (1980) with the hologram in mind, makes a provocative projection that by reversing the holographic process via integration, one might be able to reach back to the original light source—the cosmic. For the present, we may have to be contented with studying imagery in terms of the interactive relationship of the Individual and Environment.

In my recent book (Khatena, 1984) it was pointed out that to give some coherence to the study of imagery, many attempts have been made to categorize images (e.g. Hilgard, 1981; McKellar, 1972; Richardson, 1969). The classes in which images have been placed do not differ greatly, and there appears to be general agreement over three class labels: 1) after imagery, 2) eidetic imagery; and 3) memory imagery. Variation in labeling image categories, however, occurs over what Richardson (1969) has called imagination imagery. Sub-classes of imagination imagery according to Richardson and others are hypnogogic imagery, perceptual isolation imagery, hallucinogenic imagery, photic stimulation imagery, pulse current imagery, non drug-induced hallucination imagery, imagery of dreams, imaginative constructions or fantasy, and creative imagination imagery, to which may be added Ahsen's (1982) eidetic imagination imagery by which a participant enters into creative engagement with the world. In the main, differences appear not to lie in the phenomenal attributes of images reported, but in the antecedent conditions that arouse them (Richardson, 1969).

Imagery research has given much attention to the study of after imagery, eidetic imagery, memory imagery and most of the sub categories of imagination imagery with the exception of creative imagination imagery. Little research has been done in imagery as it relates to creative imagination, and until a few years ago there was almost a complete absence of experimentally based research into the relationship between imagery and creativity (Durio, 1975). The need to study creative imagination imagery was pointed out several years ago (Paivio, 1971; Richardson, 1969), and recently its importance was emphasized by Hilgard (1981) who stated that any broad discussion of imagery must give attention to the sources and nature of the products of creative imagination. What we need to bear in mind about the creative imagination and its imagery correlates is that unlike the other sub classes of imagination imagery that depend upon reduction of external stimuli activity in order to free individuals to attend to an inner world of stimulus events (Richardson, 1969), creative imagination imagery additionally requires the voluntary exercise of divergent or creative mental operations as well. This means that individuals are not just passive recipients of imagery occurrences of flow but active designers and architects of imagery in problem-solving or reflective thinking sets. We should recall Coleridge's description of imagination as "primary" and "secondary," and make note that it is the activation of imagery by the "secondary imagination" that gives it the quality we call creative imagination imagery; the "primary imagination" enters in the picture only if the cosmic is present.

Measurement of Creative Imagination Imagery

A major problem in the study of creative imagination imagery has been the lack of objective measures. The early work of Richardson (1969) and a recent paper by White, Sheehan and Ashton (1977) indicates that self-report measures are the most widely used assessment procedure. However, another paper by Sheehan, White and Ashton (1983) point to the development of several imagery assessment approaches that include the assessment of a person's consciousness. Those methods are expected to reflect experience more directly and to help detect qualitative differences in cognitive styles and characteristic modes of thought engaged in solving problems. In addition, measures of creative thinking abilities developed by Torrance, Khatena and Starkweather encourage a person via visual, auditory and tactile modalities to project in words or pictures original images.

Of these several measures, two have been used in the study of imagery and creative imagination particularly, namely *Onomatopoeia and Images* (OI) and *Sounds and Images* (SI). They are measures of originality and together comprise the test battery *Thinking Creatively with Sounds and Words.* (Khatena & Torrance, 1973; Torrance, Khatena & Cunnington, 1973).

Onomatopoeia and Images consists of onomatopoeic word stimuli. They are auditory, visual and verbal in nature, and possess both sound and sematic elements evocative of both factual and emotive meanings. The listener, when presented onomatopoeic words, is required to use creative energies (or what Coleridge calls the "secondary imagination") to break away from habitual thought patterns to produce original responses. More subtle than the meaning component of onomatopoeic words is the sound component. It strikes the listener unaware and stirs the emotional base of intellect. Together the sound and meaning of the words set in motion those intellective-emotive processes to produce the original. *Sounds and Images* consist of simple to complex auditory stimuli. Similar in rationale to *Onomatopoeia and Images,* the measure requires the listener to break away from sound sets to produce original responses. The measures are on long-playing records with instructions given to the listener to use creative imagination to produce original images. *Onomatopoeia and Images* presents five onomatopoeic words in the children's version and ten in the adult version four times, with a time interval of 30 seconds or 15 seconds between one word and the next. Both the children's and adult versions of *Sounds and Images* present four sound sets three times, with a time interval of 30 seconds between one sound set and the next. Image responses are scored for originality based on the principle of statistical infrequency and relevance with credits ranging from zero to four points.

A new procedure was developed to score the responses for creative analogies (Khatena, 1977a) such that credits of zero to three points are given for the production of direct, personal, fantasy and symbolic analogy respectively, and zero or one point for simple or complex image structure of the analogy. A combined score of from zero to four points gives a creative analogy index.

Unlike the self-report that has been widely used in imagery research, *Thinking Creatively with Sounds and Words* requires listeners to use their creative imagination to produce original images which may then be scored for originality and creative analogies. The measures have been used both as independent and dependent variables in many studies on imagery and creative imagination (Khatena, 1973a, 1978b, 1982, 1984). Of several other instruments that measure creative thinking abilities, the figural form of the Torrance Tests of Creative Thinking (Torrance, 1974) and the *Starkweather Originality Test* (Starkweather, 1971) may also be used to study imagery. The former presents stimuli in the visual mode with instructions to draw pictures using creativity, while the latter presents stimuli in the tactile mode with instruction to produce original responses. Together these instruments represent a move away from the structured introspection of self-reports to the relatively structured-unstructured projective type instrument in the three generally most used sense modalities, namely auditory, visual and tactile (Khatena, 1975a) thus providing additional instrumentation for imagery research.

About 15 years ago Richardson (1969) had observed that apart from two studies on creative imagination imagery, one in perceptual isolation, visual imagery and creativity (Kubzanski, 1961), and another on the facilitative effects of LSD on the creative problem solving process (Harman, McKin, Moger, Fadiman & Stolaroff, 1966) little else had been done. Since then, there have been a number of studies on the creative dimension of imagination imagery, among which are creativity, hyponogogic imagery and relaxation (Green & Green, 1977), aesthetic activities, imagery arousal and creativity (Lindauer, 1972), musical creativity and original imagery (Torrance & Khatena, 1969), imagery of blind and sighted children (Johnson, 1979), imagery and originality in a cross-cultural setting (Khatena & Zetenyi, 1977a, 1977b, 1983), and creativity, imagery, sex, education and socio-economic variables (Forisha, 1981).

My interest in imagery and the creative imagination found focus in several areas. These included the effects of creative training programs on production of original images, the effects of time press on production of original images, developmental patterns of original images, sense modality correlates of original images, and originality and image autonomy.

1. *Creative Thinking Training Programs*

The effects of several creative thinking programs devised to stimulate the creative imagination were studied (See Table One). The first training program consisted of five creative thinking strategies, namely, breaking away from the obvious and commonplace, restructuring, synthesis, transposition, and analogy, with exercises that used both figural and verbal content constructed for adults (Khatena, 1969a), and a second consisting of the first three strategies adapted for use with children and youth (Khatena, 1969b). The adult version used in two studies (Khatena, 1970a, 1971a) showed that in general the strategies effectively stimulated the creative imagination to produce original verbal images. A third study (Khatena & Barbour, 1972) used a modified version of the training program (Barbour, 1971) consisting of the first three strategies and Osborn's (1963) idea-spurring questions with rhythmic and melodic elements as content to stimulate the production of original images with favorable results.

Table One.

Stimulating Creative Imagination to Produce Original Images.

Investigator	Educational Level	Nature of Treatment	Measures	Findings
Khatena (1970a)	College	Creative Thinking Strategies (Adult Version)	SI & OI	Improvement in original verbal images produced with training.
Khatena (1971a)	College	Creative Thinking Strategies (Adult Version)	SI & OI	Improvement in original verbal images produced with training.
Khatena (1971b)	Preschool	Creative Thinking Strategies	TTCT (Figural)	Improvement in fluency, flexibility, originality and elaboration of figural images produced.
Khatena (1977b)	College	Analogy Training and Creative Levels	SI & OI SAM	Improvement in production of creative analogies of high and low creatives given training. All preferred to produce direct analogies and simple images.
Khatena & Barbour (1972)	College	Creative Thinking Strategies & Osborn's Idea Spurring Questions, Imaginative Manipulation of Rhythmic and Melodic Elements	SI & OI	Improvement in original verbal images produced with training.
Khatena (1973a)	College	Creative Thinking Strategies (Adult Version) & Creative Levels	SI & OI SAM	All subjects benefited from training.
Khatena & Parnes (1974)	College	Creative Problem Solving (Parnes)	OI	Improvement in original verbal images produced with training.
Khatena & Dickerson (1973)	6th Grade	Creative Thinking Strategies (Children's Version)	TTCT (Verbal)	Improvement in fluency, flexibility and originality of verbal images produced with training.
Parrish (1981)	College	Relaxation and Incubation	SI & OI	Either relaxation or incubation training but not the two combined led to improvement in production of original verbal images.
Johnson, G. M. (1981)	College	Hypnogogic Imagery Training	TTCT (Figural)	Improvement in fluency, flexibility, originality and elaboration of figural images produced.

Another study (Khatena & Parnes, 1974) using Parnes' (1967a, 1967b) creative problem solving method over a whole semester showed that experimentals produced more original images than the controls. Further, it was also found that both creative and less creative college men and women benefited from the training programs (Khatena, 1973a). The childrens' version of the Khatena creative program when used with preschool disadvantaged students (Khatena, 1971b) and sixth graders (Khatena & Dickerson, 1973) showed significant increments in figural or verbal image productions when measured by the *Torrance Tests of Creative Thinking* (Torrance, 1974) figural or verbal forms respectively.

A training program designed to encourage the use of creative analogies and images (Khatena, 1977b) was used in an experiment (Khatena, 1977c) with college adults identified as high and low creatives by *Something About Myself* (Khatena & Torrance, 1976). Experimentals were taught the use of personal, symbolic, and fantasy analogies, figures of speech, and simple-complex image structure. The findings showed that, in general, high and low creatives who were taught did significantly better than their high and low creative counterparts who were not taught. Further, all subjects used the direct analogy simple image structure more frequently than the other analogy-image types. There was, however, no obvious use of any figure of speech strategy in the analogies produced.

Kip Parrish (1981) explored the differential and combined effects of relaxation using an autogenic relaxation tape and an incubation training program (Khatena, 1981) with college adults as subjects. He found that either procedure significantly increased production of original verbal images, whereas the combined condition did not. In another study, on the effects of training college adults to use hypnogogic imagery, given time limits of 10 or 20 minutes, and where the Figural Form A of the *Torrance Test of Creative Thinking* was the measure used, G. M. Johnson (1981) found that there was improvement in the fluency, flexibility, originality and elaboration of figural images produced.

In summary, this group of studies further supports the view that expressing oneself creatively generally and in original images specifically, can be enhanced with training, that this applies to young people as well as adults, and that both high and low creatives could benefit from such training.

2. *Press Effects on Production of Original Verbal Images and Analogies*

According to Rhodes (1961) we can identify people as creative in one of four ways: by their personality characteristics, by their thinking processes, by the products they make, and by the way they respond to press. Since response to press was the least explored creative index it has been the subject of investigation by several associates and me these past few years (See Table Two).

The instrument used for the purpose has been *Thinking Creatively with Sounds and Words* (Khatena & Torrance, 1973) since each of its two components have build-in time press conditions. In the standard form of *Onomatopoeia and Images* the time interval is fixed so that between the presentation of one onomatopoeic word and the next there is a 15 second interval for adults and a 30 second interval for children. There are four presentations of each group of five or ten onomatopoeic stimuli respectively. *Sounds and Images* in the standard form has a fixed time interval of 30 seconds between the presentation of one sound and the next for both the adult and children's versions. There are three presentations of each of the same group of four sound stimuli. Experimental tapes of the *Onomatopoeia and Images* recordings alone introduce variations in the time interval such that the variable time interval relative to the four presentations is 5, 10, 15 seconds and unlimited time for the adult version, and 10, 20, 30 seconds and unlimited time for the children's versions.

Two studies on the effects of presenting onomatopoeic or sound stimuli to fixed time intervals, as in the standard conditions of the recorded text, with college adults as subjects

(Khatena, 1970b; Khatena & Torrance, 1973) showed increase in the production of original verbal images to peak in either the third or fourth presentation. Another study with children and adolescents (Khatena, 1973b) also showed progressive increase in the production of original verbal images with the greatest gains occurring between the first and second presentations. This meant that adults needed more warm-up than children and adolescents to produce better responses. Where time intervals were variable and where adults, adolescents and children were grouped as high, moderate and low creatives (Khatena, 1971c, 1972a, 1973c), high creative adults and children were generally found to produce more original verbal images when given moderate time deadlines, while high creative adolescents produced best when given as much time as they needed.

A study on the effects of timed (15 second) and unlimited time on originality and the production of creative analogies (Khatena, 1978d) found that college adults produced more original verbal images in untimed conditions, that originality increased to peak in the third presentation decreasing somewhat in the fourth presentation, and that although the production of complex images was significantly influenced by untimed conditions, the production of creative analogies was not.

Another study with educators attending a national meeting (Khatena & Parzivand, 1983) using *Sounds and Images* investigated the effects of presenting four electronically produced sounds three times, with an interval of 30 seconds between one sound and the next. Verbal images produced were scored for originality and analyzed according to differential sound effects and multiple presentations. The evidence showed no significant difference in the image evoking potential of sounds but it did confirm earlier conclusions that images improve with three repeated presentations of sound stimuli.

Four recent doctoral dissertations studied the effects of time press in association with several variables. Nananolla Yazdani (1984) did an experiment with college adults using the standard form of *Onomatopoeia and Images*. Subjects were exposed to rhythmic photic and sonic interference stimuli presented at 5 or 15 second intervals intended to stimulate right, left and both cerebral hemispheres while they were taking the test. He found that interference of 5 seconds allowed better production of original verbal images, and that auditory interference to stimulate the left hemisphere facilitated the production of original verbal images. Chungsook Bae's study (1984) of college adults hearing stimulating or sedating music before or during the presentation of onomatopoeic and sound stimuli of *Thinking Creatively with Sounds and Words* found that stimulating music enhances the production of original verbal images, and that as in other studies, this productivity increased with repeated presentation of the test stimuli. Lamon Small (1984) studied the transfer effects of positive training as a stress management technique on the production of original verbal images given the fixed time press of the standard conditions of *Thinking Creatively with Sounds and Words*. He found that more original verbal images were produced by those receiving the training, and that there was a progressive increase in their image production congruent with earlier findings. Hussein Sajjadi-Bafghi (1984) used gifted adolescents as subjects to study the effects of fixed time (30 seconds) and variable time (10, 20, 30 seconds and unlimited time) of *Onomatopoeia and Images* on these subjects classified as high moderate and low autonomous imagers (Lane, 1975). He found that image autonomy level did not affect subjects' original verbal images and creative analogy production. Further, congruent with earlier studies, a progressive increase was found for repeated presentations of stimuli with the greatest gains occurring in the third presentation, with a slight decrease in the fourth presentation of the fixed time condition, and in the fourth presentation of the variable time condition when as much time as needed was allowed.

In summary these studies generally indicate that repeated presentations of onomatopoeic and sound stimuli are needed to provide sufficient warm-up for the production of better original verbal images, that children and adolescents are most rapidly warmed-up, that given

Table Two.

Press Effects on Production of Original Verbal Images and Creative Analogies.

Investigator	Educational Level	Nature of Treatment	Measures	Findings
Khatena (1970b)	College Adults	Fixed Time (15 seconds)	OI	Progressive increase in original verbal image production – highest for presentation 3 in Form 1A & presentation 4 in Form 1B.
Khatena & Torrance (1973)	College Adults (High Creatives)	Fixed Time (15 seconds) (30 seconds)	OI & SI	Progressive increase in original verbal images.
Khatena (1973b)	Children & Adolescents	Fixed Time (30 seconds)	OI	Progressive increase in original verbal images with greatest gains between presentations 1 and 2.
Khatena (1971c)	Adolescents	Varible Time (10, 20, 30 seconds & unlimited time)	OI	High creatives produced better origin verbal images given unlimited time of presentation 4, and just as well if not better than their moderate and low creative peers in presentations 1 to 3.
Khatena (1972a)	Children	Variable Time (10, 20, 30 seconds & unlimited time)	OI	High creatives produced more original verbal images than moderate and low creatives in presentations 3 and 4; severe time press of presentations 1 and 2 affected all badly.
Khatena (1973c)	College Adults	Variable Time (5, 10, 15 seconds & unlimited time)	OI	High creatives produced better origin, verbal images than moderate and low creatives in presentation 3, with high creative men alone maintaining this superiority when given unlimited time.
Khatena (1978d)	College Adults	Fixed Time (15 seconds) Unlimited Time	OI	More original verbal images were produced in untimed conditions; originality increased and peaked in presentation 3; complexity of images produced increased but not creative analogies in untimed conditions.
Khatena & Parzivand (1983)	Educators	Fixed Time (30 seconds) & Multiple Sound Effects	SI	Progressive increase in production of original verbal images.
Yazdani (1984)	College Adults	Fixed Time (15 seconds), Rhythmic Photic and Sonic Interference at 5 or 15 seconds Intervals to Stimulate Right, Left and Both Cerebral Hemispheres.	OI	Interference of 5 seconds allowed better original verbal image production.

Table Two. *Continued*

Press Effects on Production of Original Verbal Images and Creative Analogies.

Investigator	Educational Level	Nature of Treatment	Measures	Findings
Bae (1984)	College Adults	Fixed Time (15 seconds or 30 seconds). Stimulating and Sedating Music Played Before and During the Presentation of Onomatopoeic and Sound Stimuli.	OI & SI	Stimulating music enhanced production of original verbal images; progressive increase in original verbal image production.
Small (1984)	College Adults	Fixed Time (15 seconds or 30 seconds), Positive Thinking as a Stress Management Technique	OI & SI	More original verbal images were produced by those receiving training; progressive increase in production of original verbal images.
Sajjadi-Bafhgi (1984)	Adolescents	Level of Image Autonomy and its Responsiveness to Fixed Time (30 seconds) or Variable Time (10, 20, 30 seconds & Unlimited Time)	OI	Image autonomy level did not affect production of original verbal image and creative analogies in condition of fixed or variable time; progressive increase in original verbal image production.

variable time conditions, high creative children and adults' imagination operates more effectively when given moderate time deadlines, whereas adolescents do better when given as much time as they need. Further, auditory interference to the left hemisphere, stimulating music, and positive thinking facilitate the production of original verbal images.

3. *Developmental Patterns of Original Verbal Images and Creative Analogies*

Decrements in creative thinking have been found for four periods of a child's life. These are the last six months of kindergarten and in about grades 4, 7 and 12. Productivity peaks were found between grades 3 and 4 and again in about grade 11 in several cross-sectional studies (Andrews, 1930; Torrance, 1962, 1967). Results of these studies are supported by a longitudinal study on the fourth grade slump (Torrance, 1968) as measured by the figural and verbal forms of the *Torrance Tests of Creative Thinking.*

Development of creative thinking abilities as related to originality and production of verbal images was studied with both the general population and special groups of children that included the deaf, blind, and gifted using *Thinking Creatively with Sounds and Words.* The production of original verbal images by children and adolescents between the ages of 8 and 19 and 9 and 19 was explored in two cross-sectional studies (Khatena, 1971d, 1972b) which showed that children at age 9 and 10 produced fewer original verbal images but showed a gain at age 11 years. A longitudinal study using *Onomatopoeia and Images* conducted over a four year period with a group of 8-year-olds supported the earlier findings (Khatena & Fisher, 1974).

The production of creative analogies (personal, direct, fantasy, and symbolic analogy with simple or complex image) by children, adolescents, and adults was also explored in several studies (Khatena, 1972c, 1973d, 1977c). They provided evidence that highly original men and women, and boys and girls of all age levels preferred to use the direct analogy form and simple image structure. These findings were also found applicable to a group of gifted adolescents (Sajjadi-Bafghi, 1984). Further, as highly original children grew older, they produced more complex and correspondingly fewer simple images. A Recent study (Khatena, 1983c) exploring the relationship among originality, creative analogy, and analogy-image patterns using the same measures with educators found similar results in the preference for direct analogy and simple image forms. It was also found that originality correlated significantly with creative analogy and image complexity, thus lending further support to earlier thought on the high relationship existing between creativity and preference for complexity.

A number of studies were also done with deaf and blind children. One, using *Onomatopoeia and Images*, looked at the production of original verbal images by deaf and hearing children between the ages of 10 and 19 (Johnson & Khatena, 1975) and found that hearing children produced significantly more original verbal images than deaf children. Further, although hearing children did not show any clear increase in original production as they grew older, deaf children showed significant improvement with age. Johnson (1975) tested the assumption that deaf children who were taught the factual meaning of onomatopoeic words when compared with those who were not taught would obtain higher originality scores, and found it to be the case.

Whether blind adolescents are more creative than sighted adolescents relative to the production of original verbal images when critical variables such as intelligence are taken into account was also explored using both components of *Thinking Creatively with Sounds and Words* (Johnson, 1979). The measures were administered to about an equal number of low-ability blind and sighted adolescents who were unable to record or spell their own responses. Scoring of their responses for originality provided evidence that blind adolescents produced more original verbal images, symbolic analogies and complex images than sighted adolescents who produced more personal analogies.

In summary, these studies indicate that: 1) there is a drop in the production or original verbal images at age 9 and 10 with some recovery at age 11; 2) that the production of the direct analogy simple image form was preferred by high originals of both sexes; and 3) that as high original children grow up they prefer to use the complex image. Further, hearing children when compared with deaf children and adolescents produced more original verbal images. However, the productivity of the deaf increases with age. Teaching deaf children the factual meaning of onomatopoeic words enhances their productivity. With regard to blind adolescents, they produced more original verbal images, complex images and symbolic analogies than their sighted counterparts who produced more personal analogies (See Table Three).

4. *Original Verbal Images and Sense Modality Correlates*

The view that images are indirect reactivations of earlier sensory or perceptual activity rather than the outcome of mental mechanisms at work had much to do with a renewed interest in imagery in American Psychology (Bugelski, 1970). Imagery is obviously tied to its sensory referents (Holt, 1964) and its revived sense experience in the absence of sensory stimulation (Drever, 1963). Although sensory aspects of imagery are an essential phenomenological feature of imaging, individual differences of sensory imagery are insufficiently understood and, relative to the role of sensory imagery in learning, receive little consideration (Lindauer, 1972).

Little research on various sense modality correlates of imagery relative to creativity has been done. For instance, a study by Schmeidler (1965) that used a quantifiable version of Francis Galton's original breakfast-table questionnaire (1870) found low positive correlation

Table Three.

Development Patterns of Original Verbal Images and Creative Analogies

Investigator	Educational Level	Measures	Findings
Khatena (1971d)	Children and Adolescents (8 - 19 years)	OI	Children 9 and 10 years old produced fewer original verbal images than the remaining subjects with gains at age 11.
Khatena (1972b)	Children and Adolescents (9 - 19 years)		
Khatena & Fisher (1974)	Children (8 over 4 years)	OI	
Khatena (1972 c) (1973d) (1977c) (1983c)	Adults Children & Adolescents Adults Adults	OI OI OI OI	High original men, women, boys and girls preferred the use of direct analogy simple image form over personal, fantasy and symbolic analogy complex image form; as highly original children grow up they preferred to use the complex image.
Sajjadi-Bafghi (1984)	Adolescents (gifted)	OI	
Johnson & Khatena (1975)	Children and Adolescents (deaf and hearing) 10 - 19 years)	OI	The hearing produce more original verbal images than the deaf; the productivity of deaf children increased with age.
Johnson (1975)	Children (deaf) (10 - 19 years)	OI	Deaf children taught the factual meaning of onomatopoeic words produced more original verbal images than those who were not taught.
Johnson (1979)	Adolescents (blind and sighted) (10 - 21 years)	OI	Blind adolescents produced more original verbal images, symbolic analogies and complex images than sighted adolescents who produced more personal analogies.

between imagery and creativity. Another study by Leonard and Lindauer (1973) found a significant correlation between participation in aesthetic activities (as these relate to English, art, music and theater) and imagery arousal (measured by self-rating scales). The ease and vividness of imagery production was measured in response to 45 sensory words equally distributed in five sense modalities, namely, vision, sound, touch, taste and smell. Imagery scores were found to differentiate from aesthetic participation scores.

However, not much has been done to investigate creative self-perceptions, originality, and image production, and their relationship to the several sense modalities. The study with adults (Khatena, 1975a) that explored the relationship between vividness of imagery production and creative perceptions using the short form of *Betts QMI Vividness of Imagery Scale* and *Something About Myself* found significant relationship between the two especially in the visual, auditory and tactile sense modalities. Further, vivid imagers tended to perceive themselves as highly creative. A second study (Khatena, 1976a) with adults identified by *Onomatopoeia and Images* as high, moderate, and low originals explored the use they make of the visual, auditory, tactile, gustatory, olfactory, and organic senses (according to the Betts scale) in their production of original verbal images. In general, high originals were found to use more senses when producing original verbal images.

Khatena and Bellarosa (1979) looked at sex differences of the several sense modalities used in producing original verbal images relative to *Onomatopoeia and Images* as a follow-up study. They found that college men and women do not differ significantly in their use of various single or multiple sense modalities, and that most frequently they used the auditory and auditory-visual modalities combined as well as the auditory-kinesthetic and auditory-visual-kinesthetic modalities.

Vania Carmago (1982) studied the relationship of vividness of imagery (as measured by the short form of the Betts *QMI Vividness of Imagery Scale)* to high, moderate and low creatives (identified by *Something About Myself).* Subjects who perceived themselves as high creatives tend to use the organic, auditory and kinesthetic sense modalities most frequently. Timothy Teater (1982) exposed experimentals to perceptual activities to help them become attentive and highly interested in usage of tactile or visual-auditory modalities by touching objects, by hearing tactile words, or by listening-seeing-hearing visual-auditory words. He expected that such activities would increase tactile references in their production of original verbal images using *Sounds and Images,* but did not find significant results.

In summary, these studies found that vividness of imagery, especially of the visual, auditory and tactile modalities correlated significantly with creative perceptions; that vivid imagers perceived themselves as high creatives. High originals or creatives used most frequently the visual, auditory, kinesthetic, visual-auditory and combination of two or more senses in production of original verbal images. Finally it was found that there were no significant sex differences in the use of single or multiple senses (See Table Four).

5. *Autonomy and Original Imagery Production*

Taking direction set by the early studies of Jaensch (1930) on eidetic imagery, Rosemary Gordon (1949) distinguished between autonomous and controlled imagery. Autonomous imagery according to Gordon tends to take its own course and is independent of other mental functions, whereas controlled imagery is integrated into the total personality. To study factors associated with the formation of National stereotypes, Gordon (1949) used the *Gordon Test of Visual Imagery Control,* a test which she developed. Her study showed that autonomous imagers responded to national stimulus words (like Englishman or Chinese) by producing conventional stereotyped images because of earlier life-experiences, whereas controlled imagers produced less stereotyped images. A study between these two groups (Costello, 1957) showed that dysthymics and hysterics when compared with normals were relatively just as autonomous in imagery, with dysthymics having vivid, hysterics having weak, and normals having either vivid or weak autonomous imagery.

Peter McKellar on the subject of imagination imagery (1957) and autonomy, imagery, and dissociation (1977) indicates that autonomy of imagery is fundamental and central to hypnogogic imagery. In hypnogogic imagery, images appear to follow their own course independent of the person experiencing them, and will often surprise the experiencer by their highly creative or unreproductive character. Coleridge's experience of imagination imagery

Table Four.

Sense Modality Sources of Original Verbal Images.

Investigator	Educational Level	Nature of Treatment	Measures	Findings
Khatena (1975a)	College Adults		Betts QMI SAM	Significant relationship between vividness of imagery produced and creative perceptions, especially with reference to the visual, auditory, and tactile senses.
Khatena (1976a)	College Adults		Betts QMI OI	High originals were found to use the visual, auditory, visual-auditory senses and combination of other two or more senses in producing original verbal images.
Khatena & Bellarosa (1979)	College Adults		OI	No significant sex differences in the use of single or multiple senses in production of original verbal images were found; subjects used the auditory-visual, auditory-kinesthetic, and auditory-visual-kinesthetic senses most frequently in producing of original verbal images.
Carmago (1982)	College Adults		Betts QMI SAM	Subjects who perceived themselves as high creatives tend to use the organic auditory and kinesthetic senses most frequently.
Teater (1982)	Children (8 years)	Experimentals given perceptual activities to encourage use of tactile or visual-auditory senses.	SI	No significant results were found.

immediately before and during the composition of "Kubla Khan" is a good example of this. Enid Blyton's cinematographic imagery, that provides her with ideas for the Noddy stories is another instance of autonomous imagery.

Recently, however, scientific study of image autonomy, relative to people who perceive themselves as creative, was done. Khatena (1975b), categorizing a number of college adults as less, moderate, and more autonomous imagers according to a modified scaling procedure of the *Gordon Test of Imagery Control,* found that more autonomous imagers perceived themselves as more highly creative than moderate and less autonomous imagers, and moderate imagers perceived themselves as more highly creative than less autonomous imagers. Their creative perceptions were measured by *Something About Myself.* That is to say, adults in college who perceive themselves as highly creative are more likely to have greater autonomy of imagery.

In a second study (Khatena, 1976a), college adults categorized as moderately autonomous and less autonomous imagers, were administered *Onomatopoeia and Images.* Analyses of their responses showed that moderately autonomous imagers produced significantly more original verbal images than less autonomous imagers. This suggests that more autonomous imagers are likely to produce more original images and lends support to the earlier findings relative to image autonomy and creative perceptions. An earlier study had indicated that college adults tend to use the visual, auditory, or combined visual and auditory senses most frequently in producing original verbal images and showed a preference for multiple sense modalities (Khatena, 1976a). These findings suggested a study of the production of original verbal images where a single sense modality versus multiple sense modalities would be used relative to levels of image autonomy determined by the Gordon scale (Khatena, 1978c). The results showed that autonomy of imagery does not appear to influence the use of single or multiple senses in the production of original verbal images, and that, consistent with the earlier study (Khatena, 1976a), the visual, auditory, and combined visual-auditory sense modalities are most frequently used.

In summary, these studies indicate that more autonomous imagers perceived themselves as more highly creative than moderate and less autonomous imagers, and moderate autonomous imagers perceived themselves more highly creative than less autonomous imagers. Further, moderately autonomous imagers produced more original verbal images than less autonomous imagers. In addition, it was found that autonomy of imagery was not influenced by either the use of single or multiple senses in the production of original verbal images, and that the most frequently used senses were the visual, auditory and combined visual-auditory senses (See Table Five).

Summary

The creative imagination has much to do with imagery and its language correlates. Its complexity calls for a model that is at once multi-dimensional and interactive, a model that can explain imagery in terms of the whole person, whose sources of information, influence, and mental activity are the Environment, Individual and Cosmic. An individual's access to Cosmic illumination is dependent on the interactive effects of optimum conditions of the Individual and Environment dimensions. For the present, the study of creative imagination imagery has to be thought of in terms of the interactive relationship of the Individual and Environment dimensions until the sophistication and technology to include the Cosmic becomes available.

Not much research has been done on creative imagination imagery despite its recognized importance. In studying this area, it must be noted that unlike other sub classes of imagination imagery, creative imagination imagery requires voluntary exercise of divergent thinking and transformation operations, thereby making individuals active designers and architects of imagery in problem solving or reflective thinking modes.

Lack of objective measures is seen as a major problem. Most measures that are available take the form of self-reports. Exceptions to these are measures that attempt to reach a person's consciousness. These measures are expected to reflect experience more directly and to help detect qualitative differences in cognitive styles and characteristic modes of thought engaged in solving problems. As it pertains to creativity, there are tests designed to measure this

Table Five.

Autonomy and Original Verbal Imagery Production.

Investigator	Educational Level	Measures	Findings
Khatena (1975b)	College Adults	Gordon Test of Imagery Control SAM	More autonomous imagers perceived themselves as more highly creative than moderate and less autonomous imagers, and moderate autonomous imagers more highly creative than less autonomous imagers.
Khatena (1976a)	College Adults	Gordon Test of Imagery Control OI	Moderately autonomous imagers produced more original verbal images than less autonomous imagers.
Khatena (1978c)	College Adults	Gordon Test of Imagery Control OI	Autonomy of imagery did not appear to influence the use of simple or multiple senses in the production of original verbal images; the visual, auditory, and combined visual-auditory senses were most frequently used.

dimension in the auditory, visual and tactile modalities that have been or can be used in imagery research to its advantage.

Studies done include the use of training procedures to stimulate the creative imagination to produce original images, effects of time press on originality and analogy production, developmental patterns in the production of original images and analogies, sense modality correlates of original images, and autonomy and original images.

Conclusions

The three dimensional model of Individual, Environment and Cosmic imagery system is a viable model for giving focus to new directions in research on creative imagination imagery. Taking the two interactive Individual-Environment dimensions of the model as the more feasible for present research, leads can be found to researchable problems in the following areas:

1) The nature and function of intellectual-physiological relationships and their bearing on imagery;

2) The activity of intellectual operations (beyond cognition and memory) as it processes imagery both in its original form as well as in its coded language forms;

3) Imagery functions in creative problem solving which call for the use of all five of Guilford's thinking operations;

4) Incubation in three areas, the a) problem solving mode as a vehicle to creative image production; b) incubation that relates to scientific creativity; and c) incubation in the reflective mode that relates to artistic creativity;

5) Metaphorical dimensions of imagery that are involved in scientific and artistic thoughts and works;

6) Imagery as schemas of personality differences indicative of individual character and total mental functioning;

7) Imagery functions of eminent men and women in their acts of creativity;

8) Imagery in cross-cultural situations in and out of this country;

9) Cerebral hemispherical functioning, intellectual processing and imagery correlates;

10) Intellectual operations and imagery as functions of age and sex;

11) Other important and related directions of research lie in the development of psycho-physiological measures that are sensitive to intellectual activity on imagery. These measures should go beyond self-reports to production of imagery as objective evidence that at one and the same time contain information of the subjective and private worlds of the individual at work;

12) Further, improved designs and methodology can be constructed to allow for experiment while controlling for extraneous variables; and

13) Last but not least, are areas of study that may investigate the practical application and value of theoretical findings in education, business and mental health settings, with a variety of populations along continua of mental and physical variability in different socio-cultural settings.

The intriguing dimension of the Cosmic is at present illusive to study. However, behavioral-humanistic scientists, by taking cues from the testimonies of great people whose creativity has been fired by cosmic forces, may key their energies to invent the instruments and methodologies for the exploration of this dimension of human personality. Humankind's creativity has time and again extended known parameters of knowledge not possible and put in his/her grasp what was before unknown. It may be that common pursuit of the uncommon will one day give us the ingenuity and power to transcend the tantalizing situation and place within reach, the Cosmic.

References

Ahsen, A. (1981). Image theory: Odysseus and Oedipus Rex - An essay on current image psychology and the literary technique of consciousness. (Keynote address) *5th American Imagery Conference.*

Ahsen, A. (1982). Principles of imagery in art and literature. *Journal of Mental Imagery, 6* (1), 213-250.

Andrews, E. G. (1930). The development of imagination in the preschool child. *University of Iowa Studies of Character, 3* (4).

Arieti, S. (1976). *Creativity: The magic synthesis.* New York: Basic Books.

Bae, C. (1984). Effects of time press, music type, and presentation order of music on original verbal images. (Doctoral dissertation, Mississippi State University). *Dissertation Abstracts International, 45A,* 2800 University Microfilms No. 28133).

Bagley, M. T. & Hess, K. (1982). *200 ways of using imagery in the classroom.* Woodcliff Lake, NJ: New Dimensions of the 80's Publishers.

Barbour, R. L. (1971). Exercises in creative thinking in music. Unpublished manuscript, Marshall University.

Bowra, C. M. (1969). *The romantic imagination.* New York: Oxford University Press.

Bugelski, B. R. (1970). Words and things and images. *American Psychologist, 25,* 1002-1012.

Camargo, V. B. (1982). *The relationship of vividness of imagery to low, moderate and high creative self-perceptions.* Unpublished master's thesis, Mississippi State University.

Coleridge, S. T. (1954). *Biographia litereria.* New York: E. P. Dutton. (Originally published 1817).

Costello, C. G. (1957). The control of visual imagery in mental disorder. *Journal of Mental Science, 103,* 840-849.

Drever, J. A. (1963). *A dictionary of psychology.* Baltimore, MD: Penguin Books.

Durio, H. F. (1975). Mental imagery and creativity. *Journal of Creative Behavior, 9* (4), 233-244.

Eccles, J. C. (1972). The physiology of imagination. In *Readings from Scientific American.* San Francisco, CA: W. H. Freeman. (Originally published, 1958.)

Ferguson, M. (1978). Kerl Pribram's changing reality. *Revision, 1* (3-4), 8-13.

Forisha, B. (1978). Mental imagery and creativity: Review and speculations. *Journal of Mental Imagery, 2* (2), 209-238.

Forisha, B. (1981). Patterns of creativity and mental imagery in men and women. *Journal of Mental Imagery, 5* (1), 85-96.

Galton, F. (1870). *Hereditary genius.* New York: Appleton.

Ghiselin, B. (Ed.) (1952). *The creative process.* Berkley, CA: University of California Press.

Gordon, R. (1949). An investigation into some of the factors that favor formation of stereotyped images. *British Journal of Psychology, 39,* 156-157.

Gordon, R. (1972). A very private world. In P. W. Sheehan (Ed.), *The function of imagery* (pp. 63-80). New York: Academic Press.

Gowan, J. C. (1972). *The development of the creative individual.* San Diego, CA: Robert K. Knapp.

Gowan, J. C. (1978). Creativity and the gifted movement. *Journal of Creative Behavior, 12* (1), 1-13.

Gowan, J. C. (1980). *Operations of increasing order.* West Lake Village, CA: (published by author).

Green, E. E. & Green, S. (1977). *Beyond biofeedback.* New York: McGraw-Hill.

Guilford, J. P. (1967). *The nature of human intelligence.* New York: McGraw-Hill.

Harman, W. W., McKim, R. H., Mogar, R. E., Fadiman, J. & Stoloroff, M. J. (1966). Psychedelic agents in creative problem solving: a pilot study. *Psychological Reports, 19,* 211-227.

Hilgard, E. R. (1981). Imagery and imagination in american psychology. *Journal of Mental Imagery. 5* (1), 5-19.

Holt, R. R. (1964). Imagery: The return of the ostracized. *American Psychologist, 19,* 254-264.

Holt, R. R. (1972). On the nature of mental imagery. In P. W. Sheehan (Ed.), The function and nature of imagery (pp. 3-33). New York: Academic Press.

Jaensch, E. R. (1930). *Eidetic imagery.* London: Routledge & Kegan Paul.

Johnson, G. M. (1981). An investigation of hypnagogic imagery as a vehicle for producing creativity. (Doctoral dissertation, Mississippi State University). *Dissertation Abstract International, 42B,* 4559 (University Microfilms No. DA10078).

Johnson, R. A. (1975). Word knowledge and production of original verbal responses in deaf children. *Perceptual and Motor Skills, 41,* 125-126.

Johnson, R. A. (1979). Creative imagery in blind and sighted adolescents. *Journal of Mental Imagery, 3* (1-2), 23-30.

Johnson, R. A. & Khatena, J. (1975). Comparative study of verbal originality in deaf and hearing children. *Perceptual and Motor Skills, 40,* 631-635.

Khatena, J. (1969a). Exercises in thinking creatively: Teacher's guide (adult version). In J. Khatena, *The training of creative thinking strategies and its effects on originality.* (Doctoral dissertation, University of Georgia) (University Microfilms No. 70-1172).

Khatena, J. (1969b). Exercises in thinking creatively: Teacher's guide (children's version). Unpublished manuscript, East Carolina University.

Khatena, J. (1970a). Training college adults to think creatively with words. *Psychological Reports, 27,* 279-281.

Khatena, J. (1970b). Repeated presentation of stimuli and production of original responses. *Perceptual and Motor Skills, 30,* 91-94.

Khatena, J. (1971a). A second study training college adults to think creatively with words. *Psychological Reports, 23,* 385-386.

Khatena, J. (1971b). Teaching disadvantaged preschool children to think creatively with pictures. *Journal of Educational Psychology, 62* (5), 384-386.

Khatena, J. (1971c). Adolescents and the meeting of time deadlines in the production of original images. *Gifted Child Quarterly, 15* (3), 201-204.

Khatena, J. (1971d). Production of original verbal images by children between the ages of 8 and 19 as measured by the alternate forms of "onomatopoeia and images." *Proceedings of the 79th Annual Convention of the American Psychological Association, 6* (1), 187-188.

Khatena, J. (1972a). Original verbal images of children as a function of time. *Psychological Reports, 31,* 565-566.

Khatena, J. (1972b). Development patterns in production by children aged 9-19 of original images as measured by "sounds and images." *Psychological Reports, 30,* 649-650.

Khatena, J. (1972c). The use of analogy in the production of original verbal images. *Journal of Creative Behavior, 9* (3), 209-213.

Khatena, J. (1973a). Creative level and its effects on training college adults to think creatively with words. *Psychological Reports, 32,* 336.

Khatena, J. (1973b). Production of original verbal images by college adults to variable time intervals. *Perceptual and Motor Skills, 36,* 1285-1286.

Khatena, J. (1973c). Repeated presentation of stimuli and production of original responses by children. *Perceptual and Motor Skills, 36,* 173-174.

Khatena, J. (1973d). Imagination imagery by children and the production of analogy. *Gifted Child Quarterly, 17* (2), 98-102.

Khatena, J. (1975a). Vividness of imagery and creative self-perception. *Gifted Child Quarterly, 19* (1), 33-37.

Khatena, J. (1975b). Relationship of autonomous imagery and creative self-perceptions. *Perceptual and Motor Skills, 40,* 357-358.

Khatena, J. (1976a). Original verbal imagery and its sense modality correlates. *Gifted Child Quarterly, 20* (2), 180-186.

Khatena, J. (1976b). Autonomy of imagery and production of original verbal images. *Perceptual and Motor Skills, 43,* 245-246.

Khatena, J. (1977a). "onomatopoeia and images": A preliminary scoring guide for creative imagination imagery and analogies. (Unpublished manuscript, Marshall University).

Khatena, J. (1977b). Analogy and imagination: A study guide. (Unpublished manuscript, Marshall University.)

Khatena, J. (1977c). Analogy strategies and production of original verbal images. *Journal of Creative Behavior, 11,* (3), 213.

Khatena, J. (1978a). Frontiers of creative imagination imagery. *Journal of Mental Imagery, 2* (1), 33-46.

Khatena, J. (1978b). Creative imagination through imagery: Some recent research. *Humanits, 14* (1), 227-242.

Khatena, J. (1978c). Autonomy of imagery and use of single or multiple sense modalities in original verbal image production. *Perceptual and Motor Skills, 46,* 953-954.

Khatena, J. (1978d). The effects of time press upon the production of creative analogies. *NAGCT Quarterly Journal, 4* (1), 6-13.

Khatena, J. (1979). *Teaching gifted children to use creative imagination imagery.* Starkville, MS: Allan Associates.

Khatena, J. (1981). *Creative imagination imagery actionbook.* Starkville, MS: Allan Associates.

Khatena, J. (1982). *Educational psychology of the gifted.* New York: John Wiley.

Khatena, J. (1983a). Multidimensional interactive creative imagination imagery model. (Unpublished figure, Mississippi State University).

Khatena, J. (1983b). Relationship of individual-environment dimensions illumed by the cosmic. (Unpublished figure, Mississippi State University).

Khatena, J. (1983c). Analogy, imagery and the creative imagination. *Journal of Mental Imagery, 7* (1), 127-134.

Khatena, J. (1984). *Imagery and creative imagination.* Buffalo, NY: Bearly Limited.

Khatena, J. & Barbour, R. L. (1972). Training music majors in college to think creatively with sounds and words. *Psychological Reports, 30,* 105-106.

Khatena, J. & Bellarosa, A. (1979). Sex differences, sense modality and production of original verbal images. *Perceptual and Motor Skills, 47,* 1336.

Khatena, J. & Dickerson, E. C. (1973). Training sixth grade children to think creatively with sounds and words. *Psychological reports, 32,* 841-842.

Khatena, J. & Fisher, S. (1974). A four year study of children's responses to onomatopoeic stimuli. *Perceptual and Motor Skills, 39,* 1002.

Khatena, J. & Parnes, S. (1974). Applied imagination and the production of original verbal images. *Perceptual and Motor Skills, 38,* 130.

Khatena, J. & Parvizand, A. (1983). Production of original verbal images and repeated presentation of sound stimuli. *Perceptual and Motor Skills, 56,* 221-222.

Khatena, J. & Torrance, E. P. (1973). *Thinking creatively with sounds and words: Norms-technical manual* (research ed.). Lexington, MA: Personnel Press (now available through Bensenville, IL: Scholastic Testing Service, reprinted, 1981).

Khatena, J. & Torrance, E. P. (1976). *Manual for Khatena-Torrance creative perception inventory.* Chicago, IL: Stoelting.

Khatena, J. & Zetenyi, T. (1977a). Originality of Hungarians and Americans as measured by sounds and images. *Perceptual and Motor Skills, 44,* 374.

Khatena, J. & Zetenyi, T. (1977b). Originality and perceptual set: Comparative study of Hungarians and Americans. *Perceptual and Motor Skills, 44,* 777-778.

Khatena, J. & Zetenyi, T. (1983). Production of non-sound images given sound stimuli in a cross-cultural setting. *Perceptual and Motor Skills, 56,* 505-506.

Kubzanski, P. E. (1961). Creativity, imagery and sensory deprivation. *Acta Psychologia, 19,* 507-508.

Land, G. (1973). *Grow or die: The unifying principle of transformation.* New York: Random House.

Lane, J. B. (1975). Imagination and personality: the multi-trait investigation of a new measure of imagery control. (Doctoral dissertation, University of Minnesota, 1974). *Dissertation Abstract International, 35B,* 6099. (University Microfilms No. DA 12105.)

Leonard, G. & Lindauer, M. S. (1973). Aesthetic participation and imagery arousal. *Perceptual and Motor Skills, 36,* 977-978.

Lindauer, M. S. (1972). The sensory attributes and functions of imagery and imagery evoking stimuli. In P. W. Sheehan (Ed.), *The function and nature of imagery* (pp. 131-147). New York: Academic Press.

McKellar, P. (1957). *Imagination and thinking.* New York: Basic Books.

McKellar, P. (1972). Imagery from the standpoint of introspection. In P. W. Sheehan (Ed.), *The function and nature of imagery* (pp. 35-61). New York: Academic Press.

McKellar, P. (1977). Autonomy, imagery and dissociation. *Journal of Mental Imagery, 1* (1), 93-108.

Osborn, A. F. (1963). *Applied imagination.* New York: Charles Scribners.

Paivio, A. (1971). *Imagery and verbal processes.* New York: Holt, Rinehart and Winston.

Parnes, S. J. (1967a). *Creative behavior guidebook.* New York: Charles Scribners.

Parnes, S. J. (1967b). *Creative behavior workbook.* New York: Charles Scribners.

Parrish, J. K. (1981). The effects of preparation and incubation upon production or original verbal images. (Doctoral dissertation, Mississippi State University) *Dissertation Abstract International, 42A,* 1065. (University Microfilms No. DA 19213.)

Pribram, K. H. (1978). What the fuss is all about. *Revision, 1,* (3-4), 14-18.

Rhodes, M. (1961). An analysis of creativity. *Phi Delta Kappan, 42* (7), 305-310.

Ribot, T. (1906). *Essays on the creative imagination.* London: Kegan and Paul.

Richardson, A. (1969). *Mental imagery.* New York: Springer.

Roweton, W. E. (1973). *Creativity: A review of theory and research.* Buffalo, New York: Creative Education Foundation (Occasional paper no. 7).

Rossman, J. (1931). *The psychology of the inventor.* (rev. ed.) Washington, DC: Inventors.

Rugg, H. (1963). *Imagination: An inquiry into the sources and conditions that stimulate creativity.* New York: Harper & Row.

Sajjadi-Bafghi, S. H. (1984). Effects of time press and imagery control on creativity in the production of verbal originality and analogy (Doctoral dissertation, Mississippi State University). *Dissertation Abstracts International, 45/11A,* 3311. (University Microfilms No. DA 28152.)

Schmeidler, G. R. (1965). Visual imagery correlated to a measure of creativity. *Journal of Consulting Psychology, 29,* 78080.

Sheehan, P. W., Ashton, R. & White, K. (1983). Assessment of mental imagery. In A. A. Sheik (Ed.), *Imagery: Current theory, research and application* (pp. 189-221). New York: John Wiley.

Sheikh, A. A. (1977). Mental images: Ghosts of sensations? *Journal of Mental Imagery, 1* (1), 1-4.

Simonton, D. K. (1978). The eminent genius in history: The critical role of creative development. *Gifted Child Quarterly, 22* (2), 187-195.

Small, L. H. (1984). Effects of a positive thinking approach to stress management on the production of original verbal images (Doctoral dissertation, Mississippi State University). *Dissertation Abstracts International, 45A,* 2813. (University Microfilms No. DA 28155.)

Spearman, C. (1930). *Creative Mind.* London: Cambridge University Press.

Starkweather, E. K. (1971). Creativity research instruments designed for use with preschool children. *Journal of Creative Behavior, 5* (4), 245-255.

Teater, T. F. (1982). Preceding interrupted tactile perceptual activity effects on tactile references on verbal imagery. (Doctoral dissertation, Mississippi State University.) *Dissertation Abstract International, 43A.* 739 University Microfilms No. DA 17245.)

Torrance, E. P. (1962). *Guiding creative talent.* Englewood-Cliffs, NJ: Prentice-Hall.

Torrance, E. P. (1967). Understanding the fourth grade slump in creative thinking. (Final report on cooperative research project No. 994, USDE.) Unpublished manuscript, University of Georgia.

Torrance, E. P. (1968). A longitudinal examination of the fourth grade slump in creativity. *Gifted Child Quarterly, 12* (4), 195-199.

Torrance, E. P. (1974). *Torrance tests of creative thinking: Norms-technical manual.* Lexington, MA: Personnel Press. (Now available from Bensenville, IL: Scholastic Testing Service, 1981.)

Torrance, E. P. & Hall, L. K. (1980). Assessing the further reaches of creative potential. *Journal of Creative Behavior, 14* (1), 1-19.

Torrance, E. P. & Khatena, J. (1969). Originality of imagery in identifying creative talent in music. *Gifted Child Quarterly, 13* (1), 3-8.

Torrance, E. P., Khatena, J., & Cunnington, B. F. (1973). *Thinking Creatively with sounds and words.* Lexington, MA: Personnel Scholastic Testing Service, 1981).

Treffinger, D. J., Isaksen, S. G., & Firestien, R. L. (1983). Theoretical perspectives on creative learning and its facilitation: An overview. *Journal of Creative Behavior, 17* (1), 9-17.

Vargiu, J. (1977). Creativity: The purposeful imagination. *Synthesis, 3-4, 17-53.*

White, K., Sheehan, P. W., & Ashton, R. (1977). Imagery assessment: A survey of self-report measures. *Journal of Mental Imagery, 1* (1), 145-169.

Yazdani, N. N. (1984). The effect of audiovisual interference on two cerebral hemispheres and production of original verbal images. (Doctoral dissertation, Mississippi State University.) *Dissertation Abstracts International, 45A,* 1080. (University Microfilms No. DA 15755.)

15

Creative Product Analysis: Testing a Model by Developing a Judging Instrument

Susan P. Besemer
State University College at Fredonia

Karen O'Quin
State University College at Buffalo

An artist should think of himself primarily as a craftsman, a "maker," not an "inspired" genius . . . he can or should consciously think about . . . how to make the art object as well as possible, so that it may become a durable object, permanently "on hand" in the world.

Auden, 1971

When people are being creative, they make things: inventions, works of art, soups or sonnets. While these types of products differ in many ways, they are alike in that they manifest the spark of energy and enthusiasm that characterizes the creative process. The product of the creative processes employed by creative persons or groups is the artifact remaining which proves the process.

Given the premise that everyone has a degree of creativity in his or her personality, it follows that each product made by a human being reflects the creative ability of that person. Since we are not all equally creative, our products reflect the varying degrees of our creativeness. One product might be more or less creative than the norm for a person, and the individual's norm will, of course, be more or less creative than that of others in the society. But each time a person makes something new, that creative product reflects the spark of the creative process.

It was this basic reasoning that led the early creativity theoreticians and scientists to view the creative product as a window through which they could peek at the process of creativity, and at the creative personality.

Donald W. MacKinnon (1978), in his review of studies of creative scientists, discussed the need for empirical research in the study of creativity. He pointed to the importance of studying the process, the person, the product, and the environmental setting (press) for creativity. In particular, he emphasized the need to study the product:

In a very real sense, then, the study of creative products is the basis upon which all research on creativity rests and, until this foundation is more solidly built than it is at present, all creativity research will leave something to be desired. (MacKinnon, 1978, p. 187).

However, both before and after the publication of this work, the majority of scholarly attention has continued to be aimed at efforts to clarify the process and to understand and nurture the person. More recently in the work of Amabile (1979) and others, social psychologists have considered the environmental and organizational factors that motivate persons to manifest or subdue their natural creativity.

In an initial search of the literature (Besemer & Treffinger, 1981) only a few empirical studies were discovered (Taylor & Sandler, 1972; Ward & Cox, 1974) which attempted to isolate or describe the characteristics of creative products. Many theoretical positions were discussed by experts in various disciplines regarding the characteristics which they felt made products in their field creative, but no studies were identified which attempted to focus away from the individual disciplines in order to identify the characteristics of creative products in general.

Studies are now appearing which empirically identify the characteristics of products in a single field (Pearlman, 1983a) but the need still exists for a broader view across disciplines. Pearlman devised an instrument to be used by teachers in assessing the level of creativity in products created by their sixth-grade students. He appears to set aside the need for novelty in product analysis in reaction against overemphasizing the divergent attributes of creative products. Pearlman states:

> It is argued that novelty, statistical infrequency, large numbers of responses, several types of responses, and/or associative or divergent thinking, are not adequate or sufficient as descriptors of the creative product . . . A creative product must be workable, efficient and significant in satisfying a goal. (Pearlman, 1983a, p. 215).

The criteria outlined on the instrument (which asked teachers to rank order their students in groups from high to low) were the ones cited above, "workable, efficient, and significant in satisfying a goal." Teachers, looking at the convergent side of product analysis, might overlook the importance of the novel response.

While we may be grateful for Pearlman's (1983b) empirical seriousness in attempting to test his product analysis model, it seems to be focused almost exclusively on the convergent attributes of creative products.

Interesting research continues to take place, but efforts to extend scientific validity to the theoretical constructs of the scholars interested in this field are still few. Because of the relative scarcity of such empirical research, efforts have taken place to establish first reliability and then validity of a creative product analysis model (Besemer & Treffinger, 1981).

In an effort to understand the characteristics of creative products, the model developed, The *Creative Product Analysis Matrix (CPAM),* proposed that groups of related attributes (originally called "criteria") cluster along three different, but interrelated, dimensions: 1) Novelty, 2) Resolution, and 3) Elaboration and Synthesis. The Novelty of a product refers to the degree of originality of the product in terms of new concepts, new processes, or new materials used. The Resolution of a product reflects the degree to which the product resolves the problem implied by its creation. This dimension discusses how well the product does its job and how useful the product is. The dimension termed Elaboration and Synthesis describes the stylistic attributes of the product, focusing on aspects of complexity or elaboration of the product's conception, and the refinement, synthesis and elegance shown in its manifestation.

An interesting article appeared in the British philosophical journal *Inquiry* (Briskman, 1980). The author proposed a model for evaluating creative products. Briskman identified four characteristics which seemed to him to be necessary to term a product a "creative" one. These are its novelty, its value in solving a problem, its ability to be favorably evaluated by meeting "certain exacting standards which are themselves part of the background it partially supplants," and its ability to transcend the reality of the tradition out of which it grows (Briskman, 1980, p. 97). These characteristics stress the importance of the relevance and appropriateness of the solution offered by the product.

> . . . the novelty of a product is clearly only a necessary condition of its creativity, not a sufficient condition: for the madman who, in Russell's apt phrase, believes himself to be a poached egg may very well be uttering a novel thought, but few of us, I imagine, would want to say that he was producing a creative one. So if novelty is not enough, what ingredients need to be added in order to get creativity? (Briskman, 1980, p. 95).

Briskman then points to the way that the creative product improves upon the background from which it has sprung. This is the characteristic of Resolution (Besemer & Treffinger, 1981) which is addressed as a feature sought by Rogers (1983) in his discussion of the diffusion of innovations.

Briskman (1980) used the word "creative" to denote a level of achievement which is beyond the ability of the average person. But the characteristics he identified in the product also bear an interesting similarity to the three dimensions of the *CPAM.* As Briskman stated so unequivocally, "creative people and creative process can only be identified *via* our prior identification of their scientific or artistic *products* as themselves creative" (Briskman, 1980, p. 89).

He presents a persuasive argument to support the study of the product, and presents a seemingly viable model from the point of view of the philosopher. But for the scientist, it still wants the test of empirical study.

The empirical research of Ekvall & Parnes (1984) discusses the effects of training for creativity on the ability of engineers and designers to create products that met "real life" criteria. Such criteria implied the acceptability of the products as solutions for real life industrial design problems. Using the standards of Originality, Usefulness, and Elegance, Ekvall & Parnes requested that impartial but very expert judges evaluate the products of the trained and control groups of engineers. It is interesting to note that Ekvall & Parnes selected criteria that concur with those used in the *CPAM.* Originality obviously corresponds to Novelty, Usefulness is another expression of Resolution, and Elegance, while not the whole cloth of Elaboration and Synthesis, is indeed an important part of the weave.

In his considerable research on the diffusion of innovations, Everett M. Rogers has given much study and thought to the ways that novel ideas (innovations) gain acceptance in the cultural environment. In his 1983 monograph, *Diffusion of Innovations,* Rogers defines an innovation as "an idea, practice, or object that is perceived as new by an individual or other unit of adoption" (Rogers, 1983, p. 11). Innovations, then, are creative products which by definition have an element of perceived newness about them. Rogers states five empirically-tested characteristics of innovations. These are the product's relative advantage, compatibility, complexity, trialability, and observability (Rogers, 1983, p. 15-16).

This construct is related in several ways to the *CPAM.* First, there is the notion of Novelty implicit in the innovation. This characteristic may almost go without notice because of its obvious connection. Second, several aspects of the Rogers' model have particular similarity to the dimension of Resolution. Finally, one characteristic which was cited by Rogers as influencing the rate of diffusion of innovation relates to the dimension of the *CPAM* called Elaboration and Synthesis. This characteristic is "complexity." Rogers maintains that the level of complexity of the innovation has a negative effect on the rate of acceptance of the innovation. After a more complete discussion of the characteristics of the *CPAM,* the connections between the two models will be outlined.

Teresa M. Amabile (1982), the social psychologist whose interest is in the environment which facilitates the expression of creativity, has also expressed interest in the product as a manifestation of the process and the personality. She states:

> *Thus, a product-centered operational definition is clearly most useful for empirical research in creativity.*

And from the same article:

> *Clearly, there must be particular characteristics of attitude statements of persons or products that observers systematically look to in rating them on scales . . .* (Amabile, 1982, p. 1001).

Considering the degree of consensus among experts in creativity research that the most favored approach to the study of creativity is to take place through the product, the question arises as to why so few empirical studies have been made to try to establish those "particular characteristics" of products which make them "creative." There are now approximately thirty years of creativity research, yet we still seem to be rank beginners in establishing assessments to adequately detect creativity in products.

Why is this? Is it because the problem is too difficult? It is certainly difficult. First, proposing a set of characteristics is difficult, then getting any agreement among experts about the rightness of the characteristics is difficult. Then developing and testing a judging instrument to test not people, nor process, nor even product, but to test the correctness of the characteristics themselves is a long and complex job.

Assuming agreement and the reliability of the choice of characteristics among users of the instrument, it still remains to test the validity of the instrument by comparing expert judges' responses to those gathered by other users of the instrument.

But perhaps the reason for the lack of empirical research in this area is because the problem is too easy. We all know and can recognize a creative product when we see one. MacKinnon pointed to this ironic twist when he stated:

> In short, it would appear that the explicit determination of the qualities which identify creative products has been largely neglected just because we implicitly know—or feel we know—a creative product when we see it. (MacKinnon, 1975, p. 69).

It seems that the characteristics are so well-known on an intuitive level that stating them seems unnecessary. This, of course, prevents the study from moving out of the realm of theory into that of empirical science. It also allows for some unwelcome surprises when perceived definitions are not shared by judges.

Creative Product Analysis Matrix

Because, then, of the need for a common vocabulary with which to speak, the *Creative Product Analysis Matrix* (Besemer & Treffinger, 1981) may offer a balanced approach to systematically looking at creative products.

Novelty

The most obvious cluster of characteristics or attributes in the *CPAM,* or any other schema for detecting creativity in products, is labeled Novelty.

Three facets of Novelty are proposed. The first concerns itself with the degree of Originality illustrated in the product. The second facet, termed Germinal, considers the likelihood of other products being created as spin-offs or off-shoots of this product. A third attribute or characteristic of creative products is seen only after the product has been in existence for some time. Extremely influential creative products may be termed Transformational which suggests the impact upon the culture (and perhaps on other cultures) of a creative product. See I. A. Taylor's (1975) important conceptualization of this idea. It is easy to observe Transformational qualities in a product like the printing press or the Xerox process. Still to be seen are the qualities of transforming the world view which will be put in motion by the microcomputer.

Resolution

A second dimension of the *CPAM* considers the degree of Resolution in the product. To what degree does the product as it stands respond to the needs implied by the problem solved by the product's creator? Terms describing such characteristics fall into this category. The facets proposed under the dimension of Resolution included the Adequacy of the product, its Appropriateness, its Logical qualities, its Usefulness, and its Valuable characteristics.

An Adequate product is one that answers *enough* of the needs of the problematic situation to be considered a solution. The meaning of the term Appropriate as it applies to products is the degree to which the solution or product *fits* or *applies to* the problematic situation. Logicalness is a characteristic which relates to the products following of standard conventions within the field or discipline. It is a basic level of orderliness without which it will be difficult to place a product within the group of products of the discipline. A painting, for example, must involve paint upon a surface. If an artwork does not meet these two logical rules, it is not a "painting." Usefulness is a characteristic sought in creative products. Even artworks are useful in some ways, perhaps as expressions of the artist's point of view, or as decorations. Usefulness implies applicability of the product to the world. Valuableness is the final characteristic of the dimension *Resolution.* This characteristic implies a worth based upon the ability of the product to fill a need: financial, physical, social, or psychological. When these characteristics are present in a product, the needs of Resolution are met, and the product can be seen to be more creative in the balanced sense of the word.

Elaboration and Synthesis

The final dimension of the three *CPAM* dimensions reflects the stylistic attributes of the product. This dimension, which is termed Elaboration and Synthesis, has not been explored in depth outside the area of art and aesthetics. Stylistic considerations examine how a product is presented, the way the product is manifested so that it can be used or interacted with. Rogers' (1983) final characteristic of innovations is their Complexity. This may be seen to be a feature of the dimension of Elaboration and Synthesis because it relates to the stylistic characteristics of the product. The attribute of Complexity is one which Rogers considers to be a negative factor in terms of the diffusion of innovations. Seen in another way, however, the conceptually Complex product expressed simply is a very high level creative product. In fact, many of the characteristics in the dimension of Elaboration and Synthesis express either the divergence of Complexity or the convergence of elegance. The term "Elegant" is frequently used to convey high praise of simply-expressed Complexity as in the Ekvall & Parnes (1984) studies. Parsimony of style is a frequently sought virtue.

Other attributes of successful creative products include their Attractive, Expressive and Organic qualities. The latter characteristic is suggestive of a well-integrated part-to-whole relationship. All parts of the product seem to fit well with each other. An Organic product which is well-crafted or well-made is one that has been carefully finished and at the most refined level that its creator can produce at this point in time. Products which are Attractive are those which catch the attention of the user, listener or viewer. The attraction of the product is not always that of beauty, but may involve charm or spontaneity. Humor or playfulness are equally effective indicators of the Attractive quality. Expressive products communicate their meaning quickly to the user, listener or viewer. Such products "get their message across" in a clear, direct way. This attribute helps to make the product more adoptable since it is more understandable, in contrast to Rogers' (1983) negatively "Complex" or complicated product.

Rogers' Work and the CPAM:

Four of Rogers' five characteristics of innovations bear a relationship to the *Resolution* dimension of the *CPAM.* These are the product's relative advantage, compatibility, complexity, trialability, and observability (Rogers, 1983, p. 15-16). Complexity is the only factor which may be seen as relating to the third dimension of the *CPAM* model, Elaboration and Synthesis.

Rogers' characteristic termed "Relative Advantage" considers the extent to which the product is perceived as superior to the previous one. This is related to two characteristics in the *CPAM.* The first is the attribute of Usefulness. An innovation which is Useful shows an immediate Relative Advantage. The second related characteristic is to Valuable that it fills a financial, physical, social or psychological need.

Rogers' characteristic of Compatibility is similar to the *CPAM*'s attribute termed Approp-riate. The meaning of the term Appropriate as it applies to products is the degree to which the solution or product *fits* or *applies to* the problematic situation. Rogers' meaning for Compatibility is "the degree to which an innovation is perceived as being consistent with the existing values . . . needs of potential adopters (Rogers, 1983, p. 15). A product's Observability is "the degree to which the results of an innovation are visible to others" (Rogers, 1983, p. 16). Trialability, obviously related to Observability, is for Rogers the characteristic of successful innovations that allows for limited experimental usage by the potential adopters of the inno-vation before they make a firm commitment to adopting it. Trialability and Observability seem to be related to the *CPAM*'s proposed characteristic Adequate. This attribute would certainly be identifiable through the product's "Trialability."

Characteristics like the ones now under discussion may seem to be too mundane to be considered when discussing creativity. But, as Rogers' extensive research shows, innovations lacking some of these characteristics were unsuccessful, despite other excellent characteristics. The characteristic of Logicalness is a case in point. While seemingly opposite to "creativeness," Logicalness is a characteristic without which it will be difficult to demonstrate a product's "relative advantage" over previous products. When these characteristics are present in a product, the needs of Resolution are met, and the product can be seen to be more creative in the balanced sense of the word.

Rationale

Having established the need for empirical studies to identify the attributes of creative products, we ought to apply scientific psychological techniques to the historical and theoretical schol-arship extant. The purpose of the present paper is to present empirical evidence relating to the dimensions of the *CPAM* discussed above. We sought to determine whether or not our subjects would evaluate creative products in a manner consistent with the model. We looked to determine, for instance, whether the three dimensions of the *CPAM* would actually be used in evaluating products.

We chose a variety of creative products on which to base our preliminary investigations. We wanted to examine similarities and differences among creative products. We chose three categories of products which were both readily accessible and which sampled some of the enormous variety available (letter openers, cartoons, and a well-known artwork at a local art museum).

We administered an experimental version of the judging instrument based on the model, called the *CPAM* Adjective Checklist, which contains 110 adjectives and adjectival phrases which sample the facets of the three dimensions discussed above: Novelty, Resolution, and Elaboration and Synthesis.

Overview of the Four Studies

The informed consent statement stated that the study involved describing creative products. Subjects received optical scanning sheets and rating instructions. They did not record their names, and were assured of anonymity.

Objects were rated one at a time. The rating instructions read: "For each of the following words, please indicate how well you feel the word *describes* the object which you are consid-ering. Please use this scale: 1) does not describe the object at all, 2) describes the object a little, 3) describes the object well, 4) describes the object extremely well. For instance, if you think the word "clever" describes the object a little, mark a 2 on your answer sheet. Please try to answer every item. Do not leave any blank."

The experimenter asked subjects to give their first impressions on each word, and not to spend too much time on each one. It took approximately twenty minutes to rate each object on 110 different words.

At the end of each study, subjects were given a complete explanation of the theoretical basis for the study.

Subscale Creation

The 110 words were divided, on the basis of theoretical content, into 12 subscales. Two departures from the model were made at this point. First, because of the difficulty of measuring the "expressive" facet of the Elaboration and Synthesis dimension, it was not included in the subscales. Second, it was not possible, given the measuring instrument, to differentiate between "elegant" and "organic," so they were combined into one subscale.

Table One.

Items retained in subscales after reliability analyses.

NOVELTY	**Original**	**Germinal**	**Startling**
	Novel	Trendsetting	Startling
	Unusual	Influential	Surprising
	Unique	Revolutionary	Amazing
	Original	Radical	
	Ingenious		

RESOLUTION	**Logical**	**Useful**	
	Logical	Effective	
	Makes sense	Functional	
	Correct	Feasible	
	Relevant	Durable	
	Appropriate	Operable	
		Useable	
		Useful	
		Workable	

ELABORATION & SYNTHESIS	**Elegant/Organic**	**Attractive**	**Well-Crafted**
	Harmonious	Delightful	Well-made
	Balanced	Beautiful	Well-crafted
	Restful	Charming	Interesting
	Just right	Attractive	
	Elegant	Playful	
	Deep	Spontaneous	
	Subtle		
	Unified		
	Complete		
	Refined		
	Fluent		
	Clear		
	Organic		

Table Two.

Coefficient alphas for subscales in four studies.

Object	Study 1 Openers			Study 2 Art Work	Study 3 Cartoons			Study 4 Openers			Average
	1	2	3	1	2	3	1	2	3		

Sub-Scales											
Original	.70	.79	.69	.82	.69	.76	.87	.68	.78	.74	.75
Germinal	.74	.65	.77	.59	.47	.81	.75	.73	.82	.79	.71
Startling	.69	.76	.61	.61	.81	.78	.88	.29	.83	.88	.71
Logical	.80	.77	.67	.90	.81	.70	.72	.83	.79	.53	.75
Useful	.84	.82	.74	.79	.83	.90	.80	.83	.76	.90	.82
Elegant	.86	.80	.85	.83	.79	.74	.78	.79	.83	.80	.81
Attractive	.81	.63	.86	.69	.69	.83	.61	.73	.85	.81	.75
Well-Crafted	.60	.83	.76	.81	.63	.79	.85	.75	.77	.55	.73

Averages for Studies	.76	.76	.74	.76	.72	.79	.78	.70	.80	.75	.76

Note: All cell entries are coefficient alphas (Cronbach, 1951).

The 12 subscales were subjected to reliability analyses to determine the extent to which each subscale was internally consistent. Iterative reliability analyses made clear that negative words, although they matched the subscales in theoretical content, were not used by subjects in the same complex way as positive words. In fact, the negative words in the total scale eventually formed a single "negativity" scale which yielded average internal consistencies (Cronbach's alpha; Cronbach, 1951) of .85, .97, .90 and .88 in Study 1 through Study 4, respectively. This result seemed to be an artifact of the type of measurement used; because it had no theoretical meaning, the "negativity" scale was not considered further.

Reliability analyses of the other subscales led to their condensation into eight subscales which produced, with few exceptions, consistently high reliabilities for all objects rated in the four studies. The items in the subscales are presented in Table One. Coefficient alphas (Cronbach, 1951) for each subscale are presented in Table Two. As may be seen, the reliabilities are generally quite high. Even when a coefficient is low for a particular object in a particular sample, corresponding coefficients are high for different objects in the same sample. Thus we feel confident that the eight subscales are internally consistent across different creative products in different samples.

How well do the subscales match the theoretical dimensions of the *CPAM*? They match fairly well, especially for the Novelty dimension. The corresponding facets of the Novelty dimensions are clearly represented by the Original and Germinal subscales. The Transformational facet is more problematic. The Startling subscale is relevant to the concept, defined as "the extent to which the product forces a new way of looking at the world" (Besemer & Treffinger, 1981, p. 167), yet is not identical in content.

The Resolution dimension is also fairly well supported by the structure of the subscales. Two of the five Resolution facets are represented: Logical and Useful. However, the Logical

Table Three.

Means, standard deviations, results of post hoc analyses for subscale scores.

Object	Study 1 Openers			Study 2 Art Work	Study 3 Cartoons			Study 4 Openers		
	1	2	3	1	1	2	3	1	2	3
Sub-Scales										
Original	9.53a	13.33b	8.94a	16.44	12.04	12.35	12.28	10.88	11.10	10.50
S.D.	3.35	4.09	3.39	3.90	3.31	4.03	4.66	3.24	3.77	3.71
Germinal	6.49ab	6.99a	5.60b	9.72	6.77a	8.45b	6.79a	6.18	6.64	6.52
S.D.	2.74	2.66	2.28	2.99	2.17	3.21	2.52	2.31	3.07	3.04
Startling	4.32a	5.57b	4.20a	8.39	5.20	5.68	6.00	4.28a	5.61ab	6.39b
S.D.	2.02	2.51	1.57	1.98	2.42	2.33	2.96	1.53	2.57	2.97
Logical	11.86	11.46	12.18	10.50	11.38ab	11.68a	9.74b	10.72a	9.33b	10.61ab
S.D.	3.00	3.02	2.91	4.55	3.13	3.32	2.47	2.74	2.17	3.13
Useful	23.91	24.43	25.47	17.55	16.62	17.29	15.02	23.81	21.90	22.63
S.D.	5.24	4.36	4.36	5.53	5.00	5.38	4.92	4.70	6.36	4.24
Elegant	23.21	21.78	22.85	26.99	23.43	24.42	22.06	21.99a	19.37	20.27ab
S.D.	7.16	6.25	7.00	7.45	6.38	6.31	6.30	5.80	5.56	6.35
Attractive	9.13	9.72	9.33	15.73	12.67	12.84	11.53	9.06	10.11	9.39
S.D.	3.80	3.29	3.85	3.53	3.84	4.40	3.03	3.11	3.45	3.81
Well-Crafted	6.26a	8.49b	6.97a	10.28	7.53	7.16	7.00	6.89	6.45	7.78
S.D.	2.15	2.71	2.23	2.32	2.48	2.52	2.87	2.19	1.88	2.44

Note: For each variable within each study, means with different subscripts differ at the .05 level (Tukey).

subscale in the present studies combines two of the theoretical facets (Logical and Appropriate). The Valuable subscale was not internally consistent in any of the present studies; however, it was very short (3 items). We will not completely abandon the facet until further attempts are made to improve measurement. The Adequate facet received no support in any of the present studies, perhaps for an interesting artifactual reason. We noticed that the word "Adequate" correlated with the *negative* words in the total scale. This result was especially strong for the ratings of the art work. Apparently, "Adequate" can be seen in a negative light. ("His work is merely adequate" could be a negatively critical comment on its quality.) This artifact may be dealt with in the future by using bipolar adjectives rather than absolute ratings (inadequate-adequate, for example). We will discuss this measurement change further below.

The Elaboration and Synthesis dimension was also fairly well supported. As discussed above, the Elegant and Organic facets were combined, and yielded a reliable subscale. The Attractive facet also yielded a reliable subscale which, as predicted, contained items relating to playfulness and spontaneity as well as beauty. Finally, the Well-crafted facet also yielded a subscale which was quite reliable despite its short length. Complexity did not yield a reliable subscale, but too few adjectives measuring complexity were included in the total scale.

Means and standard deviations for each subscale for objects in each of the four studies are presented in Table Three. Results of repeated-measures analyses of variance comparing means in each study will be presented below.

Although no statistical tests of means in different samples were performed, it is interesting to compare the means in Table Three across the four studies. Note, for example, that the art work is higher on Novelty than the other classes of objects: Original, Germinal and Startling are all higher for the art work. Apparently, our subjects considered the art work to be much more novel than, for example, any of the letter openers. On the stylistic facets, Refined, Attractive and Well-crafted, the art work produced higher means than those for any of the other products. Perhaps more surprising is the fact that the art work yielded means that were fairly close to the openers on the facet of Logical. It seems that even art must be logical. Note also in Table Three that the letter openers yielded higher ratings of Usefulness than the art work and the cartoons. On the Attractive subscale, the art work is highest, the cartoons intermediate and the openers lowest.

At this point, let us consider each of the four studies in more detail.

Study One

Thirty-five subjects (approximately equal numbers of males and females) were undergraduate students at the State University of New York, College at Buffalo (SUCB), 17 of whom were enrolled in creative studies courses, and 18 of whom were enrolled in an introductory psychology course. All students received participation credit for their courses.

Subjects rated three different letter openers. The first was a knife-like clear plastic letter opener with a magnifying glass in the handle. The second was a small, rectangular white plastic opener sheathing a razor blade which cut very efficiently. The third was a traditional knife-like metal opener with a slightly-decorated handle.

One-way repeated-measures analyses of variance (ANOVAS) on the 8 subscales, using the three types of objects as the independent variable, yielded significant main effects on four variables: Original, $F(2,68) = 22.24$, $p < .0001$; Germinal, $F(2,68) = 6.56$, $p < .003$; Startling, $F(2,68) = 8.92$, $p < .0005$; and Well-Crafted, $F(2,68) = 45.32$, $p < .0003$.

Means and results of the post hoc analyses are presented in Table Three. As may be seen, the razor blade opener was rated as more Original, Startling, and more Well-Crafted than the other two openers.

In order to determine the reliability of each subscale across objects, correlations were computed for each subscale for all three objects (three "interobject correlations" per subscale). The average interobject correlation for each subscale was: Original .28; Germinal .61; Startling .50; Logical .53; Useful .58; Elegant .82; Attractive .39; and Well-Crafted .17. The average correlation for Well-Crafted was low, perhaps because it is a short subscale.

These correlations, because they represent the same scale used to rate different objects, were expected to be moderately high. However, correlations that are very high would tend to obscure differences among objects. It is not true that if one rates one letter opener high on Originality that one must necessarily rate a second opener high on the same subscale. Thus, moderate correlations were seen as satisfactory.

Finally, in order to examine the extent to which the subscales were independent, a factor analysis was performed (principal factor, Varimax rotation) for each of the three objects. Factor analysis was not seen as a test of the CPAM, *per se*, because the three dimensions of the

---

Table Four.

Factor loadings after Varimax rotation for subscales for each object in Study 1 (Letter Openers).

Object 1 (Magnifying Glass Opener)

Subscale	Factor 1	Factor 2
Original	.57	.15
Germinal	.81	.30
Startling	.79	.04
Logical	.23	.79
Useful	-.07	.78
Elegant	.47	.59
Attractive	.69	.09
Well-Crafted	.53	.54

Object 2 (Razor Blade Opener)

Subscale	Factor 1	Factor 2
Original	.38	.28
Germinal	.76	.28
Startling	.78	-.16
Logical	.14	.68
Useful	.14	.63
Elegant	.67	.41
Attractive	.61	.27
Well-Crafted	.75	.44

Object 3 (Traditional Opener)

Subscale	Factor 1	Factor 2	Factor 3
Original	.62	.01	-.03
Germinal	.80	.15	.14
Startling	.83	-.06	.25
Logical	.05	.02	.87
Useful	-.22	.49	.10
Elegant	.34	.51	.60
Attractive	.56	.49	.31
Well-Crafted	.52	.77	-.09

model are not theoretically independent. Nonetheless, the analysis was seen as offering an empirical examination of the way in which the subscales were related.

The results of the analyses are presented in Table Four. Note that the three Novelty subscales, Original, Germinal and Startling, consistently loaded on the same factor. However, the subscales of the Resolution and Elaboration and Synthesis dimensions did not seem to be consistently separate from each other. There was evidence (with the notable exception of the Attractive subscale) that they tended to load on a different factor than the Novelty items.

Study Two

Subjects were 18 female docents at a large art museum in Buffalo, New York. With the cooperation of the museum, 70 docents' participation was solicited by mail; with no follow-up letter, 18 questionnaires were returned (26%).

Subjects rated a single art work in the gallery, *Le Vocifèrant* ("The Loud One") by Jean DuBuffet. The work is painted sheet metal, in white, red, blue and black, resembling a person with many arms.

A factor analysis (principal factor, Varimax rotation) was performed to examine the relationships among the eight subscales. The results are presented in Table Five. Once more, the subscales of the Novelty dimension loaded on the same factor. The Resolution and Elaboration and Synthesis dimensions were not separate from each other; Attractive and Well-Crafted loaded on the same factor as the Novelty subscales.

Study Three

Subjects were 19 students (approximately equal numbers of males and females) from introductory psychology classes at SUCB. Subjects received extra credit points for their participation.

Subjects rated three cartoons. The first was an uncaptioned picture of a snow-filled desk paper weight; inside was an unhappy-looking little man with a snow shovel. The second cartoon, also uncaptioned, portrayed two tables in a restaurant; one with the label "Reserved," seated two serious people, while a second, labelled "Rowdy" seated a carousing couple. The third cartoon portrayed a number of anthropomorphized geometric shapes in a cocktail party scenario; a sphere said to a triangular shape, "Not *the* Bermuda triangle?"

Subjects were instructed to work through the booklet one cartoon at a time. They were asked not to look ahead until each cartoon was finished. The order of the three cartoons was counterbalanced to eliminate order effects.

Table Five.

Factor loadings after Varimax rotation for subscales for each object in Study 2 (Art Work).

Subscale	Factor 1	Factor 2
Original	-.49	.75
Germinal	.27	.56
Startling	.04	.90
Logical	.83	-.02
Useful	.94	.01
Elegant	.95	.11
Attractive	.11	.59
Well-Crafted	-.44	.55

One-way repeated-measures analyses of variance (ANOVAS) on the 8 subscales, using the three types of objects as the independent variable, yielded significant main effects for these variables: Germinal, $F(2,36) = 5.14$, $p < .02$; and Logical, $F(2,36) = 4.83$, $p < .02$. Means and results of the post hoc analyses are presented in Table Three. As may be seen, the second cartoon (Reserved vs. Rowdy restaurant tables) was seen to be more Germinal than the other two cartoons. For Logical, cartoon 1 and 2 did not differ, but 2 was seen as more Logical than 3.

The average interobject correlation for each subscale was: Original .68; Germinal .55; Startling .34; Logical .53; Useful .49, Elegant .74, Attractive .34 and Well-Crafted .30. As in Study 1, Well-Crafted had the lowest correlation, perhaps because of its length.

In order to examine relationships among the subscales, a factor analysis (principal factor, Varimax rotation) was performed for each of the three objects. Results are presented in Table Six.

Table Six.

Factor loadings after Varimax rotation for subscales for each object in Study 3 (Cartoons).

Object 1 (Paperweight Cartoon)

Subscale	Factor 1	Factor 2
Original	.34	.55
Germinal	.12	.82
Startling	.06	.77
Logical	.60	-.46
Useful	.87	.19
Elegant	.70	.60
Attractive	.69	.47
Well-Crafted	.78	.11

Object 2 (Restaurant Cartoon)

Subscale	Factor 1	Factor 2
Original	.45	.36
Germinal	.45	.72
Startling	.82	.20
Logical	.12	.84
Useful	.57	.74
Elegant	.38	.73
Attractive	.79	.31
Well-Crafted	.77	.31

Object 3 (Party Cartoon)

Subscale	Factor 1	Factor 2
Original	.87	.12
Germinal	.32	.50
Startling	.80	.29
Logical	.04	.76
Useful	.39	.79
Elegant	.48	.62
Attractive	.80	.28
Well-Crafted	.76	.46

Note that for the first cartoon, there is a clear separation between the Novelty dimension and the combined Resolution and Elaboration and Synthesis dimensions. However, cartoons 2 and 3 show a different factor structure, with no clear separation among the three dimensions of the model. We should not place great weight on these differences because of the small sample size, but it is interesting to note that both cartoons 2 and 3 involved puns, while the first cartoon involved an incongruity.

Study Four

Subjects were 18 undergraduate students, approximately equal numbers of male and female students participating, 13 of whom were enrolled in creative studies courses and 5 of whom were enrolled in introductory psychology. All subjects received extra credit points for their participation.

Subjects rated three different letter openers. The first was a clear plastic letter opener with a magnifying glass in the handle. The second was a small, rectangular white plastic opener sheathing a razor blade. The third was a heavy-duty, electric letter opener used in businesses. The order of presentation of the three openers was counterbalanced to avoid order effects.

One-way repeated-measures analyses of variance (ANOVAS) on the 8 subscales, using the three types of objects as the independent variable, yielded significant main effects on these variables: Startling, $F(2,34) = 7.10$, $p < .006$; Logical, $F(2,34) = 4.00$, $p < .03$; and Elegant, $F(2,34) = 5.59$, $p < .009$. Means and results of the post hoc analyses are presented in Table Three. As may be seen, the mechanical opener was rated as more Startling than the magnifying-glass opener. The magnifying glass opener was seen as more Logical and more Elegant than the razor-blade opener.

The average interobject correlation, a measure of stability across objects for each subscale, was: Original .71, Germinal .69, Startling .53, Logical .63, Useful .52, Elegant .84, Attractive .49, and Well-Crafted .31.

The results of the factor analyses (principal factor, Varimax rotation) for each object are presented in Table Seven. Here we see less consistent evidence for the *CPAM*, although the Novelty subscales load on the same factor in two of the three analyses. The Logical, Useful and Elegant subscales loaded on the same factor in all other analyses, but in this sample, they no longer did so. Speculation about reasons for the differences are limited by the small sample size.

General Discussion

Beyond the basic concept of using factor analysis to identify the component characteristics of creative products, what are the areas at the frontier of product analysis research? The importance of the problem has been established for many years. It seems surprising that until the convergence of this topic with that of identifying the proper creative climate (Amabile, 1982), there was little promise of finding breakthroughs. When Amabile, in replying to her question, "How do you know that something is creative?" states that one must "Ask someone who knows," (an expert judge, using intuitive or explicit standards for the field) she begs the question. Regardless of the accuracy of one's intuition, the informed judgment of expert judges, or the most complete theoretical models, without empirical evidence of characteristics common among creative products, the thoughts and words lack proof.

We now have merely the tantalizing beginnings of answers to the question, "What are the characteristics of the creative product?" In some respects the *CPAM* model is supported, especially with regard to the Novelty dimension. Original and Startling consistently loaded on the same factor, as predicted by the model, and were usually accompanied by Germinal.

Table Seven.

Factor loadings after Varimax rotation for subscales for each object in Study 1 (Letter Openers).

Object 1 (Magnifying Glass Opener)

Subscale	Factor 1	Factor 2	Factor 3
Original	.84	.53	-.15
Germinal	.33	.61	.38
Startling	.78	.07	.16
Logical	.11	.03	.86
Useful	.51	.17	.29
Elegant	.60	.16	.54
Attractive	.13	.37	.48
Well-Crafted	.15	.91	.07

Object 2 (Razor Blade Opener)

Subscale	Factor 1	Factor 2	Factor 3
Original	.87	.34	-.30
Germinal	.91	.09	.28
Startling	.85	.19	-.05
Logical	-.17	.19	.82
Useful	.09	.71	.07
Elegant	.51	.01	.71
Attractive	.83	.18	.10
Well-Crafted	.31	.80	.13

Object 3 (Mechanical Opener)

Subscale	Factor 1	Factor 2
Original	.98	.15
Germinal	.71	.39
Startling	.86	.09
Logical	.07	.99
Useful	.49	.33
Elegant	.57	.58
Attractive	.50	.41
Well-Crafted	.62	.57

However, Resolution and Elaboration and Synthesis, while their subscales often loaded on a different factor or factors than Novelty, did not consistently yield separate factors. These results suggest that modification of the *CPAM* Adjective Checklist will be necessary; we will discuss possible modifications below. Three dimensions often emerge which describe differing clusters of attributes. But, while some of the subscales which clustered together are not as tied to the original proposed fourteen criteria as would be hoped, they do reflect accurately the opinions of the subjects who considered the products and selected adjectives to describe them. We now have an empirical basis to test with more products and with more subjects. Clearly, the evaluation of creative products is multidimensional, but the evidence is not sufficient as yet to specify whether we have a two-dimensional or three-dimensional structure.

The evaluation instruments derived from the *CPAM* model have gone through several versions already. (For one version close to the instrument used in the present studies see

VanGundy, 1984). The semantic ambiguity of the adjectives in each version of the instrument has continued to cause problems of meaning for subjects as they first approach the evaluation. One concerned subject (from the Docent set) took the time to attach a note to her analysis:

> . . . I must admit that I find such things terribly inadequate. For example, there can be diverse interpretations of the modifiers themselves and what they describe can also differ. Are we looking at the object physically? emotionally? psychologically? or something to be merely "viewed?" (note from an Albright-Knox Docent, 5/06/84.)

The ambiguity in the present measuring instrument is also illustrated by the "negativity" scale—subjects seemed to find it difficult to find shades of meaning in the negative words, especially when used out of context.

For our subsequent research, the concept of Osgood's (1957) technique of semantic differential holds an appealing new potential solution to the problem of words out of context. Our next instrument will propose bipolar adjective concepts where the subject will select a point for each adjective on the continuum. We feel that this will make the test easier to administer, to score, and for subjects to complete. It also will cut down the number of adjective variables from 110 to perhaps 50. Needless to say, statistical analysis of the data will be much simplified. The following example provides a few sample items:

interesting $- 1 - 2 - 3 - 4 - 5 - 6 - 7 -$ boring
novel $- 1 - 2 - 3 - 4 - 5 - 6 - 7 -$ commonplace
radical $- 1 - 2 - 3 - 4 - 5 - 6 - 7 -$ old hat
refined $- 1 - 2 - 3 - 4 - 5 - 6 - 7 -$ crude
useful $- 1 - 2 - 3 - 4 - 5 - 6 - 7 -$ useless

It is interesting to note, however that the present results do not parallel those of Osgood et al. (1957, 1971), whose Evaluation, Activity and Potency factors are more general to the language of affective description, and not specific to descriptions of creative products. However, Osgood's Novelty scale serves as an inspiring model for the future.

Developing better judging instruments is only part of the problem of creative product analysis. The real purpose for analyzing products is to be able to train or teach people to produce better products. Amabile (1979) points to the question of training subjects in the standards which would eventually be used to evaluate the products when she indicates that in one of her studies, the only group which produced better products than those who did not anticipate evaluation was the group which was told upon what standards they would be evaluated. As she points out, the threat of evaluation is a constant fact of life in the modern world.

While we agree wholeheartedly with Amabile's thesis that the way to minimize these problems is to encourage children to seek the joy of creation for its own reward, it is nonetheless only fair to allow students and workers to discover upon what basis their products will be evaluated. Asking that evaluative judgments of products be based on inspiration or special guidance from "the Muse," while consistent with the traditional alchemical approach to art, does not jibe with today's insistence on accountability. In what office, factory, or university would one be expected to perform "blind" (without the benefit of being told on what basis your work was to be judged)? Substantial litigation rests on questions like this one in modern life. We hope that the CPAM and its measuring instrument can be used to give objective feedback about the quality of students' and workers' products. We do not want to kill the Muse by overscrutinizing her, but magic as an answer in science is less than satisfactory. Perhaps it is in the area of product analysis that the arts and sciences may join forces. In doing so we may enable ordinary folk to make their products more creative by attending to established standards of judgment.

The direction for future research holds many concerns, questions, and opportunities. Some of these which seem most pressing to the authors include further validation of the CPAM model by statistically identifying the most important characteristics of creative products and then comparing evaluations done by experts with those product evaluations done by consumers or lay judges. Statistical reliability studies could establish a more succinct set of predictive variables, a situation which will greatly facilitate future development and validation efforts.

Some new directions could investigate the validity of the model across a wide breadth of types of products, while others might investigate one type of product in-depth using evaluations both by expert judges and lay judges of a limited set of products.

Other research could aim at examining the nature of the attributes of Elaboration and Synthesis. Since these attributes do not load consistently together as a separate dimension, it might be fruitful to investigate circumstances under which they load with the Novelty subscales and those where they load with Resolution.

The ultimate goal of such research, of course, is to facilitate the training of students and workers to produce products that, when compared with those created by groups which have not received the training, could be judged to be more creative than those produced by control groups.

If the field of creative product analysis is to develop, it will be necessary to move far beyond what is currently done to 1) identify the attributes of creative products, 2) incorporate valid attributes into a consistent model for understanding, 3) refine and develop the model, and 4) train users in the techniques for production of more creative products.

References

Amabile, T. M. (1979). Effects of external evaluation on artistic creativity. *Journal of Personality and Social Psychology, 27,* 221-233.

Amabile, T. M. (1982). Social psychology of creativity: A consensual assessment technique. *Journal of Social Psychology, 43,* 997-1013.

Auden, W. H. (1971, April 11). Craftsman, artist, genius. *The Observer,* p. 9.

Besemer, S. P. & Treffinger, D. J. (1981). Analysis of creative products: review and synthesis. *Journal of Creative Behavior, 15,* 158-178.

Briskman, L. (1980). Creative product and creative process in science and art. *Inquiry, 23,* 83-106.

Cronbach, L. J. (1951). Coefficient alpha and the internal structure of tests. *Psychometrika, 16,* 297-334.

Ekvall, G. & Parnes, S. J. (1984). *Creative Problem Solving Methods in Product Development–A Second Experiment.* Stockholm, Sweden: The Swedish Council for Management and Work Life Issues.

MacKinnon, D. W. (1975). IPAR's contribution to the conceptualization and study of creativity. In I. A. Taylor & J. W. Getzels (Eds.), *Perspectives in creativity (pp. 60-89).* Chicago: Aldine.

MacKinnon, D. W. (1978). *In Search of Human Effectiveness: Identifying and Developing Creativity.* Buffalo, and Great Neck, NY: Creative Education Foundation and Creative Synergetics Association.

Osgood, C. E. (1971). Exploration in semantic space: A Personal diary. *The Journal of Social Issues, 27,* 5-64.

Osgood, C. E., Suci, G. J. & Tannenbaum, P. H. (1957). *The Measurement of meaning.* Urbana, IL: University of Illinois Press.

Pearlman, C. (1983a). Teachers as an informational resource in identifying and rating student creativity. *Education, 103,* 215-222.

Pearlman, C. (1983b). A Theoretical model for creativity. *Education, 103,* 294-305.

Rogers, E. M. (1983). *Diffusion of innovations.* (3rd ed.) New York: The Free Press.

Taylor, I. A. (1975). A retrospective view of creativity investigation. In I. A. Taylor & J. W. Getzels (Eds.), *Perspectives in creativity.* (pp. 1-36). Chicago: Aldine.

Taylor, I. A., & Sandler, B. J. (1972). Use of a creative product inventory for evaluating products of chemists. *Proceedings of the 80th Annual Convention of the American Psychological Association, 7,* 311-312.

VanGundy, A. B. (1984) *Managing group creativity: A Modular approach to problem solving.* New York: Amacom, American Management Associations.

Ward, W. C. & Cox, P. W. (1974). A field study of nonverbal creativity. *Journal of Personality, 42,* 202-219.

16

Organizational Creativity and Innovation

Arthur Van Gundy
University of Oklahoma

Creativity and innovation (C&I) are widely recognized as important aspects of human functioning at all levels–individual, group, organizational, and societal. Over the last three decades, researchers and theorists from psychology (e.g., Guilford, 1959), sociology (e.g., Merton, 1957), economics (e.g., Mansfield, 1963), and many other disciplines have written about and researched the causes and consequences of C&I in a variety of settings. Rogers (1983) notes that there are over 3,000 publications (both empirical and nonempirical) on the diffusion of innovations alone.

C&I are generally considered important for a healthy national economy and for increasing the quality of life (U. S. Department of Commerce, 1980). To meet the future needs facing the U. S. and the world, large investments of resources will be required to produce and implement creative solutions. However, because of the way societies are structured, much of the impetus for C&I will have to originate within complex organizations (Quinn, 1979).

Of all the areas studied in relation to C&I, complex organizations have received considerable attention. Much of this attention can be attributed to the needs and values of organizational researchers. However, organizations themselves clearly have a stake in C&I research. Organizational growth and even survival can be tied directly to an organization's ability to produce (or adopt) and implement new services, products or processes.

The literature is replete with case studies detailing how organizations that ignored new technological advancements, for example, began a slow death spiral. Starbuck (1983) describes one case involving a manufacturer of mechanical calculators that refused to acknowledge the competitive impact of electronic calculators. The result was predictable: Profits declined steadily until the company was bought out and restructured to emphasize electronic calculators.

In spite of the importance attributed to organizational C&I, the empirical research has been somewhat spotty and less than conclusive. After reviewing close to 100 major books and articles on organizational C&I, at least ten general conclusions can be drawn:

1. The terms "creativity" and "innovation" often are used interchangeably, thus making comparative distinctions difficult. Publications that do make a distinction frequently lack agreement on how to define creativity and innovation.

2. The majority of the empirical research literature deals exclusively with organizational innovation. The literature identifying itself with organizational creativity is largely nonempirical and concerned mostly with prescriptions for needed climate variables (e.g., Cummings, 1965). The majority of empirical creativity research is limited to studies of intragroup creativity (e.g., the literature on brainstorming) and personality traits and characteristics of individuals.

3. Most of the research on organizational innovation deals either with the adoption (Aiken, Bacharach & French, 1980) or individual diffusion of innovations (Bal-

dridge & Burnham, 1975). Very few large-scale studies of the entire innovation process exist.

4. The focus of most innovation research has involved correlating structural aspects of organizations with composite measures of innovation (Becker & Whisler, 1967; Hage & Aiken, 1970).

5. Unitary models of innovation have dominated previous research (Moch & Morse, 1977). This research has largely ignored the existence of organizational C&I occurring within different organizational subsystems at different times. Instead, some research studies seem to assume that organizations are either innovative or they are not.

6. The innovation literature tends to be noncumulative and uses different dependent variables (Dill & Friedman, 1979; Downs & Mohr, 1976). There is no universally accepted theory of innovation, since many studies have not been systematically related to and built upon one another. Although there now is a trend toward some convergence, the variety of dependent variables studied has further exacerbated the theory building problem.

7. Innovation typically is considered to be a positive attribute of organizational functioning (Downs & Mohr, 1976; Knight, 1967). Although this view probably reflects the values of many researchers, the negative aspects of innovation also are important for understanding the innovation process.

8. The broad study of organizational innovation as a process similar to all organizations is giving way to the study of specific innovations in specific organizations (Downs & Mohr, 1976).

9. In most organizations, the innovation process is more evolutionary than revolutionary (Knight, 1967). Most innovations are diffused, adopted, and implemented at a relatively slow pace. Radical innovations are rare, but do occur when conditions warrant them (e.g., during situations perceived as survival-threatening, or what Knight (1967) refers to as "distress innovations").

10. Organizations designed along bureaucratic lines are highly resistant to innovations and often fail to foster conditions conducive to creativity (Mohr, 1969; Shepard, 1967; Thompson, 1965). Alternative organizational structures (such as matrix systems) and new managerial philosophies, however, are helping to counteract this resistance.

Many of these conclusions will be discussed in the remainder of this chapter. However, due to the voluminous nature of the research in this area, it will be impossible to discuss adequately all of the literature. For this chapter, I have decided to review some of the major research studies using an organizing framework to help synthesize the literature. Then, based upon this framework, I will attempt to outline a number of needed future directions. I have excluded the literature on creativity in groups and with a few exceptions, the literature on individual creativity. Before presenting the organizing framework, I will discuss some differences between creativity and innovation and then describe some major barriers to innovation.

Creativity Versus Innovation

A distinction needs to be made between creativity and innovation to clarify some differences that exist in the literature. Except for a few researchers (e.g., Pierce & Delbecq, 1977; Shepard, 1967; Thompson, 1965; Zaltman, Duncan & Holbek, 1973), definitions of organizational innovation have excluded any mention of creativity or idea generation. For example, organizational innovation has been defined as "first or early use of an idea by one of a set of organizations with similar goals" (Becker & Whisler, 1967, p. 463), "the adoption of means or ends that are new to the adopting unit" (Downs & Mohr, 1976, p. 701), "the adoption of a change which is new to an organization and to the relevant environment" (Knight, 1967, p. 478), "an idea, practice, or object that is perceived as new by an individual or other unit of adoption" (Rogers, 1983, p. 11), and "adopted changes considered new to the organization's environment" (Daft & Becker, 1978, p. 5).

Reviewing these definitions and others suggests that organizational innovation is: (1) change perceived as new to an organization, (2) something new that is adopted for use by an organization (with the implication often being that implementation will follow adoption automatically), and (3) relative to the organization adopting and using something new; what is innovative for one organization may not be innovative for another.

Organizational creativity, on the other hand, often is used to mean the same thing as organizational innovation. This usage is especially evident in the nonempirical writings on organizational creativity. Most of this work neglects to define organizational creativity precisely. However, it usually can be inferred that the writers view organizational creativity as representing the sum total of the creative traits, abilities and actions of all the organization's members (e.g., Koprowski, 1972; Mars, 1971; Steiner, 1965). It also can be inferred from this literature that an organization will be creative if the proportion of creative individuals (and their creative acts) exceed the proportion of "noncreative" individuals.

If it can be assumed that all individuals in organizations are creative and vary only in the *degree* of their creativeness, then all organizations must be considered creative. Furthermore, just as some individuals are more creative than others, some organizations should also be more creative than others. It would then follow that a creative organization is likely to be more successful at innovation than a less creative organization. That is, a highly creative organization should be better able to initiate, adopt, and implement new products, services, or processes.

Appealing as this line of logic may be, it does not seem valid when evaluated against the research on innovation. For example, Daft and Becker (1978) reviewed studies which demonstrated that organizations adopt ideas from other organizations. They concluded that "creativity is not a very reliable source of innovation (p. 153)." However, this conclusion seems to be based upon an assumption that equates creativity with idea generation.

As conceptualized by many writers in the field (e.g., Isaksen and Treffinger, 1985; Osborn, 1963; Parnes, 1967; Van Gundy, 1981), creativity might be viewed more realistically as a problem solving process with identifiable stages. One of these stages happens to be idea generation. But achievement of creative solutions cannot always be accomplished through idea generation alone. Other activities such as data-finding and problem-finding also are important.

It probably is most realistic to view creativity as a process that cuts across all aspects of the innovation process. Idea generation may be used in some stages of the process at different times and within different subsystems of a particular organization. However, other stages of the creative problem solving process also may assume equal or greater importance depending upon the needs and perceptions of individual innovators within an organization.

In some instances, an organization may generate idea proposals internally or it may decide to adopt externally-generated proposals. In either case, some degree of creative problem solving may be involved. For example, a decision to adopt an externally-generated proposal may produce new problems for an organization, any of which may require development of creative solutions. Thus, innovation and creative problem solving processes are closely intertwined. It is very difficult to consider one without considering the other.

For purposes of this chapter, the innovation process will be viewed as consisting of the following stages: (1) problem awareness and identification, (2) idea proposal, (3) idea adoption and (4) idea implementation. Such a process is very similar to the basic Osborn-Parnes five-step creative problem-solving model of Fact-finding, Problem-finding, Idea-finding, Solution-finding, and Acceptance-finding (Osborn, 1963; Parnes, 1967). The four-step model described above will be used in this chapter since the terminology is more consistent with that found in the innovation literature. Moreover, the "correctness" of models may be a moot issue. Recognition that some process exists (and should exist) is a more important issue. Any given model is not likely to be used in its entirety every time an innovation cycle is initiated. Different stages of any model usually will vary in importance over time during an organization's innovation history.

Based upon the four-step model, organizational innovation will be defined as the process of proposing, adopting, and implementing an idea (process, product, or service) new to an organization in response to a perceived problem. This definition emphasizes that innovation: (1) is a continuous, dynamic set of activities, (2) deals with the concept of newness relative to a particular organization and (3) is stimulated by a perceived gap in performance (a problem).

The act of proposing an idea can involve idea conception (generation of an idea new to the organization) as well as the act of recommending that a borrowed idea be considered for adoption. In either instance, the idea may be new to the organization. The only difference is the source of the idea.

Barriers to Innovation

The characteristics, processes, attitudes, and behaviors in organizations that have been hypothesized to impede innovation have received extensive attention in the literature. If barriers offer sufficient resistance, then innovations are not likely to be adopted or implemented. However, barriers can be a positive feature of the innovation process, since they often force innovators to plan ahead adequately and thus can help insure successful adoption and implementation.

Most of the barriers described next relate to bureaucratic dysfunctions. Some will apply more to certain stages of the innovation process, while others have significance throughout the process. Although many others could have been included, the ones chosen are fairly representative.

I have organized the barriers into five categories: (1) Structural, (2) Social/Political, (3) Procedural, (4) Resource and (5) Individual. Many of the barriers within these categories are interrelated. Consequently, the categories should be considered only rough approximations. As with most research, cause and effect determinations are difficult to make in innovation studies (Becker & Whisler, 1967; Downs & Mohr, 1976). For example, it is hard to tell if social norms "cause" structural arrangements or if structural arrangements cause social norms.

Structural Barriers.

Major barriers in this category include: (1) Stratification, (2) Formalization, (3) Centralization and, (4) Specialization. In most cases, the extent to which a structural barrier will impede innovation depends upon the innovation stage involved. For example, some barriers may be problematic during the proposal stage, but not during implementation.

Stratification has been described in terms of distribution of rewards throughout an organization (Hage & Aiken, 1970) and degree of status, congruence and ease of intraorganizational mobility (Pierce & Delbecq, 1977). Reasons for this inhibition have been attributed to: (1) a preoccupation with status differences that diverts attention and energy from idea proposals (Shepard, 1967), (2) perceived status differences create insecurity which reduces willingness to take risks (Thompson, 1965), (3) an idea proposal may suggest reducing a status differential and would be resisted by those in high status positions (Hage & Aiken, 1970) and (4) upward communication will be decreased due to fear of evaluation (Hage & Aiken, 1970).

Formalization can be defined as "the degree to which an organization emphasizes following rules and procedures in the role performance of its members" (Rogers, 1983, pp. 360-361). It is thought that formalization is detrimental to initiation of innovations (Knight, 1967; Shepard,

1967), but favorable to adoption of innovations (Evan & Black, 1967; Mohr, 1969; Pierce & Delbecq, 1977). If organizational members are expected to behave in prescribed ways and innovation is not prescribed, fewer idea proposals will be generated. However, the singleness of purpose that accompanies formalization can make it easier to adopt and implement new ideas.

The concentration of power and authority and their effect on participation in decision making will influence the degree to which an organization is centralized (Rogers, 1983; Zaltman et al., 1973). Although there are some contradictory research results, centralization may be negatively related to idea proposals (Hage & Aiken, 1967; Shepard, 1967) and positively related to adoption (Wilson, 1966). The more that power is concentrated and the less the amount of lower-level participation, the fewer will be the number of ideas that "trickle up (Daft & Becker, 1978)." If too many high-powered individuals attempt to negotiate adoption, consensus is not likely to be achieved (Wilson, 1966). Thus, centralization may inhibit initiation, but facilitate adoption. Moreover, centralization may encourage implementation (Rogers, 1983).

Specialization (sometimes referred to as differentiation or complexity) typically is defined in terms of the degree of occupational variability that exists within an organization (Pierce & Delbecq, 1977). When specialization is high (and thus diversity and cross-fertilization of ideas should be high), initiation of idea proposals (Lawrence & Lorsch, 1967; Rogers, 1983; Thompson, 1965) and idea adoption will be facilitated (Hage & Aiken, 1967; Moch & Morse, 1977). However, implementation may be inhibited due to potential conflicts (Zaltman et al., 1973), although there is some disagreement on this (e.g., Baldridge & Burnham, 1975).

Social/Political Barriers.

These barriers pertain mostly to norms and power-related influences within organizations. Although accepted standards of behavior and power may influence many organizational processes positively, some norms and power influences can have a negative influence upon innovation.

For example, many organizations have norms that reinforce conformity and engender a reluctance to "rock the boat" (Bright, 1964). Other norms include such things as a tendency to minimize conflict (which often is required to develop new ideas) (Cummings, 1965; Thompson, 1965), an attitude of secrecy and a reluctance to share ideas (Cummings, 1965), a generalized fear of criticism (Gibb, 1972), an attitude that entrepreneurial types don't fit in the organization (Quinn, 1979), a fear that any major innovation will result in elimination of jobs (Bright, 1964), and a belief that an innovation would alter a perceived uniqueness about an organization ("we're already pretty special, so why should we change?") (Havelock, 1970).

Power influences that might affect innovation negatively include a general overemphasis on power relationships and status differentials (i.e., the organization as a political system) (Thompson, 1965), a reward system that discourages idea champions to help facilitate idea adoption and implementation (Chakrabarti, 1974), and a lack of professionalism at lower organizational levels (Daft & Becker, 1978).

Procedural Barriers.

What I have classified as procedural barriers generally refer to policies, procedures, and regulations that often inhibit innovation. Also included in this category are certain procedures or managerial philosophies that, although not officially codified, nevertheless can exert a powerful negative influence.

Some examples of barriers in this category include: (1) promoting executives on the basis of their analytical skills rather than their ability to build a creative climate (U. S. Department of Commerce, 1980), (2) emphasis on short-term planning (Quinn, 1979), (3) a desire to avoid expenditures without a short-term payback (Schoen, 1969), (4) an innovation that appears in conflict with existing laws (Bright, 1964), (5) a desire to protect the status quo, to not do things differently (Cummings, 1965; Koprowski, 1972), (6) an overemphasis on an external reward system rather than internal commitment (Gibb, 1972; Havelock, 1970; Thompson, 1965), (7) expecting/demanding orderly advance during the innovation process and emphasizing planning tactics more than the innovation (Quinn, 1979), (8) exerting detailed control too early in the innovation process (Quinn, 1979) and (9) using unfamiliar jargon with decision makers (Zaltman et al., 1973).

Resource Barriers.

These barriers apply to such things as people, time, money supplies, and information. It generally is accepted that innovation will not prosper if resources are in short supply (March & Simon, 1958; Thompson, 1965). Innovation requires a certain amount of slack resources beyond those needed for routine functioning. However, resources can act as a barrier even when some slack exists. Implementing an innovation frequently requires that resources be shifted from one area to another. This shifting can, in some cases, result in internal conflicts that can be very disruptive to the innovation process (Zaltman et al., 1973).

Individual/Attitudinal Barriers.

These barriers reside within individual organizational members, but also may stem, in part, from the organization's climate. Fear of risk and failure and intolerance of uncertainty and ambiguity are commonly-cited examples of these barriers (U. S. Department of Commerce, 1980; Schoen, 1969; Quinn, 1979). Other barriers in this category would be individual characteristics that have the potential to create conflicts, thus stifling adoption or implementation. Basic differences in needs, values and perceptions would be typical examples. For instance, Hage and Dewar (1973) found that values of organizational elites who favor an innovation are more predictive of innovation than are organizational structural variables.

An Organizing Framework

As Becker and Whisler (1967) note, the innovation literature seems to be organized along the lines of simple systems elements: inputs, outputs, and processes. Inputs are variables that predispose organizations to innovate; outputs are types of innovations adopted and/or implemented; processes are sets of activities used to transform inputs into outputs. In Figure One are variables that seem to be relevant for each area.

The inputs of Structure, People, and Information Flow are somewhat analogous to the open systems perspectives of structural design, human, and work flow (Huse & Bowditch, 1977). All three of these perspectives are interrelated such that a change in one can affect either of the other two perspectives. I added the Environment input to reflect the dependency of organizations upon their environments and the crucial role that both internal and external environmental factors can have upon innovation.

The process variables have been discussed briefly earlier and will not be discussed further. There seem to be almost as many views of the innovation process as there are definitions of innovation and creativity.

The outputs have received relatively little attention in the literature. The use of innovation types as outputs has been suggested by Becker and Whisler (1967) and elaborated upon by Zaltman et al. (1973). The Products output is similar to the Outcome/Effect category of innovation types, but reflects more recent conceptualizing in this area. Many other outputs could have been included but were not due to the lack of research relating innovation to outputs.

Figure One.

A systems model of the organizational innovation process.

Inputs	Process	Outputs
I. Structure	I. Problem awareness	I. Innovation types
A. Stratification	II. Idea proposal	A. State of system
B. Formalization	III. Idea adoption	1. Programmed
C. Centralization	IV. Idea implementation	2. Nonprogrammed
D. Specialization		B. Initial focus
E. Professionalism		1. Ultimate
F. Size		2. Instrumental
II. People		C. Outcome/effect
A. Values		1. Radicalness
B. Personality		2. Variations/reorientations
C. Motivation		II. Products
D. Leadership		A. Novelty
E. Roles		B. Resolution
III. Information flow		C. Elaboration and synthesis
A. Boundary spanning		
B. Communication		
IV. Environment		
A. Uncertainty		
B. Climate		

Inputs

Structure

The effects of organizational structure upon innovation have been conceptualized and researched extensively in the literature—perhaps more than any other input variable. The most frequently mentioned structural variables are: stratification, formalization, centralization, and specialization. Professionalism sometimes is considered to be related to specialization, but is treated separately here due to the specific role it plays. Size also was included as a structural variable, since it seems to be related directly to many of the traditional structural variables.

Stratification. This variable refers to the distribution of rewards throughout the organization and the status differences that result. The literature indicates that a highly stratified power structure generally is detrimental to innovation. Thompson (1965) suggests that low stratification is needed for the freedom of communication that is conducive to innovation; Shepard (1967) states that a preoccupation with status and resulting status conflicts inhibit the innovation process; and, Hage and Aiken (1970) speculate that those in high status positions will resist change likely to jeopardize their positions and that upward communication may be inhibited due to fear of negative evaluations. This difficulty of bottom-up communication also is reflected by Zaltman et al. (1973) and by Pierce and Delbecq (1977) who hypothesize that stratification will be negatively related to the initiation of innovation proposals.

Formalization. As defined earlier, formalization assesses the degree to which an organization stresses the use of specific rules and procedures (Rogers, 1983). Formalization has been hypothesized to have a general effect on innovation as well as consequences for specific stages of the innovation process. Thompson (1965) notes that low formalization and structural looseness are essential ingredients for innovation; Knight (1967) predicts that high formalization will be associated with low creativity; and, Hage and Aiken (1967) obtained empirical results suggesting a negative relationship between job codification and rate of program change.

The effects of formalization with respect to innovation stages have been interpreted somewhat variably, although a pattern does seem evident. Low formalization has been linked with initiation of proposals (Daft, 1978; Pierce & Delbecq, 1977; Zaltman et al., 1973), while high formalization seems to be positively related to adoption and implementation (Mohr, 1969; Pierce & Delbecq, 1977; Zaltman et al., 1973). In contrast, Hage and Dewar (1973) found no significant relationship between job codification and rate of program change. Daft (1978) found low formalization to be positively associated with both initiation and adoption of innovations within the technical cores of educational systems.

Centralization. This variable deals with the degree of participation in decision making. Most of the empirical research and theory suggest that centralization is negatively related to innovation in general (or, conversely, that decentralization is positively related). The general, positive relationship between decentralization and innovation has been predicted by Burns and Stalker (1961) and confirmed in empirical research by Hage and Aiken (1967) and Daft and Becker (1978).

The majority of research and theory suggest that the effects of centralization vary according to different stages of the innovation process. For example, decentralization seems to facilitate initiation of ideas (Aiken et al., 1980; Daft, 1978; Pierce & Delbecq, 1977; Shepard, 1967; Zaltman et al., 1973) as well as the adoption of ideas (Daft, 1978; Moch & Morse, 1977; Pierce & Delbecq, 1977; Wilson, 1966). On the other hand, centralization is generally thought to ease implementation due to the coordinating and authority advantages of concentrated power structures (Pierce & Delbecq, 1977; Rogers, 1983; Sapolsky, 1967; Zaltman et al., 1973). However, other variables, such as technical versus administrative core origination of ideas (Daft, 1978; Daft & Becker, 1978) and influence of the values of organizational leaders and elites (Hage & Dewar, 1973) may play a more dominate role than centralization alone.

Specialization. This structural variable, often used interchangeably with complexity and differentiation, refers to the degree of occupational variability or diversity within organizations. It also is related closely to professionalism, which has been suggested as a better and more reliable predictor of innovation than many other structural variables (Daft & Becker, 1978).

Less than complete agreement exists as to the specific effects of specialization. Blau and McKinley (1979) and Sapolsky (1967) believe that specialization impedes innovation in general. Thompson (1965) suggests that it encourages parochialism and resistance to new ideas from outside the organization. However, specialization has been noted to be positively related to initiation (Pierce & Delbecq, 1977; Zaltman et al., 1973) and adoption (Baldridge & Burnahm, 1975; Fennell, 1984; Hage & Aiken, 1967; Moch & Morse, 1977; Pierce & Delbecq, 1977). Pierce and Delbecq (1977) conclude that specialization also is positively related to implementation, but Zaltman et al. (1973) disagree. However, Zaltman et al. note that implementation may be facilitated when complexity is high due to the increased likelihood of a large number of proposals being initiated. In an empirical study, Aiken et al. (1980) found no significant relationship between complexity and innovation proposals; Hage and Dewar (1973) concluded that, although complexity and the rate of program change appear to be correlated positively, elite values are a slightly better predictor of innovation; and, Aiken and Hage (1971) maintain that diversity affects innovation negatively. It may be that the lack of consistency in these studies can be attributed to different operational measures of specialization and innovation.

Professionalism. Although not generally considered to be a structural variable itself, professionalism often is viewed as a component of other commonly accepted structural variables, such as complexity (e.g., Hage & Aiken, 1967). Different degrees of organizational member education, training, participation in professional activities, autonomy, and the need for recognition from peers instead of the formal authority structure, all are thought to constitute professionalism as it relates to innovation (Daft, 1978). For example, Wilson (1966) and Zaltman et al. (1973) note that professionals may propose large numbers of ideas relevant to their professions, but resist proposals from others. Hage and Aiken (1967) found a weak, but positive relation between professional training and rate of program change and Pierce and Delbecq (1977) hypothesized that professionalism is positively related to initiation, adoption, and implementation of innovations. Sapolsky (1967), however, predicts that too much diversity in occupations can impede implementation.

The most promising work done in this area revolves around the "dual-core" model of innovation (Daft, 1978; Daft & Becker, 1978). In studying administrative and technical innovations within school districts, they found that high professionalism is associated with proposal initiation from the bottom up. As a result, a large number of ideas from the technical core is adopted. When professionalism is low, a top-down process is used. This process results in adoption of a greater number of ideas from the administrative core.

Size. Organizational size is one of the most widely studied innovation variables. Although it is not a "pure" structural variable, size generally is considered to be a significant determinant of many of the major structural variables discussed previously. As Pierce and Delbecq (1977) and Rogers (1983) have noted, size may not cause innovation, but it may increase the probability that more credible predictors (e.g., structure, slack resources) will be present. It is this interpretation that may account for the diversity of findings and opinions among researchers and theorists.

Blau and McKinley (1979) report that size has no impact upon innovation and Daft (1978) observes that size does not affect the process of administrative innovation, but does affect the frequency of innovations. The majority of the literature seems to support the proposition that size is positively related to adoption of innovations (Aiken & Hage, 1971; Becker & Stafford, 1967; Fennell, 1984; Mohr, 1969; Raldridge & Burnham, 1975). Ettlie (1983) found that size in the food processing industry is important up to a point (in regard to the rate of new product introductions), but then diminishes in effect as organizational growth loses its ability to stimulate change.

People

Variables related to people in the innovation process probably are the most important of all. Any number of different variables could be included in this category. I have chosen five: (1) Values, (2) Personality, (3) Motivation, (4) Leadership and (5) Roles. There is considerable overlap among these variables and no attempt is made to separate cause from effect.

Values. Values can be defined in terms of the preferences organizational members have about desired outcomes. In most organizations, values of the leaders and elites will be the primary determinants of goals and objectives. Cummings (1965) argues that values of top managers are primary determinants of an organization's ability to use its resources effectively for innovation. In fact, Hage and Dewar (1973) found that values of the organizational elite are stronger predictors of innovation than structural variables. In their study, Hage and Dewar observed that values of the elite inner circle of decision makers may be even more important than those of the top manager. Aiken et al. (1980), however, have noted that current distinctions between elites and non-elites are crude and somewhat simplistic (although such distinctions do have heuristic value). Thompson (1965) maintains that conflicts arising over value differences may be conducive to organizational creativity as long as the conflicts are not too severe or disruptive. In general, it appears that values of organizational members (especially those of elites) are reliable predictors of decisions to innovate (Mohr, 1969; Pierce & Delbecq, 1977). The role of values within different innovation stages, however, has not been studied fully.

Personality. The specific traits and characteristics of individuals involved in the innovation process have received extensive attention in the literature. Among the traits and characteristics thought to be positively associated with innovation are: (1) cognitive sensitivity—the ability to perceive a problem and develop a cognitive solution to it (Andrews & Gordon, 1970), (2) cognitive complexity—the ability to process information (Payne & Beatty, 1982), (3) general incongruity adaptation level—the amount of environmental incongruity desired by different organizational actors (Driver & Streufer, 1965; Hunsaker, 1975), (4) self-actualization (Shepard, 1967), (5) comfort with change, clarity of direction, thoroughness, a participative management style, and persuasiveness, persistence, and discretion (Kanter, 1982), (6) willingness to change (Hurt, Joseph & Cook, 1977), (7) tolerance of ambiguity, attraction to task, and communication apprehension (Comadena, 1984), (8) belief in innovation; psychological security and autonomy; good interpersonal skills, great energy, persistence, and determination; achievement orientation; a sense of timing (McGinnis & Ackelsberg, 1983), (9) risk taking ability, receptivity to different kinds of ideas, and a nonconforming, questioning attitude (Knight, 1967) and (10) innovation-adaptation—a tendency toward doing things differently as opposed to doing things better (Kirton, 1976). There also are many other variables that may be related to innovation. Moreover, the interactive effects among these variables is more or less unknown.

Motivation. Two different approaches have been used to explain the motivation to innovate: (1) Intrinsic-extrinsic rewards and (2) Performance gaps. According to Thompson (1965), a bureaucratic emphasis upon external rewards promotes conformity rather than innovation. Instead, more emphasis should be placed upon internal commitment and intrinsic rewards. This view also is reflected by Amabile (1983) who has argued for the relative importance to creativity of intrinsic motivation. Earlier, March and Simon (1958) advocated a search model of innovation in which workers look for new ways to perform as a result of job dissatisfaction. However, Hage and Aiken (1967) later found a positive relationship between job satisfaction and innovation. Their reasoning was that people who are satisfied with their jobs are more committed and more likely to seek ways to improve things. In contrast to these views, Quinn (1979) makes the point that extrinsic motivators may be needed to retain highly creative personnel. The majority of the literature, however, seems to support the validity of intrinsic motivators, while recognizing that extrinsic rewards are important up to a point.

Performance gap explanations of the motivation to innovate are based upon the assumption that perceived changes in the environment will create an undesirable gap between an existing and ideal performance state (Zaltman et al., 1973). Awareness of this gap then stimulates motivation to attempt reducing or closing the perceived gap. Duchesneau, Cohn, and Dutton (1979) found that when managers of U. S. shoe manufacturers perceived a performance gap, their perceptions were reliable predictors of the decision to adopt process innovations. However, Ettlie (1983) obtained results suggesting very little or no support for a performance gap hypothesis of innovation.

Leadership. The process involving how one person influences another has been written about and researched extensively in the literature. With respect to innovation, very little empirical research has been conducted. The one major exception would be the work of Hage and Dewar (1973). In general, it has been noted that maximizing the creative behavior of organizational members is a major responsibility of top management (Mars, 1971). In their study of managers, McGinnis & Ackelsberg (1983) state that top management leadership is needed to respond to external challenges as well as to achieve organizational goals. Siegel and Kaemmerer (1978), in a factor-analytic study of organizational climate, found that the factors correlating highest with "Support of Creativity" were those that emphasized the leadership role.

Other studies investigating the relationship between leadership and innovation have looked at opinion leadership. For example, Witteman (1976) found a positive correlation between a self-report measure of opinion leadership and individual innovation. In his study, Witteman compared self-report measures of opinion leadership among persons classified using Rogers and Shoemaker's (1971) framework of innovators, early adopters, early majority, late majority, and laggards. He found that innovators scored significantly higher on opinion leadership than the others. From a review of the literature, Rogers (1983) observes that the innovativeness of opinion leaders will depend upon the prevailing norms of the social system. When the social system is oriented toward change, the opinion leaders will be likely to innovate; when the system opposes change, the opinion leaders most likely will follow suit. In addition, opinion leaders play a unique role in an organization's communication structure, often serving as a communication center.

Roles. The innovation roles mentioned most frequently in the literature are those of entrepreneur and product or idea champion. The importance of these roles has been noted by Schoen (1969), Schon (1967), and Quinn (1979), among others. However, just performing an entrepreneurial or product champion role is rarely enough. The organizational climate also must be conducive to innovation for any change efforts to be successful (Kanter, 1982; Lawler & Drexler, 1981). In addition, the entrepreneur or product champion usually must perform roles specific to being an entrepreneur or product champion. For example, Kanter (1982) has observed that entrepreneurs act as interference handlers, momentum maintainers, secondary redesigners (to make needed readjustments), and external communicators. Chakrabarti (1974) also emphasizes that champions must perform multiple roles as well as act as a link between different phases of the innovation process.

Other roles also have been identified in the literature as being involved in the innovation process. Roberts (1980) lists five key staff roles of: (1) the creative scientist or engineer who proposes an idea, (2) the entrepreneur who promotes an idea, (3) a project manager concerned with the economic aspects, (4) a management sponsor who champions the idea to upper management and (5) a gatekeeper who gathers technical information from outside the organization and gives it to the project team. Maidique (1980) discusses the importance of combining the roles of entrepreneur, manager, and technician in order to achieve successful innovation, but Roberts (1980) believes that different roles require different types of people. Rogers and Shoemaker (1971) have identified five roles needed for each stage of the innovation process: (1) stimulator–becomes aware of the need for an innovation, (2) initiator–translates the idea into an action plan acceptable to the organization, (3) legitimizer–uses social power to sanction the idea, (4) decision maker–commits resources using formal authority and (5) executor–implements the decision to adopt the innovation. Regardless of which roles are studied, there seems to be universal agreement that top management support is necessary for any role to lead to successful innovation (Kanter, 1982; Maidique, 1980). Chakrabarti (1974), for example, found a high, positive correlation between degree of top management support and degree of success in adopting an innovation.

Information Flow

This category includes two major, related variables: (1) boundary spanning and, (2) communication. Both of these variables also are highly related to the two previously discussed input categories of Structure and People. Boundary spanning and communication are important to the innovation process, since the quantity and quality of information flows are important determinants of success during the innovation process.

Boundary spanning. In recent years, boundary spanning activity has received considerable attention in the academic literature (e.g., Adams, 1974; Brown, 1966; Leifer & Delbecq, 1978). Typically defined as the "interpersonal transfer of information across organizational boundaries" (Keller, Szilagyi & Holland, 1976, p. 700), boundary spanning has been viewed as important in regard to both external (Dill, 1958) and internal information exchanges (Tushman & Nadler, 1978). In the innovation literature, boundary spanning has played an important role in helping organizations respond to their environments as well as in communicating information needed internally during different innovation stages. For example, Utterback (1971) found that successful organizational problem solving was highly related to the existence of "technical gatekeepers" within the organization who helped acquire information vital for dealing with a rapidly changing technological environment.

Boundary spanning seems to be especially important for bureaucratic organizations desiring to innovate when their relevant task environments are essentially uncertain and complex. Callahan and Salipante (1979) report on a case study involving the establishment of temporary boundary spanning units for dealing with adoption of a major technological innovation in the health care industry. The authors concluded that the temporary units increased the flow of needed information and enabled the firm to produce a quality product and achieve sales success in a relatively short period of time. The keys to success for this project seemed to be using boundary spanning units only for dealing with relevant parts of the environment and maintaining the units for only as long as the environmental uncertainty existed. Although most innovation-related boundary spanning studies have involved the adoption of innovations, Aiken et al. (1980) report that innovation proposals from lower level personnel tended to increase in correspondence with their boundary spanning activities.

Communication. The literature on organizational communication and innovation is quite disparate. The variety of studies conducted in this area often seem to have little direct connection with one another. The emphasis seems to range from organizations' need to communicate effectively for successful innovation, to organization structure and its effects on organizational communication of innovations, to organizational social networks being analyzed to understand the innovation process fully.

Cummings (1965) notes that creative organizations are characterized by a maximum number of open channels of communication. These channels should be only those that are relevant to the particular innovation area. Zaltman et al. (1973) conclude that radical innovations require explicitly stated problems and clear-cut communication feedback networks. And McGinnis and Ackelsberg (1983) generalize that the proactive search for innovative solutions needed by organizations requires open and spontaneous communication. In a study on creative scientists, Kasperson (1978) found that the most effective channels of communication for new ideas were other people. However, Kasperson notes that interaction between people in organizations often is restricted due to the bureaucratic nature of many organizations. Hage & Aiken (1967) reinforce this view by observing that high formalization reduces the diversity of informal channels of communication. And Rogers (1983) points out that individual innovativeness is related positively to the tightness of interpersonal networks within organizations.

More specifically, the innovation literature has dealt with the effects of communication on particular stages of the innovation process. According to Zaltman et al. (1973), the existence of effective communication channels is especially important for the decision to adopt an innovation. During adoption, multiple inputs often are needed to make a high quality decision. In a study on technological innovation, Utterback (1971) found that the quantity of information during the innovation process is related positively to the effectiveness of an organization in generating, developing, and implementing new technology. The need for an innovation is often generated by external people (e.g., customers), while communication inputs during the problem solving phase of innovation arise from internal sources.

Environment

The interaction of organizations and their environments has received considerable attention in the literature (e.g., Dill, 1958; Duncan, 1972; Emery & Trist, 1965). One of the early theorists, Parsons (1956), emphasized the need for organizations to adapt to and influence their environments in order to remain healthy and survive. The importance of environments to innovation also has been recognized widely. For example, Utterback (1971) has noted that cost and technical knowledge are not an organization's major obstacles to innovation. Rather, the ability of an organization to recognize the needs and demands of its external environment is, by far, the most important consideration.

In general, the literature suggests that there is no one best way to design an organization. Instead, every organization must be designed to "fit" its environment. Burns & Stalker (1961) found that organic organizations were best suited for changing environmental conditions, while mechanistic structures were best for more stable environments; Lawrence and Lorsch (1967) obtained results suggesting that unpredictable environments require organizational designs that are high in differentiation, while more predictable environments require designs that are low in differentiation. However, both situations require a balance in the amount of collaboration among work units. With respect to innovation, Baldridge and Burnham (1975) found that the nature of an organization's environment will be related to its likelihood of adoption. Specifically, large, complex organizations with heterogeneous environments will be more likely to adopt than small, simple organizations with relatively predictable and homogeneous environments.

Uncertainty. Perhaps the one environmental variable with the greatest impact upon organizational innovation is perceived environmental uncertainty (PEU). According to Rogers (1983), uncertainty is the degree to which a number of alternatives and the probability of their occurrence with respect to an event are predictable. The majority of the theorists maintian that PEU is a stimulus for organizational innovation (e.g., Mohr, 1969; Palumbo, 1969). McGinnis and Ackelsberg (1983) assert that the perception of uncertainty causes the environment to be perceived as favorable to innovation. And Pierce and Delbecq (1977) propose that there is a positive relationship between PEU and the initiation, adoption, and implementation of innovations.

The empirical literature also seems to support an uncertainty-driven view of organizational innovation. For example, Duchesneau et al. (1979) found PEU to be positively associated with a shoe manufacturer's competitive strategy. Perceiving the environment as uncertain prompted the firm to become more future-oriented and to consider innovation as a necessary response. In a study of 54 organizations, Ettlie and Bridges (1982) found that PEU led to an aggressive technological policy for the adoption of process, product, and service innovations. Similar results were obtained by Ettlie (1983) in an investigation of the food processing industry. Perceptions of uncertainty in regard to such factors as capital supply, competition, new product needs, and customers were significantly related to innovation.

The uncertainty-innovation link also may have other effects upon organizational members. Callahan (1979) describes a situation in which adoption of innovations involved the need to consider the uncertainty organizational personnel may experience when an innovation is being studied for possible adoption. A perception of too much uncertainty can have dysfunctional consequences, such as creating undue personal insecurity. Wilson (1966) hypothesizes that when organizational members are uncertain about the linkage between expectations for rewards and performance, there will be a high frequency of innovative proposals. Thus, PEU has the potential for both negative and positive organizational effects.

Climate. The internal psychological environment of an organization can play a major role in organizational creativity, particularly in regard to the generation of innovation proposals. According to Abbey and Dickson (1983), climate can be defined as "a relatively enduring quality of an organization's internal environment that results from the behavior and policies of members of the organization, especially top management (p. 352)." From a brief review of the literature, I have identified ten interrelated climate factors.

Autonomy. Cummings (1965), Sapolsky (1967), Thompson (1965) and Wilson (1966) have argued that innovative organizations should allow employees considerable freedom and discretion to innovate. The empirical research seems to support these arguments. Andrews and Gordon (1970), and Andrews (1975) found that a low level of supervision was a positive factor in innovation among research scientists. Similar results were obtained by Abbey and Dickson (1983) among R&D personnel in the semi-conductor industry.

Performance Reward Dependency. Innovation is more likely to occur when employees perceive that their rewards are fair and appropriate and based on ability and past performance instead of luck or who you know (Abbey and Dickson, 1983). A major consideration seems to be the extent to which the reward system is based upon intrinsic motivators rather than extrinsic motivators. Employees are more likely to be creative and innovative when their motivation is internally based rather than dependent upon external rewards, such as fear of punishment or pay (Cummings, 1965; Amabile, 1983).

Risk Taking. The willingness to take risks appears to be a universally-recognized prerequisite for creative and innovative activity. For instance, Zeldman (1980) notes the need to encourage risk taking and Quinn (1979) mentions the need for top management to be willing to take personal risks as well as to allow workers the opportunity to fail. In the empirical literature, Abbey and Dickson (1983) found a significant, positive relationship between willingness to try new procedures and innovativeness.

Support for Creativity. Of all the climate variables, one of the most frequently mentioned may be the overall perception employees have about the organization's openness and willingness to support change. In a factor-analytic study, Siegel and Kaemmerer (1978) found support of creativity to be positively related with the perceived creativeness of schools they surveyed. Openness to ideas also was identified by McGinnis and Ackelsberg (1983) as a major variable in organizational innovation. Another, related factor may be the extent to which management assumes that workers are creative (Cummings, 1965).

Tolerance of Differences. Diversity among organizational members will help increase the number of innovative proposals due to the different points of view provided as well as the conflict that often accompanies diversity (Thompson, 1965). If organizational members do not perceive the organization as tolerant of individual differences, creativity is likely to be repressed (Siegel and Kammerer, 1978).

Personal Commitment. Being creative and initiating innovation proposals requires a level of personal commitment not always found in repressive work environments that emphasize external rewards. Siegel and Kaemmerer (1978) found that members of organizations judged as creative tended to be perceived as having a high level of devotion to their jobs. Being creative often is seen as going beyond routine responsibilities, and doing what is not normally expected can involve a high degree of personal commitment not always found in many organizations.

Top Management Support. It generally is agreed that support of top management is an essential ingredient of any creative climate (Chakrabarti, 1974; Schoen, 1969; Shepard, 1967). In fact, most innovation theorists believe that a creative internal climate cannot be developed in the first place without top level support. That is, all the factors normally associated with a creative climate are unlikely to exist unless some degree of management support is available to set the tone (Zeldman, 1980).

High Responsibility for Initiating Ideas. Research by Andrews and Gordon (1970), and Andrews (1975) suggests that scientists rated high in innovativeness assume that they have a responsibility to produce ideas. However, other research (Daft, 1978; Daft & Becker, 1978) suggests that sense of responsibility for idea initiation may be more a function of technical versus administrative core origination and degree of professionalism of organizational members. In any event, if employees believe that the organization supports assumption of responsibility for initiation of innovation proposals, they will be more likely to do so.

Job Security. Employees who perceive themselves as having high job security are more likely to be rated as innovative than employees who believe they have relatively low job security (Andrews, 1975; Andrews & Gordon, 1970). A sense of stability of employment may engender greater commitment which, in turn, may increase motivation to suggest new ways of doing things.

Moderate Degree of Ambiguity. McGinnis and Ackelsberg (1983) argue that a moderate degree of perceived ambiguity about the job environment will create performance gaps that are motivating to most employees. Awareness of such gaps is assumed to lead to innovation in order to help clarify cause-effect relationships. McGinnis and Ackelsberg (1983) maintain that if organizations continually present ambiguous situations to be dealt with, employees will be continually motivated to innovate. However, as mentioned previously, at least one empirical study (Ettlie, 1983) failed to find support for a performance gap theory of organizational innovation. It may be that perceived gaps may not always lead to a search for ideas to existing problems. Rather, ideas themselves may provide the stimulus for perceived performance gaps and thus prompt innovation. Some support for this view has been noted by Daft and Becker (1978).

Outputs

Innovation Types

Because the way innovation is categorized can affect its eventual adoption, several authors have developed innovation typologies. Such typologies also can be an aid to innovation research. In reviewing the literature, Zaltman et al. (1973) note that innovations can be grouped into three broad categories: (1) State of the System, (2) Initial Focus and (3) Outcome or Effect.

State of the System. These innovations include programmed and nonprogrammed types. According to Knight (1967), programmed innovations are anticipated and scheduled in advance. Adoption and implementation of such innovations usually are routine activities, although the initial idea may have been generated using creative problem solving. Nonprogrammed innovations can be characterized as either slack or distress innovations (Cyert & March, 1963; Knight, 1967). Slack innovations occur when an organization perceives itself to be successful due to excess resources over which some discretionary decision making is possible. An extended search for ideas beyond the organization occurs during slack innovation, but the organization is careful not to disturb internal processes and structures (Knight, 1967). Searching for a new product or group to add to the organization would be an example of slack innovation. Distress innovations, in contrast, occur under conditions of very little or zero slack. In this case, the search is directed inward toward internal processes or products that might be changed without undue expenditure of resources.

Initial Focus. Innovations of this type exist as either ultimate or instrumental (Grossman, 1970). Ultimate innovations are ends in themselves—e.g., the establishment of a new department in a university. Instrumental innovations are those which provide the means to achieve an end. An example might be pilot-testing a new series of courses designed to help set up the ultimate goal of a new university department.

Ultimate and instrumental innovations also can be categorized further. Knight (1967) describes four types of interrelated innovations: (1) product or service innovations (e.g., introducing a new product), (2) production-process innovations (e.g., introducing a new technology to be used internally), (3) organizational-structure innovations (e.g., changing communication channels) and (4) people innovations (e.g., hiring new personnel or modifying behavior of existing personnel).

Outcome or Effect. These innovations, the third type summarized by Zaltman et al. (1973), have been discussed in terms of radicalness or variations/reorientations. Knight (1967) distinguishes between performance radicalness—"the amount of change in output that results from one innovation when compared with a second one (p. 482)" and structural radicalness—the degree of difference between one structural arrangement and another. An example of high performance radicalness would be a new model of car that results in a large change in output; examples of structural radicalness would be a dramatic change in the physical characteristics of a product or a major alteration in an organization's authority structure.

Normann (1971) has discussed innovations in terms of reorientations (major changes) as well as variations (minor changes). Variation outcomes pertain to innovations that result in new products that are similar to earlier products of the organization (e.g., annual modifications in car models). On the other hand, reorientation outcomes involve fundamental changes, such as the deletion or addition of major product dimensions. According to Normann (1971), variations can impact the task, political, or cognitive (information acquiring) subsystems within an organization. Reorientations can be described as systematic (affecting legitimatized organizational functions, such as expanding into new markets), idiosyncratic (changes resulting from a person in authority using individual discretion without consulting others) and, marginal (innovations occurring outside the organization with little immediate impact upon the organization–although the cumulative effects could be strong).

As useful as this typology may appear to be, it may not be entirely valid. As Daft and Becker (1978) note, it fails to distinguish between innovation type and innovation attribute. By defining type as "members of a class" (p. 123) and attribute as "a characteristic of a member of a class" (p. 123), Daft and Becker propose that the only legitimate innovation types in the Zaltman et al. (1973) typology are initial focus innovations. According to Daft and Becker, these can be more appropriately classified as technical, organizational structure (administrative), and goal- (value-) centered innovations. Technical innovations then can be further divided into product and process, while people can be subsumed under organizational structure. All other types in the Zaltman et al. typology should be considered as innovation attributes (or correlates).

Products

Some preliminary research by Besemer and Treffinger (1981) suggests that creative products can be categorized into three dimensions: (1) Novelty, (2) Resolution and (3) Elaboration and Synthesis. Novelty refers to the degree to which an idea (innovation proposal) is new, either within or without the field. Three criteria contribute to Novelty: (a) Germinal, (b) Originality and (c) Transformational. Resolution involves the extent to which an idea appears capable of resolving a particular problem situation. The Resolution criteria are: (a) Adequacy, (b) Appropriateness, (c) Logical, (d) Usefulness and (e) Value. The third product dimension, Elaboration and Synthesis, can be used to evaluate stylistic considerations of creative products. Six criteria are contained in this dimension: (a) Attractiveness, (b) Complexity, (c) Elegance, (d) Expressiveness, (e) Organicness and (f) Well-craftedness. Additional information on these product variables can be found in the chapter by Besemer and O'Quin in this volume.

Future Needs

Trying to generalize about organizational innovation is probably as difficult as trying to generalize about human behavior. When people are viewed in the aggregate, there are some predictions that can be made with a fairly high degree of accuracy. However, there will always be exceptions. Something as complex as human behavior will never be 100 percent predictable. Organizational innovation, as a process involving human behavior, is certainly no different. There are certain reliable predictors of organizational behavior, but none that are 100 percent reliable. Moreover, the topic of organizational innovation has been studied much less and for a shorter period of time than has human behavior. There is still a lot to be learned about human behavior as well as the process of organizational innovation.

In the remainder of this chapter I will discuss briefly some needed future directions for the fields of organizational creativity and innovation. Most of these needs are suggested by the literature and there will be considerable overlap among them.

1. Perhaps the most frequently-mentioned future need in the innovation literature is the need for longitudinal studies (e.g., Abbey & Dickson, 1983; Becker & Whisler, 1967; Dill & Friedman, 1979). Most current research is static and *ex post facto.* This research is limited to measuring the number of innovations adopted and comparisons about the length of time necessary for adoption of an innovation. A more useful approach would be to examine the processes that occur over time in moving through a sequence of innovations (Fennell, 1984). By studying innovations as they occur, a more realistic picture is likely

to emerge. As a useful adjunct to longitudinal research, an action-research approach has been found to be beneficial to both researchers and organizational members (e.g., Pasmore & Friedlander, 1982).

2. Most innovation research treats an entire organization as the unit of analysis. However, given the complex nature and size of modern organizations, it is likely that the innovation process occurs simultaneously within many different subsystems of the same organization and involves many different innovations. By making organizational subsystems the unit of analysis, many of the inconsistent results obtained in the literature may be explained.

3. The effects of intergroup relations upon the innovation process have been neglected in the literature (Aiken et al., 1980). In addition, the effects of the innovation process at one organizational level upon the process at another level, have received relatively little attention (one major exception would be the work of Daft & Becker, 1978). For example, what effect do the rate and type of innovation proposals developed at one level have upon the rate and type of proposals at another level? How do the interpersonal relationships between members across levels affect the innovation process? Internal politics also play an important role in most areas of organizational behavior, but have been studied little in regard to innovation in organizations.

4. Most innovation theorists agree that organizational innovation needs to be planned and managed. The fit between innovation and the strategic planning process needs more study to determine how innovation will affect the organization in the long term (McGinnis & Ackelsberg, 1983). If innovation is viewed by an organization as desirable, it then must devote attention to integrating it with strategic planning.

5. The stages of the innovation process typically are conceptualized as involving initiation, adoption, and implementation. However, as Aiken et al. (1980) have noted, very little research has been conducted on the initiation or proposal development stage. This lack of research may be due to the fact that innovation in many organizations involves adoption of an idea generated by an external source. To the degree that a performance gap model of innovation is valid, the acts of becoming aware of and identifying problems also deserve attention in the innovation literature.

6. It is very difficult to generalize broadly from many innovation studies since the settings are somewhat homogeneous. Research in educational and health organizations dominated a lot of the early research, although the proportion of studies conducted in business has increased in recent years. Greater diversity in settings is needed since innovation is unlikely to be similar, even within the same types of organizations.

7. Greater conceptual clarity is required as to what constitutes an innovation. The effects of similar independent variables too often are compared using different dependent variable measures of innovation. For example, Study A may find a positive relationship between formalization and innovation, while Study B may find a negative relationship. However, Study A may have defined innovation in terms of early use, while Study B defined innovation using the number of innovations adopted during a specified time period. It would seem that innovation is organization-specific and will defy a universalistic definition until a more adequate model of innovation is developed and accepted.

8. The role of perceived environmental uncertainty in the innovation process is relatively understudied and deserves more attention. In particular, Ettlie 1983 has observed that there is a need to investigate how objective versus perceived

measures of innovation would influence the innovation process. McGinnis and Ackelsberg (1983) argue that organizations should build in some ambiguity to help stimulate innovation. Questions remain, however as to how such ambiguity should be communicated, how much should be communicated, and to whom. Furthermore, research could be useful in studying the relationship between the problem awareness/identification stage and perceptions of uncertainty. Identifying this relationship, and how it might be related to the Problem-Finding stage of the Osborn-Parnes creative problem-solving model, are additional areas for future research.

9. Most of the empirical research on innovation (as well as in other behavioral science areas) has relied upon perceptual measures. Much more research needs to be conducted using behavioral measures. What is it that innovative people actually do? How do innovative people act when compared to people in less innovative organizations? What specific actions are involved in identifying a problem, initiating a proposal, and adopting and implementing an innovation? Most perceptual studies, although useful, are fraught with problems of subjectivity. What people say they do frequently is different from what they actually do. Research using ethnomethodological procedures would seem to be indicated to add more naturalistic observational data to the literature. In addition, laboratory studies—perhaps using organizational simulations—also could contribute much to existing field experiments.

10. Most innovation studies are based upon a performance model of innovation. Such models usually are quite appropriate when emphasis is placed upon task routinization (Hunt, 1970). The bureaucratic, mechanistic approach to studying organizations would be an example of a performance model approach. However, many aspects of innovation are not concerned with routine procedures, especially durng the problem awareness/identification and initiation stages. It would seem that a problem solving approach might be more appropriate, since some form of problem solving is involved at every stage of the innovation process. An emphasis on problem solving also would make it easier to integrate the voluminous literature on individual and group creativity. Currently, little empirical research has been conducted on the role of group creativity in relation to innovation (Van Gundy, 1984).

11. Innovation usually is considered to represent positive values of organizational life. The literature suggests numerous benefits to be achieved from being innovative. However, relatively little attention has been directed toward the costs of innovation (Downs & Mohr, 1979). Both benefits and costs need to be weighed by managers when considering a decision to innovate and by researchers when conducting research.

12. Is innovation a market-push or market-pull phenomenen? Is it both? Should it be both? Are there moderating variables that might play a role? Do organizations innovate due to environmental demands or because of technological considerations, internal to the organization? What are the opportunity costs involved in internal versus external stimulation of innovation? Organizations often shun internal stimuli for ideas in favor of an emphasis upon market research results ("Find out what consumers want and give it to them"). Although such an approach has value as a short-term strategy, it may be counterproductive in the long run. There are many ideas floating around within organizations looking for problems to resolve. It was originally thought, for instance, that the telephone had little practical value. A market can be created, however. The trick is to find

the appropriate degree of balance between internal and external proposal generation and demands of the market.

13. Most research on organizational innovation could benefit from the development of a typology or model of innovation. Such a model would help provide greater consistency of dependent variables, provide for the study of interaction effects among variables and, most important, increase the generalizability of innovation research results.

Perhaps the most promising model in the literature is the one proposed by Bigoness and Perreault (1981). Their model is built around three innovation domains: (1) innovativeness, (2) content and (3) reference. Each of these domains is arrayed to present a simple, three-dimensional framework.

Innovativeness reflects the extent to which an organization has adopted a given innovation. The adoption can be measured either dichotomously (adoption or nonadoption) or continuously (using a specific adoption stage or composite measure). Time also will play a role in innovativeness, since an adoption can be static or dynamic. The content domain is used to tap the specificity of innovativeness. This domain takes into account the fact that organizations may be innovative in some areas but not in others. The content domain is very important, since it can help explain why inconsistent results have been obtained and help demonstrate that an organization's general level of innovativeness is likely to vary across a number of specific content areas. The third domain, the reference domain, provides for consideration of an organization's relevant social system. In particular, this domain identifies boundaries for specifying the social system to be used for comparing an organization's innovativeness. For example, a social system might be specified as a particular country or industry. The social system also can be either internal or external in orientation. An internal orientation would be used to compare an organization with itself at some previous point in time on the content domain; an external orientation would involve comparisons with other organizations.

Overall, the future research needs of organizational innovation seem to mirror those of other areas of organizational behavior. Identification of independent and dependent variables, interactions among variables, precision of definitions, diversity of settings, generalizability of results, perceptions versus behaviors, and many other issues characterize the research needs of a variety of disciplines in the behavioral sciences. The perception of creativity in organizations as a "fuzzy" concept, however, appears to have caused many organizational researchers to shy away from studying it. Its importance is recognized, but little empirical research is conducted, possibly due to the reward system in academe and norms pushing for conventional studies in the area of organizational innovation. Until more empirical research is conducted on creative problem solving in organizations, it is likely to lag behind research on organizational innovation. More than lip service is needed.

References

Abbey, A., & Dickson, J. W. (1983). R&D work climate and innovation in semi-conductors. *Academy of Management Journal, 26,* 362-368.

Adams, J. S. (1974). Structure and dynamics of behavior in organization boundary roles. In M. D. Dunnette (Ed.), *The handbook of industrial and organizational psychology.* Chicago: Rand-McNally.

Aiken, M., Bacharach, S. B., & French, J. L. (1980). Organizational structure, work process and proposal-making in administrative bureaucracies. *Academy of Management Journal, 23,* 631-652.

Aiken, M., & Hage, J. (1971). The organic organization and innovation. *Sociology, 5,* 63-82.

Amabile, T. M. (1983). *The social psychology of creativity.* New York: Springer-Verlag.

Andrews, F. M. (1975). Social and psychological factors which influence the creative process. In I. A. Taylor & J. W. Getzels (Eds.), *Perspectives in creativity.* Chicago: Aldine.

Andrews, F. M., & Gordon, G. (1970). Social and organizational factors affecting innovation in research. *Proceedings, 78th Annual Convention.* The American Psychology Association, *5,* 589-590.

Baldridge, J. V., & Burnahm, R. A. (1975). Organization innovation: Individual, organizational, and environmental impacts. *Administrative Science Quarterly, 20,* 165-176.

Becker, S. W., & Stafford, F. (1967). Some determinants of organizational success. *Journal of Business, 40,* 511-518.

Becker, S. W., & Whisler, T. L. (1967). The innovative organization: A selective view of current theory and research. *Journal of Business, 40,* 462-469.

Besemer, S. P., & Treffinger, D. J. (1981). Analysis of creative products: Review and synthesis. *The Journal of Creative Behavior, 15,* 159-178.

Bigoness, W. J., & Perreault, W. D. Jr. (1981). A conceptual paradigm and approach for the study of innovators. *Academy of Management Journal, 24,* 68-82.

Blau, J., & McKinley, W. (1979). Ideas, complexity, and innovation. *Administrative Science Quarterly, 24,* 200-219.

Bright, J. R. (1964). *Research, development, and technological innovation.* Homewood, IL: Richard D. Irwin.

Brown, W. B. (1966). Systems, boundaries, and information flow. *Academy of Management Journal, 9,* 318-327.

Burns, T., & Stalker, G. M. (1961). *The management of innovations.* London: Tavistock Publishing.

Callahan, R. E. (1979). A management dilemma revisited: Must businesses choose between stability and adaptability? *Sloan Management Review, 21,* 25-33.

Callahan, R. E., & Salipante, P. (1979). Boundary spanning units: Organizational implications for the management of innovation. *Human Resources Management, 18,* 26-31.

Chakrabarti, A. K. (1974). The role of champion in product innovation. *California Management Review, 17,* 58-62.

Comadema, M. E. (1984). Brainstorming groups: Ambiguity tolerance, communication apprehension, task attraction, and individual productivity. *Small Group Behavior, 15,* 251-264.

Cummings, L. (1965). Organizational climates for creativity. *Academy of Management Journal, 3,* 220-227.

Cyert, R. M., & March, J. G. (1963). *A behavioral theory of the firm.* Englewood Cliffs, NJ: Prentice-Hall.

Daft, R. L. (1978). A dual-core model of organizational innovation. *Academy of Management Journal, 21,* 193-210.

Daft, R. L., & Becker, S. W. (1978). *Innovation in organizations.* New York: Elsevier North-Holland.

Dill, W. R. (1958). Environment as an influence on managerial autonomy. *Administrative Science Quarterly, 2,* 409-443.

Dill, D. D., & Friedman, C. P. (1979). An analysis of frameworks for research on innovation and change in higher education. *Review of Educational Research, 49,* 411-435.

Downs, G. W. Jr., & Mohr, L. B. (1976). Conceptual issues in the study of innovation. *Administrative Science Quarterly, 21,* 700-714.

Downs, G. W. Jr., & Mohr, L. B. (1979). Toward a theory of innovation. *Administration and Society, 10,* 379-408.

Driver, M. J., & Streufert, S. (1965). *The general incongruity adaptation level (GIAL) hypothesis, an analysis and integration of cognitive approaches to motivation.* Paper 114, Purdue University Institute for Research in the Behavioral, Economic and Management Sciences, West Lafayette, IN.

Duchesneau, T. D., Cohn, S. F., & Dutton, J. E. (1979, January & December). A panel study of the determinants of innovation in the U. S. footwear industry. *A study of innovation in manufacturing: Determinants, processes, and methodological issues, I, II.* Orono, ME: The Social Science Research Institute, University of Maine at Orono.

Duncan, R. B. (1972). Characteristics of organizational environments and perceived environmental uncertainty. *Administrative Science Quarterly, 17,* 313-327.

Emery, R. E., & Trist, E. (1965). The causal texture of organizational environments. *Human Relations, 18,* 21-31.

Ettlie, J. E. (1983). Organizational policy and innovation among suppliers to the food processing sector. *Academy of Management Journal, 26,* 27-44.

Ettlie, J. E., & Bridges, W. P. (1982). Environmental uncertainty and organizational policy. *IEEE Transactions on Engineering Management, EM-29,* 2-10.

Evan, E. M., & Black, G. (1967). Innovation in business organizations: Some factors associated with success or failure of staff proposals. *The Journal of Business, 40,* 519-530.

Fennell, M. L. (1984). Synergy, influence, and information in the adoption of administrative innovations. *Academy of Management Journal, 27,* 113-129.

Gibb, J. R. (1972). Managing for creativity in the organization. In C. W. Taylor (Ed.), *Climate for creativity,* (pp. 23-32). New York: Pergamon.

Grossman, J. B. (1970). The Supreme Court and social change. *American Behavioral Scientists, 13,* 535-552.

Guilford, J. P. (1959). Traits of creativity. In H. H. Anderson (Ed.), *Creativity and its cultivation.* New York: Harper & Row.

Hage, J., & Aiken, M. (1967). Program change and organizational properties: A comparative analysis. *American Journal of Sociology, 72,* 503-519.

Hage, J., & Aiken, M. (1970). *Social change in complex organizations.* New York: Random House.

Hage, J., & Dewar, R. (1973). Elite values versus organizational structure in predicting innovation. *Administrative Science Quarterly, 18,* 279-290.

Havelock, R. G. (1970). *Planning for innovation.* Ann Arbor, MI: Center for Research on Utilization of Scientific Knowledge, University of Michigan.

Hunsacker, P. L. (1975). Incongruity adaptation capability and risk preference in turbulent decision-making environments. *Organizational Behavior and Human Performance, 14,* 173-185.

Hunt, R. G. (1970). Technology and organization. *Academy of Management Journal, 13,* 235-252.

Hurt, H. T., Joseph, K., & Cook, C. D. (1977). Scales for the measurement of innovativeness. *Human Communication Research, 4,* 58-65.

Huse, E., & Bowditch, J. (1977). *Behavior in organizations: A systems approach to managing* (2nd ed.). Reading, MA: Addison-Wesley.

Isaksen, S. G., & Treffinger, D. J. (1985). *Creative problem solving: The basic course.* Buffalo, NY: Bearly Limited.

Kanter, R. M. (1982, July-August). The middle manager as innovator. *Harvard Business Review,* 95-105.

Kasperson, C. J. (1978). An analysis of the relationship between information sources and creativity in scientists and engineers. *Human Communication Research, 4,* 113-119.

Keller, R. T., Szilagyi, A. D., & Holland, W. E. (1976). Boundary-spanning activity and employee reactions: An empirical study. *Human Relations, 29,* 699-710.

Kirton, M. (1976). Adaptors and innovators: A description and measure. *Journal of Applied Psychology, 61,* 622-629.

Knight, K. (1967). A descriptive model of the intra-firm innovation process. *Journal of Business, 40,* 478-496.

Koprowski, E. J. (1972). Creativity, man, and organizations. *The Journal of Creative Behavior, 6,* 49-54.

Lawler, E. E., & Drexler, J. A. (1981, February). Entrepreneurship in the large corporation: Is it possible? *Management Review,* 8-11.

Lawrence, P., & Lorsch, J. (1967). Differentiation and integration in complex organizations. *Administrative Science Quarterly, 12,* 1-47.

Leifer, R. P., & Delbecq, A. (1978). Organizational/environmental interchange: A model of boundary spanning activity. *Academy of Management Review, 3,* 40-50.

McGinnis, M. A., & Ackelsberg, M. R. (1983). Effective innovation management: Missing link in strategic planning? *Journal of Business Strategy, 4,* 69-76.

Maidique, M. A. (1980). Entrepreneurs, champions, and technological innovation. *Sloan Management Review, 2,* 59-76.

Mansfield, E. (1963). The speed of response of firms to new techniques. *Quarterly Journal of Economics, 77,* 290-311.

March, J., & Simon, H. (1958). *Organizations.* New York: John Wiley.

Mars, D. (1971). The role of the middle manager in nurturing creativity. *The Journal of Creative Behavior, 5,* 270-278.

Merton, R. K. (1957). *Social theory and social structure.* New York: Free Press.

Moch, M., & Morse, E. (1977). Size, centralization and organizational adoption of innovations. *American Sociological Review, 42,* 716-725.

Mohr, L. (1969). Determinants of innovation in organizations. *American Political Science Review, 63,* 111-126.

Normann, R. (1971). Organizational innovativeness: Product variation and reorientation. *Administrative Science Quarterly, 16,* 203-215.

Osborn, A. F. (1963). *Applied imagination* (3rd ed.). New York: Scribner's.

Palumbo, D. (1969). Power and role specificity in organization theory. *American Political Science Review, 29,* 237-248.

Parnes, S. J. (1967). *Creative behavior guidebook.* New York: Scribner's.

Parsons, T. (1956). Suggestions for a sociological approach to the theory of organizations. *Administrative Science Quarterly, 1,* 63-85.

Pasmore, W., & Friedlander, F. (1982). An action-research program for increasing employee involvement in problem solving. *Administrative Science Quarterly, 27,* 343-362.

Payne, S. K., & Beatty, M. J. (1982). Innovativeness and cognitive complexity. *Psychological Reports, 51,* 85-86.

Pierce, J. L., & Delbecq, A. L. (1977). Organization structure, individual attitudes and innovation. *Academy of Management Journal, 2,* 27-37.

Quinn, J. B. (1979). Technological innovation, entrepreneurship, and strategy. *Sloan Management Review, 20,* 19-30.

Roberts, E. B. (1980, October). In: Putting innovation to work. *Duns Review,* 72-81.

Rogers, E. M. (1983). *Diffusion of innovations* (3rd ed.). New York: Free Press.

Rogers, E. M., & Shoemaker, F. F. (1971). *Communication of innovations: A cross-cultural approach.* New York: Free Press.

Rowe, L. A., & Boise, W. B. (1974). Organizational innovation: Current research and evolving concepts. *Public Administration Review, 34,* 284-293.

Sapolsky, H. M. (1967). Organizational structure and innovation. *Journal of Business, 40,* 497-510.

Schoen, D. R. (1969). Managing technological innovation. *Harvard Business Review, 47,* 156-167.

Schon, D. A. (1967). *Technology and change.* New York: Delacorte Press.

Shepard, H. A. (1967). Innovation-resisting and innovation-producing organizations. *Journal of Business, 40,* 470-477.

Siegel, S. M., & Kaemmerer, W. F. (1978). Measuring the perceived support for innovation in organizations. *Journal of Applied Psychology, 63,* 553-562.

Starbuck, W. H. (1983). Organizations as action generators. *American Sociological Review, 48,* 91-102.

Steiner, G. (Ed.). (1965). *The creative organization.* Chicago: University of Chicago.

Thompson, V. A. (1965). Bureaucracy and innovation. *Administrative Science Quarterly, 5,* 1-20.

Tushman, M. S., & Nadler, D. A. (1978). Information processing as an integrating concept in organizational design. *Academy of Management Review, 3,* 613-624.

U. S. Department of Commerce. (1980). *Learning environments for innovation.* Washington, DC: U. S. Government Printing Office.

Utterback, J. M. (1971). The process of technological innovation within the firm. *Academy of Management Journal, 14,* 75-88.

Van Gundy, A. B. (1981). *Techniques of structured problem solving.* New York: Van Nostrand Reinhold.

Van Gundy, A. B. (1984). *Managing group creativity: A modular approach to problem solving.* New York: AMACOM.

Wilson, J. Q. (1966). Innovation in organizations: Notes toward a theory. In J. D. Thompson (Ed.), *Approaches to organizational design,* (pp. 195-218). Pittsburgh: University of Pittsburgh Press.

Witteman, H. (1976). *The relationship of communication apprehension to opinion leadership and innovativeness.* Unpublished master's thesis, Department of Speech Communication, West Virginia University.

Zaltman, G., Duncan, R. & Holbek, J. (1973). *Innovation in organizations.* New York: John Wiley.

Zeldman, M. I. (1980). How management can develop and sustain a creative environment. *Advanced Management Journal, 45,* 23-27.

17

Philosophical Perspectives on the Study of Creativity

Carl R. Hausman
The Pennsylvania State University

Not long ago, Albert Rothenberg (1984), with whom I have worked and been in contact for some twenty years, published a commentary on a series of papers on the topic, "Creation and Interpretation." Although his chief purpose was not to criticize the papers, he did call to task many of the authors for failing to reflect on their own preconceptions of the concept of creativity. He pointed out that the authors play fast and loose with the terms "creation," "creative process," and "creativity," sometimes applying them inconsistently and almost invariably using them without attention to the ways the other writers in the series used the same terms.

My choice of Rothenberg's criticism as a way to start my comments is based on my own dismay over the fact that the lack of care in using the term "creativity" and its variations is not confined to the authors whom he was discussing. Such thoughtlessness is fairly widespread. Many writers who are fascinated with the phenomenon of creativity seem to take for granted that everyone will understand how they conceive the topic. Sometimes they apparently take for granted assumptions about which they themselves have not thought. This is evident when the key terms are not used consistently. For instance, it is implied, if not asserted outright, that creating is something extraordinary and is the province of genius. Yet creating is also thought to be something we all engage in. Creating is sometimes equated with making something physical, such as exemplified in painting, sculpture, and architecture; yet creating is also construed as any process of self-actualization. Creating is doing something valuable; yet creating is simply doing anything that has not been done before.

Unfortunately, ignoring one's presuppositions about what it is to create, may infect one's conclusions about the topic. For example, one assumption that has guided some theorists is that creativity must be dissociated from originality. A consequence of this assumption is to deny the attribute of newness to what is said to be created. But the assumption itself is unnecessary and misguided, for what the one who separates creating from being original seems to want to do is exclude eccentricity or what is bizarre from created outcomes. This motive is well taken. But it does not require our denying newness to what we consider to be a creation. What this motive does require is a bit of reflection on how the idea of creating is normative. That is, we need to consider the possibility that we expect a created outcome to be valuable. Thus, although simply being new is not sufficient to guarantee that a product is a creation, neither is being valuable without being new. It is surely possible that being a creation requires both newness and value.

Formulating these requirements, or criteria, however, is still not enough. What do we mean by "newness?" Is anything that is different new in the sense that is required if something is to be regarded as a creation? What sort of value do we expect? Is being useful for some purpose all that is needed? These questions need to be asked in order to highlight the importance of acknowledging and reflecting on the assumptions about creativity before discussion proceeds as if these assumptions were self-evident. In short, it seems only proper to begin a study of creativity with a consideration of what some would call "the concept of creativity."

The call for, and analysis of, the concept of creativity has been a kind of battlecry for some of the few philosophers who have turned their attention to our topic. Their insistence on the need for such an analysis appears to be the expression of rigor and thoughtfulness, and they are right, I think, in asking for some kind of examination of the term, "creativity." However, there is something curious about the request—something that suggests that reflection has not gone far enough. It may be that creativity is not the kind of power or condition that is amenable, wholly or even in part, to conceptualization. It may not be a concept. In any case, it is fair to ask what is expected of an activity that is to be called "creative." What criteria do we believe must be met if an act is to be called "creative" and its outcome is to be called a "creation?" If the answer to this is not a clarification of "the concept of creativity," it should at least be a step in exploring some of our assumptions about creativity.[1]

Expectations for Creativity

The following remarks will be a sketch of what I believe is expected of creativity whenever and wherever it is encountered. The summary will be based on some of my previously published discussions, though I shall here present these in a somewhat different form. As a word of caution, it should be emphasized that I do not intend to define creativity—such an intention would be a commitment to the assumption that creativity can be understood as a determinate concept. Instead, the discussion should indicate what I think most of us, at least in Western Civilization, assume must take place when creativity takes place. There may be additional conditions, not known to us, that would guarantee that a certain process is creative. If these were known, perhaps creativity could be controlled. It could, that is, if these conditions could be realized when and where creative achievement seemed desirable. I doubt that such knowledge is possible. Reasons for saying this should be obvious later. But the point here is simply that it is possible to state what is expected of an act if it is to be creative without thereby implying that creativity can be fully defined or explained. Indeed, an examination of these expectations should show in what sense gaining complete knowledge, and thus controlling creativity, is impossible.

Our expectations for creativity can be condensed into the following statement: an act that is considered creative must have as its outcome something that is new with respect to the way in which it is both intelligible and valuable. To say that the thing must be intelligible means that the new thing must have a character, an identifiable principle or quality, and that this character is identifiable because it seems to be something we may in the future be able to connect with other things. For example, when Cézanne created one of the paintings that represented the style which helped make his reputation, that painting was intelligible. It made visual sense for at least some of its viewers. It made sense in the way it exhibited color patches that built up forms in the painting—forms such as houses, trees, a mountain. In using color patches in this way, the painting showed the viewer an identifiable way of seeing in terms of painting. This characteristic way of painting—or what perhaps should be called "this style"—was recognized as being related, is some, though not all, respects to other, previous styles, such as those of the impressionist painters. It was also recognized as potentially connected with styles that might come in the future, one of which we now know was *cubism*.

At the same time, the outcome of a creative act is expected to be new or novel. But what does it mean to say that it is new? We can distinguish at least two kinds of newness or novelty. First, newness or novelty may be found in anything that is simply different from its past. We should notice that if it is only difference that counts for newness, then everything in the world is new. Every single thing is different from all things in its past, if for no other reason than because each thing has a specific place in time when it came into existence and, if it is a physical thing, it has its own unique spatial location. Each crayon in a box, no matter how much it may look like other crayons—of the same color, of course—is new in the sense of coming into existence at a specific, unique time. In addition, it has its own spatial location. But this kind of difference is trivial with respect to what is intelligible and significant about the "new" crayon. This kind of difference of particularity is not what we expect of the newness of an outcome of creativity. However, there is a second kind of newness. We may be able to see this if we notice first that the Cézanne painting referred to a moment ago may itself be considered to be new in the trivial sense. It can be regarded as being different from all the Cézanne paintings and the impressionist paintings done earlier. But it was also different in a more important way: difference with respect to its intelligibility or character. This kind of difference from other paintings is more fundamental than the kind of difference attributable to one of the crayons in relation to the other crayons. It is not just being in a different place, and being produced at its own moment in time, that marks it as new. Its newness is newness of what is intelligible. Its newness pertains to what is understandable in bringing about a style in painting that was not known before. It thus has a second radical kind of newness—what I have called "Novelty Proper" (Hausman 1984). In contrast, the trivially "new" crayon is not new in its intelligibility: it is still understood as a crayon and also as like any other crayon of the same color. It is still the same kind of thing as the crayons that preceded it. On the other hand, the more basic new style of Cézanne is exemplified in a new type of painting. While it is not new because it is a painting, just as the crayon is not new because it is a crayon, Cézanne's painting is new as a different kind of painting—or, better, it exhibits a new type.

Not only must the outcome of a creation be radically new, it must also be valuable. Value is not easy to define, if indeed it is definable. Yet, however we understand value, I think it is safe to say that some values, or normative conditions—which function as demands on our attention—are expected of creations. These demands are encountered as compelling requirements, as something that beckons us to judge that the new thing ought to exist. Furthermore, there are two ways these normative conditions call attention to themselves. According to the first way, what we recognize is valuable for the sake of something else. We see that the thing is valuable, or ought to exist, in order that something else may exist. Thus, the values we recognize are goods for something. A knife, for example, is recognized as valuable, as something good, because it can cut food for our nourishment. The knife is thus instrumentally valuable.

The second way a value demands recognition is in showing that something ought to exist for its own sake. What ought to exist is something that ought to be, just because it is what it is. Regardless of whether it is also instrumentally valuable for something else, it still is seen as good in itself. It is then intrinsically good. If the knife seems to be designed in a way that we find attractive, even though what is attractive about it does not make it cut better, then the knife is also regarded as having intrinsic value.

The reason for paying so much attention to instrumental and intrinsic value is that the distinction is important for the value expected of the outcome of creative acts. Most, if not all, examples of creativity are expected to have instrumental value—value for the sake of something. Most new, intelligible things probably would not be considered creations if their newness and intelligibility were not considered valuable instrumentally, as good for some other values. Cézanne's new style was valuable instrumentally for the tradition of painting. It contributed directly to the future of painting—in particular, to cubism. However, we should observe that it would not have contributed in this way—that is, it would not have been worthy of being sustained and influential—if it had not had a value for its own sake. Cézanne's style then, also must have been intrinsically valuable if it was and is considered to be the outcome of a creative act.

These expectations for the outcome of creative acts suggest further expectations which we also have for the acts that lead to created results. I shall not take the space to develop this point in depth. Suffice it to say for our purposes here that if created outcomes are radically new, they must be unpredictable on the basis of what was known at the time they were created. Thus, the activity that leads to created results or outcomes must include some principles or conditions that were not present until the activity succeeded in bringing about the radically new and valuable outcome. Such an activity includes unexpected turns—unexpected, unpredictable, and surprising moments. Thus, it is generally recognized that creative people, as well as their audiences, are surprised about at least some of the things that happen when they create. Archimedes is said to have shouted "Eureka" in expressing such surprise. What creators accomplish often seem to them as much discoveries as they seem to be developments of processes completely under their control. Creations are surprising to them not simply because they and we have limited knowledge about how they succeed, but also because the nature of what they do is to bring new intelligibilities, new types, into the world.

If this account of creativity is adequate, or if it is at least not too far off the mark, then two overlapping consequences follow for those who study creativity with the hope of explaining and controlling the phenomenon. These consequences are: (1) the requirement of radical newness raises the question whether an explanation could be found that would specify and predict newness of intelligibility rather than the trivial newness of simple difference; (2) the requirement of value also raises the question whether an explanation could be found which could foresee the values that contribute to created outcomes. The presence of radical newness and value contradicts the view that an explanation which is based on a model that incorporates the criterion of predictability can be found. One obvious reason for denying such explanations follows from the expectation that creative acts include valuable surprises. This is sometimes referred to as *serendipity*. If the new and valuable type or intelligible character is to some extent surprising, then the creator of that character could not have predicted it. But neither could anyone else predict it, unless what is said to be new is not new after all, but is antecedently known at the time of the prediction.

Some Possible Objections

There are two kinds of objections, which, I think, are most likely to be raised against the acceptance of the above criteria. Someone might question the idea that serendipity occurs, saying that the creator must have the created outcome in mind, at least in some relatively indeterminate form, before articulating it in a medium. The general outlines of a painting or poem or musical composition, or the basis of a logically formulated scientific hypothesis, must be available if the creator is to externalize a created outcome and make it public. But no one I know, who affirms the presence of spontaneity and newness of intelligibility, would deny that there is some envisaged, insipient idea or image present to the creator when the creative act begins. Even Croce and Collingwood, two of the strongest advocates of spontaneity as against preconception in creativity, acknowledge that impressions and formed experiences are present to the creator at the beginning of the creative act. However, the point is that these incipient creations are transformed through the creative act. Furthermore, even if someone were to insist further that the creator could predict the outcome before completing the work or creation, we would still face the problem that the creator could not have predicted his or her own prediction. As Vincent Tomas (1958) said, the creative artist does not have a ready-made target with a bullseye at which to aim before the creative act is completed. That is why there is an element of surprise at some point, even if the moment of surprise arises in the mind of the creator as an insight to be elaborated. Certainly, we are surprised if the outcome is new in the sense mentioned, that is, new in intelligibility and value.

Another objection that might be raised concerns what might be thought to be the program of science. The aim of science, it may be said, is to find the laws and conditions for making predictions; thus, our expectation that there must be surprise is precisely what is at issue.

Give science more time and we will be able to predict the growth of new value and intelligibility—new styles and new theoretical advances in science itself. This objection raises a question of metaphysics, as well as epistemology, since it assumes a metaphysical conception of the nature of reality, or of the fundamental conditions of our experiences.

The objection in question, that our limits in understanding such phenomena as creativity are only temporary, presupposes a metaphysical determinism. This view asserts that everything, including every event and every object, is connected by laws or regularities with every other thing in the universe. All such connections among all things could be known if we had sufficient information and knowledge about all the laws of nature and the kinds of conditions according to which they function. Given such knowledge, we could predict everything in the future, at least to the extent of assigning probability ratios to the things predicted. On the basis of what happened in the past, we could fully explain everything that did occur and which is occurring in the present. If the objector who defends the possibility of predicting instances of creativity were to acknowledge such a presupposed determinism, then he could claim that the conception of creativity as unpredictable is not true in principle. Unpredictability is only a matter of ignorance. Thus, given time, scientists will come to know all that is necessary to know about how information is processed and about the rules by which patterns of connected data are replaced by higher order patterns. With this knowledge, they could predict what in the future will be valued and thus what will be valued as the work of genius.

In response, it should be admitted first that if determinism is true, then the expectation that there must be newness of intelligibility and value must be abandoned. Determinism, in short, implies that "There is nothing new under the sun,"—or, better, with the qualification I have suggested already, "There is nothing intelligible (predictable and relatable to what is known) that is new under the sun." For this view, in principle we can foresee every change in the future. Thus, the idea that creativity is the power to overturn basic assumptions and generate radically new intelligibility must be rejected. Instances of serendipity are only appearances of the emergence of radically new intelligibility. Given time, the underlying connections among circumstances, regularities, and results will be known. Furthermore, the idea that there is value in the results of genius—or value anywhere, for that matter—must be modified, if not dropped. No result could be better or worse than another, since all results would be just whatever they happen to be within the patterns according to which everything must happen. Of course, some things may please and some things displease sentient creatures, but the pleasure too must be predictable in principle, if determinism holds. Further, the view that values are nothing but conditions of pleasure is challengeable. If value is more than what is pleasureable, then whether other value conditions are predictable is surely at issue for the determinist. In any case, the presence of value implies that it could have been absent, that it could have been otherwise, and if we wish to be determinists, we must revise the expectations for creativity that were sketched above.

One serious problem determinism faces is that it is based on a presupposition, which is, after all, a postulate—that is, a view or principle which is not itself proven. As C. S. Peirce (1934a) says, a postulate is only a hope. Peirce goes on to present one of the most thoughtful critiques of determinism in print. I cannot review his entire argument. Suffice it to say here that he points out that when we look around, we see diversity and disconnected things, as well as things in connections and which are apparent instances of laws. We may try to connect the things that appear to be disconnected. We may try to "make sense" of diversity by reducing it to laws or regularities. But if we claim that we do this because everything is necessarily lawfully connected with everything else, we are simply expressing a hope.

Furthermore, if we look at determinism with respect to its most basic frame of reference, we could object that it cannot escape from its own limitation on how much we can understand about our experience. The reason for saying this is that if we ask the determinist what laws and conditions could explain the entire universe, he has only two kinds of answers. The first answer is that the whole universe, which is determined in all its details, is infinite. Thus no finite investigator, or finite group of investigators, could understand the universe so as to predict every detail in it. Only a divine mind could do this. The other answer is not that the universe is infinite but rather that it is bounded or finite. Consequently, it is possible in principle to gain enough knowledge to predict everything in the universe, past, present, and future. Given this answer, the universe as a whole is left unpredicted and unpredictable; there is nothing independent of it that could be known as conditions by virtue of which it could have been predicted. Thus determinism on this alternative, as well as the first, is limited and open to a fundamental condition of unintelligibility, or a limit to the rules of intelligibility laid down by the determinist. In this respect, from the point of view of determinism, the universe is as, if not more, unintelligible than the universe of those who hold the view that there is real spontaneity. The difference is that the determinist gets his unintelligibility all in one dose, at the boundaries of his universe, while the spontaneitist has his unintelligibility in small doses as the universe evolves through moments of spontaneity. What this controversy shows is that neither determinism nor spontaneitism—if the reader will excuse this invention of a label—can be demonstrated. Both views are speculative extrapolations from data to which both proponents assent: there is both order and disorder in the universe. It seems to me that spontaneitism remains closer to this data than does determinism, and it grants the relevance of knowledge that requires predictability. But its presupposition is that this requirement is limited now and in the future. Its postulate, then, is not a hope, as Peirce says determinism is, but is a recommendation, which has heuristic consequences, to remain open minded about future deviations—deviations that are sometimes radical overhaulings of the laws which theories have given us—from the successful predictions available to us up until now.

Devoting so much attention to determinism should make it clear that determinism should not be taken lightly. Determinism is a powerful view, and in a sense it needs to be reflected on carefully by both the determinist and his opponent. The choice between these two views will depend, at bottom, on where one believes the limitations on human knowledge should be placed. I choose mine within the world of diversity and growth.

Directions for the Future

The foregoing discussion might be interpreted as a cry of despair over the possibility of understanding creativity. Long ago, Plato spoke of the creative artist as one who was driven by divine madness, something beyond our understanding. Later, Freud said that the analyst must lay down his arms before the creative artist. More recently, John Hospers (1985) expressed a similar despair when, after reviewing some of the reasons why our understanding of creativity is limited, he asked, "What *can* one say [about artistic creativity]?" Although this way of regarding the study of creativity is not always expressed explicitly, the reason for the despair does, I think, infect much of the discussion of creativity on the part of those who approach creativity from philosophical perspectives. It is the lingering hope of the determinist that lies behind the doubt that anything *can* be said about creativity. It is the expectation that everything must be made predictable and assimilable to what is familiar, if things are to be made intelligible, that haunts many of those who look at creativity philosophically.

However, there are very few philosophical discussions in writing that concern creativity as a distinct topic, at least if we compare these with studies in psychology and biographical writings of artists and scientists. This is not to say that philosophers generally have taken no interest in the phenomenon. Rather, it seems that creativity of the radical kind I tried to sketch above often has been taken for granted or assumed in discussions of other issues such as those that occur in existentialists affirmations of human freedom, in the relation of art processes to non-aesthetic conditions, in understanding concept formation or theory change in the sciences, in theorizing about the nature of thought, or in the development of a metaphysics. When the topic is distinguished, as it has been occasionally in the past decade or so, the result is usually either an analysis of the problems of coming to grips with the phenomenon of creativity or an attempt to propose an explanation that tacitly or explicitly presupposes that understanding is to trace what remains to be understood to what is already known. It should be useful to comment briefly on two examples. In these cases, it can be seen that some form of determinism—or the hope of prediction—lurks in the background of those who claim to offer non-traditional ways of hypothesizing about creativity, just as it haunts those who recognize the limits of determinism when it is directed toward creative achievement.

In a relatively recent book devoted to the topic, *The Concept of Creativity in Science and Art,* R. Harre (1981), whose essay, "Creativity in Science," was written specifically for the volume, begins by acknowledging that to create is to produce something novel—something "of a new and hitherto unknown kind." Yet a few lines later, he reintroduces the spectre of determinism—to be sure, not in the standard form in which it is usually identified, but under the guise of analogical relations. He says,

> So novelty must be tempered by connection with the known, or at least with that amongst the known which we take to be intelligible. . . . But the only possible connection that would allow both intelligibility and novelty is that of analogy. New things and processes must be like known things and processes in some ways, but must be unlike them in others.

Of course, the focus and function of unlikenesses are crucial, and Harré seems to agree, since he spends the remainder of the paragraph in suggesting the origin of them. However, this issue seems to drop out of sight in the subsequent discussion. And well it might, since "novelty must be tempered by connection with the known," and what is known must, presumably, be found in the likenesses that give analogies intelligibility. It is interesting that Harré does not introduce the possibility that a creative achievement might be a "connection that would allow both intelligibility and novelty." I shall return in a moment to this possibility.

The second example of how determinism hovers in the background of twentieth century philosophically oriented approaches to creativity is the work of Arthur Koestler. The extent to which Koestler is bound by determinism is, however, limited. Koestler seems well aware of the limits of a deterministic framework when it is applied to creativity. In what may be thought of as his major work on creativity, *The Act of Creation,* Koestler (1964) proposes a theory that tries to integrate considerations drawn from psychology, biology, and genetics, as well as from his own literary, poetic way of articulating his ideas. His key concept is "bisociation," which refers to a pattern of thinking that is at the basis of creative achievement in all fields, including the art of humor (which for Koestler springs from the same root as all creative expression), all theoretical sciences and the arts, literature, and poetry. Bisociation is the intersection of two dissociated patterns of thinking and feeling, and it yields complexes that are new.

Koestler's concept of bisociation is quite appropriate as a descriptive label for at least a necessary part of creative activity. But a descriptive term is not itself an explanation. The explanation must include an account of the conditions under which bisociation occurs. Koestler's richly developed discussion of these conditions, of course, cannot be set forth adequately here. However, the most fundamental principle can be identified. It is this principle which illustrates the point of taking up Koestler's view, since it shows how a writer who is sensitive to the intricacies of creativity and who affirms the requirement of newness must restrict the explanatory power of his account of creativity.

At the foundation of Koestler's conditions for bisociation is genetic coding. A fully successful understanding of creativity would depend upon identifying an overall rule according to which genetic codes are broken—which would be a rule for the occasions of bisociations. But for Koestler, chance must play an integral role in bisociation, in part because of the place of environmental factors. Thus, there is an overall rule that no rule is final. Creative acts, then, cannot be subsumed under a general rule that enables an inquirer to predict bisociations.

If an account of creativity cannot properly include a principle for predicting creative acts, then what is the proper aim of a study of creativity? Koestler, of course, shows us that conceptual understanding is possible up to a point—in finding connections among various aspects of the phenomenon and providing a system of knowledge drawn from different disciplines and making them complementary to one another. In this way, he treats creativity as a "connection," to use Harré's term, that allows for both intelligibility and novelty.

It seems to me that the kind of account illustrated here may be regarded as a picture—a verbal picture that gives us a perspective on the phenomenon in question. Koestler's is a highly conceptual, discursive picture, though the literary character of his writing is integral to and an enhancement of the discursive presentation. To the extent that the account is discursive and systematic, it places creativity within a general systematic framework, a framework that is the beginning of a metaphysics. To the extent that the account is literary or figurative, involving metaphor, it offers insight that could not be introduced if the account were purely discursive and literal. For instance, the key term, bisociation, itself functions this way. It is a neologism and more. It exhibits in one (figurative) stroke the paradoxical structure of creative acts and shows that structure to be embedded in ordinary yet transforming patterns of thinking.

The idea of pursuing creativity studies with the aim of constructing what I have called a picture is another way of expressing a suggestion I made some time ago in other contexts (see footnote 1). I proposed that an appropriate way to study creativity is through a study of metaphor. Metaphors not only may exemplify creations, but they are also integral to sustained attempts to interpret and understand creative achievements. This is especially evident in interpretations and criticisms of works of art. I did not claim that the study of metaphor could lead to explanation that would fall under the aims of some form of determinism. The paradoxical character of creative acts is just as inescapable in metaphor as in all creations. In fact, I have proposed that metaphor is at the root of all creativity, as its structure—Koestler's idea of bisociation, I think, is one way of indicating this structure—and as a verbal linguistic technique in scientific creativity. Our concern at the moment, however, is to consider the kind of picture that might result from a study that incorporated the outcomes of the study of metaphor and that made use of theoretical studies in the sciences as well as the humanities.

The form and content of a picture of creativity would depend upon the maker's competence, that is, upon the field and training of the inquirer and specific talent for articulating the writer's thought. Koestler's was a rich and broad competence that led to a rather comprehensive picture. But if it were to be joined to an even more comprehensive endeavor, its power as a picture would be greater. The outcome would be a metaphysics with some fundamental teleological structure.

Charles S. Peirce (1934b) sought an architectonic that might have been congenial to the outcome I have in mind. Peirce proposed what he called a developmental teleology, a theory that included purposive activity, teleological process, on a cosmic as well as human scale, that left room for spontaneity, room for the breaking of rules. For him no rule, no law, was final. The fundamental operative principle of the world in which developmental teleology reigned was evolutionary love, or a kind of force or drive toward the future which was open to deviations. However, this is not the place to explore Peirce's or any other philosophical view in terms of the picture building I think is appropriate to creativity study. I only want to hint at the kind of general philosophical view, the overall perspective, that might be appropriate for creativity study undertaken from the approach of philosophy.

It would be a mistake to think that developing a picture into which to fit creativity should be undertaken from above. One of the failures of philosophical views to do justice to creativity in the tradition was the result of beginning with metaphysical inclinations and giving expression to these first, letting whatever might be called "creative" find its place afterward. Thus, some form of radical creativity was taken for granted or it was denied in favor of a determinism that left no room for radical novelty. Insufficient attention was given to what can be meant by "creativity" and the consequences of such meanings. My proposal is that picture building begin with a close examination of the notion of creativity. The ensuing picture should then be developed without contradicting the initial conclusions about creativity.

In conclusion, I should like to raise two general questions about the way to attack the problem of delineating the notion of creativity. The first, in a sense, should not, it seems to me, arise; yet sometimes it occurs as a stumbling block—a constriction on what one undertakes in studying creativity—that may stand in the way of inquiry if it is not addressed. The question concerns whether a study of creativity should be about the process or the product of creativity. My own view, it will be recalled, has been that we must start with the product. It is by their fruits that we shall know them. We recognize that a process is creative because it shows us something that we are willing to call a creation. Thus, we need to look for the conditions necessary and sufficient, if we can find them for an outcome to be deemed a creation. Once some understanding of what there is in an outcome or expression that invites the attribution, "a creation," attention can—must be, if the account is to approach anything approximating completeness—be turned to the process or activity that seems to be responsible for the creation. I see no way of offering an approximation to an adequate picture unless both product and process are studied. To focus on process while ignoring the product is to risk studying processes that are not creative. To focus on the product exclusively is to exclude consideration of the autonomous source responsible for the outcome and which is integral to the conditions for the created character of the outcome.

The second general question concerns suggestions about the particular direction philosophical inquiry about creativity may take in addition to what has been said about picture building. The suggestions I have in mind have to do with the possible component disciplinary findings that might contribute to a philosophy of creativity. I think the most pregnant component is to be found in biology, particularly in genetics as it bears on evolutionary processes. That biology and genetics are fruitful places to look was seen by Koestler. That a general theory of evolution is a fruitful place to find a framework that gives a role to radical creativity while admitting a limited determinism (a developmental teleology) was shown by Peirce.

One conclusion seems inescapable. Future inquiry into creativity should be interdisciplinary. Representatives of various disciplines, from the sciences and humanities, need to cooperate with one another. Debunking the approach of an inquirer who approaches the topic in a way that is different from one's own must be rejected. Of course, my own perspective leads me to think that a philosophical picture-building approach—a metaphysics—offers the most comprehensive, if not most fruitful way of gaining a general understanding of creativity. This is not to belittle the approach of anyone else. I would like to think of this suggestion as a plea for cooperative inter-disciplinary work in the future.

Footnote

1. I have discussed the possibility of stating the conditions of creativity most extensively in; Hausman, C. R. (1984). A paper concentrating exclusively on this issue was published as; Hausman, C. R. (1979, 1981).

References

Harre, R. (1981). Creativity in science. In D. Dutton & M. Krausz (Eds.), *The concept of creativity in science and art*. The Hague: Martinus Nijhoff Publishers.

Hausman, C. R. (1979). Criteria of creativity. *Philosophy and Phenomenological Research, 40,* 237-249.

Hausman, C. R. (1981). Criteria of creativity. Reprinted in D. Dutton & M. Krausz (Eds.), *The concept of creativity in science and art.* The Hague: Matinus Nijhoff publishers.

Hausman, C. R. (1984). *A discourse on novelty and creation.* Albany, NY: New York University Press.

Hospers, J. (1985, Spring). Artistic Creativity. *The Journal of Aesthetics and Art Criticism, 43* (3), 243-255.

Koestler, A. (1964). *The act of creation.* New York: The Macmillan Company.

Peirce, C. S. (1934a). The doctrine of necessity examined. *Collected papers of Charles Sanders Peirce,* Vol. 6 (pp. 35-65). Cambridge, MA: The Belknap Press of Harvard University Press.

Peirce, C. S. (1934b). The law of mind. *Collected Papers of Charles Sanders Peirce,* Vol. 6 (pp. 102-163). Cambridge, MA: The Belknap Press of Harvard University Press.

Rothenberg, A. (1984). Commentary on creation and interpretation. *New Literary History, 15* (2), 397-410.

Tomas, V. (1958). Creativity in art. *Philosophical Review, 67* (7).

18

Needed Research in Creativity for Business and Industrial Applications

Min Basadur
MacMaster University

In an article entitled "Research in Creative Problem-Solving Training in Business and Industry" (Basadur, 1982), I described both how I had learned to apply creative problem solving methodology on an ongoing basis in a large industrial organization and the research that work had spawned. As the application of processes and techniques of creative problem solving penetrated throughout this organization, opportunities for further research began to emerge. The organization became a laboratory of its own, consisting of real people learning to apply creative processes in ongoing everyday business and technical situations. Since that time, my "laboratory" has grown much larger, extending to many varied organizations. New knowledge has been gained and many new questions raised.

A trained practitioner can be of great help to any organization in a variety of creative problem-solving applications. The design of each application opportunity must be developed uniquely and creatively. A thorough consulting diagnosis involving the client(s) and the practitioner is required to develop an appropriate creative plan. The plan includes the selection, development and sequence of creativity techniques to be used. It may include pre-meeting work. It always includes provisions for post meeting action planning and follow-up.

The first part of this paper describes some aspects of implementing and consulting in small group creativity. Specific different types of applications and techniques that I have found successful are identified. Also described is an original piece of research that provides evidence that creativity training does work. It also provides some theoretical models of how it may work in an organization. The research is a field experiment indicating that training in a complete process of creative problem solving can improve attitudes and behaviors associated with creativity.

The second part of this chapter reviews six broad issues relating to practical concerns of using creative problem solving in organizations. Some research findings are shared and directions for future research are suggested.

PART ONE

I have long felt that the success I achieved in my career in new product development and product management had less to do with my formal engineering training than with other skills. These include such things as an ability to get things done, to initiate new ideas and projects, and to "keep many balls in the air" at once. I usually felt quite comfortable with the ambiguity of unstructured situations, and found the many differing aspects, both technical and non-technical, of any particular problem or question stimulating. This led to the realization that I had in some way acquired or developed a set of divergent thinking and feeling qualities in addition to the standard qualities emphasized in engineering school. Many of these thoughts and feelings were confirmed for me during my first exposure to creativity in a formal sense

Figure One.

Complete Process of Creative Problem Solving: Simplex.

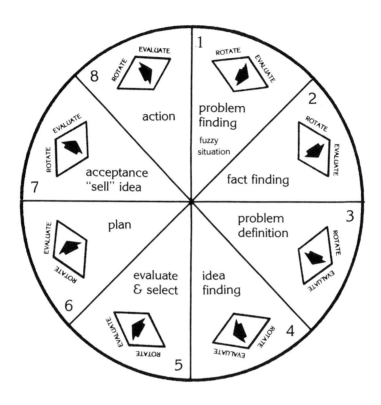

---

at the Creative Problem-Solving Institute at Buffalo, New York in 1971. The week had a dramatic effect on me, and upon my return to work, I resolved to begin developing and implementing creative processes and concepts more deliberately in myself and within the large corporation where I was employed.

My first two steps were to (1) announce informally to the company's R & D community that I was available as a part-time consultant to try to help people or teams solve real world technical problems, and (2) begin using a model of the creative process deliberately and systematically on my own laboratory projects both alone and in conjunction with teams of peers and subordinates. Many of these applications proved quite successful in moving all kinds of projects ahead. These applications included developing new ideas for patentable products, circumventing process patents held by competitors, and meeting test market and national expansion deadlines.

A particular approach to creative problem solving began to evolve and prove itself very useful. The model is called *Simplex* (see Figure One).

Each step of the Simplex approach contains a divergent thinking component followed by a convergent thinking component. This is termed the two-step "ideation-evaluation" process. Ideation is defined as the generation of ideas, information, and opinions without evaluation. Evaluation is defined as generation of judgments relating to these ideas, and performs a filtering function, selecting out the more important ideas. The model is circular, indicating problems once solved merely create new opportunities and challenges, and many problems require an iterative attack.

My consulting process began to evolve into a pattern. The pre-consultation period was the key. The client (the person owning the problem), would meet with me to plan the creative meeting. During this planning meeting I would familiarize the client with the Simplex model including the ideation-evaluation principle. Then we would use the model for the planning process, beginning with the first step. Treating the client's apparent objective as a "fuzzy situation" would allow me to ask fact-finding questions (step two) and to develop a specific meeting objective (problem definition, step three). Often the final meeting objective would turn out to be quite different and more insightful from the one held by the client originally. I soon realized the importance of these first three diagnostic steps for the success of the process. From this base, the client and I would then generate some ideas (step four) of how to best organize the upcoming creative meeting, what specific techniques to employ, and whether or not to ask the group to repeat the first three steps. This is important to consider. The client and I needed to decide whether it would be best for the group to develop their own problem definition or to continue directly with generating solutions (step four). Except in the most straightforward of problems, it is almost always vital to begin in step one again. It is also possible that we would decide that the session should begin in step five (evaluation and selection of alternative solutions) or in any of the following steps. This would depend on the project's development to date.

The client and I also would determine at this time who should participate and where the meeting would be held. I prefer an off-site location to remove the participants from familiar surroundings and increase the probability of novel output. Attendees are notified by a letter inviting their participation. The criteria for selecting participants is based on contribution potential and, where appropriate, team building considerations. Also desirable is the right blend of technical knowledge and "blissful ignorance." This blend allows fresh viewpoints and a certain novel perspective on the problem. The invitation letter always provides a statement of the objective of the meeting, and may also provide some simple imaginative prework to be brought to the meeting. Such prework provides a starting point for ideas, and allows participants to incubate on the problem ahead of the meeting time. The pre-meeting period is usually one to three weeks.

As time went on, the consulting sessions began to "spill over" from R & D to other corporate functions such as engineering, marketing, advertising, and confidential personnel problems. The marketing and advertising problems ranged from complex name brand strategy formulation sessions to more simple brand promotion and new brand name idea-generation sessions. The personnel problems ranged from "how to make our team more effective" to "what to do with a 20-year employee who no longer seems to be productive" or "is no longer seen as fitting in with new and evolving organizational directions and needs." The engineering problems ranged from "how to attach the string to the tampon in the most efficient way" to "how to map out a strategy for a staff engineering group to help line engineering groups improve their cost improvement programs."

The complex brand strategy meetings often ran two days or more in length and primarily focused on the fact-finding and problem definition steps of the Simplex process. They almost always involved representatives of a complete team such as product development, the advertising agency, marketing, packaging development, and sales. In strategy formulation work, it was much more important to determine the best problem definition, that is the *question* to be considered, rather than the subsequent solutions and actions. Since each functional group had its own insular point of view to contribute, it was vital to get all of these views represented.

The less complex, more straight forward brand promotion and new brand name idea generation meetings often ran shorter, about three to six hours. Simple brainstorming was a very effective tool for predetermined specific challenges. An example of such a challenge would be, "how might we entice more New Yorkers to get excited about purchasing Oxydol?" Each small group (six to seven people) would be asked to pause every 40 minutes or so to evaluate their ideas up to that point and report their best five or so. At the end of the session the "very best" of the best would be selected by the participants. An action plan, specifically detailing who would do what came out of every meeting to ensure that action (step eight of Figure One) would take place.

The work on generating new brand names evolved the following theory and practice. New brand names for products were found to range on a spectrum as follows:

Highly Descriptive Names	Secondary Meaning Names	Fabricated Names
Mellow Yellow (soda) (soda)	Escort (car)	Crisco (shortening)
Head & Shoulders (anti-dandruff shampoo)	Downy (fabric softener)	Prell (shampoo)

Simple brainstorming for new brand names was found to lead to a long list of "highly descriptive" names. Highly descriptive names were easily imitated by other companies and were sometimes found wanting in this respect. Imagery techniques were found an excellent way of obtaining "secondary meaning" names. For example, imaging various scenes of refreshment might give rise to a "sea coast" analogy concept which might (and did) lead to the brand name "Coast" for a new "refreshment" bar soap.

The third kind, "fabricated" names, are often the ones most highly desired because they are the most difficult to copy by competitive companies. Here a variation of the "forced relationships" technique of idea generation was found highly effective. "Headline" words pertaining to the product's important properties or benefits or qualities (e.g., softness, absorbency, etc.) are listed across the top of newsprint pages. Participants write in words under each headline which they associate with that quality or benefit. Then participants take two or more columns of these words and start forcing syllables or other parts of words together to form nonsense words. For example:

	Benefit: Soft	Benefit: Absorb
Associated words:	Fluffy	Soak
	Pillowy	Slurp
	Mushy	Drain
	Gentle	Inhale
	etc.	etc.

Forcing pieces of the words above together might produce names such as Sopil, Pip, Sluffy, Pif, Drillo, Gain, Murain, Slush, etc. Forcing together portions of words like "Crisp" and "Corn" might provide a name for a good-frying (Benefit No. one), all vegetable (Benefit No. two) shortening, for example, such as "Crisco" (It probably didn't really happen that way, but it *could* have!).

During this period of time, 1971-1974, I began to believe a full-time corporate-wide position was justifiable for consulting in creative processes and so proposed this to the company. This led to a position for me as "Methods Consultant" within the corporate-wide "Management Systems Division" (a hybrid of data processing and industrial engineering personnel). This base permitted the expansion of applications of small group creativity to manufacturing (e.g. cost improvement, plant modernization, energy conservation, etc.), engineering (new plant and process design), qualitative market research (using consumers as participants), systems analysts (how to consult with clients more effectively), R & D matrix team formation, critical path scheduling, and strategic planning from corporate level to project team levels. Also, an increasing demand for training in creative problem solving began to develop, largely by word of mouth. For example, some of the sales departments began to find such training not only highly pertinent to gaining new business (by more creatively solving customers' problems), but also highly motivational. This led to training sessions of various duration for new sales employees, seasoned sales veterans and entire sales districts.

By this time, I had learned how to incorporate both ideational and evaluative techniques such as metaphors, psychodrama, music and paired comparison analysis into Simplex on the job. Thus the eight-step model had demonstrated itself to be very versatile.

I had become convinced that deliberate, planned, individual and small group creativity process application was a powerful tool in industry for at least two reasons. First, it could be applied to virtually any situation or function across the corporation. Second, it was an excellent way of getting a great deal more depth out of problem solving than was possible by traditional methods. By depth, I refer to breaking through superficiality. For example, often group members would dig up and share information they might normally "hide" in a competitive business environment. This occurred because of the trust level built up in the group by the process. Also, the tendency of the group members to see the same problem from differing viewpoints brought forward information that members were not even consciously aware of as individuals. This caused more imaginative and risky ideas to flow forth.

It was important to get participants to *internalize* the deferral of judgment principle as opposed to having a simple understanding of it. I would often help achieve this by modeling the opposite of this principle. I would ask the members for an idea related to the objective. Then when someone volunteered such an idea I would immediately proceed to destroy it with various "killer phrase" remarks (i.e. "yes, but . . . "). This vividly demonstrated the negative effect of premature judgment on idea flow. Another technique I found valuable involved asking participants to choose a partner from a different department or section with instructions to exchange information they felt was relevant to the session. This increased the tendency to share differing ideas and thoughts. Finally, as the process leader, I continually would demonstrate that I would enforce the deferral of judgment principle (at all times) and that sharing any thoughts occurring to any participant at any time during the session was most desirable and welcome. There were *no* wrong answers.

The Effectiveness of Training

During this period, I became highly intrigued with the possibility of obtaining a better theoretical understanding of the mechanics of these creativity applications and training sessions in addition to being a practitioner. However, when I reviewed the literature on creative problem solving, I found the scientific support to be sparse. There was a particular scarcity of research evaluating real-world applications of creativity training. I found myself desiring more theoretical and scientific grounding in many of the small group dynamics principles and teaching techniques I was employing. As a result, in 1974, I enrolled in a Ph.D. program at the University of Cincinnati, majoring in Organizational Behavior and minoring in Social, Cognitive, and Educational Psychology. Over a period of time, this led to my being able to blend together the theoretical understandings and concepts I was learning in my classes with my work as a creativity practitioner. I found myself feeling much more confident as an "expert" consultant in subsequent sessions and training.

In late 1977, a golden opportunity came my way to convert a company project into my dissertation research because of two unrelated happenings: (1) I was asked to consult with an R & D staff group interested in exploring the question, "Can engineers and scientists be trained to increase their creativity on the job?" and (2) an applied research organization within the company asked me to provide Creativity training to its members. I found a way to combine the above two events into one project which eventually became a controlled field experiment on which my dissertation was based. (The dissertation was designed to be both a direct test of the value of training in creativity in an organizational setting and an attempt to understand the mechanics by which such training might work.) Over the next two years, with considerable cooperation from many people within the large corporation I was employed at, the University of Cincinnati, the Creative Education Foundation, and other organizations, I was able to conduct a controlled field experiment whose results scientifically supported the belief that training in creativity results in positive on-the-job performance improvement.

A particular problem with this kind of research is the difficulty of measurement. In fact, a primary feature of the dissertation turned out to be the development, application and analysis of many different ways of measuring creativity training effects. These went far beyond "paper-and-pencil" tests and "trainee reaction" data, yet they remained compatible with environmental constraints. These measurements were developed gradually during pilot testing with three cooperative R & D project teams over a nine-month period in 1978.

In addition to the measurement difficulty, previous industrial training effectiveness research in general (i.e., not only creativity training research) seemed to be characterized by other problems and inadequacies (Goldstein, 1980; Hinrichs, 1976). The literature contained vigorous debate as to whether or not it was even appropriate to try to evaluate any organizational behavior training (Campbell, Dunnette, Lawler, & Weick, 1979; Campbell, 1971). Other problems included shortcomings in methodology, such as inadequate control or being overly mechanistic, and a lack of investigation of real-world portability effects. Thus, the field experiment was carefully designed to minimize all of the above inadequacies.

The research below was presented at the 1980 annual convention of the American Psychological Association. Participants in the study were engineers, engineering managers, and technicians of a large engineering department. This department was involved in applied research and wanted more new projects initiated and completed. An experimental (trained) group was compared to two control (placebo and non-placebo) groups. The training employed was described as a three-stage "complete process" of Problem Finding, Problem Solving and Solution Implementation (Figure Two). This was actually the 8 step Simplex approach described earlier in Figure One, but simplified for research reporting purposes.

Six hypotheses were tested, both immediately after training and later back on the job. There were three methods of measurement (questionnaire, tape recorded task, and interview) and 22 different measures. The hypotheses were as follows:

In an applied research setting, given a sample that has a relatively low ideation tendency, training in a "complete process of creative problem solving" emphasizing the ideation-evaluation process in all stages (see Figure Two) will lead to:

H1A: An increase in preference for ideation in problem *finding*
H1B: An increase in preference for ideation in problem *solving.*
H2A: An increase in the practice of ideation in problem *finding*
H2B: An increase in the practice of ideation in problem *solving*
H3A: Improved performance in problem *finding*
H3B: Improved performance in problem *solving*

Fundamental to the above hypotheses was a firm belief, based on experience, that group members (or individuals working alone) must be able to internalize the "ideation-evaluation" and the "deferral of judgment" principles. In other words, the creative model proposed is successful only when actual separation of ideation and evaluation is achieved in thinking, attitude, and behavior. Cohen, Whitmeyer and Funk (1960) show that given a substantial

Figure Two.

A "Complete Creative Problem – Solving Process" Emphasizing Ideation – Evaluation as a two step process in each of three stages.

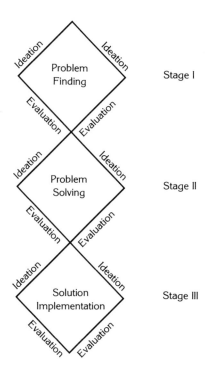

training period, trained subjects provided better ideas then untrained subjects. However, Rickards (1975), with training confined to only a warm-up activity, found little or no difference between the output of trained and untrained groups. Training must be of sufficient duration and intensity to bring about increased preference for the two-step ideation-evaluation process. Thus, the process is not simply cognitive but also affective in nature. It is due to the fact that changes are experienced at both of these levels that results are significantly improved.

Summary of Field Experiment Results

Thirty-two out of a total possible of 44 supportive contrasts were statistically significant. None of the 22 contrasts between placebo and untreated groups were significant. Moreover, each of the six hypotheses was supported by at least one significant contrast.

Overall, the results strongly supported four of the six hypotheses. In particular, individuals receiving such training in an applied research setting, especially if they are relatively low in ideation tendency, seem to show significant differences compared to controls in:

1. Preference for ideation in problem *solving* (H1B), but maybe not in problem *finding* (H1A);

2. Practice of ideation in both problem *finding* and problem *solving* (H2A and H2B); and

3. Problem *finding* performance (H3A), but maybe not in problem *solving* performance (H3B).

The effects of the training appear to be fairly "generalized." That is, there was evidence of changes in cognitive (e.g., openness to ideas), and behavioral (e.g., number of negative judgments made on ideas; and not jumping to conclusions) processes. Both arenas (cognitive and behavioral) seemed actively involved by this training. Our belief that the effects of training are more likely to be long lasting when several aspects of behavior are influenced was encouraged by this evidence.

Some changes in the behavior patterns of trainees were readily observable by co-workers even back on the job. Thus, the training appears to translate (at least in the short run) into actual changes in job behavior. This relationship was stronger for the "practice of ideation" than for "problem-solving performance."

One interesting anomaly in the results is that preference for ideation in problem finding was only weakly affected by the treatment, yet "practice of ideation" and performance in problem finding showed strong effects. It may be the case that training can get participants to *do* problem finding (cognitive and behavioral) yet still not *like* it (affective or attitudinal). Problem finding for many people in our culture appears to be a somewhat unfamiliar chore, especially for people who tend to operate more in problem solving or solution implementation modes (e.g., business people in more programmed jobs and engineers in applied work).

Future Directions for Research

One future direction is to test the elements of the model (Figure Two) more completely, particularly the evaluation steps and implementation stage. Furthermore, creativity talent identification research could be integrated into empirical tests of the model (Gough, 1976; Guilford, 1967; MacKinnon, 1962, 1977; Roe, 1976). For example, it remains to be shown whether this training influences different personality or cognitive traits differentially, or whether one can identify more creative people by their behavior during such training. Perhaps greater gains in organizational creativity could be realized by focusing training only on people possessing certain traits.

A second research direction involves generalizability. One of the limitations of this study is that it concerns only one organization sample. Future studies should cover different types of organizations, different organizational functions and other organizational levels.

A third research direction would be to attempt to clarify and replicate the training effects discovered in this study. Increasing base size and strengthening the internal consistency and reliabilities of measures, especially for some of the on-the-job observational measures, is in order. Further, developing improved methods to measure all hypothesized constructs would appear to be a fruitful opportunity for some creative methodological work.

A fourth research direction would be to negotiate opportunities to study transferability of effects for longer periods, say ten weeks, six months, one year or several years.

Finally, an interesting line of research would be to explore the relative contributions of ideation and evaluation at each of the three stages of the process (Figure Two). Also, one might question whether these relative contributions differ by task. For example, perhaps in high implementation-oriented jobs the contribution or importance of evaluation is relatively higher than ideation. Perhaps there are optimum "ideation-evaluation" ratios which differ by stage for any job or organization.

In conclusion, it appears that creativity, in the narrow sense of this research, can be influenced by training. As always, more new questions have been raised than answered as understanding has deepened. Sockman's saying, "the larger the island of knowledge, the longer the shoreline of wonder" is supported by this experience.

PART TWO

Since the original research, six broad practical issues have guided my selection of research projects from the wide array of options. The summaries that follow are organized around these six issues.

The six broad issues are: (1) inducing more managers, professionals and other organizational members to try using creative problem solving processes and techniques in their daily work; (2) increasing understanding among all parties interested that a systems approach is a must; (3) increasing understanding of how problem solving processes overcome inadequacies in real world human problem solving and decision making processes; (4) furthering understanding of how creative problem solving processes and techniques can serve to operationalize various new management tools; (5) using the extended effort principle for idea generation; and (6) gaining a better understanding of the exogenous factors which may increase organizational creativity and effectiveness.

1. *Inducing the use of processes and techniques.*

One of the major problems to be solved in bringing more creativity into organizations is inducing the key managers and professionals to try using creative problem solving processes and techniques in their daily work and to model the necessary attitudes and thinking skills consistent with creativity. Because of their previous traditional training, many managers and professionals tend to have a negative view of creativity. For example, in two recent studies, Basadur and Finkbeiner (1983a; 1985) identified four managerial attitudes relating to ideation in organizations. One attitude is "preference for ideation," confirming the construct developed in the research described earlier. This is a positive attitude, as is one other of the four attitudinal factors uncovered, "valuing new ideas." However, the other two were both negative; "tendency to make premature critical evaluations of ideas," and "belief that creative thinking is bizarre." Experience confirms that such negative attitudes are held by many managers and professionals in business and industry. More is said of their study later in this section.

Methods of inducing managers to try creative problem solving processes and techniques on-the-job include improving their understanding of such processes and techniques, providing scientific research evidence that they are valuable to use in their jobs, and improving their attitudes toward such processes and techniques. The following is one example of research into attitude change (Basadur, Graen, and Scandura, 1985).

The purpose of the research was to find out if training of manufacturing engineers in a complete process of creative problem solving will result in a positive change in attitudes which are associated with the effective use of creative problem solving techniques on the job. Below are the hypotheses for the effects of the training.

1. Training manufacturing engineers in creative problem solving will lead to the following attitude changes which will persist five weeks after the training:

    H1a: An increase in preference for ideation (active divergence)
    H1b: A decrease in tendency to make premature critical evaluations
        of ideas (premature convergence)

2. Training manufacturing engineers in creative problem solving as members of a natural work group which returns to work to the same location as a unit all

having experienced the same training compared to members that come to the training from different work groups then return to diffuse work locations following the training will lead to the following attitude changes which will persist five weeks after the training:

H2a: A greater increase in preference for ideation (active divergence)
H2b: A greater decrease in tendency to make premature critical evaluations of ideas (premature convergence)

The participants were drawn from a large consumer goods manufacturing organization. These manufacturing engineers were known to be "efficiency minded," achieving excellence in performing their routine work assignments. However, this same tough-minded orientation toward optimizing the day-to-day routine was working against the manufacturing engineers attempting to also be "innovation-minded," that is, using creativity to develop new routines, anticipate new opportunities and find new problems (opportunistic surveillance) (Simon, 1960), and solve old persistent problems in new ways.

From this manufacturing organization, 65 manufacturing engineers from eight different locations were invited to a three day (24 hours) intensive training program in this complete process of creative problem solving as described above. A second similar group of 47 manufacturing engineers were invited to a second training program five weeks later. The only major difference was that the second group of manufacturing engineers were all from the same single location.

The design is a field experiment using non-equivalent groups (Cook and Campbell, 1976). The procedures of this research were such that the experimental design and measures were meshed with organizational events. The measures were introduced to the participants as non-evaluative aids to developing future training.

The six item "preference for ideation" scale was used to measure the "active divergence" attitude and the eight item "tendency to make premature critical evaluations of ideas" scale was used to measure the "premature convergence"/"not deferring convergence" attitude. The two scales were randomly mixed into one 14-item questionnaire identical to the procedure used by Basadur and Finkbeiner (1985).

The overall multivariate analysis of variance demonstrated significant ($p < .001$) time and treatment by time effects for both self-report and supervisor report. All gains over both five-week periods were significant (time effects). In contrast, the differences between the gains of the two groups (treatment x time effects) were not all significant. The gains in preference for ideation measures taken from both self and supervisor reports failed to show significant differences between groups for the period from the pretest to post-test one. Though these two treatment x time effects were insignificant, the remaining six treatment x time effects were significant (five at .001 and one at .05).

Thus, the results showed support for the effectiveness of training on both preference for ideation and reduction in the tendency to make premature critical evaluations under family-type training. However, under missionary-type training only the tendency to make premature critical evaluations yield significant results.

Thus, this field experiment illustrated that training in a complete process of creative problem solving improves attitudes toward creativity even among subjects likely to be highly skeptical. Trained manufacturing engineers were found to be significantly higher in preference for ideation and significantly lower in tendency to make premature evaluations of ideas than untrained engineers five weeks after return to their jobs. That is, from before to after the training, the engineers increased their preference for generating different points of view and new or novel solutions to problems and increased their preference for keeping an open mind on ideas until they can be further explored and developed.

This study demonstrates that training can positively influence manufacturing engineers' attitudes toward creative problem solving and identifies an important aspect of the training situation, the use of intact work groups. Attitudes are important antecedents to the use of creative problem solving on the job. The results of this research point to methods of training that can positively change those attitudes and therefore enable the development of more creative organizations.

2. *Increasing understanding among all interested parties.*

The next study represents the approach of improving understanding of creative problem solving processes and techniques as a method of inducing trial. The above research was made possible in part because of the previous efforts of Basadur and Finkbeiner (1983 a, b, 1985) to develop reliable, and valid measures of two attitudes associated with ideation: (1) preference for ideation and (2) low tendency to make premature critical evaluations of ideas. These two attitudes were identified and measures developed in a study attempting to "sharpen up" a "deferral of critical judgment" scale as an early measure of "preference for ideation."

The research is presented here and directed specifically at furthering the understanding of attitudes apparently related to ideation. Effective ideation may require specific attitudes favoring this kind of thinking, perhaps to help participants truly "let loose" and use more fully their unencumbered imagination. Thus, for training to succeed, it may have to have sufficient impact to increase such attitudes.

The research explored this question: What attitudes may be associated with the ideation thinking process? Basadur (1979) and Basadur et al. (1982) identified one such attitudinal construct "preference for ideation," and offered a preliminary seven-item scale to measure it. The research discussed here attempted to strengthen the internal consistency, reliability, and external validity of that scale. Thus, one purpose of this research was to construct a new scale with additional items that could provide better internal consistency. We call this Study Number One.

In Study Number One, a group of 36 middle managers and professionals, drawn from across all the functions of a large industrial company and familiar with creative problem-solving concepts such as ideation and deferral of judgment, were asked to suggest scale items to add to the two strong items from the original preference-for ideation scale. This exercise produced 101 new items. A questionnaire including the total 103 items was sent out to a broad cross section of 186 middle managers and professionals from several companies, who were asked to evaluate the items on a five-point scale, ranging from "strongly agree" to "strongly disagree." This latter sample included both people who had and had not been exposed to training. We extracted four factors.

We examined the four factors for item content and labelled them accordingly. One factor, which included the two original scale items, was identified as "preference for ideation"; we designated it factor number one to indicate we considered it of primary interest. Then, to construct a meaningful and relatively pure measure of factor number one, we selected only those six items that loaded solely on it and higher than 0.30 to comprise the first scale. We tentatively named the other three factors "tendency for premature critical evaluation of ideas"; "valuing new ideas"; and "belief that creative thinking is bizarre," designating them factors number two, three and four respectively.

Study Number Two was an independent study to establish the internal validity, reliability, and external validity of Scale Number One ("preference for ideation") from Study Number One. A new sample of 238 managers and professionals from a variety of industrial, business, and hospital organizations completed a 14-item questionnaire derived by combining in random order the six items from Scale Number One with eight items selected from factor number 2. We chose the eight items constituting Scale Number Two, "tendency for premature critical evaluation of ideas," by using a procedure similar to that used for Scale Number One.

The data from the 238 panelists were factor analyzed to confirm that the two sets of items indeed constituted two separate factors, as Study Number One had led us to believe. We used factor analysis procedures identical to those of Study Number One. A two-factor solution emerged. All six items from Scale Number One loaded on one factor and all eight items from Scale Number Two loaded on the other factor. The Cronbach alpha reliability estimate was then calculated for each scale (Cronbach, 1951). Thus, internal validity and reliability had been assessed.

Next, to assess external validity, the panelists' response scores in each of the two scales were calculated. From the large sample, we selected two nearly equal, smaller "known" groups. These consisted of panelists whom two independent expert judges had identified as being either high or low in their preference for ideation on the job (the judges were two people familiar with both the concept of ideation and also with the individuals' on-the-job attitudes and behaviors.

A significant difference occurred in the hypothesized direction between the "known high" and "known low" group mean scores on the "preference for ideation" scale. There was no evidence of a significant difference between the same groups on the "tendency for premature critical evaluation of ideas" scale. Thus, significant evidence indicated that the "preference for ideation" scale can discriminate between the two groups while the other scale does not. This supports the idea that the "preference for ideation" scale agrees with the expert judges in identifying participants' preferences for ideation. Thus, we found evidence of the external validity of the "preference for ideation" construct.

In discussing these results, Basadur and Finkbeiner proposed that the instrument described as Scale Number One acts as a valid and reliable measure of the "preference for ideation" of an individual in an organizational setting. Factors number two, three and four, tentatively identified as possible valid and useful constructs on their own, are particularly intriguing for future research.

The above concepts may help clarify the attitudes and cognitions relating to Osborn's four brainstorming operations: (1) defer judgment, (2) strive for quantity, (3) welcome freewheeling, and (4) hitchhike. The first operation seems more passive, the latter three more active. Speculatively, a high "preference for ideation" appears associated with performing the latter three operations well–and thereby "triggering ideation"–while a low "tendency for premature critical evaluation of ideas" might be associated with performing the first operation well, thereby allowing "freedom for ideation." An examination of the items in factors number three and four (Basadur and Finkbeiner, 1983a) suggested that the attitudes of low "belief that creative thinking is bizarre" and high "valuing new ideas" might be similarly associated with the "welcome freewheeling" and "hitchhike" operations, respectively. How the attitudes actually relate to the thinking processes is a matter for further research (See Figure Three).

In summary, we have identified four separate attitudinal factors relating to ideation and have developed a reliable and valid measure for one of them. This differentiation may prove particularly useful in helping organizations and individuals better understand specific attitudes and thinking processes affecting creative behavior–and understand how training in creative problem solving works, thereby increasing its effectiveness. For example, an organization may seek to preferentially target its training to modify whichever of these four attitudes it diagnoses as most critically needed. Also, when such training is provided, the concept of ideation may now be better and more completely explained to participants. At the beginning of training, organization members are likely to have substantially different interpretations of the meaning of constructs associated with creative problem-solving training such as "ideation." This research may thus reduce some of the "mystery" of creativity training.

3. *Increasing the understanding of the value of process for solving real-world problems.*

Both organizational adaptability and efficiency are important for organizational effective-

Figure Three.

Revised model of Creative Problem-Solving Training emphasizing Ideation and differentiating between "Ideation Freeing" and "Ideation Triggering".

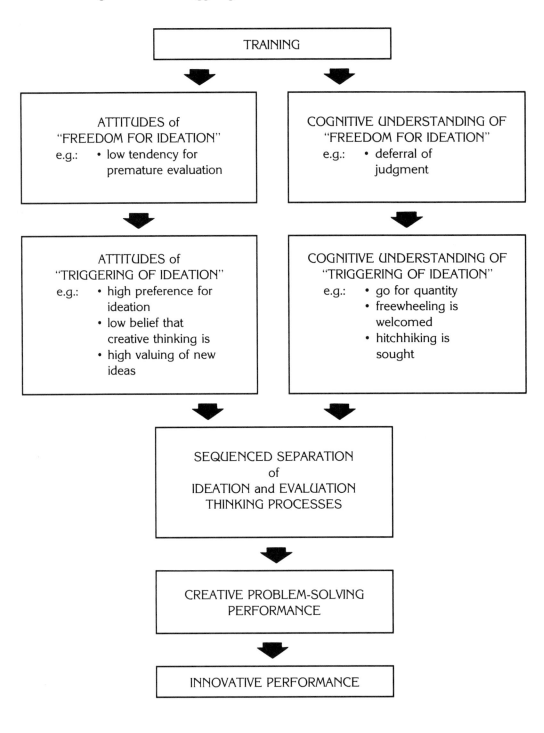

ness. Clarifying these two as distinct components of effectiveness represents another approach to increasing managerial understanding of the need for creativity. For example, Basadur (1986) described the concepts of adaptability, efficiency, and effectiveness as well as horizontal and vertical leadership for members of business and industry.

In many companies which have thrived on functional excellence and organizational efficiency, the need to expand managerial competence in the following new ways is being increasingly recognized:

- More idea generation and thought leadership
- More horizontal leadership and team work
- More strategic thinking

In the following section, a unique, proven, managerial productivity process is described which helps maintain profits in spite of inflationary and market pressures. The centerpiece of this productivity process is a trainable thinking process called a "Complete Process of Creative Problem Solving" (See Figure Two). This process is action-oriented, facilitates teamwork and team leadership, and develops thinking skills and attitudes for taking problem solving initiative and idea generation. It is a practical, research-based process. It expands the kind of thinking skills and attitudes prevalent among most North American managers.

There are two very different kinds of problems and decisions people encounter in business, industry, and their personal lives. The first kind is of a more "programmed" nature. Solutions to this first kind are based on rigorous training, experience, analytical skills and knowledge of rules and procedures. The second kind are of a more "non-programmed" nature. Solutions require additional skills such as problem sensing, problem defining, fact gathering, seeing different points of view, and creating and selecting from diverse options. They require the use of the imagination, non-linear thinking and some risk-taking. They usually have never been encountered before and have no pre-set rules and procedures to guide their handling. They are sometimes caused by changing circumstances. Such problems are typically less structured, more unpredictable, and ambiguous as to "what is wanted." Often the main job is to discover and define "what is wanted" because no one really knows. Often sensing, anticipating and defining the problem is much more difficult than solving it.

In today's rapidly changing business environment, managerial skills in *both* of the above kinds of problems are vital for effective performance. Unfortunately, our traditional formal training addresses primarily the former, the more "programmed" kind of problem. We tend to learn formulas, problem "types" and rules and procedures. The focus of the "Complete Process of Creative Problem Solving" is to help with the second kind of problem which is less structured and less programmed and where higher level initiative, imagination and tolerance of ambiguity is vital. The process enhances problem initiation, solution, and implementation skills in non-programmed decision-making.

Research (Mott, 1972) shows that highly productive organizations have three major characteristics in common:

1. Efficiency (the ability to organize for routine production)
    - High quantity of "product"
    - High quality of "product"
    - High output/input (0/I) ratio

2. Adaptability (the ability to organize to change routine)
    - Anticipating problems
    - Staying abreast of new technology
    - Prompt and prevalent acceptance of new solutions

3. Flexibility (the ability to organize to cope with temporary emergencies and main-
    tain the routine)

Efficiency is the ability to organize for routine production. A routine is something that
we do over and over again. In addition to being efficient, productive organizations are also
flexible, that is that they have the capacity to cope with, to respond to and react to temporary
changes or interruptions and maintain the routine. They can deal with interruptions and get
back to normal routine and highly productive work. Flexibility thus can be lumped in with
efficiency. They are both necessary in the short run.

Adaptability is a longer-range characteristic. It refers to an organization's capacity to
intentionally change its routines and to find new, ongoing, better ways to do the business that
it does. Adaptability requires no more programmed thinking skills and tends to be consistant
with problem *finding* performance. Efficiency requires more programmed thinking skills and
tends to be consistent with solution *implementation* performance. Flexibility is more of a
blend, and tends to be consistent with problem *solving* performance.

Non-programmed thinking skills become more vital as the amount of change confronting
the organization increases. To summarize:

High efficiency means excellent mastery of the routine while high adaptability means
a high rate of change in the routine.

In pursuing high efficiency, we are highlighting and measuring absolute performance. In
pursuing adaptability, we are highlighting and measuring progressive rate of change. The
most effective organization would be the one which combined highest efficiency (e.g., as
measured by lowest cost) with highest adaptability (e.g., as measured by highest progressive
rate of lowering cost).

The problem-solving process used in training (See Figure Two) is based on two major
concepts. First, it is seen as having three different stages. It separates problem finding from
problem solving and from solution implementation. The second important feature of the
process is that within each of the three critical stages, there is a common fundamental process.
This is a two-step process called "ideation-evaluation." Both aspects are believed essential
to creativity.

There are three major premises underlying training based on this view. First, for most
people, the ideation step is more difficult than the evaluation step of the ideation-evaluation
process. Our society, general training and school systems tend to reward and hone our
evaluation capabilities and preferences and promote their use virtually to the exclusion of
ideation. (MacKinnon, 1962, 1977; Osborn, 1963; Thurstone, 1950; Wallach, 1971). Over a
period of time, evaluation starts to dominate. For example, some research has shown that
engineering students upon graduation are less able to use their imaginations than when they
entered four years earlier (Altemeyer, 1966; Doktor, 1970). Second, even within the above
context, there are individual differences. People differ in their relative preferences, aptitudes,
and/or abilities in the two steps of the ideation-evaluation process (Guilford, 1967). Some
people may be relatively better in ideation or evaluation. Third, while the training is designed
to strengthen both steps of the ideation-evaluation process, it is expected to have the most
effect on that step of the ideation-evaluation process that is least developed in each trainee.

In practice, the three stages are reshaped into a circular eight-step process (Figure One).
The process must be "learned by doing" and therefore the training is experiential. The training
is accomplished by a series of diverse tasks and then direct application to real world problems.

Training in the "Complete Process of Creative Problem Solving" encourages people to
explore new territory, to find new ideas and to continually bring new energies to problem
solving. New breakthroughs are more likely to occur under this process of different points of
view, relaxed supportiveness and increased energy. The process is trained to be used on the

job both by individuals and groups in day to day business activities as well as in formal problem solving meetings.

In summary, the use of the "Complete Process of Creative Problem Solving" and supportive environments result in the kinds of corporate behaviors exhibited by employees who:

- Search for new opportunities and new problems;
- Have a positive attitude that problems can be solved;
- Value interfunctional problem solving activities;
- Rely on different points of view;
- Appreciate the value of investing time in identifying the "real problem" before searching for solutions, believing that "a problem well stated is half solved."

4. *Problem solving as new management tools.*

There are three keys to assure the success of the process corporate wide. First, it is vital that top management makes sure everyone knows the "business need." Top management planners must calculate and present the business need to the function heads in a "bullet-proof" case for adaptability improvement at the very beginning of the process. Furthermore, the function heads need to be involved in the planning and tailoring of the overall approach and receive training first. At least one high ranking member of management should be present at virtually every training program to share the overall company business need and position the particular local business need. Cost and profit data should be openly shared with employees at all levels. People want to help, but they can't solve cost and profit problems without the cost and profit facts. Before a training program is designed, an extensive "preconsultation" with the leaders of the organizational sub-unit should be conducted to ensure the appropriate business need is addressed. Corporate strategy decisions and commitments need to be openly shared with employees. Anticipated cost improvements are calculated directly into next year's budget. Successful realization is thus expected. In essence, just as good management sets efficiency goals, it must also set adaptability goals.

Second, interfunctional profit improvement teams need to be formed to attack specific problems. The idea is to leverage traditional functional performance. This is because the problems of sustaining profit in today's accelerated competitive arena require an interdisciplinary approach. Most times the problems require knowledge about several parts of the business. Furthermore, the best solutions often affect or require the cooperation of other functions (e.g., a manufacturing idea to reduce cost may cause sales to have an additional "headache," yet the net result is very positive).

One example of how the use of the "Complete Process of Creative Problem Solving" expanded the range of thinking follows. A manufacturing management interfunctional team was concerned with crewing a new process designed to improve the way seasoning was applied to a snack food product. As originally perceived, the problem was "how might we crew the new seasoning loop?" With further fact finding and shifting of points of view, the problem was redefined first as "how might we minimize cost and maximize output labor when crewing the loop?", and finally sharpened to "how might we obtain 'crew buy-in' for how we crew the new seasoning loop?" Several good ideas were generated and an action plan developed as soon as this new problem definition was recognized. For most teams, the problem sensing and redefinition process is the most powerful aspect of the Complete Process of Creative Problem Solving. Investing creative effort in fact finding and in problem definition always pays off in saving time by finding superior solutions which can be implemented more quickly.

Third, there must be training provided in the new attitudes, behaviors and thinking skills expected. However, it is not sufficient to simply train members in the "Complete Process of

Creative Problem Solving." All key managers must also receive training in how to manage the organizational factors to make the training "stick." Some of these factors are listed below:

    (a) Help organizational members understand the business need and the adaptability concept.
    (b) Give teams the right tools and attitudes to perform creatively.
    (c) Provide expertise in the thinking skills and attitudes to help members find and solve tough, important problems.
    (d) Train higher management how to nurture adaptability and horizontal leadership performance via structural methods.

In summary, the complexities of managing a successful business in the 1980's and beyond are increasing. National markets are now international markets. Regional competitors are being merged to form national competitors. Inflation wanes and waxes but never disappears. Consumers demand more value and will continue to do so. Planned productivity and the employment of minds, as well as bodies may have been optional in the past . . . it's mandatory today. The process provides a method of aligning business need, teamwork and creative problem solving to improve key business results *and* at the same time, deepen and strengthen the partnership between a company and its employees. The development of increased adaptability will no doubt dictate the survival and continued profitability of many a well-known firm over the years ahead.

5. *The extend-effort principle*

Several theorists have suggested that extending effort in idea generation improves creative problem solving performance and skills. Extended effort involves generating additional possible solutions to a problem beyond the first crop of ideas that come to mind, deferring the impulse or tendency to "quit early" when a good idea may seem to be already in hand. For example, extended effort is one of the four operational rules of Osborn's (1963) brainstorming process ("quantity breeds quality"). Gordon (1956) writes of the principle of "deferment," the capacity to discard the glittering "immediate" in favor of a shadowy but possibly richer "future."

There has been empirical support for this extended effort principle in laboratory research in solving non-real world problems. Parnes, (1961), showed that when effort was deliberately extended under Osborn's four rules, the number of good ideas generated was greater in each of the two latter thirds of the idea generation time period than in the first third of the time period. These results, plus Gordon's theory of deferment led Parnes to speculate that under extended effort, the *single best idea* might occur more often in the chronologically latter part of the series of ideas generated.

If there were empirical evidence that the best idea frequently would come later (rather than earlier) in a series of ideas produced by deferment, that is, by extending effort to pile up a list of ideas prior to selecting one, perhaps more managers could be induced to try these principles of deferment and extended effort. Ultimately they could become skilled at these non-sequential thinking techniques and thus boost their managerial decision making effectiveness. They would less often "grab the first idea and run with it" and more often develop several ideas prior to selecting one as the "best bet." The research reported here represents an attempt to provide such empirical evidence.

These hypotheses, as tested in this field research, were specifically worded as follows:

In creative problem solving, when extended effort is used to generate a series of ideas to solve a meaningful real world technical or managerial problem, the most preferred idea:

    H1:   Will occur more often among the *latter two thirds* of the ideas in the series than among the first third.

H2:   Will occur more often among the *last third* of the ideas in the series than the first two thirds.

Two studies were conducted to test the above hypotheses. One study involved individual problem solving, the other involved group problem solving.

In the first study, participants received four hours of training, then applied the training (See Figure One) individually to a common real problem. Participants devoted five minutes to each of the three steps preceding idea generation (total 15 minutes). They shared their work at the end of each step. At the end of the third step one common problem definition was selected as useful and meaningful to everyone. The idea generation step was then done individually for five minutes on this common problem definition. Individuals then chose their most preferred idea (MPI) from the series (list) of ideas they had just generated. No formal evaluation criteria were used. The total number of ideas in the series and the chronological or serial position in the series of the MPI were reported by each individual.

In the second study, managers and professionals were trained for one to two days (8 to 16 hours) in the same "Complete Process of Creative Problem Solving" described above and applied it to their own individual problem from the beginning. (There was no common agreed problem or problem definition). Each individual received help from a small group comprised of three other trainees. Individuals chose the MPI individually from the list generated for their problem definition using their own criteria selected from the list of potential criteria. As in the first study above, individuals then reported their total number of ideas in the series and the chronological (serial) position in the series and the chronological (serial) position in the series of the MPI.

The base size in the first study was 101, and 264 in the second. The training groups involved 10 to 30 participants each. There were 6 training groups in the first study, and 14 in the second.

The research design was a field study in which the data were gathered by questionnaire following the problem solving activity. Each participant reported three numbers:

1. the total number of ideas that were generated for the problem selected;
2. the chronological number (serial position) of their four MPI's generated;
3. the chronological number (serial position) of their single MPI generated.

The data for both studies were analyzed by tabulating how frequently the MPI occurred in the first third, middle third, and last third of the serial list of ideas generated for each problem. This analysis follows Parnes' approach (1961). The data collection procedure is described above. The hypotheses were tested as follows:

H1 was tested by calculating if significantly more often the MPI was to be found among the latter two thirds of the ideas listed serially rather than among the first third.

H2 was tested by calculating if significantly more often the MPI was to be found among the last third of this idea listed serially rather than among the first two thirds.

In addition, in the second study only, the data were also analyzed by using the *four most preferred ideas* rather than the *single* most preferred idea. H1 and H2 tested again accordingly.

These data were not available from the first study because many of the idea lists were not sufficiently long to permit four ideas to be selected as "most preferred" in a meaningful way.

To summarize, in Study Number One, 39.6% of the participants chose their MPI from the first third of their serial list of ideas, while 25.7% chose it from the middle third, and 34.7% from the last third. For the tests of hypothesis, this meant that 39.6% chose their MPI from the first third and 60.4% from the latter two thirds. Conversely, 65.3% chose it from the first two thirds, 34.7% from the last third.

In study Number Two, 42.7% of the *four* MPI's came from the first third, 33.4% from the middle third, and 23.9% from the last third. Thus, for the tests of hypotheses, 42.7% were chosen from the first third, and 57.3% from the latter two thirds, while 76.1% chose from the first two thirds, and 23.9% from the last third.

In both studies, there is firm support for H1. In all three comparisons, the frequency of occurrence of the MPI's in the combined latter two thirds was higher than for the first third. In two of the three comparisons the difference was statistically significant.

Neither study provides any support for H2. In none of the three comparisons was the frequency of occurrence of the MPI's in the last third higher than the combined first two thirds. In fact, the reverse was true in all three cases.

The above results support the belief that extended effort is useful in creative problem solving for real world managerial and technical problem solving. While it does not appear that the most preferred ideas are more likely to come more often at the very end than at the very beginning of the idea series, nevertheless, it does appear that they are more likely to occur in the later two-thirds that is after the first early burst of ideas (first third). The apparent difference in dispersion pattern between the two studies may be important to consider (there is some evidence of a downward trend in Study Number Two in frequency of occurrence of the MPI with serial position). A very interesting future research direction would be to explore the reasons for the difference. For example, the possible causes of the difference may have to do with any or all of the following:

1. Group vs. individual idea generation ("normal group" effect?) See Taylor, Berry, and Block, 1985: Do groups inhibit extended effort effects?)

2. Duration of training (4 hours vs 8-16 hours)

3. Length of time of idea generation (5 min. vs 10 min.)

4. Greater use of a "complete process of creative problem solving," that is, more time spent on problem finding, fact finding and problem definition before idea generation (2 hours vs. 15 min.).

For the author, possibility number four above is perhaps the most intriguing. The literature attributes the following sayings to John Dewey and Albert Einstein respectively: "a problem well-stated is half solved," and "the formulation of a problem is much more important than its solution" (Parnes, et al., 1977). Einstein is further quoted as saying if he were asked to solve a problem of world wide importance (to save the world) in only one hour, he would spend the first 55 minutes defining the problem and the last five minutes solving it. Thus, is it possible that the most preferred idea should come earlier when significantly more attention is paid to developing a good problem definition? This would lead to research testing the hypothesis such as "the greater the time/effort devoted to defining the problem using a complete process of problem solving, the earlier the occurrence of the most preferred idea in a serial list of ideas."

Overall, the results of this study are consistent with the previous research in supporting the usefulness of the extended effort principle in training and application of processes of creative problem solving. In particular, these results indicate it is worthwhile for an individual or a group to use extended effort when generating ideas on real world managerial and technical problems. Significantly more people will find their most preferred idea in the combined latter two thirds of their idea list than in the first third. Thus, "quitting early" in idea generation reduces the chances of obtaining the idea that would be most preferred if given the opportunity to surface.

In summary, Parnes and Meadow (1959) and Parnes (1961) found that extended effort provided significantly more good ideas in a given time period. Cohen et al. (1960) and Basadur et al. (1982) found better ideas result from extended effort in a given time period. In this study, we have found that extending effort significantly increases the odds of finding a more preferred idea than the early ideas in a given time period. All of these findings suggest that quality and quantity are related positively in idea generation when the ideation principle is employed.

6. Exogenous organizational factors

The foregoing series of research efforts was focused on increasing awareness in business and industry that there are tools available to increase organizational creativity and effectiveness. The tools can be learned and systematically applied with training. However, increasing the creative performance of an organization requires more than just training. To sustain such increases over time requires the managing of many mediating variables, which if unattended, can totally undo training effects.

These other variables could be termed exogenous factors. These are factors outside the individual which affect his or her creative behavior. The way these exogenous factors are managed has tremendous potential for affecting the short and long term use of creativity training in the organization as a whole. We know we can build individual skills in creative problem solving by training. Now the question is how do we ensure those increased skills? First, key exogenous variables must be identified and second, skills must be developed in managing them. What might this "system" look like?

The conceptual model in Figure Four could serve as a starting point. The research summarized earlier in this chapter indicated the internal mechanisms for increasing creative problem solving performance. The exogenous factors can be categorized as being either organizational, group or individual in scope. What do we know about these exogenous factors and what more needs to be known? The following attempts to throw light on these questions from practical experience and research.

Basadur, Graen & Scandura (1985) shows the positive impact of returning to a supportive home base populated by co-workers, superiors and subordinates who have undergone similar training. Cohen, et al. (1960) found that work group cohesiveness importantly enhances the impact of creativity training. Experience shows that when senior managers visibly model the attitudes and thinking skills associated with creative problem solving training, subordinates are much more likely to try using them on the job. This is to differentiate modelling from supporting. It is not enough to support the new attitudes and thinking skills. They must be used visibly by higher managers. Mott (1972) found that more adaptable organizations had higher levels of rational trust—the extent to which higher managers are seen as "practicing what they preach."

Baker et al. (1976) made an extensive review of the empirical literature relating organizational, structural and behavioral variables to the enhancement or inhibition of idea generation at the individual and work group level in R&D organizations. The most important organizational influences found can be placed into three categories: (1) Diversity of Information (enhancing effective divergence in problem finding and problem solving); (2) Clarifying Information, Organizational Goals, Needs, and Opportunities (enhancing effective convergence in problem finding and problem solving); and (3) Flexibility of Organizational Resources (enhancing solution implementation).

Diversity of information refers to the availability to organizational members of a wide array of information about diverse factors in the environment and is the result of two factors: (a) frequent contact with many diverse colleagues (diverse interests and backgrounds) especially "gatekeepers" and (b) variety of work activity. Gatekeepers are people who differ from their colleagues in the degree to which they expose themselves to sources of information outside their organization about their fields. Diversity of information is enhanced by factors such as participation in extra-organizational professional activity, increased number of occupational specialties within the organization, low formalization of tasks or jobs and high participation in organizational decision making.

Figure Four.

Model for training individual creative behavior in an organization.

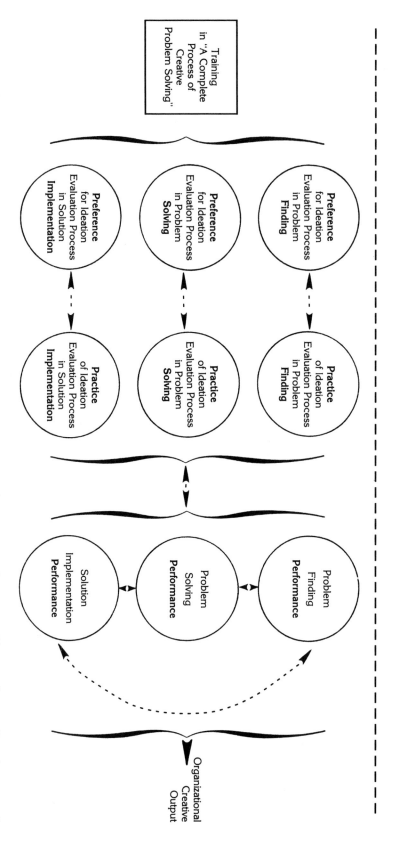

* Exogenous Influences of Group, Organizational, and External Individual Work Related Factors

* For example, Group Cohesiveness; Diversity of Information; Organizational Values and Norms such as Time Pressures, Resources, and Incentive Systems; Commitment to and Familiarity with the Work or Problem.

Clarifying information, organizational goals, needs and opportunities refers to specific detailed information which helps organizational members to effectively evaluate and select from alternative opportunities for problem solving and form alternative solutions to problems. The availability of such information is enhanced by: (1) formal statements of the firm's goals and objectives; (2) by appropriate attitudes of the primary work group and ample interaction with the group; (3) by appropriate supervisory behavior and attitudes including quality of perceived enthusiastic receptivity to and helpful evaluation of ideas offered; (4) facilitation of problem solving activities; (5) and influence both upward and downward organizationally to assure the appropriate rewards, resources, and work environment to make individual contributions available and assessable; (6) by an appropriate organizational incentive system rewarding creative performance; (7) by appropriate time pressures permitting enough time for divergence activity and also encouragement for convergence; and (8) by providing a system of control which permits a proper balance of freedom and direction to organizational members in their work.

Flexibility of organizational resources refers to the availability of uncommitted resources and funds available to help organizational members respond more quickly to new opportunities, do more long range planning and research, feel less risk of failure, and less need to compete for resource allocation thus reducing internal friction with other organizational members.

The above variables are quite general, and need to be researched and developed into much more specific factors. For example, a sample of engineers and scientists from private industry identified the specific factors in Table One as the most significant organizational factors affecting their creative performance.

Such preliminary data above need to be made more broadly based, prioritized, categorized, validated and developed into an integrated conceptual model. Also it must be determined

---

Table One.

Innovation barriers cited in a private industry R&D organization.

---

1. LIMITED TIME AVAILABLE TO SPEND ON BEING INNOVATIVE.

2. OVER-MANAGEMENT BY IMMEDIATE SUPERVISOR
   * Too many guidelines/lack of freedom
   * Over critique of new ideas
   * Early killing of fledgling ideas
   * Over-censorship of both "good" and "bad" ideas

3. LIMITED OR INVISIBLE INCENTIVES TO BE INNOVATIVE

4. INADEQUATE UPWARD COMMUNICATION OF IDEAS VIA PYRAMIDAL HIERARCHY
   * Need more direct communication between staff and upper management

5. INADEQUATE DOWNWARD COMMUNICATION FROM UPPER MANAGEMENT ON RESEARCH AND MARKETING STRATEGIES
   * Poor or so screened by pyramid that full message not received by staff

6. PHYSICAL ENVIRONMENT NOT CONDUCIVE TO INNOVATION

7. INADEQUATE CONTACT WITH OUTSIDE TECHNICAL ACTIVITIES VIA MEETINGS AND PUBLISHING

8. ORGANIZATION STRUCTURE NOT OPTIMUM FOR INNOVATION

9. LACK OF TECHNICAL CRITIQUE BY PEER EXPERTS

10. LOW RISK-TAKING BY MANAGEMENT

11. LACK OF SUPPORT FOR USE OF CREATIVITY/INNOVATION PROCESSES AND TRAINING

how such general variables and specific factors may be different in organizations other than R&D. For example, what about manufacturing operations attempting to become more profitable or to improve the quality of work life by tapping the creative potential of its employees? What management and organizational factors enhance the likelihood of individuals' using creative behavior? What factors cause manufacturing teams to be successful in creative problem solving? Similarly, what about hospitals, department stores, sales and distribution organizations, and other kinds of industries?

At a group level, what exogenous factors other than cohesiveness affect creativity? The literature on small group structure and dynamics provides considerable information on variables that affect various aspects of group performance. Some of these, include sources of tension and conflict, mix, size, goal clarity, time pressures, trust, openness of communication, competition-creating conditions, power and authority influences, social stratification and complexity of task. These variables now need to be explored more specifically in their impact on and interaction with creative processes and performance.

Finally, at an *individual* level, what are the exogenous factors affecting creativity and application of creative processes and techniques in the business and industrial setting? Experience and some empirical work indicate that two such variables are: (1) problem significance to the individual (ego-involvement) and (2) familiarity with the problem. Cohen et al. (1960) and Basadur et al. (1982) showed positive results for creative process application when there was more broadly based ego-involvement and familiarity with the problem being addressed among the problem solving participants. This is in contrast to a study by Rickards (1975). Each problem brainstormed in the Rickards study was chosen by "one or more" of the group participants, raising the possibility that the other group members were not very familiar with or ego-involved in each problem. In contrast, the Cohen et al. and Basadur et al. studies used problems of high interest and general knowledge to all subjects.

What other factors impact individual creative performance and success in applying creative processes in business and industry? The personality and cognitive identification work spearheaded by MacKinnon (1962) and Guilford (1967) needs to be integrated into performance models. We need to discover other individual variables that exist to fill out or change or deepen the model in Figure Four.

Miscellaneous Areas for Research

It would be valuable to learn if and why there are specific learnings from training in processes such as the "complete process of creative problem solving" which are considered relatively more significant and useful by members of different occupational groups (e.g.: engineers, accountants, etc.), organizational functions (e.g.: manufacturing, marketing, etc.), organizational designs (bureaucratic, organic, tall/flat structures, etc.), organizational types (electronics, chemicals, engineers, accountants, etc.), and organizational levels (e.g.: vice-president, first-line supervisor, hourly worker, etc.). How and by what mechanisms do skills in creative processes and techniques improve the basic fundamental work processes in the classic business and industry functions, such as product development, market research, and engineering? For example, can such skills increase the effectiveness of market research focus groups by increasing openness among group members? In focus group interviews, members usually limit themselves to discussing problems which they believe are possible to solve, rather than expressing their true wants and needs. Companies should rather have them defer judgment as to feasibility and creatively express how they would like to see their world—a more problem *finding* mode than problem solving. As a further example, can multi-functional critical path scheduling meetings be made more productive if participants are trained to use creative attitudes and thinking skills to increase trust and risk-taking among themselves in the face of uncertainty about future events?

Summary

Most of the literature pertaining to creativity in business and industry consists of non-empirical articles attempting to convince managers to learn to use creative problem solving processes and techniques. There are also a few theoretical pieces organizing previous knowledge and ideas about creativity in organizations. These are designed to help managers increase their awareness about the role of creativity in organizations. Such literature is useful, but what is sorely needed is more empirical work. From the author's perspective the following are the five most important areas for such new research.

First, new and improved instruments must be developed to measure and identify attitudes and thinking skills associated with the successful application of creative problem solving processes and techniques by individuals and groups. Constructs and systems models describing the mechanisms by which organizational members can perform more creatively need to be built. Attitudes and thinking skills associated with solution implementation and evaluation within the complete process of creative problem solving are specific examples of concepts needing exploring (Basadur, Graen & Green, 1982). Can the model in Figure Two be validated? The external validities and reliabilities of the attitudinal concepts "valuing new ideas" and "belief that creative thinking is bizarre" need to be established and measured reliably. Is there any such thing as an optimum ideation-evaluation ratio for a given field of endeavor or stage of creativity? The internal relationships of Figure Two modelling the complete process of creative problem solving need to be tested and further developed. How does training in such a process actually work to increase individual creative performance? Are the three stages, problem finding, problem solving and solution implementation and the ideation-evaluation two step process within each stage sufficient as a basic model?

Answering such questions will serve many additional purposes. It will increase awareness and understanding so more people will learn the process. It will improve the quality yet reduce the mystery of training in the process. It will help potential trainers realize the importance of behavioral *change* in the form of new attitudes and thinking skills such as increased deferral of judgment, preference for ideation, and cognitive ideation skill before any short or long term impact of training can be expected. It will help remove some of the misunderstandings developed over the years concerning terms like "brainstorming." It is one thing to "go through the motions" of following Osborn's four rules; it is totally another thing to *learn* the ideation-triggering skills of piling up a quantity of ideas, deliberately free wheeling, and skillfully building ideas from fragments of other ideas. Some researchers have confused "brainstorming" with "group brainstorming," attempting to show that pooling the brainstorming responses of untrained individuals (kept apart) is better than using interacting brainstorming groups of untrained individuals (Taylor, Berry & Block, 1958). The issue is not individuals versus groups, but rather, can we train individuals to really increase ideation attitudes and thinking skills? Can we isolate and identify the group effects that affect the exercising of such skills and teach individuals how to maximize ideation in groups and minimize negative impacts on individual ideation skill? You cannot get something for nothing. Unless there is sufficient training and follow-up to produce significant attitudinal thinking skill improvements in trainees, no on-the-job improvements in creativity will result. The kind of research described above will help people in business and industry understand this and manage training opportunities accordingly.

Second, what kinds of support from higher management best help insure that trained creative problem solving attitudes, behaviors and thinking skills will become permanent in the organization? How can we best get higher managers to understand those support variables once identified? What blend of reward systems, boss-subordinate interface behaviors, managerial behavior-modelling, and other extrinsic and intrinsic variables are important to be managed so that trained skills and attitudes will be transformed into on-the-job habitual usage? A much better understanding of the exogenous factors that moderate short-term impact and long-term stickability of training in creative problem solving is needed by both the managers and the trainers. Otherwise, valuable attitudes and thinking skills will continue to be left in the classroom. Trainers of processes of creative problem solving must see themselves as organizational consultants. Their work begins long before the training begins and continues long after it ends. Their job is to help their managerial clients learn how to make the new *habits* about to be trained stick permanently on the job. Their job is to transform the daily attitudes, behaviors and thinking skills of the organization. How this can be done needs thorough research and documentation.

Third, the improvement of ongoing work processes in business and industry (including the implementation of new human resource managerial concepts and techniques) by creative problem solving processes needs to be better understood and documented. It is not sufficient that trainers and consultants go into such organizations promising that training in creative problem solving will somehow "increase creativity in the organization." What does this actually mean? Such training must be preplanned with a view toward impacting selected processes and concepts. Then the training effects and mechanisms must be documented and models developed. Experience shows that the attitudes and thinking skills of the "Complete Process of Creative Problem Solving" can serve to operationalize most new and old managerial processes. Now, *how* this occurs needs understanding and documentation.

Fourth, the whole field of managerial problem solving and decision-making needs to be "de-fragmentized" and pulled together into a coherent model or systematic set of models. The complete process of creative problem solving needs to be made more visible to theorists and researchers. It offers the opportunity to incorporate many other models within it. Getting terms such as "analytical problem solving," "econologic model," "bounded rationality model," "implicit favorite model," and "programmed thinking and non-programmed thinking" systematized would be a valuable contribution to managerial and organizational science. It would provide the basis for a much more systematic approach to improving managerial thinking and decision making skills. In addition, it would help explain much better what it is that training in processes of creative problem solving can do to improve such skills.

Fifth, there is a great deal of research to be done to understand and document the effects of training and application of creative processes across different types of business and industry, different organizational designs, functions and levels, different occupational groups, and different work processes including managerial/non-managerial and professional/non-professional. Concepts such as optimum ideation-evaluation ratio by field of endeavor would fit neatly into such investigations. Developing instruments to measure individual, group and organizational thinking and problem solving styles in terms of relative preferences for various parts and stages of the complete process of creative problem solving would also be valuable. Comparing such styles across international boundaries in business and industry could be most informative. For example, most literature attempts to explain Japanese vs. North American differences in managerial problem solving and style are anecdotal or at best qualitative in nature. Solid quantitative concepts and measures are needed to make any real headway in understanding those differences.

References

Altemeyer, R. (1965). *Education in the arts and sciences:* Divergent paths. Unpublished doctoral dissertation, Carnegie Institute of Technology.

Baker, N. R., Winkofsky, E., Langmeyer, L. & Sweeney, D. J. (1976, June 28). *Idea generation: A procrustean bed of variables, hypotheses and implications.* College of Business Administration. University of Cincinnati.

Basadur, M. S. (1979). *Training in creative problem solving: Effects of deferred judgment and problem finding and solving in an industrial research organization.* Unpublished doctoral dissertation, University of Cincinnati.

Basadur, M. S. (1982). Research in creative problem-solving training in business and industry. In S. S. Gryskiewicz & J. T. Shields (Eds.), *Proceedings of Creativity Week IV* (pp. 40-59). Greensboro, NC: Center for Creative Leadership.

Basadur, M. S. (1986). The catalyzing interfunctional efforts to find and creatively solve important business problems. *McMaster University Research and Working Paper Series, 261.*

Basadur, M. S. & Finkbeiner, C. T. (1983a). Identifying attitudinal factors related to ideation in creative problem solving. *McMaster University Research and Working Paper Series, 207.*

Basadur, M. S. & Finkbeiner, C. T. (1983b). Measuring preference for ideation in creative problem solving. *McMaster University Research and Working Paper Series, 208.*

Basadur, M. S. & Finkbeiner, C. T. (1985, February). Measuring preference for ideation in creative problem-solving training. *Journal of Applied Behavioral Science, 21* (1), 37-49.

Basadur, M. S., Graen, G. B. & Green, S. G. (1982). Training in creative problem solving: Effects on ideation and problem finding and solving in an industrial research organization. *Organizational Behavior and Human Performance, 30,* 41-70.

Basadur, M. S., Graen, G. B. & Scandura, T. A. (1985). Improving attitudes towards creative problem solving among manufacturing engineers. *McMaster University Research and Working Paper Series, 237.*

Campbell, J. P. (1971). Personnel training and development. *The Annual Review of Psychology,* 565-602.

Campbell, J. P., Dunnette, M. D., Lawler, E. E., III & Weick, K. E., Jr. (1979). *Managerial behavior, performance and effectiveness.* New York: McGraw-Hill.

Cohen, D., Whitmeyer, J. W. & Funk, W. H. (1960). Effect of group cohesiveness and training upon creative thinking. *Journal of Applied Psychology, 44* (5).

Cook, T. D. & Campbell, D. T. (1976). The design and conduct of quasi-experiments and true experiments in field settings. In M. D. Dunnette (Ed.), *Handbook of Industrial and Organizational Psychology* (pp. 223-326). Chicago: Rand McNally.

Cronbach, L. J. (1951). Coefficient alpha and the internal structure of tests. *Psychometrika, 16,* 297-334.

Doktor, R. (1970). *The development and mapping of certain cognitive styles of problem solving.* Unpublished doctoral dissertation, Stanford University.

Goldstein, I. L. (1980). Training in work organizations. *The Annual Review of Psychology, 32,* 229-272.

Gordon, W. J. J. (1956). Operational approach to creativity. *Harvard Business Review, 34* (6), 41-51.

Gough, H. (1976). Personality and personality assessment. In M. D. Dunnette (Ed.), *Handbook of Industrial and Organizational Psychology* (pp. 571-607). Chicago: Rand McNally.

Guilford, J. P. (1967). *The nature of human intelligence.* New York: McGraw-Hill.

Hinrichs, J. R. (1976). Personnel training. In M. D. Dunnette (Ed.), *Handbook of Industrial and Organizational Psychology* (pp. 829-860). Chicago: Rand McNally.

MacKinnon, D. W. (1962). The nature and nurture of the creative talent. *American Psychologist, 17,* 484-495.

MacKinnon, D. W. (1977). Foreword. In S. J. Parnes, R. B. Noller & A. M. Biondi (Eds.), *Guide to Creative Action, XIII.* New York: Scribner's.

Mott, P. E. (1972). *Characteristics of effective organizations.* New York: Harper & Row.

Osborn, A. F. (1963). *Applied Imagination.* New York: Scribner's.

Parnes, S. J. (1961). Effects of extended effort in creative problem solving. *Journal of Educational Psychology, 52* (3), 113-122.

Parnes, S. J. & Meadow, A. (1959). Effects of brainstorming instruction on creative problem solving by trained and untrained subjects. *Journal of Educational Psychology, 50* (4), 171-176.

Parnes, S. J., Noeller, R. B. & Biondi, A. M. (1977). *Guide to Creative Action.* New York: Scribner's.

Rickards, T. (1975). Brainstorming: An examination of idea production rate and level of speculation in real managerial situations. *R&D Management, 6* (1), 11-14.

Roe, A. (1976). Psychological approaches to creativity in science. In A. Rothenberg & C. R. Hausman (Eds.), *The creativity question* (pp. 165-174). Durham, NC: Duke University Press.

Simon, H. A. (1960). *The new science of management decision.* Englewood Cliffs, NJ: Prentice Hall.

Taylor, D. W., Berry, P. C., & Block, C. H. (1958). Does group participation when using brainstorming facilitate or inhibit creative thinking? *Administrative Science Quarterly, 3,* 23-47.

Thurstone, L. L. (1950). *Psychmetric Laboratory,* 61, University of Chicago.

Wallach, M. A. (1971). *The intelligence/creativity distinction.* Morristown, NJ: General Learning Press.

19

Creativity Research at the Crossroads:
A 1985 Perspective*

Morris I. Stein
New York University

The occasion of this book provides an opportunity for a bit of stock-taking. In the 35 years since Guilford's (1950) presidential address to the American Psychological Association, researchers have been prolific (Barron and Harrington, 1981) and contributed significantly to the understanding of creativity—the creative individual and the creative process.

Much has been accomplished, but there is still much to be done. I will therefore address myself to the future and cite the past or the present only to indicate where we stand with respect to baseline data. My aim is to share ideas and suggestions that stem from a review of the current state of the art* to facilitate our getting to where we want to be in the future.

The Prediction of Creativity

To date the outstanding feature of creativity research is that it has been devoted primarily to the *description* of the characteristics of persons regarded as creative. Life history, cognitive and personality characteristics of creative persons in various fields of endeavor have been published. This work has to continue for we have not exhausted the different psychological and social variables that need to be studied or the different scientific and artistic groups that still require study. Nor have we done enough in studying women as well as men, children as well as adults, different ethnic groups in the United States, groups in different cultures, etc.

Descriptive studies are invaluable for understanding the creative individual and the creative process, but, they are insufficient. It is critical that we undertake major long-term *predictive* studies. Until we can predict creativity, we will be working with limited knowledge of the creative person and the creative process.

There are numerous issues involved in the prediction problem and neither time nor space allow us to consider them all here. Here are two for starters. One is: To what extent are the psychological variables which we now know to be characteristic of manifestly creative persons valid for the prediction of the creativity of persons who have not yet manifested their creativity? A person's self-perceptions, self-evaluations and their underlying psychological characteristics may well change after manifesting creativity and being regarded by others as creative. The feedback one gets after a creative work, can produce changes in one's self esteem and one's behavior.

Such changes may not occur in all individuals. Nor may they occur in all persons with regard to the same psychological variables and to the same extent for each of these variables.

---

*This chapter is based on: A book I have just completed reviewing the literature on gifted, talented and creative children (Stein, 1986); an analysis of research-based findings that can be used for the selection and management of creative persons in industry (Stein, 1984d); two previously published works on stimulating creativity (Stein, 1974 and 1975) and an earlier review of the psychiatric and psychological literature on the individual and creativity (Stein and Heinze, 1960).

Nevertheless, they occur. Therefore, data collected on persons with already acknowledged creativity may not be good predictors of the creativity of others who have yet to make their contributions.

The second issue is: To what extent does one need to know the characteristics of the environment in which the individual will work before one can predict his/her creativity? In the vast majority of studies conducted to date, the concern is with the characteristics of the individual and not the characteristics of the environment in which he/she works or in which the creativity will be manifest. It is as if we believed that man/woman made history and that the context in which he/she worked and the environment in which he/she lived had little to do with the creative process. But we know better.

Behavior is a function of the transactional relationships between an individual and his/her environment (Lewin, 1935). Is creative output any different? The validity of behavioral predictions is enhanced when one knows the characteristics of the individual and the environment against which predictions are to be made (Stern, Stein and Bloom, 1956). What are we losing when we do not have data on environmental characteristics? We may be losing some very vital data.

To investigate the predictability of creativity is a formidable undertaking. In most situations, e.g., the prediction of college success, the goal is to predict a common and probable event. In predicting creativity, one is confronted with the prediction of the improbable, the unique event.

To cope with this problem will take the efforts of a good many people to collect and store the data over long periods of time. It is an enormous job but we should not despair. Let us remember Terman's contributions as he followed his subjects over extended periods of time. His achievements were attained without the advantages of computer technology, telecommunications, and the statistical developments which we possess today.

The Need for Theoretically Based Studies

Contemporary creativity research is largely atheoretical. Studies are based on empirically derived questionnaires in which the typical hypothesis is that one group rated higher than another on a creativity criterion. It will be significantly different from that other group on a specific set of psychological variables. The kind of empiricism underlying this approach characterized some of the work at IPAR, the Institute for Personality Assessment and Research at the University of California, Berkeley, where it yielded much valuable data on the creativity of writers, scientists, architects, etc. It was also at IPAR that much good use was made of the Ego-Strength Scale (Barron, 1953), the California Personality Inventory (Gough, 1957) and the Adjective Check List (Gough & Heilbrun, 1965).

Who has not profited from these empirically derived and easily administered self-report measures? When a student needed a quick and ready measure for a thesis what better suggestion could one make than to use one of these derived scales? The tests, in my experience, almost always "worked." They almost always yielded some statistically significant results. I am a fan of these tests because I have used them.

If all this is so positive then why do I raise questions? Because, although these measures "work," it is not always clear why. Just why a questionnaire based on whether an individual will or will not stay in psychotherapy for a short period of time (Barron's Ego-Strength Scale [Barron, 1953]) works in studies of creativity I am not absolutely certain. Was it really ego strength that helped the persons in the original sample stay in therapy? If it was, was it the same ego strength that is involved in creativity?

And, when it comes to Gough and Heilbrun's (1965) Adjective Check List I am fascinated with the number of adjectives that differentiate between more and less creative persons. But

I often wonder, if the list would have contained the adjective *creative*, which for some reason it does not, whether it would always have differentiated between criterion groups. I also wonder, if the list had contained the word *creative*, how investigators would have interpreted their results if this adjective would have appeared with and without the word *intelligent* (which is part of the list of adjectives) in the characterization of their creative subjects. How would they square their results with data reported by some who are concerned about the relationship between intelligence and creativity?

Dustbowl empiricism need not smother good theory. Just as IPAR reaped good results with empirically derived tests so it has also been the home of a valuable paper on creativity which *is* derived from theory. MacKinnon (1976) used Rankian theory for a superb integration of the IPAR data on architects and we would do well to emulate it in future works.

Knowledge of the Field's Literature and History

Not only may one characterize this field as atheoretical but one may also characterize it as ahistorical. With all the technology and resources available for bibliographic surveys it is surprising how frequently papers are published in which there seems to be little awareness of what has already been accomplished and published. For example, if ever there was a finding that has been worked and re-worked it is that evaluation has a negative effect on creativity. Researchers have reported this, philosophers (*e.g.,* Schiller as reported in Freud [1938]) have reported this, and certainly so have Osborn (1963) in his work on Brainstorming and Parnes and his co-workers (Noller, *et al.,* 1976; Parnes, *et al.,* 1977) on Creative Problem-Solving. It is therefore surprising when contemporary investigators make this such a central point in their research.

That evaluation can have a negative effect on creativity is old hat. A person who evaluates too early in the creative process may inhibit the development of hypotheses. But it is quite salient during the hypothesis testing and communication phases of the creative process (Stein, 1974). The effects of evaluation depend, in all likelihood on the context in which it occurs, the way in which it occurs, the evaluator, the creative person, etc. Evaluation cannot be avoided. To make certain that it does not destroy creativity and even helps it we have to learn how to give it and how to receive it.

As an aside it should be noted that Amabile's (1983) work on evaluation has been cited in a recent edition of an Introductory Psychology textbook (Zimbardo, 1985). In this citation students are informed of its negative effects. One can only wonder what impression this finding might have on students if they took it seriously. If they did, might they not think that the creative process is a relatively simple one? One has only "to be inspired." Ideas alone—good or bad—are all that creativity is about. We do such students and ourselves an injustice if evaluation is not given its appropriate place and appropriate weight in the creative process.

The ahistorical approach is also reflected in the work of others who are important contributors to the field. Howard Gardner (Gardner, 1982) and his colleagues call their studies of giftedness and creativity *Project Zero* because they believe that nothing much has been accomplished in the field before they came on the scene.

Terman found that a sub-group of "creativity" tests did not correlate with intelligence and he therefore dropped them from his intelligence test. Would knowledge of this fact have had any effect on the vast amount of energy that has gone into the creativity-intelligence controversy? Are people who use so-called creativity tests aware of the pros and cons in the literature on this matter?

There are problems in getting good bibliographic surveys. They are expensive and not always easy to come by. Such serious problems have to be dealt with so that the process is more efficient and is easily used. And, while we do so, let us give more adequate coverage to the foreign literature.

Studies of the Whole Person

Contemporary mainstream psychology is largely cognitive. Human beings, thanks to the computer and the information explosion, are now studied as an information processing organism. The problem, in this context, is that they are fallible. Research therefore focuses on how man/woman goes astray or the conditions under which he/she can become a high-fidelity system.

Cognitive emphases in the studies of creativity focus only on one set of psychological characteristics. But individuals also have personalities. These have to be studied in their own right and in their transactional relationships with cognitive characteristics.

The human organism has a history. It develops over time. We have to know about critical historical developments in a creative person's life. And, we also need to gather more first hand information on the parents of creative adults and gifted, talented and creative children (Colangelo and Dettman, 1983). We need to remember that *Even the Muses Had Parents* (Stein, 1984b).

The creative individual is a complex organism. It is surprising how little of what is reported in the contemporary creativity literature does justice to this fact. In another context (Stein, 1984c) I called attention to this point by citing Hofstadter (1979) who said, "The pearl is prized for its luster and simplicity; the oyster is a complex living beast, whose innards give rise to this mysteriously simple gem, the pearl." Elegant solutions in creative works appear *simple* and *obvious* as the poet Milton said (Holton, 1953 as quoted in Stein, 1984c) but such solutions can only be produced by complex creative persons to whom we have to do justice in the presentation of their psychodynamics.

In the past, a study of creative persons that would include a host of relevant variables would have been a formidable task. However, with computers and the software currently available the problem is much less formidable. Moreover, there is some very valuable help that one can get from the use of typologies (Kirton, 1982; Myers and Briggs, 1962; Myers and McCaulley, 1985 and Stein, 1966, 1971). As we make use of current technology and developments we will come closer and closer to more complete and valid pictures of creative persons.

Creativity—Big C and Little c

I hesitate to discuss the issue of *Creativity—Big C (high level creativity) and Little c (day to day creativity)* for fear that the reader may think that it deals solely with the definition of creativity and the criterion. Surely these are involved but let us not open Pandora's box.

My point here is simple. We should not assume that the psychological characteristics associated with *Creativity Little c* are the same as those associated with *Creativity Big C* until it has been proven to be so.

Studies of creativity cover a wide range of persons. At one extreme persons are studied who have made very significant creative contributions to society. Amongst them are those whose works are responsible for paradigmatic shifts (Kuhn, 1970). At the other extreme are those whose creativity represents "the creativity of normal people." It is reasonable to assume that the psychological characteristics of both groups may overlap but they will not be the same in all instances. It is important that we know the communalities as well as the differences.

My point may be more clear with an example from the field of intelligence testing. One of Terman's (1925) purposes in his studies of genius was to counteract the effects of the pathographers of genius—those who focused solely, if not primarily on what they regarded as the pathology in genius. One of Terman's contributions was that children with IQ's in the area of 140 were generally healthy, robust, all-around kids. From this finding some persons then maintained that high intelligence and psychological health were highly correlated. This, however, was not substantiated in the studies of children of IQ's of 180, 190 and above (Hollingsworth, 1942).

Similarly in the field of creativity, we may find that a test of divergent thinking relates positively to the creativity of school children which has been evaluated by their teachers. The same test however, may not correlate positively with the creativity of adults in research and development organizations. It would be an error to say that divergent thinking and creativity are correlated without specifying the kind of creativity, or the kinds of subjects and the kinds of situations involved.

Studies of creativity should not be limited to one group or the other. But results should be stated with clarity and specificity. It might be well to consider the suggestion that every creativity study should specify in a subscript the kinds of persons and the kinds of creativity studied. For example, $Creativity_1$ would stand for those who have creatively contributed to paradigmatic shifts and $Creativity_n$ would stand for those who write what are regarded as creative poems in the fourth grade.

To set up such standards may be a laborious and time-consuming task. If so, the task may be worthy of a Bureau of Standards. The time and effort devoted to such work would be very much worthwhile for it would clarify confusion and provide structure to our work.

It is unlikely that the distinctions I suggest will be easily instituted. At the present time there is much pressure to think that everyone is creative in the same way. Such thinking may have arisen in reaction against the effects of hereditary and aristocratic values that limited the opportunities for creative expression to a privileged few. But current emphasis on equal opportunity to manifest and fulfill one's potentialities should not lead us to adopt equally erroneous orientations. The realities of life are such that even when equal opportunity is available, it does not necessarily result in the same behavior.

By applying the same word, *creative,* to every little thing that is novel or every minor deviation from the *status quo,* we risk the danger of erecting a tower of Babel. Just as inflationary pressures have made serious inroads into our economy, so it is apparent that they have made serious inroads in the field of creativity as well. Hopefully, my suggestion if adopted, might help reduce some of these pressures.

In the context of this discussion it is worthwhile to remember some of the usages of the word *creative* over time. In the Book of Genesis a clear linguistic distinction is made between God's and man's creativity. Baráh is used solely and exclusively for God's creativity. It denotes to create *ex nihilo,* to create out of nothing. For man's creativity there are other words like asáh, yatzár, and the like.[1] Man does not create out of nothing but rather makes or brings forth new things by making combinations out of those things that already exist. Man, therefore, *transforms*[2] that which exists into something new but he does not create out of nothing.

Later in history, along about the second half of the 17th century, a distinction was made between *copying* a work and being *original.* Many who we might have regarded today as creative were then called original. But then the difference between "copying" and "originality" was not sufficient for desired distinctions. Dryden felt that the word *original* might not have been sufficient to describe some of Shakespeare's work. To remedy this situation Dryden felt that a word better than original was necessary and he chose *creative.* (Smith [1924] presents a full discussion of this matter and readers who cannot find this source might want to read Stein [1984a].)

Distinctions as to level of creativity have always been made in this field. If, on the current scene, there are strong forces in favor of extending the use of the term to a wide range of works, then, in doing so, let us be careful to specify our referents or else our discussions and communications will be confusing.

On Factor Analysis and Convergent-Divergent Thinking

The use of factor analysis has resulted in some very important contributions to test development. There is hardly a student of creativity who does not know Guilford's (1967, 1977) cube and the 120+ factors derived from it and tested for. There is hardly a person in this field who does not know Guilford's distinction between divergent and convergent thinking and of the contributions of Getzels and Jackson (1962), Wallach and Kogan (1965) and certainly of Torrance's tests of creativity (1972, 1974). Moreover, although the data are not yet all in on the validity and predictive utility of convergent-divergent thinking for purposes of creativity as well as the many other Guilford factors, there is a program already in existence that provides children with training for these factors (Meeker, 1969 and 1976).

Factor analysis is a very potent statistical technique, but it and especially the findings that stem from it, should not be abused. The assumptions underlying various factor analytic procedures need to be kept in mind. There are important disagreements in this field (Vernon et al., 1977), and before we settle on any existing set of factors let us maintain an open mind as we wait for the contributions of Gardner (1983) and Sternberg (1977).

When one lines up the contributions to the intelligence-creativity controversy based on divergent and convergent thinking together with the criticisms thereof (Stein, in press a), then one becomes aware of the extent to which our field has been carried away by a distinction that is not as complete or as deserving as some think—at least in terms of the operations used in those studies. There is a lesson to be learned from all this and it may stand us in good stead to learn it. Santayana (1905) once said, "Those who cannot remember the past are condemned to fulfill it."

Some day historians will consider the intelligence-creativity controversy and the divergent-convergent matter and hopefully they will put it in a perspective from which we will learn for the future. In such a perspective an important role will have to be assigned to the *zeitgeist* of the 60's and the extent to which some of our values may have distorted our perception of the results.

The 60's with its emphasis on non-conformity and autonomy provided a fertile environment for orientations and data which stressed the importance of unlimited freedom and the importance of overcoming any possible restriction placed on us by society. In this context there were no single correct answers to any question. And just as this orientation was to hold in the socio-political arena so it was to hold in test construction. Convergent thinking was to become inferior to divergent thinking. When it came to intelligence and creativity, then the baby was thrown out with the bath. Intelligence and creativity were not related, they were independent of each other. Was it possible that creativity was possible even without intelligence?

What is especially curious about the creativity-intelligence research is the attitude that investigators had towards statistical analyses and statistical techniques. The initial work by Getzels and Jackson was founded on the statistical argument about the independence of intelligence and creativity. It wasn't long before this study was regarded as a classic. It is acknowledged as responsible for a real turnaround in the field and a spurt in research. But soon after its publication, statistical arguments were presented that the tests which made up the creativity battery were no more highly correlated with each other than they were with the tests in the intelligence battery; the same could be said about the intelligence tests. Correlations, a fairly simple statistical procedure, were used both in the initial work and in the criticisms. The arguments could be quite clear. But, for all intents and purposes the arguments were largely ignored and the ground swell of research in this area continued.

In due time there was a feeling that independence could truly be obtained between creativity and intelligence if one used appropriate testing conditions. Indeed, this is what Wallach and Kogan (1965) did and this is what they found. Now investigators interested in the difference between intelligence and creativity had another variable to play with—the test conditions. Research on these issues continued unabated and many studies found supporting results. But then Cronbach asked for and obtained the Wallach and Kogan data for reanalysis. On the basis of his analysis Cronbach (1968) argued the Wallach and Kogan results were not supported. No matter. Cronbach's paper was largely ignored.

Another item for future historians is the overemphasis on divergent thinking and the relative lack of attention paid to other factors related to creativity. Guilford, whose very work was basic to their development and use, had pointed out (Guilford, 1967) that divergent thinking was only *one* factor among several that was important for creative thinking. But despite such an assertion by such an important figure as Guilford no one seemed to bother much about the use of these other tests.

A side matter that seemed to reinforce the use of the concepts *divergent thinking* and *convergent thinking* and pushed them to forefront of visibility and popularity was the fact that they began to turn up in a technique for stimulating creativity. The proponents of Creative Problem-Solving (Parnes, 1975; and Parnes, *et al.,* 1977 and the newer Isaksen & Treffinger, 1985) began to use the terms–diverge and converge. Anyone acquainted with the books on Creative Problem-Solving or whoever has attended a Creative Problem Solving Institute (CPSI) is well-acquainted with the sequence of diamond shapes with a separate diamond for each stage in the creative problem-solving process. Mess-Finding, Data-Finding, Problem-Finding, Idea-Finding, Solution-Finding, and Acceptance-Finding each has its separate diamond. The lines of the first vertical half of each diamond move *out* and the lines of the second vertical half move *in*. Thus, in a training session when an individual starts an activity indicated in a diamond (*e.g.,* Data-Finding), the person is encouraged to *diverge*–meaning in this instance to come up with as many ideas as possible since, as in *Brainstorming* (Osborn, 1963) so here *Quantity Breeds Quality*. Then, after the person has engaged in this activity and completed it he/she is asked to *converge*–in this context the word means to select one idea among the many that the individual came up with which the person would like to work on further because he/she thinks it best. There is no certainty, of course, that this one selection is in fact the *one* best answer as it would be in a test where the questions do have one best answer and involve convergent thinking.

The words *convergent* and *divergent,* as words, are the same in both Guilford's system and in creative problem-solving training. As *concepts* they may be similar but not the same. If anything the similarity between the two is primarily that of a clang association. Nevertheless, to anyone who was not aware of these matters it might well have appeared that *divergent thinking* and *convergent thinking* as concepts had received some reinforcement from persons like Parnes and others who were teaching creative problem-solving.

Thus there were many pressures in favor of the use of divergent thinking as a measure of creativity. On the positive side the divergent thinking factor had been isolated by a very important factor analyst and tests for that factor had been developed. Some researchers had already begun to publish studies in which intriguing results were presented; prestigious trainers in creative problem-solving used words that sounded as if they gave support to the concept; a training program in the further development of the concept was underway. On the negative side, however, there were statistical arguments against the early research which alleged that the measures of creativity and the measures of intelligence that were used were not really independent of each other; Guilford, who had found the divergent thinking factor and started the differentiation between convergent and divergent thinking, had pointed out that the divergent thinking factor was not the only factor involved in creative thinking; divergent thinking tests were not as valid as one might hope in studies of creative adults.

None of the negative characteristics were sufficient to stem the tide–the use of divergent thinking tests as measures of creativity continues unabated. Are we possibly doing as much injustice to those we test with so-called tests of creativity as we have done to those we tested in the past with tests of intelligence?

British investigators (Haddon & Lytton, 1968; Hudson, 1962; Marsh, 1964) appear to caution their countrymen that when they read the American literature on divergent thinking they should remember that these tests are what they are—tests of divergent thinking. We in the United States would do well to bear this caution in mind. The tests are tests of divergent thinking but not yet tests of creativity. Moreover, for a sobering and depressing evaluation of so-called tests of creativity one should read Richert et. al. (1982).

Test users, because they frequently are not as schooled in the use of advanced statistical techniques such as factor analysis are dependent on researchers, test constructors, editors and publishers to provide them with direct, easily understandable and complete information. Just as this was always important so will it continue to be important as we await future developments by Gardner, Sternberg and others. Let us learn from the past. Just as it was true then so it is true now and in the future—*Caveat emptor! Let the buyer beware!*

On Scientism

The motivation in the field is very high to be scientific and "hardheaded." But, sometimes the effort is misplaced and distortions develop so that instead of science there is scientism—the orientation and the work smack of science but the final result is misguided and not really very scientific.

The most recent experience in this regard was the work and emphasis on the split brain. For years everyone knew that creativity depended on imagination, capacity to engage in non-linear thinking, the use of imagery and the like. But after Roger Sperry's (1968) work on the split brain was published a new fad developed. It was as if everyone heaved a sigh of relief for they now had a basis in brain physiology for all of their suggestions. All of their previously good ideas now became even better because desirable functions could be localized in specific locations in the brain. The desirable functions were always in the brain. Now localization was "precise."

It was not long, however, before the pendulum began to swing extremely. If one were naturally left brain dominant one had better not show up at a conference—the right side was in and that was that. The best that a naturally left brain dominant person could do was go to a training program where he/she could learn how to shift and become right brain dominant. In one instance I was told by a mother that her daughter could tell when she shifted from one side of the brain to the other because she heard a click! Maybe so.

Things got so bad that people had to be reminded that they had two major parts to their brain and that they had better make use of both of them. Specifically, right-brained people, who were in the group had to be cautioned: "Your left brain, don't leave home without it."

Hopefully, we have learned some valuable lessons about scientism from right and left brain research. May this knowledge stand us in good stead with future work.

Procedures for Stimulating Creativity

There are now numerous procedures available for stimulating creativity (Van Gundy, 1982; Stein, 1974, 1975). The time has come to start evaluating just how effective these are. In so doing the goal should not be such simplistic general statements as "those who have used the procedure were able to solve more problems than those who did not." While this information is desirable it does not go far enough. We need to know what *kinds* of people should use what *kinds* of procedures with what *kinds* of problems. A comparison of several procedures has already begun (Ekvall, 1981; Ekvall & Parnes, 1984; Nęcka, 1984a). It is important to go further and especially is it important to be able to recommend procedures for different kinds of people so that each type (Myers & Briggs, 1962; Myers & McCaulley, 1985; Kirton, 1982; Stein, 1966, 1971) can become more effective. Forehand (cited in Stein, 1975) pointed out that persons who were autonomous and independent could be expected to profit from a cognitive skill-oriented approach while persons who were dependent could profit most from a personality-insight approach.

Previous work evaluating creativity stimulating procedures were faulted because the evaluation session utilized a procedure that was very much the same as one used in training. Thus, it was not unusual to find someone suggesting that a program in which training to come up with as many ideas as possible and which contained a practice problem such as "How many ideas can you think of for ways to use a coat hanger?" was tested for its effectiveness with the question "How many ideas can you think of for ways to use a brick?" Training and evaluation procedures should be different from each other. If training is to be at all meaningful then evaluation should involve a carryover or a transfer of training to significant problems. Moreover, the expectation should also be that training should not only result in shortlived effects of one or two weeks duration but should yield effects that may be long lasting if not permanent.

A Consortium

It is apparent that the issues and suggestions discussed in this chapter are of such proportions that to put a dent in them is beyond the efforts of any one person. Their solution requires the combined efforts of numbers of individuals working together cooperatively. Only through our combined efforts and our combined resources can we divide the problem domain amongst ourselves and then share in the utilization of the results.

On a previous occasion (Stein, 1983a) I suggested the value of a consortium for just such a purpose. The suggestion fell on the ears of others who had already heard similar suggestions in the past. A meeting of several interested persons was held and reported on in the literature (Isaksen, Stein, Hills and Gryskiewicz, 1984). The ball has been carried by Isaksen at the Center for Studies in Creativity of the State University College at Buffalo. This program deserves all of our support because only through our combined effort will we come close to making the future what we want it to be.

Conclusion

In 1986 we can look back at more than three and a half decades of inordinate and impressive productivity in the area of creativity research. Like all good research it has provided us with valuable findings but it has also raised more questions than it started with. The path ahead is full of challenges which together, we can solve creatively.

Footnotes

1. For these and other distinctions see Stein (1983b).
2. For discussions of man the transformer there is an audiotape (Stein, 1984d), a videotape (Stein, 1985) as well as a small monograph which discusses the matter with reference to the management of creative individuals in government and industry (Stein, in press b).

References

Amabile, T. M. (1983). *The social psychology of creativity*. New York: Springer-Verlag.

Barron, F. (1953). An ego-strength scale which predicts response to psychotherapy. *Journal of Consulting Psychology, 17*, 327-333.

Barron, F. & Harrington, D. M. (1981). Creativity, intelligence and personality. *Annual Review of Psychology, 32*, 439-476.

Colangelo, M. & Dettman, D. F. (1983). A review of research on parents and families of gifted children. *Exceptional Children, 50,* 20-27.

Cronbach, L. J. (1968). Intelligence? Creativity? A parsimonious reinterpretation of the Wallach-Kogan data. *American Educational Research Journal, 5,* 491-511.

Ekvall, G. (1981). *Creative problem-solving methods in product development: A comparative development.* Report 1. Sweden: The Swedish Council for Management and Organization Behavior.

Ekvall, G. & Parnes, S. (1984). *Creative problem-solving methods in product development: A second experiment.* Report 2. Sweden: The Swedish Council for Management and World Life Issues.

Freud, S. (1938). *The basic writings of Sigmund Freud.* A. A. Brill (Ed. and trans.) New York: Random House.

Gardner, H. (1982). *Art, mind and brain: A cognitive approach to creativity.* New York: Basic Books.

Gardner, H. (1983). *Frames of mind.* New York: Basic Books.

Getzels, J. W. and Jackson, P. W. (1962). *Creativity and intelligence: Explorations with gifted children.* New York: Wiley.

Gough, H. G. (1957). *Manual for the California Psychological Inventory.* Palo Alto, CA: Consulting Psychologists Press.

Gough, H. G. & Heilbrun, A. B. Jr. (1965). *The adjective check list manual.* Palo Alto, CA: Consulting Psychologists Press.

Guilford, J. P. (1950). Creativity. *American Psychologist, 5,* 444-454.

Guilford, J. P. (1967). *The nature of human intelligence.* New York: McGraw Hill.

Guilford, J. P. (1977). *Way beyond the IQ.* Buffalo, NY Creative Education Foundation.

Haddon, F. A. and Lytton, H. (1968). Teaching approach and development of divergent thinking abilities in primary schools. *British Journal of Educational Psychology, 38,* 171-180.

Hofstadter, D. R. (1979). *Godel, Escher, Bach: An eternal golden braid.* New York: Basic Books.

Hollingworth, L. S. (1942). Children above 180 IQ Stanford-Binet: origin and development. Yonkers, NY: World Book Company.

Hudson, L. (1962). Intelligence, divergence and potential originality. *Nature, 196,* 601-602.

Isaksen, S. G., Stein, M. I., Hills, D. A., & Gryskiewicz, S. G. (1984). A proposed model for the formulation of creativity research. *Journal of Creative Behavior, 18,* 67-85.

Isaksen, S. G. & Treffinger, D. J. (1985). *Creative problem solving: The basic course.* Buffalo, NY: Bearly Limited.

Kirton, M. J. (1982). *Kirton adaption-innovation inventory (KAI).* Hertfordshire, England. Kirton, Director, Occupational Research Centre, Hatfield Polytechnic.

Kuhn, T. S. (1970). *The structure of scientific revolutions.* (2nd ed. en.). Chicago: University of Chicago Press.

Lewin, K. (1935). *A dynamic theory of personality.* New York: McGraw-Hill.

MacKinnon, D. W. (1976). *In search of human effectiveness.* Buffalo, NY Creative Education Foundation; and Great Neck, NY Creative Synergetic Associations.

Mansfield, R. S., Busse, F. V. and Krepelka, E. J. (1978). The effectiveness of creative training. *Review of Educational Research, 48,* 517-536.

Marsh, R. W. (1964). Statistical re-analysis of Getzel's and Jackson's data. *British Journal of Educational Psychology, 34,* 91-93.

Meeker, M. N. (1969). *The structure of intellect, its interpretation and uses.* Columbus, OH: Charles E. Merrill.

Meeker, M. N. (1976). *Learning to plan, judge and make decisions, advanced: A structure of intellect evaluation workbook.* El Segundo, CA: SOI Institute.

Myers, I. B. and Briggs, K. C. (1962). *Myers-Briggs type indicator, Manual.* Palo Alto, CA: Consulting Psychologists Press.

Myers, I. B. & McCaulley, M. H. (1985). *Manual for the Myers-Briggs type indicator: a guide to the development and use of the MBTI.* Palo Alto, CA: Consulting Psychologists Press.

Nęcka, E. (1984). The effectiveness of synectics and brainstorming as conditioned by socio-economic climate and type of problem. *Polish Psychological Bulletin, 15,* 41-50.

Noller, R. B., Parnes, S. J. & Biondi, A. M. (1976). *Creative action book.* New York: Scribner's.

Osborn, A. F. (1963). *Applied imagination.* (3rd ed.) New York: Scribner's.

Parnes, S. J. (1975). CPSI–a program for balanced growth. *Journal of Creative Behavior, 9,* 23-29.

Parnes, S. J., Noller, R. B. & Biondi, A. M. (1977). *Guide to Creative Action.* New York: Scribner's.

Richert, E. S. with Alvino, J. J. and McDonnel, R. C. (1982). *National report on identification: Assessment and recommendations for comprehensive identification of gifted and talented youth.* Sewell, New Jersey: Educational Improvement Center-South.

Santayana, G. (1905). *Life of reason.* Vol. 1, New York: Scribner's.

Smith, L. P. (1924). *S.P.E. Tract No. XVII four words: Romantic, originality, creative and genius.* London: Oxford University Press.

Sperry, R. W. (1968). *Mental unity following surgical disconnection of the cerebral hemispheres.* The Harvey Lectures, Series 62. New York: Academic Press.

Stein, M. I. (1966). *Volunteers for peace.* New York: Wiley.

Stein, M. I. (1971, June 17-18). Ecology of typology. In *Proceedings of the Conference on Personality Measurement in Medical Education.* Des Plaines, IL: Association of American Medical Colleges.

Stein, M. I. (1974). *Stimulating creativity: Vol. 1 individual procedures.* New York: Academic Press.

Stein, M. I. (1975). *Stimulating creativity: Vol. 2 group procedures.* New York: Academic Press.

Stein, M. I. (1983a, June). State of the art: Research on gifted/talented/creative children. Paper presented at the 29th annual CPSI, Buffalo, New York.

Stein, M. I. (1983b). Creativity in Genesis. *Journal of Creative Behavior, 17,* 1-8.

Stein, M. I. (1984a). Creative: The adjective. *Creativity and Innovation Network, 10,* 115-117.

Stein, M. I. (1984b). Even the muses had parents. *Journal of Creative Behavior, 18,* 185-186.

Stein, M. I. (1984c). *Making the point: Anecdotes, poems and illustration for the creative process.* Buffalo, N.Y.: Bearly Limited.

Stein, M. I. (1984d). *Homo Transformare,* Greensboro, NC: Center for Creative Leadership. Audiotape.

Stein, M. I. (1985). *The creative process.* Greensboro, NC: Center for Creative Leadership. Videotape.

Stein, M. I. (1986). *Gifted, talented & creative young people: A guide to theory, teaching and research.* New York: Garland Publishing.

Stein, M. I. & Heinze, S. J. (1960). *Creativity and the individual: summaries of selected writings in the psychological and psychiatric literature.* New York: The Free Press.

Stern, G. G., Stein, M. I. & Bloom, B. S. (1956). *Methods in personality assessment.* New York: The Free Press.

Sternberg, J. (1977). *Intelligence: Information processing and analogical reasoning.* Hillsdale, NJ: Lawrence Erlbaum Associates.

Tannenbaum, A. J. (1983). *Gifted children: Psychological and educational perspectives.* New York: Macmillan.

Terman, L. (1925). *Mental and physical traits of a thousand gifted children. Genetic studies of genius.* In L. Terman (Ed.) Stanford, CA: Stanford University Press.

Torrance, E. P. (1972). Predictive validity of the Torrance tests of creative thinking. *Journal of Creative Behavior, 6,* 236-252.

Torrance, E. P. (1974). *Torrance tests of creative thinking: Norms-technical manual.* Bensenville, IL: Scholastic Testing Service.

Torrance, E. P. (1981). *Administration, scoring and norms–technical manual for: Thinking creatively in action and movement.* Bensenville, IL: Scholastic Testing Service.

Van Gundy, A. B. (1982). Training your creative mind. Englewood Cliffs, NJ: Prentice-Hall.

Vernon, P. E., Adamson, G. & Vernon, D. F. (1977). *The psychology and education of gifted children.* Boulder, CO: Westview Press.

Wallach, M. A. & Kogan, N. (1965). *Modes of thinking in young children.* New York, NY: Holt.

Zimbardo, P. (1985). *Psychology and life.* (Eleventh ed.) Glenview, IL: Scott, Foresman & Co.

Author Index

Subject Index